D1608343

MONEY AND FINANCE

A FLOW-OF-FUNDS APPROACH

THE IOWA STATE UNIVERSITY PRESS / AMES

JACOB COHEN

PROFESSOR OF ECONOMICS AND FINANCE
DEPARTMENT OF ECONOMICS
UNIVERSITY OF PITTSBURGH

MONEY AND FINANCE

A FLOW-OF-FUNDS APPROACH

© 1986 The Iowa State University Press, Ames, Iowa 50010

Composed by The Iowa State University Press
Printed in the United States of America

First edition, 1986

Library of Congress Cataloging-in-Publication Data

Cohen, Jacob, 1918–
   Money and finance.

   Includes bibliographical references and index.
   1. Money.   2. Finance.   3. Flow of funds.
I. Title.
HG221.C68   1986   332   86–7338
ISBN 0–8138–1166–X

CONTENTS

PREFACE

Every author of a money and banking text must offer some apologies for adding to the great number of available books. One justification is that events are so fast moving that new books are continually needed just to keep up. The second justification has to do with vision. Each author has a unique slant and is convinced it will help the reader. This author's vision is that the flow of funds (the transaction) underlies economics and that spelling out the implications is the best approach to the subject. We all speak the language of the flow of funds—about money flowing in and money flowing out—and, like Ogden Nash, may lament its flowing out so much faster than it flows in. The transaction has a fundamental architecture, which is introduced in the very first chapter, and involves some simple accounting rules that can be applied throughout.

A flow-of-funds framework is comprehensive without loose ends. Many familiar discussions fit into it easily, such as a discussion of the mechanics of money creation, the balance of payments, or borrowers and lenders interacting in credit markets.

An accounting framework imposes the discipline of numbers. It is not possible to avoid qualitative descriptions using such words as "some" or "many." But wherever possible I have tried to say "how much." Thus we have a goodly number of tables and charts. This has the side benefit of providing data sources for the student's future use. The most complex kind of table (matrix) plots "from whom to whom" transactions, but they should be no more difficult than reading a baseball schedule.

Quantitative thinking means that relations between variables must be expressed symbolically and ultimately tested with numbers. The regression equation has become a staple of modern economics and we have made use of it. How much of an effect one variable will have on another is a satisfying bit of information. Econometric models consist of a set of such equations, and they provide a fitting climax to the study of money and finance.

The contemporary economist describes the decision maker as responding to relative prices and to stocks of assets and liabilities. Such decision making must be consistent with the decision maker's sources and uses of funds. Behavior is constrained by flows. The idea of constraints in this text goes beyond flow constraints to include the many inhibiting factors that influence central bank behavior. The first 12 chapters can be considered expository. The remainder suggest the constraints under which the Federal Reserve operates, beginning with political constraints (the politics of money). Some readers may regard the tone of the text as overly critical. But the life of a central banker is not an easy one, and the difficulties must be spelled out even on a textbook level.

More than a set of constraints, the flow of funds suggests a theory. It might be called "creditist" because it focuses on credit markets. The behavior of borrowers and lenders in financial markets becomes the key to spending activity. The flow of credit as the link has advantages over interest rates and money, the commoner linkages. Money matters, but the dynamics of disturbances in the modern economy are best understood by focusing on the demand and supply of credit.

In common with most texts I have tried to "cover the waterfront." So the monetarist and Keynesian theories together with offshoots such as rational expectations are given their due. An attempt has been made in these 25 chapters to deal with every major topic in the field of money and finance. Review questions at the end of each chapter suggest key topics. The detailed citation of sources should help the student in following up a topic of interest.

This book was first used in the University External Studies Program, University of Pittsburgh, and the cooperation of the staff through many drafts is greatly appreciated. I am indebted to Nancy Bohlen of Iowa State University Press for her painstaking editing.

MONEY AND FINANCE

A FLOW-OF-FUNDS APPROACH

1

Players in the game
and the moves they make

Economic activity is a game carried on by a set of players. The players in the game are members of the various sectors of the economy. To build a framework for economic analysis, these sectors must be identified. Players carry on their business via transactions with players in other sectors or with players in their own. Transactions cause a flow of money between sectors corresponding to the flow of goods and services. Pieces of paper (financial claims that promise future income) also underlie transactions between sectors. These flows of goods and services, financial claims, and the corresponding money payments provide the basic architecture of economic activity. If one person pays out money to another, this implies that exactly the same amount will be received by the second party. At the same time, the value of goods and services and/or financial claims bought by one player will equal the value of goods and services and/or financial claims sold by the other.

Thus there are four sides to every transaction. To assist in understanding and quantifying transactions between sectors, we shall introduce the flow-of-funds accounts in this chapter. In this accounting system sectors are tied together by their transactions.

The different sectors

In the economic game players vie for prizes according to set rules and enjoy the sport. We do not identify individual players (the U.S. population in 1984 was 235 million) but classify them instead into sectors. The end purpose of economic activity is consumer welfare, so the consumer sector is the logical beginning point. As workers, consumers are sellers of productive services. They work in myriad occupations, delivering productive services that are incorporated into the millions of products they help to produce. As consumers, they purchase final as opposed to productive services, e.g., the services of a doctor or a barber (consumed at the moment they are delivered). A broader term (and one we shall use) covering both the buying and selling activities of consumers is the household sector.

The business sector combines the productive services provided by the household sector with the firm's capital goods and the intermediate inputs (raw materials, semifinished goods) provided by other firms into finished goods.

The reciprocal relation between business and households is responsible for a circular flow of economic activity. Households sell their productive services to business and in turn buy back the latter's products. Within the business sector, raw materials and intermediate products flow between business firms. The government sector regulates the economy by taxes, spending, and legislation. Financing these nonfinancial sectors (households, business, government) and in turn depending on them for its own financing is the financial sector, two major subcategories of which are commercial banks and financial intermediaries—e.g., savings and loan associations (S&Ls), mutual savings banks, insurance companies, and security brokers and dealers. Finally, we should identify a sector that is more of a geographical unit than a separate decision-making sector. The rest of the world represents all the transactions that the domestic economy carries on with economic units in other countries.

The growing importance of the rest of the world for every country probably makes its current textbook treatment out of date. Contemporary texts focus on the national economy, with the rest of the world being relegated to a few chapters somewhere at the end. In the years to come when more thought has gone into this approach, a global framework will no doubt replace a national framework. As we point out in Chapter 23, an advantage of the flow-of-funds accounts is its portrayal of the national economy as an integral part of the world economy.

Motives and transactions

All these sectors have different motives, which are reflected in their transactions. We think of households attempting to maximize their utility or satisfaction, while business attempts to maximize profits. Recent economic analysis, however, also applies the term "utility" to business because its decisions are affected by risk considerations. In choosing a path between profits and risk, business maximizes its expected utility. Financial institutions are a form of business and have the same motivations. The government (particularly the federal government) presumably maximizes social welfare. The aspects of government in which we shall be most interested are the functions performed by the U.S. Treasury and the policymakers in the Federal Reserve System. Fiscal policy includes the taxing, spending, and debt management policies of the Treasury. The controls exercised by the Board of Governors of the Federal Reserve System and the Federal Reserve Banks over money and credit constitute monetary policy. A convenient nickname for these policymakers is to refer to them as the "Fed."

The different motivations of the various sectors show up in the transactions or moves the players make. Households sell their labor services for wages and salaries, lend money at interest, and rent out physical assets (e.g., house rent). Households may operate unincorporated businesses (as farmers or small retail merchants) and thus can earn profits, which in fact may contain an indistinguishable wage payment. Such business activities of households are usually separated and included in the statistics of business as unincorporated business.

As consumers, households spend income from the sale of productive services. They buy nondurable goods (e.g., clothing, food) and final services (e.g., dental work), all of which are subsumed under current expenditures. They purchase durables such as houses and cars, which yield their services over an extended period. Such expenditures are called capital expenditures or physical investment. Capital investment is to be contrasted with financial investment—the third type of buying (current expenditures and capital expenditures are the first two). Financial investment is investment in financial claims, pieces of paper that yield interest or dividends. Households, for example, may put money in S&Ls or buy stocks and bonds. Financial claims are referred to as intangibles as compared to the tangible quality of current and capital expenditures. The prices of such intangibles when they are marketable (some financial claims can only be redeemed and are non-marketable, e.g., U.S. government savings bonds) may rise or fall, yielding capital gains or losses to their owners.

Households are not only lenders of funds (when they acquire financial claims) but at the same time may be borrowers, issuing their own promises to pay (IOUs). This is a second major financial source of purchasing power, the first being the sale of financial assets (claims) acquired at some previous time; e.g., a household may sell its stock in General Motors to buy a new car. Most commonly, households borrow or sell off financial claims to finance "big ticket" items (cars, major appliances, houses). Households are encouraged to borrow to consolidate their debts arising from doctor and dentist bills or for vacation purposes. Such current expenditure financing is ordinarily not as important as capital expenditure financing.

In sophisticated households and large business corporations, the two activities of lending and borrowing are tied together. Households and corporations borrow in one market for the sake of lending in another. In the high-interest days of 1974, households even borrowed at low rates against the cash value of their life insurance and invested the money in time deposits or open-market securities yielding higher interest returns.

Businesses use funds to hire productive services, to buy outputs of other firms, and for capital (physical) and financial investment. Their sources of funds come from selling goods and final services and borrowing or from selling off their holdings of financial assets. Both businesses and households will hold cash assets, which are either money or readily convertible into money with little chance of capital loss from their sale. Being liquid in this way is a major objective of decision-making sectors. Otherwise, if their inflow of cash is below expectations, households or business firms with insufficient cash assets will find themselves in financial difficulties. One economic unit's lack of liquidity will thereby be transmitted to a second unit. The latter now will find itself short of cash unless its liquidity is adequate. This ripple effect can potentially affect an entire economy. As the lender of last resort the Fed attempts to frustrate such a ripple effect, as discussed in Chapters 13 and 22.

While dealing in financial claims is only part of the business of nonfinancial sectors (households, business), such claims are the exclusive interest of the financial sector. Their business is to lend borrowed funds. They are also able to follow a strategy not available to nonfinancial sectors. They can borrow short and lend long; i.e., they can promise to pay their creditors on short notice at the same time they lend for long periods. In contrast, nonfinancial sectors will generally match the maturities of their assets and liabilities; e.g., when businesses borrow short, it is for the purpose of acquiring short-term physical assets such as inventories. When the goods are sold, the loan is paid off. On the other hand, when they acquire fixed investments (plant and equipment) that pay for themselves only over a long period, they will issue stocks and bonds that have no maturity or long maturities respectively. Financial institutions would therefore seem to be inviting a serious liquidity problem when their sources of funds are cash assets for their creditors at the same time they are lending for fixed periods, sometimes 25–30 years (in the case of mortgage money). The safety cushion is that some of their creditors will be redepositing funds while others are making withdrawals. Financial institutions also have sufficient discretion over their assets and financial liabilities to remain liquid. As we shall see in Chapters 6 and 7, banks engage in asset and liability management to control the inflow of funds.

Flow-of-funds accounts

We have seen that sectors engage in transactions that bring in money and then spend it in another set of transactions. Between sectors, whenever one sector receives goods or money another is selling goods or paying out money. This interconnectedness disciplines our study of money and finance. We must build it into our analysis or there will be loose ends somewhere. These relations, called identities, are quantitative (can be represented numerically) and always hold. They underly the presentation of national and international transactions in the flow-of-funds accounts.

SOURCES AND USES OF FUNDS, DEBIT AND CREDIT ENTRIES   The transactions for a given player in the game are recorded in the statement for sources and uses of funds. This is a series of bookkeeping entries, each one a part of some transaction. For the word "uses," one might better substitute the word "debit" and for the word "sources," the word "credit." The language of debit and credit is preferred because sources and uses do not adequately describe the payment side of the transaction. The implication of uses of funds is that someone is getting rid of money, which is opposite to the idea of money being held. For this reason, uses of funds cannot accurately describe an increase in the money balances held by a sector. The word "debit," however, does apply to an increased holding of money because the latter represents an increase in a sector's assets. Uses of funds and an increase in money holdings are therefore both covered by the debit term. Similarly, a reduction in cash holdings is not adequately covered by sources of funds, since cash is flowing out and not in, as sources implies. The term "credit" encompasses both sources of funds and cash outflows, since the latter represents a reduction in assets and thus a credit (as discussed immediately below). The terminology of debit and credit records both the substantive part of the transaction (e.g., the sale of goods) and the receipt of payment for the goods (the increase in money balances).

The comprehensiveness of flow-of-funds statements in depicting the economic activities of a sector is a result of the statement combining the debit and credit transactions found in two ultimate financial statements, the income statement and the balance sheet. The former describes the current economic activities of an economic unit, the latter its financial position.

Debit entries on these two statements encompass expense items on the income statement and two types of balance sheet entries. If a person increases assets (including money holdings), the increase is a debit. One year's balance sheet will then show more assets than the previous year's. If you reduce your indebtedness, which is shown on the liabilities side of the balance sheet, this makes you better off in the same way as an increase in assets and it is also a debit entry. The word debit causes confusion because it has a different connotation when referring to the income statement than to the balance sheet. It is not a "nice" word when referring to the income statement because expenses make you worse off. But when the balance sheet is involved, the word has pleasant "vibes", indicating the acquisition of assets or the reduction of one's debts.

Corresponding to the three categories of debits are three kinds of credit transactions (with opposite overtones to the debit concept). The sale of a product or a productive service (such as wage income) will be a credit transaction on the income statement; but if you reduce your holdings of assets or borrow (increase your liabilities), these will appear as credit entries on the balance sheet. These six categories of debit and credit transactions exhaust all possible entries on the flow-of-funds statement. No matter what the entry is (whether we are recording the substantive part of the transaction or the means-of-payment side of the transaction), it can be recorded in one of these six ways.

To summarize, the six exhaustive types of entries in flow-of-funds statements are:

DEBIT	CREDIT
1. Purchase of goods and final services or purchase of productive services	1. Sales of goods and final services or sale of productive services
2. Increase in assets	2. Reduction in assets
3. Reduction or retirement of indebtedness	3. Borrowing (increase in financial liabilities)

The flow-of-funds statement for a single sector consists then of these six types of debit and credit entries. When joined to similar statements for other players, it produces a set of interlocking accounts. One sector's transaction entries lead to corresponding entries on the opposite side of the flow-of-funds statement for a second sector.

Let us say that one sector sells a radio worth $100 to a second sector. As illustrated in Table 1.1 when sector A sells to sector B, the sale will be a source of funds (credit) for sector A and a use of funds for sector B (debit). At the same time, A's cash holdings will increase (debit) and B's cash holdings will decrease (credit). The four bookkeeping entries explain why the flow of funds is called a quadruple-entry bookkeeping system.

Table 1.2 shows how the published flow-of-funds accounts would treat transactions between two sectors, A and B. Sector A sells $300 of goods and borrows $500. On the debit side it buys $400 of goods and lends $200. Each of these entries

Table 1.1. The flow of funds: A quadruple-entry accounting system

| Sector A | | | | Sector B | | |
Debit		Credit		Debit		Credit
Increase in money holdings from sale of radio	$100	Sale of radio to B	$100	Purchase of a radio from A	$100	Decrease in money holdings to pay for radio	$100
Total	$100	Total	$100		$100	Total	$100

Table 1.2. Flow-of-funds statement for two transactions between two sectors

| Sector A | | | | Sector B | | |
Debit		Credit		Debit		Credit
Purchase of goods	$400	Sale of goods	$300	Purchase of goods	$300	Sale of goods	$400
Acquisition of financial claims (lending)	200	Sale of financial claims (borrowing)	500	Acquisition of financial claims (lending)	500	Sale of financial claims (borrowing)	200
Net change in money holdings	200			Net change in money holdings	-200		
Total	$800	Total	$800		$600	Total	$600

describes the substantive part of a single transaction; so sector A has engaged in four transactions, each of which (if fully spelled out) would have a counterpart entry for changes in money holdings. Only one entry ($200) is shown for the change in money holdings. This is the net change and is arrived at by summing all the credit entries and subtracting the sum of the debit entries (except for the money item).

The story is similar for sector B. Only the substantive part of all its four transactions are recorded, with the net change in money holdings being the sum of the credits less the sum of the debits. Since the former exceed the latter by $200, the net change in money holdings for sector B is a minus $200. Unlike Table 1.1, we record this net change on the debit side but with a minus sign, which makes this entry equivalent to an entry on the credit side. This treatment is in keeping with the published accounts treatment.

Without the spelling out of the money side of each transaction, we may forget that each transaction has been settled for money. As a result, we may incorrectly interpret the published accounts as describing barter transactions between sectors. In barter, goods and financial claims would be swapped for goods and financial claims without benefit of money payments. Ours is a money exchange economy in which, for the most part, we sell something for money and then use the money to buy something else. This is what is meant by saying that money is a medium of exchange.

Nonetheless, the existence of barter must be recognized. We refer, not to the kind of goods swapping that takes place in flea markets, but to the swapping of financial claims for goods when goods are bought on credit. In this case, goods are acquired (bought) by one sector (a debit entry for this sector) and a financial liability incurred (credit). For the seller the entries are reversed; the sale of goods is a credit, and the financial claim (e.g., an increase in accounts receivable) is a debit entry. The two parties have swapped goods for financial claims. Sellers are willing to do this because they earn a return on the claim. Moreover, had they not accepted the financial claim, they might not have been able to sell the goods.

The kinds of transactions we have been discussing are bona fide, since they all involve two sectors. In addition, we must talk about "fake" transactions (i.e., internal bookkeeping transactions); e.g., when a business estimates the depreciation on its equipment, this expense item is an imputed (estimated) transaction, since no second firm is involved. Similarly, in calculating profits a business firm will (or should) consider what could have been earned on an alternative use of funds. This imputed amount is offset against accounting profits to arrive at an estimate of true economic profits. Thus economic profits can be negative when accounting profits are positive. To understand economic behavior, we must consider such imputed values.

STOCK (BALANCE SHEET) DIMENSION   The flow-of-funds statement is in part derived from changes in the balance sheet. Economic reasoning in balance sheet terms has probably been commoner than emphasis on the flow dimension. Balance sheets show the economic position of a transactor at a point of time, in contrast with the flow of funds depicting transactions taking place over a period of time. Thus one can think of every flow-of-funds statement as sandwiched between an opening and closing balance sheet. The difference between the two balance sheets will reflect flow-of-funds transactions.

A hypothetical opening balance sheet (Table 1.3) has been constructed with Table 1.1 in mind. The end-of-period (closing) balance sheet values reflect the transactions of Table 1.1.

Table 1.3.   Balance sheets for two sectors

	Sector A			Sector B	
Assets		Liabilities and net worth	Assets		Liabilities and net worth
Physical assets (PA)	$1000	Financial liabilities (FL)	$ 500	PA	$3000	FL	$ 400
Financial assets (FA)	400	Net worth (NW)	900	FA	500	NW	3100
Total	$1400	Total	$1400		$3500	Total	$3500
End-of-period values							
PA	$ 900	FL	$ 500	PA	$3100	FL	$ 400
FA	500	NW	900	FA	400	NW	3100
Total	$1400	Total	$1400		$3500	Total	$3500

The balance sheet records levels of assets (A) and liabilities (L) and their difference, net worth (NW); i.e. $A - L = NW$. In the simplified example of Table 1.3 the totals and net worths for each sector remain unchanged. One sector's financial assets have increased at the expense of its physical assets and vice versa for the second sector. A more comprehensive flow-of-funds statement would include a sector's productive activity, with the resultant profits affecting net worth. We illustrate this in Table 1.4 for a single sector.

The flow-of-funds statement has now been broken into a current account and

Table 1.4. An increase in net worth, sector A (business firm)

Opening balance sheet, January 1, 1985

Assets		Liabilities	
Physical assets	$1000	Financial liabilities	$ 500
Financial assets	400	Net worth	900
Financial claims $300			
Money holdings $100			
Total	$1400	Total	$1400

Flow-of-funds statement, 1985, current account

Debit		Credit	
Inputs (labor, raw materials, etc.)	$1000	Sales	$2000
Saving	1000		

Capital account

Assets		Liabilities	
Increase in physical assets	$ 100	Saving	$1000
Increase in financial claims (lending)	1200	Increase in financial liabilities (borrowing)	500
Net increase in money holdings	200		

Closing balance sheet, December 31, 1985

Assets		Liabilities	
Physical assets	$1100	Financial liabilities	$1000
Financial assets	1800	Net worth	1900
Financial claims $1500			
Money holdings 300			
Total	$2900	Total	$2900

a capital account. The former records transactions found on the income statement; the latter shows changes in balance sheet items. The chief advantage of this separation is that it identifies increases in net worth with current saving. The latter in turn represents a residual value, the difference between expenses and income from sales. A similar flow-of-funds statement could be drawn up for any sector (e.g., the household sector). In this case current household expenses would replace business expense.

The disadvantage of the saving concept is that in the theoretical literature (following the work of the illustrious British economist John Maynard Keynes) it has taken on the meaning of a leakage. As can be seen from the capital account statement, saving and borrowing are allocated to physical assets and financial claims. Only to the extent that it results in increases in money holdings would we regard saving as a leakage. (This is extensively discussed in Chapters 2 and 19.) It should be noted that if one consolidated the current and capital account, the saving item would be eliminated and only legitimate transactions would be recorded.

The economic significance of the balance sheet is that players in the game are influenced by balance sheet values. Such influence, when it concentrates on the household's net worth figure, is called the wealth effect. The greater the household's net worth, the greater its spending on current consumption or the acquisition of physical assets. Either the household will add less to financial assets out of current income, will sell off some financial assets, or even increase its borrowing because of the wealth effect. In any case the sources of funds for increased spending are expanded. For business sectors an increase in net worth may similarly stimulate an increase in expenditures.

However, we should stress that the wealth effect must work through a flow-of-funds effect. The credit side of the flow-of-funds statement will be enlarged, thus increasing the supply of finance for current or capital expenditures. Or alternatively, the wealth effect works via the debit side; the decision maker adds less to financial assets than before, thus facilitating greater expenditures out of current income.

Accounting matrix

To appreciate the architecture of the flow of funds, we must consolidate sectors and their transactions into a single table. The table must be drawn up in such a way that it satisfies a number of rules (identities). These constraints provide us with sufficient information to determine the values of some transactions from the known values of others. We also know that in predicting values for some future period the identities must be satisfied. The forecast must be consistent.

In Table 1.5, transaction categories are shown across the rows, sectors down the columns. This is a summary table, even though more detailed than earlier ones.

Table 1.5. An abbreviated flow-of-funds table with numerical values (hypothetical data; $bil.)

Transaction category	Private domestic nonfinancial sector		Government sector		Financial intermediaries sector		Rest-of-the-world sector		Totals		Memo: domestic totals	
	Dr[a]	Cr[a]	Dr	Cr	Dr	Cr	Dr	Cr	Dr	Cr	Dr	Cr
Nonfinancial												
1. Saving		179	-18 [10]			5		4 [-4]		170		166 [174]
2. Capital outlays	170		...		...		...		170		170	
Financial												
3. Net financial investment	9		-18 [-10]			5		4 [-4]		0		-4 [4]
4. Total financial uses and sources (line 5 + line 6)	69	60	5	23 [15]	70	65	11 [3]	7	155 [147]	155 [147]	144 [144]	148 [140]
5. Deposits at financial intermediaries	50			3		55	2		55	55	53	55
6. Loans and securities	19	60	2	23 [15]	70	10	9 [1]	7	100	100	91	93

Source: Based on FRB 1980a Table 1.3. Brackets indicate original figures found in the source.
[a]Dr = debit; Cr = credit.

The initial nonfinancial transactions of saving and investment are rearrangements of the saving and investment figures found in the more familiar national income and product accounts. Saving for each sector is reached by subtracting its outlays for consumption or operating expenses (the latter apply to business and government) from current income receipts (which, for the government sector, would largely be taxes).

Capital outlays equal the sector's physical investment (housing, consumer durables, plant and equipment, inventories). Saving and capital outlays are equal for the entire economy, including the rest-of-the-world sector. This equality of saving and capital outlays over all sectors, which is a major tenet of the income and product accounts, is our first identity. Thus saving, $179 + (-18) + 5 + 4 = 170$, which equals capital outlays, 170.

The saving for the rest of the world (4) reflects the net value of transactions between the rest of the world and the domestic economy. This value tells us that the U.S. domestic economy was making $4 bil. less financial investment in the rest of the world than the latter was making in the U.S. domestic economy. If we exclude the positive saving of the rest of the world, we arrive at the domestic total (in the last column), which consequently will be $4 bil. lower ($166 bil.).

A second identity underlying the matrix is the equality of credits (sources of funds) and debits (uses of funds) for each sector. Alternative totals can be estimated depending on the degree of netting (the extent to which credit and debit values are offset against each other); e.g., on a gross basis, total financial uses for the private domestic nonfinancial sector would be 69, which added on to capital outlays gives a total of 239. This total is equal to saving (179) plus financial sources (60). If financial sources are offset against financial uses in line 4 to give net financial investment of 9, this amount plus capital outlays of 170 equals 179, which is the smaller amount of sources of funds via saving.

The saving-investment identity for individual sectors (the netted version of the second identity) differs from that for all sectors combined. Now net financial investment must be added on to a sector's capital outlays for the identity with saving to hold for the individual sector. For all sectors, net financial investment is zero, as can be seen by totaling the values across line 3. Thus for all sectors, saving equals capital outlays (the initial identity).

Lines 5 and 6 of Table 1.5 spell out the lender-borrower characteristics of each sector; e.g., the nonfinancial sector was a net lender, but at the same time it was a borrower via loans and securities of 60. This borrowing is offset against the total of financial uses, deposits at financial intermediaries (50), and loans and securities (19).

Unlike the nonfinancial sector (which subtracts only current outlays from income in estimating saving), for the government sector the prevailing accounting practice is to subtract all outlays. The deficit of 18 (saving $= -18$) shown for the government sector thus overstates the true deficit, since some government outlays deserve to be treated as capital outlays (e.g., highway construction, new government buildings).

Corresponding to negative saving of -18 for the government sector is -18 of net financial investment. Thus the underlying sector identity holds, with net financial uses of funds being -18 and net sources (saving) being a similar amount. Despite its deficit position, the government lends directly (line 6) and indirectly via financial institutions (line 5). Its total borrowing (including borrowing to finance the deficit) exceeds its lending, thus explaining the negative overall value of -18.

The saving ($5 bil.) of the next sector (financial intermediaries) makes it possible for them to lend $5 bil. more than they borrow $(70 - 65)$. Finally, the rest-of-the-world sector, like the government sector, acquires financial assets in excess of its surplus (saving) as shown in lines 5 and 6.

The equality of sources and uses across financial transaction rows (lines 5 and

6 and summary line 4) makes a third category of identities. This identity follows from a financial debit being a corresponding credit on another sector's account. In an overall sense, taking all sectors together (considering them as one huge sector), finance cancels out. Financial uses and sources would be internal to this consolidated sector, so they lose their character as financial claims. Zero net financial investment for all sectors combined as shown in the second-to-last total column (line 3) is another way of seeing that finance disappears.

Net financial investment is a key line for checking on the accuracy of any flow-of-funds matrix. Whether we begin with financial flows (below line 3) and work up to line 3 or begin with nonfinancial flows and work down, we should secure the same answer for this row.

A good way of seeing the interrelationship of sectors and their transactions is to change one of the cell values in the matrix. It will quickly be discovered that many more cell values must be changed if the constraints are to be satisfied. Changing a cell value will throw a transaction and sector balance out of kilter, requiring compensating adjustments along the transaction row and down the column sector, which in turn will lead to other transactions and sectoral adustments. Table 1.5 illustrates these adjustments. The bracketed figures suggest that saving by the rest of the world is negative, which is a misleading picture of today's world. By changing the figures for the government deficit (-18 instead of -10) at the same time that rest-of-the-world saving is increased by 8 (from -4 to $+4$), adjustments in the cells are reduced to a minimum. While these are the easiest adjustments to make, they also have the ring of truth. In part, a growing U.S. deficit has been financed by increased rest-of-the-world purchase of the U.S. government debt (line 6).

Looking at the economy as a whole, the temptation is to say that finance does not matter because it cancels out. At best, it might be claimed that the financial strip shows how saving finances other sectors' expenditures. To this extent, the identities underlying the accounts are misleading. The level of economic activity itself and thus the volume of saving and investment will depend on some financial stimulus. Finance creates income and wealth rather than being a mere conduit for saving. To understand the dynamic role of finance, we must interpret the flow of funds. We must formulate hypotheses and develop an analytical framework. We begin doing this in Chapter 2.

Keeping abreast of the times

The world is one gigantic communications network, and if the sphere was too much with us in bygone days, it is much more so today. The pressing problem might seem to be one of fending off the news rather than being on top of every daily crisis. But there is no escaping reality, and in keeping up with money and finance we should try to minimize our information costs.

NEWSPAPERS   The daily press is the logical beginning point. From newspapers we get a sense of new disturbances and the ripple effects from previous ones. Oil prices, petrodollar recycling, inflation, interest rates, the stock market, unemployment, bank failures, depression, cities on the verge of bankruptcy, and growth in the money supply are familiar topics. Most city newspapers do a creditable job of informing, but the *New York Times* is in a class by itself. Each weekday edition devotes several pages to financial news. The weighty Sunday edition has an entire section devoted to finance. The Sunday *Magazine* of the *New York Times* frequently has articles dealing with the economic situation or leading personalities. The *Wall Street Journal* is a well-known financial daily with more comprehensive data on commodity and financial markets. A great amount of coverage is given to individual firms. Nevertheless, many articles deal with macro aspects of money and finance.

ECONOMIC LETTERS AND REVIEWS   Publications with less pressing deadlines than newspapers have more analysis. The major banks publish regular economic letters, although many are now beginning to charge for them because of rising costs. Still available free upon written request is Manufacturers Hanover Trust, *Economic Report.*

The greatest riches are bestowed by the 12 Federal Reserve Banks and the Board of Governors of the Federal Reserve System (Federal Reserve Board). The Fed generously dispenses financial wisdom to anyone interested. Spending money on the widespread dissemination of financial information and analysis is the alternative to returning Fed profits (from holdings of U.S. government securities) to the U.S. Treasury. The U.S. Treasury imposes a tax on the Federal Reserve notes issued by the 12 Banks, so calculated that most of the profits earned are turned over to the U.S. government. Each Bank publishes its monthly, bimonthly, or quarterly *Review.* A *Weekly Letter* is published by the San Francisco Bank on a single topic such as inflation or deposit insurance. Cleveland publishes *Economic Commentary,* again on a single topic.

The Federal Reserve Board (at the pinnacle of the Federal Reserve System) publishes the monthly *Federal Reserve Bulletin* containing formal statements by Board members, descriptive articles, and extensive financial statistics. The latter are graphed in the current and historical *Chart Books*. The *Bulletin* and the *Chart Books* have a cost, but article reprints for the *Bulletin* and other materials prepared by the Board are free. The Board's current publication list will be found in the back of each monthly issue.

The uniqueness of the *Reviews* is due to a felicitous blend of scholarship and good writing. Most of the articles are written by Ph.D.s and readability is assured by tough editing. The *Reviews* initially had a regional interest with an emphasis on regional data. They were designed to keep member banks posted on district developments. Now the regional data mainly gets published separately. While a regional interest continues, all the *Reviews* discuss national issues. In part the articles are conduits for scholarly literature; they make technical economic ideas more accessible. The *Reviews* also contribute to this scholarly literature. Perhaps the *Review* of the Federal Reserve Bank of St. Louis and the *New England Economic Review* (Federal Reserve Bank of Boston) are the most original.

In addition to its *Review,* the Federal Reserve Bank of St. Louis publishes a useful series of statistical releases. These cover the federal budget, the balance of payments, U.S. financial data (interest yields), annual U.S. economic data (compounded rates of change for monetary and business indicators), monetary trends, rates of change in economic data for ten industrial countries, and national economic trends (prices, production, employment). On the international level a comparable publication to the *Reviews* is *Finance and Development,* published quarterly by the International Monetary Fund and the World Bank group.

Addresses for obtaining free publications are given at the end of the References.

SCHOLARLY JOURNALS   More rigorous than the *Reviews* but with longer lead time between the event and its analysis are the scholarly journals, although their increasingly mathematical quality might discourage the student. This reflects the maturing of economics rather than any intellectual snobbery. It is hoped the student will take the time to look through some of the main journals. These include the *Journal of Money, Credit and Banking, Journal of Finance, Journal of Financial and Quantitative Analysis,* and *Journal of Monetary Economics.* Major journals that are more general in their coverage but have many articles in the money and finance area are the *American Economic Review, Journal of Political Economy, Quarterly Journal of Economics, Economic Journal* (British), *Economic Enquiry, Southern Economic Journal,* and *Brookings Papers on Economic Activity.* The latter is noteworthy because it is a scholarly journal consciously attempting to overcome the long lead time characteristic of the others.

A useful guide to the scholarly literature is the extensive bibliography found in the quarterly *Journal of Economic Literature.* Books and journal articles in all branches of economics, including monetary economics, are cited and annotated in this journal. A quarterly annotated bibliography limited to books is *Economic Books,* published at the University of Pittsburgh. With an even longer lead time are books on money and finance. Here we suggest browsing through the appropriate section of the library.

Review questions

1. Identify the economic sectors by name and recognize the major role or function of each.

2. Identify the three kinds of debit and credit entries and explain why the language of debit and credit is superior to that of sources and uses of funds.

3. Distinguish between the income statement and the balance sheet. How are they combined into a flow-of-funds statement?

4. List the identities underlying the flow-of-funds matrix in Table 1.5.

5. How does net financial investment function as a bridge between a sector's financial and nonfinancial transactions?

6. Why is finance important even though it cancels out for the economy as a whole?

7. Define:

Assets	Identities
Liabilities	Interlocking accounts
Current expenditures	Quadruple entry accounting system
Physical investment	Imputed transactions
Financial investment	Barter
Liquidity	

2

Genesis of the
gross national product

The gross national product (GNP) refers to the nation's output of goods and services. This is made up of household purchases (current and capital expenditures), business purchases (capital expenditures such as plant and equipment, inventories), government expenditures, and net exports. As stressed in Chapter 1, such expenditures depend on sources of funds (credits) that fall into three categories: income (receipts from the sale of productive services in the case of households, receipts from the sale of products in the case of business), borrowing, and the sell-off of assets. The income source is generated by the sector's own economic actions and for this reason is referred to as internal finance. The other two sources are referred to as external finance.

Expenditures in general depend on these sources of funds. Expenditures can also increase at the expense of increases in financial assets (a debit item). Instead of adding a given sum to financial investment, we may add less. With sources of funds staying the same, we can thereby increase our spending. Particular categories of expenditures can increase at the expense of others (e.g., travel expenditures at the expense of education).

Our hypothesis is that credit (external finance) is the key to spending on the GNP. While income is a major condition for spending, income, we assert, can only increase in the first place because of an extra shot of credit. First, we explore the possible linkages among sources and uses of funds. Next, we discuss the role of credit in a growing economy. This forces us in turn to go behind external finance and enquire into the role of money as the ultimate disturbance factor. The empirical evidence for a relationship between external finance and spending is explored in separate sections.

Establishing a linkage between credit and expenditures leaves the question of discretion unanswered. A brief discussion of the respective possibilities that lenders and borrowers exercise discretion leads us into a final discussion of borrowers substituting among alternative financial sources of funds.

16

Linking sources and uses of funds

The possible linkages between sources and uses of funds of the nonfinancial sector are illustrated in Figure 2.1 (using the figures of Table 1.5). Arrow 1 shows that the nonfinancial sector's saving may finance its capital outlays directly. This is referred to as internal finance. Arrow 2 links saving with increases in financial assets (sector lending). This link indicates that the sector is financing its lending out of its saving, a second case of internal finance. Arrow 3 relates external finance (sector borrowing) to its capital expenditures. Arrow 4 demonstrates the possibility that a sector may borrow to acquire financial assets. Lending is financed externally.

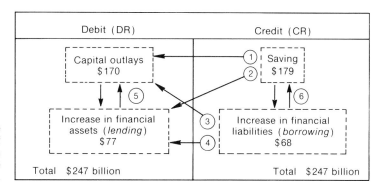

2.1. Linking the credits (sources of funds) and the debits (uses of funds) of the nonfinancial sector.

Other linkages on the debit and credit sides can affect expenditures. Capital outlays can increase at the expense of lending (linkage 5). A decrease in lending (less being added to financial assets than formerly) means that more spending is possible. On the other hand, an increase in saving may be at the expense of current borrowing, implying less expenditures than suggested by the increase in saving (linkage 6).

Figure 2.1 can be expanded in two substantial directions. First, we can substitute decreases in financial asset holdings (which we call financial dissaving) for increases in financial liabilities and repeat the analysis. Now we are talking about the selling of financial assets, not simply adding less to financial assets. Less important would be the sell-off of physical assets. Second, in the place of capital outlays we could substitute expenditures in general (including current expenditures), requiring that we substitute the broader concept of income in the place of saving.

Money in a growing economy

Assume a growing economy whose productive capacity is expanding, with expenditures steadily growing. Financial flows must also be growing steadily to finance the necessary increase in expenditures. What is the source of additional finance? It must be new money creation or a more active use of existing money. Money is the unique disturbance variable and also the unique leakage variable. The borrower may swap IOUs for additional purchases of goods and services, but increased production at some point in the process will require business firms to make additional cash outlays for the inputs (e.g., labor) that they hire.

Three different growth states can be distinguished. The first, the no-growth state, would be stationary where lending and borrowing could take place for consumption purposes only. The second would have constant net investment so that growth would be taking place at a steady pace. Borrowing would finance investment, and the nonfinancial sector would be lending out of current income. But the level of income increases with the capacity expansion caused by investment. The higher level of transactions associated with this higher level of income will increase the demand for money balances. Unless prices fall so that the same money buys a larger output, additional money will be demanded. This is the significance of the banking system; banks have a unique capacity for self-finance through money creation. Finally, the demand for money becomes more intense if the investment rate is a growing one. This represents the third growth state. Both income and money demand are growing at an increasing rate.

When increased expenditures are financed by banks, they subsequently become income for another transactor, who in turn spends or lends income. But one other allocation takes place. Each economic unit adds to the average holdings of money for the purpose of financing the additional transactions. Such additions on the average must be seen as leakages from the payment stream; funds are not being transmitted to another economic unit. The process of economic expansion will continue until desired increases in money holdings for all spending units match the initial monetary disturbance.

The following sequence of flow-of-funds statements illustrates the multiplier effects of the money disturbance. Two sectors are shown in Table 2.1, the nonfinancial and the bank. The bank sector performs an intermediary function, as shown by its borrowing (e.g., time deposits), and also a money-creating function. In period 1 the nonfinancial sector is assumed to spend 80% of its income of $100 and to lend 20% to the bank sector, which then relends it to members of the nonfinancial sector. The latter's borrowing finances nonfinancial expenditures.

Table 2.1. Flow-of-funds adjustment after a monetary disturbance

	Nonfinancial sector				Bank sector	
	Debit		Credit		Debit	Credit
Period 1	Expenditures (E)	100	Income (Y)	100		
	Loans (L)	20	Borrowing (B)	20	Loans (L) 20	Borrowing (B) 20
Period 2	E	100	Y	100	L 30	B 20
	L	20	B	30		ΔM 10
	ΔM	10				
Period 3	E	110	Y	100	L 20	B 20
	L	20	B	20		
	ΔM	-10	or (ΔM 10)			
Period 4	E	119	Y	110	L 22	B 22
	L	22	B	22		
	ΔM	-9	or (ΔM 9)			
Period 5	E	127.1	Y	119	L 23.8	B 23.8
	L	23.8	B	23.8		
	ΔM	-8.1	or (ΔM 8.1)			
Period n	E	200	Y	200	L 40	B 40
	L	40	B	40		
	ΔM	-0	or (ΔM 0)			

This steady state is disturbed in period 2 by an extra $10 of lending by the banking sector, financed by an increase in the money supply. The credit entry ΔM may stretch credulity at this point but nonetheless is an accurate way of describing the process of bank lending. Banks do indeed make paper bookkeeping entries that function as money. Chapter 6 explains the process. The corresponding entries in the nonfinancial sector account are an increase in borrowing and an increase in money holdings.

In period 3 the nonfinancial sector dishoards the extra $10 of money holdings, since the purpose of its borrowing was to increase spending. In period 4 income has increased (the expenditures of one period become the income of the next). Nonbank lending and borrowing expand to $22, intermediated by the banking sector. Desired money holdings now increase. Assume that the nonfinancial sector wishes to hold 10% of its income in the form of additional money holdings (to finance additional transactions). Additional desired money holdings equal $1 (10% of the increased income of $10). As a result, in period 4 excess money holdings (the difference between the extra $10 of money holdings and the extra $1 this sector wishes to hold) will decline to $9. Nine dollars of dishoarding in period 4 increase spending by the same amount. Period 5 is a further illustration of the process, and period n indicates the long-run adjustment. Expenditures have reached an equilibrium level, since the initial increase in money holdings of $10 is voluntarily held by the nonfinancial sector. With no further dishoarding taking place, income stays at the $200 level. The simple rule of thumb to determine the limits to income expansion is to multiply the $10 money increase by the reciprocal of the desired ratio of money to income, which is 10%. Thus income will rise by 10 × $10 above its original $100 level.

This analysis is based on a one-shot increase in the money supply. If the money supply grows by $10 in every period, after n periods the cumulative effects of money increases will be responsible for expenditures and income increasing by $100 in every single period. In each period, borrowing and lending (apart from the $10 of bank lending financed in every period by money creation) will regularly grow by $20.

If money becomes more active, the effect is the same as if the money stock increases. In Table 2.1 replace the banking sector with a nonbank institution, say an insurance company. In period 2, ΔM stands for financial sector dishoarding (a reduction in money balances). Such dishoardings are a credit entry in the same way as an increase in the money supply. The period analysis proceeds as before. Again, regular dishoarding of $10 in every period would ultimately be responsible for expenditures and income increasing by $100 in every single period. Similarly, borrowing and lending (apart from the $10 of nonbank lending financed by dishoarding) will regularly grow by $20 in every period.

More realistically, dishoarding would originate in the nonfinancial sector. Now the expenditure effect is quicker. What is shown in Table 2.1 as a period 3 effect occurs in the disturbance period (period 2). Members of the nonfinancial sector finance increased spending ($110) by reducing their money holdings. The same sequence beginning with former period 4 (now period 3) follows.

The nonfinancial sector (households, businesses), instead of financing expenditures by dishoarding, may increase the amount loaned. They may lend to each other, or they may lend through a financial intermediary. In the first case, the entries for period 2 for the nonfinancial sector will be as follows:

Debit		Credit	
E	100	Y	100
L	30	B	30
ΔM	10	ΔM	10

Dishoarding of $10 on the credit side finances extra lending of $10, which means that borrowing goes up by this amount. Corresponding to this increased borrowing will be increased money holdings of $10. The sequence is then as described beginning with period 3.

With financial intermediation the entries in period 2 are as follows:

Debit		Credit		Debit		Credit	
E	100	Y	100	L	20	B	30
L	30	B	20	ΔM	10[a]		
		ΔM	10				

[a] This entry is literally correct if a nonbank financial institution is the intermediary. In the case of a commercial bank, effective reserves will be increased (rather than money holdings) with similar consequences.

Now the period 2 entries in Table 2.1 become period 3 entries, and all the periods are moved back in this way.

We can rank monetary disturbances in terms of the speed of impact on the GNP. The quickest route is when households and businesses deplete their cash balances. Banks lending on the basis of money creation and direct lending by the nonfinancial sector financed by dishoarding are tied for second. The least rapid would be dishoarding by the nonfinancial sector intermediated by the financial sector.

Equation of exchange

The significance of monetary disturbances is the basis of the famous equation of exchange. It should be distinguished from the quantity theory, which is derived from the equation; it is an identity as opposed to a theory. The equation of exchange brings together four key variables: output (Y), prices (P), money (M), and the velocity of money (V). Output equals income on the national level, so the same symbol Y can be used for both variables. Velocity measures the rate of turnover of money and is an average applied to the entire money supply. Velocity is customarily more than one in value, which means that a dollar gets spent more than once on the national output. The equation takes the form $MV = PY = GNP$. The quantity of money times its velocity (left-hand side of the identity) equals total spending, which equals the monetary value of output and income (right-hand side). The equation highlights the financial side of economic activity. Money and its turnover are necessary conditions for physical output to have a certain monetary value.

To illustrate this important identity we apply it to 1983 data. The total GNP in 1972 dollars was $1572 bil. The money stock was $535 bil. The index number of prices was 2.186 (1972 base year). The income velocity of money was ($1572 bil. × 2.186)/$535 bil. = 6.423.

$$MV = PY$$
$$(\$535 \text{ bil.})(6.423) = (\$1572 \text{ bil.})(2.186) \text{ or } \$3436 \text{ bil.}$$

A stronger statement would be that money and its velocity are sufficient conditions for the GNP. Now a theory is being asserted. Such a statement says that MV is always responsible for PY without the possibility of the reverse being true (i.e., an increase in GNP leading to an increase in MV). It therefore denies that the producing and consuming sectors of the economy can exert their own effects on MV. Since it can be wrong, the sufficient condition statement is a theory rather than an identity.

The well-known quantity theory of money makes an even stronger statement. The quantity theory assumes that the quantity of money determines PY. Stated mathematically, PY is a function of M: $PY = f(M)$. Not only is the influence of PY on MV denied, but also the influence of velocity. The stability of velocity is maintained by monetarists, the quantity theorists of our day. As previously indicated, however, dishoarding by the nonfinancial sector has the effect of making money more active (i.e., increasing its velocity). The data on velocity demonstrates considerable variability over the business cycle, rising in recovery periods and declining in recession (see Higgins 1978:15ff.). The long-run upward movement in GNP velocity is shown in Figure 2.2.

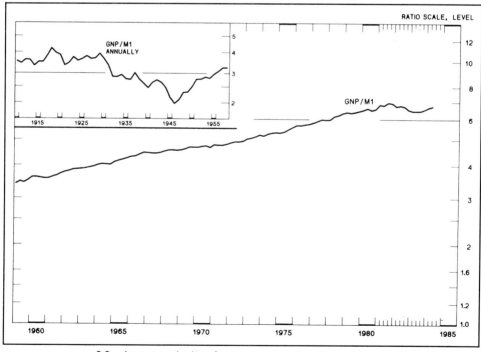

2.2.   Income velocity of money, seasonally adjusted quarterly. (FRB 1984a:5)

Accepting *MV* as a necessary condition means that a growth in money flows depends on a growth in the money supply or an increase in its velocity. Without an increase in physical output, however, increases in money flows will be nominal rather than real. This describes inflation, i.e., higher price tags for the same volume of goods and services.

Borrowing-spending linkage

Our own theory asserts a strong positive relation between borrowing and spending. When sectors borrow, they do so to increase their spending (arrow 3 in Fig. 2.1). The statistical data bear this out; borrowing moves with spending.

Figure 2.3 depicts the relationship between private net capital outlays (business investment in plant and equipment and inventories, residential construction) and borrowing (household and business). The figure is based on quarterly data that has been massaged to clarify the underlying relationships. The per capita growth trend in the GNP has been eliminated from all the series so that a rising curve means a growth rate faster than the per capita GNP trend rate; a falling curve means that the time series is increasing at a slower pace than the GNP trend rate. The data is further adjusted for seasonal variations and price changes. The quarterly figures are multiplied by four to give an annual seasonally adjusted rate (FRB 1980a:11, 23). *P* and *T* denote peaks and troughs in the business cycle as chronicled by the National Bureau of Economic Research.

Our theory suggests that borrowing and net capital outlays will be closely related. Figure 2.3 illustrates the parallel movements in both series. The changed relationship between the curves after 1975, when the borrowing curve rises above

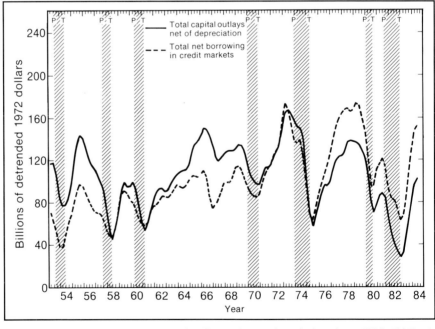

2.3. Borrowing and capital outlays. (FRB 1985b:13)

22

the net capital outlay curve, suggests an increase in purely financial transactions (e.g., business takeovers), borrowing by households (e.g., to finance consumption expenditures), and a sharp increase in depreciation charges.

Money and spending

Our theory also suggests that money and spending will be closely related. This is borne out by Figure 2.4, which covers 70 years. During this period, $M1$ is the narrowly defined money supply, including demand deposits and currency outside banks. The data in Figure 2.4 are highly aggregative, contributing to the appearance of parallel movement. A more detailed scale would better reveal disparities in movements owing to variations in income velocity. As earlier discussion in this chapter indicates, additions to the money supply exert their influence on income primarily through the influence of money on external finance.

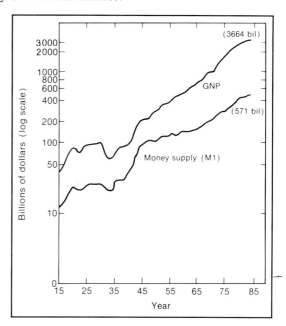

2.4. Gross national product and money supply, 1915–84. (Eastburn and Hoskins 1978:4; *Fed. Res. Bull.* 1985a:A13, A51; President 1984:242, 291)

A more precise way of relating spending and borrowing: The regression equation

Figure 2.3 evaluated the relationship between borrowing and spending by drawing curves for each of these variables. Each curve showed the behavior of a variable (a measurable quantity that can change in value) over time. Depending on the closeness of the movements in the curves, the variables are strongly or weakly related.

TECHNIQUE   But we would like to know more than this. By how much will one variable change when a second variable changes first? This can be determined by fitting a regression equation to the data. A regression equation begins with an economic theory or hypothesis. This hypothesis is next formulated in mathematical form. Finally, by statistical analysis the mathematical symbols are converted into numbers. By means of these numbers one can measure the effect of the right-hand variables in the equation on the left-hand variable. The right-hand variables are called independent variables; the left-hand variable is called the dependent variable.

Suppose one theorizes that consumption expenditures by households depend on their income. This can be stated in mathematical form. Thus we may first state that C is a function of Y: $C = f(Y)$, where C = consumption and Y = income. (This is the famous Keynesian consumption function discussed in Ch. 19.) However, this equation is not explicit, since it does not show the way in which changes in income change consumption. We can state the equation in explicit form: $C = a + bY$. The relationship between income and consumption is linear in this statement. The a and b symbols are parameters or coefficients. The a coefficient tells us what the value of consumption is if the value of income is zero. The b coefficient tells us how much consumption would change if income changed by $1 or $1 bil. If we measure the change in income in billions or trillions, consumption must also be measured in those amounts.

The a and b coefficients can next be quantified by fitting the explicit mathematical equation to the statistical data. This is done by regression analysis and the result is a regression equation. The resultant equation may be $C = 50 + 0.8Y$, which states that when income is zero, consumption (in a given period) would be $50 bil. If income was $1 tril., consumption would be 0.8 of $1 tril. or $800 bil. plus $50 bil., or $850 bil. The b coefficient, as previously stated, has the additional function of measuring the changes in the dependent variable with a given change in the independent variable. Thus a $1 bil. change in income will lead to an $800 mil. change in consumption expenditures.

REGRESSION EQUATION   The following regression equation expresses GNP as a function of borrowing by the private nonfinancial sectors (RTC) and by the government sectors (RTG). The values of the variables have been deflated for price changes so they are real values.

$$\text{RGNP} = 135.825 + 3.90372 \text{ RTC} + 2.41391 \text{ RTG}$$

	[22.6247]	[14.3395]	[5.53106]
1952:1–1976:2	$R^2 = 0.7432$	D/W = 1.2843	

The figures in brackets below the coefficients are the t-ratios, which are the ratios of the coefficients to the standard errors of the variables. The lower the value of the standard errors, the more reliable the coefficients. In contrast to the interpretation of the standard errors, the larger the t-ratios, the more confidence we can have in these coefficients. A rule of thumb is that the t-ratios should have at least a value of 2 before taking them seriously.

The equation presents the average relationship for the period of 1952 first quarter to 1976 second quarter. On the average, a $1 bil. increase in private borrowing will increase output by $3.9 bil. and a $1 bil. increase in public borrowing will increase output by $2.4 bil. The fact that the coefficients exceed 1 in value indicates that credit has a multiplier effect on income. The growth in income generated by credit will feed on itself in a circular flow fashion.

The ability of the right-hand variables to explain variations in the left-hand variable is summarized in the value R^2, the coefficient of multiple determination. The value cannot exceed 1, and the closer it is, the better the explanation. The value here (0.7432) is respectable.

The D/W statistic (named after its authors Durbin and Watson) measures the correlation between the successive residuals of the equation (this is called serial correlation). The residuals are the difference between the values of the dependent variable as estimated by the equation and their actual values. Serial correlation poses a problem in interpreting econometric equations. Low values of this statistic (below 2) suggest that some important explanatory variables may have been left out. Since the econometricians would have put them in if they knew them, they typically shrug their shoulders and move on.

Regression equations are now a standard tool in monetary economics. The ultimate kind of understanding we want is quantitative, and it is provided by these equations. Regression equations with independent variables that are dependent variables in a second equation constitute an econometric model. The explained variables in such a model are referred to as endogenous variables. The disturbances that trigger the model and cause the endogenous variables to change in value are known as the exogenous variables. Chapter 25 will consider such models.

Cyclical behavior of borrowing and spending

The GNP spending and sums raised in credit markets rise and fall with the business cycle. The ratio of borrowing to spending also rises in expansion times and declines in recession as shown in Figure 2.5. Net new equity issues are included in borrowing.

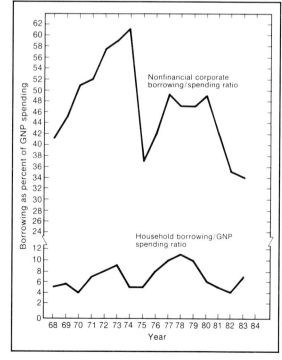

2.5.   Household and business borrowing ratios. (FRB 1984d)

Behind the cyclical behavior of the borrowing-spending ratio lie two different ratios, that of capital expenditures to GNP spending and of borrowing to investment. Both ratios move in the same direction in most years, thus intensifying the relationship between borrowing and GNP. The corporate ratio, while declining in the expansion year 1983 because of a sharp increase in internal funds (depreciation charges), turns up in 1984, joining the household sector in the expansion (not shown in Fig. 2.5).

Although only clearly visible in 1974 and 1975 in the annual data in Figure 2.5, there are several reasons why an earlier decline might be expected in the household ratio as compared with the business ratio. Business initially formulates its investment plans on the basis of favorable business sales. When cash flows slump because of consumer retrenching, business must maintain its borrowing in the short run. Monetary policy offers a supplementary explanation. Policies that are expansionary and restrictive have their initial effects on household borrowing. Flow of funds into financial institutions that accompany easier financial conditions benefit households buying homes or consumer durables. When credit gets tighter, business is a favored financial customer and is better able to absorb higher interest costs for inventories and fixed investment (Cacy and Hamblin 1974:9–10).

Question of discretion

So far our interest has been in relating external finance to GNP spending. External finance is generated by the interaction of borrowers and lenders. On the borrowing side, plans to borrow are conditioned by plans to spend. Some of the influences are expectations as to the future state of the economy, recent changes in saving flows, the price level, and the cost of borrowing. On the supply-of-credit side of the market, the volume of lending is chiefly influenced by saving flows, i.e., high-powered money (bank reserves) supplied through the central bank, and again the interest rate. These influences can be stated in symbolic form:

$$TCd \overset{+\quad -\quad\;-\quad+\;-}{=\; f(EXP,\ HS1,\ BS1,\ P,\ r)}$$

$$TCs \overset{+\quad\;+\quad+}{=\; f(GS,\ BR,\ r)}$$

where TCd = demand for credit
EXP = expectations
$HS1$ = change in household saving in the previous period
$BS1$ = change in business saving in the previous period
P = price level
r = market rate of interest
TCs = supply of credit
GS = gross saving flow
BR = change in bank reserves

The variables on the right-hand side are expected to influence the left-hand dependent variable in the direction shown by the sign above the symbols. The demand for credit is expected to increase when business expectations become more

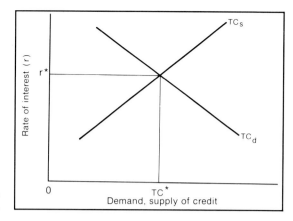

2.6. Determination of the flow of credit.

favorable, decrease when saving increases in an earlier period, increase with increases in the price level, and decrease with increases in the market rate of interest. A higher saving rate means that more funds are available internally. Increases in the price level mean that more dollars are required for given projects, and a higher interest rate makes the project more expensive.

On the supply-of-credit side, the supply of credit should increase with increases in gross saving and increase with an increased flow of reserves and increases in the market rate of interest. Bank reserves make it possible for banks to create money, which in turn finances their lending as depicted in Table 2.1. In familiar demand-and-supply fashion (Fig. 2.6) the flow of credit (and the common explanatory variable, i.e., the rate of interest) will be determined by these two equations and by the market-clearing equality of TCd and TCs. The independent variables influencing TCd and TCs (except for the interest rate variable) are called shift variables. If their values change, the curve will shift accordingly; e.g., a higher price level will cause the TCd curve to move to the right.

Whether the hypothesized signs are indeed the correct ones depends on empirical testing. This is the task of quantitative modeling. If we get the "wrong" sign in certain cases, all is not lost; the underlying hypothesis can readily be revised. This applies, for example, to the change-in-saving variable in the first equation. Underlying the negative sign is the substitute relation between saving and borrowing; the greater is internal finance, the lesser will be borrowed. But saving also has a net worth effect. Transactors may borrow more because they feel more solvent as a result of increased wealth. A positive relationship then also makes sense.

GROWTH-INDUCING VS. GROWTH-INDUCED FINANCE   Discretion in credit markets lies with either borrowers or lenders, depending on which curve does the most shifting. If the borrower side of the market is the more volatile, the flow of credit responds to the demand for credit, and finance is growth induced. On the other hand, if discretion lies with the lender, shifts in the supply of finance would be growth inducing.

Economic historians have unsuccessfully studied many different countries for an answer (e.g., see R. Cameron 1967). Our later analysis of financial markets and econometric modeling should throw light on this central question. Locating discretion is a matter of determining which exogenous shift variable dominates financial markets; e.g., if business expectations on the borrowing side call the tune, finance is growth induced. On the lending side, if the provision of bank reserves is at the discretion of the central bank and bank reserves are the key market influence, finance would be growth inducing.

HOUSEHOLD BALANCE SHEET   Table 2.2 presents a comprehensive balance
sheet for the household sector with detail on assets, liabilities, and net worth.
Tangible assets (such as homes, cars), reflecting current market values, approached

Table 2.2. Household balance sheet with tangible assets at current cost

Item	Year-end outstandings 1982 ($ mil.)	1983
1 Tangible assets	4533,000	4812,355
2 Reproducible assets	3417,261	3586,520
3 Residential structures	2119,564	2227,886
4 Owner-occupied housing	2094,506	2202,618
5 Nonprofit institutions	25,058	25,268
6 Nonprofit plant and equipment	200,970	207,622
7 Consumer durables	1096,727	1151,012
8 Land	1115,739	1225,835
9 Owner-occupied	1048,510	1156,374
10 Nonprofit institutions	67,229	69,461
11 Total financial assets	7528,884	8276,814
12 Deposits and credit market instruments	2781,342	3043,075
13 Checkable deposits and currency	307,299	338,682
14 Small time and savings deposits	1322,901	1532,234
15 Money market fund shares	206,607	162,552
16 Large time deposits	145,922	141,490
17 Credit market instruments	798,613	868,117
18 U.S. government securities	376,986	424,970
19 Savings bonds	68,346	71,485
20 Other Treasury issues	223,440	257,768
21 Agency issues	85,200	95,717
22 State and local obligations	128,993	159,992
23 Corporate and foreign bonds	64,540	58,644
24 Open-market paper	41,603	40,205
25 Mortgages	186,491	184,306
26 Corporate equities	1322,311	1519,547
27 Mutual fund shares	89,451	129,442
28 Other corporate equities	1232,860	1390,105
29 Life insurance reserves	246,799	262,584
30 Pension fund reserves	932,586	1105,644
31 Equity in noncorporate business	2144,526	2234,419
32 Security credit	16,044	19,333
33 Miscellaneous assets	85,276	92,212
34 Total assets	12061,884	13089,169
35 Total liabilities	1740,939	1922,968
36 Credit market instruments	1674,364	1832,206
37 Home mortgages	1100,957	1199,482
38 Other mortgages	36,428	38,917
39 Installment consumer credit	344,798	387,927
40 Other consumer credit	85,871	96,910
41 Bank loans n.e.c.	33,326	32,294
42 Other loans	72,984	76,676
43 Security credit	28,840	47,830
44 Trade credit	22,220	26,486
45 Deferred and unpaid life insurance premiums	15,515	16,446
46 Net worth	10320,945	11166,201

Memo:
| 47 Total owner-occupied real estate | 3143,016 | 3358,992 |
| 48 Home mortgages as percent of owner-occupied real estate | 35.028 | 35.709 |

Source: FRB 1984d:24-25.

$5 tril. at the end of 1983 (line 1, Table 2.2). Financial assets (to be discussed in more detail in later chapters) exceeded $8 tril. (line 11). The resultant net worth (the difference between total assets and total liabilities) is in excess of $11 tril. (line 46). Net worth is the accumulation of past saving and marks the household sector as the leading sector in the economy for savings.

Spending units have alternatives in borrowing; e.g., households can choose between a personal loan, a credit card, an installment loan, or a mortgage. Borrowings outstanding for the household sector begin with line 35 of Table 2.2. The total at the end of 1983 is seen to be an impressive $1923 bil. Since 1945 when the figure was $34.5 bil., liabilities have risen 55-fold.

Home mortgages and installment consumer credit are the largest items. As can be seen from memo lines 47 and 48, mortgages contributed 36% of the value of owner-occupied real estate. Other consumer credit (line 40) refers to noninstallment credit including single-payment loans, charge accounts, and service credits such as doctors' bills. Bank loans n.e.c. means loans not elsewhere classified in the banking data. Security credit measures loans from banks or brokers and dealers in securities, which are secured by stocks and bonds. Trade credit is the business debt of nonprofit organizations (those such as churches and universities are included in the household flow-of-funds sector).

The major categories of installment credit are spelled out by lender in Table 2.3. The "other" category includes home improvement and personal loans. Credit cards and check credit plans (overdraft privileges) are revolving credits. A line of credit is run down by purchases and built up by repayment. Nonbank credit cards issued by retail stores and oil companies are roughly equal to bank credit cards in the size of debts generated.

The widespread use of credit cards is suggested by Table 2.4, which describes the growth of credit card holding by type of card. Seventy percent of the families surveyed had some type of card in 1982, with retail store cards having the largest incidence.

Table 2.3. Consumer installment credit, total outstanding

Holder and type of credit	1982	1983
	($ mil.)	
1 Total	355,849	396,082
By major holder		
2 Commercial banks	152.490	171,978
3 Finance companies	98,693	102,862
4 Credit unions	47,253	53,471
5 Retailers[a]	32,735	35,911
6 Savings and loans	15,823	21,615
7 Gasoline companies	4,063	4,131
8 Mutual savings banks	4,792	6,114
By major type of credit		
9 Automobile	131,086	142,449
10 Commercial banks	59,555	67,557
11 Indirect paper	34,755	(b)
12 Direct loans	23,472	(b)
13 Credit unions	22,596	25,574
14 Finance companies	48,935	49,318
15 Revolving	69,998	80,823
16 Commercial banks	36,666	44,184
17 Retailers	29,269	32,508
18 Gasoline companies	4,063	4,131
19 Mobile home	22,254	23,680
20 Commercial banks	9,605	9,842
21 Finance companies	9,003	9,365
22 Savings and loans	3,143	3,906
23 Credit unions	503	567
24 Other	132,511	149,130
25 Commercial banks	46,664	50,395
26 Finance companies	40,755	44,179
27 Credit unions	24,154	27,330
28 Retailers	3,466	3,403
29 Savings and loans	12,680	17,709
30 Mutual savings banks	4,792	6,114

Source: *Fed. Res. Bull.* 1984a:A38.
Note: The Board's series cover most short- and intermediate-term credit extended to individuals through regular business channels, usually to finance the purchase of consumer goods and services or to refinance debts incurred for such purposes, and scheduled to be repaid (or with the option of repayment) in two or more installments.
[a]Includes auto dealers and excludes 30-day charge credit held by travel and entertainment companies.
[b]Not reported after December 1982.

Table 2.4. Credit card holding (families holding cards as percent of all families)

Type of credit card	Year			
	1977	1978	1981	1982
Any	63	64	66	70
Gasoline	34	34	30	35
Bank	38	40	45	51
General purpose[a]	8	10	14	14
Retail store	53	50	57	63
Other[b]	6	5	7	n.a.[c]

Source: FRB 1983b.
[a]Travel and entertainment cards.
[b]Includes airline cards, car-rental cards, and others not classified elsewhere.
[c]Not available. Data collected for the Federal Reserve Board by the Survey Research Center, University of Michigan.

The dominance of commercial banks in lending is quickly noted. Commercial banks, surprisingly, became a factor in installment credit only after World War II. Before that only self-liquidating loans to business were regarded as safe.

While the net change for 1982–83 in consumer installment credit (line 39, Table 2.2) was large ($43 bil.), it underestimates the economic impact of installment credit. Net change is the difference between extensions and liquidations; e.g., in 1977 extensions amounted to $226 bil. and liquidations to $195 bil. (*Fed. Res. Bull.* 1978:Table A43). The extensions figure should be linked to consumer spending rather than net change. At the same time, liquidations should be linked to saving (arrows 3 and 2 respectively of Fig. 2.1).

HOUSEHOLD SUBSTITUTION   Borrowers can be expected to minimize the cost of loans, but another major consideration is loan maturity. Spending units with long-term projects requiring many years before the investment or consumption good wears out will prefer to borrow long. On the other hand, borrowers may have short-term demands for funds, as in the case of inventory financing. Depending on the term structure of interest rates (the relationship between interest cost and maturities), a borrower may be able to both minimize interest costs and choose the desired maturity. This relationship is the topic of Chapters 5 and 16.

For households, we associate mortgages with home purchases and consumer durables with consumer credit, but substitution among sources of funds is possible (see Ch. 15 for empirical estimates). It is most likely for consumer durable financing. For example, by funding higher equity values in homes, consumers have spent more on current consumption, including consumer durables (Balatsos 1978). Internal and external finance are also substitutes. When borrowing declines relative to housing expenditures, this indicates that expenditures are being more largely financed internally (by saving).

BUSINESS BALANCE SHEET   Nonfinancial corporate business is the main producing sector of the economy. This is reflected in the character of their reproducible assets (Table 2.5, lines 2–5). The investment in plant and equipment contrasts with the household sector's investment in housing and consumer durables. The net worth of this sector is ultimately owned by the household sector via the ownership of equity securities.

The financial liabilities for the nonfinancial corporate business sector are

```
Table 2.5.  Nonfinancial business balance sheet with tangible assets
           at current cost
                                                    Year-end outstandings
Item                                                  1982          1983
                                                          ($ mil.)
   1 Tangible assets                               3219,925      3312,992

   2    Reproducible assets                        2718,043      2774,822
   3       Residential structures                    60,929        64,895
   4       Nonresidential plant and equipment      1980,952      2024,709
   5       Inventories                              676,162       685,218

   6    Land                                        501,882       538,170

   7 Total financial assets                        1080,569      1203,932

   8    Liquid assets                               225,135       263,410
   9       Demand deposits and currency              78,555        82,974
  10       Time deposits                             60,029        71,845
  11       Security repurchase agreements            26,643        30,488
  12       Foreign deposits                          12,129        15,400
  13       U.S. government securities                 8,435        13,624
  14       State and local obligations                3,536         4,201
  15       Open-market paper                         35,808        44,878

  16    Consumer credit                              32,255        35,868
  17    Trade credit                                489,232       545,892
  18    Miscellaneous assets                        333,947       358,762
  19       Foreign direct investment               226,468       237,228
  20       Insurance receivables                     50,030        52,889
  21       Equity in sponsoring agencies               714           723
  22       Other                                     56,735        67,922

  23 Total assets                                  4300,494      4516,924

  24 Total liabilities                             1567,094      1684,667

  25    Credit market instruments                  1086,350      1143,251
  26       Tax-exempt bonds                          74,466        83,838
  27       Corporate bonds                          406,017       421,037
  28       Mortgages                                 76,727        79,652
  29          Home mortgages                          4,352         6,986
  30          Multifamily                            40,766        41,726
  31          Commercial                             31,609        30,940

  32       Bank loans n.e.c.                        383,026       400,053
  33       Commercial paper                          38,184        37,731
  34       Acceptances                                9,833         9,476
  35       Finance company loans·                    86,714       100,464
  36       U.S. government loans                      11,383        11,000

  37    Profit taxes payable                          2,384         5,220
  38    Trade debt                                  376,516       425,660
  39    Foreign direct investment in U.S.          101,844       110,536

  40 Net worth                                     2733,400      2832,257
          Source:   FRB 1984c:44-45.
```

presented in the lower section of Table 2.5. The leading obligations of this sector
are seen to be bonds, mortgages, and bank loans. Commercial paper (the IOUs of
major corporations) and finance company loans have become increasingly important as financial sources.

BUSINESS SUBSTITUTION   The usual borrowing-spending linkages are assumed to be between inventories and bank loans and fixed investment and corporate bonds. Study of the underlying data suggests a weakening of the inventory–bank loan relationship after 1966. This weakening resulted from the
substitution of bank loans for other sources of funds in the financing of fixed
investment and from the substitution of other sources of funds for bank loans,

such as commercial paper and finance company loans in the financing of inventories.

The substitution of short-term debt for long-term debt is a part of a liquidity cycle. Business corporations increase short-term debts in expansion periods and retire them in slower economic times. At the same time, liquid asset holdings (e.g., deposits, government securities) decline in boom times in relation to short-term liabilities. Despite cyclical movements, the long-run trend over the last 25 years is toward less liquidity in the balance sheet—relatively more short-term debt and relatively less liquid assets (FRB 1983c:9–10).

Instead of substitutability, the relation between internal and external sources of funds is one of complementarity when capital expenditures are expanding. Borrowing supplements internal sources at such a time.

The extent of substitution has its implications for the likely effectiveness of selective credit controls. The potential for controlling particular kinds of expenditures by controlling specific kinds of lending (borrowing) will be greatest when substitution possibilities are the least. This question is more fully discussed in Chapter 18.

Summary

In this chapter economic activity is traced back from spending to borrowing to money. The linkage between borrowing and spending is emphasized as a key bond among the flow of funds of the nonfinancial sector. Borrowing in turn is traced back to money creation by commercial banks. The importance of money as the unique disturbance variable and unique leakage variable is illustrated by hypothetical examples. Monetary dishoarding, which affects the velocity of money, is shown to be the equivalent of new money in its economic effects. Dishoarding could affect spending directly in addition to affecting it indirectly via the lending-borrowing process.

The borrowing-spending-money linkages are examined empirically by means of graphs and regression equations. Household and business borrowing-spending patterns are seen to differ over the business cycle.

The discretion for borrowing may originate on either the borrowing or lending side of the market. A methodology for locating discretion is briefly discussed. Finally, we present the balance sheets of the two leading nonfinancial sectors and discuss the possibility of substitution among different sources of funds. Substitution has its implications for the potential effectiveness of selective credit controls, a future topic.

Review questions

1. Describe the possible linkages between sources and uses of funds for the nonfinancial sector and identify the linkages relating to internal and external finance.

2. Explain how an initial equilibrium state, given a nonfinancial sector and a banking sector, is disturbed by an extra $10 of lending by the banking sector. When will equilibrium again be reached? How is the value of the multiplier determined?

3. Rank each type of monetary disturbance in terms of its speed of impact on the GNP.

4. Define the variables in the "equation of exchange."

5. Describe the theories associated with the "equation of exchange."

6. How does the ratio of borrowing to spending differ over the business cycle?

7. What influences the demand for credit and the supply of credit in financial markets?

8. What is a regression equation?

9. Distinguish between growth-induced and growth-inducing finance.

10. What are the main categories of assets and liabilities in the balance sheets of the household and business sectors?

11. Which is larger, the net worths of households or business? Why?

12. What determines the extent of borrower substitution among financial sources?

13. Define:

Internal finance	Velocity
External finance	Dependent variable
Dishoarding	Independent variables
Monetary disturbance	

3

Inflation: Measurement and costs

The previous chapters have either ignored prices (Ch. 1) or corrected for prices (Ch. 2). Correcting for prices means that our discussion is in real values rather than nominal values. In a world where the dollar is steadily losing its value, real values are always less than nominal values.

The dollar losing its value is the other side of prices going up. If the dollar buys half as much as before, prices have doubled. With millions of goods and services in the market, how do we get an estimate of prices overall? And once measured, what are the consequences of inflation for economic well-being? These questions are the concern of this chapter. They deserve early attention in a study that will later try to explain the whys of inflation and what to do about it.

Price indexes

Price indexes offer a way of measuring changes in the general price level. The paradox of price indexes is that, while they are indispensable, they must always be wrong ("arbitrary" is a politer word) because construction of a price index requires introducing quantities, the mythical "basket" of purchases. Once introduced, the basket must be held constant. When year 2 is compared with year 1, the same basket must be assumed, even though we know it is never the same in both years. Otherwise, if we allow quantities to change, we are no longer measuring prices alone but the effect of quantity changes as well. The standard of living instead of the cost of living is being measured.

Since the basket is changing and we must hold it constant, alternative strategies are to take either the first year's or the final year's basket. These indexes are respectively called Laspeyres and Paasche (after their authors), the former taking the weights of the base (first) year, the latter the weights of the current year. The base year in both versions is represented by 1 or 100.

The Laspeyres index for prices in year 2 as compared with year 1 takes the following form:

$$I_{12} = \Sigma P_2 Q_1 / \Sigma P_1 Q_1$$

where I_{12} = price index in year 2 based on year 1
P = prices
Q = quantities

For simplicity let us say that we are determining price level changes represented by two commodities, meat and bread. The values assumed are:

	YEAR 1			YEAR 2	
	Price	Quantity consumed		Price	Quantity consumed
Meat	$1.00/lb	100 lb	Meat	$1.60/lb	80 lb
Bread	.10/loaf	1000 loaves	Bread	.20/loaf	1600 loaves

Using our formula, the price index in year 2 based on year 1 is:

$$\frac{(1.60)(100) + (0.20)(1000)}{(1.00)(100) + (0.10)(1000)} = 1.80$$

Ordinarily, index numbers are multiplied through by 100, eliminating the decimals. An index number of 180 tells us that prices in year 2 were 180% of year 1 or that prices had gone up by 80%.

In contrast, the Paasche index uses the current year's basket as weights. Now the formula reads:

$$I_{12} = \Sigma P_2 Q_2 / \Sigma P_1 Q_2$$

Applying the formula, the index is:

$$\frac{(1.60)(80) + (0.20)(1600)}{(1.00)(80) + (0.10)(1600)} = (1.87)(100) = 187$$

The larger price increase as measured by the Paasche index is due to the greater weight (1600 vs. 1000) given bread and the lower weight given meat (80 vs. 100). Thus the greater percentage increase in the price of bread as compared with meat gets more attention.

Which index is correct? As previously intimated, one cannot say because the weights are arbitrary. Nor is the arbitrariness avoided by averaging weights. The Fisher and Edgeworth indexes are examples of such attempts. But their average basket is less representative of any single period than the conventional indexes they are designed to replace. (For an elementary discussion of these index numbers, construction of index numbers, and the weaknesses of statistical sampling procedures, see Wallace and Cullison 1979:27.)

The Laspeyres and Paasche choice of weights gives each index a built-in bias. The Laspeyres index exaggerates price increases by taking the first year's weights. Thus it ignores the effect of buyers shifting into lower priced goods in the face of inflation. The Paasche index understates price increases because it ignores the choice of lower priced goods in the base year. These biases apply only when consumers respond to relative prices. In our example they respond to absolute prices. In year 2 bread prices rose relative to meat prices (0.20 to 1.60 is greater than 0.10 to 1.00). With a response to relative prices the example should substitute a larger figure than 100 for meat in year 2, say 120, and a smaller figure for bread than 1000, say 800. With these figures the Laspeyres index of 180 would be greater than the Paasche index of 176.

The Laspeyres index, however, does have one redeeming feature compared with the Paasche. We can compare year 2, year 3, etc., with year 1 and year 2 with year 3 because the weights are always the same—those of year 1. In the Paasche, we can compare year 2 with year 1, year 3 with year 1, but not year 2 with year 3. For example, if the Paasche index for year 3 was 200 and that for year 2 was 150, we cannot say that prices had gone up 33% between year 2 and year 3 because the baskets of years 2 and 3 are not the same.

Major price indexes

The major price indexes in the United States are the consumer price index (CPI), the wholesale price index, and the gross national product (GNP) deflator, all prepared by the Bureau of Labor Statistics, U.S. Department of Labor. The first two are Laspeyres-type indexes; the latter is a Paasche index. The U.S. Department of Commerce publishes a fixed-weight GNP deflator based on 1972 weights, transforming it into a Laspeyres index. The problem of interyear comparisons has also been overcome by the preparation of a chain price index (*Survey of Current Business,* June issues).

CONSUMER PRICE INDEX   Sampling techniques are employed; thus sampling errors are inevitable. They show up in the choice of items sampled in retail stores, the period selected for checking prices, and the geographic areas chosen. As a result, changes in the CPI (in either direction) are not statistically significant unless the change exceeds 0.2 of 1% (certainly not a problem nowadays with large price increases).

The constancy of the basket creates problems associated with quality changes and changes in tastes (Wallace and Cullison 1979:33–34, 40). The index makers take quality changes into account in calculating the CPI. If old- and new-style items are both available (say television sets), the new item will be introduced into the index at the old item's price if this is the same, with quality assumed to explain the higher price on the new item if the price is higher. Differences in manufacturers' costs are consulted when both old and new are not available at the same time in the same market. Automobile prices are adjusted yearly to eliminate quality improvements. Medical care is another area where undeniable quality changes have taken place, offsetting its rising cost.

Changes in tastes create similar problems. Garters, bed warmers, and washtubs have been replaced by panty hose, electric blankets, and automatic washers. Updating the base year and thus weights is the most satisfactory way of handling the problem. Currently, the CPI retains the 1967 base year but employs 1972 weights. These replace weights based on an earlier survey of consumer expenditures in 1960–61. The weight changes for major CPI components are shown in Table 3.1.

Table 3.1. Relative weights of major price index components							
	Wage earners and clerical workers					All urban consumers 1972-73[d]	All urban consumers Dec. 1977[e]
Major group	1935-39[a]	1952[b]	1963[c]	1972-73[d]	Dec. 1977[e]		
Food and alcoholic beverages	35.4	32.2	25.2	20.4	20.5	18.8	18.8
Housing	33.7	33.5	34.9	39.8	40.7	42.9	43.9
Apparel	11.0	9.4	10.6	7.0	5.8	7.0	5.8
Transportation	8.1	11.3	14.0	19.8	20.2	17.7	18.0
Medical care	4.1	4.8	5.7	4.2	4.5	4.6	5.0
Entertainment	2.8	4.0	3.9	4.3	3.9	4.5	4.1
Personal care	2.5	2.1	2.8	1.8	1.8	1.7	1.8
Other goods and services	2.4	2.7	2.9	2.7	2.6	2.8	2.6

Source: Wallace and Cullison 1979:37.
[a]Relative importance for the survey period 1934-36 (updated for price change).
[b]Relative importance for the survey period 1947-49 (updated for price change).
[c]Relative importance for the survey period 1960-61 (updated for price change).
[d]Relative importance for the survey period 1972-73.
[e]Relative importance for the survey period 1972-73 (updated for price change).

It is of interest that the 1972 weights are themselves revised on the basis of prices (see footnotes to Table 3.1). Weights increase (e.g., see columns for 1972–73 and December 1977) when relative expenditures increase because of rising prices. Thus the weight for food and alcoholic beverages and housing increases and the weight for apparel declines.

The CPI is calculated by multiplying the price relatives by their respective weights and summing them. For example, suppose food prices in a given year are 50% higher than in the base year and housing prices 75% higher, etc. The price relative is then 1.5 (150) for food and 1.75 (175) for housing. The price relative of 1.5 will be multiplied by 20.5% (December 1977 column of Table 3.1) and 1.75 by 40.7%, and so on for other components. The products of price relatives and their weights are then summed for the cost of living.

Two versions of the CPI have been prepared since 1978; before then the index reflected expenditures for urban wage earners and clerical workers (CPI-W). Now the regularly published version (see Table 3.2, n. b) covers expenditures for all urban consumers (CPI-U), adding another 35% to the 45% expenditures coverage of the old index (CPI-W is still published in the *Survey of Current Business*). The weights for all urban consumers in the last column of Table 3.1, when compared with the last column under wage earners and clerical workers, show more weight being given to housing and medical care and less to food and transportation in the all-urban index.

The CPI-U was revised in one respect in 1983 (Runyon 1983). Instead of measuring the costs of purchasing and financing homeownership, the new index measures the rental equivalent (see Table 3.2, n. b). The double counting of home expense (by counting both the purchase price and the related mortgage interest payments) gave a weight of 43.9% to housing in the old index (Table 3.1, CPI-U, final column). The new index reduces the inflationary bias when home prices and interest rates are rising sharply.

Table 3.2. Consumer and producer prices (percentage changes based on seasonally adjusted data, except as noted)

Item	Change from 12 months earlier 1983 March	Change from 12 months earlier 1984 March	Index level March 1984 (1967 =100)[a]
Consumer prices[b]			
1 All items	3.6	4.7	307.3
2 Food	2.7	4.0	302.2
3 Energy items	-1.5	4.6	418.1
4 All items less food and energy	4.7	5.0	296.7
5 Commodities	6.1	4.5	249.9
6 Services	3.6	5.3	350.7
Producer prices			
7 Finished goods	2.2	2.9	291.7
8 Consumer foods	1.6	6.1	277.0
9 Consumer energy	-4.9	-1.8	759.8
10 Other consumer goods	3.8	2.8	244.8
11 Capital equipment	3.6	2.5	292.7
12 Intermediate materials[c]	-0.4	3.0	324.2
13 Excluding energy	0.7	3.5	302.5
Crude materials			
14 Foods	0.5	8.7	270.7
15 Energy	1.6	-2.6	780.7
16 Other	-1.7	12.4	274.6

Source: *Fed. Res. Bull.* 1984a:A47.
[a]Not seasonally adjusted.
[b]Figures for consumer prices are those for all urban consumers and reflect a rental equivalence measure of homeownership after 1982.
[c]Excludes intermediate materials for food manufacturing and manufactured animal feeds.

Table 3.2 gives recent percentage changes and index numbers for consumer and producer (wholesale) prices. The March 1984 index number of 307.3 (final column, line 1) indicates a percentage rise in consumer prices of 207% since 1967. The components showing the greatest increases are energy items and service. Services include medical care, which has sharply increased in cost over this period.

Table 3.2 shows changes of 3.6 and 4.7% over recent 12-month periods. This contrasts sharply with the double-digit inflation of 1973–74 and 1980–82 (Fig. 3.1).

3.1. Comprehensive price measures, change at annual rates; seasonally adjusted quarterly. (FRB 1983d:37)

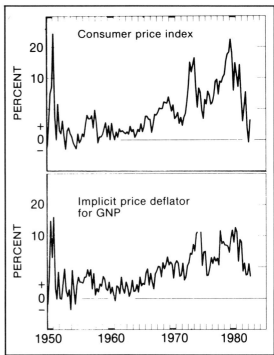

PRODUCER PRICES   The former wholesale price index is now called the producer price index, which is a better description of its coverage (Wallace and Cullison 1979:42). The purpose of the index is to measure commodity prices at the stage of their most important commercial transaction. The weights are the net value of shipments of producers in particular industries. These are shown in Table 3.3. They are given by both industry and stage of processing. Consumer finished goods in the latter category are at wholesale, making this the only strictly wholesale price in the classification.

Table 3.3. Relative importance of commodities included in the producer price index

Commodities	1972 weights
Broken down by industry	
Farm products	8.40
Processed foods and feeds	14.37
Textile products and apparel	5.78
Hides, skins, leather, and related products	0.76
Fuels and related products, power	10.34
Chemicals and allied products	7.17
Rubber and plastic products	2.80
Lumber and wood products	2.23
Pulp, paper, and allied products	5.28
Metals and metal products	13.00
Machinery and equipment	11.84
Furniture and household durables	3.44
Nonmetallic mineral products	2.82
Transportation equipment	8.61
Miscellaneous products	3.19
Broken down by stage of processing	
Crude materials for further processing	11.33
Foodstuffs and feedstuffs	6.97
Nonfood materials except fuel	3.15
Crude fuel	1.21
Intermediate materials, supplies, and components	47.11
Materials and components for manufacturing	25.59
Materials and components for construction	7.94
Processed fuels and lubricants	4.85
Containers	1.39
Supplies	7.35
Finished goods (including raw foods and fuel)	41.56
Consumer goods	29.71
Producer finished goods	11.85

Source: Wallace and Cullison 1979:44.

Comparison of Table 3.2 with one for an earlier period would reveal a marked slowing in the pace of inflation. Thus finished goods in the 12-month period from June 1979 to June 1980 jumped 13.8 and 10.2% in the following year from June 1980 to June 1981. This compares with 2.2 and 2.9% in the two years shown in line 7, Table 3.2. The decline in consumer energy prices (line 9) is a major reason for the slowing of inflation.

IMPLICIT GNP DEFLATOR   The most comprehensive measure of price change is the GNP deflator, which measures price changes in the major GNP components and subcomponents, as shown in Table 3.4. Indexes for the change in inventories and thus the broader category of gross private domestic investment are not estimated. It is assumed that price movements are the same as fixed investment.

The GNP deflator is constructed in a roundabout way using previously determined consumer and producer price indexes. Components of the GNP in current

Table 3.4. GNP implicit price deflators

Component		1983, 4th quarter index (1972=100)
Personal consumption expenditures		216.3
Durable goods	180.4	
Nondurable goods	215.5	
Services	229.1	
Fixed investment		217.9
Nonresidential structures	264.5	
Producers' durable equipment	184.9	
Residential structures	251.2	
Exports		246.0
Imports		274.0
Government purchases of goods and services		239.3
Federal	235.8	
State and local	241.6	
Total GNP		218.5

Source: President 1984:224-25.

dollars (in as fine a detail as possible) are deflated by the appropriate price in-dexes. Once deflated, the components are aggregated to obtain wider GNP totals, and finally the GNP itself, in constant dollars. The GNP in current dollars for these categories is then divided by constant dollar values to obtain the implicit price deflators; e.g., total expenditures on steel reinforcing bars in 1980 will be divided by the index number of bar prices, using 1972 as the base year (a compo-nent of the producer price index—a Laspeyres-type index). Steel reinforcing bar production in 1980 is thus being estimated in 1972 prices. Similar calculations will be carried out for all components of the GNP, and the deflated estimates will be added together. This deflated total is then divided into the GNP total in current dollars to yield the implicit GNP deflator.

The implicit deflator for personal consumption expenditure (PCE) has been regarded as a better measure of inflation than the CPI, because it has always used the revised CPI approach to measuring housing costs. In addition, the current expenditure weights of PCE allow for consumers who cut their consumption of energy in response to higher energy prices. The CPI uses fixed expenditure weights. As a result, the implicit deflator for PCE in recent years shows considera-bly less inflation (Gordon 1981:48–49).

When prices are rising, real values are lower than nominal values. Real values are nominal (dollar) values deflated for price changes. (This means that the effect of price changes is taken out. We say a magnitude—purchase of cars, personal income—is being expressed in constant dollars.) For example, GNP in nominal dollars was $3310 bil. in 1983. The GNP in 1972 dollars (meaning that the nominal figures are deflated by the 1983 price index) in the same period was $1535 bil. The GNP deflator must have been 215.6 ($3310 ÷ 215.6 = $1535), indicating that the price of the comprehensive GNP basket more than doubled between 1972 and 1983.

What is wrong with inflation?

If we can allow for price changes by expressing nominal magnitudes in real terms, why the concern with inflation? Why not just make all our comparisons in real rather than nominal terms? First, rising prices may affect real magnitudes and make us all worse off. Second, and on this we are on surer ground, inflation may make some of us worse off and some of us better off.

So far inflation has not been a real threat to the size of the national pie. If we correct for prices, population growth, and personal taxes, real per capita disposable personal income fell only slightly in 1974 and 1982 (President 1984:249). Several reasons may be given for persons feeling worse off despite the growth in real income. First, the rate of growth in real per capita disposable income has slowed since 1973. Rising aspirations have been disappointed. Second, because money income has risen faster than real income, people are frustrated because they can imagine what life would be like if the rise in money incomes had not been accompanied by an almost equal rise in prices. This suggests an absence of "money illusion." People are aware that higher prices make them worse off. Third, the unemployed, whose numbers have risen with inflation since 1970, face a double whammy with inflation.

The growth in disposable (after-tax) personal income took place despite a progressive tax structure. The latter makes real incomes fall after taxes even if incomes keep up with inflation. With inflation, individuals move into higher income tax brackets. Real take-home pay suffers. Assume income before tax of $25,000, which with a 20% inflation rate increases to $30,000. On the basis of 1980 tax rates, taxes before and after would be $5952 and $7962. Nominal incomes after tax are $19,048 and $22,038 respectively. Allowing for 20% inflation, real incomes after tax are $19,048 and $18,365. The loss in real income is $683 despite before-tax real earnings remaining constant (Maisel 1982:492).

Tax decreases enhanced by inflation are called "bracket creep." The Economic Recovery Tax Act of 1981 aims at eliminating this effect beginning in 1985. This will be done by indexing the bracket ranges according to the CPI.

The most familiar argument against inflation has to do with its distributional effects — some people being made better off while others are made worse off. Keeping up with inflation requires two distinct abilities: anticipating it and adjusting for it. A wage earner may forecast an increase in prices of 10% next year but is unable to negotiate a similar increase in her personal "price" (wage). The result is that some prices go up faster than others and income is redistributed. Conventional wisdom places pensioners, widows and orphans, and nonunion workers in the fixed income class that will suffer from inflation. But periodic increases in social security benefits and cost-of-living escalator clauses have put the first two categories into the variable income class. The wages of nonunion workers seem to move in tandem with union wages.

Another candidate for being made worse off is the poor. Defining the poor is a matter of some contention now that the government spends almost twice as much in noncash benefits to low-income families as in cash payments. In 1983 the poverty threshold (based on U.S. Census Bureau data) of cash income alone was estimated to be $10,178 for a family of four. On this basis the Bureau reported a poverty population of 35.3 mil. equal to a poverty rate of 15.2%. When allowance is made for food stamps, free or reduced price school lunches, public or other subsidized housing, and Medicaid and Medicare, the percentage of poor drops as low as 10% depending on what programs are considered (Pear 1984:1, 28). The poverty rate of 15.2% was the highest such rate since the start of President Johnson's antipoverty campaign in 1965.

Overall figures fail to give an impression of the personal impact of inflation. Reporters of the *New York Times* (1978) interviewed consumers, business managers, and state and local government officials in the middle of 1978 to find out how they were reacting to inflation. A suburban family in Montclair, N.J., makes $20,000 a year. The father of two holds three jobs. His figuring shows that he has $6500 to "live on" after deducting $4000 for federal taxes; $700 for property taxes; $3400 for mortgage, heat, and utility bills; $1000 on loans; $1000 for social security; $600 toward a pension; and auto bills of $1000. They do not eat steak and have not taken a vacation in three years. This family represents the economic middle class. Further down the economic ladder an inner-city family of five making $139 a week copes with inflation by letting utility and rental bills pile up and walking a few blocks further to buy milk. Recently, they applied for public assistance.

Wealth effect of inflation

Assessing the effects of inflation is complicated by the balance sheet. The real net worth of economic units will be affected because the value of individual items on the balance sheet are affected differently by inflation. Thus inflation has distributional effects via its effect on personal wealth.

Table 3.5 illustrates the hypothetical effects of inflation on net worth for a single household. A flow statement (limited to capital account items) links an initial and final balance sheet.

Part A of the table describes the no-inflation case. The household begins with fixed price assets (FPA) of $1000 and variable price assets (VPA) of $2000. The FPA yield fixed dollar incomes and have fixed redemption prices, e.g., money, savings deposits, and savings bonds. (Bonds, corporate or government, fit this category except they can be sold before maturity at variable market prices.) The VPA are those with variable incomes and without fixed redemption prices, Examples are corporate common stock and physical assets such as gold, Chinese

Table 3.5. Effect of inflation on household net worth

A. No inflation

Initial balance sheet				Capital account flow statement				Final balance sheet			
Debit		Credit		Debit		Credit		Debit		Credit	
Fixed price assets	$1000	Fixed price liabilities	$ 500	ΔFPA	$ 300	Saving	$ 500	FPA	$1300	FPL	$1500
Variable price assets	2000	Net worth	2500	ΔVPA	1200	Borrowing	1000	VPA	3200	NW	3000
Totals	$3000		$3000		$1500		$1500		$4500		$4500

B. Inflation (100% rate)

Initial balance sheet				Flow				Final balance sheet			
Debit		Credit		Debit		Credit		Debit		Credit	
Fixed price assets	$1000	Fixed price liabilities	$ 500	ΔFPA	$ 600	Saving	$1000	FPA (real value)	$1600 800	FPL (real value)	$2500 1250
Variable price assets	2000	Net worth	2500	ΔVPA	2400	Borrowing	2000	VPA (real value)	6400 3200	NW (real value)	5500 2750
Totals	$3000		$3000		$3000		$3000	Total (real)	$8000 4000	Total (real)	$8000 4000

ceramics, homes, and automobiles. Another term for FPA is monetary assets.

On the credit side the balance sheet shows fixed price liabilities (FPL) such as mortgages or consumer debt. (From the standpoint of the lender they are FPA.) The final balance sheet item is the net worth (NW), $2500.

The flow statement indicates that the household had savings of $500 and had borrowed $1000. These sources of funds were allocated between FPA and VPA. The final balance sheet adds these flow values to the initial balance sheet. The final net worth is $3000, equal to the initial net worth plus the year's saving.

In Part B of Table 3.5 the flow values double on the assumption that they keep pace with the 100% inflation rate. Our hypothetical transactor suffers from inflation. The final balance sheet cannot be derived in the same straightforward fashion as in the no-inflation case. Now the VPA reflect not only the $2400 of flows but also the doubling of the initial $2000 value of VPA. This explains the $6400 figure. The net worth figure is derived residually according to the balance sheet identity $(A - L = NW)$. The closing balance sheet shows a real net worth of $2725 compared with a value of $3000 before inflation (the dollar value before inflation is also the real value). The reason for this decline is the household owning more monetary assets originally than the amount it owes. It stays even with inflation in flow terms, but when the initial balance sheet values are deflated because of inflation, the downward correction is severest for the larger amount of FPA. For real net worth to be maintained with inflation, monetary assets initially must equal liabilities. To get ahead, monetary liabilities should exceed monetary assets. Alternatively, household borrowing on the flow statement should more than double to compensate for the initial shortfall of liabilities.

Investors would be even better off if the market value of their variable assets outran the pace of inflation. This is not an easy task. For generations, common stock purchases were recommended as the ideal hedge against inflation, and this is justified on a long-run basis. Over a 55-year period (1926–80) the mean return on common stocks was 11.7%, greatly in excess of the returns on fixed income securities and the inflation rate of 3% (Ibbotson et al. 1984:369). But fixed income securities over shorter time spans have done better than variable income securities. An excellent basis for comparison is the respective return on TIAA and CREF, pension fund investments for university faculty. The former represents funds invested in fixed income securities, the latter a fund invested in equities (common and preferred stock). In the 1960s and 1970s, a dollar invested in TIAA generally brought higher retirement benefits than CREF (see Reif 1978a:16–18; 1978b:124–26).

Until the stock market took off in 1982, an investor would have had higher returns by investing in Chinese pottery. The compound rate of return was 23.1% compared with inflation's 6.2% average over the 1968–78 period (Rukeyser 1978:12). Other investments that beat inflation in this time frame are old masters (13%), rare nongold coins (12.3%), farmland (11.1%), and houses (8.6%). Gold was in a class by itself, advancing from $35 an ounce to over $800 in 1980, a 25-fold increase. Once stock market prices started jumping, however, it provided an excellent hedge against inflation. Common stock prices on the New York Stock Exchange rose on average 58% between August 1982 and January 1984 (*Fed. Res. Bull.* 1983a:A29; 1984d:A25).

Is the net worth effect of inflation (positive or negative) as real as the income (flow) effect? In the sense of being potential purchasing power it is not. Only if the balance sheet is liquidated in part or in whole (assets sold off, debts repaid) or the allocation of income between consumption and saving changed will wealth influence consumption.

Debtors and creditors: Households

The previous balance sheet example implies that inflation redistributes wealth from creditors to debtors. Households with net monetary debts (monetary liabilities greater than monetary assets) benefit; those with net monetary assets lose.

A study of debtors and creditors identifies them by income and occupation and net worths (Bach and Stephenson 1974). The poor and the rich are more vulnerable to inflation than the middle-income groups. At these extremes the percentage of assets in monetary form is relatively high and debts are low. As a result the leverage ratio (the ratio of VPA to total assets minus debts) is lowest for these income groups. The lower the leverage ratio, the greater the loss of real wealth as a result of inflation.

In terms of occupations the retired are seen to have the lowest leverage ratio. Those with the lowest net worths have the highest leverage ratio because low net worths are due to high debts. These results for net worth are not inconsistent with those for income, since low-income families are not high-debt families.

More recent evidence emphasizes the adverse effect of inflation on the wealthy. In Figure 3.2 the hypothetical effects of a persistent 2% inflation rate are measured in terms of cash income ("census income") and in terms of a more comprehensive income concept, accrued comprehensive income (ACI). The first includes wages, salaries, business income, interest, dividends, rents, royalties, pension benefits, government cash transfers, and private cash benefits—all before deduction of taxes (Minarik 1978:8). ACI adds on income in kind (including employer-financed employee benefits and government in-kind transfers), balance sheet changes (such as the depreciation in the cash value of bonds and appreciation in home values) and subtracts taxes on all government levels.

Figure 3.2 measures the ratio of real income with inflation to real income

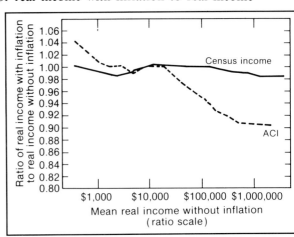

3.2. Effects of 2% increase in the inflation rate during the sixth year. (Used with permission from Minarik 1978:9)

without inflation for households in different real-income brackets (the horizontal scale). The results are startlingly different for the two income concepts. Under the narrower concept, households with incomes ranging from $10,000 to $100,000 hold their own with losses for lower income groups and wealthier households. But the wider concept shows low-income categories benefiting (probably because of homeownership), with only a small range of families ($10,000–$20,000) holding their own. As income levels rise, the effects of inflation become more adverse, with the very wealthy being hardest hit as a result of the effect of inflation on the market value of financial instruments. The effect of inflation on asset values via interest rates was not considered in the example of Table 3.5.

The same approach can be taken to a study of the effect of inflation on the aged. Figure 3.3 compares the initial effects of a 2% inflation rate on the aged and nonaged, using the ACI concept.

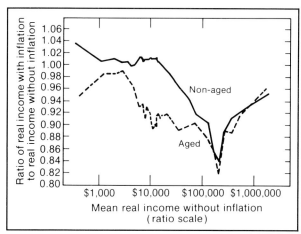

3.3. Effects of 2% increase in the inflation rate on aged and nonaged. (Used with permission from Minarik 1978:9)

The intensified effect of inflation on the poorer aged as compared to the nonaged is due to dependence of the aged on income from intangible property. Since at higher levels of income (over $100,000) both aged and nonaged depend primarily on such property income, the two curves come together.

Inflation and the business sector

Discussion of the effects of inflation on the business sector is complicated by the effect of accounting practices on tax liabilities. Tax liabilities increase in real terms with inflation because conventional rules for calculating depreciation expense and cost of goods sold understate these costs in inflationary times and thus increase taxable income (Kopcke 1978:56). Allowable depreciation expense for tax purposes is based on original cost, thus underestimating these expenses when the time comes to replace fixed investment. When businesses follow FIFO accounting rules for business inventories, goods first in are assumed to be the goods first out. With rising prices, the firm's closing inventory (the goods it bought last) will cost more than the beginning inventory. As a result, materials cost will be understated (beginning inventory costs will determine costs of goods sold), profits overstated, and tax liability increased.

Increases in the effective tax rate (calculated as a percent of true income) are responsible for declining after-tax rates of return on corporate income since 1965 (Kopcke 1978:56). In turn, such declining rates of return may have adverse consequences on investment spending and real GNP growth. The Economic Recovery Tax Act of 1981 offered businesses many tax concessions, including accelerated depreciation and low corporate tax rates on income below $50,000.

In theory (as was true of the household sector) we should expect that net debtor firms would fare better than net creditor firms. Future tax saving resulting from depreciation deductions can also be treated as a monetary asset. The loss from inflation is then estimated by multiplying potential tax saving by the inflation rate. The study found, however, that rates of return on investment and stock market gains were not significantly different for firms with positive exposure (net creditors including depreciation accounts) than for firms with negative exposure (net debtors after depreciation) (Bach and Stephenson 1974:9, 11).

A possible explanation offered by Bach and Stephenson is that the stock market recognizes the real effects of inflation only with a lag. The market may wait until the firm replaces worn-out capital with more dollars than the original cost or retires its debt with cheap dollars before passing judgment. A later chapter will discuss the important theory of rational expectations. This doctrine implies that stock market values reflect all available information so that no one can outguess the market. A serious criticism shows up here: market valuations may be based on misleading accounting statements stated in nominal rather than real terms. If this is the case, the stock market is not an efficient market (Bach and Stephenson 1974:12).

Additional reasons why the hypothesis was not confirmed may be suggested. Earnings and their variability are probably more influential factors on stock market performance. Bach and Stephenson's study allowed for variability but not for the average level of earnings. The results of their study are consistent with the famous Modigliani-Miller theory that the market value of a company is not affected by the mix of bonds and equity (leverage) but depends solely on the expected earnings from the firm's assets (Modigliani and Miller 1958:26–77; 1963:433–42).

INTEREST RATE EFFECTS   Debtors and creditors are affected by changes in interest rates as discussed above for households. Net debtors will benefit from rising interest rates since the market value of their financial liabilities will fall. Higher interest rates mean that investors will only buy existing debt instruments if their price falls. In this way an old security will give the same effective return as a new one. (The underlying mathematics of finance are taken up in Ch. 5.)

On the other side of the market, holders of old securities will suffer when market interest rates go up. These gains and losses may be unrealized if debtors do not buy back their debt at lower market prices before debts mature and if creditors hold their securities to maturity instead of selling them off at current market prices. (We did not consider this interest rate effect in discussing the net worth effect of inflation.) In 1974, a year of sharply rising interest rates, it is estimated

that the potential gain to nonfinancial corporations from the market decline in
their financial liabilities was $26 bil. (Shoven and Bulow 1976:40–41).

Interest rates and the inflation premium

Inflation may be an important reason for rising interest rates and thus for the
distributional effects just discussed. It can be argued that lenders will demand an
inflation premium if they anticipate inflation. Borrowers will be willing to pay it
because of similar anticipations.

The nominal market interest rate according to this hypothesis is the sum of an
inflation premium and a basic real interest rate return. The hypothesis is known as
the Fisher effect after the famous American economist Irving Fisher (see Fisher
1930). Stated symbolically:

$$i = r + \dot{P}$$

where i = nominal (observed) market rate of interest
$\quad\;\; r$ = real rate of interest
$\quad\;\; \dot{P}$ = percentage change in prices, measured by some price index and equal
$\qquad\quad$ to prices at the end of the current period minus prices at the beginning
$\qquad\quad$ of the current period, all divided by the price level at the beginning of
$\qquad\quad$ the period; symbolically, $\dot{P} = (P_{t+1} - P_t)/P_t$

For this equation to be correct, however, the demand and supply for loanable
funds must mirror anticipated inflation.

The curves L and B in Figure 3.4 stand for the lending and borrowing curves
before inflation. Planned borrowing and lending are equal at a rate of interest of
3%, which is both the nominal and the real rate. Assume perfect anticipation –
lenders know that prices are going to go up by 4%, and similarly for borrowers.
Both curves will shift upward by the same distances. The result will be a new
clearing of the loanable funds market at the interest rate of 7%, equal to the real
rate of 3% and an inflation premium of 4%.

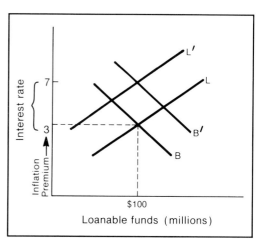

3.4. Anticipated inflation
and the rate of interest.

Question: In a successive period, if prices continue to go up by 4%, will nominal interest rates also go up by 4%? The answer is no, as can be seen from the equation. The inflation premium does not have to keep pace with inflation, only with changes in the percentage increase in prices. As long as prices are advancing at the same rate, the same nominal interest return will protect both the real wealth of the investor and the real rate of return.

Let us say that in period 1 the real rate of interest is 4%, the price change is zero, and thus the nominal rate is 4%. Now in period 2 the inflation rate goes to 6%. The nominal rate must rise to 10% if it is to cover the inflation premium. Despite price rises in every period of the same 6%, the lender (as we shall see) is protected.

Assume that a lender has loaned out $100 for one year at 10%. At the end of the year she will receive back $110. She can spend $4 as before and her real wealth will remain $100 ($106 deflated by 1.06). For simplicity's sake the nominal interest rate is based on the equation shown rather than the "correct" equation, which is $i = r + \dot{P} + r\dot{P}$. The correct equation is derived from $1 + i = (1 + r)(1 + \dot{P})$. Had the correct interest rate of 10.24% been used, $4.24 instead of $4 could have been allocated to current spending in the second period so that real spending would have been exactly $4. To preserve real wealth in our simplified example, real spending is off one period. The example has the investor spending $4.24 in the third period instead of the second.

The lender will relend this $106 the next year, receiving a return of $10.60 plus the original principal of $106. Now $4.24 can be spent (the same real purchasing power as before), leaving a principal of $112.36. In dollars of purchasing power of the initial year, this amount is equivalent to $100. The real wealth of the lender has not suffered because of continued inflation as long as the inflation premium part of the nominal interest rate equals the (constant) inflation rate.

The wealth effects of inflation according to this analysis are traceable to the long-term nature of debt contracts. If lenders and borrowers had one-year contracts that had to be renegotiated annually, with interest rates keeping pace with inflation, the real value of debt obligations need not fall and wealth redistribution would not occur.

Interest rates fail to keep pace exactly with inflation, however. As Figure 3.4 suggests, equal shifts in the demand-and-supply curves are necessary for this to happen. It is likely that the borrower curve will shift more than the lender curve. Borrowers may be more alert to inflation and thus more willing to pay the higher nominal rate that affords them the same real return. Households lend in part on a contractual basis (e.g., life insurance, pension funds) and as a result are less responsive to inflationary expectations. Further, lenders may react to some average of past price increases (this is called adaptive expectations) rather than anticipating the extent of next period's inflation.

The demand curve, too, may not respond appropriately. Borrowers may doubt that inflation will continue throughout the lifetime of the asset they are financing or that their competitors will similarly be willing to pay the inflation premium (Ackley 1978:514).

Lenders do not consistently earn an inflation premium. Looking at the statistics for prices and interest rates in Table 3.6, the change in interest rates rarely matches the change in the percentage increase in prices as the theory requires. (The

Table 3.6. Price and interest rate movements

Year	(1) Percent increase in prices (CPI)	(2) Change in percentage change	Year	(3) Interest rate on 3-month Treasury bill	(4) Change in interest rates
1971	4.3	-1.6	1971	4.35	-2.11
1972	3.3	-1.0	1972	4.07	-0.28
1973	6.2	2.9	1973	7.04	2.97
1974	11.0	4.8	1974	7.89	0.85
1975	9.1	-1.9	1975	5.84	-2.05
1976	5.8	-3.3	1976	4.99	-0.85
1977	6.4	0.6	1977	5.26	0.27
1978	7.6	1.2	1978	7.22	1.96
1979	11.5	3.9	1979	10.04	2.82
1980	13.5	2.0	1980	11.51	1.47
1981	10.2	-3.3	1981	14.08	2.57
1982	6.0	-4.2	1982	10.69	-3.39
1983	3.0	-3.0	1983	8.63	-2.06

Source: Data before 1982 from U.S. Dep. Commer., *Bus. Stat. 1982*, suppl., *Surv. Curr. Bus.* November 1983:24,72; data for 1983 from *Surv. Curr. Bus.* May 1984:s-6, s-16.

short-term rate used better measures of short-run inflationary expectations than the long-term rate.) When the value in col. 2 exceeded the value in col. 4, the borrower benefited, with the reverse being true when 4 exceeded 2. In the first case, the real interest rate and the real cost of borrowing declined. In the second, the real return to the lender increased.

For most of the period shown, the real interest rate was negative or close to zero (col. 3 minus col. 1, Table 3.6). Since 1981 the real interest has been positive and rising. The recession of 1981–82 has been attributed to this increase in the real rate of interest, but the revival in economic activity in 1983–84 points out either the limitations of the real interest rate as an economic indicator or the difficulties in measuring the real rate of interest. If expected inflation rates are subtracted from the interest rate (rather than current inflation rates), inflationary expectations will result in a lowering of the real rate of interest.

The real interest rate takes precedence over the nominal rate in financial decision making. Similarly, the after-tax real interest rate takes precedence over the real interest rate. Assume a nominal rate of 20%, an inflation rate of 10%, and a marginal tax rate of 40% for both borrowers and lenders; the after-tax real interest rate is then 6%. An increase in the marginal tax rate (say to 50%) will have the same effect as an increase in inflationary expectations. The demand for funds will increase (the after-tax cost of borrowing declines, since interest cost is a tax deduction), and the supply of funds will decrease (lenders require additional compensation), the effect being an increase in the nominal rate of interest.

Government as beneficiary

The major creditor sector is the household sector. The net debtor sectors are unincorporated business, nonfinancial corporations, and the government. The loss of real asset value by households as a result of inflation is matched by gains of the debtor sectors. But this is illusory, since the ultimate ownership of both unincorporated and incorporated business belongs to households. If we consolidated all business and household balance sheets, the claims that these sectors have on each other would cancel out.

Government (particularly the federal sector) is a major beneficiary of inflation. Tax revenues rise faster than inflation (because of a progressive tax structure and fixed tax exemptions), and major payments such as interest on the public debt are fixed in dollar terms unless the deficit increases. While households "own" the government, it is doubtful if they appreciate this other side of the coin. The increased government spending made possible by increased tax dollars probably has less utility for the average taxpayer than private spending. If this is correct, the government is a distinct entity and the primary beneficiary from inflation.

Inflation and output

Distribution effects, on which we have been focusing, are of secondary importance to output effects. The size of the national "pie" is more important than the way it is sliced.

Colorful terms such as "menu costs" and "shoe leather costs" describe the output costs of inflation. New menus have to be printed, pay phones adapted, etc., when prices go up. High inflation rates induce people to economize on cash balances by making more trips to the bank. Shopping becomes more difficult because a good buy now requires more information. Automatic teller machines probably minimize shoe leather cost (N. Miller 1983:19–20; Maisel 1982:489).

Output can decline because of efficiency costs. Economic agents cannot be sure if price supports represent a shift in demand (a relative price change) or a nominal change in all price tags. The market mechanism now works less efficiently because it takes longer for firms and workers to move to more productive efforts when there is a genuine change in demand. Managerial talent may be shunted from production management to speculative activities (Ackley 1978:515).

Economic growth may be adversely affected by low after-tax real rates of interest, discouraging saving. Increased uncertainty as to future inflation rates may offset lower real borrowing costs and discourage investment. In particular, investment in longer lived equipment suffers (N. Miller 1983:20–23).

Indexation as the antidote

"If you can't beat 'em, join 'em" summarizes the argument for indexation. Having all prices move with the general price level would stem the inequities of inflation. Interest rates moving up with inflation are part of indexation. Automatic adjustments in tax brackets would also be included in any universal scheme.

Indexation would extend the scope of present COLAs (cost-of-living adjustments); 8.5 mil. union workers were covered in 1978 by COLA. To this number should be added social security recipients, millions of federal civilian and military retirees and their survivors, and over 20 mil. food stamp recipients. Wage contracts negotiated on the basis of expected price increases are tantamount to the COLA arrangements (Cloos 1978:6).

The argument against indexation is the obvious one – that it accelerates and perpetuates inflation. Since indexation fails to increase output, the only effect can be higher prices. If income taxes were indexed, the ultimate effect would be higher prices as spendable income increased. The present system of tax revenues increasing faster than income is a built-in stabilizer (if the government just does not spend more money because of increased taxes). In an open economy, indexation by one country will lead to serious trading difficulties.

Indexation conjures up visions of hyperinflation. The case history of Germany in the 1920s is that the payments mechanism broke down and production suffered when the players spent their time trying to beat the game of runaway prices. This is apart from the wiping out of the German middle class by inflation. By 1923, 1 tril. marks were needed to buy what one bought before the war. The German hyperinflation had its origins in the government printing of money rather than raising taxes when it had to make reparations payments to the winning Allied side in World War I (cf. Mansfield 1977:281).

Falling prices

If rising prices are so bad, falling prices should be great. No, says the economist, this creates problems of its own. What attracted attention in 1984 was the convergence of a wide variety of falling prices exceeding anything economists had seen in a generation. Midwestern farmers were hard hit by the twin prongs of deflation—a decline in the value of farmland often used for collateral for loans and declines in the prices of major farm crops. Merchants who had accumulated high-priced inventories (such as fuel oil dealers) took losses when they are forced to sell for less than cost. The situation of pockets of falling prices is not as worrisome, however, as the sharp and widespread fall in prices in the Great Depression (1929–33) when the general level of prices fell at a rate close to 7% a year, throwing borrowers into bankruptcy and banks out of business (Kilborn 1984a:1, 22).

THE MISERY INDEX   From the standpoint of consumers, falling prices make them better off. This offsets the effect of unemployment, which may be rising at the same time that prices are falling. A misery index (the simple sum of the inflation and unemployment rates) suggests a value to the index of just over 10% in 1984, a decline of nearly one-half since 1981 (Chandrasekhar 1984:56). The fall in the misery index parallels a rise in a second measure of well-being, per capita disposable income in 1972 dollars. The subjective response of voters confirms these data. A mid-1984 poll showed that 55% of those polled thought that the country was better off than it was 4 years earlier and 54% said they were personally better off (Clymer 1984:1, 10).

Summary

We live in an inflationary world. This chapter has suggested how we measure inflation and what its consequences are. Inflation has income and wealth effects. These are exerted directly and also indirectly by the effect of inflation on interest rates. So far in the United States, the consequences have been distributional— some economic agents fare better than others. Among sectors, the federal government appears to be the clearest beneficiary. Output may be affected by a series of factors such as menu, shoe leather, and efficiency costs. In addition the economic growth rate may be adversely affected. The remedy most closely associated with the study of price indexes is indexation. Results are dubious because of its perpetuation of inflation.

1. Describe the differences between the Laspeyres and the Paasche indexes. Why are all price indexes arbitrary?

2. Identify the downward and upward biases of Laspeyres and Paasche price indexes.

3. Distinguish between the major price indexes in the United States. Which are Laspeyres- and which are Paasche-type indexes?

4. Describe how the effects of inflation are complicated by the balance sheet.

5. State the meaning of distributional effects and list those who suffer from inflation and those whose incomes keep pace with inflation.

6. Why do people feel "worse off" in recent years?

7. Explain how inflation, complicated by the effects of accounting practices, affects the business sector.

8. How does inflation affect the government budget?

9. State symbolically the hypothesis that the nominal market interest rate is the sum of an inflation premium and a "real" interest rate.

10. Explain why the nominal interest rate does not have to rise when prices increase at a constant rate equal to the inflation premium.

11. Are decisions in financial markets by lenders and borrowers made on the basis of (a) the nominal interest rate, (b) the real interest rate, (c) the after-tax real interest rate?

12. Explain the argument against indexation as a remedy for inflation.

13. Define:

Consumer price index	Inflation premium
Wholesale price index	Nominal market interest rate
Implicit GNP deflator	Indexation
Leverage ratio	Net worth
Census income	Monetary assets
Accrued comprehensive income	Variable price assets
	Bracket creep

Financial intermediation

Here we discuss how financial markets improve the use of resources for consumption and investment purposes. (This is a separate question from the stimulating effect of money and finance on the gross national product discussed in Ch. 2.) This chapter also covers the routing of credit flows between lender and borrower.

Making choices without financial markets

CONSUMER SATISFACTION   In a world without financial markets, preference for future goods over present goods is exercised by holding cash for future spending. Time preference works only in this one direction. A preference for present goods over future goods cannot be exercised at all.

These restrictions on consumer behavior are illustrated in Figure 4.1. The

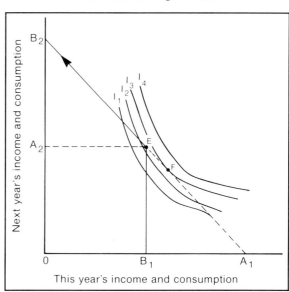

4.1. Spending allocations without finance.

horizontal scale measures this year's income and consumption, and the values for next year are shown on the vertical axis. The concentric lines are called indifference curves. Each curve shows different combinations of consumption this year and next that will yield the consumer the same amount of well-being. The convex (from below) shape of these curves tells us that goods become more valuable as they get scarcer. Moving down the curves, one can see that it takes more consumption this year to compensate for the loss of a unit of consumption next year as next year's consumption is cut back (if total satisfaction is to remain constant). Moving up the curves, the reasoning is similar. As current consumption is cut back, progressively more is required next year if total consumer satisfaction is to stay the same. The shape of the curves tells us that this year's consumption is not a perfect substitute for next year's. If it was, the indifference curves would be straight lines sloping downward from left to right. Higher curves represent higher levels of satisfaction, since they obviously represent more goods. The rational consumer aims at the highest possible indifference curve.

The catch is that consumption choices must be consistent with available income. The income constraint is represented by the solid opportunity line identified with an arrow (EB_2). Where it meets the vertical axis at $0B_2$ measures next year's income $0A_2$ plus this year's income $0A_1$. (Interest on the first year's income is neglected.) The consumer's opportunity is to spend both years' income next year, if choosing to spend zero income this year. Such an extreme choice is unlikely, but it allows us to define the alternatives. The direction of the arrow signifies the one-way choice open to the consumer, who can allocate this year's income to next year but cannot do the reverse.

Given the contours of the consumer's indifference curves and the necessity that one make contact with the opportunity line, the best that can be done is to achieve the indifference level I_2, consuming $0A_1$ income this year and $0A_2$ income next year, as shown by point E.

If we extended the opportunity line so that it met the horizontal axis (shown by the dashed segment), this would signify that next year's income could be spent this year. (It neglects the interest rate on money. As drawn, $0B_1$ equals $0B_2$, which implies that all of next year's income could be spent this year. Considering this interest deduction, maximum consumption this year will be less than the sum of both years' incomes.) Now a higher indifference curve I_3 is tangent to the opportunity line at F. Such tangency gives the highest level of satisfaction consistent with the income constraint. It is only possible if the consumer has the option to borrow against future income.

INVESTMENT OPPORTUNITIES   In a world without finance, better investment opportunities go neglected. Two sectors are represented in Figure 4.2 (cf. Friedland 1966:305). The saving flows in every period are shown by the vertical S curves, signifying that regardless of the interest yield, the same amount of saving will be forthcoming. Such unresponsiveness may be due to lack of financial alternatives, but the curves will be assumed to stay the same even with them.

The FC lines measure the dollar value of the extra output resulting from additional investment, expressed as a percent of this investment. As investment increases, marginal productivity declines (the law of diminishing returns). The yields on the vertical axis measure this decline.

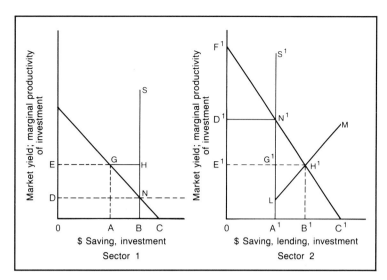

4.2. Investment decisions before and after financial markets.

When the sectors are isolated, saving is automatically reinvested. Sector 1 saves and invests $0B$; sector 2 saves and reinvests $0A^1$. The yield on the marginal investment of sector 2 is $0D^1$, much higher than $0D$. The economic imperative is that sector 2 should invest more and sector 1 should invest less, a situation that only lending and borrowing make possible.

This may bother the reader. Increasing investment will lower yields. Aren't higher yields better than lower yields? Marginal analysis (the economist's stock-in-trade) points out that total product will keep increasing as long as the additions to product in sector 2 (measured by yields down the F^1C^1 curve) exceed the losses in product in sector 1 (by moving up the FC curve). When losses and gains are equal, investment is optimal. No further increase in total output results from reallocating investment.

LENDING AND BORROWING   Lending and borrowing introduces the LM line in sector 2. Sector 1 is now willing to lend to sector 2 because prospective yields from financial investment exceed possible returns from own real investment. $0D$ is the minimum rate at which sector 1 will lend to sector 2 since $0D$ marks the return that can be earned in its own sector. Above that rate the saving curve in sector 2 is supplemented by sector 1 lending. Earnings on such lending must always exceed what sector 1 could have earned in self-investment. As interest yields rise, more is loaned to sector 2, since less investment will earn this return in sector 1. The horizontal distances between LS^1 and LM are the mirror image of the distances between NF and NS.

Equilibrium is reached at the $0E$ yield with $0A$ investment in sector 1 and $0B'$ investment in sector 2. The latter investment is financed by $0A$ saving of sector 2 and sector 1 loans equal to G^1H^1. The resultant gain in total output is measured by areas under the investment curves. The output loss in sector 1 as a result of lending instead of investment is equal to the area $GABN$. The output gain in sector 2 is equal to $N^1A^1B^1H^1$, obviously greater than $GABN$.

Assume that consumers of the first section of this chapter are the owners (shareholders) of the business firm making investment outlays. Consumers have a strong preference for present goods (dividends) versus future goods (via reinvestment). At the same time, rational decision making calls for plowing back earnings. Such conflicts of interest are resolved by resorting to external finance. It will be shown that the shareholders "can have their cake and eat it too." They can enjoy high current income and high future income via the investment-borrowing process.

Figures 4.3 and 4.4 bring back the consumer indifference curves of Figure 4.1. These diagrams follow the logic of the figure in Smith (1971:15). The new PP curve, which can be called an investment opportunity curve, is similar to the previous marginal productivity curve of Figure 4.2 except the total returns on investment are measured on the vertical axis. The marginal productivity of investment is now measured by the slope of the curve at any selected level of investment. In interpreting this curve begin at point $0A_1$, which stands for this year's corporate income. If this amount is reinvested, the return would be $0B_1$ in the following year. As another example, if A_2A_1 was reinvested, the following year's return would be $0B_2$ and so on. Note that the volume of investment is measured leftward from A_1 rather than the origin.

A single indifference curve is drawn tangent to the investment opportunity curve at E. In financial isolation the corporation should invest A_1A_3, leaving $0A_3$ for current dividends. Next year's return will be $0B_3$, which can be paid out to stockholders. (Unlike the indifference curve analysis of Fig. 4.1, next year's income

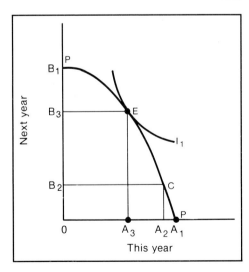

4.3. Introducing the investment opportunity line.

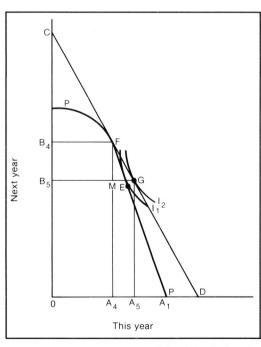

4.4. Introducing the market opportunity line.

is dependent on this year's investment.) In this way, the relative preferences of shareholders for present versus future consumption are consistent with the corporate income constraint. The shareholder is on the highest possible indifference curve.

Now it can be shown that corporate borrowing makes shareholders better off. Figure 4.4 introduces the market opportunity line CD whose slope measures the market rate of interest. More precisely, the slope is $-(1 + r)$, where r is the market rate of interest. When the investment opportunity curve is tangent to the market opportunity line at F, marginal returns from investment equal the marginal opportunity cost of investment. (The cost may be an implicit one – what the company could have earned had it loaned out money instead of borrowing it – or an explicit one – what borrowed money costs; the term "opportunity" permits both meanings.) This equality marks the ideal amount of investment. It could be financed by reducing current consumption to $0A_4$. But such a choice would place shareholders on a lower indifference curve (not drawn).

The market rate of interest is also the key to consumption allocation. When the shareholder's preference for goods this year as opposed to goods next year (measured by the slope of the indifference curve) corresponds to the slope of the market opportunity line CD, present goods are valued at their true market cost in terms of future goods (point G). Borrowing to reach this amount of consumption is warranted. The amount of goods that must be sacrificed next year (in repayment) for the extra unit of consumption this year is consistent with shareholder preferences. Any more borrowing for present consumption will cost more than it is worth. (The indifference curve beyond G going to the right is flatter than the market curve.) Thus A_4A_5 is the right amount of borrowing. This places shareholders on the indifference curve I_2 with $0A_5$ of consumption this year and $0B_5$ next year, both amounts exceeding values at E. This may puzzle the reader, who has been taught that borrowing finances investment, and now it seems to finance consumption. In fact, there is no inconsistency. The other side of borrowing to finance investment is that consumption is higher than it otherwise would be. To relate investment directly to borrowing, the investment distance on Figure 4.4 $A_4A_1 = (0A_1 - 0A_5) + A_4A_5$; i.e., investment equals the first year's income less consumption plus borrowing. The term $0A_1 - 0A_5$ represents internal finance, which can also be written as A_5A_1. Thus investment equals retained earnings plus borrowing.

The B_4B_5 of next year's output is used to repay the loan at interest. Everything works out neatly because of the triangle FMG. MG equals A_4A_5, the amount of borrowing. The $-(1 + r)$ slope of the CD line guarantees that FM ($= B_4B_5$) will be greater than MG by the amount of interest r. The total output next year will be $0B_4$. When B_4B_5 repayment of the loan plus interest is subtracted, the amount of consumption next year is $0B_5$.

To draw Figure 4.4 correctly, the investment opportunity line must be tangent with the market opportunity line above and to the left of tangency of the second indifference curve with the market opportunity line. One author (Smith 1971:15) meets the challenge by drawing the market opportunity line with a slope of less than one, implying a negative rate of interest. Drawing the curves properly has interesting economic implications. The investment opportunity line is drawn very steeply, implying high marginal returns. The shareholder indifference curve must also be steep, implying a high rate of time preference for present versus future goods.

Direct versus indirect finance

Lending and borrowing may be direct or indirect. Lenders may lend directly to borrowers or they may acquire financial claims on intermediaries who in turn lend to ultimate borrowers. Table 4.1, using hypothetical figures from Chapter 1, brings out the distinction. An alternative terminology is to talk of surplus and deficit units. Surplus units experience net financial investment; deficit units, negative net financial investment. Typically, households fall into the first category, the business sector into the second. This can be misleading terminology, however, because surplus units may be both borrowers and lenders and the same is true of deficit units. For this reason, we prefer the less ambiguous concepts of lending and borrowing.

Table 4.1 begins with the funds raised by nonfinancial sectors. These amount to $92 bil., with $70 bil. constituting indirect borrowing. Direct borrowing of $22 bil. is determined residually. Funds advanced by the nonfinancial sector include $22 bil. of direct lending and $65 bil. of indirect lending and are $5 bil. less than indirect borrowing by nonfinancial sectors, since $5 bil. of indirect lending by financial intermediaries is financed by saving.

Funds advanced by financial intermediaries in Table 4.1 are indirect ($70 bil.). They exceed their indirect borrowing by the amount of the intermediary saving of $5 bil. listed last.

Members of the nonfinancial sector issuing claims against themselves are primary borrowers and the claims are primary claims. Any sector buying these claims is a primary lender. So by this nomenclature the nonfinancial sector is a primary direct lender and financial intermediaries are both primary and indirect lenders. The deposit claims issued by intermediaries are secondary claims; thus depositors are purchasers of secondary claims.

Table 4.1.	Estimating direct and indirect finance	
Line	Transaction	
		($ bil.)
1 [6]	Funds raised by nonfinancial sectors	92
2 [1-3]	Direct borrowing (credit market borrowing)	22
3 [4] = 7	Indirect borrowing	70
4 1-13	Funds advanced by nonfinancial sectors	87
5 2	Direct lending	22
6 7-13	Indirect lending	65
7 [4]	Funds advanced by financial intermediaries	70
8 [4]	Indirect lending	70
9 [4] + [1]	Funds raised by financial intermediaries	70
10 [4]	Indirect borrowing	65
11 [5]	Deposits at financial intermediaries	55
12 [6]	Loans and securities (credit market borrowing)	10
13 [1]	Saving	5

Note: Bracketed line references are to Table 1.5. Other line references are to lines in table.

CLASSIFICATION OF FINANCIAL MARKETS   The problem with use of primary and secondary with respect to claims is that these terms also apply to financial markets in which primary securities are traded. When they trade for the first time, such trading is said to take place in the primary market. Subsequent trading takes place in the secondary market.

The idea of a market is confusing because it conjures up an image of a fixed spot where buyers and sellers confront each other. In part, this is true of financial markets. The best example might be the New York Stock Exchange. But buyers and sellers the world over may constitute a market via electronic linkages. The term over-the-counter market applies to such electronic markets and is to be contrasted with the type of organized market represented by New York.

Markets can also be characterized by the maturity of the debt they handle. The term money market is applied to short-term instruments (one year or less), capital market to longer term maturities. Money market has a narrower meaning for the monetary theorist who restricts it to the demand for and supply of money.

THE DATA ON DIRECT AND INDIRECT FINANCE   Comprehensive data on direct and indirect flows are regularly published in the *Federal Reserve Bulletin* and sample figures are reproduced in Table 4.2. Line 1, total funds advanced to the nonfinancial sector, is equivalent to funds raised in the skeleton outline of Table 4.1. The nonfinancial sector includes public agencies, the foreign sector, and private domestic nonfinancial investors. Lines 3–6 indicate the financial instruments involved in lending by the public and foreign sectors, and lines 7–10 identify the amounts advanced by these sectors. Lines 14–18 list the main financial instruments for domestic lending. The heading private financial intermediation measures indirect lending. Direct lending in credit markets (line 33) is broader than the concept of direct lending in Table 4.1 by including credit market borrowing by financial intermediaries (line 27). If the nature of the debt instrument used is the criterion, this treatment is justified, since the credit market instruments (bonds, stocks) issued by intermediaries are similar to those issued by the nonfinancial sector. Financial intermediaries with this treatment have direct borrowing, indirect borrowing, and saving as sources of funds.

The rationale of indirect finance

What stands out in the data on direct and indirect finance is the importance of the latter (line 49, Table 4.2). Financial institutions extend credit in one market, the credit market, and borrow in another, the deposit market — a term being used in a comprehensive enough way to include insurance and pension fund premiums. In the credit market, they are dealing with borrowers who are buying illiquidity (deferral of debt payment) at the price of higher interest costs. In the deposit market, they are dealing with lenders who are buying liquidity at the sacrifice of interest. Financial institutions on the basis of their own trade-offs aim at reaching an equilibrium with both parties. In equilibrium, the interest spread covers the costs of intermediation.

The magic of the financial intermediary is in its transforming illiquid claims into liquid ones. Instead of ultimate lenders buying illiquid securities, they let

Table 4.2. Direct and indirect sources of funds to credit markets ($ bil., except as noted)

Transaction category, or sector	1982	1983
1 Total funds advanced in credit markets to domestic nonfinancial sectors	395.3	509.5
By public agencies and foreign		
2 Total net advances	109.3	114.8
3 U.S. government securities	17.9	27.7
4 Residential mortgages	61.1	75.9
5 Federal Home Loan Bank (FHLB) advances to savings and loans	0.8	-7.0
6 Other loans and securities	29.5	18.3
Total advanced, by sector		
7 U.S. government	16.7	9.8
8 Sponsored credit agencies	65.3	68.9
9 Monetary authorities	9.8	10.9
10 Foreign	17.6	25.2
Agency and foreign borrowing not in line 1		
11 Sponsored credit agencies and mortgage pools	64.9	68.1
12 Foreign	15.7	19.2
Private domestic funds advanced		
13 Total net advances	366.6	482.0
14 U.S. government securities	207.9	227.0
15 State and local obligations	50.5	44.3
16 Corporate and foreign bonds	15.4	12.1
17 Residential mortgages	-3.3	44.6
18 Other mortgages and loans	96.8	146.9
19 Less: FHLB advances	0.8	-7.0
Private financial intermediation		
20 Credit market funds advanced by private financial institutions	271.2	368.5
21 Commercial banking	108.5	135.3
22 Savings institutions	30.6	128.6
23 Insurance and pension funds	94.2	102.1
24 Other finance	37.9	2.6
25 Sources of funds	271.2	368.5
26 Private domestic deposits and repurchase agreements (RPs)	173.4	200.3
27 Credit market borrowing	4.4	20.5
28 Other sources	93.5	147.7
29 Foreign funds	-27.7	17.2
30 Treasury balances	6.1	-6.0
31 Insurance and pension reserves	85.9	88.0
32 Other, net	29.2	48.4
Private domestic nonfinancial investors		
33 Direct lending in credit markets	99.7	134.0
34 U.S. government securities	58.1	89.8
35 State and local obligations	30.9	31.9
36 Corporate and foreign bonds	-9.4	-6.1
37 Open-market paper	-2.0	7.7
38 Other	22.1	10.8
39 Deposits and currency	179.4	217.5
40 Currency	8.4	13.9
41 Checkable deposits	13.0	22.5
42 Small time and savings accounts	137.0	216.6
43 Money market fund shares	24.7	-44.1
44 Large time deposits	-5.2	-2.3
45 Security RPs	3.8	7.5
46 Deposits in foreign countries	-2.4	3.3
47 Total of credit market instruments, deposits and currency	279.1	351.6
48 Public holdings as percent of total	26.6	21.7
49 Private financial intermediation (%)	74.0	76.5
50 Total foreign funds	-10.2	42.5
Memo: Corporate equities not included above		
51 Total net issues	35.4	69.2
52 Mutual fund shares	18.6	32.6
53 Other equities	16.8	36.6

Table 4.2. (continued)

Transaction category, or sector	1982	1983
54 Acquisitions by financial institutions	27.9	54.4
55 Other net purchases	7.5	14.8

Source: *Fed. Res. Bull.* 1984a:A41.
Notes by line number:
1. Line 1 of Table 1.58 in source.
2. Sum of lines 3-6 or 7-10.
6. Includes farm and commercial mortgages.
11. Credit market funds raised by federally sponsored credit agencies and net issues of federally related mortgage pool securities.
13. Line 1 less line 2 plus line 11 and 12. Also line 20 less line 27 plus line 33. Also sum of lines 28 and 47 less lines 40 and 46.
18. Includes farm and commercial mortgages.
26. Line 39 less lines 40 and 46.
27. Excludes equity issues and investment company shares. Includes line 19.
29. Foreign deposits at commercial banks, bank borrowings from foreign branches, and liabilities of foreign banking agencies to foreign affiliates.
30. Demand deposits at commercial banks.
31. Excludes net investment of these reserves in corporate equities.
32. Mainly retained earnings and net miscellaneous liabilities.
33. Line 12 less line 20 plus line 27.
34-38. Lines 14-18 less amounts acquired by private finance. Line 38 includes mortgages.
40. Mainly an offset to line 9.
47. Lines 33 plus 39, or line 13 less line 28 plus 40 and 46.
48. Line 2/line 1.
49. Line 20/line 13.
50. Sum of lines 10 and 29.
51, 53. Includes issues by financial institutions.

institutions do this. Lenders can have their cake and eat it too; they can earn interest and yet own monetary assets that are easily convertible into cash. The law of large numbers keeps intermediation costs down and explains their success. Specialization gives expertise in lending, and the law of averages permits risky loan making financed by liquid claims. It is not surprising then that financial intermediaries have shown tremendous growth. The average share in external finance was less than 45% in 1901–29, 60% in 1934–49, and 81% in 1974–83 (Goldsmith 1958:301; *Fed. Res. Bull.,* various issues). At the same time, there are year-to-year swings in the intermediation ratio. A decline in the channeling role of financial intermediaries is referred to as "disintermediation." The ebb and flow of intermediation are discussed in Chapter 14.

WHY DIRECT FINANCE PERSISTS   In extolling the prowess of the intermediary, one can succeed only too well. Why does any direct finance take place, since both borrowers and lenders appear to benefit from intermediation? In addition to the liquidity feature, the intermediary saves search and information costs for both borrowers and lenders. This impression of overwhelming superiority is given by Kaufman (1977:59–63).

Direct finance persists (and increases with disintermediation) for several reasons. Individual lenders are willing to assume greater risk in exchange for a greater return. Some lenders are more knowledgeable than other investors and do not have to depend on the expertise of the intermediary. Their search and information costs are low. When rates on credit market instruments are rising, deposit rates fail to keep in step for various reasons (legal restraints, fixed interest returns on intermediary portfolios).

In Table 4.2, private financial intermediation (lines 20–24) includes commercial banks, savings institutions (savings and loans, mutual savings banks, credit unions), insurance and pension funds, and other finance. Their chief sources of funds are private domestic deposits and credit market borrowing (lines 26, 27). It is convenient to consider commercial banks as intermediaries because deposits are a common source of funds for them and savings institutions.

But treating demand deposits and currency as moneys advanced to the bank sector (as financial intermediation implies) is misleading. Holders of money cannot be advancing it to someone else. Increases in the money stock are not sources of funds for the bank sector. (The money item in Ch. 1 was for this reason identified as a debit or a credit entry and not a use or source of funds.) The dilemma is that the individual bank does indeed see an increase in its demand deposits as a source of funds—the funds being its reserves. But from the standpoint of all banks (the bank sector) deposits are created as part of the lending process.

For the banking sector, as far as money is concerned, the intermediation is between the central bank and the nonbank public. The central bank provides commercial banks with reserves, which lead to the advance of funds on a multiple basis to the public. Similarly, it intermediates in the currency process. In the United States, currency is largely a credit entry for the central bank. The currency is shipped to the banks who pay it out to their depositors as they demand it. Since 1980 when an important banking act was passed (see Ch. 6), deposit-type thrift institutions share the money-creating features of commercial banks. Commercial banks are now members of the wider category of depository institutions.

Nondepository financial intermediaries can be classified into several distinct groups. Insurance-type intermediaries include insurance companies and pension funds. Investment bankers, brokers, and dealers perform closely related functions in underwriting the issue of new securities. The federal government is an important lender. The amounts advanced by the U.S. government and sponsored credit agencies are shown in lines 7 and 8 of Table 4.2. Public agencies and foreign lending accounted for 22% of total funds advanced in 1983 (line 48). Other financial institutions include investment-type intermediaries and consumer-oriented intermediaries. Mutual funds and bank-administered personal trusts fall into the former category, sales and personal finance companies into the latter.

Summary

Lending and borrowing make it possible for saving to be allocated to its most productive use. At the same time, borrowing reconciles shareholder time preference with the investment preferences of corporate management. To a considerable and growing extent the financial process is intermediated by financial institutions because of their unique ability to convert illiquid claims into liquid ones. Nevertheless, direct finance persists and disintermediation can rise sharply in tight-money periods. Banks are a unique form of financial intermediary because of their ability to create money. Banking legislation has resulted in the more comprehensive category of depository institutions with a similar capacity.

1. Explain how consumers choose beween present consumption and future consumption in the absence of finance.

2. Describe how lending and borrowing induce optimal amounts of investment, assuming two sectors with sharply different marginal productivity schedules but with identical saving schedules.

3. Show by means of indifference curve analysis how the optimal amount of investment makes it possible for shareholders to reach the highest possible satisfaction level.

4. Distinguish between indirect and direct finance and explain the rationale behind intermediation.

5. Has indirect finance become progressively more or less important in this country? Why?

6. Are commercial banks (depository institutions) financial intermediaries in the same way as other financial institutions?

7. Define:

Indifference curves	Primary market
Opportunity lines	Secondary market
Marginal productivity of investment	Primary claims
Marginal opportunity cost of investment	Secondary claims
Direct versus indirect finance	Money market
Intermediation	Capital market
Disintermediation	

5

Mathematics of finance

Lenders must calculate and so must borrowers. They must decide whether an investment (real or financial) pays. A series of comparisons are involved. The financial lender must be able to compare alternative returns. The borrower must compare alternative costs.

The theory

The ingredients of decision making are four related variables: nominal interest rate, market price of the financial instrument, market rate of interest, and time to maturity of the instrument.

The nominal rate of interest is the rate stated on a fixed income security. A bond may promise to pay 6% annually. If the face value of the bond (the amount to be repaid when the bond matures) is $1000, the owner will clip a $60 coupon annually. Thus the 6% rate is called the coupon rate.

The market price of the bond is what the buyer must pay for it. The market rate of interest is the effective rate of interest, what the lender is in fact earning on the investment. The time to maturity is the length of time before the obligation is repaid.

Representing these variables symbolically:

FV = face value of the bond
C = value of the coupon
$c = C/FV$ = the coupon (nominal) rate of interest
r = market rate of interest
n = number of years to maturity
PB = market price of the bond

PERPETUITIES   The easiest way to begin is with perpetuities, which have no fixed maturity date. (The British issued their debt in this form until 1947.) We can initially concentrate on three variables: the dollar value of the coupon, market rate of interest, and market price of the bond. The following equation shows their relationship: $PB = C/r = cFV/r$, or $r = C/PB$.

The inverse relationship between the market price of the bond and the market rate of interest is revealed in these equations. The higher the market rate of interest, the lower the market price of the bond, given the coupon (nominal) rate of interest. The reasoning is intuitive: if a bond pays a fixed number of dollars a year, say $60 (a coupon rate of 6% times a face value of $1000) and investors can earn 10% on a new bond, they will only pay $60/0.10, or $600, for the right to $60 in perpetuity from an old one. In this way returns are equalized. Conversely, given the market price of $600, a would-be investor can determine the prospective yield to be 10%.

Suppose an investor holds a bond bought originally for $1000. Would it pay to sell it and buy a new security paying the higher market rate? The answer is that it never pays to do so because the investor can be considered as earning the going market yield on the depreciated security. Apart from tax considerations, it would not pay to sell and reinvest in another bond. By holding on to the security, the extra transaction costs of selling the first security and buying a second one will be avoided.

FIXED MATURITIES   The mathematics become more complicated in the case of a fixed maturity. The market price is now determined by the present value of a series of future interest returns and the future repayment.

Present value is the other side of accumulation and can most easily be explained by beginning with an example of accumulation. Whether we take advantage of it or not, the interest clock keeps ticking away. A sum today accumulates to a larger value tomorrow. A sum of $100 this year will accumulate to $106 next year, given a market rate of 6%. Expressed symbolically, $S = A(1 + r)$, where S is the future sum and A is the present sum. The $1 + r$ indicates that the future sum is the return of principal plus the interest on it. Suppose now that the future sum S is known (as is true of future interest payments). We can then reverse the equation and solve for A, the present value of this future sum. Thus $A = S/(1 + r)$. The future sum is discounted at 1 plus the market rate. (It makes a considerable difference when the denominator is $1 + r$ instead of r alone. The latter is appropriate for a perpetuity—a sum to be paid regularly ad infinitum but not for a single future sum.) In similar fashion, present values of later future returns can be calculated. For example, a payment due in 2 years' time, $S2$, is equal to $A(1 + r)$ $(1 + r)$. Knowing $S2$ and r, we can again solve for A, the present value of a sum due in 2 years' time. A bond paying S regularly for n years and paid back at the end of n years will have a market price equal to the present value of all these payments. Thus:

$$PB = \frac{S1}{(1 + r)} + \frac{S2}{(1 + r)^2} + \cdots + \frac{Sn}{(1 + r)^n} + \frac{FV}{(1 + r)^n}$$

The introduction of a fourth dimension (time to maturity) makes calculation of one variable (given the value of the other variables) more complex. Solving r, for example, is a tedious chore requiring the use of logarithms. Happily, bond tables are available for reading present values or market yields. In Table 5.1 present values of a $100 bond paying 15% nominal interest are shown for different combinations of yields (the rows) and maturities (the columns). Suppose you want to determine the market price of a 14-year bond when the market yield is 13%. Going down the rows on the left-hand side of the table, locate this yield and proceed across the row to the 14-year column. The present value of the bond is $112.75. Conversely, starting with a 9-year maturity and a present value of $138.38, we read off a market yield of 8.75%.

In the absence of bond tables, bond salespeople's methods give rough approximations to market yields. The current yield can be calculated by dividing the regular interest payment by the market price; e.g., an annual payment of $10 on a bond selling for $70 represents a 14.3% current yield.

The formula for calculating the yield to maturity is:

$$r = \frac{C + (FV - PB)/n}{(PB + FV)/2}$$

The difference between the purchase price BP and the maturity value FV measures the capital gain or loss on the bond. When divided by the number of years to maturity n, the gain is put on an annual basis. The average return shown in the numerator is divided by the average investment in the bond; e.g., a bond purchased for $70, paying 10% nominal interest with a value at maturity of $100 in 5 years, will have a yield to maturity (shortcut method) equal to 18.8%.

When a security is sold before maturity, its yield is referred to as the holding-period yield. The expected holding period can be calculated by using the above formula, with the expected selling price replacing the face value of the bond in both numerator and denominator. Retrospectively, a realized holding-period yield can be calculated using the actual selling price. For a more accurate formula, one that allows for present values of future returns, see Kaufman (1977:192).

BUSINESS INVESTMENT   A business firm contemplating a capital expenditure can exploit the present-value equation in two alternate ways. On the basis of an estimate of future returns from the investment, its scrap value (equivalent to FV in the present-value equation), and the market rate of interest, the firm can estimate the present value of the investment. (Because the market rate of interest is usually thought of in terms of a riskless security, the rate will be the market rate plus a premium based on risk in the firm's own line of business.) The present value will be compared with the cost of the capital good (building, machines). A positive net present value (present value less the cost of the capital good) signals the profitability of the investment.

Alternatively, on the left-hand side of the equation, the cost of the capital good can be substituted for present value. Now the discount factor becomes the unknown. The name now given to r is the internal rate of return or the marginal efficiency of investment. A return in excess of the cost of capital is a signal to go ahead with the investment. The cost of capital is more complex than the interest cost. Tax credits, depreciation, and the inflation rate must all be considered (see Ch. 15).

The third main variable, time, can also be the criterion for decision making. Management may be interested in the payback period, i.e., how long it takes before an initial investment is recouped. Assume that the net present value is the same for two different projects. The project with the shorter payback period (as

Table 5.1. Bond value table, 15% nominal rate

Yield	1 yr	2 yr	3 yr	4 yr	5 yr	6 yr	7 yr	8 yr	9 yr	10 yr	11 yr	12 yr	13 yr	14 yr	15 yr	16 yr
0.0	115.00	130.00	145.00	160.00	175.00	190.00	205.00	220.00	235.00	250.00	265.00	280.00	295.00	310.00	325.00	340.00
1.00	113.90	127.65	141.27	154.76	168.11	181.33	194.42	207.38	220.21	232.91	245.49	257.94	270.27	282.47	294.56	306.52
2.00	112.81	125.36	137.67	149.74	161.56	173.16	184.52	195.67	206.59	217.30	227.79	238.08	248.17	258.06	267.75	277.25
3.00	111.74	123.13	134.18	144.92	155.33	165.45	175.26	184.79	194.04	203.01	211.72	220.18	228.39	236.36	244.10	251.60
4.00	110.68	120.94	130.81	140.29	149.40	158.16	166.58	174.68	182.46	189.93	197.12	204.03	210.67	217.05	223.18	229.08
4.25	110.42	120.40	129.98	139.16	147.97	156.41	164.50	172.26	179.70	186.84	193.68	200.24	206.53	212.56	218.34	223.88
4.50	110.16	119.87	129.16	138.05	146.55	154.68	162.45	169.89	177.01	183.81	190.32	196.54	202.50	208.19	213.64	218.85
4.75	109.90	119.34	128.35	136.94	145.15	152.97	160.44	167.56	174.36	180.85	187.03	192.94	198.57	203.95	209.08	213.97
5.00	109.64	118.81	127.54	135.85	143.76	151.29	158.45	165.28	171.77	177.95	183.83	189.42	194.75	199.82	204.65	209.25
5.25	109.38	118.28	126.74	134.77	142.39	149.63	156.50	163.03	169.22	175.11	180.69	186.00	191.03	195.81	200.36	204.67
5.50	109.12	117.76	125.95	133.70	141.04	147.99	154.58	160.82	166.73	172.33	177.63	182.65	187.41	191.92	196.18	200.23
5.75	108.87	117.24	125.16	132.64	139.71	146.38	152.69	158.65	164.29	169.61	174.64	179.39	183.88	188.13	192.13	195.92
6.00	108.61	116.73	124.38	131.59	138.39	144.79	150.83	156.52	161.89	166.95	171.72	176.21	180.45	184.44	188.20	191.75
6.25	108.36	116.21	123.60	130.55	137.08	143.23	149.00	154.43	159.54	164.34	168.86	173.11	177.10	180.85	184.38	187.70
6.50	108.10	115.70	122.83	129.52	135.80	141.68	147.20	152.38	157.24	161.79	166.07	170.08	173.84	177.36	180.67	183.78
6.75	107.85	115.20	122.07	128.50	134.52	140.16	145.43	150.36	154.98	159.29	163.34	167.12	170.66	173.97	177.07	179.97
7.00	107.60	114.69	121.31	127.50	133.27	138.65	143.68	148.38	152.76	156.85	160.67	164.23	167.56	170.67	173.57	176.28
7.25	107.35	114.19	120.56	126.50	132.02	137.17	141.96	146.43	150.58	154.46	158.06	161.42	164.54	167.45	170.17	172.69
7.50	107.10	113.69	119.82	125.51	130.80	135.71	140.27	144.51	148.45	152.11	155.51	158.67	161.60	164.33	166.86	169.21
7.75	106.85	113.20	119.08	124.53	129.59	134.27	138.61	142.63	146.36	149.81	153.02	155.98	158.73	161.28	163.65	165.84
8.00	106.60	112.70	118.35	123.56	128.39	132.85	136.97	140.78	144.31	147.57	150.58	153.36	155.94	158.32	160.52	162.56
8.25	106.35	112.21	117.62	122.61	127.20	131.45	135.36	138.97	142.29	145.36	148.19	150.81	153.21	155.44	157.48	159.37
8.50	106.11	111.73	116.90	121.66	126.04	130.06	133.77	137.18	140.32	143.21	145.86	148.31	150.56	152.63	154.53	156.28
8.75	105.86	111.24	116.18	120.72	124.88	128.70	132.21	135.43	138.38	141.09	143.58	145.87	147.97	149.89	151.66	153.28
9.00	105.62	110.76	115.47	119.79	123.74	127.36	130.67	133.70	136.48	139.02	141.35	143.49	145.44	147.23	148.87	150.37
9.25	105.37	110.28	114.77	118.87	122.61	126.03	129.15	132.01	134.61	137.00	139.17	141.16	142.98	144.63	146.15	147.53
9.50	105.13	109.81	114.07	117.95	121.49	124.72	127.66	130.34	132.78	135.01	137.04	138.89	140.57	142.11	143.51	144.78
9.75	104.89	109.34	113.38	117.05	120.39	123.43	126.19	128.70	130.99	133.06	134.95	136.67	138.23	139.64	140.93	142.11
10.00	104.65	108.86	112.69	116.16	119.30	122.16	124.75	127.09	129.22	131.16	132.91	134.50	135.94	137.25	138.43	139.51
10.25	104.41	108.40	112.01	115.27	118.23	120.90	123.32	125.51	127.49	129.29	130.91	132.38	133.71	134.91	136.00	136.98
10.50	104.17	107.93	111.33	114.40	117.16	119.66	121.92	123.96	125.80	127.46	128.95	130.31	131.53	132.63	133.62	134.52
10.75	103.93	107.47	110.66	113.53	116.11	118.44	120.54	122.43	124.13	125.66	127.04	128.28	129.40	130.41	131.32	132.13
11.00	103.69	107.01	109.99	112.67	115.08	117.24	119.18	120.92	122.49	123.90	125.17	126.30	127.32	128.24	129.07	129.81
11.25	103.46	106.55	109.33	111.82	114.05	116.05	117.84	119.45	120.89	122.18	123.33	124.37	125.30	126.13	126.88	127.55
11.50	103.22	106.10	108.67	110.98	113.03	114.87	116.52	117.99	119.31	120.49	121.54	122.48	123.32	124.07	124.75	125.35
11.75	102.98	105.65	108.02	110.14	112.03	113.72	115.22	116.56	117.76	118.83	119.78	120.63	121.39	122.07	122.67	123.21

Table 5.1. (continued)

Yield	1 yr	2 yr	3 yr	4 yr	5 yr	6 yr	7 yr	8 yr	9 yr	10 yr	11 yr	12 yr	13 yr	14 yr	15 yr	16 yr
12.00	102.75	105.20	107.38	109.31	111.04	112.58	113.94	115.16	116.24	117.20	118.06	118.83	119.50	120.11	120.65	121.13
12.25	102.52	104.75	106.73	108.50	110.06	111.45	112.68	113.78	114.75	115.61	116.38	117.06	117.66	118.20	118.68	119.10
12.50	102.28	104.31	106.10	107.69	109.09	110.34	111.44	112.42	113.28	114.05	114.73	115.33	115.86	116.34	116.76	117.13
12.75	102.05	103.87	105.47	106.88	108.13	109.24	110.22	111.08	111.85	112.52	113.12	113.64	114.11	114.52	114.88	115.20
13.00	101.82	103.43	104.84	106.09	107.19	108.16	109.01	109.77	110.43	111.02	111.54	111.99	112.39	112.75	113.06	113.33
13.25	101.59	102.99	104.22	105.30	106.25	107.09	107.83	108.48	109.04	109.55	109.99	110.37	110.72	111.02	111.28	111.51
13.50	101.36	102.55	103.60	104.52	105.33	106.04	106.66	107.20	107.68	108.10	108.47	108.79	109.08	109.33	109.55	109.74
13.75	101.13	102.12	102.99	103.75	104.42	105.00	105.51	105.95	106.34	106.69	106.99	107.25	107.48	107.68	107.85	108.01
14.00	100.90	101.69	102.38	102.99	103.51	103.97	104.37	104.72	105.03	105.30	105.53	105.73	105.91	106.07	106.20	106.32
14.25	100.68	101.27	101.78	102.23	102.62	102.96	103.26	103.51	103.74	103.93	104.11	104.25	104.38	104.50	104.60	104.68
14.50	100.45	100.84	101.18	101.48	101.74	101.96	102.15	102.32	102.47	102.60	102.71	102.81	102.89	102.96	103.03	103.08
14.75	100.22	100.42	100.59	100.74	100.86	100.97	101.07	101.15	101.22	101.29	101.34	101.39	101.43	101.46	101.49	101.52
15.00	100.00	100.00	100.00	100.00	100.00	100.00	100.00	100.00	100.00	100.00	100.00	100.00	100.00	100.00	100.00	100.00
15.25	99.78	99.58	99.42	99.27	99.15	99.04	98.95	98.87	98.80	98.74	98.69	98.64	98.60	98.57	98.54	98.52
15.50	99.55	99.17	98.84	98.55	98.30	98.09	97.91	97.75	97.62	97.50	97.40	97.31	97.24	97.17	97.12	97.07
15.75	99.33	98.75	98.26	97.83	97.47	97.16	96.89	96.65	96.45	96.28	96.14	96.01	95.90	95.81	95.73	95.66
16.00	99.11	98.34	97.69	97.13	96.64	96.23	95.88	95.57	95.31	95.09	94.90	94.74	94.60	94.47	94.37	94.28
16.25	98.89	97.94	97.12	96.43	95.83	95.32	94.88	94.51	94.19	93.92	93.69	93.49	93.32	93.17	93.05	92.94
16.50	98.67	97.53	96.56	95.83	95.02	94.44	93.91	93.47	93.09	92.77	92.50	92.27	92.07	91.90	91.75	91.63
16.75	98.45	97.13	96.00	95.04	94.23	93.53	92.94	92.44	92.01	91.64	91.33	91.07	90.84	90.65	90.49	90.35
17.00	98.23	96.72	95.45	94.36	93.44	92.66	91.99	91.42	90.94	90.54	90.19	89.90	89.65	89.43	89.25	89.10
17.25	98.01	96.33	94.90	93.69	92.66	91.79	91.05	90.43	89.90	89.45	89.07	88.75	88.47	88.24	88.05	87.88
17.50	97.79	95.93	94.35	93.02	91.89	90.94	90.13	89.45	88.87	88.38	87.97	87.62	87.33	87.08	86.87	86.69
17.75	97.58	95.53	93.81	92.35	91.13	90.09	89.22	88.48	87.86	87.34	86.89	86.52	86.21	85.94	85.72	85.53
18.00	97.36	95.14	93.27	91.70	90.37	89.26	88.32	87.53	86.87	86.31	85.84	85.44	85.11	84.83	84.59	84.39
18.25	97.15	94.75	92.74	91.05	89.63	88.44	87.44	86.60	85.89	85.30	84.80	84.38	84.03	83.74	83.49	83.28
18.50	96.93	94.36	92.21	90.40	88.89	87.63	86.56	85.67	84.93	84.31	83.78	83.34	82.98	82.67	82.41	82.20
18.75	96.72	93.98	91.68	89.77	88.16	86.82	85.70	84.77	83.99	83.33	82.79	82.33	81.95	81.63	81.36	81.14
19.00	96.51	93.59	91.16	89.13	87.44	86.03	84.86	83.88	83.06	82.38	81.81	81.33	80.94	80.61	80.33	80.10
20.00	95.66	92.08	89.11	86.66	84.64	82.97	81.58	80.44	79.50	78.72	78.07	77.54	77.10	76.73	76.43	76.18
25.00	91.60	84.97	79.73	75.59	72.32	69.73	67.68	66.08	64.80	63.79	63.00	62.37	61.87	61.48	61.17	60.92
30.00	87.81	78.59	71.62	66.35	62.36	59.35	57.07	55.34	54.04	53.06	52.31	51.75	51.32	51.00	50.76	50.57

Source: Used with permission from David Thorndike, The Thorndike Encyclopedia of Banking and Financial Tables, pp. 27-100, copyright © 1980, Warren, Gorham, and Lamont, Boston.

measured by the number of terms in the present-value equation) is to be preferred. In a world of uncertainty, the quicker an investment is recouped the better. In its simplest form, the payback period is estimated by dividing the cost of the machine by the annual cash flow; e.g., if the cash flow is $100 for 5 years and the machine cost is $300, the payback period is 300/100 = 3 (Friedland 1978:28).

COMPOUND INTEREST   Interest is earned on interest. The more frequently interest is paid, the higher the effective yield in relation to the nominal rate of interest. To convert nominal rates into effective rates, the following equation is used:

$$(1 + j) = [1 + (i/m)]^m \quad \text{or} \quad j = [1 + (i/m)]^m - 1$$

where j = effective rate
$\quad i$ = nominal annual rate
$\quad m$ = number of times the nominal rate is compounded in a year

Table 5.2 compares nominal rates and effective rates for different compounding periods. Thus a nominal rate of interest of 10% compounded quarterly is equivalent to an effective rate of 10.38%. The principal of compounding is well advertised by savings institutions. Continuous compounding has considerable appeal but surprisingly only raises the effective rate to 10.52%. The formula for continuous compounding is $j = e^i - 1$, where e has the value of 2.71828. What limits j is the value of i being ordinarily less than one. Assume, for example, that the nominal rate was 100%; the effective rate would be a very high 172%.

Table 5.2.   Effective rate when nominal rate is compounded

Nominal rate of interest	Annually	Half yearly	Quarterly	Bimonthly	Monthly	Continuously
.02	.0200	.020100	.020151	.020167	.020184	.020201
.03	.0300	.030225	.030339	.030378	.030416	.030455
.04	.0400	.040400	.040604	.040673	.040742	.040811
.05	.0500	.050625	.050945	.051053	.051162	.051271
.10	.1000	.102500	.103813	.104260	.104713	.105171
.20	.2000	.210000	.215506	.217426	.219391	.221403
.30	.3000	.322500	.335469	.340096	.344889	.349859
.40	.4000	.440000	.464100	.472897	.482126	.491825
.50	.5000	.562500	.601807	.616489	.632094	.648721

Source: Used with permission from James E. Howell and Daniel Teichroew, *Mathematical Analysis for Business Decisions*, copyright © 1963, Richard D. Irwin, Homewood, Ill.

Borrower costs

The great variety of methods used by retailers and financial institutions to calculate interest costs results in effective rates to the borrower being at variance with nominal rates (cf. Laporte 1973:3–11). "Truth in lending" legislation was inspired by this confusion. The act of 1968 required creditors to make clear to consumers the exact amount of the finance charge to be paid for the extension of credit (J. B. Cohen 1979:344–48).

From the standpoint of the borrower, the present value of a loan is the sum actually borrowed. Loans at discount lend less than the principal of the loan. This makes the effective rate higher than the nominal (discount) rate. The repayment schedule also influences the effective rate. The more often the borrower must make payments on the principal, the shorter the average time for use of borrowed funds. The effect of both these factors can be caught in a present-value formula.

An illustration would be a $1000 loan at a discount of 10% that must be repaid in two semiannual installments: $900 = [500/(1 + r)] + [500/(1 + r)^2]$. We know the effective rate is more than 10% because at 10% (using present-value tables), the present value of the two installment payments is $476 + $453.50 = $929.50. This greater amount ($929.50 as compared with $900) would have to be borrowed originally for an effective rate of 10%.

Consumer installment loans are an example of add-on interest, where the total interest due is allocated with principal over scheduled repayments. Assume that the consumer has borrowed $1000 on a 12-month installment basis with add-on interest of $60. Applying a shortcut formula developed for this purpose (e.g., see Block and Hirt 1978:180):

$$\text{Rate on installment loan} = 2\frac{(\text{annual number of payments})(\text{interest payment})}{(\text{total number of payments} + 1)(\text{principal})}$$

$$\frac{(2)(12)(60)}{(13)(1000)} = \frac{1440}{13,000} = 11.08, \text{ almost twice the nominal rate of 6\%}$$

Tables are available for calculating the annual percentage rate. Suppose, for example, the finance charge (add-on interest) is $65.11 and the amount financed is $332.20. The finance charge for $100 of purchases is $19.60. With 24 monthly payments, read across Table 5.3 on the 24-payment line to the value nearest $19.60. This is $19.53 in the 17.75% column, which is the annual percentage rate.

In contrast to level installment payments, a loan contract might call for a final payment greatly in excess of preceding installments. This is known as a balloon contract and must be so labeled under the Truth in Lending Act. It is to be avoided because the necessity of refinancing possibly two or three times makes for exorbitant interest costs (J. B. Cohen 1979a: 342–43).

Not all consumer borrowing has the potential deception of loans at discount or add-on interest. Mortgages are customarily calculated on a declining balance method. Interest is charged only on the unpaid principal. The nominal rate is the effective rate.

The homeowner (mortgagor) makes uniform monthly payments on the mortgage. As the interest portion of the level payment declines, the payment of principal increases. Given the nominal interest rate, mortgage loan, and present value of $1 monthly for the life of the mortgage, it is possible to determine the mortgagor's monthly payment:

$$MORT = S \frac{1 - (1 + r)^{-n}}{r} \quad \text{and} \quad S = \frac{MORT}{[1 - (1 + r)^{-n}]/r}$$

where $MORT$ = value of the mortgage loan
S = monthly payment
$[1 - (1 + r)^{-n}]/r$ = present value of $1 payable for n periods

Table 5.3. Annual percentage rate table for monthly payment plans

Number of payments	Annual percentage rate															
	14.00%	14.25%	14.50%	14.75%	15.00%	15.25%	15.50%	15.75%	16.00%	16.25%	16.50%	16.75%	17.00%	17.25%	17.50%	17.75%
	(Finance charge per $100 of amount financed)															
1	1.17	1.19	1.21	1.23	1.25	1.27	1.29	1.31	1.33	1.35	1.37	1.40	1.42	1.44	1.46	1.48
2	1.75	1.78	1.82	1.85	1.88	1.91	1.94	1.97	2.00	2.04	2.07	2.10	2.13	2.16	2.19	2.22
3	2.34	2.38	2.43	2.47	2.51	2.55	2.59	2.64	2.68	2.72	2.76	2.80	2.85	2.89	2.93	2.97
4	2.93	2.99	3.04	3.09	3.14	3.20	3.25	3.30	3.36	3.41	3.46	3.51	3.57	3.62	3.67	3.73
5	3.53	3.59	3.65	3.72	3.78	3.84	3.91	3.97	4.04	4.10	4.16	4.23	4.29	4.35	4.42	4.48
6	4.12	4.20	4.27	4.35	4.42	4.49	4.57	4.64	4.72	4.79	4.87	4.94	5.02	5.09	5.17	5.24
7	4.72	4.81	4.89	4.98	5.06	5.15	5.23	5.32	5.40	5.49	5.58	5.66	5.75	5.83	5.92	6.00
8	5.32	5.42	5.51	5.61	5.71	5.80	5.90	6.00	6.09	6.19	6.29	6.38	6.48	6.58	6.67	6.77
9	5.92	6.03	6.14	6.25	6.35	6.46	6.57	6.68	6.78	6.89	7.00	7.11	7.22	7.32	7.43	7.54
10	6.53	6.65	6.77	6.88	7.00	7.12	7.24	7.36	7.48	7.60	7.72	7.84	7.96	8.08	8.19	8.31
11	7.14	7.27	7.40	7.53	7.66	7.79	7.92	8.05	8.18	8.31	8.44	8.57	8.70	8.83	8.96	9.09
12	7.74	7.89	8.03	8.17	8.31	8.45	8.59	8.74	8.88	9.02	9.16	9.30	9.45	9.59	9.73	9.87
13	8.36	8.51	8.66	8.81	8.97	9.12	9.27	9.43	9.58	9.73	9.89	10.04	10.20	10.35	10.50	10.66
14	8.97	9.13	9.30	9.46	9.63	9.79	9.96	10.12	10.29	10.45	10.62	10.78	10.95	11.11	11.28	11.45
15	9.59	9.76	9.94	10.11	10.29	10.47	10.64	10.82	11.00	11.17	11.35	11.53	11.71	11.88	12.06	12.24
16	10.20	10.39	10.58	10.77	10.95	11.14	11.33	11.52	11.71	11.90	12.09	12.28	12.46	12.65	12.84	13.03
17	10.82	11.02	11.22	11.42	11.62	11.82	12.02	12.22	12.42	12.62	12.83	13.03	13.23	13.43	13.63	13.83
18	11.45	11.66	11.87	12.08	12.29	12.50	12.72	12.93	13.14	13.35	13.57	13.78	13.99	14.21	14.42	14.64
19	12.07	12.30	12.52	12.74	12.97	13.19	13.41	13.64	13.86	14.09	14.31	14.54	14.76	14.99	15.22	15.44
20	12.70	12.93	13.17	13.41	13.64	13.88	14.11	14.35	14.59	14.82	15.06	15.30	15.54	15.77	16.01	16.25
21	13.33	13.58	13.82	14.07	14.32	14.57	14.82	15.06	15.31	15.56	15.81	16.06	16.31	16.56	16.81	17.07
22	13.96	14.22	14.48	14.74	15.00	15.26	15.52	15.78	16.04	16.30	16.57	16.83	17.09	17.36	17.62	17.88
23	14.59	14.87	15.14	15.41	15.68	15.96	16.23	16.50	16.78	17.05	17.32	17.60	17.88	18.15	18.43	18.70
24	15.23	15.51	15.80	16.08	16.37	16.65	16.94	17.22	17.51	17.80	18.09	18.37	18.66	18.95	19.24	19.53
25	15.87	16.17	16.46	16.76	17.06	17.35	17.65	17.95	18.25	18.55	18.85	19.15	19.45	19.75	20.05	20.36
26	16.51	16.82	17.13	17.44	17.75	18.06	18.37	18.68	18.99	19.30	19.62	19.93	20.24	20.56	20.87	21.19
27	17.15	17.47	17.80	18.12	18.44	18.76	19.09	19.41	19.74	20.06	20.39	20.71	21.04	21.37	21.69	22.02
28	17.80	18.13	18.47	18.80	19.14	19.47	19.81	20.15	20.48	20.82	21.16	21.50	21.84	22.18	22.52	22.86
29	18.45	18.79	19.14	19.49	19.83	20.18	20.53	20.88	21.23	21.58	21.94	22.29	22.64	22.99	23.35	23.70
30	19.10	19.45	19.81	20.17	20.54	20.90	21.26	21.62	21.99	22.35	22.72	23.08	23.45	23.81	24.18	24.55
31	19.75	20.12	20.49	20.87	21.24	21.61	21.99	22.37	22.74	23.12	23.50	23.88	24.26	24.64	25.02	25.40
32	20.40	20.79	21.17	21.56	21.95	22.33	22.72	23.11	23.50	23.89	24.28	24.68	25.07	25.46	25.86	26.25
33	21.06	21.46	21.85	22.25	22.65	23.06	23.46	23.86	24.26	24.67	25.07	25.48	25.88	26.29	26.70	27.11
34	21.72	22.13	22.54	22.95	23.37	23.78	24.19	24.61	25.03	25.44	25.86	26.28	26.70	27.12	27.54	27.97
35	22.38	22.80	23.23	23.65	24.08	24.51	24.94	25.36	25.79	26.23	26.66	27.09	27.52	27.96	28.39	28.83

Table 5.3. (continued)

Number of payments	Annual percentage rate (Finance charge per $100 of amount financed)															
	14.00%	14.25%	14.50%	14.75%	15.00%	15.25%	15.50%	15.75%	16.00%	16.25%	16.50%	16.75%	17.00%	17.25%	17.50%	17.75%
36	23.04	23.48	23.92	24.35	24.80	25.24	25.68	26.12	26.57	27.01	27.46	27.90	28.35	28.80	29.25	29.70
37	23.70	24.16	24.61	25.06	25.51	25.97	26.42	26.88	27.34	27.80	28.26	28.72	29.18	29.64	30.10	30.57
38	24.37	24.84	25.30	25.77	26.24	26.70	27.17	27.64	28.11	28.59	29.06	29.53	30.01	30.49	30.96	31.44
39	25.04	25.52	26.00	26.48	26.96	27.44	27.92	28.41	28.89	29.38	29.87	30.36	30.85	31.34	31.83	32.32
40	25.71	26.20	26.70	27.19	27.69	28.18	28.68	29.18	29.68	30.18	30.68	31.18	31.68	32.19	32.69	33.20
41	26.39	26.89	27.40	27.91	28.41	28.92	29.44	29.95	30.46	30.97	31.49	32.01	32.52	33.04	33.56	34.08
42	27.06	27.58	28.10	28.62	29.15	29.67	30.19	30.72	31.25	31.78	32.31	32.84	33.37	33.90	34.44	34.97
43	27.74	28.27	28.81	29.34	29.88	30.42	30.96	31.50	32.04	32.58	33.13	33.67	34.22	34.76	35.31	35.86
44	28.42	28.97	29.52	30.07	30.62	31.17	31.72	32.28	32.83	33.39	33.95	34.51	35.07	35.63	36.19	36.76
45	29.11	29.67	30.23	30.79	31.36	31.92	32.49	33.06	33.63	34.20	34.77	35.35	35.92	36.50	37.08	37.66
46	29.79	30.36	30.94	31.52	32.10	32.68	33.26	33.84	34.43	35.01	35.60	36.19	36.78	37.37	37.96	38.56
47	30.48	31.07	31.66	32.25	32.84	33.44	34.03	34.63	35.23	35.83	36.43	37.04	37.64	38.25	38.86	39.46
48	31.17	31.77	32.37	32.98	33.59	34.20	34.81	35.42	36.03	36.65	37.27	37.88	38.50	39.13	39.75	40.37
49	31.86	32.48	33.09	33.71	34.34	34.96	35.59	36.21	36.84	37.47	38.10	38.74	39.37	40.01	40.65	41.29
50	32.55	33.18	33.82	34.45	35.09	35.73	36.37	37.01	37.65	38.30	38.94	39.59	40.24	40.89	41.55	42.20
51	33.25	33.89	34.54	35.19	35.84	36.49	37.15	37.81	38.46	39.12	39.79	40.45	41.11	41.78	42.45	43.12
52	33.95	34.61	35.27	35.93	36.60	37.27	37.94	38.61	39.28	39.96	40.63	41.31	41.99	42.67	43.36	44.04
53	34.65	35.32	36.00	36.68	37.36	38.04	38.72	39.41	40.10	40.79	41.48	42.17	42.87	43.57	44.27	44.97
54	35.35	36.04	36.73	37.42	38.12	38.82	39.52	40.22	40.92	41.63	42.33	43.04	43.75	44.47	45.18	45.90
55	36.05	36.76	37.46	38.17	38.88	39.60	40.31	41.03	41.74	42.47	43.19	43.91	44.64	45.37	46.10	46.83
56	36.76	37.48	38.20	38.92	39.65	40.38	41.11	41.84	42.57	43.31	44.05	44.79	45.53	46.27	47.02	47.77
57	37.47	38.20	38.94	39.68	40.42	41.16	41.91	42.65	43.40	44.15	44.91	45.66	46.42	47.18	47.94	48.71
58	38.18	38.93	39.68	40.43	41.19	41.95	42.71	43.47	44.23	45.00	45.77	46.54	47.32	48.09	48.87	49.65
59	38.89	39.66	40.42	41.19	41.96	42.74	43.51	44.29	45.07	45.85	46.64	47.42	48.21	49.01	49.80	50.60
60	39.61	40.39	41.17	41.95	42.74	43.53	44.32	45.11	45.91	46.71	47.51	48.31	49.12	49.92	50.73	51.55

Source: FRB n.d., Reg. Z Tables:104.

This formula sums up the series $[1/(1 + r] + [1/(1 + r)^2] + \ldots + [1/(1 + r)^n]$, which we have previously discussed (see Howell and Teichroew 1963: 196–97). Further simplification is possible by replacing $(1 + r)^{-n}$ with v^n.

Bond tables provide an easy solution; e.g., a homeowner takes out a $20,000 mortgage to run for 20 years at 8.4% interest. The present value of $1 payable monthly for 20 years at this interest rate is $116.07. Dividing $20,000 by this figure gives a monthly payment of $172.31.

Long- and short-term interest rates

Important mathematical relationships exist between time to maturity, market prices, and market yields of securities. The longer the term of the security for a given change in the market yield, the greater the change in the market price. Long-term government securities such as 15-year Treasury bonds change much more in price than 3-month U.S. Treasury bills. The basic inverse relationship between bond prices and market yields still holds, but it is modified by the maturity factor.

The present-value formula helps to explain the systematic way market prices vary with market yields. A short-term security has fewer coupon payments to discount at the market rate than a long-term security. As a result, the loss in market price from an increase in market yield is less than for a long-term security. This relative immunity of short-term securities from price fluctuations explains their liquidity. A Treasury bill will return its owner approximately the purchase price if sold before maturity.

The behavior of market prices is not inconsistent with a greater volatility in short-term yields as compared with long-term yields. The comparative liquidity of short-term securities was predicated on a given change in market yields. In fact, changes in market yields will be different for short-terms and long-terms. Over time, short-terms fluctuate more widely than long-terms, as shown in Figure 5.1. Why this is so goes beyond mathematics into monetary theory.

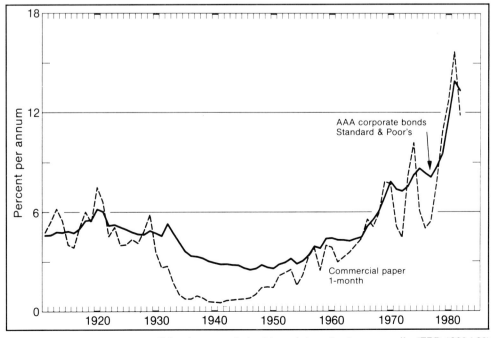

5.1. Long- and short-term interest rates, annually. (FRB 1983d:96)

TERM STRUCTURE OF INTEREST RATES   A mathematical relationship exists between long- and short-term rates at any given time. This will be the basis for later theorizing about the term structure of interest rates.

Let us contrast a two-year security and two consecutive one-year securities and indicate the circumstances under which an investor will be indifferent between them. Beginning with a two-year security $R2$, the accumulated value after two years will be $(1 + R2)^2$. The rates on the two consecutive one-year securities are $R1$ and $r2$. The R notation indicates that the rate at time t is known. The r rate, which is the rate on a one-year security to be purchased a year from now (time $t + 1$), is not known. Investing successively in these two one-year securities will result in a total sum of $(1 + R1)(1 + r2)$ at the end of two years.

It should be a matter of indifference to the investor which option is elected, as long as the total returns at the end of two years are the same. In such a case, $(1 + R2)^2 = (1 + R1)(1 + r2)$. The two-year case can readily be generalized to an n-period case: $(1 + R_n)^n = (1 + R_1)(1 + r_1)(1 + r_2)(1 + r_3)...(1 + r_{n-1})$. Returning to the two-year case, since R_2 and R_1 are known, we can solve for r_2. Thus:

$$1 + r2 = (1 + R2)^2/(1 + R1) \qquad r2 = [(1 + R2)^2/(1 + R1)] - 1$$

This is the future short-term rate that an investor would agree to accept in the present. It is called the implicit forward rate, since it is implicit in the long-term rate. We can see this by solving for $R2$ instead of $r2$:

$$1 + R2 = [(1 + R1)(1 + r2)]^{1/2} \qquad R2 = [(1 + R1)(1 + r2)]^{1/2} - 1$$

The long-term rate is the geometric average of the known short-term rate $R1$ and the implicit forward rate $r2$; e.g., if $R1$ is 10% and $r2$ is 15%, $R2$ will have a value of $[(1.10)(1.15)]^{1/2} - 1 = 12\%$. An investor will be indifferent between a 12% yield on a two-year security and yields of 10% and 15% on two successive one-year securities. The higher yield on the two-year security as compared with the 10% yield on the one-year security constitutes the term structure of interest rates. The explanation for the difference in yields lies in the implicit forward rate being higher than the short-term rate. The term structure can readily be generalized for n periods with differing yields for each maturity.

Comparison of the formula for R_n with the earlier market price (PB) equation raises the question of whether they give consistent solution to the long-term interest rate (r as compared to R_n). The R_n formula assumes that interest is automatically reinvested at varying short-term rates. The PB formula assumes that interest is regularly paid out to the bondholder. Only under very stringent assumptions can the two equations be expected to give the same answer.

Algebra leaves off and theory comes in with the interpretation of the implicit forward rate. The unbiased expectations theory to be discussed in Chapter 16 argues that the implicit forward rate is a reliable estimate of the short-term rate that will prevail in the future. This goes beyond a mathematical statement of short- and long-term rates that are equally acceptable to an investor. The theory says in effect that the implicit forward rate is the expected short-term rate.

Summary

Financial decision making is founded on the mathematics of finance — on the relationship between market interest rates, coupon rates, market prices, and time to maturity. The basic equation is the present-value equation that reduces future returns to a present value by a discounting process. Anyone lending or borrowing money who neglects present-value considerations is likely to be ignorant of the true return or costs. Fortunately, financial information on yields and bond prices abounds.

Market yields and prices vary differently for short- and long-term securities. Short-terms fluctuate more in yields, long-terms more in price. At any given time, the term-structure equation relates short-term rates to long-term rates. From this equation one can derive equivalent returns for an investor by investing either in a long-term security or a series of successive short-term securities. The implicit forward rates in this relation are the basis for predictions of the future behavior of interest rates.

Review questions

1. Identify the relationship between market interest rates, coupon rates, market prices, and time to maturity.

2. In the case of fixed maturities, explain how the market price is determined. How does this compare with the determination of the market price of perpetuities?

3. Write the equation that converts nominal rates into effective rates when interest is compounded.

4. Describe three ways in which business firms can exploit the present-value equation to aid management in decision making.

5. What does "add-on" interest mean, and give an example of a type of loan that falls into this category. According to the example in the text, how is the effective interest rate affected by "add-on" interest?

6. Explain why mortgages do not have the potential deception of loans at discount or "add-on" interest.

7. Explain how borrowing at discount and the repayment schedule affect the effective interest rate.

8. Write the equation showing the relationship between long-term and short-term rates at a given time.

9. Define:

Market interest rates	Holding period yields
Coupon rates	Present value
Market prices	Implicit forward interest rate
Time to maturity	

6

Mechanics of money creation

The connection between spending and borrowing is a major theme of Chapters 1 and 2. A second theme is that variations in external finance are triggered by changes in money and its velocity. Depository institutions, or DIs, which include commercial banks and thrift institutions, are responsible for changes in the money supply. The mechanics of money creation is the principal interest of this chapter.

Money stock measures

There is no unanimity about the definition of money. In monetary policy deliberations a series of alternative measures serve as targets. Three versions of increasing breadth are illustrated in Table 6.1. The narrowly defined money supply is $M1$ and has the components listed in lines 6–9. $M1$ balances are known as transactions balances because they are used to pay for purchases and to settle debts. Most important are checkable deposits (lines 28 and 29). $M2$ and $M3$ add on nontransactions components to $M1$ and $M2$ respectively. The nature of these nontransaction components (such as savings deposits) are detailed in lines 12–19. Liquid assets (L) add on mainly short-term financial instruments to the previous $M3$ total. The most comprehensive aggregate is the debt aggregate, which measures indebtedness of the nonfinancial sectors of the economy rather than their asset holdings. For this reason the assets of the financial sectors are counted rather than deposit liabilities (which measure asset holdings of the nonfinancial sector). Money market mutual funds are a nontransaction component of $M2$ and $M3$. This is controversial because above a certain minimum amount ($250 or $500) they can be checked against and so constitute transaction balances.

From the components in Table 6.1 it is seen that, at the end of 1983, currency of $150.5 bil. was 28% of the total $M1$ money supply of $537.8 bil. Currency is further broken down in Table 6.2. The effects of inflation are clearly evident in the trend to larger denominations of paper money between 1970 and 1982.

Table 6.1. Money stock measures and components ($ bil., averages of daily figures, not seasonally adjusted)

Item	Dec. 1982	Dec. 1983
1 *M*1	491.9	537.8
2 *M*2	1967.4	2197.9
3 *M*3	2466.6	2712.8
4 *L*	2876.5	3184.7
5 Debt	4710.1	5244.8
*M*1 components		
6 Currency	136.4	150.5
7 Travelers checks	4.1	4.6
8 Demand deposits	247.3	251.6
9 Other checkable deposits	104.1	131.2
Nontransactions components		
10 *M*2	1475.5	1660.1
11 *M*3 only	499.2	514.8
Money market deposit accounts		
12 Commercial banks	26.3	230.0
13 Thrift institutions	16.6	145.9
Savings deposits		
14 Commercial banks	162.1	132.0
15 Thrift institutions	195.5	176.5
Small denomination time deposits		
16 Commercial banks	380.1	351.0
17 Thrift institutions	472.4	437.6
Money market mutual funds		
18 General purpose and broker/dealer	185.2	138.2
19 Institution only	48.4	40.3
Large denomination time deposits		
20 Commercial banks	266.2	229.0
21 Thrift institutions	66.2	100.7
Debt components		
22 Federal debt	991.4	1177.9
23 Nonfederal debt	3718.7	4066.80

Source: *Fed. Res. Bull.* 1984b:A13,A14.
Note: For details on composition of the money stock measures and debt, see source.

Table 6.2. Money in circulation, by denomination (in $ mil. as of December 31)

Denomination	1970	1973	1974	1975	1976	1977	1978	1979	1980	1981	1982
Total[a]	57,093	72,497	79,743	86,547	93,717	103,811	114,645	125,600	137,244	145,566	156,158
Coin and small currency	39,639	48,288	51,606	54.865	57,645	62,543	66,693	70,693	73,893	76,517	79,632
Coin	6,281	7,759	8,332	8,959	9,483	10,071	10,739	11,658	12,419	13,084	13,597
$1[b]	2,310	2,639	2,720	2,809	2,858	3,038	3,194	3,308	3,499	3,613	3,682
$2	136	135	135	135	637	650	661	671	677	680	684
$5	3,161	3,614	3,718	3,841	3,905	4,190	4,393	4,549	4,635	4,797	4,810
$10	9,170	10,226	10,503	10,777	10,775	11,361	11,661	11,894	11,924	11,824	11,677
$20	18,581	23,915	26,197	28,344	29,987	33,233	36,045	38,613	40,739	42,519	45,180
Large currency	17,454	24,210	28,137	31,681	36,072	41,269	47,952	54,907	63,352	69,049	76,527
$50	4,896	6,514	7,444	8,157	9,026	10,079	11,279	12,585	13,731	14,889	16,785
$100	12,084	17,288	20,298	23,139	26,668	30,818	36,306	41,960	49,264	53,807	59,392
$500	215	185	179	175	172	169	167	164	163	161	159
$1,000	252	216	209	204	200	197	194	192	189	187	185
$5,000	3	2	2	2	2	2	2	2	2	2	2
$10,000	4	4	4	4	4	4	4	4	3	3	4

Source: *U.S. Stat. Abstr.* 1984:519.
[a]Outside Treasury and Federal Reserve banks.
[b]Paper currency only; $1 silver coins reported under coin.

Money creation

For the purpose of this discussion, we shall follow an *M*1 definition of money, focusing on the checkable deposits component. Before 1980 the discussion could have been confined to commercial banks. Since then, as a result of the

Depository Institutions Deregulation and Monetary Control Act (DIDMCA), the discussion applies to savings and loans (S&Ls), mutual savings banks (MSBs), and credit unions (CUs).

Money is created by DIs; this takes place when they acquire financial claims (lend money). The bank simultaneously adds to its assets (the IOUs of the borrowers) and credits the deposit liabilities of the borrower. We remind the reader that making entries on a DI balance sheet is equivalent to making entries on a flow-of-funds account under the headings of debit and credit. Changes in assets and liabilities are debit and credit entries respectively when the changes are positive in value. When the asset change is negative, it is a credit entry; when the liability change is negative, it is a debit entry. The credit entry can either be made on the asset side with a minus sign or listed on the credit side of the flow-of-funds account without such a sign. Similarly, the liability debit entry can be made either on the liability side with a minus sign or on the debit side of the flow-of-funds account. Because of the T silhouette, tables showing bank transactions are referred to as T accounts.

As shown in Table 6.3, money has been created by means of an entry on the books of the bank. Money is no more than that. If the student regards this as a kind of magic, so be it. A bookkeeping entry is the way the money supply expands. Someone owns more checking accounts than before. Nobody else holds less checking accounts. Nor is it any different if the borrower asks for cash instead of a checking account. The borrower will still have more money. No one else will have less money as a consequence. We cannot show this on the bank's statement because currency is not a liability of a commercial bank. All currency in existence is issued either by the Fed or the Treasury.

Table 6.3. The basic entries on a bank statement showing how money is created	
Assets	Liabilities
The bank acquires the IOUs of a borrower (an asset for the bank) $100	The bank in payment for the asset (the borrower's IOU) credits the borrower with a demand deposit $100
Total $100	Total $100

A third way in which a loan can be extended (besides crediting an account or handing out cash) is by the bank writing a check on itself. The magic of money creation is not so apparent in this case because the check will probably be deposited in another DI. Among the three methods at the present time, the crediting of a borrower's account is commonest for commercial banks; for other DIs the loan is made by writing checks on themselves. The former method has the advantage from the lender's point of view of temporarily delaying the loss of reserves to other institutions.

One recent textbook concentrates on the third method because the first approach gives the impression that DIs do something magical when they "create" increases in these accounts (Pierce 1984:331; author's quotes). But they do indeed credit depositors' accounts and the magic cannot be denied.

Is there a limit to this sleight of hand? Yes, the reserves that DIs must keep against their deposits. Reserves are the DI's deposits in a Federal Reserve Bank and to a much lesser extent the cash (currency) that it has on its premises (cash in the vault). Till money is placed in the bank vault at night; therefore, it is appropriately part of cash in the vault. The two chief liabilities of the Federal Reserve Bank are reserve balances (deposits) and notes (see Table 6.4).

Table 6.4. Federal Reserve Bank liabilities

Assets	Liabilities	
	DI reserve deposits	$___
	Federal Reserve Notes outstanding	$___

DIs have deposits in the Fed just as an individual or business has at a DI. Corresponding to the entry on the liability side of the Fed balance sheet is the same entry on the balance sheet of DIs but now on the asset side (item b, Table 6.5).

Table 6.5. Selected items on the balance sheet of a commercial bank (DI)

Assets		Liabilities	
Loans	$___	Deposits	$___
Reserves			
a. Cash in vault	$___		
b. Deposits in the Federal Reserve	$___		

Banks are required by law to have reserves as a certain percentage of their "reservable deposits." This is one reason why collectively they cannot expand their loans and deposits indefinitely unless their reserves change. A bank's reserves, and thus its ability to lend, will decline when a customer asks for currency. The customer's deposit (a liability) will be reduced (debited) on the books of the bank, and cash in the vault for the bank will go down (will be credited) (stage 1, Table 6.6). (If we showed the entries on the customer's books, they would be reversed: cash would be debited and deposits credited. Remember: this use of debit and credit is consistent with the ground rules of Ch. 1.) Assuming the bank wishes to maintain its cash level, it will cash in its deposit at the Fed for currency. Thus bank reserves will go down (be debited on the balance sheet of the Fed), and the Fed's liabilities for Federal Reserve notes outstanding will increase by a like amount (stage 2, Table 6.6).

Table 6.6. The bookkeeping entries when a bank customer asks for cash

Bank (DI)		Federal Reserve Bank	
Assets	Liabilities	Assets	Liabilities
Stage 1			
Cash in vault -$100	Deposits -$100		
Stage 2			
Bank reserves -$100			DI reserves -$100
Vault cash +$100			Federal Reserve Notes outstanding +$100

The money-creating activities of the individual DI are obscured by the existence of other depository institutions. The more than 14,000 commercial banks compete with 4700 S&Ls, 500 MSBs, and 23,000 CUs. When one DI acquires IOUs (makes a loan), a borrower, assuming he takes the loan in the form of a checking account (the most probable way), will soon write checks on the newly created account. He is paying interest on the loan and will not let the deposit stay idle long. Making the assumption that the person at the other end of the transaction deposits the check in a second DI, deposits and reserves will decline in the lending DI and go up in the second DI. The switching of reserves between DIs involves a process for clearing checks between them. Fed offices, as discussed in Chapter 9, play a leading role in the clearing process.

The accounting entries resulting from the check clearance are shown in Table 6.7. The reserve-gaining, DI-lending, and deposit-creating processes are summarized in Table 6.8. DI A first gains reserves of $100 through an increase of $100 in deposits, as shown in line 1. The arrow suggests the causal direction. Deposits bring reserves to the DI. How much is loaned? DI A is going to anticipate a loss of reserves as a result of making a loan. It will lend less than available additional reserves so that those remaining are just sufficient to meet required reserves. Required reserves equal deposit liabilities times the reserve requirement against deposits. The reserve requirement is a percentage, one which reserves must be of deposits. Assuming a 10% reserve requirement, DI A loans $90 (line 2, Table 6.8). The loan leads to a temporary deposit for the borrower; DI A's anticipations turn out correctly. Deposits and reserves increase in DI B to the extent that they decline in DI A (line 3). The remaining reserves of $10 are 10% of the original deposit of $100. Thus actual reserves equal required reserves (for this deposit increase of $100 and neglecting any previous values on the balance sheet). From the standpoint of DI A, when looking at the three steps retrospectively, it might be argued that the DI has loaned the customer's deposit, and less than these deposits at that, because of the reserve requirement (and thus required reserves) against the original deposit.

Table 6.7. The effect of a transfer of deposits between DIs

DI A		DI B	
Assets	Liabilities	Assets	Liabilities
Reserves -$90	Deposits -$90	Reserves +$90	Deposits +$90

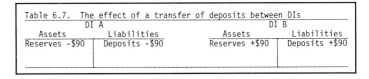

Table 6.8. DI A's transactions

Assets		Liabilities	
1. Reserves	+$100 ←	Original deposit	+$100
2. Loan	+$ 90 →	Temporary deposit	+$ 90
3. Reserves	-$ 90	Temporary deposit	-$ 90
(to DI B)		(to DI B)	

DI A does not, however, lend out the customer's deposits (even if the customer thinks so). The original deposits were $100 and they are still $100. The initial depositors have not been deprived of funds. More accurately, we should say that DI A lends the excess reserves — the difference between initial reserves of $100 and required reserves of $10 against the deposit of $100.

But DI A might still query whether money has been created. The books show no increase in deposits. The answer is to be found on the books of DI B. DI A's

Table 6.9. An open-market purchase by the
  Fed increases DI reserves

Assets		Liabilities	
U.S. government		DI reserve	
securities	$1000	deposits	$1000

loan of $90 shows up as an additional deposit of $90 in DI B. Money creation is reflected in the balance sheet entries of the second DI.

Now if DI A got its reserves in the same way as DI B — from another DI (say DI C) — then taking all three DIs together, money would not have been created. The loans made by DI A would be offset by a reduction in loans by DI C, whose deposit liabilities were transferred to DI A. DI C would find itself with deficient reserves; i.e., its actual reserves would be less than required reserves. It works this way: assume that DI C lost $100 of deposits and $100 of reserves to DI A. Only $10 of the $100 of reserves would have been earmarked against the lost $100 deposits (the required reserves for $100 of deposits are $10). When the full $100 of reserves are lost, $90 of this amount must have been earmarked for DI C's remaining deposits. Its deficient reserves (or negative excess reserves) are thus $90. Another way of calculating deficient reserves is to take the difference between reserves lost ($100) and the reduction in required reserves ($10), which equals $90.

For money creation to take place, some DI in the system must secure reserves from outside the banking system. This is where the Fed comes into the picture; it supplies these reserves. (The various instruments for supplying reserves and the rationale of central banking policy are the subject matter of Chs. 10, 11, and 12.) The chief way is by purchasing government securities (an open-market operation), as shown in Table 6.9. The Fed pays for the purchase of an interest-bearing security by crediting the reserves of a DI. Just as the DI creates money for the nonbank public by crediting the deposit accounts, so the Fed creates high-powered money for DIs by crediting their accounts. (Thrift-type institutions may have their accounts credited at member banks, who in turn have their accounts credited at the Fed. This is known as a pass-through of reserves.)

Once DI reserves increase, a process of multiple expansion of loans and money takes place throughout the DI system. DI B now makes loans so that deposits and reserves go up in DI D and so on. This repetitive process is described in Table 6.10, now assuming a reserve requirement of 15%. Thus through stage

Table 6.10. Multiple deposit expansion

	Assets				Liabilities
		Reserves		Loans and	Checkable
Stage	Total	Required	Excess	investments	deposits
Initial reserves provided	1000	150	850	...	1000
Expansion:					
Stage 1 (DI A)	1000	278	722	850	1850
Stage 2 (S&L B)	1000	386	614	1572	2572
Stage 3 (MSB C)	1000	478	522	2186	3186
Stage 4 (CU D)	1000	556	444	2708	3708
Stage 5 (S&L E)	1000	623	377	3125	4152
Stage 6 (DI F)	1000	680	320	3529	4529
Stage 7 (MSB G)	1000	728	272	3849	4849
Stage 8 (CU H)	1000	769	231	4121	5121
Stage 9 (DI I)	1000	803	197	4352	5352
Stage 10 (DI J)	1000	833	167	4549	5549
⋮	⋮	⋮	⋮	⋮	⋮
Stage 20 (S&L K)	1000	961	39	5448	6448
⋮	⋮	⋮	⋮	⋮	⋮
Final stage (DI Z)	1000	1000	0	5667	6667

Source: Fed, Chicago 1975:11.

after stage of expansion, money can grow to a total of 6⅔ times the new reserves supplied to the DI system as the new deposits created by loans at each stage are added to those created at all earlier stages and to those supplied by the initial reserve-creating action.

Limits of DI expansion

Is there any shortcut way of determining the amount of DI expansion without working out the process bank by bank? Yes, by applying a basic equation (identity). The limit of expansion is reached when the required reserves RR of the DI system become equal to actual reserves AR, sometimes referred to as legal reserves, since they meet legal reserve requirements. The underlying identity that must be satisfied is $AR = RR$. Required reserves in turn will equal deposits D times the legal reserve requirement r. Thus substituting for the term RR, the equation becomes $rD = AR$. In terms of change, rather than levels of values, $r\Delta D = \Delta AR$, where Δ stands for change. Solving for ΔD, $\Delta D = \Delta AR/r$.

If we know the change in legal (actual) reserves of the DI system and the reserve requirement, we can solve for ΔD; i.e., we can determine the amount of deposits after expansion takes place. For example, if the change in legal reserves is $100 and the reserve requirement is 10%, the potential change in deposits will be $1000. The reciprocal of the reserve requirement is referred to as the deposit multiplier. This is r upside down, or $1/r$. It has a value of 10 and indicates the extent to which deposits will change with a $1 increase in actual reserves. If we let $1/r = k$, the deposit multiplier, $\Delta D = k\Delta AR$.

The potential expansion in loans can also be worked out by introducing the balance sheet identity for DIs. Loans L plus the reserves on the asset side of the balance sheet will equal deposits on the liability side: $L + AR = D$. In terms of changes, $\Delta L + \Delta AR = \Delta D$. Taking AR over to the right-hand side, $\Delta L = \Delta D - \Delta AR$. We know from previous discussion that $\Delta D = \Delta AR/r$. Substituting $\Delta AR/r$ for ΔD, we have $\Delta L = \Delta AR/r - \Delta AR$. The multiplier, k, can be substituted for $1/r$; thus $\Delta L = k\Delta AR - \Delta AR$. Factoring out ΔAR, $\Delta L = \Delta AR(k - 1)$. Thus the change in loans for all DIs will be potential deposit expansion $k\Delta AR$ less the change in actual reserves ΔAR. Using our previous values in the equation ($k = 10$ and $\Delta AR = 100), potential loan expansion is $900.

Loan and deposit expansion comes to an end when additional reserves have all "leaked out" into required reserves against demand deposits. This is the elementary version of multiple expansion and is based on the simplest multiplier, frequently called the textbook multiplier.

A number of other leakages are at work, affecting required reserves. They cause the change in actual (legal) reserves to come into equality with required reserves with less deposit and loan expansion than in the simple textbook multiplier case. Three leakages will now be distinguished. First, banks may desire to keep excess reserves. This means they wish to hold reserves in excess of those required by law. Instead of required reserves, a more general term covering both leakages will be reserves absorbed. Thus we now write the identity that must be satisfied as $\Delta AR = \Delta RA$ (reserves absorbed). ΔRA now includes excess reserves in addition to legally required reserves. We express the DIs' desired excess reserves as a percentage of deposits. Let e represent this percentage:

e = (desired excess reserve ER)/(demand deposits D)

$eD = ER$

Substituting now for ΔRA, the limit to deposit expansion will be reached when $\Delta AR = r\Delta D + e\Delta D$. Now solving for ΔD, $\Delta D = \Delta AR/(r + e)$.

We can convert $1/(r + e)$ into a multiplier by taking its reciprocal and calling in $k1$. Potential deposit expansion is written as $\Delta D = k1\Delta AR$. The value of $k1$ will be smaller than k because of the addition of e. Let us say that e has a value of 0.05 meaning that for every additional \$1 in deposits banks wish to keep \$.05 in excess reserves. Thus $k1$ will be equal to $1/(0.05 + 0.10)$, which is below the value of the first deposit multiplier (10). In each round (or stage) of loan expansion, DIs loan less than in the first example because more reserves leak into required reserves and less excess reserves are available for further lending. Now "excess reserves" means reserves they hold in excess of desired excess reserves (measured by eD) and required reserves (measured by rD). Assuming an increase in \$1 of actual reserves, the potential expansion in deposits would be \$6.6.

A third leakage (the first was required legal reserves, the second desired excess reserves) results if we allow for the public's holding hand-to-hand currency C. Let us assume that the public holds cash in some fixed proportion of their checkable deposits; call this percentage c, where $c = C/D$. Thus desired currency holdings are $C = cD$.

In terms of the $AR = RA$ identity, the change in actual reserves will now have to equal the changes in reserves absorbed by all three leakages.

Substituting for ΔRA:

$$\Delta AR = e\Delta D + r\Delta D + c\Delta D$$
$$\Delta D = \Delta AR/(e + r + c)$$

Again we can take the reciprocal of $1/(e + r + c)$ and call it $k2$. Thus potential deposit expansion is $\Delta D = k2\Delta AR$.

If we give c the value of 0.25, then $e + r + c$ will total 0.40. The value of $k2$ will be $1/0.40$, or 2.5. The deposit multiplier has declined sharply in value when we allow for currency drains. Now \$1 increase in DI reserves will increase deposits by \$2.5.

Since currency holdings are part of the money supply, the deposit multiplier understates the increase in the money supply associated with an increase in reserves. We require a money multiplier, which adds c on to the numerator of the fraction used in estimating the deposit multiplier. The algebra is ΔM (change in the money supply) $= \Delta D + c\Delta D = \Delta D(1 + c)$. Substituting for ΔD, $\Delta M = [(1 + c)/(e + r + c)]\Delta AR$. Thus the money multiplier, call it m, is equal to $(1 + c)/(e + r + c)$. Using previous values for these ratios, the multiplier will have a value of $1.25/0.40 = 3.1$. Writing the equation for the change in the money supply, $\Delta M = m\Delta AR$: A \$1 increase in actual reserves will cause the money supply (checkable deposits plus currency) to increase by \$3.1.

A fourth leakage distinguishes between interest-bearing time deposits ($M2$) and checkable deposits. If loans result in an increase in time deposits, to that extent money expansion (as we define money) will be reduced.

Let us call t the public's desired ratio of time to checkable deposit holdings T.

Thus $t = T/D$ or $T = tD$; e. g., if the public wishes to keep \$1 in time deposits for each \$1 they hold in checkable deposits, t has a value of one and $T = D$. Time deposits are subject to reserve requirements that are lower than those against checkable deposits. Two symbols are now necessary for reserve requirements, r_1 for checkable deposits and r_2 for time deposits. Reserves will be absorbed by checkable deposits $r_1 D$ and time deposits $r_2 tD$. For each \$1 of time deposits tD, the required reserves will be r_2, thus explaining the three symbols in $r_2 tD$.

Solving for ΔD, potential checkable deposit expansion is:

$$\Delta AR = r_1 \Delta D + r_2 t \Delta D + e \Delta D + c \Delta D$$
$$\Delta D = \Delta AR/(r_1 + r_2 t + e + c)$$

The $k3$ multiplier will be $1/(r_1 + r_2 t + e + c)$. Assuming values for the coefficients given previously and a 4% reserve requirement against time deposits ($r_2 = 4\%$), the $k3$ multiplier value will be $1/(0.10 + 0.04 + 0.05 + 0.25) = 1/0.44 = 2.27$. A dollar extra in reserves will now generate \$2.27 in new checkable deposits. Potential money expansion (with $1 + c$ in the numerator) will be $1.25/0.44 = 2.84$.

An alternative simplified presentation would substitute a weighted average reserve ratio r for the two individual ratios r_1 and r_2: $r = r_1[D/(T + D)] + r_2[T/(T + D)]$. The multiplier is now $1/[r(1 + t) + e + c]$. The simplification becomes more apparent when additional terms are introduced in the denominator, such as the ratio of Treasury deposits to checkable deposits. It is now no longer necessary to introduce a separate reserve requirement for each depository liability.

The banking system's ability to lend is substantially greater than its ability to expand checkable deposits. The volume of loans will be reflected in time and currency drains as well as checkable deposits. (Later, we shall see there are other sources of funds that have to be considered in estimating bank lending potential.) Time deposits add to the liability side of the balance sheet (or, in flow-of-funds terms, they are credit entries or sources of funds). Currency lost to depositors cashing in their accounts are a credit item on the bank's flow-of-funds statement, showing that they also finance the bank's loans. The change in loans of the bank are the sum of the change in deposit liabilities plus the reduction in reserves from currency drains.

Let us assume an accretion of \$1000 in reserves for the banking system. Using the last formula above for deposit expansion, this increase will be associated with an increase in checkable deposits of \$2272.73. Since t has a value of one, the increase in time deposits will be of like value. Currency drain is 25% of the increase in checkable deposits. This means a loss of reserves of \$568.18, with the banks collectively retaining \$431.82 of the original \$1000 in reserves. This amount (\$431.82) will equal 10% of \$2272.73 ($r_1 D$) plus 4% of \$2272.73 ($r_2 tD$) and 5% of \$2272.73 (eD). The remaining balance sheet item (the change in loans) will be $\$2272.73 + \$2272.73 + \$568.18 - \$431.82 = \$4681.82$ (see Table 6.11).

The above results can be checked using a formula for explaining the increase in bank assets. The formula is the same as the previous one except now we will add t and c to the numerator.

$$\Delta A \text{ (change in bank assets)} = [(1 + t + c)/(r_1 + r_2 t + e + c)] \Delta AR$$

Table 6.11. Change in balance sheet items for DI system following an increase in DI reserves with four leakages: required reserves against checkables and time deposits; excess reserves and currency drain

Assets		Liabilities	
Loss of reserves (currency drain)	-$ 568.18	Checkable deposits	$2272.73
Net change in reserves	431.82	Time deposits	2272.73
Increase in loans	4681.82		
Total	$4545.46	Total	$4545.46

Having c in both the numerator and denominator points to its dual role. In the denominator, c is a leakage limiting bank asset expansion. In the numerator it is a means of financing bank lending, thus contributing to bank asset expansion.

Using the previous values for the ratios, the asset multiplier will be 5.11364. A $1 increase in reserves results potentially in an increase of bank assets of $5.11364. An increase in $1000 in reserves will increase assets by $5113.64 (1000 × 5.11364). Of this increase in assets, required reserves (as previously calculated) will absorb $431.82. Thus the increase in loans will be $5113.64 − $431.82 = $4681.82 as shown on the balance sheet (Table 6.11). The asset expansion of $5113.64 is not inconsistent with the footings of $4545.46 in Table 6.11. If the currency drain of $568.18 is taken to the other side of the account, the total will be $5113.64.

VARIABLE MULTIPLIERS   The multiplier terms (which determine multiplier values) are not constant but vary with such diverse factors as market interest rates, the degree of urbanization, and levels of real income. As these items vary in value, so do the multipliers; e.g., the desired time deposit ratio (T/TD) depends on relative interest returns. As own rates on time deposits rise, the ratio will increase. It will fall as rival interest rates advance. The multipliers are stable rather than constant if the parameter values can be predicted on the basis of change in the explanatory variables.

The monetary base

The money multiplier shows the effect of a $1 increase in reserves on the money stock. The money multiplier could also be based on a $1 increase in the monetary base—the sum of DI reserves and currency in the hands of the public. At any given time during the expansion process, the monetary base will be the sum of reserves still in the hands of the DIs (either required reserves or excess reserves) and the currency increase in the hands of the public. Reserves are supporting deposit expansion; currency (on a one-to-one basis) is supporting the currency part of the money expansion. The round-by-round description of the expansion process goes beyond that of Table 6.10 by allowing for the allocation of the proceeds of loans to time deposits and currency in addition to checkable deposits.

This process is outlined in Table 6.12 (see Weintraub 1970:124). A Fed open-market purchase initially generates an increase in reserves of $1000. Banks gain these reserves on the basis of their sales of government securities to the Fed. Table 6.12 records values at the end of each time period (round). Banks lend their excess reserves at the beginning of each period. (Desired excess reserves are assumed to be zero.) Initially, excess reserves are $1000 (equal to the sale of government securities), so this is the amount loaned. We could also work out the expansion process, assuming that bonds were sold to the Fed by the nonbank public. In this case, round 1 values of Table 6.12 show the distribution of proceeds among currency, demand, and time deposits by sellers of $1000 of government securities. Now bank lending begins in the second period and is equal to the excess reserves of the first period, $804.44. Every subsequent period's lending will in a similar way be equal to the excess reserves indicated in the previous period. Assuming this alternative in place of the bank selling securities to the Fed, total loans (col. 9) will be $1000 less than the total shown there, or $4113.44.

Table 6.12. The expansion process featuring an increase in base money of $1000

	(1)	(2)	(3)	(4)	(5)	(6)	(7)	(8)	(9)
					Required reserves	Excess	Money = currency + checkable	Base money = reserves +	
Round	Reserves	Currency = $0.25 \times DD$	Checkable deposits	Time deposits	$(0.14 \times DD)$ + $(0.05 \times TD)$	reserves $(1) - (5)$	deposits $(2) + (3)$	currency $(1) + (2)$	Total loans
1	$ 888.88	$ 111.11	$ 444.44	$ 444.44	$ 84.44	$ 804.44	$ 555.55	$1000.00	$1000.00
2	799.50	200.49	801.97	801.97	168.89	630.61	1002.46	1000.00	1804.44
3	718.22	270.56	1082.24	1082.24	214.15	504.07	1408.88	1000.00	2435.05
⋮									
N	431.84	568.16	2272.64	2272.64	431.84	0.00	2840.80	1000.00	5113.44

Source: Used with permission from Robert E. Weintraub, *Introduction to Monetary Economics*, p. 124, copyright © 1970, Ronald Press, New York.

Knowing the values of the coefficients, increases in checkable and time deposits and currency outside banks are predictable. While checkable deposits initially increase with increases in bank loans, their owners shuffle them between checkable and time deposits and currency until the desired ratios are reached. These amounts are shown in cols. 2, 3, and 4. The figure for reserves in col. 1 in the round 1 row is the amount at the end of round 1 after the currency loss of $111.11. Required reserves in col. 5 are calculated on the basis of known reserve requirements for checkable (14%) and time deposits (5%). The difference between required reserves (col. 5) and total reserves (col. 1) in col. 6 measures the banking system's excess reserves at the end of round 1, which are the basis of lending in round 2. Initial loans of $1000 result in an increase in the money stock of $555.55 ($111.11 + $444.44) plus increases in time deposits of $444.44 (col. 4). Base money in col. 8 is the sum of currency and reserves at the end of each period. The process repeats itself round by round, with the figures shown being the cumulative values. The key to the values in each row is first to solve for D, using the relation $0.25D + (1)(D) + D = $ loans = excess reserves of the previous period. The first term stands for the currency increase, the second for the time deposit increase, and the third for the checkable deposit increase associated with bank lending. Collecting terms and solving for D: $D = ER/2.25$. To get the first row, substitute $1000 for loans or excess reserves. The solution is $D = $444.44. To get second-row values, substitute $804.44 (excess reserves in the first row) for ER. D then equals $357.53. Once D is known, other values in the row are readily determined from a knowledge of the currency–checkable deposit and time deposit–checkable deposit ratios. The values shown in Table 6.12 are cumulative.

Expansion comes to an end when the banking system's excess reserves are zero. The expansion of money is equal to initial excess reserves of $1000 times the multiplier of 2.84. (This is the earlier $k3$ multiplier, assuming e has a value of zero). Base money is constant in every round. The composition keeps changing with an ever increasing proportion consisting of cash and a decreasing percentage of reserves.

The money base is the trigger variable in monetarist descriptions of the money supply process. (The pioneers are Brunner and Meltzer 1968. The Federal Reserve Bank of St. Louis is closely identified with popularization of this concept and developing a statistical series; e.g., see Jordan 1969:10ff.). The transformation is a simple one. All that is entailed is adding currency outside banks to DI reserves. The monetary base makes more sense than the reserve concept for multiplier analysis once we introduce currency as a leakage. In the same way that actual reserves satisfy bank demand for required and excess reserves, currency outside banks satisfies the demand for currency. Equilibrium in the money expansion process is reached when the demand for reserves and currency, M/m — measured by the ratio of the money stock to the new money multiplier m — equals the supply of reserves and currency B. Thus we write the new money supply equation as $M = mB$, where B (the monetary base) $= AR + C$. Our previous multiplier analysis for k is not wrong as long as we assume that actual reserves equal initial reserves. Statistically, however, we have data only for actual reserves, not initial reserves. At any given time, assuming that the value of the multiplier stays unchanged, the level of the monetary base will be a better predictor of the money supply than the level of reserves, since a change in reserves as a result of currency drain implies a change in the money supply at the same time that a stable monetary base would correctly imply no change. (Using the money multiplier equation with $l + c$ in the numerator is no help since the problem is with the multiplicand, AR.)

The monetary base has a practical advantage from the standpoint of policy-making. Bank reserves and currency are the so-called uses of the monetary base and are explained by the sources of the monetary base. (Their organization in a T account is discussed in Ch. 10.) On a daily basis, the Fed has knowledge of the total sources rather than of the individual uses — reserves and currency. Considering reserves and currency collectively (via the daily knowledge of the sources of the monetary base) is a matter of expediency for policymaking purposes (see Burger 1971:188).

Despite its apparent usefulness, the Fed authorities only began to acknowledge the monetary base concept in their statistics in March 1979. It still is given less weight than the reserve concept in policy implementation. One reason is that an underforecasting error for currency has more serious consequences when the monetary base is the target. When currency, the principal component of the base, is running stronger than anticipated, the shortfall in reserves will have a multiple effect on deposits. On the other hand, with a reserve target, the money supply would be stronger than targeted, but only by the amount by which currency is stronger than expected (FRB 1980b). The experience of the early 1930s might support this point of view. At that time, the monetary base increased but the money supply declined because the public (because of distrust of banks) cashed their deposits, thus converting bank reserves into currency (see Thomas 1979:214ff.).

The money supply is the product of the multiplier times reserves, or the monetary base. Reserve requirements affect the value of the multiplier. The higher the reserve requirements, the lower the multiplier values. The rationale of reserve requirements and their structure are discussed below.

LIQUIDITY AND RESERVE REQUIREMENTS   Initially, the purpose of required reserves, which are a dollar figure (reserve requirements times deposit liabilities), was to make banks liquid, i.e., enable them to meet demands for cash from their depositors. But required reserves immobilize bank reserves and reduce bank liquidity. It is as if a city ordinance always required a taxicab to be in front of a cab stand or a fire engine to be in the station house. One cab or one fire engine is permanently out of service.

Let us illustrate the illiquidity of reserve requirements by assuming that DI A is fully "loaned up" with legal reserves of $100 and deposits of $1000. This tells us that the reserve requirement is 10% and also that the DI's loans will be $900. Now it is faced with deposit withdrawals of $50. It will supply cash out of its reserves (either from its own vault or from the central bank). (We rule out the possibility of the bank borrowing additional reserves; borrowing rather than reserves alone would be the basis for liquidity.) The paradox is that it now must dip into its reserves earmarked for the remaining $950 of deposits. Only $5 of reserves are available for the $50 that has been withdrawn. Thus the bank suffers deficient reserves equal to $45. Instead of the required reserve ratio of 10%, the actual reserve ratio is 5.3% (50/950). The bank will be forced to reduce its loans by $45 to restore the required reserve ratio.

The repayment of a bank loan of $45 will increase reserves by $45. The borrower repaying the $45 probably raises the money by a transaction (e.g., sale of goods) involving a second DI. The buyer keeps the deposits at a second DI, and reserves are transferred between DIs. The sequence of balance sheet changes is shown in Table 6.13.

Table 6.13. Effects of a deposit withdrawal on DI liquidity

Assets			Liabilities	
Stage a.	Initial balance sheet			
	Reserves	$100	Deposits	$1000
	Loans	900		
Stage b.	Balance sheet after $50 withdrawal			
	Reserves	50	Deposits	950
	Loans	900		
Stage c.	Balance sheet after loan repayment			
	Reserves	95	Deposits	950
	Loans	855		

Contrast this situation with an absence of reserve requirements. All the $100 in reserves are excess and thus available to meet withdrawals. Without legal compulsion and at its leisure the DI can cut back on its loans and restore the 10% customary reserve ratio. Legal reserve requirements thus make a bank less liquid rather than more so. If a bank did not keep any reserves when reserve ratios are self-imposed, it would have to scramble for cash to meet withdrawals. Our assumption has to be that the bank keeps the same amount of reserves in the absence of formal reserve requirements.

HISTORY OF RESERVE REQUIREMENTS   The rationale for legal reserve requirements must be sought elsewhere, i.e., in the possibilities they offer for monetary control. Money and credit multipliers will vary in size depending on the level of reserve requirements; in this way they affect the money supply. Historically, reserve requirements have been related to bank size. They hark back to the National Banking Acts of the 1860s when big-city banks were expected to be the depositories for country banks. The liquidity of the big-city banks was crucial to that of the banking system. Central reserve city and reserve city banks (based on geographic location) had higher reserve requirements than country banks. Until 1887 New York was the only central reserve city bank, with St. Louis and Chicago being added in that year. The major U.S. cities fell initially into the reserve city category. St. Louis was subsequently dropped from the central reserve city category, and over time the number of reserve cities continued to increase, with the nucleus being the head and branch offices of the Fed. (For an excellent short history of reserve requirements, see Knight 1974a:3–20.)

This tradition persisted until 1972 when deposit size rather than location became the basis for differential requirements. As shown in the left-hand side of Table 6.14, reserve requirements against net demand deposits were graduated by demand deposit intervals. In this way, larger banks had higher average reserve requirements than smaller banks. After 1980 (right-hand side, Table 6.14) this discrimination still lingered, with lower reserve requirements against the first $28.9 mil. of transaction accounts and the exemption of $2 mil. of reservable liabilities.

Table 6.14. Reserve requirements of DIs (percent of deposits)

Type of deposit and deposit interval	Member bank requirements before implementation of the Monetary Control Act		Type of deposit and deposit interval	DI requirements after implementation of the Monetary Control Act	
	Percent	Effective date		Percent	Effective date
Net demand			*Net transaction accounts*		
$0 mil.–$2 mil.	7	12/30/76	$0–$28.9 mil.	3	12/29/83
$2 mil.–$10 mil.	9-1/2	12/30/76	Over $28.9 mil.	12	12/29/83
$10 mil.–$100 mil.	11-3/4	12/30/76			
$100 mil.–$400 mil.	12-3/4	12/30/76	*Nonpersonal time deposits*		
Over $400 mil.	16-1/4	12/30/76	By original maturity		
			Less than 1-1/2 years	3	10/6/83
Time and savings			1-1/2 years or more	0	10/6/83
Savings	3	3/16/67			
Time			*Eurocurrency liabilities*		
$0 mil.–$5 mil., by maturity			All types	3	11/13/80
30–179 days	3	3/16/67			
180 days to 4 years	2-1/2	1/8/76			
4 years or more	1	10/30/75			
Over $5 mil., by maturity					
30–179 days	6	12/12/74			
180 days to 4 years	2-1/2	1/8/76			
4 years or more	1	10/30/75			

Source: *Fed. Res. Bull.* 1984b:A7.
Note: For details on reserve requirements, see notes to table in source.

Unlike the single set of reserve requirements for member banks, nonmembers of the Fed were subject to a variety of state requirements until DIDMCA. Reserve requirements for state nonmember banks are detailed in Knight (1974a:App.) and Gilbert and Lovati (1978:23–27). Their effective level was generally lower compared with member bank reserve requirements. The chief reason was the eligibility for reserve purposes of interest-bearing assets (such as U.S. government bonds). Moreover, nominal reserve requirements were not enforced as strictly as for member banks (Gilbert and Lovati 1978:28ff.). (Later discussion of Fed structure in Chs. 9 and 10 will comment on the exodus from the system owing to reserve differentials and their policy implications.)

The cash reserves of nonmember banks consisted of holdings of vault cash and deposits in other banks. The result was a considerable flexibility in the size of money and credit multipliers as checkable and time deposits shifted between member and nonmember banks. An increase in deposits in nonmember banks increased the excess reserves of nonmember banks. At the same time, however, the required reserves of member banks were not affected. Their deposit liability totals stayed the same; only the composition had changed. Nonmember banks owned deposits in place of the nonbank public. If nonmember banks kept required reserves in other nonmember banks, the reserve base was expanded even further. This is known as pyramiding of reserves. Nonmember banks, because their reserves were not limited to cash and Fed deposits, magnified the size of the money multiplier (the ratio of the money stock to the monetary base).

Monetary Control Act of 1980

RESERVE REQUIREMENTS   The Monetary Control Act of 1980 is Title 1 of what has been called the most significant banking legislation since passage of the Federal Reserve Act in 1913 (Senator William A. Proxmire, quoted in Fed, Chicago 1983:7). The full act, the Depository Institution Deregulation and Monetary Control Act, was signed into law on March 31, 1980. The new banking law has revolutionized the regulatory structure and competitive environment among banking and financial institutions.

Effective November 1980 all DIs were made subject to the same federally imposed reserve requirements. Nonmember banks, S&Ls, MSBs, and federally insured CUs are now in the same boat as member banks. The membership tax on member banks, because of higher reserve requirements, has thus been eliminated.

Each DI now must maintain 3% on its transaction accounts of $28.9 mil. or less plus 12% on the amount over $28.9 mil. (right-hand side, Table 6.14). Reserve requirements are being phased in for nonmember banks and thrift institutions until 1987. Transaction accounts are net (similar to demand deposits before the Monetary Control Act) because cash items in process of collection (checks forwarded for collection) and demand balances due from domestic banks are subtracted in estimating reservable deposits.

DIs know precisely what their required reserves will be in any reserve period because of a lag between the computation period and the maintenance period. The lag was greatly shortened in February 1984 when the Fed shifted from lagged reserve accounting to contemporaneous reserve accounting for transaction deposits. As Figure 6.1 shows, until the change, required reserves for the reserve week (Thursday through Wednesday) were based on deposit liabilities two weeks earlier. Now during a given two-week reserve maintenance period, which begins on

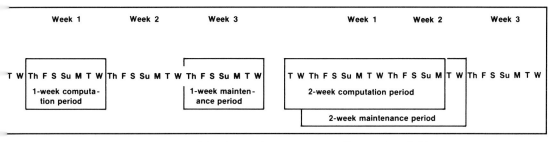

6.1. Lagged reserve accounting system (left); contemporaneous reserve accounting system, transaction deposits only (right). (Judd and Motley 1984)

a Thursday and ends on the second Wednesday, a bank's required reserves depend on its checkable deposits in the two-week reserve computation period that ended on the preceding Monday. With the exception of a lag of two days, the computation and maintenance periods overlap. That this change will improve monetary control as intended is doubtful (see Ch. 11 for discussion).

On the nontransaction accounts, a 3% requirement applies to nonpersonal time deposits (such as large CDs) and Eurocurrency liabilities. Reserve requirements against savings and personal time deposits (left-hand side, Table 6.14) have been eliminated.

DIs will satisfy their reserve requirements with vault cash or a Fed account. Additionally, nonmember institutions may pass through their required reserves via a correspondent reserve account held with another institution that maintains required reserve balances with the Fed, a Federal Home Loan Bank, or the National Credit Union Administration's central liquidity facility (Cacy and Winningham 1980:4–5).

The average required reserve ratios on deposits included in the various monetary aggregates have fallen over the past 20 years because of the declining importance of member bank deposits and the rising importance of deposits other than checkable deposits. Because of the uniformity of the new requirements, average required ratios will now be stabilized, thus contributing to better monetary control (Cacy and Winningham 1980:10ff.). Member banks will enjoy a windfall as required reserves at the Fed decline from about $32 to $14 bil. (Fed, Chicago 1980:7).

OTHER KEY PROVISIONS   Among its other key titles, DIDMCA (1) authorized the Fed to collect data needed to monitor and control the money and credit aggregates; (2) required the Fed to price its services and grant all DIs access to such services that include Fed borrowing privileges; (3) provided for the orderly phase-out of deposit interest rate ceilings—the Depository Institutions Deregulation Committee (DIDC), consisting of the heads of the major federal financial regulatory agencies, was charged with implementing the phase-out; (4) overrode state usury ceilings on certain types of loans; and (5) broadened the asset powers and permissible activities of thrift institutions. Finally, the wider category of checkable deposits superseded demand deposits because NOW (negotiable orders of withdrawal) accounts were authorized nationwide together with certain other interest-bearing balances at both banks and thrift institutions, which can be used for transactions purposes (Fed, Chicago 1983:8; *Fed Res Bull* 1984c:A7,n.7). Further discussion of various features of DIDMCA appear in Chapters 8, 14, and 17.

The Garn–St. Germain Depository Institutions Act of 1982

The financial innovation of DIDMCA was carried forward two years later in the Garn–St. Germain Depository Institutions Act of 1982. Its best known provision was the authorization of the money market deposit account (MMDA). The account was to be in competition with money market mutual funds. This account, which has been widely available since December 14, 1982, is federally insured, pays an interest rate restricted only by the discretion of the institution (minimum balances were eliminated on January 1, 1986), and has limited transaction features (six transfers per month of which no more than three may be by check). MMDAs can be owned by corporations, which is not the case for NOW accounts. On personal accounts, MMDAs do not carry required reserves, but a 3% reserve requirement is imposed on nonpersonal accounts (Fed, Chicago 1983:31). As of the middle of 1984, MMDAs amounted to $393 bil. or 17% of $M2$ (FRB 1984g).

Another new account was authorized by the DIDC in January 1983. The Super NOW account is restricted like NOW accounts to individuals and nonprofit organizations. Unlike the NOW accounts, which have a ceiling interest rate of 5¼%, interest rates are unregulated. As a transactions account it is subject to the 12% reserve requirement.

An overriding concern of the act was the plight of thrift institutions after 1980 due to sharply rising market interest rates; but in creating a level playing field, the two acts may have exacerbated the financial problems of thrifts (see Ch. 14).

Summary

Our central purpose has been to explain the stock of money as the product of a multiplier and a multiplicand. The multiplicand is either depository reserves or the monetary base. The multipliers estimate how much of an increase in the money supply or total bank assets is made possible by a $1 increase in reserves or the monetary base. The extent of the leakages as the DI lending process takes place (the denominator of the multiplier) and the corresponding increases in money (the terms in the numerator) determine the size of the multiplier. As an expansion proceeds, the multiplicand is absorbed into required reserves, desired excess reserves, and currency in the hands of the public. The broader the monetary or DI asset concept, the larger the value of the multiplier. The leakages remain the same, but additional expansion terms are introduced into the numerator. Two multipliers were considered in depth—those for $M1$ and bank loans. Additional money stock measures were listed early in the chapter.

The cumulative process of money and credit creation is described by equations such as $D = AR$ or $M = mB$, where D denotes checkable deposits; $M,$ the money stock; $AR,$ reserves; and $B,$ the monetary base. Behind these formulas lies the participation of thousands of individual financial institutions in the expansion process. The spillover of deposits from the expanding DI transfers reserves to a second DI, and the step-by-step process continues.

In the basic textbook multiplier, reserve requirements are the sole factor setting limits to the expansion process. In more detailed multipliers, additional leakages are added. The function of reserve requirements is monetary control rather than one of assuring bank liquidity. The graduated structure of reserve requirements in effect until recently has its roots in the mistaken notion of liquidity.

While the multipliers are represented by fixed coefficients, their values can change because of variations in the underlying parameters. Multipliers vary because of changes in reserve requirements, currency-deposit ratios, time deposit ratios, etc. These changes in turn are explained by such influences as market interest rates, service charges on checking accounts, household wealth, deposit variability, and recreation travel.

Momentous changes have taken place, which have affected the concept and measurement of the money stock. DIDMCA in 1980 expanded the potential for money creation beyond commercial banks. Now thrift institutions are members of a wider category of depository institutions whose transaction accounts are subject to uniform reserve requirements. Transaction accounts (checkable deposits) go beyond demand deposits and embrace interest-bearing deposits, most notably NOW accounts. The Garn–St. Germain Act in 1982 added MMDAs, which fall into the $M2$ category despite their (limited) use for transaction purposes, and also Super NOWs ($M1$ aggregate).

Review questions

1. Do DIs create money? How is this done?

2. Explain why DIs cannot expand their loans and deposits indefinitely.

3. Distinguish between the four types of leakages: reserve requirements on checkable deposits, reserve requirements on time deposits, excess reserves, and currency withdrawal. Explain the relationship of leakage to a bank's ability to lend.

4. Differentiate between monetary base and reserves and describe the advantages and disadvantages of the base concept.

5. Describe the new types of deposit accounts created by DIDMCA and the Garn–St. Germain Act.

6. Do reserve requirements make a bank more liquid?

7. Identify the coefficients determining the money multiplier. Are the coefficients constant? Show by means of an equation how potential checkable deposit expansion can be determined if we know the reserve requirements, desired excess reserves, and currency drain.

8. Explain why an individual banker (who has not had a course in money and banking) might deny that he creates money when he makes loans.

9. What are the bookkeeping entries on the books of the Federal Reserve when it buys a government security?

10. What is the underlying identity for the limit to DI deposit expansion?

11. Define:

Money stock	Multiplier
T accounts	Monetary base
Required reserves	Contemporaneous reserve requirements
Actual reserves	Lagged reserve requirements
Excess reserves	Money market deposit accounts
Deficient reserves	NOW accounts
Open-market purchases	Super NOW accounts

7

Bankers in action

The mechanics of money creation are only part of the banking story. To understand the banking process, we have to dig into the portfolio behavior of banks (i.e., how bankers manage their assets and liabilities).

Bankers, like other business firms, are interested in making profits. To a greater extent than is true of other business firms, profit making is tempered by considerations of liquidity and safety. Liquidity is the ability to meet cash withdrawals on demand. Safety is maintaining asset values in excess of liabilities. Banks have a cushion in the size of their capital accounts (surplus and undivided profits), but if the balance sheet balances only by writing down the stated value of the bank's common stock, the bank is insolvent. (Action may be taken by the regulatory authorities against the bank before such technical insolvency is reached.) Because of banking's strategic role in a money economy, banks are a highly regulated industry.

Financial statements

BALANCE SHEET   The financial statements of a bank summarize its activities. The main classes of items found in bank balance sheets are given in Table 7.1. Bank debits (uses of funds) are broken down into four categories: cash assets or

Table 7.1. Main balance sheet items, insured commercial banks (values in $ bil. as of Dec. 31, 1983)

	Assets		Liabilities		
11.2%	$ 225.1	Cash assets (primary reserves)	Demand deposits	$ 388.1	19.2%
12.8	259.1	Secondary reserves[a]	Time deposits	1138.7	56.4
54.0	1090.0	Net loans	Borrowed funds	351.6	17.4
22.0	444.2	Investments[b]	Capital accounts	140.0	7.0
100%	$2018.4			$2018.4	100%

Source: *Fed. Res. Bull.* 1984b:A70, A71.
[a]Secondary reserves is the sum of federal funds sold, and repurchase agreement and U.S. Treasury securities.
[b]Investments include total securities, excluding those of the U.S. Treasury, which are included in secondary reserves, lease-financing receivables, bank premises and other bank-owned real estate, and other assets.

primary reserves, secondary reserves, loans, and investments. On the credit side (sources-of-funds side), we show deposits, borrowed funds, and capital accounts. When the balance sheet is converted into a flow-of-funds statement, additional inflows of funds result from repayments of loans and net profits (mainly interest income less operating expenses but also capital gains or losses on the sale of financial assets). Net loans dominate the asset side, followed by investments. On the liability side, time deposits are the largest single item, followed by demand deposits.

INCOME STATEMENT   The earnings and expenses of insured commercial banks are given in some detail in Table 7.2 for 1978–82. The primary source of operating income is interest on loans, and the primary operating expense is interest paid on deposits and other borrowed funds. Security interest income is much less important than loan income, with the percent reaching a low of 18% in 1981. Wages and salaries follow interest as the next major expense.

Table 7.2. Report of income for all insured commercial banks

Item	1978	1979	1980	1981	1982
			($ mil.)		
Operating income, total	113,170	149,795	190,109	247,932	257,188
Interest, total	102,706	137,364	174,416	228,675	235,121
Loans	75,948	101,942	126,663	163,171	166,589
Balances with banks	6,662	10,561	16,035	23,935	23,857
Federal funds sold and securities purchased under					
resale agreement	3,664	6,106	8,750	12,236	11,316
Securities (excluding trading accounts)					
Total income	16,432	18,755	22,968	29,333	33,359
U.S. Treasury and U.S. government agencies and corporations	9,335	10,630	13,400	18,037	21,022
States and political subdivisions	6,003	6,928	8,131	9,671	10,612
Other[a]	1,094	1,197	1,437	1,635	1,725
Trust department	2,138	2,375	2,738	3,179	3,604
Direct lease financing	862	1,073	1,371	1,746	1,943
Service charges on deposits	2,039	2,517	3,173	3,905	4,573
Other charges, fees, etc.	2,930	3,635	4,352	5,302	6,203
Other operating income	2,495	2,831	4,059	5,116	5,715
Operating expenses, total	98,104	131,950	170,675	227,714	238,016
Interest, total	59,198	87,570	119,758	169,268	168,553
Time and savings deposits	50,054	71,693	98,130	138,977	141,097
Time certificate of deposits of $100,000 or more issued					
by domestic offices	11,693	18,105	24,753	39,034	37,359
Deposits in foreign offices	14,559	24,523	34,941	46,696	41,746
Other deposits	23,802	29,065	38,436	53,248	62,029
Federal funds purchased and securities sold under					
repurchase agreement	7,247	12,218	16,707	23,786	20,618
Other borrowed money[b]	1,452	3,162	4,380	5,894	6,188
Capital notes and debentures	445	497	541	611	650
Salaries, wages, and employee benefits	18,654	21,465	24,565	27,927	31,218
Occupancy expense[c]	5,559	6,255	7,325	8,566	9,960
Loan-loss provision	3,499	3,764	4,453	5,059	8,291
Other operating expenses	11,194	12,796	14,573	16,962	19,953
Income before taxes and securities gains or losses	15,067	17,843	19,435	20,149	19,172
Applicable income taxes	4,155	4,736	5,009	4,611	3,639
Net securities gains or losses (-) after taxes	-225	-350	-492	-861	-661
Extraordinary charges (-) or credits after taxes	45	39	17	54	68
Net income	10,731	12,797	13,950	14,731	14,940
Cash dividends declared	3,714	4,449	5,091	5,831	6,529
Memo					
Number of banks	14,380	14,352	14,421	14,400	14,121
Average fully consolidated assets ($ bil.)	1,418	1,593	1,768	1,933	2,101

Source: *Fed. Res. Bull.* 1984d:501.
[a]Includes interest income from other bonds, notes and debentures, and dividends from stocks.
[b]Includes interest paid on U.S. Treasury tax and loan account balances, which were begun in November 1978.
[c]Occupancy expense for bank premises net of any rental income plus furniture and equipment expenses.

The leading importance of interest income on loans is explained by two factors: their dominance in portfolios and the greater average return as compared with securities. Between 1979 and 1982, for example, loans were over 55% of interest-earning assets when the highest percentage of securities was 17% (*Fed. Res. Bull.* 1983b:502). As can be seen from Table 7.3, the average return on securities in 1982 was 9.96%, while the return on loans was 15.20% (before loan-loss provisions).

Table 7.3. Rates of return on fully consolidated portfolios, all insured commercial banks			
Item	1980	1981	1982
		(%)	
Securities, total	7.88	9.27	9.96
U.S. government	9.38	11.38	12.19
State and local government	6.03	6.72	7.19
Other	10.55	11.54	11.64
Loans, gross	13.71	16.37	15.20
Net of loan-loss provision	13.19	15.83	14.39
Taxable equivalent			
Total securities	10.23	11.73	12.49
State and local government	11.13	12.15	12.93
Total securities and gross loans	12.88	15.26	14.57

Source: *Fed. Res. Bull.* 1984d:490.
Note: Calculated as described in *Fed. Res. Bull.* 1979:704. For each bank with profits before tax greater than zero, income from state and local obligations was increased by $[1/(1-t)-1]$ times the lesser of profits before tax or interest earned on state and local obligations (t is the marginal federal income tax rate). This adjustment approximates the equivalent pretax return on state and local obligations.

The sources of noninterest income are shown in Table 7.2, beginning with "trust department." This is income from the fiduciary activities of banks. Bank trust departments administer trust funds on behalf of their clients. Such financial assets do not show up on bank balance sheets, since the assets are not owned by the banks. At the end of 1982, personal trusts and estates administered by banks amounted to $257 bil. (see also Ch. 14). Banks are involved in the leasing business as evidenced in the income item of direct lease financing. By buying airplanes, computers, railroad cars, etc., and then leasing them to firms, banks can reduce their taxable income by taking advantage of depreciation allowances and investment tax credits. Bank service charges account for most of the remaining noninterest income.

Finally, operating income is supplemented by capital gains or losses on security transactions to yield net income (see net securities gains or losses, Table 7.2). Capital losses will be less when bond yields are falling (1982) and greater when they are rising (1981). The persistent capital losses in 1978–82 despite periods of declining yields suggest that such losses were the result of selling off "old" low-yielding bonds in order to finance a demand for loans.

How profitable are banks? Table 7.4 expresses net income (income after taxes) as a percent of assets and average equity for 1978–82 for banks of different sizes.

Compared with previous years, returns fell in 1982 in terms of returns on assets and as a percent of equity. The decline in profitability occurred despite a widening of the net interest margin—the difference between interest income and interest expense relative to average assets. This widening continued in 1983 (Keeley

Table 7.4. Profit rates of insured commercial banks					
Type of return and size of bank[a]	1978	1979	1980	1981	1982
	(%)				
Return on assets[b]					
All banks	0.76	0.80	0.79	0.76	0.71
Less than $100 mil.	1.04	1.15	1.18	1.15	1.08
$100 mil. to $1 bil.	0.90	0.96	0.96	0.91	0.85
$1 bil. or more					
Money center banks	0.53	0.56	0.56	0.53	0.50
Others	0.68	0.72	0.66	0.68	0.63
Return on equity[c]					
All banks	12.9	13.9	13.7	13.2	12.2
Less than $100 mil.	13.2	14.1	14.2	13.6	12.7
$100 mil. to $1 bil.	13.2	13.9	13.7	12.8	12.0
$1 bil. or more					
Money center banks	12.8	14.0	14.4	13.4	12.3
Others	12.5	13.5	12.7	12.9	11.9

Source: *Fed. Res. Bull.* 1984d:498.

[a]Size categories are based on year-end fully consolidated assets.
[b]Net income as a percent of the average of beginning- and end-of-year fully consolidated assets net of loan-loss reserves.
[c]Net income as a percent of the average of beginning- and end-of-year equity capital.

and Zimmerman 1984). Expectations that deregulation would lead to a higher cost of retail time deposit accounts and a fall in the margin did not materialize. The breakdown by bank size suggests that bigness is not always the key to profitability; e.g., returns on assets and equity for banks with less than $100 mil. in assets exceeded returns for larger sized banks in all years.

COMPARISON WITH MANUFACTURING   How profitable are banks in comparison with other industries? Table 7.5 suggests that they are not as profitable as the manufacturing industry. Looking at insured commercial banks, rates of return are either approximately the same or lower than for manufacturing. An exception is 1982 when the impact of the recession on manufacturing resulted in higher returns for banking.

Table 7.5. Rates of return in banking and manufacturing				
	(1)	(2)	(3)	(4)
Year	Manufacturing corporation profits after taxes	Manufacturing corporation stockholders equity	Profits to equity (1) ÷ (2)	Insured commercial bank net income to equity
	($ bil.)	($ bil.)	(%)	(%)
1973	48.1	374	12.9	12.9
1974	58.7	395	14.9	12.5
1975	49.1	423	11.6	11.8
1976	64.5	463	13.9	11.6
1977	70.4	497	14.2	11.8
1978	81.2	541	15.0	13.1
1979	98.7	600	16.4	14.3
1980	92.4	665	13.9	14.1
1981	101.3	743	13.6	13.0
1982	71.0	770	9.2	12.1

Sources: Cols. 1, 2--*U.S. Stat. Abst.* 1984:549; col. 4--(1973-80) FDIC 1979:191; 1980:277; (1981-82) FDIC 1982:74-75.

ANNUAL REPORT   It might be difficult to recognize a "flesh and blood" bank in this discussion of bank behavior even though we are attempting to describe individual banks. Going through a financial report of a bank gives us a greater feel for bank activity. The annual report for the Mellon Bank N.A. (national association), which we shall review, is not the report for a typical bank, since Mellon is the thirteenth largest U.S. banking company (over $30 bil. in total assets in 1985). The annual report for 1983 is a glossy 76-page publication illustrated with many colored photographs and done with obvious professionalism. The holding company, Mellon Bank Corporation, is a multinational financial services organization carrying on its securities trading, consumer finance, mortgage banking, and lease financing through a number of subsidiaries. The 27 directors of the corporation (and bank) are current or retired chairs of other leading corporations.

The report reviews Mellon's community financial services, which are greatly widened as a result of a series of mergers, institutional financial services (domestic lending activity), and trust and investment services (Mellon is now the country's largest personal trust institution). The overall impression of recent reports is of a bank expanding rapidly in a highly competitive environment by means of mergers, attracting loan customers by setting up representative offices throughout the world, and making extensive use of computer technology as a way of expanding both retail (consumer) and wholesale (business) services.

Financial statements and supplementary financial data occupy two-thirds of the report. As now requested by the Financial Accounting Standards Board, selected financial data are adjusted for inflation in one table. In 1983 the net income per common share was $7.44. When expressed as a percent of shareholders' equity of $53.62 at the year's end, this amounts to a return of 13.9%. The earnings-price ratio was slightly higher, since the common stock at the end of the year was selling for $51. Not unusual for bank stocks, market value was below book value (the equity per share of $53.62). Investors may put more weight on dividends than on retained earnings, explaining this high earnings-price ratio. Dividends as a percent of net income were 33% in 1983. The average yield on interest-earning assets was 11.62%, considerably below the 1979–83 high of 15.83% in 1981. The cost of funds was 8.02%, again a fall from a high of 12.61% in 1981. The net rate of return on interest-earning assets was the difference, 3.6%, which compares with a five-year high return of 3.72% in 1979.

Banking strategy

Banks manage their flow of funds for the purpose of maximizing profits subject to the twin constraints of liquidity and safety. Some financial items are more subject to banker control than others. In terms of Table 7.1, banks have least control over their deposits and cash assets. Reserve requirements or time lags in the collection process mainly determine cash assets. Deposits move among banks at the discretion of depositors. Deposits as a whole (for the banking system) depend on the central bank providing a reserve base. Banks exercise discretion via management of loans, investments, and their borrowing activity.

RESPONDING TO THE DEMAND FOR CREDIT   The key to banking strategy is the loan portfolio. Once liquidity requirements are taken care of, banks give the highest priority to satisfying their customers' demand for credit. The customer relation is paramount in banking strategy. (The classic study is Hodgman 1963.) In contrast to loans, investments are impersonal transactions being conducted in the open market. Business borrowers in particular are favored customers not only because of the relatively higher return on loans as compared with investments but because they are major depositors. From the standpoint of the individual bank, such deposits are a source of reserves.

The profitability of business loans is enhanced by related increases in deposit balances. Not all the proceeds of a loan will be withdrawn from a given bank, since creditors of the borrower may also use the same bank. (This is less likely the case for bank purchases of securities.) Borrowers also are required to keep compensating balances (minimum average balance requirement imposed by the bank and calculated as a percent of the loan), further increasing deposits and lending capacity.

A simple model of bank behavior illustrates profit maximization subject to limitations imposed by "footings" (totals on the balance sheet), liquidity requirements, and accommodation to loan demand. The bank maximizes:

$$P = r_l L + r_s S - N$$

subject to

$$L + S + C = G + K \qquad r_s < r_l \qquad r_c = 0$$
$$S + C = h(L + S + C) \qquad \text{or} \qquad S + C = [h/(1 - h)]L$$

where P = bank profits in a given time period
L = loans made at interest rate r_l
S = securities paying interest rates r_s
C = cash assets whose rate of return $r_c = 0$
G = deposits
K = bank capital
N = fixed expenses
h = desired liquidity ratio (including legal reserve requirements)

For convenience in portraying a graphic solution in two dimensions, securities have been coupled with cash assets. They have been expressed as a percentage of loans rather than total balance sheet values for the same reason.

Dollar value of loans are measured on the horizontal axis of Figure 7.1 and on the vertical axis, dollar value of securities and cash. The A lines measure the total footings of the balance sheet expressed either as loans or securities plus cash. Since they represent equal values, the lines have a slope of -1. The $0B$ line measures desired liquidity for alternative loan values. Alternate levels of loan demand are represented by the vertical L lines. The I lines can be given various names (market opportunity lines, objective function). Every point on these lines represents the same amount of income (after subtraction of fixed expenses N). This income is obtainable by different combinations of loans and securities and cash. Since the return on loans is greater than that on the combination of securities and cash, adding one unit of loans means that more than one unit of securities and cash must be withdrawn from the bank's portfolio if total income is to remain constant. Stated algebraically, $r_l \Delta L = -r_s \Delta S$ (neglecting cash), $\Delta L / \Delta S = -r_s/r_l$. The slope of the line $(\Delta L / \Delta S)$ is thus the reciprocal of respective rates of return, r_s/r_l. The slope of the I lines is therefore greater than -1.

A series of I lines must be drawn, representing different possible profit levels.

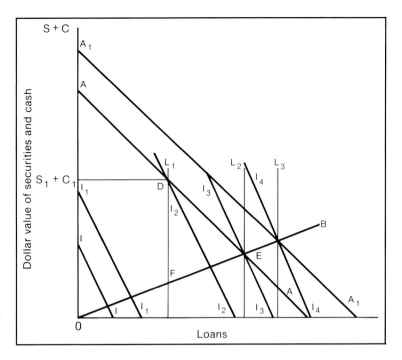

7.1. Bank profit-maximizing behavior.

Subject to the liquidity, footings, and loan demand constraints, the bank will attempt to get on the highest income curve. Assume first that loan demand is L_1. Since the bank accommodates to this loan demand, L_1 dictates the amount of loans made. The remainder of asset holdings will be $S_1 + C_1$. The triangular area *DEF* is called the feasible region, since any portfolio within this triangle satisfies all three constraints.

Each point on the *AA* line indicates a possible combination of assets that will exhaust balance sheet totals. Under these circumstances, the highest possible income is represented by the I_2I_2 line.

Next we assume that loan demand is pushed to the maximum level permitted by the other constraints. The intersection of I_3I_3 with $0B$ and AA denotes the new portfolio. It is conceivable that when the loan demand is L_1, banks, by actively soliciting loans (taking on riskier loans), can succeed in pushing L_1 over to L_2.

The third possibility is that loan demand (L_3) exceeds available resources. Banks must now seek more deposits, pushing out the balance sheet line to A_1A_1. If the new composition of deposits places less of a liquidity burden on banks by consisting of relatively more time deposits, an increase in deposits might shift the $0B$ line downward (not shown). Meeting the L_3 loan demand under these circumstances would require less of an increase in deposits than otherwise. The intersection of the A and B lines would occur at the same L_3 loan level but below the present intersection (cf. Broaddus 1972:3–11). It is assumed, of course, that the extra (interest) costs associated with additional deposits are less than the interest earned on additional loans.

Numerical examples are easily given. Assume that loans earn 10%; cash and securities, 5%; and that total footings are $100 mil. Assuming that L_1 has a value of $30 mil., gross income will be [($30 mil.)(0.10)] + [($70 mil.)(0.05)] = $6.5 mil. In a similar way the increase in gross income from an expansion in loans to either L_2 or L_3 can be calculated. The possibility of a corner solution, when security yields are above loan yields, should be pointed out. The I lines would be flatter than the A lines in these circumstances, so that intersection with an A line would occur at the vertical axis, with the entire portfolio being invested in securities and cash. The balance sheet constraint is the only constraint when all investments are in securities and cash, since obviously the liquidity constraint is being met automatically.

CYCLICAL BEHAVIOR   Viewing bank behavior from a dynamic or cyclical perspective, the demand for credit will increase in periods of economic expansion and subside in recession. Looking at the adjustment process in more detail, in buoyant times banks will reduce their secondary reserves, increase borrowings, and sell off securities. An optimal portfolio policy is one that equates marginal cost and marginal revenue. Assets and liabilities will be adjusted from this standpoint. Thus the optimal balance sheet will change from one phase of the business cycle to another.

As the demand for credit increases, the marginal revenue curve from loans shifts upward. The marginal cost of such lending is the return sacrificed on investments and the cost of borrowing. The investment loss is measured by the sum of the interest return and the capital loss on the liquidated investment. Since secondary reserves have shorter maturities and the potential capital loss is less, it is likely that secondary reserves will be liquidated before long-term investments. Banks will also engage in liability management. They will increase their borrowing by issuing large-denomination negotiable certificates of deposit (CDs) (included in time deposits on the bank balance sheet). Increased borrowing will also take place at the Fed's discount window and from other banks in the federal funds market. Free reserves (the difference between excess reserves and borrowings) will become negative in times of expanding bank credit. Instead of free reserves, we can speak of net borrowed reserves.

One can speculate on the likely sequence on the way up: loans increase, secondary reserves decline, investments decline, borrowing increases. On the way down, following a decline in the demand for credit, borrowing can be expected to fall off first, with secondary reserves being built up before long-term investments.

It is difficult to test for these relationships empirically because other factors may be at work affecting the observed data; e.g., reserves and deposits may be simultaneously increasing or effective reserve requirements may be varying. Nevertheless, theoretical a priori expectations as to how the series will move appear to be verified by the data.

Figure 7.2 plots balance sheet ratios for total loans, cash and securities, and commercial and industrial loans (1950–83) for all commercial banks. The cyclical movements punctuate the long-run trends. Over the period as a whole, total loans have risen (more so than the component category commercial and industrial loans) and cash and securities have fallen. If borrowing (as previously defined) had been plotted, it would show a long-run upward movement paralleling the movement in loans and securities. Time and savings deposits move in the opposite direction to demand deposits over the 1950–83 period (Fig. 7.3) (Ch. 14 discusses these trends). Close examination of both figures indicates the short-run cyclical movements. Now cash and securities increase when loans fall off. Time and savings

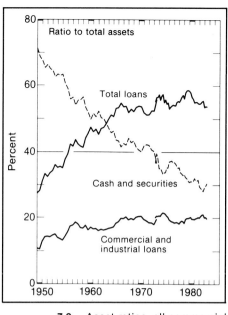

7.2. Asset ratios, all commercial banks. (FRB 1983d:83)

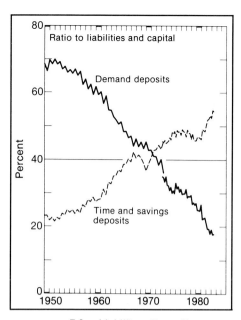

7.3. Liability ratios, all commercial banks. (FRB 1983d:83)

deposits are the mirror image of movements in demand deposits because of substitution in response to changes in transactions requirements.

REACTION TO AN INCREASE IN DEPOSITS   Another shock to a bank's portfolio can be an exogenous increase in checkable deposits. Again loans are pivotal in bank decision making, but now the adjustment process takes longer. Banks first must seek out and screen loan applicants who were unaware of the greater availability or lower cost of credit.

The likely time sequence in the adustment process of various assets and liabilities is now depicted in Figure 7.4. Cash assets immediately rise by the amount of

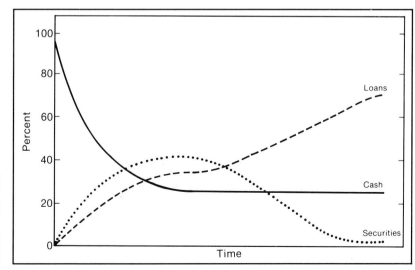

7.4. Dynamic portfolio adjustment paths. (Used with permission from Hester and Pierce 1975:70)

the deposit increase and subsequently decline until some minimum level is reached. As cash assets fall, security holdings rise synchronously, reaching a peak and then subsequently declining. With a slower start, loans begin to rise and continue to do so over the period.

The hypothetical relationship shown in Figure 7.4 can be estimated by means of an input-output model. If we treat demand (checkable) deposits as inputs and assets as outputs, the coefficients attached to demand deposits show how much of an initial dollar increase in them will show up in cash, securities, and loans in the first, second, third month, etc. (Hester and Pierce 1975:Ch. 6). Similar linkages can be established for increases in time deposits; the difference will be more mortgage lending.

Does this kind of mechanical relationship between the inflow of deposits and the allocation of funds mean that banks do not attempt to maximize their profits? This is not the case. Banks move cautiously into higher yielding loans because this is the way to maximize their profits. The costs of lending are less if banks take their time in choosing their loan portfolio (Hester and Pierce 1975:69–71).

RESPONSE TO OTHER DISTURBANCES   Bankers have been pictured as responding to an exogenous demand for credit and to an exogenous increase in their checkable deposits. They also respond to other policy instruments, e.g., the discount rate—the borrowing rate the Fed charges depository institutions (DIs). An increase in the discount rate will discourage bank borrowing. Another policy instrument is the level of reserve requirements. Higher reserve requirements increase required cash assets on which no interest is earned. This will reduce a bank's profitability and may lead it to substitute loans for secondary reserves. In this way, the policy objective of the Fed (to restrict credit expansion) might be frustrated (Ascheim 1959:697–704).

Summary

This chapter goes a step beyond the previous one by taking a closer look at commercial bank operations (other DIs are studied in Ch. 14). Commercial banks engage in a wide variety of lending activity, with the objective of profit maximization but subject to the constraints of safety and liquidity. Liquidity is a more measurable type of constraint (one can take for granted that banks intend all their loans to be safe) and is the one on which we have concentrated.

Bankers respond to shocks from the outside. They respond to an exogenous increase in the demand for credit and to various nuances of monetary policy, particularly those affecting bank reserves. When loan demand increases, loans replace other assets and liabilities increase. The heightened importance of liabilities other than demand deposits since the 1960s is the result of liability management.

Attention is given to the portfolio response to an increase in reserves (deposits). Relying on an input-output or flow-of-funds approach to portfolio choice, various assets are linked to demand and time deposit increases, with the relationships changing over time.

Review questions

1. List the main assets and liabilities on banks' balance sheets. What are the largest items?

2. Distinguish balance sheet items in terms of bank control over these items.

3. What are the primary sources of operating income and operating expense for insured commercial banks?

4. Develop a simple model of bank behavior both algebraically and by means of a diagram. What are the chief constraints on bank behavior?

5. Discuss the dynamic (cyclical) aspects of bank behavior.

6. How profitable are banks? What is the relationship between size and profitability?

7. Describe the typical annual report of a major bank holding company.

8. Define:

Net income	Capital gains and losses in securities
Net interest margin	Feasible region
Direct lease financing	Corner solution

8

Banking as a regulated industry

Banking is a highly regulated industry. In previous chapters the discussion is chiefly concerned with reserve requirements. But regulation goes far beyond this, running the gamut from the initial charter of incorporation and legal form of organization to mergers, loan and investment practices, maximum rates that can be charged or paid, and finally to dissolution. Regulation has the effect of restricting competition. Whether the social costs of restricting competition exceed the social benefits of conferring greater safety on the banking system is a central question. As a result of financial legislation in 1980 and 1982 (see Ch. 6), a major effort has been made to induce more competition among financial institutions and create a level playing field.

Banking structure

The present banking structure is the end product of a series of piecemeal changes made in response to specific problems ever since the republic was founded. The first epoch of state banking roughly covers the period from 1791 to the Civil War. It was a chaotic period, with a number of attempts on the state level to provide safety to currency holders. A safe and uniform currency did result from the National Banking Acts of 1862–63. National banks newly chartered by the comptroller of the currency issued national bank notes with their own bank names and collateraled by government bonds. (The National Banking Acts had the clever idea of tying the financing of the Civil War to the currency problem.) The National Banking System lasted until 1913 when the Federal Reserve Act ushered in another era. The Federal Reserve System established a central bank, which was designed to cure the ailments that developed after the Civil War—an elastic currency, pyramiding of reserves (see Ch. 6), roundabout methods for collecting checks (which also created fictitious reserves), and lack of a lender of last resort. It perhaps succeeded in all these objectives (see Ch. 9) except the last. It failed to prevent the Great Depression and bank failures. Many economists blame the Fed for these calamities. The Fed, it is alleged, was too much concerned with its own liquidity to safeguard that of the economy. Two major banking acts were passed in 1933 and 1935 – the response of Congress to financial collapse. Among the major provisions of these acts were deposit insurance, prohibitions of interest payments on demand deposits, setting of ceilings on interest rates on time and savings deposits (Regulation Q), and separation of investment banking from commercial banking. The latter restriction was to prevent banks lending to companies they were underwriting, an obvious conflict of interest.

A third important act of the 1933–35 period was the Securities Act of 1934, which established margin requirements for stock market lending. The stock market crash of 1929 was blamed on excessive speculation financed by bank credit. Margin requirements limited the amount of borrowing for such purposes (e.g., 60% requirement meant that the borrower could only borrow 40% of the purchase price). Since the 1930s other important legislation has aimed at controlling bank concentration. These include the Bank Holding Company Act of 1956 as amended in 1970 (discussed below) and the Bank Merger Act of 1960. The Comptroller of the Currency, the Fed, and the Federal Deposit Insurance Corporation (FDIC) were empowered to approve or deny proposed mergers on the basis of banking factors and the effect on competition. A subsequent 1966 law brought the Department of Justice into the process. If the department did not file a suit within 30 days after the appropriate banking agency had approved the merger, the merger was exempt from further attack under the antitrust laws (Horvitz 1974:123–41). Through the 1966 law more attention is given by the regulatory authorities to the effects of the merger on competition.

Two acts in 1978 made this a significant year for legislation (Waage 1979:12). One of these will be discussed (the International Banking Act). The other (Financial Institutions Regulatory and Interest Rate Control Act) established a Federal Financial Institutions Examination Council for coordinating bank examinations and permitting automatic transfers from savings accounts.

CHARTERING AND MEMBERSHIP   The United States has a dual banking system. Banks are chartered and regulated on both the federal and state level. Banks chartered by the federal government have national bank or N.A. (national association) in their titles. Banks are also chartered by the individual state governments. National banks are required to become members of the Federal Reserve System; state banks are not. The distribution of banks by number and by dollar value of assets according to chartering authority and membership in the Fed and the FDIC is shown in Figure 8.1.

Most banks hold state charters (68%). State banks are chiefly nonmember banks, which explains why 60% of all banks are this type. The assets of member banks are disproportionate to their numbers. While making up 40% of all banks, they hold 75% of all assets. Virtually all banks are members of the FDIC, which insures individual deposits up to $100,000. The percentage of banks belonging to the Fed dropped from 52% in 1947 to 35% in 1979. In this time the share of deposits dropped from 86% to 71%. This was a matter of concern to the Fed, and finally the Depository Institutions Deregulation and Monetary Control Act (DIDMCA) was passed in 1980 to stop this attrition. Since 1980 the percentage of Fed membership has increased to 40%, with the share of assets increasing to 75%.

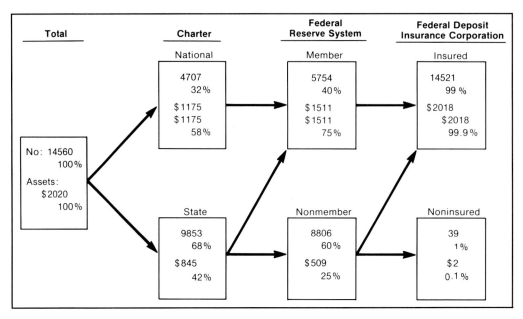

Total	Charter	Federal Reserve System	Federal Deposit Insurance Corporation
	National	Member	Insured
	4707 32% $1175 $1175 58%	5754 40% $1511 $1511 75%	14521 99 % $2018 $2018 99.9%
No: 14560 100% Assets: $2020 100%			
	State	Nonmember	Noninsured
	9853 68% $845 42%	8806 60% $509 25%	39 1% $2 0.1%

8.1. Structure of banking, number of banks, anc amount of assets ($ bil.), June 30, 1983. Noninsured assets is a 1982 figure. (FDIC 1983; FRB 1984b:A70)

BANK OFFICES   The number of bank offices that a state sanctions determines whether the banking structure is unit banking, limited branching, or statewide branching. Federal regulations defer here to state regulations: national banks are subject to the same regulations governing state banks. Figure 8.2 suggests a geographic pattern, with western states permitting statewide branching; the Midwest, single bank offices; and the East, limited branching. Limited branching can take various forms, with limitation of branches to the same city or county or to tiers of counties contiguous to the one in which the head office is located. As would be expected, statewide and limited branching states account for the bulk of bank offices, with 47,810 offices in 42 states out of a total of 54,892 offices nationwide.

The trend is toward states liberalizing their branching laws (Savage 1982:79). Statewide branching has recently been permitted in erstwhile limited branching states (New Jersey, New York, New Hampshire, Massachusetts). West Virginia, Oklahoma, and Nebraska have moved from unit to limited branching. In Pennsylvania, branching is now permitted in a second tier of counties beyond contiguous counties.

HOLDING COMPANIES   An increasingly visible feature of bank structure is the holding company. Holding companies are corporations whose assets consist of the stock of operating companies (see Fig. 8.3). By this ownership (25% or more of the stock) they can control the activities of a single bank (one-bank holding company, OBHC) or several banks (multibank holding company, MBHC) plus nonbank enterprises. The four possibilities are no explicit law, state laws permitting holding companies, states restricting operations, and prohibition of holding companies. States can move between categories. In 1982 Pennsylvania relaxed its re-

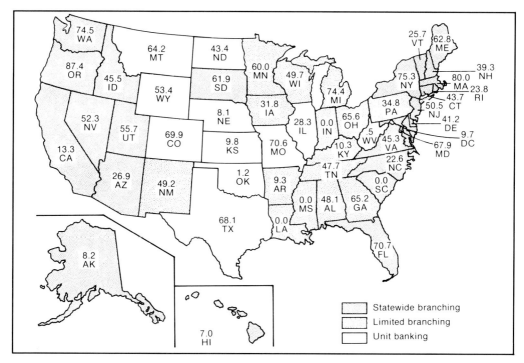

8.2. Percent of commercial banking deposits held by multibank holding companies, end of 1982. (*Fed. Res. Bull.* 1982:81, with updated percentages supplied by the FRB)

strictions on MBHCs. Before that, OBHCs were allowed. In 1982 Illinois permitted MBHCs for the first time (Gregorash 1983:13).

The growing importance of holding companies is gauged by the percent of bank deposits under their control. By the end of 1982, 82% of domestic commercial banking assets were held by subsidiary banks of holding companies. MBHCs held 50% of these assets, an increase from 19% at the end of 1969. Figure 8.2 shows the percentages of deposits held in subsidiary banks by state. Since 1970 the

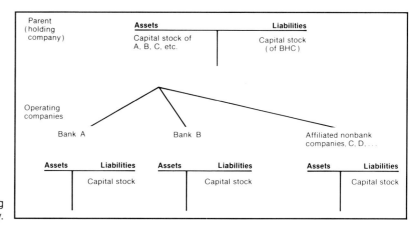

8.3. Bank holding company.

bulk of the increase in MBHCs has been concentrated in a small number of unit banking or limited branching states – Texas, Florida, Missouri, Michigan, Ohio, Colorado, Wisconsin, and Alabama.

Control of the Fed was extended to OBHCs in 1970 (MBHCs have been subject to regulations since 1956) because of their great growth in the 1960s. The 1970 act made OBHCs subject to the 1956 law limiting related business activities, but the list of allowable activities was extended (Horvitz 1974:120–21).

Table 8.1 describes the activities approved and denied by the Fed as of December 1983. The large number of activities permitted by regulation and by order suggests that BHCs can engage in a broad scope of nonbank activities. No geographic limitation is placed, so a BHC in Chicago may provide trust services through an office in Phoenix, Miami, or Anchorage (Gregorash 1983:3).

Banks set up certain nonbank subsidiaries to avoid regulation. Setting up a subsidiary, for example, circumvents the Glass-Steagall Act of 1933, which barred banks from being in the security business (Pierce 1984:268). By acquiring discount brokerage firms, they can actively solicit business and meet the competition of financial conglomerates (combinations of brokerage firms, insurance companies, and money market mutual funds plus nonfinancial entities), which offer attractive financial services to the public. Nonbank subsidiaries bypass the limits on the number of loan offices in unit banking states. Finance company subsidiaries, for example, lend to consumers wherever the bank chooses to operate.

On the borderline of BHC expansion is the legality of acquiring nonbank banks, which differ from banks (as defined by the Bank Holding Company Act of 1956) by not engaging in commercial lending and/or demand deposit functions. The difference from banks means that they are not subject to the restrictions of the act against interstate banking (Johnston 1983:1). The attraction exists not only for BHCs but also extends to nonbank entities as diverse as oil, pen, furniture, and mutual funds companies.

The result has been increased competition for commercial banks. They find themselves faced with new competitors – manufacturers such as Sears Roebuck and Company and diversified financial companies such as Merrill Lynch and American Express (Rosenblum et al. 1983:1). Among the nation's largest banking firms only three had earnings that exceeded the financial service earnings of General Motors and Sears in 1981. Inroads on the dominant position of commercial banking have been made in consumer lending, business lending, and deposit taking. Banks have fought back, mainly by acquiring subsidiaries (see Rosenblum et al. 1983:10).

The geographic freedom of nonbank competitors is also being successfully challenged. Interstate banking is slowly becoming a reality through mergers, acquisitions, affiliations, relaxations of some state laws, and technological advances. The chronology of change is described in Rosenblum et al. (1983:10).

Sears Roebuck acquires Dean Witter Reynolds. Shearson, another brokerage firm, merges with American Express and later they take over investment bankers Lehman Brothers Kuhn Loeb, now Shearson/Lehman Brothers (American Express). The emergence of financial supermarkets raises the question of whether this will tilt the level playing field. Will banklike institutions (approximately 43,000 in number since the passage of DIDMCA in 1980 and the Garn–St. Germain Act in 1982) need to be financial supermarkets to survive? Some observers

Table 8.1. Permissible nonbank activities for bank holding companies under Section 4(c)(8) of the Bank Holding Company Act and Regulation Y (Dec. 1983)

Activities permitted by regulation
1. Extensions of credit[a]
   Mortgage banking
   Finance companies: consumer, sales, and commercial
   Credit cards
   Factoring
2. Industrial bank, Morris Plan bank, industrial loan company
3. Servicing loans and other extensions of credit[a]
4. Trust company[a]
5. Investment or financial advising[a]
6. Full-payout leasing of personal or real property[a]
7. Investments in community welfare projects[a]
8. Providing bookkeeping or data processing services[a]
9. Acting as insurance agent or broker primarily in connection with credit extensions[a]
10. Underwriting credit life and accident and health insurance
11. Providing courier services[a]
12. Management consulting to all depository institutions
13. Sale at retail of money orders with a face value of not more than $1000, travelers checks, and savings bonds[a,b]
14. Performing appraisals of real estate[b]
15. Issuance and sale of travelers checks
16. Providing securities brokerage services and related securities credit activities[b]
17. Arranging commercial real estate equity financing[b]
18. Underwriting and dealing in government obligations and money market instruments[b]
19. Foreign exchange advisory and transactional services[b]
20. Acting as a futures commission merchant[b]

Activities permitted by order
1. Issuance and sale of travelers checks[a,c]
2. Buying and selling gold and silver bullion and silver coin[a,d]
3. Issuing money orders and general-purpose variable denominated payment instruments[a,b,d]
4. Futures commission merchant to cover gold and silver bullion and coins[a,b,c]
5. Underwriting certain federal, state, and municipal securities[a,b,c]
6. Check verification[a,b,d]
7. Financial advice to consumers[a,b]
8. Issuance of small denomination debt instruments[b]
9. Arranging for equity financing of real estate[c]
10. Acting as futures commissions merchant[c]
11. Discount brokerage
12. Operating a distressed savings and loan association
13. Operating an Article XII investment company
14. Executing foreign banking unsolicited purchases and sales of securities
15. Engaging in commercial banking activities abroad through a limited purpose Delaware bank
16. Performing appraisal of real estate and real estate adviser and real estate brokerage on nonresidential properties
17. Operating a pool reserve plan for loss reserves of banks for loans to small businesses
18. Operating a thrift institution in Rhode Island
19. Operating a guaranty savings bank in New Hampshire
20. Offering information and transactional services for foreign exchange services

Activities denied by the Board
1. Insurance premium funding (combined sales of mutual funds and insurance)
2. Underwriting life insurance not related to credit extension
3. Sales of level-term credit life insurance
4. Real estate brokerage (residential)
5. Armored car
6. Land development
7. Real estate syndication
8. General management consulting
9. Property management
10. Computer output microfilm service
11. Underwriting mortgage guaranty insurance[e]
12. Operating a savings and loan association[b,f]
13. Operating a travel agency[a,b]
14. Underwriting property and casualty insurance[b]
15. Underwriting home loan life mortgage insurance[b]
16. Investment note issue with transactional characteristics
17. Real estate advisory services

Source: Gregorash 1984:4-5.
[a]Activities permissible to national banks.
[b]Added to list since January 1, 1975.
[c]Subsequently permitted by regulation.
[d]To be decided on a case-by-case basis.
[e]Board orders found these activities closely related to banking but denied proposed acquisitions as part of its "go slow" policy.
[f]Operating a thrift institution has been permitted by order in Rhode Island, New Hampshire, California, and Illinois.

have argued that a massive merger movement is required to avert widespread bank failures. Specialization, however, may be a workable alternative to one-stop financial shopping (Rhoades 1984). Just as specialty shops have survived in competition with department stores, so customers may have preferences for a bank specializing in retail operations or a broker offering stock market advice. In the light of the short-run success and later failure of industrial conglomerates in the 1960s, financial supermarkets may not even work. Casual and anecdotal incidents concerning financial conglomerates suggest that they have not been any more successful than their nonfinancial counterparts (Kaufman et al. 1984:789–803).

The unimportance of economies of scale (higher unit costs are only prevalent among the smallest banks) (Rhoades 1984:2) argues against the dominance of the playing field by a few financial giants. However, little is known (either way) about the economies of scope. Economies of scale refer to the saving in costs by expanding the output of a single product. Economies of scope result when the total cost of producing two goods jointly is less than the combined cost of producing the same amount of each good separately (Kane 1984:761). It has been maintained that a financial intermediary's computer, communications network, and branch-office system should make it cheaper for it to offer standardized deposit, loan, brokerage, investment banking, money management, and insurance products in combination than a series of specialized producers providing the same products on a stand-alone basis. (These services will be discussed in detail in Ch. 14.)

International banking

International banking refers to business with nonlocal residents. A dollar loan might be arranged in the United States or outside (offshore). Offshore banking in

Table 8.2. Assets and liabilities of overseas branches of member banks, year-end 1982

Item	United Kingdom and Ireland	Continental Europe	Bahamas and Cayman Islands	Latin America	Far East	Near East and Africa	U.S. overseas areas and Trust Territories
				($ mil.)			
Assets							
Cash and balances with banks	37,681	11,241	41,102	2,205	10,517	2,289	1,493
Loans, net	44,796	19,970	37,912	12,711	36,627	4,849	5,456
Due from other non-U.S. branches of own bank	30,970	3,540	7,778	204	2,773	390	1,500
Due from head office and U.S. branches	12,912	231	16,800	222	89	157	167
Due from consolidated subsidiaries	7,149	939	1,267	944	1,698	78	494
Other assets	8,318	4,442	3,395	2,450	9,292	396	1,034
Total	141,827	40,365	108,256	18,734	60,995	8,159	10,147
Liabilities							
Deposits of other banks	54,366	17,560	25,912	4,876	10,049	3,047	1,235
Other deposits	66,347	8,151	43,480	4,362	17,079	2,973	6,419
Due to other non-U.S. branches of own bank	6,837	5,388	7,450	3,299	17,070	1,402	1,653
Due to head office and U.S. branches	7,137	3,015	27,496	2,543	5,816	184	79
Due to consolidated subsidiaries	248	2,864	2,040	1,292	1,181	97	254
Other liabilities	6,892	3,387	1,978	2,363	9,800	457	507
Total[a]	141,827	40,365	108,256	18,734	60,995	8,159	10,147
Number of branches	64	119	168	240	207	49	53

Source: *Fed. Res. Bull.* 1983c:697.
[a]Amounts may not add to totals because of rounding.

dollars constitutes the Eurocurrency market. Banks outside the United States (most prominently in London) take dollar deposits and lend dollars. In 1981 the Fed permitted the establishment of international banking facilities (IBFs) in the United States. They do not represent new physical facilities but only a separate set of books within existing banking institutions (Chrystal 1984b:5). Their business in deposits and loans is limited to nonresidents of the United States. Offshore banks are now onshore and part of the Eurocurrency market. Because the Eurocurrency market has been extended to the United States, international lending no longer can be classified as lending U.S. dollars (onshore) and lending offshore in Eurodollars. A more useful distinction is between international banking that is subject to regulation and the growing proportion that is free of it (Terrell and Mills 1983:1). Offshore banking arose to avoid bank regulations. By dealing in Eurodollars, offshore banks avoid reserve requirements on deposits, FDIC assessments, and interest-rate ceilings. Similarly, IBFs are free of the regulations that apply to domestic banking activity.

Increasingly, banks are crossing international borders. U.S. banks go abroad and foreign banks establish themselves in the United States. U.S. banks have gone abroad as the combined result of the regulatory environment and the rise of the multinational corporation (Frankel 1974:4). Attempts to stem the outflow of capital funds (1964–65) encouraged overseas branching. Several programs to which banks responded were initiated by the federal government: the Foreign Direct Investment Program (FDIP), the interest equalization tax (IET), and the Voluntary Foreign Credit Restraint (VFCR) program. The FDIP limited the amount of funds that U.S. corporations could transfer to their corporate affiliates overseas. The IET reduced net yields to U.S. citizens, thus reducing foreign flotations in the United States. Finally, under VFCR, head offices of U.S. banks were restricted to historic levels of foreign lending. The effect of these programs was to make U.S. corporations dependent on external sources of funds to finance their foreign investments. Branch banking was the logical response, with foreign branches raising funds abroad that could be loaned to the U.S. multinational corporations (Frankel 1974:3).

U.S. banks carry on international banking from domestic offices, foreign branches, Edge corporations, and foreign subsidiaries. Edge corporations (named after a 1919 amendment to the Federal Reserve Act sponsored by Senator Walter Edge) are bank branches in the United States outside the home state involved in the financing of foreign trade. Foreign branches are legally integral parts of the parent banks. Foreign subsidiaries, in contrast, are separate legal entities (Houpt and Martinson 1982:1).

Table 8.2 provides a summary of assets and liabilities of U.S. member bank branches overseas. They numbered 900 at the end of 1982, with total assets and liabilities of $389 bil. This amount represents about 65% of total foreign assets of U.S. insured commercial banks. The bulk of claims were located in branches in the United Kingdom and Ireland, followed by the Caribbean branches (Bahama and Cayman islands).

It will be noted that most balance sheet items consist of claims between bank offices. Depending on the relative demands and supplies of funds in the United States and overseas, the head offices of major member banks lend to or borrow from their foreign branches. Other overseas banks also are involved on both the

otals[a]
06,531
62,322
47,155
30,580
12,567
29,327
388,484
17,045
48,811
43,099
46,270
7,976
25,284
388,484
900

lending and borrowing side. Additional deposits are secured from the nonbank public as shown on this balance sheet under liabilities.

In 1966 and 1969–70, individual banks experienced a runoff in their deposits as interest rates reached ceiling levels. Branch banks (particularly in London) became a source of dollar funds, since they attracted dollars from corporate and government clients.

In the 1970s after the 1969 credit crunch, a dramatic reversal of flows took place, with head offices lending to their foreign branches. This reversal is explained by the suspension in the United States of interest ceilings on longer term big denomination certificates of deposit (CDs) and by the U.S. imposition of a 10% reserve requirement on increases in foreign borrowing. Branch banks increasingly engaged in a brokerage rather than a banking business, with the placement of funds in the foreign interbank market (Brimmer and Dahl 1976:295ff.). The growth in the interbank market is an interesting commentary on market imperfections. Bank A attracts Eurodollar deposits but lacks the knowledge of would-be borrowers that Bank B has. Interbank lending is profitable to both banks. The rate at which banks borrow from each other in the London Eurodollar market is known as LIBOR (London interbank offering rate).

The geographic distribution of branches also underwent significant changes. Between 1960 and 1965 the United Kingdom dominated European growth, but thereafter the Continent became more important. Latin American branches show a steady growth over the entire period. The most dramatic geographic development is establishment of "shell branches" in the Caribbean in the 1970s. Shell branches derive their name from the skeleton requirements for establishing a foreign branch. Approval from the Fed for such a bank is given provided there is no contact with the local public at the branch and its quarters, staff, and bookkeeping are, at least in part, supplied under contract by another party (Frankel 1974:7). The favorable tax treatment such banks received encouraged U.S. banks to set up such branches, mainly in Nassau in the Bahamas, and to channel as much of their foreign lending through Caribbean offices as could pass legal scrutiny. Once IBFs were permitted, the raison d'être of Caribbean branches for business with foreigners disappeared. Claims and liabilities were shifted to the United States from offshore centers. Shell branches, however, continue to be important for business with U.S. residents (Chrystal 1984b:10).

The importance of banks located in the United States in total international lending and borrowing has increased as a result of IBFs. As Table 8.3 shows, in September 1981, banks located in the United States held 15% of total international banking assets of banks reporting to the Bank for International Settlements and 11% of the liabilities. By December 1982, these percentages had risen to 21 and 15% respectively. Banks in the United States and U.S. branches in offshore centers are roughly responsible for one-third of all international lending.

PROFIT AND LOSS FROM FOREIGN LENDING: THE INTERNATIONAL DEBT CRISIS   U.S. bank lending has greatly increased since the 1973 oil crisis. In a period of three and one-half years following the crisis, claims on foreign borrowers, primarily government, virtually doubled from $100 bil. to $200 bil. It was an extremely profitable business for major U.S. banks. For example, for Citibank in New York in 1983, foreign lending accounted for more than 70% of net income.

Table 8.3. External assets and liabilities of Bank for International Settlements reporting banks

Item	1981 Sept.	1982 Dec.[a] adjusted
	($ bil.)	
Total assets	1424	1713
Banks in the United States	215	361
U.S.-chartered banks[b]	133	233
International banking facilities	...	71
Other U.S. offices	132	162
Foreign banks	82	128
International banking facilities	...	73
Other U.S. offices	82	55
U.S. branches in offshore centers	168	173
Banks in the United Kingdom	400	1179
Banks in other locations	641	
Total liabilities	1414	1640
Banks in the United States	155	245
U.S.-chartered banks[b]	93	142
International banking facilities	...	65
Other U.S. offices	93	77
Foreign banks	62	103
International banks	...	59
Other U.S. offices	62	44
U.S. branches in offshore centers	173	179
Banks in the United Kingdom	412	1216
Banks in other locations	674	

Source: Terrell and Mills 1983:3.
Note: Banks in the United Kingdom and in other locations include U.S. branches and subsidiaries.
[a]Effects of appreciation of U.S. dollar on nondollar asset values (applies to last two bank categories) have been eliminated.
[b]Includes Edge Act agreement corporations.

International business contributed about one-third of consolidated net income of U.S. banks with foreign offices in 1982, slightly less than in 1981 (Opper 1983:500, 507).

The profitability of international banking in 1982 masks the beginnings of the international debt crisis in that year. The problem dates from late 1981 when Poland rescheduled its debts. About eight months later Mexico postponed debt repayment to foreign banks. Since then, other countries (most notably Argentina and Brazil) have had similar difficulties. The magnitude of the problem for nonoil developing countries is suggested by Table 8.4. At the end of 1984 the estimated debt will be $711 bil. (line 1). Most of the $388 bil. owed to private creditors is to commercial banks. The U.S. share was approximately 37% (Barth and Pelzman 1984:1, 11). The debt and debt service ratios based on exports of goods and services and domestic output in lower lines of the table suggest how great a burden the debt has been for less developed countries.

Bail-out operations dominated the financial news in 1983 and 1984. The International Monetary Fund increased its lending but exacted a price in austerity programs that increased social unrest in Latin America. The U.S. banks cooperated in lending to Argentina so that country could meet its interest payments. Debt repayments were rescheduled. Financial headlines speculated on the implications of third-world debt repudiation (e.g., see Sandler 1984:1).

Rescue packages helped U.S. banks, since debtor nations were now able to meet their obligations. The alternative would have been to let the banks suffer for the sins of imprudent lending. This interpretation of the international debt crisis has been rejected. Instead, problems have been blamed on the integration of the world's financial markets that have resulted from the expansion of international banking activities over the last 20 years (Cheng 1983:1). Integrated markets transmit economic disturbances throughout the world, turning well-diversified portfo-

Table 8.4. Nonoil developing countries: External debt outstanding

Debt	1977	1978	1979	1980	1981	1982	1983	1984
					(U.S. $ bil.)			
Nonoil developing countries	280.3	334.3	395.3	475.2	559.6	633.3	668.6	710.9
Short-term debt	43.2	51.6	59.1	84.5	103.8	125.1	102.2	88.2
Long-term debt	237.2	282.7	336.2	390.8	455.8	508.2	566.4	622.8
Type of creditor								
Official creditors	97.6	116.3	133.4	153.2	170.2	189.3	211.9	235.0
Governments	68.3	80.5	90.1	101.8	111.5	123.2	138.3	153.3
International institutions	29.3	35.8	43.2	51.4	58.6	66.1	73.7	81.7
Private creditors	139.6	166.4	202.8	237.6	285.6	318.9	354.5	387.8
Unguaranteed debt	50.4	51.7	62.4	75.2	94.2	102.0	104.2	103.4
Guaranteed debt	89.2	114.7	140.4	162.4	191.4	216.9	250.2	284.4
Financial institutions	63.1	83.7	108.0	128.9	154.7	176.4	209.6	243.2
Other private creditors	26.1	31.0	32.4	33.5	36.7	40.5	40.6	41.2
Value of debt service payments	32.8	47.5	61.0	73.4	97.2	107.7	96.6	103.4
Interest payments	12.7	18.1	25.9	39.0	54.7	63.0	59.2	63.7
Amortization[a]	20.2	29.4	35.1	34.3	42.5	44.6	37.4	39.7
Debt service ratio[b]	14.8	18.1	18.1	17.2	21.3	24.5	21.6	21.1
Interest payments ratio	5.7	6.9	7.7	9.1	12.0	14.3	13.2	13.0
Amortization ratio[a]	9.1	11.2	10.4	8.0	9.3	10.2	8.4	8.1
Ratio of external debt to								
exports of goods and services[c]	126.1	127.7	117.2	111.2	122.5	144.1	149.5	144.7
Ratio of external debt to GDP[c]	23.7	24.1	23.3	23.9	27.1	32.5	36.7	37.5

Source: IMF 1984c:205, 206, 209.
Note: Does not include debt owed to the International Monetary Fund.
[a]Excludes, for purposes of this table, eight oil-exporting countries: the Islamic Republic of Iran, Iraq, Kuwait, the Libyan Arab Jamahiriya, Oman, Qatar, Saudi Arabia, and the United Arab Emirates.
[b]Percentage of exports of goods and services.
[c]Ratio of year-end debt to exports or gross domestic product for year indicated.

lios into risky ones. Oil price increases in 1979–80 followed by world recession, falling commodity prices, and high real interest rates are some of the leading shocks.

Pushing the panic button   Despite rescue packages, U.S. international banks have not gone unscathed. When portfolios turn sour, foreign depositors can push the electronic button and empty deposits out overnight (Hertzberg et al. 1984:6). The Continental Illinois Bank of Chicago became insolvent as foreign depositors reacted to the bank's exposure to the debt of weak firms and to a lesser extent to weak countries. As discussed below under Regulators, the bank run culminated in the biggest government rescue in banking history. More closely linked to fallout from the international debt crisis was the decline in stock prices of leading money center banks with large holdings of Latin debt (Bennett 1984b:25). A major factor in the decline of stock prices was a fall in earnings. The Fed imposed tighter accounting rules on international bankers in 1984. Delay in receiving interest payments beyond 90 days now required greater loss provisions for nonperforming loans and smaller recorded interest earnings.

The Fed is the chief regulator of U.S. banks and their foreign affiliates, but the other regulatory authorities also exercise jurisdiction (Frankel 1974:4). The underlying philosophy is to allow U.S. banks to do abroad what they can do at home. This conflicts with the philosophy of letting U.S. banks overseas be subject to the national laws of the countries in which they are operating—a liberal approach. The conservative approach is most evident in the treatment of overseas branches. The reasoning is that a branch is an integral part of the bank itself and thus a threat to bank solvency. With respect to the activities of nonbank subsidiaries, the Fed generally permits activities similar to those allowed nonbank subsidiaries in the United States. In some instances, however, additional activities are permitted for competitive purposes in the foreign bank market.

FOREIGN BANKING IN THE UNITED STATES   Until 1978 foreign banks in the United States had privileges that domestic banks did not enjoy. Under the McFadden Act of 1927, interstate branch banking was prohibited to United States–chartered banks. But foreign-owned banks were permitted such activity. Similarly, foreign banks could engage in both commercial and investment banking. In this way they escaped the prohibitions of both the Glass-Steagall Act of 1933 and the Bank Holding Company Act of 1956 (Segala 1979:19).

Table 8.5 shows foreign banking offices in the United States by country of the parent bank, organizational form, and U.S. location. Branches and agencies are legal extensions of the parent bank, while subsidiaries are separate legal entities with their own capitalization. Agencies, unlike branches, are not allowed to accept deposits from citizens or residents of the United States. Foreign banks have also

Table 8.5. Location of foreign banking institutions in the United States as of June 30, 1984

Country of parent bank and state of reporter	Agency	Branch	Subsidiary commercial bank	Investment co.	Agreement corp.	Total
Japan						
New York	0	24	4	0	0	28
California	21	1	8	0	1	31
Illinois	0	6	0	0	0	6
All others	2	6	0	0	2	10
Total	23	37	12	0	3	75
Canada						
New York	1	8	5	0	0	14
California	7	0	2	0	0	9
Illinois	0	3	0	0	0	3
All others	6	8	0	0	0	14
Total	14	19	7	0	0	40
United Kingdom						
New York	0	13	3	1	1	18
California	4	2	4	0	0	10
Illinois	0	4	0	0	0	4
All others	7	6	0	0	4	17
Total	11	25	7	1	5	49
Continental Europe						
New York	3	65	5	5	1	79
California	26	5	3	0	0	34
Illinois	0	17	2	0	1	20
All others	22	4	1	0	7	34
Total	51	91	11	5	9	167
Rest of the world						
New York	27	79	7	3	4	120
California	34	16	8	0	1	59
Illinois	0	13	0	0	1	14
All others	17	9	1	0	11	38
Total	78	117	16	3	17	231
All reporters						
New York	31	189	24	9	6	259
California	92	24	25	0	2	143
Illinois	0	43	2	0	2	47
All others	54	33	2	0	24	113
Total	177	289	53	9	34	562

Source: FRB 1984h.

established a small number of investment companies, representative offices, and Edge Act corporations. Investment companies deal in securities, extend loans, and accept credit balances (associated with the securities transactions), but are not allowed to accept deposits. Representative offices cannot conduct any banking business but serve to publicize the parent organization (White 1982:49). Japan, Canada, the United Kingdom, and continental Europe are the main countries or areas of origin. Foreign banking operations are concentrated in New York, San Francisco, Los Angeles, and Chicago. Table 8.5 shows a grand total of 562 offices in mid-1984.

A comparison of agency and branch balance sheets with those of subsidiaries would show a sharp contrast between the focus of subsidiaries on retail operations and the focus of agencies and branches on the wholesale market. Subsidiaries raise funds from nonbank depositors and do most of their lending to domestic borrowers. Agencies and branches rely heavily on the interbank market for funding— two-thirds of their liabilities are to financial institutions (White 1982:51–52). Loans to foreigners are more important than for subsidiaries. Subsidiaries enter retail banking markets through the acquisition of domestic banks with already established retail branch networks. By December 31, 1983, the assets and liabilities of agencies and branches had risen to $228 bil. (*Fed. Res. Bull.* 1984d:A72). Assuming the same rate of increase of 32% for subsidiaries since 1981 (direct data are not available), their totals would have been $108 bil. for a grand total of $336 bil.

The motivation for foreign banks to penetrate the U.S. market centers on the key role of the U.S. dollar in international transactions and the influx of foreign direct investment. Having a banking office in the U.S. with access to dollar deposits and borrowings provides protection against Eurodollar deposit withdrawals at home. With major foreign corporations moving into the United States, foreign banks followed their corporate customers (in the same way as U.S. banks trailed the U.S. multinational corporation) (Kvasnicka 1976:3–11). Before 1979, bargain prices (the decline in the value of the dollar and depressed bank prices) enhanced the attractiveness of buying into local banks (Bennett 1978:D1, D2).

Keen competition in the business loan market has made domestic banks well aware of the presence of foreign banks; $56 bil. of the assets of branches and agencies were in business loans at the end of December 1983. This was 20% of the total for large commercial banks nationwide (national member banks).

The growth in competition from banks in the 1970s brought mounting clamor for their regulation. The International Banking Act of 1978 was enacted to close the gap between the regulation of these institutions and the regulation of domestic banks at the federal level. The act decided in favor of nondiscrimination or national treatment versus the principle of reciprocity.

Foreign banks were to be treated on an equal footing with domestic banks instead of being offered the same range of activities that the home country offered U.S. banks. The act prohibited multistate banking except for a "grandfathering" of bank operations before July 27, 1978. Nevertheless, a bank could have agencies outside the home state. The Fed now assumed major responsibility for the supervision of foreign banks whether they were branches or agencies, provided their worldwide assets exceeded $1 bil. (invariably the case). The Fed's authority included the setting of reserve requirements and control over nonbank activities.

The act made foreign branches eligible for FDIC insurance (Segala 1979:18–19, 21). Modification of the McFadden Act forbidding interstate branching is also possible as a result of the banking study called for by the act. The authorization of IBFs in 1981 gave foreign banks the opportunity to escape the newfound regulations. As can be seen from Table 8.3, assets and liabilities at foreign bank IBFs rose sharply after their introduction at the same time that they declined at other U.S. offices.

The regulators

STRUCTURE AND PROBLEMS   Currently, seven federal agencies regulate U.S. depository institutions: five agencies supervise banks, one monitors savings and loans (S&Ls), and one regulates federal credit unions (CUs) (Pianalto 1984:1–4; Carron 1984:12–21). The comptroller of the currency, head of a bureau of the Treasury Department, supervises all national banks. The Fed supervises state-chartered banks that are members of the Fed system and bank holding companies (the Fed in Washington examines the 12 Federal Reserve Banks and their 25 branches). The FDIC supervises insured state banks that are not members of the Fed system. The Federal Home Loan Board (FHLB) regulates federally chartered S&Ls and savings banks. The Federal Savings and Loan Insurance Corporation (FSLIC) is a subsidiary of the Federal Home Loan Bank System (which includes both the FHLB and district banks) and performs an insurance function only. Deposits up to $100,000 in many state-chartered S&Ls as well as in all federally chartered S&Ls are insured by the FSLIC. Deposits up to $100,000 in federally chartered savings banks and in many state-chartered savings banks are insured either by the FDIC or FSLIC (Fed, New York 1984). The National Credit Union Administration charters, regulates, and insures federal CUs and state-chartered CUs. The Securities and Exchange Commission and the Department of Justice are involved in the regulation of bank holding companies and antitrust enforcement respectively.

On the state level, agencies in each of the 50 states supervise state-chartered banks and state savings banks, S&Ls, and CUs. Figure 8.4 presents the existing regulatory structure for banks and thrifts (Carron 1984:14). The potential for overlap is suggested by duplicating arrows to the regulated institutions. As the functions of the regulatory agencies were described above, some of these agencies cooperate to minimize duplication. Thus, while national banks could be examined by both the Fed and the comptroller of the currency, these examinations are conducted only by the comptroller. Sharing exists for the state member banks and insured nonmember banks. State examiners join with the Fed in examining the former category (only one arrow is shown) and with the FDIC in examining non-member banks. The arrows suggest the most overlap for holding companies.

Nevertheless, the overlapping powers and divided authorities inherent in the structure often result in inconsistencies in enforcement. The rules for thrift institutions, for example, with respect to nonbank activities are more permissive than for bank holding companies. The sharing of responsibility for regulation in the case of bank holding companies has resulted in transactions between holding company affiliates "falling between the cracks" with subsequent failures. A major difficulty is that the agencies have different primary goals, which are not necessarily consist-

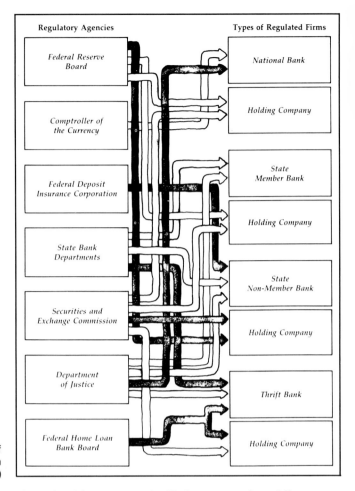

Regulatory Agencies

Federal Reserve Board

Comptroller of the Currency

Federal Deposit Insurance Corporation

State Bank Departments

Securities and Exchange Commission

Department of Justice

Federal Home Loan Bank Board

Types of Regulated Firms

National Bank

Holding Company

State Member Bank

Holding Company

State Non-Member Bank

Holding Company

Thrift Bank

Holding Company

8.4. Existing regulation of banks and thrifts. (Carron 1984:14)

ent. The comptroller aims at a solvent banking system, the Fed at economic stability, the FDIC at preserving its insurance fund. This has resulted in conflicts over liberality in chartering banks and permission to enter new lines of business (Carron 1984:13,16).

REACTION TO REGULATION   Bank regulation attempts to make banks behave differently than they would otherwise. If this was not so, why regulate? The effect is that the variable constrained by regulation now assumes a value different from its optimal value from the standpoint of bank profit maximization (Fallek and Nelson 1978:7). The bank attempts to compensate, however, by adjusting the values of other decision variables. The adjustment mechanisms employed by banks will also have their implications for the effectiveness of regulation. Since compliance and adjustment to regulation have their costs, the wisdom of regulation depends on a consideration of such costs.

INTEREST RATE CEILINGS   Interest rate ceilings are imposed on member bank time and savings deposits by Regulation Q (and a companion ceiling is set by the FDIC on nonmember banks and mutual savings banks). The authorization goes back to the banking acts of 1933–35, passed after the bank failures of 1930–33. Congress blamed the collapse on the reaching out for risky loans. (This interpretation of bank runs and bank holidays is now controversial.) For many years, ceiling rates were above market rates, so the ceiling was inapplicable. In the 1960s, however, the market rates rose above the ceiling. While in the early 1960s the ceilings were raised in step with rising market rates, a different policy was followed in 1966 (Kaufman 1977:124). Instead of raising them, ceilings were also applied to the S&Ls (via Federal Home Loan Bank Board regulations). The rationale was to safeguard and nurture the home building industry. S&Ls were a leading conduit of funds into home building. Rising market rates gave rise to outflows from such institutions. This move seemed to call for higher interest rates. Another consideration, however, was the financial squeeze that this would put on S&Ls. Higher rates would have had to be paid on all deposits, whereas higher mortgage rates would only be earned on new ones. As a result, ceiling rates were fixed for S&Ls with a 0.25% advantage over commercial banks.

Holding ceilings constant after 1963 was a deliberate policy instrument for controlling bank credit (Ruebling 1969:25). But banks thwarted such attempts at credit control by resorting to other sources of funds. The outstanding instances are 1966 and 1969. Rising market yields in 1966 resulted in a runoff of maturing negotiable CDs. Instead of renewing them in August 1966, holders moved into Treasury bills or commercial paper. Banks faced with a strong demand for loans restructured their portfolios by liquidating municipals. A liquidity crisis developed in the municipal bond market. When the monetary restraint was maintained, banks reduced their business loans. These are the characteristics of the credit crunch of 1966 (Burger 1969:13, 24).

The circumstances making for a credit crunch repeated themselves with greater intensity in 1969. Banks had begun substantial borrowing in the Eurodollar market after 1966. Most of these funds were borrowed from their overseas branches. In 1969, CDs in commercial banks declined by close to $13 bil. During the same year Eurodollar borrowing rose by $7 bil. and bank-related commercial paper by $6 bil. (FRB 1970:21). Banks borrowed from their parent holding companies, who in turn raised funds by selling commercial paper (their short-term IOUs). Figure 8.5 shows the relationship between dollar movements in these liabilities (upper section) and the movement of open-market interest rates (represented

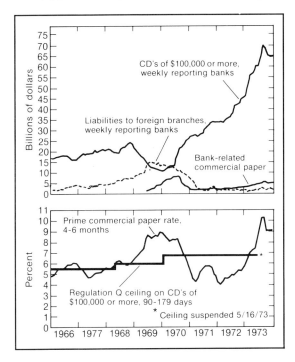

8.5. Growth of liability management banking, 1966–73. (DePamphilis 1974:19)

121

by the prime commercial paper rate) above the ceiling rate on CDs (lower section). When open-market rates rose above the ceiling (1968–69), CDs fell off sharply and Eurodollar borrowing and bank-related commercial paper increased. A reverse movement occurred in 1970–72 when open-market rates fell below the ceiling rate. The ceiling (as indicated on the chart) was suspended in the middle of 1973. As a result a credit crunch was avoided.

Ceilings have persisted until the present, with significant modifications. In 1973, Regulation Q ceilings were suspended on large-denomination CDs. In 1978 introduction of money market certificates (in $10,000 denominations) with yields tied to the Treasury bill rate succeeded in a stratification of savings so that higher interest rates had only to be paid on new savings. To a substantial extent, savings depositors simply converted deposits into certificates so that no new funds were forthcoming. Automatic transfer service accounts were introduced in the same year and small-saver certificates in June 1979. These and subsequent steps in the phase-out of Regulation Q are detailed in Table 8.6. Since DIDMCA in 1980, the Depository Institutions Deregulation Committee has been responsible for phasing out ceilings, with the terminal date being 1986. On April 1, 1986, the 5½% ceiling on passbook saving deposits was lifted and the committee went out of business.

Table 8.6. Steps in the phase-out of Regulation Q

Effective date of change	Nature of change
June 1978	Money market certificates established with minimum denomination of $10,000, 26-week maturity, and ceiling rates based on the 6-month Treasury bill rate.
Nov. 1978	Automatic transfer service (ATS) savings account created, allowing funds to be transferred automatically from savings to checking account when needed.
June 1979	Small saver certificates established with no minimum denomination, maturity of 30 months or more, and ceiling rates based on the yield on 2-1/2-year Treasury securities, with maximums of 11.75% at commercial banks and 12% at thrifts.
June 2, 1980	Ceiling rates on small saver certificates relative to yield on 2-1/2-year Treasury securities raised 50 basis points (maximums retained).
June 5, 1980	Maximum ceiling rate on money market certificates raised to the 6-month Treasury bill rate plus 25 basis points when the bill rate is above 8.75%. Other ceilings apply below 8.75%.
Jan. 1, 1981	NOW accounts permitted nationwide. On the previous day, ceiling rates on NOW and ATS accounts set at 5.25%.
Aug. 1, 1981	Caps on small saver certificates of 11.75% at commercial banks and 12% at thrifts eliminated. Ceiling rates fluctuate with 2-1/2-year Treasury security yields.
Oct. 1, 1981	Adopted rules for the All Savers Certificates specified in the Economic Recovery Act of 1981.
Dec. 1, 1981	New category of IRA/Keogh accounts created with minimum maturity of 1-1/2 years, no regulated interest rate ceiling, and no minimum denomination.
May 1, 1982	New time deposit created with no interest rate ceiling, a required denomination of $500 (but no specified minimum), and an initial minimum maturity of 3-1/2 years. New short-term deposit instrument created with a $7500 minimum denomination, 91-day maturity, and a ceiling rate tied to the 91-day Treasury bill discount rate. Maturity range of small saver certificate adjusted to 30-42 months.
Sept. 1, 1982	New deposit account (7- to 31-day account) created with ceiling rate based on 91-day Treasury bill discount rate, minimum daily balance of $20,000, and either a fixed term or a required notice period of 7-31 days.
Dec. 14, 1982	Money market deposit account (MMDA) created with minimum balance of not less than $2500, no interest ceiling, no minimum maturity, up to six transfers per month (no more than three by draft), and unlimited withdrawals by mail, messenger, or in person.
Jan. 5, 1983	Super NOW account created with same features as the MMDA, except that unlimited transfers are permitted. Interest rate ceiling eliminated and minimum denomination reduced to $2500 on 7- to 31-day account. Minimum denomination reduced to $2500 on 91-day accounts and money market certificates of less than $100,000.
Apr. 1, 1983	Minimum maturity on small saver certificates reduced to 18 months.
Oct. 1, 1983	All interest rate ceilings eliminated except those on passbook savings and regular NOW accounts. Minimum denomination of $2500 established for time deposits with maturities of 31 days or less (below this minimum, passbook savings rates apply).
Jan. 1, 1984	Rate differential between commercial banks and thrifts on passbook savings accounts and 7- to 31-day time deposits of less than $2500 eliminated. All depository institutions may now pay a maximum of 5.50%.
Jan. 1, 1985	Minimum denominations on MMDAs, Super NOWs, and 7- to 31-day ceiling-free time deposits will be reduced to $1000.
Jan. 1, 1986	Minimum denominations on MMDAs, Super NOWs, and 7- to 31-day ceiling-free time deposits will be eliminated.

Source: Gilbert and Holland 1984:6.

Removal of ceilings has made it possible for thrifts specializing in mortgage lending to compete for funds in the open market. So far, however, they have been caught between the squeeze of higher costs for money and fixed returns on old mortgages (see Ch. 14). Title IV of DIDMCA increases the flexibility of thrift institutions on the asset side. It permits S&Ls to invest funds in consumer loans, commercial paper, and corporate debt (up to 20% of their assets) and to issue credit cards.

NONDEPOSIT SOURCES OF FUNDS   How controls lead to avoidance and to further control is the lesson of liability management in the 1960s. Banks moved to nondeposit sources of funds when Regulation Q became effective as discussed above. What can also be detailed is the strategy of move and countermove, as each attempt by the banks to secure new funds was countered by the Fed (see DePamphilis 1974:19; Broaddus 1984:9). When banks increased their Eurodollar borrowing in 1969 under Regulations D and M, 10% marginal reserve requirements were established. "Marginal" means that the requirement was imposed only on amounts in excess of base period values. In 1970, federal funds were redefined so that borrowing deposits from nonbank sources were to be considered as deposits for reserve purposes. Previously, when banks borrowed these deposits, required reserves declined along with deposits. In 1970 the deposit concept was further extended to include long-term promissory notes, and reserve requirements were imposed on funds secured through the issuance of commercial paper.

COSTS OF COMPLIANCE   What are the costs of compliance? From the standpoint of the banks, seeking out new sources of funds has extra costs or they would have been exploited in the first place. Depositors are also worse off because they are beguiled by gift premiums instead of cash. There is an adverse distributional effect between low- and high-income depositors. When market rates rise, the large investor can jump the financial barrier faced by the small investor. This situation was seen in 1968 when the minimum denomination of Treasury bills was raised to $10,000 from $1000, frustrating the small depositor.

Another cost of interest regulation is resource misallocation. The economist's credo is that funds should flow where the return is highest. Keeping down rates on mortgage loans (the rationale for controlling deposit rates) results in more funds for housing than would be allocated in a free market. Housing construction has marginal private returns below true marginal cost. If subsidies are desirable, they should be explicit and not hidden in artificially low interest rates.

The remaining defense of ceilings is their use as an instrument of monetary restraint. It can be contended, however, that past control of bank sources of funds was too heavy-handed an instrument (Burger 1969:30).

Deregulation

UNDERLYING FORCES   Deregulation in the 1980s should be seen as a consequence of accelerated innovation in the 1970s, which in turn can be explained by high rates of interest associated with inflation and by rapid technological progress in the computer and communications industries. A case in point is the money market mutual fund (MMMF) (to be discussed further in Ch. 14). Such funds promised the public interest rates far above prevailing ceiling rates at the same time that they permitted third-party transactions. The enormous competitive pressure that the growth of MMMFs put on U.S. banks resulted in their putting pressure on the regulatory agencies and Congress for relief. Beginning with the authorization of money market certificates (MMCs) in June 1978 (see Table 8.6), the pressure for further deregulation continued to build up and culminated in DIDMCA in March 1980 Broaddus 1985:2–22).

GAINERS AND LOSERS   Interest ceilings to all intents and purposes are a thing of the past, and deregulation has resulted in intense financial competition among financial firms. A financial services industry has emerged with depository institutions, brokerage firms, and insurance companies invading each other's turf. At the same time, nonfinancial firms are expanding their product lines by acquiring financial units. In the few years experience since deregulation some gainers and losers can be distinguished. The losers have been identified as small businesses, low-balance depositors, aggressive banks, old-line industries, and bank employees (Bennett 1983:1, 35). Small businesses bear the brunt of higher interest rates paid on consumer deposits. In the past many local businesses and farmers had been insulated from rising interest rates because of the availability of low-cost savings deposits. Bank service charges (e.g., on checks returned for insufficient funds) have risen sharply. For people with relatively low balances the increases in bank charges may have been greater than the increase in interest earned. The higher cost of deposits has increased the risk factor for banks as they make riskier loans to earn higher returns (see the following section on bank safety). As banks enter new fields such as stock brokerage, they pose new competition for old-line companies. Personnel layoffs and expense cuts were the order of the day at dozens of brokerage houses in mid-1984 (Bleakley 1984:27, 32). Higher costs have stimulated automation in banks, displacing personnel.

The winners have been identified as high-balance depositors, buyers of financial services, convenience seekers, and bank employees (again). High-balance holders are beneficiaries of the higher rates of interest available to individuals. Lower cost brokerage services have resulted from the entry of banks into the discount brokerage business. Customers can now have the convenience of transacting diverse lines of financial business in a single statement framework (Kane 1984:759). The ubiquitous computer that made this possible has also created new job opportunities in finance. Higher interest costs to financial lenders as a result of deregulation evidently mean higher interest costs for their customer borrowers. Deregulation was intended to help the home building industry, but instead, higher mortgage rates may have restrained residential construction. This average cost approach to mortgage interest rates has its challengers, however. Resorting to marginal cost and marginal revenue analysis, they demonstrate that elimination of Regulation Q ceilings should result in lower mortgage rates (Gilbert and Holland 1984:7–8; Keeley 1984). The increase in the cost of small-denomination deposits with deregulation should be more than offset by the decline in the cost of large-denomination deposits. Depository institutions attract more small-denomination deposits by paying higher interest rates, which reduces their dependence on the more expensive, large CDs. The marginal cost curve now intersects the marginal revenue curve at a greater volume of funds and a lower mortgage rate. The empirical test would seem to be how mortgage rates have moved in relation to government bonds (always unregulated) since deregulation. It is contended that while the spread has increased (mortgage rates increasing after deregulation by more than government bonds) the pattern is not due to deregulation. Instead, it is blamed on more variable interest rates and the economic downturn in the early 1980s. The first factor caused a higher interest premium for the option of prepaying a mortgage loan. The second factor raised the premium for the risk of default on mortgages (Gilbert and Holland 1984:8, 15).

The benefits of deregulation are a matter of continued controversy. A wide-ranging survey of bankers, economists, and regulators in 1985 reveals deep dis-agreements (*Wall Street Journal* 1985b:1, 8).

A within the System review of the impact of financial deregulation has recently appeared (Evanoff 1985:3–79). The discussion includes the Fed's impact on correspondent banking, the pricing of federal deposit insurance, and bank and thrift performance since DIDMCA.

SYSTEM SAFETY   The sensational collapse in mid-1984 of the Continental Illinois National Bank and Trust Company of Chicago (CINB), the nation's sixth largest bank, raised questions about the adverse consequences of deregulation and put the spotlight on the FDIC. (For the chronology of the bank's troubles, see Bennett 1984a:3.1, 3.8.) Deregulation's responsibility has been denied, and the blame is placed on bad energy loans, particularly to the Penn Square Bank of Oklahoma, which failed in 1982. At the end of July 1984 the FDIC committed itself to a $4.5 bil. rescue package (Bennett 1984c:1, 41). It purchased bad loans for $3.5 bil. and injected fresh capital by acquiring preferred stock for $1 bil. An ironic twist is that this action was a replay of the dramatic rescue of CINB by the Reconstruction Finance Corporation in 1933. This federal agency was set up during the depression of the 1930s to bail out banks and other companies.

The CINB debacle exposes the underlying fragility of the financial system. With a fractional reserve system (see Ch. 6), a loaned-up bank is immediately short of required reserves if a depositor asks for cash. The experience of the 1930s suggests that such withdrawals can quickly mushroom, leading to mass bank failures. In an electronic one-world financial market (as already mentioned in connection with the international debt crisis), the potential is there for history to repeat itself.

Because this possibility was recognized, the government (FDIC in consultation with the administration and other bank regulatory agencies) saw no alternative but to guarantee all depositors in CINB that their funds were safe. Before the final rescue package was assembled, the Federal Reserve Bank of Chicago made extensive loans to the bank to assure its liquidity. Opening the discount window (the metaphor for Fed lending) resulted in $3.6 bil. of reserves being pumped into the banking system. By August 1984 the amount of lending had increased to $7 bil. The lender-of-last-resort function of the Fed clashed with its monetary control function (see also Ch. 13).

The dilemma of deposit insurance is exposed by the CINB debacle. On the one hand, it could be argued that insurance coverage was inadequate because CINB troubles were caused by the flight of large uninsured depositors. Almost three-quarters of its deposits were over $100,000 (Mayer et al. 1985:1). The absence of a small-deposit base is explained by the lack of branch offices under Illinois unit banking laws. On the other hand, full insurance would increase moral hazard (irresponsible risk taking) on the part of bank management. With insured depositors staying put because of their protected status, bank management need not fear bank runs. This makes for risky loan practices. Bank shareholders are still wiped out when the bank fails. But this is not enough to make for conservative loan practices. Bank profits depend on the leverage provided by deposits and not on the capital supplied by stockholders.

Deregulation has also contributed to moral hazard by encouraging risky lending on the part of depositors. The rise and fall of the deposit broker (1982–84) is a chronicle of the fruits of deregulation and subsequent efforts at control. The deposit broker is a financial go-between who solicits funds from clients and funnels the money in $100,000 units to federally insured banks and thrifts (Muir 1984:1). By 1984 this had become a $50 bil. business. Depositors, since they are insured, need only concern themselves with the highest return. The highest rates will be offered by the most desperate institutions with the riskiest loans and the weakest capital positions (Furlong and Keran 1984:1–4). The FDIC and FSLIC have responded by limiting insurance on brokered deposits to $100,000 per broker per institution but their efforts have foundered in the courts.

In contrast to the bail-out of CINB stands the enforcing of market discipline on lesser banks, which makes the bank shareholders and large depositors pay for bank losses. There is inequity in the treatment of large versus small banks. The universal guarantee on deposits was waived in the Penn Square failure in 1982 and two bank failures in California and Texas in the winter of 1984 (Hertzberg 1984:14). The new policy has been formalized in a modified payout plan. Under this plan, holders of large-denomination deposits (over $100,000) will receive only pro rata shares of what the FDIC thinks it can recover from the liquidation of assets immediately after a bank has failed (Furlong 1984:1–4).

A weakness of the plan is that putting large depositors at risk might make the depository system even more susceptible to bank runs. To avert bank runs and promote economic stability, all liquid (checkable) deposits (as opposed to time deposits) should be insured (Furlong 1984:2–3). The onus of risk could be placed on financial lenders by relating insurance premiums to the riskiness of their assets. The FDIC has backed legislation giving them the authority to introduce a system of risk-based insurance premium rebates (Furlong and Keran 1984:2). Another solution frequently mentioned in the academic literature is the substitution of private for government insurance. Safeguards would be necessary, however, against the profit-maximizing insurer canceling insurance policies in anticipation of insolvency leaving depositors unprotected (Horvitz 1984:786).

FDIC finances   The costs to the FDIC of taking over CINB represented a significant portion of its resources of $15.4 bil. (end of 1983). Concern with its resources in the aftermath of the rescue may lead to an increase in insurance premiums (Noble 1984:25–26). This concern is a recent development, although FDIC assets have always been a small percentage of insured deposits, currently 1%. Insured deposits in turn are 75% of total deposits of $1.7 tril. in insured banks at the end of 1983 (FDIC 1984:58). The FDIC has been a model of success for most of its history since incorporation in 1934 following the collapse of 2274 banks between 1930 and 1933 (11.6% of the total number). Depositors suffered losses estimated to have been $1.5 bil. (Kaufman 1977:104). By contrast, depositors lost only $17 mil. between January 1, 1933, and the end of 1980 in 81 bank cases (FDIC 1980:293). Deposit liabilities are either assumed by another bank or the FDIC makes direct payoffs to depositors in failed banks. Until recently this meant that uninsured depositors as well as insured depositors have been paid off virtually in full. The amount of deposit insurance (covering all deposits, whether time or checkable) began in 1934 at $2500 and is currently $100,000 per deposit account.

The number of bank failures jumped sharply after 1981. In 1984, 78 banks failed. In 1985, by November, 100 banks had failed, an unprecedented number since the 1930s (Nash 1985: 21, 23). The FDIC's list of problem banks included 690 institutions in mid-1984, over double the figure 18 months earlier (Keran and Furlong 1984:1).

The increase in FDIC expenses to pay off depositors in failed banks has reduced the rebates formerly paid to banks on their insurance premiums. The statutory insurance premium is one-twelfth of 1% of a bank's total deposits. In 1980 the agency rebated $521 mil. or 54.8% of premiums received. By 1983 the rebate had fallen to $164 mil. or 13.5% of premium income (Noble 1984:26).

Because of the FDIC's limited resources at a time of increased losses, the prevention of bank failures takes on added significance. For this reason, the regulators have a great interest in the net worth of banks. A bank's equity is a buffer against insolvency. The higher the capital-asset ratio, the greater the leeway for a decline in asset values before a bank exhausts its equity capital and goes broke. But the catch is that the more highly leveraged a bank (i.e., the higher the ratio of deposits to equity capital), the higher the expected value (in a mathematical sense) of risky loans and the higher the return on stockholder's equity (Furlong and Keran 1984:1–2). The regulator and the regulated in terms of their interests are on opposite sides of the fence.

Leveraging depends on the insurance of deposits. Fixed rate insurance premiums and low capital-asset (deposit) ratios jointly contribute to institutional risk taking and the FDIC's problems. Along with the comptroller of the currency it has proposed a rule that would require banks to maintain a primary ratio of capital assets of 5.5% and a secondary capital minimum, including some convertible debt and the value of intangible assets in the definition of capital of 6% (Furlong and Keran 1984:3). This rule is directed at the major banks (those with assets over $5 bil.), since lower sized groups have ratios in excess of these requirements (Talley 1983:2–3).

Regulatory reform

Deregulation has taken place within a regulatory structure largely unchanged over 50 years. During this time countless proposals have been made for centralizing regulatory and supervisory functions (for a complete listing and discussion of the history of reform proposals, see Carron 1984:18–19). The only tangible result was the establishment of an interagency Federal Financial Institutions Council in 1978. Its efforts at achieving greater uniformity in examination and supervisory procedures and reporting forms have not succeeded (Johnston 1984:3).

The most recent set of recommendations was issued by the Task Group on Regulation of Financial Services chaired by Vice President Bush in 1984. A blue ribbon committee, it consisted of the heads of the various regulatory agencies. While a centralized authority is not proposed, the suggested plan does attempt to reduce overlap and duplication. Its main recommendation is that the office of the comptroller of the currency be renamed the Federal Banking Agency and have authority over most BHCs in addition to its current functions vis-à-vis national banks. The Fed would give up its regulation of BHCs except for some 50 in the so-called international class. At the same time the Fed would inherit the FDIC's supervisory and examination powers over state-chartered banks. A simpler plan would have had all the Fed's regulatory powers transferred to the new banking agency, but Chairman Paul Volcker of the Fed objected; monetary and regulatory policies are necessarily intertwined. Ultimately, through a certification program, state agencies would assume examination and supervision authority over state-chartered banks and BHCs. The FDIC would be limited to activities related to its deposit insurance function with examination focusing on troubled banks. The proposed regulatory structure is shown in Figure 8.6.

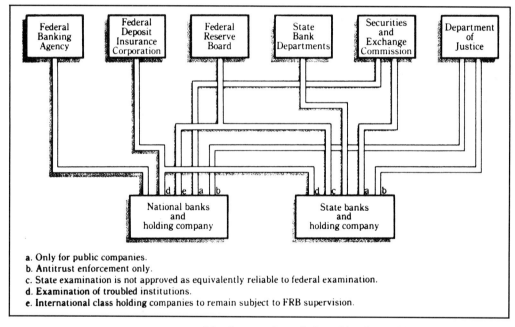

a. Only for public companies.
b. Antitrust enforcement only.
c. State examination is not approved as equivalently reliable to federal examination.
d. Examination of troubled institutions.
e. International class holding companies to remain subject to FRB supervision.

8.6 Proposed regulation of banks and their holding companies (includes thrifts with identical bank portfolios). (Pianalto 1984:3)

In the light of past treatment of reform proposals and the lukewarm reception given the Bush proposals it is not likely that Congress will soon implement them in legislation. The dominant view is the traditional view, "if it ain't broke don't fix it" (Johnston 1984:3).

Summary

The outstanding impression that this chapter should convey is that we now think of a financial services industry instead of banks, thrifts, brokers, and insurance industries. Even this is not satisfactory because of the invasion of financial territory by nonfinancial firms. All that one can be sure of is that the contours of the industry are not likely to stay put long enough for a mapping of boundaries. Behind the dynamics of financial expansionism may lie the effect of inflation on interest rates and the computer revolution. Prospective economies of scope join economies of scale in explaining the expansion and fusion of services, although there is no hard evidence that such economies exist. Deregulation has quickened the pace of financial competition by the removal of interest rate ceilings.

Financial competition has become worldwide as U.S. banks go abroad and foreign banks enter the U.S. market. Such crossing of borders has helped to forge a worldwide financial market, with events in one geographic area quickly sending shock waves through the entire system. The international debt crisis of recent years is testimony to the fragility of the world financial system.

There have been both losers and gainers from deregulation. The losers are those who have to pay higher interest costs or higher service fees. The gainers are those who find their interest going up or enjoy a wider range of services.

An increase in the riskiness of lending caused by increased cost of funds and sensitivity to world economic shocks has placed the FDIC under its greatest strains since deposit insurance was established more than 50 years ago.

The stability of the regulatory structure is remarkable in contrast to the protean nature of the financial services industry. Countless proposals for structural change have been made beginning in the 1930s down to the Bush proposals of 1984, but they have all failed to muster support in Congress.

Review questions

1. Why is banking a highly regulated industry?

2. Why is it more appropriate to speak of a financial services industry today than a banking industry?

3. Describe the present regulatory structure and the Bush proposals for reform.

4. Discuss the growth of international banking.

5. Discuss the step-by-step elimination of Regulation Q and some of the consequences of its virtual removal.

6. Who are the losers and gainers from deregulation?

7. Will economies of scale and scope result in a concentration of firms providing diversified financial services? Will this increase or decrease competition?

8. Has the housing industry benefited from financial deregulation?

9. How do the interests of regulators and regulatees differ in the case of capital adequacy?

10. What is meant by a dual banking system?

11. Describe briefly the major banking acts enacted since the Civil War.

12. What are the present difficulties facing the FDIC?

13. What is the magnitude of the international debt crisis and how does it affect U.S. banks?

14. Describe the steps taken to rescue the Continental Illinois National Bank.

15. What is moral hazard? What reforms does it suggest for deposit insurance?

9

The Federal Reserve at work: Service functions

Member banks are the base of the pyramid that constitutes the Federal Reserve System. A reference to the Federal Reserve is a reference to the administrative levels of the system — the 12 Federal Reserve Banks, the Board of Governors, and the Federal Open-Market Committee.

Structure

Figure 9.1 presents the organization of the Federal Reserve System. The system has five main parts — the Board of Governors, the Federal Open-Market Committee (FOMC), the 12 Federal Reserve Banks, the member banks, and three

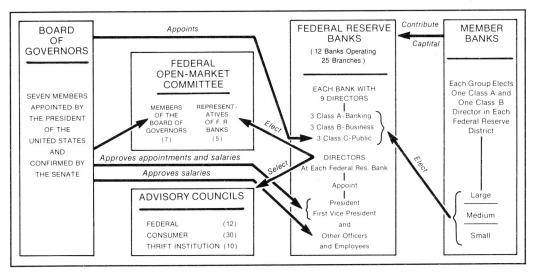

9.1. Organization of the Federal Reserve System. (Adapted from FRB 1974:18)

advisory councils (Federal, Consumer, and Thrift Institutions). The president of the United States appoints members of the Board of Governors to 14-year terms, which are staggered so that a new appointment is made every two years (barring appointments to fill vacancies). One of the seven appointees is designated as chairman for a four-year renewable term. A permanent representative on the 12-person FOMC is the president of the Federal Reserve Bank of New York. The other four Bank representatives (usually presidents) are drawn from the remaining 11 Banks on a rotating basis. Representatives of all the Banks, including nonvoting members, attend the open-market meetings.

While publicly administered, the Federal Reserve Banks are owned by the member banks, showing the quasi-public nature of the Fed. Member banks invest 3% of their capital and surplus in their district Bank stock and can be called on to subscribe to another 3%. The commercial banks, as owners, elect six of the nine members of the board of directors of each Bank. (The branches have a lesser number of directors.) The member banks are divided into three categories on the basis of size and elect one class A and one class B director each. The class A directors are bankers; the class B directors represent business interests.

The more important directors are the class C directors appointed by the Board. They include the Bank chair and the deputy chair. Frequently, class C directors are drawn from the ranks of academics and journalists as well as business. The Federal Advisory Council consists of 12 bankers, one from each district. It is required by law to meet at least four times annually in Washington, D.C., and advises the Board on all matters falling within its jurisdiction. The Thrift Institutions Advisory Council is made up of representatives of thrifts and advises the Board on issues pertaining to the thrift industry. A recent addition to the system is the Consumer Advisory Council. It is appointed by the Board and advises and consults with it on consumer-related matters such as truth in lending. The presidents and vice-presidents of the 12 Banks are organized into conferences and meet from time to time to consider matters of common interest.

CENTRALIZATION IN THE FED   The allocation of policymaking powers is suggested by Figure 9.2. Except for a nominal sharing of discretion over discount rate, power resides in Washington. The Banks set the discount rate every two weeks, but this power is severely limited by the Board's necessary approval of the rate. The Banks do administer the discount window, however, which means they approve or reject loan applications. While loans are now arranged over the phone, the banks still have tellers' cages at which loans were once negotiated. The metaphor for borrowing has persisted despite the change in lending practices.

This centralization in Washington was not always the case. The intent of the framers of the Federal Reserve Act (passed in 1913) was to establish a set of regional banks with loose coordination by Washington. It has not worked out that way because economic pressures, most notably those of the Great Depression, jumped over regional boundaries. The Banking Act of 1935 formalized the mechanism for policymaking on a national basis. The Board of Governors, which replaced the old Federal Reserve Board, was given power to approve Bank presidents and the final say as to the discount rate. Most importantly, the FOMC was created and centralized the responsibility for open-market operations.

In this centralized setting one can be somewhat cynical about the role of the

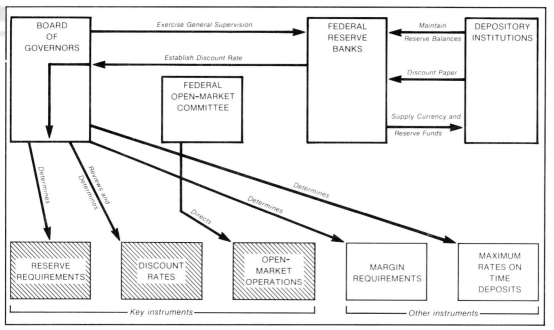

9.2. The Federal Reserve System — relation to instruments of credit policy. (FRB 1974:50)

Bank directors. While they set the discount rate every two weeks, this is done after consultation with Washington. One former Bank chair has commented on the anomaly of prestigious members having little to do. Their largely ceremonial role reflects the activities of the personnel of the Banks; 95% are engaged in operational activities relating to the flow and storage of money and credit, with only 5% or less being concerned with issues of monetary and credit policy. Policy discussions center on the discount rate. What is lacking, however, is an information loop, i.e., input into the FOMC from the board of directors and feedback to the board. The presidents of the Banks have no obligation to follow instructions of their boards nor to report back to them on their deliberations (Winn 1970:241ff.).

```
Table 9.1.  Regulations by subject matter
  A--Loans to depository institutions
  B--Equal credit opportunity
  C--Home mortgage disclosure
  D--Reserve requirements
  E--Electronic fund transfers
  F--Securities of member banks
  G--Margin credit extended by parties other
       than banks, brokers, and dealers
  H--Membership requirements for state-chartered
       banks
  I--Member stock in Federal Reserve Banks
  J--Check collection and funds transfer
  K--International banking operations
  L--Interlocking bank relationships
  M--Consumer leasing
  N--Relationships with foreign banks
  O--Loans to executive officers of member banks
  P--Member bank protection standards
  Q--Interest on deposits
  R--Interlocking relationships between securities
       dealers and member banks
  S--Reimbursement for providing financial records
  T--Margin credit extended by brokers and dealers
  U--Margin credit extended by banks
  V--Guarantee of loans for national defense work
  W--Extensions of consumer credit (revoked)
  X--Borrowers who obtain margin credit
  Y--Bank holding companies
  Z--Truth in lending
 AA--Consumer complaint procedures
 BB--Community reinvestment
     Source:  FRB 1981.
```

FED REGULATIONS The Board of Governors of the Federal Reserve System and the Banks administer more than two dozen regulations from A to Z and beyond as shown in Table 9.1. They deal with the functions of the central bank and its relationships with financial institutions, with the activities of commercial banks and bank holding companies, and with consumer credit transactions. They are the Fed's way of carrying out congressional policies embodied in various banking laws (FRB 1981:preface).

MAP OF THE FED   Figure 9.3 shows the boundaries of the Federal Reserve
Districts, their branch territories, and head-office cities. Bank size as measured by
assets varies widely; Minneapolis is the smallest with $3.3 bil. and New York is the

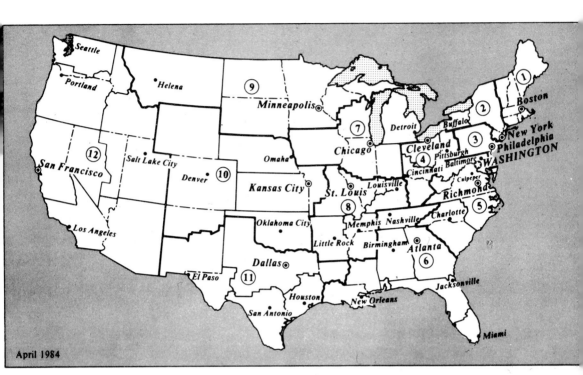

April 1984

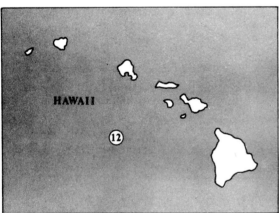

9.3. Boundaries of Federal Reserve districts and their
branch territories. (*Fed. Res. Bull.* 1985b:80)

━━ Boundaries of Federal Reserve districts
── Boundaries of Federal Reserve branch territories
⊘ Board of Governors of the Federal Reserve system
◉ Federal Reserve bank cities
• Federal Reserve branch cities
· Federal Reserve bank facility

largest with \$62.7 bil. at the end of 1983. About 60% of total assets of \$198.6 bil. were held by the three largest banks (New York, Chicago, and San Francisco).

STAFF ORGANIZATION OF BOARD OF GOVERNORS   The table of organization of the Washington Fed is shown in Figure 9.4. The offices and divisions listed in the first, third, and fourth columns deal with routine operations or internal administration. The Office of Board Members is a special resource of the Board. The Division of Consumer Affairs monitors consumer credit protection laws such as the Truth in Lending Act.

The scope of monetary research in the system is suggested by the Office of Monetary and Financial Policy in the second column of Figure 9.4 with its divisions of research and statistics and international finance. The scholarly caliber of the published research of staff members compares favorably with any major university. In this respect the Fed is a unique Washington institution.

ederal Reserve Board of Governors and Official Staff

AUL A. VOLCKER, *Chairman*	HENRY C. WALLICH	EMMETT J. RICE	MARTHA R. SEGER
RESTON MARTIN, *Vice Chairman*	J. CHARLES PARTEE	LYLE E. GRAMLEY	

FFICE OF BOARD MEMBERS
EPH R. COYNE, *Assistant to the Board*
NALD J. WINN, *Assistant to the Board*
EVEN M. ROBERTS, *Assistant to the Chairman*
ANK O'BRIEN, JR., *Deputy Assistant to the Board*
THONY F. COLE, *Special Assistant to the Board*
LLIAM R. JONES, *Special Assistant to the Board*
OMI P. SALUS, *Special Assistant to the Board*

EGAL DIVISION
CHAEL BRADFIELD, *General Counsel*
VIRGIL MATTINGLY, JR., *Associate General Counsel*
LBERT T. SCHWARTZ, *Associate General Counsel*
HARD M. ASHTON, *Assistant General Counsel*
ANCY P. JACKLIN, *Assistant General Counsel*
ARYELLEN A. BROWN, *Assistant to the General Counsel*

FFICE OF THE SECRETARY
LLIAM W. WILES, *Secretary*
RBARA R. LOWREY, *Associate Secretary*
MES MCAFEE, *Associate Secretary*

VISION OF CONSUMER
ND COMMUNITY AFFAIRS
IFFITH L. GARWOOD, *Director*
RAULD C. KLUCKMAN, *Associate Director*
ENN E. LONEY, *Assistant Director*
OLORES S. SMITH, *Assistant Director*

IVISION OF BANKING
UPERVISION AND REGULATION
HN E. RYAN, *Director*
ILLIAM TAYLOR, *Deputy Director*
EDERICK R. DAHL, *Associate Director*
N E. KLINE, *Associate Director*
CK M. EGERTSON, *Assistant Director*
OBERT S. PLOTKIN, *Assistant Director*
DNEY M. SUSSAN, *Assistant Director*
URA M. HOMER, *Securities Credit Officer*

OFFICE OF STAFF DIRECTOR FOR
MONETARY AND FINANCIAL POLICY
STEPHEN H. AXILROD, *Staff Director*
DONALD L. KOHN, *Deputy Staff Director*
STANLEY J. SIGEL, *Assistant to the Board*
NORMAND R.V. BERNARD, *Special Assistant to the Board*

DIVISION OF RESEARCH AND STATISTICS
JAMES L. KICHLINE, *Director*
EDWARD C. ETTIN, *Deputy Director*
MICHAEL J. PRELL, *Deputy Director*
JOSEPH S. ZEISEL, *Deputy Director*
JARED J. ENZLER, *Deputy Director*
ELEANOR J. STOCKWELL, *Associate Director*
DAVID E. LINDSEY, *Deputy Associate Director*
FREDERICK M. STRUBLE, *Deputy Associate Director*
HELMUT F. WENDEL, *Deputy Associate Director*
MARTHA BETHEA, *Assistant Director*
ROBERT M. FISHER, *Assistant Director*
SUSAN J. LEPPER, *Assistant Director*
THOMAS D. SIMPSON, *Assistant Director*
LAWRENCE SLIFMAN, *Assistant Director*
STEPHEN P. TAYLOR, *Assistant Director*
PETER A. TINSLEY, *Assistant Director*
LEVON H. GARABEDIAN, *Assistant Director*
  (Administration)

DIVISION OF INTERNATIONAL FINANCE
EDWIN M. TRUMAN, *Director*
LARRY J. PROMISEL, *Senior Associate Director*
CHARLES J. SIEGMAN, *Senior Associate Director*
DALE W. HENDERSON, *Associate Director*
ROBERT F. GEMMILL, *Staff Adviser*
SAMUEL PIZER, *Staff Adviser*
PETER HOOPER, III, *Assistant Director*
DAVID H. HOWARD, *Assistant Director*
RAYMOND LUBITZ, *Assistant Director*
RALPH W. SMITH, JR., *Assistant Director*

OFFICE OF
STAFF DIRECTOR FOR MANAGEMENT
S. DAVID FROST, *Staff Director*
EDWARD T. MULRENIN, *Assistant Staff Director*
STEPHEN R. MALPHRUS, *Assistant Staff Director for Office Automation and Technology*
PORTIA W. THOMPSON, *EEO Programs Officer*

DIVISION OF DATA PROCESSING
CHARLES L. HAMPTON, *Director*
BRUCE M. BEARDSLEY, *Deputy Director*
GLENN L. CUMMINS, *Assistant Director*
NEAL H. HILLERMAN, *Assistant Director*
RICHARD J. MANASSERI, *Assistant Director*
ELIZABETH B. RIGGS, *Assistant Director*
WILLIAM C. SCHNEIDER, JR., *Assistant Director*
ROBERT J. ZEMEL, *Assistant Director*

DIVISION OF PERSONNEL
DAVID L. SHANNON, *Director*
JOHN R. WEIS, *Assistant Director*
CHARLES W. WOOD, *Assistant Director*

OFFICE OF THE CONTROLLER
GEORGE E. LIVINGSTON, *Controller*
BRENT L. BOWEN, *Assistant Controller*

DIVISION OF SUPPORT SERVICES
ROBERT E. FRAZIER, *Director*
WALTER W. KREIMANN, *Associate Director*
GEORGE M. LOPEZ, *Assistant Director*

OFFICE OF STAFF DIRECTOR FOR
FEDERAL RESERVE BANK ACTIVITIES
THEODORE E. ALLISON, *Staff Director*
JOSEPH W. DANIELS, SR., *Advisor, Equal Employment Opportunity Programs*

DIVISION OF FEDERAL RESERVE
BANK OPERATIONS
CLYDE H. FARNSWORTH, JR., *Director*
ELLIOTT C. MCENTEE, *Associate Director*
DAVID L. ROBINSON, *Associate Director*
C. WILLIAM SCHLEICHER, JR., *Associate Director*
WALTER ALTHAUSEN, *Assistant Director*
CHARLES W. BENNETT, *Assistant Director*
ANNE M. DEBEER, *Assistant Director*
JACK DENNIS, JR., *Assistant Director*
EARL G. HAMILTON, *Assistant Director*
* JOHN F. SOBALA, *Assistant Director*

9.4.   Federal Reserve Board of Governors and official staff. (*Fed. Res. Bull.* 1985b:A70, 71)

The payments mechanism

CHECK PROCESSING   The Fed has responsibility for ensuring an efficient and effective payments mechanism (Brundy et al. 1979:97). It does this mainly by supervising the clearing of checks. Most transactions in the United States are settled by check, emphasizing the importance of the check-clearing process. While no one has ever offered hard evidence for the figure, the oft-repeated percentage for transactions settled by check is 90%.

THE CHECK   Writing a check involves three parties – the writer or drawer of the check, the drawee bank, and the recipient of the check (the payee). Figure 9.5 explains the various codes on the check; magnetic ink character recognition numbers at the bottom have led to computerized handling. A reliable system of check clearing is necessary before anyone will accept a check. Prior to the Fed, clearinghouse arrangements had developed for clearing checks between banks in the same city. The simplification this brings about is illustrated in Figure 9.6.

Before the clearinghouse arrangement, six payments and six separate round trips by messengers would be necessary between any three banks. The number of round trips and payments for three hypothetical banks is cut in half by the clearinghouse. Moreover, net payments are handled by bookkeeping entries at the local Federal Reserve Bank head office or branch (37 in number). The development of regional check-processing centers has extended the clearinghouse arrangement to other areas. Local banks still serve as clearinghouses in the absence of Federal Reserve Banks or processing centers. Net payments are settled by posting the accounts of local clearinghouse members at the clearinghouse bank. It is, of course, possible for local banks to hold reciprocal accounts and exchange checks on each other (Brundy et al. 1979:98).

The outstanding weakness in the clearing process prior to the Federal Reserve System was the clearing of out-of-town checks. Figure 9.7 illustrates the roundabout system of check collection that developed to avoid exchange charges, which were fees levied by the receiving (drawee) bank and deducted from the draft remitted to the sending bank. (The draft was drawn on the drawee's correspondent bank in the city in which the presenting bank was located.) The delays meant that anyone accepting a check in payment for a sale would have to wait a long time before having checkable funds. (Banks would not give the seller credit until they were paid.) The reluctance of sellers to accept checks on out-of-town banks is understandable.

The Fed virtually eliminated this roundabout system of check collection. Banks still may use correspondent banks in the check-clearing process (the sending bank is the correspondee bank), but this is for reasons other than avoiding exchange charges. The Fed effectively eliminated exchange fees by establishing a par clearing list. All member banks had to be on this list, and other banks had to agree to remit at par to have their checks accepted for collection through the Fed. Virtually all banks in the United States are now on the par clearing list; as of June 1976, there were 64 nonpar banks located chiefly in Louisiana, South Carolina, and Texas (*Fed. Res. Bull.* 1976:481–82). In this way the Fed administers a national clearing system. In 1983, the Banks handled 16.6 bil. commercial check items, individually or in presorted bundles, with a total dollar value close to $11 tril. (FRB 1983a:234). Such check handling is a fraction of this country's "paper avalanche." In 1984, 40.6 bil. checks are expected to be written on the basis of an annual 5% growth rate (Berger et al. forthcoming). Besides check bundling, the difference between the two totals is explained by the many checks being redeposit-

CHECKS ARRIVE AT THE NEW YORK FED IN BUNDLES. ATTACHED TO EACH BUNDLE IS A TAPE LISTING THE AMOUNT OF EACH CHECK.

EACH BANK ALSO SENDS A "CASH LETTER" WHICH BEARS THE TOTAL OF ALL THE PACKAGES. THE FEDERAL RESERVE BANK VERIFIES THIS AMOUNT AND ADDS IT TO THE DEPOSITING BANK.

CHECK PROCESSING IS AUTOMATED. HIGH-SPEED ELECTRONIC MACHINES SORT CHECKS BY "READING" THE SORTING INSTRUCTIONS PRINTED IN MAGNETIC INK CHARACTERS ALONG THE BOTTOM OF CHECKS...AT A SPEED APPROACHING 100,000 CHECKS AN HOUR.

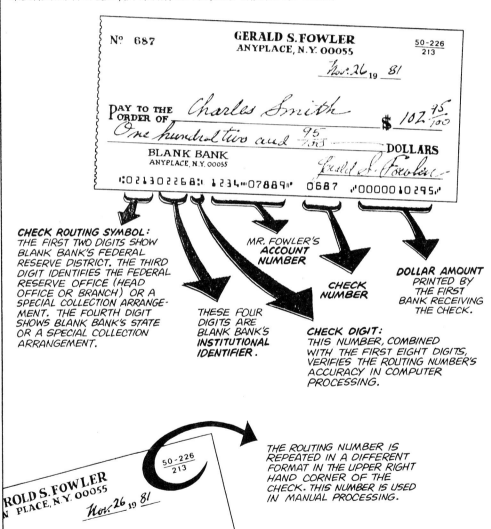

CHECK ROUTING SYMBOL:
THE FIRST TWO DIGITS SHOW BLANK BANK'S FEDERAL RESERVE DISTRICT. THE THIRD DIGIT IDENTIFIES THE FEDERAL RESERVE OFFICE (HEAD OFFICE OR BRANCH) OR A SPECIAL COLLECTION ARRANGEMENT. THE FOURTH DIGIT SHOWS BLANK BANK'S STATE OR A SPECIAL COLLECTION ARRANGEMENT.

THESE FOUR DIGITS ARE BLANK BANK'S INSTITUTIONAL IDENTIFIER.

MR. FOWLER'S ACCOUNT NUMBER

CHECK NUMBER

CHECK DIGIT:
THIS NUMBER, COMBINED WITH THE FIRST EIGHT DIGITS, VERIFIES THE ROUTING NUMBER'S ACCURACY IN COMPUTER PROCESSING.

DOLLAR AMOUNT PRINTED BY THE FIRST BANK RECEIVING THE CHECK.

THE ROUTING NUMBER IS REPEATED IN A DIFFERENT FORMAT IN THE UPPER RIGHT HAND CORNER OF THE CHECK. THIS NUMBER IS USED IN MANUAL PROCESSING.

9.5. Explanation of various codes on checks. (Fed, New York 1983:15)

9.6. How the clearing house works. (Fed, New York 1983:7)

ed in the same bank (these are called "on us" checks) and correspondent banks collecting checks directly on behalf of their correspondee banks.

The interdistrict clearing process is shown in pictorial form in Figure 9.8. The cast of players includes the drawer of the check (Mrs. Henderson), the payee (the art dealer), two commercial banks, and two Banks. As pointed out, the two Banks settle between themselves by transfers of ownership of assets in the Interdistrict Settlement Fund. Until 1976 the asset consisted of Bank holdings of gold certifi-

TO AVOID THE EXCHANGE CHARGES, BANKS WOULD SEND OUT-OF-TOWN CHECKS TO CORRESPONDENT BANKS RATHER THAN BY THE MOST DIRECT ROUTE. CORRESPONDENTS WOULD IN TURN SEND THE CHECKS TO THEIR CORRESPONDENTS...THE RESULT--CHECKS SOMETIMES TOOK A LONG TIME TO BE COLLECTED AND WENT A ROUNDABOUT WAY...

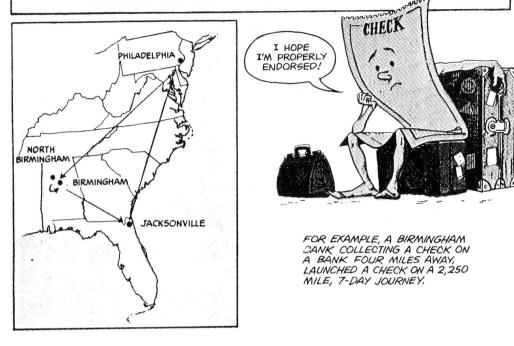

I HOPE I'M PROPERLY ENDORSED!

FOR EXAMPLE, A BIRMINGHAM BANK COLLECTING A CHECK ON A BANK FOUR MILES AWAY, LAUNCHED A CHECK ON A 2,250 MILE, 7-DAY JOURNEY.

WHEN PRESIDENT WILSON SIGNED THE FEDERAL RESERVE ACT IN 1913, A NEW ERA IN THE STORY OF CHECKS BEGAN IN THE UNITED STATES. THE ACT ESTABLISHED FEDERAL RESERVE BANKS AND THEIR BRANCHES AS CHECK CLEARING AND COLLECTING CENTERS FOR THE BANKS THAT BELONGED TO THE FEDERAL RESERVE SYSTEM.

WOODROW WILSON

THIS NEW NATIONWIDE CHECK CLEARING FACILITY WENT A LONG WAY TOWARD ENDING LENGTHY ROUTING AND EXCHANGE CHARGES ON CHECKS.

9.7. Roundabout check collection. (Fed, New York 1983:9)

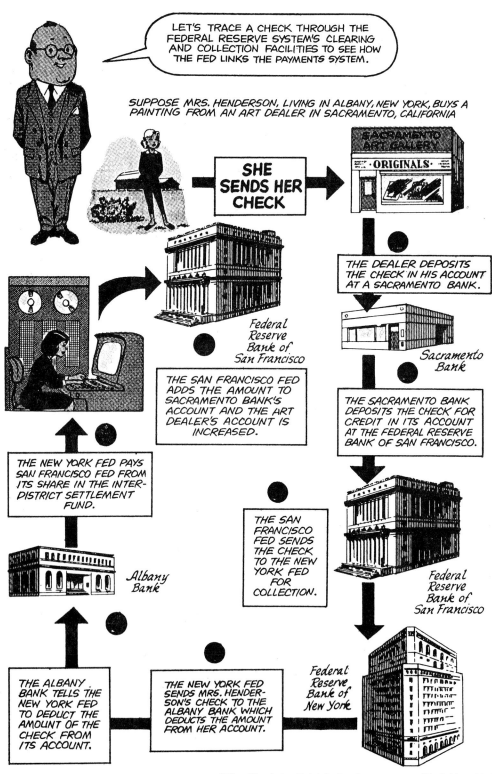

9.8. The interdistrict clearing process. (Fed, New York 1983:13)

cates. Since 1976, settlement has been accomplished by reallocating the ownership of U.S. government securities among the banks. The fund is no more than a name for centralized recording of interdistrict checks received by each Fed office.

The final debit and credit entries for interdistrict clearings are indicated in Table 9.2 (assuming a $1000 transaction).

Table 9.2. Entries for interdistrict clearing

Sacramento Bank			Federal Reserve Bank of San Francisco		
Debit	Credit		Debit	Credit	
Reserves $1000	Deposits $1000		U.S. government securities $1000	Bank reserves $1000	

Albany Bank			Federal Reserve Bank of New York		
Debit	Credit		Debit	Credit	
Reserves -$1000	Deposits -$1000		U.S. government securities -$1000	Bank reserves -$1000	

The clearing process can be short-circuited if the Sacramento bank sends the check directly to the Federal Reserve Bank of New York. Major banks do this and are known as direct sending banks. The importance of direct sending is illustrated in the matrix given in Table 9.3. In 121 of the 132 interdistrict sending combinations in Table 9.3, the share of items sent by direct-sending banks exceeds 50% of

Table 9.3. Percentage distribution of number and dollar value of interdistrict deposits at Federal Reserve offices sent by Federal Reserve offices (daily average, May 1978)

Receiving Federal Reserve district	Boston (1)	New York (2)	Philadelphia (3)	Cleveland (4)	Richmond (5)	Atlanta (6)	Chicago (7)	St. Louis (8)	Minneapolis (9)	Kansas City (10)	Dallas (11)	San Francisco (12)
Boston	...	18.1	13.6	33.3	29.6	44.0	19.0	17.0	48.7	42.5	8.5	10.5
		(6.4)	(5.0)	(10.9)	(22.3)	(35.4)	(5.2)	(17.2)	(32.0)	(31.5)	(3.5)	(4.6)
New York	8.7	...	9.1	31.5	15.9	46.1	18.5	16.1	45.7	44.2	5.2	4.5
	(3.6)		(5.3)	(10.1)	(9.0)	(25.3)	(4.9)	(9.0)	(19.0)	(25.3)	(1.3)	(2.2)
Philadelphia	16.9	10.7	...	19.6	19.5	47.3	19.9	14.8	46.7	40.5	8.5	10.8
	(5.1)	(3.3)		(6.5)	(12.7)	(40.3)	(6.0)	(12.1)	(20.9)	(24.3)	(2.2)	(3.7)
Cleveland	13.4	17.5	14.2	...	29.5	49.8	18.0	6.9	51.2	39.7	7.7	12.4
	(4.7)	(2.7)	(12.2)		(30.8)	(33.0)	(4.6)	(6.2)	(38.7)	(24.1)	(2.7)	(4.9)
Richmond	20.9	16.5	12.4	28.3	...	34.0	21.5	34.7	50.4	36.4	8.3	10.8
	(7.3)	(3.8)	(10.6)	(11.3)		(14.9)	(5.9)	(30.9)	(22.7)	(19.5)	(2.2)	(5.0)
Atlanta	23.1	18.0	22.9	55.9	21.3	...	26.6	18.1	69.2	38.8	5.5	15.5
	(10.6)	(2.5)	(7.4)	(9.5)	(17.1)		(5.3)	(12.9)	(32.9)	(22.1)	(1.6)	(8.4)
Chicago	14.2	14.5	11.5	26.9	35.8	52.2	...	13.1	32.4	26.6	9.2	10.4
	(4.7)	(.9)	(4.0)	(11.4)	(16.6)	(33.1)		(11.3)	(23.0)	(13.8)	(2.4)	(4.6)
St. Louis	19.3	15.5	14.0	32.6	42.0	37.4	21.6	...	41.1	15.2	5.7	13.7
	(6.5)	(2.7)	(8.3)	(14.4)	(32.3)	(23.4)	(4.8)		(41.1)	(15.2)	(2.6)	(3.7)
Minneapolis	14.7	29.5	12.2	47.5	32.0	64.4	19.0	30.7	...	41.4	16.1	19.5
	(.5)	(9.2)	(18.5)	(24.7)	(39.2)	(59.6)	(6.5)	(21.2)		(26.9)	(13.2)	(33.3)
Kansas City	27.4	14.9	11.9	47.8	46.7	62.3	17.7	24.5	64.1	...	4.8	15.8
	(13.5)	(3.5)	(8.8)	(13.2)	(36.1)	(44.2)	(3.9)	(13.0)	(34.8)		(1.6)	(14.5)
Dallas	20.0	14.9	13.2	46.5	36.6	52.5	20.5	21.4	67.8	33.1	...	11.1
	(7.9)	(3.6)	(8.6)	(10.0)	(32.2)	(38.1)	(5.3)	(11.5)	(44.9)	(15.2)		(5.1)
San Francisco	23.2	8.8	19.5	41.7	24.9	33.4	11.5	31.7	30.9	25.1	18.6	...
	(18.3)	(3.3)	(6.7)	(16.1)	(17.3)	(19.5)	(6.6)	(29.5)	(18.0)	(29.4)	(13.2)	

Source: Brundy et al. 1979:102.
Note: The percentages for dollar value appear in parentheses. This table tells, for example, that 29.6% of the number of items (and 22.3% of the dollar value) sent from the Richmond district and received in the Boston district were sent by Richmond district Federal Reserve offices (row 1, col. 5). Thus, the balance, 70.4% of the items (and 77.7% of the dollar value), were from direct-sending banks. These data do not cover clearings outside the Federal Reserve system.

the total deposits received by Fed offices (Brundy et al. 1979:103). The motivation for direct sending is to increase the flow of items out of the sending bank on any given day; e.g., the Pittsburgh branch of the Federal Reserve Bank of Cleveland has an early-morning mailing deadline for forwarding checks. Pittsburgh banks, by waiting until the end of the day, can send more checks for collection. They notify the Pittsburgh branch and are reimbursed for ordinary first-class mail charges. The maximum two days deferred availability begins with notification of the local Bank. Minimizing deferred availability time on the greatest possible volume of items is the motive, then, for direct sending. Deferred availability is discussed below.

FLOAT   The entries in Table 9.2 simplify the clearing process by ignoring float, which refers to checks in limbo, i.e., in the collection process. First, there is mail float when the art buyer tells the art dealer that the check is in the mail. The float in this case is equal to the discrepancy between the banking system's record of deposits and the depositor's own records. The writer of the check will show a lower total than the bank records. If she writes checks on the basis of what is left in her checking account, the bank records are misleading. Of course, to the extent that the art seller anticipates additional funds and writes checks beyond current deposits, bank records are not so misleading. The practice of writing checks in advance of receipts is called floating. A study of payments in Atlanta estimated that between 70 and 80% of consumer accounts are likely to float checks at least once during the course of the year (Knight 1974b:17–18). Check floating is not illegal as long as the checks are covered in time. A related practice that is illegal is check kiting. Here checks written on an account are covered by writing checks on a second account in another bank, which in turn are covered by writing checks on the first or some other bank. Because there is a pattern to this check writing, bankers usually catch on and halt such schemes. Check kiting on a massive scale was practiced by the well-known brokerage firm, E. F. Hutton & Company, over 1980–82. Anyone who has had checks bounce for insufficient funds will be happy to know that the firm was found guilty and required to make substantial restitution (Bleakley 1985:31, 34; Pasztor 1985:6).

Closely allied to the E. F. Hutton practices are "daylight overdrafts." It is estimated that every day banks electronically make more than $120 bil. in payments for corporate customers without funds to cover them (Zweig 1985:6). Fed concern for a possible domino effect from corporate defaults (failing to settle accounts by the end of the day) has led to new guidelines to go into effect in 1986. Caps will be placed on a bank's daily overdrafts.

Mail float is replaced by bank float once the check reaches the banking system. Bank float results from the crediting of the depositor's account before the payer's account is debited. It is measured by the bank asset account, cash items in process of collection. Cash items is a broader category than checks and includes postal money orders, food coupons, and other items payable on demand, such as travelers checks. While customer's accounts are credited when these items are deposited, they may not be allowed to write checks for a specified time, presumably to allow for collection. Abuse in delaying customer access to check deposits has been of interest to Congress (Corrigan 1984:418–19).

Finally, when banks pass cash items on to the Fed, Federal Reserve float is created. This is the difference between the Fed's holdings of cash items in process of collection and the increase in reserves for the sending banks. Fed float thus measures double counting of reserves; the sending bank's reserves are credited before the receiving bank's reserves are debited. The Fed credits sending banks according to a deferred availability schedule. Depending on the time that the Fed expects to receive payment from the bank on which the check is drawn, the sending bank is given reserve credit either on the day of deposit, one day later, or at the most two days later. Clearly, this is an act of generosity for many out-of-town checks, even in the absence of winter snowstorms and equipment malfunctions or work stoppages.

This generosity came to an end with the Depository Institutions Deregulation and Monetary Control Act of 1980 (DIDMCA) which required the Fed to price its services. As a result, by the end of 1983, total costs for Fed check services of $438 mil. were virtually all recovered (FRB 1983a:200). The Fed charged on the basis of estimated interest earnings from float, using the federal funds rate as the yardstick. The pricing of float is more complicated than this, however, depending on whether it is the result of a transportation problem or a holdover problem at the Fed, in the latter case becoming the Fed's fault (see FRB 1983e). Charging for float along with a successful program to accelerate check collection sharply reduced the volume. Banks had an incentive to use alternative channels for check collection and to bypass the Fed. The large correspondent banks have accused the Fed of unfair competition in the pricing of payments (clearing) services. On the other hand, small banks see the Fed as a check on potential correspondent bank abuses (U.S. Congr. 1984: 16–21)

At the end of May 1984, the consolidated balance sheet of the Banks showed the following entries:

DEBITS		CREDITS	
Cash items in process of collection	$10.9 bil.	Deferred availability cash items	$9.5 bil.

The amount of float was the difference between these items ($1.4 bil.), a great reduction from float averaging $4.5 bil. in 1980. The task of monetary policy has been complicated by float, which in the past was highly volatile because of a seasonal pattern in the volume and value of payments by check (Thomas 1982: 184). The Fed has to predict float to offset its effect on the targeted level of reserves. (We discuss float in relation to monetary policy in Ch. 10.)

The Fed's efforts at reducing float antedates DIDMCA. The modification of Regulation J (which deals with check collection) in 1972 was for the purpose of reducing float. Regional Check Processing Centers were set up to supplement the 37 Fed offices. As of 1984, 12 such centers had been established. By having these centers (some of them use Bank facilities) and speedy transportation, checks on banks outside the centers are presented the next day instead of one or two days later as before. Now out-of-town banks have their accounts debited the day after city banks deposit them with the center, at the same time that the city banks receive credit. No float results in such circumstances (Knight 1972:14–24).

Currency (paper money and coin) gets into circulation via the Banks. Each Fed district issues its own notes identifiable by the name of the Bank and its number. District Federal Reserve notes now circulate nationally. Once it was illegal for one Bank to reissue the notes of another. In keeping with national circulation, a current proposal is for elimination of the district seal. Substantial savings in the printing and distribution of currency would result (FRB 1978a:374).

The Banks secure paper money from the U.S. Treasury's Bureau of Engraving and Printing and distribute it to depository institutions (DIs). The Federal Reserve Banks turn over 100% collateral to the chair of each. In the role of Fed agent he or she is the Board's representative at each of the 12 Banks. The collateral consists primarily of gold certificates and government securities. This 100% collateral requirement is the vestigial remains of various reserve requirements historically imposed on the Fed. Until the 1960s the Fed was required to keep gold certificates against its note liabilities and also against member bank deposits. This anomaly of tying the hands of a central bank has now disappeared except for the collateral requirement.

Federal Reserve notes are the principal form of paper money in circulation. Until 1963 the paper money component of Treasury currency included $1 and $5 silver certificates. To free the silver behind the silver certificates with the upsurge in market demand, silver certificates were replaced by Federal Reserve notes in $1 denominations. The disappearance of silver coins with the rise in the market price of silver led to legislation in 1965 and 1970 reducing and finally eliminating silver from circulating coins. In 1967 the Treasury stopped sales of silver and also silver certificate redemptions in silver. As a result, the market price of silver shot above its monetary value of $1.29 per ounce (Horvitz 1974:35–36). The monetary value of silver is the price the Treasury paid beginning in 1792. With the dollar defined as 372.25 grains of pure silver, an ounce of silver was valued at (480 grains/372.25 grains) ($1) = $1.29.

The Fed is also a conduit for coins minted at the U.S. mints in Denver and Philadelphia. A routine Fed duty is sorting incoming coins and screening out slugs and counterfeits. Some idea of the scope of currency activity is given by the physical volume handled. In 1983 the Banks received and counted 11.5 bil. pieces of paper money and 17 bil. coins (FRB 1983a:234). Unlike Federal Reserve notes, which are a liability of the Banks when issued, their holdings of coins are an asset.

Electronic funds transfer

FED WIRE NETWORK   The paper avalanche may be propelling us toward a checkless society. The Fed has been active in this movement; its wire network pioneered in the paperless transfer of funds. In 1918 the Fed installed a private Morse code system (*Fed. Res. Bull.* 1976:486–87), which was converted into a teletype system in 1937. The relay station or switch concept was introduced in 1940 and further elaborated in 1953. Now a central switch facility is maintained in Culpeper, Va. The Banks, branch offices, Treasury, and a number of member banks are interconnected nationwide through this facility. The system transfers deposits, reserve balances, U.S. government securities, and administrative and research information.

A computerized network for electronic funds transfer (EFT) of international dollar payments linking about 100 DIs that have offices or subsidiaries in New York is coordinated by the Federal Reserve Bank of New York. The CHIPS network (Clearing House Interbank Payments System) handles on a daily basis about 70,000 interbank transfers valued at $185 bil. This represents about 90% of all interbank transfers relating to international dollar payments (Fed, New York 1982).

CONSUMER USE OF EFT   Compared to the pioneering of the Fed, EFT has come to the consumer only recently. Rapid improvement in electronic data processing and the development of low-cost, high-speed telecommunications has made widespread use possible. The signs of growth are summarized by Schroeder (1983:395–96):

1. A Board-sponsored survey conducted in April 1983 found that of the households with a checking, savings, NOW, or share draft account, more than 68% had an account with an EFT feature and used it at least occasionally. In March 1981 the proportion was 54%.

2. A recent survey of automation by commercial banks confirms the trend toward expansion of EFT services. Many small banks offer EFT services, and nearly all banks engage in computerized operations, a necessary condition for the spread of EFT.

3. The number of automated teller machines (ATMs) in use has grown rapidly. At the end of 1982, financial institutions were operating an estimated 36,000 ATMs, 38% more than at the end of 1981. The average annual volume of transactions, excluding inquiries about balances, rose 32% to 86,000 transactions per machine. Total volume increased 74% to an annual rate of 3.1 bil. transactions at the end of 1982.

4. The number of financial institutions offering ATM access increased dramatically during 1981. According to a recent survey, 29% of the nation's 14,400 commercial banks were offering ATM services in 1982, up from 19% a year earlier; and 14% planned to offer ATM services. Of banks offering such services, more than half were engaged in some form of ATM sharing with other institutions.

5. Telephone bill payment services were offered by more than 450 financial institutions in 1982, compared with 403 in 1981. These providers accounted for about one-fifth of the assets of all DIs in the nation. Telephone bill payments grew approximately 20% in 1982 to an annual rate of 72 mil. transactions.

6. The volume of transactions through automated clearinghouses (ACHs) continued to grow substantially during 1982. Of the more than 49 mil. payments of federal salaries and benefits in December 1982, nearly 18 mil., or 36%, were made by EFT. Another 16 mil. electronic payments were originated each month by about 20,000 private organizations. Total ACH volume reached an annual rate of 408 mil. electronic transactions, an increase of 30% over the year.

7. Surveys indicate that 71% of all households now have at least one account at a financial institution that offers ATM access, and that at least one person in 32% of all households used an ATM in November 1982.

8. Point-of-sale EFT and home banking systems are developing at an increasingly rapid pace. Of commercial banks with total deposits exceeding $500 mil., 13% supported some form of EFT at point of sale, and 14% more planned to support such a system. Of banks with deposits between $100 mil. and $500 mil., 3% supported and 10% planned to support point-of-sale EFT. Experiments with home banking systems are spreading: in 1980, 2 institutions operated pilot projects; by 1982, 80 institutions had pilots. About 25 systems are expected to be in full operation by 1986.

The possibilities of EFT still lie largely in the future, since consumer EFTs collectively account for less than 1% of all payments in the economy. There are no technical barriers in the way of EFTs replacing cash, checks, and credit cards as the chief method of payment. Dramatic increases are likely because EFT costs are considerably below alternative means of payment. For example, checks deposited by mail in 1981 had an estimated processing cost for the banking system of $.59 as compared with a cost of $.07 for preauthorized direct deposits by EFT (Schroeder 1983:1). Consumers also prefer the convenience and the opportunity to serve themselves.

There are currently two principal forms of EFT: transfers through automated clearinghouses and transfers through computer terminal systems. The latter encompasses automated teller machines (ATMs), telephone bill payment, point-of-sale payments, and check truncation.

Automated clearinghouses   ACHs are distinguished from check-clearing operations by the exchange of payment information by magnetic tape instead of paper checks. Instead of a paycheck, the employee receives a notice that a certain number of dollars has been deposited in his or her checking account. The magnetic tape goes first to the company's own bank. The bank takes off its entries and forwards the tape to the ACH. The ACH prepares computer tapes for the other participating banks so that the remaining employees can have their accounts credited. The originating bank and the receiving banks will have their reserves debited and credited respectively.

In 1976 the Fed provided clearing and settlement facilities in 24 ACH offices (*Fed. Res. Bull.* 1976:485). Direct deposit of federal salaries and benefits are an example of ACHs working internally through Fed ACH offices. The Fed, however, is not the sole processor of automated payments, e.g., in New York and Chicago ACHs are being set up independently.

Public reaction to automatic payroll depositing has been mixed and probably explains its relatively slow progress. Employees have a strong psychological desire to see their paychecks (Knight 1974b:13). Companies are unhappy because they lose the float. They no longer can benefit from a delay in check cashing. While percentage increases are very substantial, they may be misleading because of low base figures.

On the debit side of ACH operations, customers can authorize a utility or insurance company to charge their demand deposit accounts for the amount of the utility bill or insurance premium. The company then turns over a magnetic tape to its bank. After stripping off its own customers, the originating bank forwards the tape to the ACH for distribution to other DIs (Taggart 1978:86). Preauthorized debits of this kind preceded ACHs, but only a small percentage of customers have given this authorization.

Computer terminal systems   The age of electronic banking is most visible in the ATM. Teller machines are always open for business and provide most of the services available at the teller's window. These include cash deposits, withdrawals from checking or savings accounts, transfers of funds between accounts, advances drawn against a line of credit, and responses to balance inquiries. These machines are activated with a plastic card (such as a MasterCard plate) and the supplying of a personal identification number. ATM networks (e.g., Cirrus, Cashstream) are growing rapidly, forming a national system of telecommunication.

In April 1975, telephone transfers of funds from savings accounts of member banks were authorized by the Fed. They had previously been allowed by thrift institutions since the 1960s (Simpson et al. 1979:15). A customer can transmit instructions directly to the bank computer by using a Touch-Tone telephone. An alternative is to talk to someone at the financial institution by ordinary phone. In the case of a bank holding the payee's account (a merchant or a utility company), one account would be debited and the merchant's account would be credited. A thrift institution would have its checking account debited, transferring payment to the seller.

Point-of-sale (POS) terminals feature the use of a debit card that permits the seller's checking account to be credited at the seller's bank and the purchaser's bank account to be debited. (The debit and crediting does not have to be simultaneous. The computer can handle the transaction after business hours.) ATM networks are now realizing their POS possibilities. For some time card holders in Cirrus could get cash from any of its 5300 ATMs. In mid-1984 customers could start using their cards to pay for purchases at the point of sale outside their home regions. The incentive for merchants is the cost saving. A POS transaction costs a retail store $.15 to $.20, compared with $.47 to process a check or $.29 for a cash transaction (L. Friedman 1984:36).

On the horizon is the smart card. These are credit cards containing a micro-chip that allows a range of uses, including cashless shopping, data storage, and the placing of telephone calls. It is also more tamperproof than magnetic cards (*Wall Street Journal* 1985a:43).

Check truncation does not eliminate checks but shortens their passage through the banking system. The first bank receiving the check captures all the data electronically. The check is retained at the point of interception but the information flows through the banking system. Credit unions have been national pacesetters in influencing their members to forego receiving their physical checks.

Congress anticipated headaches along with convenience when consumer EFT was evolving. It passed the Electronic Fund Transfer Act in November 1978. The act had as its primary purpose the establishment of consumer rights and protections (Schroeder 1983: 397). Suppose a user withdraws $50 from her ATM but the account is debited for $500. Fed Regulation E, which implements the act, calls for notifying the bank within 60 days of noticing the problem; the bank then has 45 days to resolve it. If it is not resolved within 10 business days, however, the bank credits the customer with the discrepancy (Donoghue 1984:B5).

EFT AND THE MONEY SUPPLY   Innovations in the payments mechanism have significant implications for the money concept. The line between $M1$ (avowedly transaction balances) and $M2$ becomes blurred. Time deposits in $M2$ can be quickly and conveniently converted into transactions balances by EFT. Defining the money supply becomes more difficult. Retaining a narrow definition of money ($M1$), the effect of EFT is to reduce average holdings of money balances in relation to income and spending, thereby increasing the velocity of money.

The Banks act as fiscal agents of the U.S. government. The Treasury makes payments by writing checks on its deposits in the Banks. Such funds are first transferred from tax and loan accounts in commercial banks built up from tax and debt revenues. Commercial banks willing to pledge government securities as collateral against such deposits qualify as special depositories. An advantage of being a special depository is that tax payments or debt purchases by bank customers do not result in an immediate loss of deposits and reserves. The Treasury redeposits these checks in the banks on which they were drawn and gives advance notice to the banks before calling these deposits. The Treasury times its withdrawals to synchronize with its expenditures. In this way it minimizes the disturbing effect on bank reserves.

The Treasury drastically changed its cash balance procedures in 1974 and again in November 1978. Because of high interest rates in 1974 the Treasury began to quickly shift funds deposited in Treasury, tax, and loan (TTL) accounts to its accounts at the Banks. The intention was to indirectly increase Treasury interest earnings on Fed holdings of government securities. The Fed would have to take defensive actions to offset the loss of bank reserves by open-market purchases, thus increasing its portfolio of government securities. The record after 1974 does indeed show much greater average weekly swings in Treasury balances at the Fed and in Fed holdings of government securities (Lang 1979:3,6). The increased volatility of the Treasury's balance at the Fed also made prediction of bank reserves more difficult for the Fed.

In November 1978 banks were given the option of transferring funds deposited in TTL accounts to interest-bearing note accounts not subject to reserve requirements. In their freedom from reserve requirements, TTL note accounts resembled Treasury deposit accounts between 1917 and 1935. In the latter year, these accounts were made subject to the same reserve requirements as imposed on private demand deposits (Lang 1979:3). Although TTL accounts are payable on demand, the Treasury has a regular pattern of withdrawals similar to the pattern in effect before 1974. The introduction of note accounts has greatly reduced the volatility of Treasury balances at the Fed and the size of defensive open-market operations.

The Banks, as fiscal agents, handle the Treasury's public debt transactions. They redeem government securities as they mature, pay the interest coupons, handle sales of new securities, and conduct transactions in the market for various Treasury accounts. The Banks are not compensated for handling the Treasury's checking accounts and redeeming its coupons but are reimbursed for most other fiscal agency functions performed (Fed, Richmond 1974:5–6).

The Fed also acts as fiscal agent and depository for foreign governments and international organizations. Marketable U.S. government securities held in custody for foreign and international accounts at the Banks amounted to $114 bil. at the end of May 1984 (*Fed. Res. Bull.* 1984b:A107). This total does not include nonmarketable securities and gold held in custody. The gold is stored in New York and is earmarked for about 150 foreign governments, central banks, and international organizations. Governments may settle international debts with this earmarked gold, in which case its ownership changes but it stays in the New York

Federal Reserve Bank's vaults. It may be of interest that a payment of $5 mil. in gold weighs 4 tons, involves moving 300 construction-size bricks weighing about 27 pounds each. Five people help make the transfer, two gold stackers and three overseers from the divisions responsible for earmarked gold. The bars will be moved from one central bank compartment to another, with the compartment doors securely locked. The massive door to the vault offers final security (Fed, New York 1974:23–24).

Cost of operations

Most of the Banks' service functions were performed free of charge until recently, and they account for the bulk of operation costs. The current expenses of the Fed in 1983 amounted to $1 bil. (FRB 1983a:204). To these outlays must be added the $224 mil. (1983) spent by the Board of Governors, which is financed by assessments levied on the Banks. Almost 70% of this amount represents expenditures for printing, issuing, and redeeming Federal Reserve notes on behalf of the Banks. Policymaking, although the most important of the Fed's activities, absorbs but a small fraction of total Bank outlays.

Operating expenses of the Banks were more than covered by their earnings. In 1983 the total earnings of all Banks was $16.1 bil., most of which was from their holdings of U.S. government securities (FRB 1983a:204). The bulk of earnings after expenses reverts to the Treasury. In this way it does not really cost the Treasury the stated interest amount when the Banks hold its debt. The Treasury recovers the interest paid on its debt by charging interest on Federal Reserve notes outstanding. Payments to the Treasury calculated as interest on Federal Reserve notes amounted to $14.2 bil. in 1983.

With the passage of DIDMCA, free bank services have become a thing of the past. Title I requires that the Board publish a set of pricing principles and a proposed schedule of fees based on them (Fed, Chicago 1980:10ff.). Services to be priced include currency and coin, check clearing and collection, wire transfer, ACH services, settlement, securities safekeeping, and Fed float. Prices are based on costs and a profit margin so that the Fed can compete on a free-market basis, with the private sector offering the same services. As previously discussed, the Banks now recover virtually all costs of services.

DIDMCA meant a tremendous increase in the workload of the Banks. Their basic constituency of member banks has been extended to nonmember banks and thrift institutions. Bank personnel have had to design computer systems to handle new pricing and billing functions and process reports from DIs.

Summary

Following a description of the organizational structure, the role of the Fed in the payments mechanism and currency issuance has been discussed. An important reason for the formation of the Federal Reserve System was to improve the payments mechanism. The growing importance of EFT suggests how the economy will cope in the future with the paper avalanche. Finally, the fiscal agency functions of the Fed are considered. The Fed once subsidized the member banks by performing its service functions free of charge. By the end of 1982 this was no longer the case. The Fed has large profits through its interest earnings on holdings of U.S. government securities.

Review questions

1. Describe the organization of the Federal Reserve System.

2. What is the role of the Fed in ensuring an efficient payments mechanism?

3. Differentiate between mail float, bank float, and Fed float.

4. Describe the role of the Federal Reserve Banks in the circulation of currency.

5. Are we moving toward a checkless society? Identify the various EFT innovations.

6. Explain the role of the Fed as the fiscal agent of the United States government.

7. Discuss the pricing of Fed services since DIDMCA.

8. How does "direct sending" short-circuit the check-clearing process?

9. How does EFT affect the definition of money?

10

The Federal Reserve at work: Determination of the monetary base

This chapter tracks down depository reserves and the monetary base (high-powered money). In Chapter 6 high-powered money was the driving force behind deposit expansion. While the focus was on commercial banks, the analysis applies to all depository institutions (DIs). This chapter explains how reserves are influenced by Fed action. We may be surprised to find that there are other influences on reserves that the Fed must offset if it is to have a discretionary policy.

Fed balance sheet

We start with an analysis of the Fed balance sheet shown in Table 10.1. Only the items found on this statement explain reserve deposits at the Fed (line 22). The determination of reserve deposits is then absurdly simple. Any increase on the asset side, holding all other liabilities constant, will cause reserve deposits to increase. Similarly, holding assets constant, an increase in any liability other than reserves will cause them to decline. We can think of asset items as factors supplying reserves and liabilities as factors absorbing reserves. Of course, if changes in these items in any period are negative, they will have reverse effects. A negative change in an asset item acts as a factor of decrease, and a negative change in a liability item acts as a factor of increase. The balance sheet explains reserves in stock terms. Changes in the items explain changes in reserves over a certain period.

GOLD CERTIFICATE ACCOUNT   Gold certificates are assets of the Banks and a liability of the Treasury. Later, when we bring together Treasury monetary accounts and the Fed balance sheets, gold certificates disappear and are replaced with gold on the consolidated statement. Gold certificates for the Banks replaced gold in 1933 when the United States went off a convertible gold coin standard and

Table 10.1. Federal Reserve Banks (condition and Federal Reserve note statements)

Account	End of month, May 1984
	($ mil.)
Assets	
1 Gold certificate account	11,104
2 Special drawing rights certificate account	4,618
3 Coin	443
Loans	
4 Depository institutions	2,832
5 Other	0
Acceptances, bought outright	
6 Held under repurchase agreements	426
Federal agency obligations	
7 Bought outright	8,515
8 Held under repurchase agreements	336
U.S. government securities, bought outright	
9 Bills	65,814
10 Notes	63,870
11 Bonds	22,061
12 Total bought outright[a]	151,745
13 Held under repurchase agreements	3,124
14 Total U.S. government securities	154,869
15 Total loans and securities	166,978
16 Cash items in process of collection	8,770
17 Bank premises	553
Other assets	
18 Denominated in foreign currencies[b]	3,794
19 All other[c]	3,840
20 Total assets	200,100
Liabilities	
21 Federal Reserve notes	158,727
Deposits	
22 To depository institutions	21,686
23 U.S. Treasury--General account	4,855
24 Foreign--Official accounts	295
25 Other	416
26 Total deposits	27,252
27 Deferred availability cash items	8,182
28 Other liabilities and accrued dividends[d]	2,593
29 Total liabilities	196,754
Capital accounts	
30 Capital paid in	1,531
31 Surplus	1,465
32 Other capital accounts	350
33 Total liabilities and capital accounts	200,100
34 *Memo:* Marketable U.S. government securities held in custody for foreign and international account	114,495
35 Federal Reserve notes outstanding	185,998
36 Less: Held by bank[e]	27,271
37 Federal Reserve notes, net	158,727
Collateral held against notes net	
38 Gold certificate account	11,104
39 Special drawing rights certificate account	4,618
40 Other eligible assets	0
41 U.S. government and agency securities	143,005
42 Total collateral	158,727

Source: *Fed. Res. Bull.* 1984b:A10.

[a]Includes securities loaned (fully guaranteed by U.S. government securities pledged with Federal Reserve Banks) and excludes (if any) securities sold and scheduled to be bought back under matched sale-purchase transactions.

[b]Assets shown in this line are revalued monthly at market exchange rates.

[c]Includes special investment account at Chicago of Treasury bills maturing within 90 days.

[d]Includes exchange-translation account reflecting the monthly revaluation at market exchange rates of foreign exchange commitments.

[e]Beginning September 1980, Federal Reserve notes held by the Reserve Bank are exempt from the collateral requirement.

the Banks surrendered their gold holdings to the Treasury in exchange for gold certificates. Today, gold certificate transactions are bookkeeping entries. The only gold certificates extant are those the Banks use for public education displays.

Gold (via gold certificates) still played a role in the domestic banking system after 1933 (Fed, New York 1981:6). It was not until 1965 and 1968 respectively that gold reserve requirements were abolished against Fed deposit liabilities and Federal Reserve notes.

For most of the initial gold standard period beginning in 1792, the monetary value of an ounce of gold was $23.22; i.e., this is what the mint would pay for gold of a specified fineness. In 1934 when gold was officially devalued, the price was increased to $35. Subsequently, the official gold price reached $42.22 in the United States in 1973. Market prices of gold have soared astronomically since 1968, reaching over $800 an ounce in 1980. As a result of gold losses to foreign central banks in the 1960s and 1970s, the gold stock valued at official prices fell from $24 bil. in 1950 to its current value of $11 bil. At market prices of $354 in mid-1984, its value was around $92 bil. Past international crises involving gold are discussed in Chapter 24.

The decline in the gold stock also resulted from the Treasury (1975–79) auctioning off gold at market prices. Such gold auctions did not affect the money stock, but under certain circumstances they could affect both the money stock and the monetary base (Burger 1975:18–22).

The gold stock increased rapidly in the 1930s, since foreign countries regarded the United States as a safe financial haven. Let us trace the mechanics of gold purchased by the Treasury, showing how reserves increased by such purchases (Table 10.2). The seller of gold is assumed to maintain a deposit account in a member bank. Deposits go up as a gold seller (foreign country or a domestic mine) deposits a check drawn on the Fed (the Treasury's bank). When the member bank sends on the check to the Fed (its Bank), the member bank's account is credited and the Treasury's account is debited. The Treasury then replenishes its account by issuing gold certificates to the Fed as shown by the second set of entries. The Treasury thus acquires gold without cost. If a foreign central bank sold the gold to

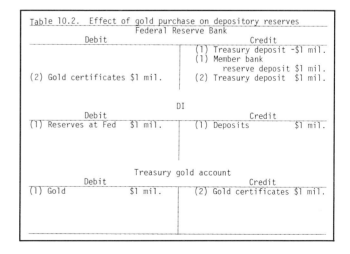

Table 10.2. Effect of gold purchase on depository reserves

Federal Reserve Bank

Debit	Credit
	(1) Treasury deposit -$1 mil.
	(1) Member bank reserve deposit $1 mil.
(2) Gold certificates $1 mil.	(2) Treasury deposit $1 mil.

DI

Debit	Credit
(1) Reserves at Fed $1 mil.	(1) Deposits $1 mil.

Treasury gold account

Debit	Credit
(1) Gold $1 mil.	(2) Gold certificates $1 mil.

the Treasury and deposited the check in its account at the Fed (line 24, Table 10.1), foreign deposits would be credited instead of member bank reserves. Assuming, however, that foreign deposits are run down to their original level, reserves would still increase.

SPECIAL DRAWING RIGHTS   The International Monetary Fund (IMF) allocates special drawing rights (SDRs) to its members. The Treasury monetizes them by issuing SDR certificates to the Banks. In return the Treasury's Exchange Stabilization Fund (ESF) is credited with an equal number of dollars. This deposit is included in line 25 in Table 10.1. The ESF was established in 1934 for purposes of stabilizing foreign exchange rates. If the ESF maintains its new deposit level in a way similar to foreign deposits, member bank reserves will not be affected.

COIN   More appropriately, this item is cash, since it might include some U.S. notes (issued by the Treasury). Formerly, it included silver certificates, but these are retired now when they reach the Fed. Deposits of newly minted coins with the Fed are credited to the Treasury. When the Treasury runs down its account, reserves will go up again. The profit the Treasury makes from issuing coins whose face value exceeds production costs is termed "seignorage."

LOANS   The former title of the loan account was discounts and advances. Since the mid-1930s virtually all borrowing has consisted of advances that are loans made on the basis of promissory notes collateralized chiefly by government securities (Fed, New York 1981:9). Discounts employed before the mid-1930s are really rediscounts, with the customer's promissory note being rediscounted at a Bank by the borrowing commercial bank. The discount rate as charged by the Fed is an interest rate, with interest being paid at maturity on the face value of the loan rather than in advance (subtracted from the full value of the loan), which is the technical definition of a discount rate. The discount rate is expressed in annual terms (i.e., a 365- or 366-day year), and interest charges are computed on the basis of the number of days funds are actually advanced.

Under current discount window regulations, borrowing by DIs is divided into two main categories—adjustment credit including seasonal credit and extended credit (Table 10.3). Extended credit includes that provided to a particular institution under exceptional circumstances and credit to institutions experiencing serious liquidity problems that affect a broad range of DIs. Adjustment and seasonal credit are designed to provide a short-term cushion to balance unexpected outflows from reserve accounts. (Sellon 1984:10). A fifth possible category of loans (not classified in Table 10.3) is advances to individuals, partnerships, and corporations other than DIs ("other" Table 10.1, line 5). The effect of loans on depository reserves is depicted in Table 10.4. (For pre-1980 loan regulations see Fed, New York 1981:4–5.)

The regional character of the Federal Reserve System survives in the range of interest rates charged by the Banks. As the lower half of Table 10.3 shows, while the range is narrow, it nonetheless has existed, followed two or so days later by adjustment of rates to uniformity.

ACCEPTANCES   Acceptances fall under the general legal heading of bills of

Table 10.3. Federal Reserve Bank interest rates (percent/annum)

Current and previous levels

Federal Reserve Bank	Short-term adjustment credit and seasonal credit			Extended credit[a]						Effective date for current rates
				First 60 days of borrowing		Next 90 days of borrowing		After 150 days		
	Rate on 4/30/84	Effective date	Previous rate	Rate on 4/30/84	Previous rate	Rate on 4/30/84	Previous rate	Rate on 4/30/84	Previous rate	
Boston	9	4/9/84	8-1/2	9	8-1/2	10	9-1/2	11	9-1/2	4/9/84
New York	↑	4/9/84		↑		↑		↑		4/9/84
Philadelphia		4/9/84								4/9/84
Cleveland		4/10/84								4/10/84
Richmond		4/9/84								4/9/84
Atlanta		4/10/84								4/10/84
Chicago		4/9/84								4/9/84
St. Louis		4/9/84								4/9/84
Minneapolis		4/9/84								4/9/84
Kansas City		4/13/84								4/13/84
Dallas	↓	4/9/84	↓	↓	↓	↓	↓	↓	↓	4/9/84
San Francisco	9	4/13/84	8-1/2	9	8-1/2	10	9-1/2	11	9-1/2	4/13/84

Range of rates in recent years[b]

Effective date	Range (or level)-- all F.R. Banks	F.R. Bank of N.Y.	Effective date	Range (or level)-- all F.R. Banks	F.R. Bank of N.Y.	Effective date	Range (or level)-- all F.R. Banks	F.R. Bank of N.Y.
In effect Dec. 31, 1973	7-1/2	7-1/2	1978--July 3	7-7-1/4	7-1/4	1981--May 5	13-14	14
1974--Apr. 25	7-1/2-8	8	10	7-1/4	7-1/4	8	14	14
30	8	8	Aug. 21	7-3/4	7-3/4	Nov. 2	13-14	13
Dec. 9	7-3/4-8	7-3/4	Sept. 22	8	8	6	13	13
16	7-3/4	7-3/4	Oct. 16	8-8-1/2	8-1/2	Dec. 4	12	12
			20	8-1/2	8-1/2			
1975--Jan. 6	7-1/4-7-3/4	7-3/4	Nov. 1	8-1/2-9-1/2	9-1/2	1982--July 20	11-1/2-12	11-1/2
10	7-1/4-7-3/4	7-1/4	3	9-1/2	9-1/2	23	11-1/2	11-1/2
24	7-1/4	7-1/4				Aug. 2	11-11-1/2	11
Feb. 5	6-3/4-7-1/4	6-3/4	1979--July 20	10	10	3	11	11
7	6-3/4	6-3/4	Aug. 17	10-10-1/2	10-1/2	16	10-1/2	10-1/2
Mar. 10	6-1/4-6-3/4	6-1/4	20	10-1/2	10-1/2	27	10-10-1/2	10
14	6-1/4	6-1/4	Sept. 19	10-1/2-11	11	30	10	10
May 16	6-6-1/4	6	21	11	11	Oct. 12	9-1/2-10	9-1/2
23	6	6	Oct. 8	11-12	12	13	9-1/2	9-1/2
			10	12	12	Nov. 22	9-9-1/2	9
1976--Jan. 19	5-1/2-6	5-1/2				26	9	9
23	5-1/2	5-1/2	1980--Feb. 15	12-13	13	Dec. 14	8-1/2-9	9
Nov. 22	5-1/4-5-1/2	5-1/4	19	13	13	15	8-1/2-9	8-1/2
26	5-1/4	5-1/4	May 29	12-13	13	17	8-1/2	8-1/2
			30	12	12			
1977--Aug. 30	5-1/4-5-3/4	5-1/4	June 13	11-12	11	1984--Apr. 9	8-1/2-9	9
31	5-1/4-5-3/4	5-3/4	16	11	11			
Sept. 2	5-3/4	5-3/4	July 28	10-11	10			
Oct. 26	6	6	29	10	10			
			Sept. 26	11	11			
1978--Jan. 9	6-6-1/2	6-1/2	Nov. 17	12	12			
20	6-1/2	6-1/2	Dec. 5	12-13	13			
May 11	6-1/2-7	7	8	13	13	In effect		
12	7	7				Apr. 30, 1984	9	9

Source: *Fed. Res. Bull.* 1984b:A6.

[a]Applicable to advances when exceptional circumstances or practices involve only a particular depository institution and to advances when an institution is under sustained liquidity pressures. See section 201.3(b)(2) of Regulation A.

[b]Rates for short-term adjustment credit. In 1980 and 1981, the Federal Reserve applied a surcharge to short-term adjustment credit borrowings by institutions with deposits of $500 mil. or more that had borrowed in successive weeks or in more than 4 weeks in a calendar quarter. A 3% surcharge was in effect from Mar. 17, 1980, through May 7, 1980. There was no surcharge until Nov. 17, 1980, when a 2% surcharge was adopted and was subsequently raised to 3% on Dec. 5, 1980, and to 4% on May 5, 1981. The surcharge was reduced to 3% effective Sept. 22, 1981, and to 2% effective Oct. 12. As of Oct. 1, the formula for applying the surcharge was changed from a calendar quarter to a moving 13-week period. The surcharge was eliminated on Nov. 17, 1981.

Table 10.4. Effect of DI borrowing on reserves

Federal Reserve Bank

	Debit		Credit	
Loans		$1 mil.	D.I. reserves	$1 mil.

DI

	Debit		Credit	
Reserves		$1 mil.	Borrowing from Fed	$1 mil.

exchange, as do checks. In the case of a check, the payer takes the initiative. In the case of an acceptance, the initiative is taken by the payee. The draft created orders the buyer, or more likely the buyer's bank, to pay a certain sum, typically in connection with some export transaction. A draft drawn on a bank is more readily acceptable than one drawn on a business firm, explaining why banks are usually designated as the drawees in the instrument. The importer pays the bank a service charge for accepting the draft and covers its face value. Upon acceptance, the draft is known as a banker's acceptance.

A facsimile of a banker's acceptance is shown in Figure 10.1. It is drawn on the Fifth National Bank of Boston by an Australian wool exporter, A. J. Ashton, under conditions laid down in a letter of credit. The bank's stamp of acceptance is visible across the face. By having the acceptance payable to the order of the Boston bank instead of the exporter, the bank gains control over all the shipping documents it releases to the importer. The Australian exporter is paid the discounted value of the draft, since the wool is shipped before payment.

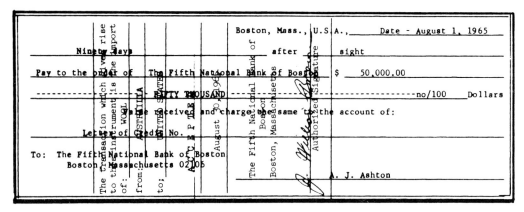

10.1. A banker's acceptance. (McCarthy 1975:46)

In the case of acceptances and two other assets (federal agency obligations and government securities), a distinction is made between "bought outright" and "held under repurchase agreement." The repurchase agreement ("repo") is a buy-sell arrangement between the Fed and securities dealers (including dealers in acceptances). The dealers make commitments for buying back the instrument, usu-

Table 10.5. Reserve effect of Fed repurchase agreement for bankers' acceptances

Federal Reserve Bank			
Debit		Credit	
Bankers' acceptances	$1 mil.	DI reserves	$1 mil.

DI			
Debit		Credit	
Reserves	$1 mil.	Deposits	$1 mil.

ally within 15 days. For them, it is a "reverse repo." In effect, the dealers are getting short-term loans. The Federal Reserve Bank of New York, which conducts all open-market operations, buys bankers' acceptances for its own account (rather than the System account). Since the dealer deposits the check in a commercial bank, DIs gain reserves at the Fed (see Table 10.5). As Table 10.1 shows, the Fed owned no acceptances outright but held $426 bil. bought under repurchase agreement as of the end of May 1984 (line 6). One reason for the discontinuance of outright purchase (in 1977) was the highly developed nature of the secondary market for acceptances. Fed purchases and sales were no longer required for support (Hervey 1983:25).

FEDERAL AGENCY OBLIGATIONS   Since 1971 Banks have been authorized to buy federal agency obligations outright, thus widening the base of open-market operations. These are securities issued by federal agencies primarily involved in the government's farm and home lending programs. They are direct obligations of the agencies, although in some cases the securities may also be guaranteed by the U.S. government. In 1977 the FOMC restricted System Open-Market Account purchases to agencies that were not eligible to borrow from the Federal Financing Bank. This bank began operations in 1974 (Fed, New York 1981:9). The mechanics of reserve creation are the same as for bankers' acceptances.

The Fed carries on all its open-market operations (which include bankers' acceptances and federal agency and U.S. government securities) through approved dealers. They number 36 (mainly located in New York), of which one-third are commercial banks. The proceeds of a sale to the Fed are deposited in the dealer's commercial bank. It makes a difference to excess reserves whether the dealer replenishes an inventory by a purchase from a commercial bank or from another member of the nonbank public. The dealer's deposit in the commercial bank declines to its original level (before sale to the Fed) when buying the security from a commercial bank. In this way, total depository reserves represent an increase in excess reserves, since deposits and therefore required reserves have not increased. Table 10.6 depicts the reserve effects of a Fed purchase when the primary seller is a bank (transactions 1 and 2). On the other hand, when the dealer replenishes inventory by buying a security from a fellow bank depositor while the dealer's deposit goes down, some other depositor's deposit goes up by the same amount (it replaces transaction 1 dealer deposits). It is as if transaction 2 did not take place. In this case, required reserves increase, and DI excess reserves go up by less than the increase in their legal reserves.

Table 10.6.   Fed open-market purchase when the primary seller is a bank

Federal Reserve Bank

Debit		Credit	
(1) Federal agency securities	$1 mil.	(1) DI reserves	$1 mil.

DI

Debit		Credit	
(1) Reserves	$1 mil.	(1) Dealer deposits	$1 mil.
(2) Federal agency securities	-$1 mil.	(2) Dealer deposits	-$1 mil.
		Net change	0

U.S. GOVERNMENT SECURITIES   U.S. government securities are the largest and best known Fed assets and the main vehicle for open-market operations. Securities are carried on the books at their maturity value. Bills, certificates, etc., are distinctions based on the maturity of the obligation. Treasury bills have maturities of three months, six months, and one year and are sold at a discount. Certificates also have maturities of less than one year but, unlike bills, they carry an interest coupon. Notes have maturities running from one to ten years, and bonds generally have longer maturities. Most marketable U.S. government securities are in book-entry form. Computer entries at the Fed and Treasury replace paper certificates (Fed, New York 1981:7). By 1986 this will be true of all government securities (Martin 1985:15–16). Special certificates are issued when the Treasury borrows directly from the Banks. Such borrowing is infrequent, with no amounts being shown in Table 10.1. When this does take place, it is because the Treasury is running short just before a tax date. Note 1 to "total" on line 12 needs further explanation. The reference is to government securities loaned to dealers, made to facilitate their delivery of securities. The Fed has other dealers' securities as collateral.

FED FLOAT   In Table 10.1, line 16 (cash items in process of collection) minus line 27 (deferred availability cash items) constitutes Fed float as discussed in Chapter 9. At the end of May 1984 the total was $1.4 bil.

BANK PREMISES   The imposing edifices occupied by the Banks and their branch offices had a value of $553 mil. at the end of May 1984 (line 17, Table 10.1). This is after estimated depreciation.

OTHER ASSETS   Assets denominated in foreign currencies include those acquired through "swap" drawings. The Fed swaps dollars for a line of credit on foreign central banks. Increases in line 18 of Table 10.1 are thus accompanied by a corresponding increase in line 24 (foreign deposits). The "all other" assets category is a miscellany including accrued interest (interest earned but not yet collected) on government securities and other interest-bearing assets.

ALLOCATING ASSETS   Table 10.1 is a consolidation of the balance sheets of the 12 Banks. Allocation formulas are then necessary for dividing assets acquired for the System. Gold certificate credits are assigned on the basis of distribution of Federal Reserve notes and government and federal agency securities on the basis of the capital account at the 12 Banks.

FEDERAL RESERVE NOTES   Federal Reserve notes are the largest single item on the liability side of the statement (line 21, Table 10.1). All Federal Reserve notes in circulation are included—those held by DIs and the Treasury plus the private nonbank sector. Notes held in the Banks' own vaults are not counted. DI reserves are debited and Federal Reserve notes are credited when DIs withdraw currency to pay out to their depositors (see Table 10.7). Entries are reversed when currency is redeposited in DIs.

DEPOSITS   Deposit accounts affecting DI reserve deposits are those of the

Table 10.7. Effect of currency withdrawals on reserves

	Federal Reserve Bank	
Debit	Credit	
	(1) DI deposits	-$1 mil.
	(1) Federal Reserve notes	$1 mil.

	DI		
Debit		Credit	
(1) Vault cash	$1 mil.		
(1) DI reserve deposits	-$1 mil.		
(2) Vault cash	-$1 mil.	(2) Deposits	-$1 mil.

Treasury, foreign central banks and governments (foreign deposits), and miscellaneous accounts (other deposits). Included in the latter are international organizations such as the IMF, the Treasury's Exchange Stabilization Fund, and some U.S. government agency accounts, including the Post Office.

The way Treasury deposits affect DI reserves is shown in Table 10.8. A payment to the Treasury (taxes, bond purchases) will build up its tax and loan account in DIs (primarily commercial banks) and reduce private deposits. When Treasury deposits are transferred to the Bank prior to Treasury disbursement, DI reserves are debited and Treasury deposits credited. The guide to reserve effects is to keep one's eye on the check. When checks drawn on DIs are deposited in the Fed, member bank reserves will be debited and the depositor's account will be credited.

Table 10.8. Effect of Treasury deposits on reserves

	Federal Reserve Bank	
Debit	Credit	
	(2) Treasury deposits	$1 mil.
	(2) DI reserve deposits	-$1 mil.

	DI		
Debit		Credit	
		(1) Tax and loan account	$1 mil.
		(1) Private deposits	-$1 mil.
(2) Reserves at Fed	-$1 mil.	(2) Tax and loan account	-$1 mil.

OTHER LIABILITIES   Other liability accounts include accrued discount on securities (the difference between the maturity value and the price paid by the Fed) and accrued dividend (the future liability for 6% dividend payments on Bank stock). Accrued discount on securities compensates for listing the maturity value of government securities on the asset side when this is higher than market value.

CAPITAL ACCOUNTS   Capital paid in is the purchase of Bank stock equal to 3% of member bank and surplus accounts. Such purchases have an equal and opposite effect on member bank reserves (Table 10.9). The capital accounts belong to mem-

Table 10.9. Member bank purchase of Federal Reserve Bank stock

	Federal Reserve Bank	
Debit	Credit	
	Member bank reserve	
	deposits	-$1 mil.
	Capital paid in	$1 mil.

	Member bank		
Debit		Credit	
Federal Reserve Bank			
stock	$1 mil.		
Reserves	-$1 mil.		

ber banks, so this is one place in the Fed statement where, since 1980, DIs do not replace member banks.

Bank surplus represents the plowing back of net earnings by the Fed. End-of-year figures would show capital paid in (line 30, Table 10.1) and surplus (line 31) to be equal (see, e.g., FRB 1983a:215). This is not accidental. Since 1964 the Board has specified this equal relationship. At the end of the year, any net earnings remaining after dividends and additions to surplus equal to changes in paid-in capital are turned over to the Treasury (line 23) under the guise of an interest payment on Federal Reserve notes outstanding. The value of other capital accounts in line 32 is zero at the end of the year. At other times, however (as shown in Table 10.1), the account will contain earnings to be transferred later to dividends (line 28) or to the Treasury (line 23).

The final item shown in Table 10.1 is not part of the balance sheet but a memorandum item indicating that as of the end of May 1984 the Federal Reserve Bank of New York held $114.5 bil. of U.S. government securities in custody for foreign and international accounts. This amount has implications for the government securities market. First, it shows that a considerable amount of interest is paid to nonresidents, since the debt is not owed entirely to ourselves. Second, purchases by foreign central banks has the effect of strengthening the government securities market. The dollars acquired by foreign central banks in support operations (when the U.S. dollar was weak vis-à-vis foreign currencies) were reinvested in U.S. government securities, with the Fed acting as custodial agent.

The Federal Reserve note statement below the balance sheet spells out the collateral held against Federal Reserve notes outstanding. This archaic reminder of more extensive reserve requirements shows government securities as the main collateral. One never has to worry about the collateral requirement being met because increases in Federal Reserve notes necessarily increase eligible assets.

Fed discretion

Of the many influences on reserve deposits, only open-market operations (transactions in acceptances, U.S. agency securities, U.S. government securities) qualify as an outright policy instrument. Loans have a mixed character. In part, they represent Fed discretion. The Fed sets the discount rate and controls access to the discount window, shutting the window (diplomatically, of course) when it questions the borrower's motives. On the other hand, DIs must approach the discount window before the Fed can take action.

All other factors influencing reserves reflect the initiative of other players. The Treasury influences reserves through its gold policy and deposit account. Foreign deposits are at the discretion of the foreign sector. The public exerts an influence via its demand for currency. Member banks affect reserves by their capital subscriptions. Vicissitudes of weather, strikes, equipment, etc., explain variations in float.

For the conduct of policy, the Fed must first forecast and offset these other factors of change (defensive behavior) before it can exercise active discretion (dynamic behavior).

Introducing Treasury monetary accounts

A broader context for discussing DI reserves results from integrating Treasury monetary accounts (gold, silver, Treasury currency) with Fed accounts. Now we are able to explain DI reserves, a broader concept than member reserve deposits. For such estimation it is necessary to know total currency holdings of member banks, i.e., holdings of Treasury currency in addition to Federal Reserve notes.

Regularly published in the *Federal Reserve Bulletin* is a table, Reserve Balances of Depository Institutions and Reserve Bank Credit, formerly entitled factors affecting member bank reserves (see Table 10.10). In factors supplying reserves, four main categories are shown: reserve bank credit, gold stock, SDRs certificate account, and Treasury currency outstanding. Reserve bank credit is a generic heading for the interest-earning assets of the Fed plus float. Gold stock replaces gold certificates with the consolidation of the Treasury gold account with Fed holdings of gold certificates. Treasury currency outstanding replaces the previous item of "coin."

The gold stock (line 12) shown in Table 10.10 refers to the Treasury gold stock. The terms "monetary gold stock" and "total gold stock" of the United States have been synonymous since December 1974. At that time the ESF gold holdings were monetized. Monetization means that the Treasury increases its Fed account

Table 10.10. Factors affecting reserve funds	
Factors	Monthly averages of daily figures, Feb. 1984
Supplying reserve funds	*($ mil.)*
1 Reserve Bank credit	166,904
2 U.S. government securities	148,137
3 Bought outright	148,137
4 Held under repurchase agreements	0
5 Federal agency obligations	8,573
6 Bought outright	8,573
7 Held under repurchase agreements	0
8 Acceptances	0
9 Loans	588
10 Float	1,100
11 Other Federal Reserve assets	8,506
12 Gold stock	11,118
13 Special drawing rights certificate account	4,618
14 Treasury currency outstanding	15,813
Absorbing reserve funds	
15 Currency in circulation	167,179
16 Treasury cash holdings	485
Deposits, other than reserve balances, with Federal Reserve Banks	
17 Treasury	4,669
18 Foreign	214
19 Service-related balances and adjustments	1,452
20 Other	549
21 Other Federal Reserve liabilities and capital	5,492
22 Reserve balances with Federal Reserve Banks	18,414
Deriving total reserves	
23 Total vault cash	22,269
24 Vault cash used to satisfy reserve requirements	17,951
25 Surplus vault cash	4,318
26 Total reserves	36,365
27 Required reserves	35,423
28 Excess reserve balances at Reserve Banks	942
29 Total borrowings at Reserve Banks	567
30 Seasonal borrowings at Reserve Banks	103
31 Extended credit at Reserve Banks	5
Source: *Fed. Res. Bull.* 1984f:A4-A5.	
Note: For more detailed information see notes to tables in source.	

by issuing gold certificates. While such monetization made gold a part of the monetary gold stock, gold can be in that stock without being monetized. This was the case again until December 1974. The Treasury held some gold (besides ESF holdings) against which gold certificates had not been issued. Such gold was included in the monetary gold stock on the left-hand side and in Treasury cash holdings (line 16) on the reserve-absorbing strip of Table 10.10.

Treasury currency outstanding (line 14) on the reserve-supplying strip was easier to understand when the Treasury held silver bullion (metal in noncoin form) against silver certificates outstanding. The physical asset in the Treasury currency monetary account was distinct from the paper liability. But even then, the asset side of this account contained items that also appeared on the liability side. The best example might be U.S. notes, whose legal authority goes back to the Civil War period. To the extent that they are not lost or destroyed, the liability for $323 mil. of such notes will correspond to a similar amount shown on the asset side. Similarly, coins issued by the Treasury will have identical entries on the asset and liability side.

The widening of the currency concept beyond the Fed's holdings means that the absorbing side of the balance sheet must be correspondingly expanded. In the place of Federal Reserve notes, we substitute currency in circulation (paper currency and coin held outside the Treasury and the Fed) and introduce a new category, Treasury cash holdings (TCH).

Line 22 in Table 10.10 brings us to the residual value of reserve balances with the Fed, which corresponds to the category of DI deposits (line 22, Table 10.1), less required clearing balances and other adjustments, line 19). The additional lines in Table 10.10 convert reserve balances with the Fed into a total reserve concept (line 26) by adding on line 24, vault cash used to satisfy reserve requirements. If vault cash of DIs is subtracted from currency in circulation, it provides a measure of currency in the hands of the public. Remaining lines in the table detail excess reserve balances at the Fed and also give amounts of borrowings. Such borrowing contributes to total reserves. Another reserve concept, free reserves, is derived by subtracting borrowings from total reserves.

Summarizing all the factors supplying and absorbing reserves, the reserve equation takes the following form:

$$
\begin{aligned}
DIRES &= DEP + VC \\
&= GSEC + FAS + A + L + F + OA + GS + SDR + TCO \\
&\quad - (CIP + TCH + TD + FD + OD + CA)
\end{aligned}
$$

where $DIRES$ = DI reserves
$\quad DEP$ = reserve deposits
$\quad VC$ = vault cash
$\quad GSEC$ = government securities
$\quad FAS$ = federal agency securities
$\quad A$ = bankers' acceptances
$\quad L$ = loans to DIs
$\quad F$ = float
$\quad OA$ = other assets
$\quad GS$ = gold stock

SDR = special drawing rights
TCO = treasury currency outstanding
CIP = cash in the hands of the public
TCH = treasury cash holdings
TD = treasury deposits
FD = foreign deposits
OD = other deposits
CA = capital accounts

The change in DI reserves equals the sum of change in factors supplying reserves minus the sum of change in factors absorbing reserves.

The monetary base

We have already introduced the monetary base in Chapter 6 but not in full balance sheet terms. Instead of factors supplying and absorbing reserves, the terminology now is "uses and sources of the monetary base." As in the rearranged balance sheet shown in Table 10.11, uses of the monetary base include DI reserves and a former factor absorbing reserves, CIP. The remaining factors absorbing reserves are transferred to the sources side where they are offsets to the factors supplying reserves. The terminology of sources and uses differs from its previous meaning when it was applied to a decision-making sector (with sources on the right-hand side and uses on the left-hand side). Now the context is a "market" with the sources indicating the supply of the monetary base and uses indicating the demand for the monetary base.

Table 10.11. Monetary base balance sheet, Feb. 1984 (averages of daily figures, in $ bil.)

Sources of the base		Uses of the base	
Reserve Bank credit outstanding:			
U.S. government securities	$148.1	DI reserves	$ 36.4
Federal agency securities	8.6		
Bankers acceptances	0		
Loans	0.6		
Other Federal Reserve assets	1.1	Currency in the hands	
Float	8.5	of the public	149.2
Gold stock	11.1		
Special drawing rights	4.6		
Treasury currency outstanding	15.8		
Total	$198.4		
Less:			
Treasury cash holdings	- 0.5		
Treasury deposits	- 4.7		
Foreign deposits	- 0.2		
Other deposits	- 0.5		
Other Federal Reserve			
liabilities and capital	- 5.5		
Required clearing balance	- 1.4		
Sources of the base total	$185.6	Uses of the base total	$185.6

Source: Table 10.10.

A modification of the monetary base (adjusted monetary base) allows for changes in reserve requirements over time. When reserve requirement ratios change, either because legal reserve ratios are changed or deposits are shifted between deposit categories subject to different reserve requirements, the effective size of the monetary base is altered. Lower average reserve requirements are equivalent to the Fed pumping more reserves into the system. The Federal Reserve Bank of St. Louis has for some time published a reserve adjustment magnitude, which is added on to the source base to get the adjusted monetary base. On the uses of the base side of the statement, adjusted reserves replace reserves. The Fed also publishes an adjustment for changes in reserve requirements (see the monthly table in the *Fed. Res. Bull.*, various issues). The two reserve series differ because of different methods used to seasonally adjust the series, differences in the methods used to account for vault cash, and the lack of adjustment in the Fed series for zero reserve requirements against money market deposit accounts (Gilbert 1983:16–25).

Summary

The basis of money creation and credit expansion by DIs is the high-powered money supplied by the Fed. This chapter begins by explaining DI reserve deposits at the Fed. The remaining items on the Fed balance sheet (Table 10.1) identify the relevant factors. Only these items can affect reserve deposits. It is thus easy to expose error in an understanding of the determinants; e.g., if one said that personal saving influences reserve deposits, we can see that this is incorrect, since personal saving is not an entry on the balance sheet. Or if one said that holding checking accounts in DIs is a factor, this again would be incorrect.

The next step is to move from an explanation of DI reserve deposits to an explanation of DI reserves. This means being able to explain the VC holdings of the DIs. To do this, the monetary accounts of the Treasury must be introduced and consolidated with the Fed statement. Gold replaced gold certificates, Treasury currency outstanding replaced coin. Treasury cash holdings are added to the factors absorbing reserves. Factors supplying and absorbing reserves are regularly published in this consolidated form. Unfortunately, as illustrated in Table 10.10, two separate *Federal Reserve Bulletin* tables have to be integrated to explain reserves.

The transition to the balance sheet for the monetary base is a simple one, with the offsetting of factors supplying reserves with factors absorbing reserves except for CIP. The uses of the monetary base on the right-hand side of the statement now consist of DI reserves and CIP. Adding a reserve adjustment magnitude to both sides gives a second version of the monetary base, the adjusted monetary base.

Review questions

1. Describe the Fed balance sheet and how it can be used to explain DI reserve deposits.

2. How do we move from a financial statement explaining DI reserve deposits to a financial statement explaining reserves?

3. How do we move from a financial statement explaining DI reserves to a financial statement explaining the monetary base?

4. What is the reserve equation?

5. By means of T accounts, show the effects of an increase in (a) currency in the hands of the public, (b) Treasury deposits, (c) open-market Fed purchases, (d) gold auction sales on DI reserves.

6. What types of borrowing are permitted by the Fed?

7. Studying the tables of this chapter, what are recent magnitudes of DI reserves, the Fed discount rate, Fed government security holdings, Treasury deposits, the monetary base, currency in circulation, currency in the hands of the public?

11

Tools and targets
of monetary policy

In Chapter 10 we discussed the determination of the monetary base. Influencing the monetary base, or depository institution (DI) reserves, is crucial to carrying out monetary policy. Here we turn to the instruments available to the Fed for influencing reserves. The instruments of policymaking go beyond the quantitative instruments of Chapter 10 to include selective instruments. Ultimately, the Fed wishes to influence economic activity, but it does this indirectly by affecting a series of operational and intermediate targets. Figure 11.1 provides a brief introduction to monetary policy.

Means and ends

Two different types of instruments are distinguished: general or quantitative controls and selective or qualitative controls. The former affect the volume of legal and required reserves (thus the volume of excess reserves, which is the difference between legal and required). Selective controls affect specific categories of sources and uses of DI funds, which is why they are so called.

The Fed varies its instruments to reach operational targets; these are the financial variables most sensitive to changes in the instruments. As shown in the second box, the Fed has two alternative strategies it can follow. It can attempt to control money market conditions as reflected in DI borrowing, the federal funds rate, or other interest rates. The alternative strategy is to control some reserve aggregate such as reserves or the monetary base.

The operational targets are designed in turn to influence intermediate targets or monetary indicators (third box). These are financial variables that have an identifiable relation with economic activity. Again we suggest two alternative strategies that the Fed could follow. As shown on the left-hand side of the box, market interest yields could be controlled. The Treasury bill rate (interest yield on short-term government securities) may be the key rate. Monetary aggregates are the alternative targets. These include narrowly defined money ($M1$) and broadly defined money ($M2$).

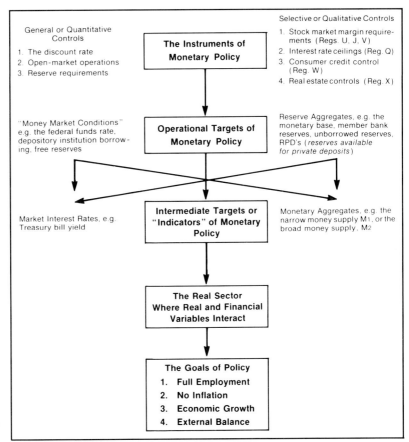

General or Quantitative
Controls

1. The discount rate
2. Open-market operations
3. Reserve requirements

Selective or Qualitative Controls

1. Stock market margin requirements (Regs. U, J, V)
2. Interest rate ceilings (Reg. Q)
3. Consumer credit control
   (Reg. W)
4. Real estate controls (Reg. X)

**The Instruments of
Monetary Policy**

"Money Market Conditions"
e.g. the federal funds rate,
depository institution borrowing, free reserves

**Operational Targets of
Monetary Policy**

Reserve Aggregates, e.g. the
monetary base, member bank
reserves, unborrowed reserves,
RPD's (*reserves available
for private deposits*)

Market Interest Rates, e.g.
Treasury bill yield

**Intermediate Targets or
"Indicators" of Monetary
Policy**

Monetary Aggregates, e.g. the
narrow money supply M1, or the
broad money supply, M2

**The Real Sector
Where Real and Financial
Variables Interact**

The Goals of Policy
1. **Full Employment**
2. **No Inflation**
3. **Economic Growth**
4. **External Balance**

11.1.
The way monetary
policy works.

An emphasis on the left-hand side, most notably keeping the federal funds rate or the Treasury bill rate at a certain level, is not necessarily inconsistent with controlling reserves and the monetary targets on the right-hand side (the crossed arrows in Fig. 11.1 suggest this). The lower the interest rate aimed at, the greater must the amount of reserves provided be and the greater the monetary aggregates. The difference, however, is in what is the means and what is the end.

The effect of the Fed on the real economy is indirect. The variables in the first three boxes are financial variables. The real economy is affected by the intermediate targets, not directly by the exercise of instruments (the first box). For this reason monetary policy is to be contrasted with fiscal policy (tax-expenditure policies of the Treasury). The latter have a direct effect on the real economy because taxes and expenditures have a direct effect on income, sales, and production (the real variables).

The financial variables affected by the Fed interact with the nonfinancial variables, output and spending. Enough interaction takes place among the set of real (nonfinancial) variables to fill a course in macroeconomics. When we talk about investment multipliers, for example, we are talking about the impact that an exogenous (unexplained) increase in investment has on income via its effect on consumption. A $1 increase in investment will have a greater than $1 effect on income because it leads to more household income, which in turn leads to more spending, and so on. Such increase in income can also induce investment so that investment and income interact.

In a course in monetary economics we wish to understand the effect of the financial variables (influenced by Fed policy) on the nonfinancial variables. The way these variables exert this effect is called the transmission mechanism or the channels of monetary influence.

Each strategy sees the transmission mechanism in a different light. A "money market conditions" approach fancies the interest rate as the key linkage variable. Low interest rates encourage investment, which starts off the multiplier process. In addition, low interest rates may have a wealth effect. The lower the interest rate, the greater the value the market places on the right to a given amount of income from a financial instrument. Thus, for example, the market will value the right to a regular income of $1 at $10 when the market interest rate is 10%. Should the market rate fall to 5%, the market value will rise to $20. The owner of the credit instrument will be that much richer and will spend income more freely. However, the choice of reserves or the monetary base as the strategic variable implies the quantity of money as the linkage variable. When the public holds more money than it desires for expenditure purposes, it will spend the excess, causing the gross national product to increase.

The final box lists the ultimate goals of monetary policy. The Fed wishes to avoid inflation and achieve full employment. The goal of economic growth is related to full employment except that it emphasizes a growth in investment so that productive capacity can increase. Another goal has to do with the nation's balance of payments (external equilibrium). The Fed wishes to minimize the deficit in the balance of payments. Just what the balance of payments is and what can be done about a deficit will be treated in Chapters 23 and 24.

Quantitative controls

DISCOUNT MECHANISM   The discount rate is the oldest instrument of general control and the only one discussed in the original Federal Reserve Act of 1913. The preamble to the act reads: "To provide for the establishment of Federal Reserve Banks, to furnish an elastic currency, to afford means of rediscounting commercial paper, to establish a more effective supervision of banking in the United States, and for other purposes." Behind this preamble are the difficulties that beset the National Banking System. More hand-to-hand money was required during crop-moving seasons but was not forthcoming because the note issue was tied to government bonds. A decline in the public debt after the Civil War meant less collateral for national bank notes. Bank credit was also inelastic (even if borrowers chose checking accounts rather than currency) because of the inflexibility of the monetary base. The problem was particularly acute when financial panic hit New York City. Reserves gravitated to New York because of interest paid on interbank deposits. When New York banks were losing gold to local depositors, outlying banks found it impossible to borrow, let alone cash in their deposits. The financial crisis of 1907 was the most notable of many. It led to the appointment of the National Monetary Commission (known as the Aldrich Commission after Senator Aldrich, the chairman) whose findings in turn spawned the Federal Reserve Act.

The protagonists in the legislative battle (Congressman Carter Glass of Virginia is the best known name) envisioned a central bank that would provide for flexibility in bank credit and the note issue. The New York banks were de facto central banks, but they did not function like a bank of last resort was supposed to function. As profit-making banks, they strove to be fully "loaned-up," leaving no slack for emergency lending to other banks. President Wilson, sitting in his study recuperating from pneumonia and flanked by major protagonists of the legislation, applauded the elasticity feature. (One of the better films on the Fed, produced by the Federal Reserve Bank of Cleveland, reenacts this historic signing.) When the demand for currency increases, banks will go to the Fed and rediscount the promissory notes of their customers who are securing Federal Reserve notes. When seasonal demand for currency abates, currency will flow back to the banks.

Initially, the bank customer was seen as discounting a promissory note based on the legitimate needs of trade. The borrower receives an amount less than the face value of the note. The bank takes the paper to its Federal Reserve Bank for rediscount. The amount of reserves or currency obtained would also be less than the face value of the promissory note. Since the rediscount rate was likely to be less than the discount rate, the bank would be credited with a larger sum than the bank borrower.

The automatic way the note issue got its backing caught the president's fancy. The Federal Reserve note had to be backed by at least 40% in gold and the rest in eligible paper. The Federal Reserve Act reflected contemporary banking theory expressed in the "real bills" doctrine. As long as banks made productive loans that gave rise to eligible paper, the loans would be self-liquidating and no harm could come to the banking system.

Very quickly, however, the character of the Fed changed. In 1916 the Fed began lending to member banks on the basis of their own promissory notes secured by government securities and eligible paper. Such advances had several advantages for the borrowing bank. The borrower-customer did not have to know that the bank had made a parallel trip to the Fed. The promissory note could be written for the specific amount of funds desired by the bank. However, it was not until 1933 that advances were granted the same maximum maturity of 90 days enjoyed by discounted paper.

The eligibility of government securities as collateral for advances marked a transition to a government bond–based monetary system. The continued expansion in the public debt avoided the earlier problems of collateral. The current dominance of open-market operations carried on in government securities underscores the return to a bond-based monetary system, originally ushered in by the National Banking Acts of the Civil War period.

The real bills doctrine was further eroded in the emergency situation of the 1930s. With a scarcity of eligible paper, the Glass-Steagall Act of 1932 allowed the Banks to make loans to member banks secured to the satisfaction of the Banks (Fed, Philadelphia 1964:11). This act also made the issuance of currency easier by adding government securities to the list of assets eligible as collateral for Federal Reserve notes. In 1933 Bank notes were authorized (but never issued), backed solely by government securities.

At such a time of widespread bank failures, all inhibitions on Bank lending should have been removed (apart from carrying on more vigorous open-market operations). The Banks and Congress deserve a large share of the blame for the Great Depression. Whether banks did in fact lack eligible paper is challenged in a monumental study by Friedman and Schwartz. Moreover, banks owned substantial amounts of government securities that could have provided collateral for their advances. The truth of the matter is that the Banks feared for their own solvency (gold was a required reserve against Federal Reserve notes and deposit liabilities) if they fulfilled their lender-of-last-resort function (Friedman and Schwartz 1963:11,405).

The importance of loans dropped off after the early 1930s, not recovering until the early 1950s (see Fig. 11.2), but they have never approached their importance in the first 20 years of the system. Exceptions are 1974, when member bank borrowings exceeded $3 bil. in the fourth quarter of the year, and 1984, when Continental Illinois bank borrowing rose to $7 bil. in August (not shown in Fig. 11.2).

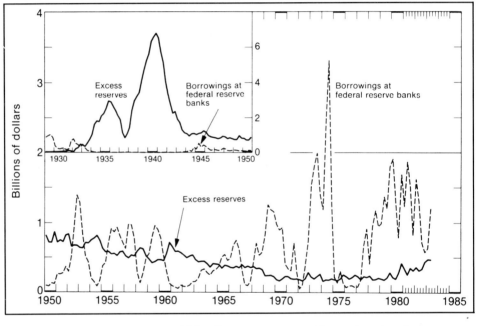

11.2. Excess reserves and borrowings (quarterly averages of daily figures). (FRB 1983d:3)

The desired price effect of raising the discount rate and tightening loan standards at the discount window is to have banks pay off their indebtedness to the Fed and charge higher interest rates to their customers, who are expected to reduce their borrowings. But customers may borrow more and banks may increase their borrowing at a time when the discount rate is increasing and borrow less when it falls. This is because banks respond to the spread between the discount rate and other short-term rates. Since short-term rates go up faster and fall faster than the discount rate, borrowing from the discount window tends to run in a counterdirection to changes in the rate.

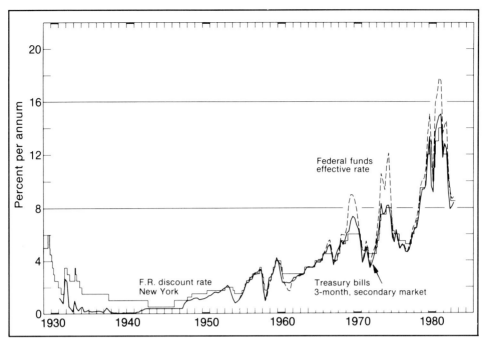

11.3. Short-term interest rates, money market. (FRB 1983d:98)

Figures 11.3 and 11.4 show the movement in the discount rate, compared with the Treasury bill and federal funds rates, and the relationship between the interest differential on federal funds and the discount rate and the level of discounts and advances. Figure 11.3 shows that until 1952 the discount rate was a penalty rate, being consistently above the Treasury bill rate. Variations in the rate and the interest spread as indicated by comparison with Figure 11.2 were ineffective in influencing borrowings. Banks could consistently shun the discount window be-

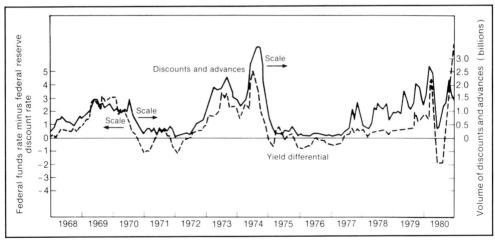

11.4. Relationship between the volume of discounts and advances and the incentive to borrow. (Lloyd B. Thomas, Jr., *Money, Banking, and Economic Activity*, 2nd ed., ©1982, p. 257. Reprinted by permission of Prentice-Hall, Inc., Englewood Cliffs, N.J.)

cause of their large holdings of excess reserves. After 1952 a positive relation is noted between the discount rate and borrowing. Figures 11.3 and 11.4 suggest that this positive relation is to be explained by the interest differential. Borrowing increases when market rates (Treasury bills, federal funds) rise more than the discount rate, with the reverse being true when market rates fall relative to the discount rate. This held true even when a surcharge on the discount rate was imposed in 1980–81 (Sellon and Seibert 1982:3–18).

The influence of market interest rates on DI borrowing from the Fed belies the formal categories of permissible short-term and long-term borrowing outlined in Chapter 10. Evidently market interest rates are much more relevant than sanctioned borrowing (e.g., for seasonal reasons). This suspicion is reinforced by the Fed policy of forcing banks to the discount window by restraining the growth in unborrowed reserves (see Ch. 12). The view that the discount mechanism provides a safety valve for open-market operations is thereby threatened. If banks are forced to the discount window by such operations, causing the federal funds rate to jump, it is black humor to say that they have a friend at the Fed.

The discount rate may have a signaling role apart from its intended effect on member bank borrowing. This is referred to as the announcement effect. By raising the discount rate, the Fed is signaling the financial community that higher interest rates are on the way. By generating expectations of this kind, the Fed can achieve higher interest rates at less cost in terms of direct intervention. In theory, borrowers and banks will now take the supply side in financial markets, selling off securities in anticipation of higher interest rates. Market prices fall and market yields rise.

The problem with the announcement effect is one of misinterpretation. First, the public may have more confidence in the Fed's forecast than its effectiveness in combating expected economic trouble. Thus a higher discount rate may lead to just the kind of behavior the Fed is trying to discourage. The sale of securities by would-be borrowers, which succeeds in raising interest rates, may be for the purpose of buying ahead to beat price increases. Second (except in isolated instances such as 1978 when the discount rate increase was a clear signal of a firm antiinflation policy), the discount rate generally follows market rates, so the change may be no indication of a policy change (Mayer et al. 1984:376–77).

The Depository Institutions Deregulation and Monetary Control Act of 1980 (DIDMCA) broadened discount window access to all DIs. Thrift institution borrowing has generally been confined to borrowing under the extended credit program. (When thrifts were under financial pressure in 1981–82, they borrowed from both the Fed and the Federal Home Loan Banks.)

RESERVE REQUIREMENTS   The function of reserve requirements is to control the money supply (as originally discussed in Ch. 6). Raising reserve requirements will restrict the lending ability of DIs. Expressed in T-account form, excess reserves decline from $0.8 mil. to $0.6 mil. when average reserve requirements are doubled from 10 to 20% (see Table 11.1). In terms of the money multiplier formula of Chapter 6, the effect is to reduce the size of the multiplier by increasing the value of r.

The modern era of reserve requirements begins in 1936 when as a result of the Banking Act of 1935 the Fed was permitted to vary reserve requirements. Details

Table 11.1. Excess reserves before and after an increase in reserve requirements (r)			
Debit		**Credit**	
Before (r: 10%)		Deposits	$2 mil.
Reserves	$ 1 mil.		
Required reserves	.2 mil.		
Excess reserves	.8 mil.		
Loans	1 mil.		
After (r: 20%)			
Required reserves	.4 mil.		
Excess reserves	.6 mil.		

on changes in reserve requirements from 1917 to the present are given in a regularly published table (see FRB 1983a:236–39). Reserve requirements were used in a restrictive way in 1936–37 and 1942–51. The Fed acted as it did in 1936–37 because it feared the expansionary effects of gold inflows on the reserve base. In the wartime period, Fed support of the government securities market through open-market operations meant massive increases in the monetary base. Requirements were raised to the maximum, with supplementary reserve requirements added in 1948. Thinking in terms of the money equation, $M = mB$, the Fed attempted to reduce m as an offset to wartime increases in the monetary base B.

Since the early 1950s, average reserve requirements on total deposits have fallen steadily. In addition to lower reserve requirements on demand deposits, a major reason has been the increased importance of time deposits. Average reserve requirements were revised downward in 1972 to compensate for the reduction of float when regional check-processing centers were established. The departure of banks from the system until 1980 probably made the Fed reluctant to use reserve requirements for monetary control. (The bluntness of the instrument – having to change the percentage requirements by 0.5% – is given as an argument against the use of reserve requirements. In this age of computers the argument is specious.)

The new structure of reserve requirements introduced by DIDMCA enhanced Fed control over the narrowly defined money stock ($M1$) consisting of currency, demand deposits, and other transactions accounts. Nominal reserves could no longer turn into a large volume of effective reserves by banks leaving the system and becoming subject to lower nonmember reserve requirements. Shifts between member and nonmember bank checkable deposits in a similar way would not affect excess reserves. Finally, shifts between transactions accounts included in $M1$ and personal time and savings deposits included in $M2$ have less impact on $M1$. The initial reduction in $M1$ when deposits are shifted frees reserves, since personal time and savings deposits are nonreservable. Expansion on the basis of excess reserves then restores $M1$. Previously, leakages in $M1$ resulted from reserve requirements against such time and savings deposits.

However, control over the broader aggregates ($M2$ and $M3$) may be weakened (Sellon 1984:9–10) because reserve requirements have either been lowered or eliminated on many of the components. Shifts into $M2$ and $M3$ components take on significance with multiple targeting. Since the mid-1970s the Fed has set targets for a variety of monetary aggregates (see Ch. 12). In 1982 and 1983 the primary target $M1$ was deemphasized because of problems with its interpretation. Focusing on the so-called nontransactions accounts is warranted because many components (e.g., money market funds) may serve as means of payments. Moreover, increases in $M2$ and $M3$ finance a credit expansion. The importance of DI lending in understanding economic activity has been stressed in Chapter 2.

Reserve requirements take on more importance when the operational target is reserves rather than interest rates. In the latter case the supply curve of money does not play an independent role in determining the money stock. As will be discussed in Chapter 12, the supply curve can be considered to be horizontal, paralleling the horizontal supply of reserves by the Fed at the targeted federal rate. When, instead, reserves are targeted, the supply of money will be a positively sloping curve that can be shifted to the left by raising reserve requirements. The effect will be a reduction in the money supply.

Similarly, the discount rate plays a more dynamic role in monetary management under a reserve-targeting strategy (Meek 1982:105). A rise or fall in the discount rate is now accompanied by a corresponding change in the federal funds rate rather than a narrowing of the spread with the discount rate, the latter being the result of stabilizing the federal funds rate under an interest rate target.

The regulatory move from lagged reserve requirements (LRR) to contemporaneous reserve requirements (CRR) in 1984 was intended to improve the monetary control process. The reasoning is that banks have short horizons (the grasshopper rather than the ant) and do not respond to reserve pressure with a two-week lag but will feel it with only two days to adjust reserves (see Ch. 6). But as long as the discount window is open and there is no penalty rate, banks would seem as likely to borrow under CRR as under LRR. Pressure to liquidate assets and curtail the money stock will be no greater now than before. If anything, forecasting required and excess reserves and the implementation of monetary policy have become more difficult for the New York Fed (Sternlight 1985:43–46).

Falling reserve requirements have their implications for the distribution of profits between DIs and the Fed (Thomas 1979:286–87). Higher reserve requirements entail increases in the monetary base consistent with larger required reserves. This is accomplished by the Fed purchasing government securities. At the same time, higher reserve requirements result in less DI profits per dollar of deposits.

A "wrong" interpretation of the relation between reserve requirements and profits underscores the "right" way to view the mechanics of deposit expansion. The misunderstanding runs this way. Higher reserve requirements mean larger bank deposits at the Fed, greater Fed security purchases, and thus greater profitability. Therefore, higher reserve requirements make the increase in the monetary base possible and are responsible for increased Fed profits. The reader does not have to be reminded that the acquisition of securities by the Fed increases DI reserve deposits. Periodically, however, the Fed finds it necessary to remind bankers that this is how the system works. The Banks do not acquire assets with the deposits provided by DIs (see *Fed. Res. Bull.* 1940:99–100; Nichols 1977:7–8).

OPEN-MARKET OPERATIONS   The hit and miss way that open-market operations developed illustrates the learning process. What we now take for granted was not understood at the time the Federal Reserve System was established. The Federal Reserve Act contained no provisions for coordinated open-market operations. The act authorizes open-market operations by individual Banks, but until 1922–23 they were conducted for the sake of bank earnings rather than as a means of influencing reserves (Klise 1955:225ff). It is not going too far to say that initially the Banks (mistakenly) saw themselves as lending the pooled reserves provided by banks joining the system. When the reserve effect was understood, an effort at coordination of open-market operations resulted in establishment of an open-market committee that administered the open-market investment account. For several years the committee represented five Banks only, but the smaller Banks insistence on representation led to reorganization in 1930 with representatives of all the Banks. The present-day Federal Open-Market Committee (FOMC) was established by the banking acts of 1933 and 1935. In 1942 the Federal Reserve Bank of New York was given permanent representation, with rotation for the other 11 Banks. By tradition the chair of the Board is chair of the committee; the President of the New York Bank is the vice-chair.

Federal Open-Market Committee

The focus of the media on the FOMC has made its procedures and deliberations well known not only to professional Fed watchers but beyond. The committee currently meets eight times a year. Attending the meetings in an ornate boardroom in Washington are not only 5 Board members and 7 Bank representatives but also the presidents (or their alternates) of the remaining 5 Banks. They participate in the discussion but do not vote. Senior research officers of the Banks and the Board also attend (mainly economists) as shown in Figure 11.5 (for a full discussion see Meek 1982:Ch. 5). Economic presentations and advice are mainly the preserve of Board economists. This gives the chairman of the Board and the FOMC power to influence the flow of economic information in his favor (Pierce 1984:690).

Those in the room are aware of influences from outside. An economist who served as a Board member has estimated the distribution of power both within and without the Federal Reserve System, 1965–73 (Maisel 1973:Ch. 6). Within the

---

FEDERAL OPEN MARKET COMMITTEE

PAUL A. VOLCKER, *Chairman*   ANTHONY M. SOLOMON, *Vice Chairman*

EDWARD G. BOEHNE	LYLE E. GRAMLEY	J. CHARLES PARTEE
ROBERT H. BOYKIN	KAREN N. HORN	EMMETT J. RICE
E. GERALD CORRIGAN	PRESTON MARTIN	NANCY H. TEETERS
		HENRY C. WALLICH

STEPHEN H. AXILROD, *Staff Director and Secretary*   RICHARD G. DAVIS, *Associate Economist*
NORMAND R.V. BERNARD, *Assistant Secretary*   DONALD L. KOHN, *Associate Economist*
NANCY M. STEELE, *Deputy Assistant Secretary*   RICHARD W. LANG, *Associate Economist*
MICHAEL BRADFIELD, *General Counsel*   DAVID E. LINDSEY, *Associate Economist*
JAMES H. OLTMAN, *Deputy General Counsel*   MICHAEL J. PRELL, *Associate Economist*
JAMES L. KICHLINE, *Economist*   CHARLES J. SIEGMAN, *Associate Economist*
EDWIN M. TRUMAN, *Economist (International)*   GARY H. STERN, *Associate Economist*
JOSEPH E. BURNS, *Associate Economist*   JOSEPH S. ZEISEL, *Associate Economist*
JOHN M. DAVIS, *Associate Economist*

PETER D. STERNLIGHT, *Manager for Domestic Operations, System Open Market Account*
SAM Y. CROSS, *Manager for Foreign Operations, System Open Market Account*

11.5. Federal Open Market Committee. (*Fed. Res. Bull.* 1985b:A72)

system the chairman is assigned the most power. It is not just a question of first among equals on the Board. The chairman's voice is more persuasive than other governors. The Fed staff is given 25% of power right behind the chairman. In practice, however, because predictions have a wide band of error, the Board's confidence in recommendations is limited.

Despite its nominal independence, the Fed is well aware of White House and congressional pressures; the Board reads the daily newspapers. In 1979 the chairman made clear his support for higher interest rates in line with the president's antiinflationary stance. The Fed responded to Democrat pressures in 1972, an election year, to expand money growth (Pierce 1984:723). (But see pp. 366–67 for conflicting opinions.) Between Congress and the administration, 60% of the outside influence is accounted for. The public, financial interests, foreign interests, and regulatory agencies in that order explain the remaining 40% (see Table 11.2) (the politics of the Fed are discussed further in Ch. 13).

The purpose of the meetings is to appraise the economic situation and to draw up a directive to the manager of the Open-Market Account (also referred to as the Open-Market desk), who operates out of the New York Bank and is instructed as to the broad objectives of policy, including the desired ranges of $M1$, $M2$, and the federal funds rate. If the monetary aggregates go beyond their ranges, the federal funds rate is to be allowed to vary to offset the growth in the aggregates (Meek 1982:Ch. 5).

At the FOMC meeting held March 26–27, 1984, the operational instructions concluding the domestic policy directive to the Federal Reserve Bank of New York were as follows: "In the short run the Committee seeks to maintain pressures on bank reserve positions judged to be consistent with growth in M1, M2, and M3 at annual rates of around 6½, 8, and 8½ percent, respectively, during the period from March to June. Greater reserve restraint would be acceptable in the event of more substantial growth of the monetary aggregates, while somewhat lesser restraint might be acceptable if growth of the monetary aggregates slowed significantly; in either case, such a change would be considered in the context of appraisals of the continuing strength of the business expansion, inflationary pressures, and

Table 11.2. Degree of monetary power 1965-73	
The Federal Reserve System	*(%)*
The chairman	45
The staff of the Board and Federal Open-Market Committee	25
The other governors	20
Federal Reserve Banks	10
Outside influences	
The Administration	
President	
Treasury	
Council of Economic Advisers	35
Office of Management and Budget	
All other nonfinancial	
The Congress	
House and Senate committees on banking	
Joint Economic Committee	25
Senate Finance Committee	
House Ways and Means Committee	
The public directly	
Unorganized	
Press	20
Economists	
Lobbyists	
The financial interests	
Banks	
S&Ls	10
Stockbrokers	
Other	
Foreign interests	5
Other regulatory agencies	
Federal Deposit Insurance Corporation	
Comptroller	5
Federal Home Loan Bank Board	
Securities and Exchange Commission	

Source: Maisel 1973:110. Reproduced from *Managing the Dollar* by Sherman J. Maisel, by permission of W. W. Norton & Company, Inc. Copyright © 1973 by Sherman J. Maisel.

the rate of credit growth" (*Fed. Res. Bull.* 1984c:513). The instructions close with the proviso that the chairman may call for committee consultation if it appears to the manager for domestic operations (also called the manager of the open-market account) that the federal funds rate will fall outside the 7.5–11.5% range.

The committee's growth ranges for the broader aggregates, fourth quarter 1983 to the fourth quarter 1984 were 6–9% (*M*2 and *M*3), and were 4–8% for *M*1. The March 1984 instructions leaned toward the upper half of the ranges and thus suggest relative easing of restraint. One Board member voted against the directive because of too much restraint. Two voted against the directive because they preferred one calling for more reserve restraint and a lower growth in *M*1. The vote was 9–3, with all the Bank presidents siding with the remaining four Board members.

The delay in the publication of FOMC deliberations is a matter of controversy. A summary of the above meeting of March 1984 was released after the following FOMC meeting in May. It was then published in the *Federal Reserve Bulletin* for June 1984 and was subsequently published in the annual report. The more than one month of delay has been defended because of time necessary for the staff to prepare and the committee to approve the policy record. The more substantive argument is that it avoids the abrupt effects that might follow a more immediate announcement of significant changes, permitting decisions to be implemented in an orderly and sometimes conditional manner (Meek 1982:26). The conclusions of one study are that there are economic advantages to more immediate disclosure (Erb 1978:12). A recent study, however, concludes that immediate disclosure of FOMC policy directives after 1979 would not have been of much value to market participants in projecting near-term levels of interest rates (O'Brien 1984:151–64).

Criticism regularly comes from a private "shadow open-market committee" that holds meetings several times a year coinciding with the FOMC meetings. At these meetings, monetarist recommendations are made and publicized without fear of announcement effects. In September 1984 they called for slowing down money growth and criticized the Fed for bailing out failing banks.

VIEW FROM THE TRADING DESK   The FOMC directive is implemented by the manager for domestic operations working out of the eighth floor trading room of the Federal Reserve Bank of New York. First, the directive is translated into reserve paths. This discussion of reserve targeting is deferred until Chapter 12, since it is part of the theory of Fed policy. Here we wish to take a look at a day at the Fed trading desk and the vast information network that this entails. The activities of the trading room have a daily rhythm (Fig. 11.6).

The officers of the trading desk begin the day at 9 A.M. with a series of meetings with government securities dealers. This gives them a feel of the market, a concern of the desk first given expression in a classic study by Roosa (1956) and now updated by Meek. The information flow is one-way at the briefing. The Fed officers are poker faced in the spirit of FOMC deliberations. This secretiveness has spawned a new profession of Fed watchers who try to divine the Fed's intentions. Being a graduate of the Fed is almost a must for becoming a money market economist (Meek 1982:146).

At 10 A.M. the figures for the previous day's total and unborrowed reserves

9:00 A.M.

Discussing the market with dealers.

10:00

Reviewing market developments in the trading room.

10:15

Consulting the Treasury by phone about its balances at the Reserve Banks.

10:45

Developing a plan of action for the day.

11.6. A day at the trading desk. (Meek 1982:128–29)

are reviewed, and the research staff projects the reserve outlook for the current week. Float and currency in the hands of the public will receive special attention in the projection. If a holiday is coming up, allowance will be made for sharp increases in float. The manager or an associate discusses with the Treasury how it plans to manage its Fed accounts in the days ahead. This provides information on the likely behavior of Treasury deposits.

By 11 A.M. a program of open-market operations has been formulated. The 11:15 A.M. telephone conference call informs one of the Bank presidents serving on the FOMC and the staff at the Board of plans for the day. Soon after the call, the go-around begins. Traders sit at individual desks before a large board displaying bid quotations for each of the traded issues outstanding. Each trader faces a

11:15

Conferring by phone with FOMC representatives on the day's program.

11:45

Buying bills from dealers in a market go round.

4:15P.M.

Sizing up market reactions to the Friday money supply data.

Photos by Arthur Krasinsky

telephone console with direct lines to federal fund brokers, the money desks of major New York banks, primary securities dealers and senior officers of the Bank's securities and foreign departments. The buttons on the telephone turrets light up as traders make their calls to dealers (Meek 1982:100, 139).

Offers to buy or sell and commitments on repurchase agreements RPs (temporary injection of reserves) or the reverse short-term arrangement of matched sales and purchases (MSPs — temporarily absorbing reserves) are secured from all dealers before the Fed notifies dealers of acceptances and rejections. By 1:30 P.M. reserves have been determined for the day and the accountants and clerks in adjoining rooms do the paper work. On Thursday (Friday, briefly, before 1984) at 4:15 P.M. the Board releases estimates of the money supply ending on Wednesday of the previous week, and the New York Bank studies financial market reaction to the release of these figures.

Selective controls

Selective controls are distinguished from general controls by being imposed on specific uses and sources of funds. One of these has already been discussed (regulation Q in Ch. 8). By setting interest rate ceilings, it controls the amount of funds that banks can raise through savings deposits. Another selective control is margin requirements. Controls on consumer and real estate credit will also be discussed. Certain buyers may be subsidized when they buy a home, or corporations may be restricted in the amount of securities they can sell. Here the impact is on the borrower. Finally, the control may center on the financial instrument. The selective controls we shall discuss fall into this category: margin requirements relating to corporate stock, Regulation Q relating to savings deposits in commercial banks, consumer credit control being based on installment sales contracts, and mortgage regulation on the mortgage instrument. Since the lenders and borrowers are linked by the financial instrument, the selective control is on both a use and a source of funds.

MARGIN REQUIREMENTS   The statutory authorization for margin requirements was the Securities Exchange Act of 1934. Four Fed regulations apply to use of credit for purchasing or carrying securities. Brokers and dealers are regulated by Regulation T, banks by Regulation U, and other lenders by Regulations G and X. Margin requirements apply to corporate stocks and bonds convertible into stocks registered on national exchanges or identified as over-the-counter margin stocks (FRB 1974:87). Margin requirements were the first selective control granted the Fed. Another first was the power to control organizations (brokers and dealers, nonbank lenders) outside the Federal Reserve System.

Margin refers to the portion of the market value of the stock that the borrower finances. Thus if the margin requirement is 60%, the buyer of the stock can only borrow 40% of its value. Table 11.3 shows the historical margin requirements on stocks.

Behind the passage of margin requirements were the calamitous events of the late 1920s and early 1930s — the stock market crash of October 1929 and the Great Depression. The stock market crash was attributed to excessive speculation fueled by bank borrowing. Inadequate margins on the part of borrower-speculators meant that their stocks were sold out with slight market declines, thus adding to selling pressures. Slim margin requirements (imposed by the banks before they became mandatory) made for easy financing of purchases, leading to sharp increases in stock market prices followed by the sharp decline in the fall of 1929. It was believed that the stock market crash was a major factor in the Great Depression, thus

Table 11.3. Margin requirements on stocks

Date of change, Apr. 1, 1936[a]	Percentage requirement (%)
Nov. 1, 1937	40
Feb. 5, 1945	50
July 5, 1945	75
Jan. 21, 1946	100
Feb. 1, 1947	75
Mar. 30, 1949	50
Jan. 17, 1951	75
Feb. 20, 1953	50
Jan. 4, 1955	60
Apr. 23, 1955	70
Jan. 16, 1958	50
Aug. 5, 1958	70
Oct. 16, 1958	90
July 28, 1960	70
July 10, 1962	50
Nov. 6, 1963	70
June 8, 1968	80
May 6, 1970	65
Dec. 6, 1971	55
Nov. 24, 1972	65
Jan. 3, 1974	50

Source: *Fed. Res. Bulls.*
[a]Prior to Apr. 1, 1936, a sliding scale was used, the amount of loan value depending on the extent to which the current market price had recovered from its lowest price for the 36 months preceding (Klise 1955:242).

increasing the clamor for margin requirements.

The evidence is not strong that margin requirements have produced more stable stock prices (J. Cohen 1965a; Moore 1966:158ff.). This may be an instance of perverse "announcement effects." Higher margin requirements will be interpreted as a forecast by the Fed of rising stock market prices, leading investors to buy *now*. The margin requirement has been at 50% for more than 10 years. Margin requirements may lead borrowers to misstate the purpose of their stock-secured loan. Such requirements do not apply to business loans, for example, meaning that a bank could lend in excess of the maximum loan value if the borrower stated the loan to be a nonpurpose loan. This would also weaken the relationship between changes in margin requirements and stock market behavior.

The flow-of-funds side of the debate is whether the stock market absorbs funds, thus depriving legitimate business of necessary finance. It is difficult to demonstrate, however, that funds are indeed absorbed in the stock market. Funds that flow in also flow out. The rapid turnover of money in stock market transactions means that a relatively small amount of financial balances can take care of a rising volume of dollar transactions. The classic analysis of this question, prompted by the rising stock market of the 1920s, is Machlup (1940); (J. Cohen 1965b:882ff.).

CONSUMER CREDIT CONTROLS   General controls may have specific sector effects requiring selective controls for their amelioration. On the other hand, a strong demand in one industrial sector may trigger inflationary prices. Again, selective controls might be in order; e.g., restrictive monetary policy via general instruments may have a discriminatory effect on housing finance and expenditures. Selective measures such as Regulation Q might then be a way of minimizing this effect. In the second case a strong demand for durables at a time when civilian production is being curtailed (e.g., World War II) had threatening implications for inflation. As a result, on August 9, 1941, an executive order of the president gave the Board of Governors the power to regulate consumer credit, and shortly thereafter Regulation W was issued. Minimum down payments were one-third, and installment contracts could not run for longer than a year. Consumer credit controls expired in November 1947 and were renewed in 1948–49 and during the Korean War (September 1950–May 1952). Under the terms of the Credit Control Act of 1969, the president can authorize the Board to control any and all extensions of credit (FRB 1974:90). As discussed in Chapter 18, the act was invoked in 1980 by President Carter.

Evidence on the effectiveness of consumer credit control in World War II is clouded by the curtailment of automobile and other durable goods production and simultaneous increases in consumer income. Consumer credit did indeed fall drastically (from $6 bil. in 1941 to $2 bil. in 1943), but these other factors could have been responsible. (The conditions required for selective controls to be effective are extensively discussed in Ch. 18.)

MORTGAGE CREDIT CONTROLS   Regulation X was issued in October 1950 during the Korean War for the purpose of reducing excess aggregate demand. This regulation no longer applies to mortgage credit but extends Regulations U, T, and V to certain borrowers and certain types of credit extensions not specifically covered by those regulations (see FRB 1978b:16).

Ordinarily, restrictive monetary policy has a dampening effect on the housing industry. But the Fed at this time was supporting the Treasury bond market, thus inhibiting conventional monetary policy. For this reason, minimum down payments for both new and existing homes were set as high as 50% on houses having a value higher than $24,000 (Klise 1955:244–45). Regulation X was thus a companion measure to Regulation W in its objective of curbing excess demand. When the Treasury reached its accord with the Fed in March 1951, the Fed's responsibility for maintaining the government bond market came to an end. Shortly thereafter interest rates rose sharply and residential mortgage credit declined (Guttentag 1975:51). To all intents and purposes, Regulation X expired in June 1952 when minimum down payments and maturity terms were relaxed (Klise 1955:245).

Summary

Working toward an understanding of Fed monetary policy, this chapter has dealt with the tools at the Fed's disposal. The major classes are variously contrasted as general and selective, quantitative and qualitative, indirect and direct, impersonal and personal.

General or quantitative controls are the more familiar tools, and among them open-market operations are the dominant instrument. The discount mechanism shares with open-market operations a reliance on U.S. government securities. The money supply is bond based, since both instruments are responsible for variations in the reserves of DIs. The irony is that the Federal Reserve Act was designed to divorce government bonds from the creation of high-powered money. This was a reaction to the National Banking Act under which national bank notes were collateraled by government securities, creating an inelasticity in the currency.

The discount mechanism has two distinct elements, the window and the rate. While the rate is clearly at the discretion of the Fed, this is not the case for resort to the window. When the private sector demand for credit is strong, DIs will increase their borrowing at the window despite increases in the discount rate, since it is the spread between the market rate and the discount rate that influences borrowing. On the other hand, the Fed may exercise discretion and force banks to resort to the discount window by restraining reserve growth through open-market sales. As discussed in Chapter 12, the intention is to reduce the rate of DI lending to the public. The "announcement effects" of the discount rate, separate from its cost-of-credit effect, may be perverse.

The third main quantitative instrument (reserve requirements) has been drastically altered by DIDMCA. Now uniform reserve requirements apply against transactions deposits of all DIs. This has improved control of the narrow money aggregate $M1$. However, the absence of requirements (or nominal requirements) against other deposit categories has reduced control of the wider $M2$ and $M3$ aggregates. Reserve requirements and the discount mechanism may have taken on greater significance when the proximate target of policy shifted from the federal funds rate to unborrowed reserves in 1979. As will be discussed in Chapter 12, however, it is questionable whether the federal funds rate has receded in importance, even as compared with the 1950s and 1960s when the money market conditions dominated policymaking. Contemporaneous reserve requirements that replaced lagged reserve requirements in 1984 have so far not improved monetary control.

The strategy of monetary policy centers around the trading desk of the Open-Market Account. Here government securities are bought and sold in accordance with directives from the FOMC. The desk is the hub for a vast information-gathering network.

The range of selective controls exercised by the Fed varies depending on how we define them. The least ambiguous way is to limit them to those that affect the magnitude of specific fund flows, i.e., sources of funds of borrowers and the corresponding uses of funds of lenders. Thus, raising down payment requirements and shortening loan maturities aims at restricting borrowing for consumer durable expenditures (Regulation W) or borrowing for home purchases (old Regulation X). Margin requirements (Regulations U, T, V, and the new X) have the same effect of increasing the down payment on stocks. A wider meaning for selective controls is to include those that affect the price or cost of a given fund flow. Thus Regulation Q limits the return on time deposits in commercial banks, and reserve requirements increase the cost to the bank of specific sources of funds.

The effectiveness of selective credit controls depends on maintenance of a one-to-one relation between specific kinds of spending and specific financial instruments (see Ch. 18).

Review questions

1. Distinguish between the quantitative and qualitative instruments of Fed policy.

2. Distinguish between instruments, operational targets, intermediate targets, and the ultimate goals of policy.

3. What is the leading instrument of monetary policy? How does the choice of operational targets (interest rates vs. reserves) affect the importance of the discount rate and reserve requirement as policy instruments?

4. How did the Depository Institutions Deregulation and Monetary Control Act of 1980 improve monetary control?

5. The discount mechanism has two separate arms: the rate itself and the discount window. Explain.

6. What are the weaknesses of the discount mechanism as a policy instrument?

7. What are the advantages of multiple targeting and target ranges from the standpoint of the Fed?

8. How is the FOMC policy directive arrived at and what is its significance?

9. Describe a day at the trading desk of the Federal Reserve Bank of New York.

10. Explain the rationale of selective controls. Identify the main types of selective controls that have been tried in the United States. Which are still in effect?

11. "The United States has a bond-based money supply." Do you agree with this statement?

12

Theory of monetary policy

The stage is now set for a discussion of the theory and strategy of policymaking. We now fill in the gaps between instruments and ultimate objectives. This means exploring the preference or social welfare function of the Fed. (Still other names are objective, disutility, and utility function.) Policy is carried on subject to the constraints imposed by the economy. The effects of different economic models must be considered together with the effects of economic policies carried on by other branches of government. The Fed reaches its goals by an indirect route. Policy instruments help to reach operational targets, and operational targets are the stepping stones to intermediate targets. This has been called a two-stage decision process. Intermediate targets in turn affect the economy. The Fed has been reporting its choice of monetary targets to Congress. Despite the recent emphasis on the monetary aggregates, the central question remains whether the Fed still inclines more toward money market conditions than the aggregates in making policy.

The immediate problems confronting the policymaker are taken up here. In a more fundamental way, for many reasons policymaking runs the risk of ineffectiveness. The remaining chapters in one way or another document the difficulties besetting central bankers.

The Fed's preference function

The ultimate targets of the Fed are full employment without inflation, economic growth, and equilibrium in the balance of payments. These are the better known goals associated with Fed policy. Maintaining orderly markets for government securities may be thought of either as a constraint on the Fed's seeking these goals or as another main goal.

The Fed tries to come as close as it can to its target values. This means it wishes to minimize deviations from these objectives. If the policymaker hits all targets, the deviations of outcomes (actual values) from target values will be zero as will disutility. The disutility (dissatisfaction) arising from missing targets may have a linear or quadratic relation to these deviations. In the first case, the disutility is in proportion to the miss, regardless of its size. In the second case, disutility increases by the square of the deviation. Larger deviations cause relatively more dissatisfaction than smaller ones. Examples of these functions follow:

$$DIS_t = F(P_t, U_t, BP_t, y_t) \tag{12.1}$$

where DIS_t = disutility in period t
$\quad\quad P_t$ = the price index in period t
$\quad\quad U_t$ = unemployment rate in period t
$\quad\quad BP_t$ = the balance of payments surplus in period t
$\quad\quad y_t$ = real output per capita in period t (economic growth)

Eq. 12.1 lists the goals of policy; Eqs. 12.2 and 12.3 express the disutility function in linear and quadratic form respectively:

$$DIS_t = w_1(P_t - P_t^*) + w_2(U_t - U_t^*) + w_3(BP_t - BP_t^*) + w_4(y_t - y_t^*) \tag{12.2}$$

$$DIS_t = w_1(P_t - P_t^*)^2 + w_2(U_t - U_t^*)^2 + w_3(BP_t - BP_t^*)^2 + w_4(y_t - y_t^*)^2 \tag{12.3}$$

The $w_1 \ldots w_4$ coefficients weigh the different objectives according to their varying importance for the policymaker. Inflation, for example, may be viewed as a more serious problem than unemployment so that w_1 has a higher value than w_2.

Eqs. 12.2 and 12.3 state that departures from targeted goals in either direction are equally unsatisfactory to the policymaker. But the policymaker will actually be less unhappy if the growth rate in income exceeds targeted values than if it falls short and, similarly, will prefer the unemployment rate to fall below the targeted value and the balance-of-payments surplus to grow. Symmetry in the social welfare function may obtain only for price changes or changes in interest rates (the latter measuring disorderly financial markets) (cf. Wood 1967:138). Eq. 12.4 takes account of these asymmetries, adds disorderly markets as a target, and now maximizes utility:

$$SAT = -w_1(P_t - P_t^*)^2 - w_2U_t + w_3BP_t + w_4y_t - w_5r^2t \tag{12.4}$$

where SAT = utility
$\quad\quad r^2t$ = change in interest rates in period t, squared

Now the policymaker's "happiness" declines with fluctuations either above or below targeted price changes, fluctuations in interest rates, and increases in the unemployment rate and goes up with a rise in real per capita income and the balance-of-payments surplus.

Policies are taken in an uncertain world. This means that the policymaker can never be sure as to how the economy works but must assign probabilities to alternative economic models, these probabilities being an estimate of the true state of nature. Examples are such obvious ones as the Keynesian and monetarist models. The former emphasizes the interest rate as the linkage between policy and the real sector; the latter emphasizes the quantity of money.

On the basis of these probabilities we can calculate the expected value of a given monetary policy, which will be the sum of probabilities of the different outcomes, each multiplied by the value of these outcomes. "Outcomes" are to be understood as the weighted sum of the actual (realized) values of the targeted variables. Expected values can be calculated in this way for every different policy (Culbertson 1968:401). Figure 12.1 describes the decision-making process given E possible economic models and M possible monetary policies. Within the cells of the matrix, p_i denotes the probabilities of a given economic model being the true one (they sum to 1 along the row), and the x_{mn} denote the outcomes from policy decisions. The summations on the right-hand side are the expected values of a given policy. One expected value may be higher than another (e.g., the expected value of M_2 may be higher than the expected value of M_1), but, nevertheless, a policymaker will choose M_1 because he is more comfortable with the riskiness of outcomes from M_1. So, in addition to the expected value of a given policy, the risk associated with that policy must be considered. Risk is measured by the distance of outcomes from their targeted value. One policymaker will follow a maximax rule, i.e., choose the policy that has the better best outcome. It also runs the risk of the worst possible outcome. A more conservative policymaker, on the other hand, will follow a minimax rule favoring the policy with the better worst outcome, which loses a chance for the best possible outcome. Their choices are dictated by disutility (loss) functions. The first policymaker will have a linear loss function—he will minimize the sum of the differences between the xs and the target values, x^*, with these differences weighted by the relative frequency of the outcomes (p_i): thus, $\sum_{i=1}^{2} p_i(x^* - x_i)$ for two outcomes. On the other hand, the second policymaker, who follows a minimax rule, has a quadratic loss function—she is minimizing the expected value of the squared deviation, $\sum_{i=1}^{2} p_i(x^* - x_i)^2$, giving a higher weight to the worst possible outcome (Culbertson 1968:403).

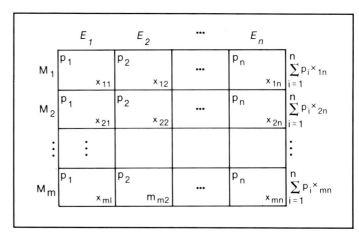

12.1. Monetary policy decisions in matrix form.

We can illustrate the difference in risk and risk preferences in a world consisting of two economic models and two policies. The first subscript to M in Table 12.1 indicates the policy, the second, the economic model. The x^* value is 100. The policymaker who is averse to risk and follows the minimax rule chooses the M_1

Table 12.1.	Estimating the riskiness of monetary policy				
Policy	Probability(p) (1)	$x^* - x$ (2)	$(x^* - x)^2$ (3)	$p(x^* - x)$ (4)	$p(x^* - x)^2$ (5)
M_{11}	0.70	40	1600	28	1120
M_{12}	0.30	35	1225	10.5	367.5
Total	1.00			38.5	1487.5
M_{21}	0.40	70	4900	28	1960
M_{22}	0.60	10	100	6	60
Total	1.00			34	2020

monetary policy. The values in col. 5 are the relevant ones for the quadratic loss function. Comparison of the values in this column shows that the sum of the squared deviations weighted by their probabilities is lower for M_1, 1487.5 as against 2020 for the M_2 policy. The policymaker with a linear loss function is interested in col. 4. The sum of the differences ($x^* - x$) weighted by their probabilities is 34 for M_2, less than the 38.5 associated with an M_1 policy; M_2 is then the policy chosen.

DIMENSIONS OF CHOICE   Besides evaluating the effects of different economic structures, the policymaker must reckon with many other interactions. The choice matrix goes beyond the two dimensions of Table 12.1. Perhaps the most obvious addition is fiscal policy. Table 12.2 illustrates a minimax strategy for monetary policy when Congress is responsible for different tax rates.

Table 12.2. A minimax strategy for alternative fiscal policies		
If		Then
Interest rate (r)	Tax rate (t)	Income deviation from target ($ bil.)
4%	10%	25 (high)
	12%	70 (low)
8%	10%	0
	12%	93 (low)
Source: Miller and Kaatz 1974:12.		

The instrumental variable for the Fed is the interest rate. It can set the interest rate at 4 or 8%. The tax rate (beyond the control of the Fed) can be either 10 or 12%. Which interest rate should the Fed select if it wishes to avoid the worst possible outcome? The final column tells us the outcomes in terms of missing the target income level. The worst possible outcome results if the interest rate is set at 8%. The target is missed on the low side by $93 bil. A minimax strategy will opt for a 4% interest rate rather than 8%.

If we distinguish debt management from fiscal policy, this introduces another variable. Debt management refers to the Treasury's borrowing, refunding, and debt retirement activities. We may think of such activities as affecting the nation's liquidity. The more short-term debt the Treasury issues, the more liquid the economy. Finally, there is the spectrum of political systems. The choice of monetary policy will be different whether the economy is market oriented or centrally directed. The matrix for monetary policy decisions is now of the order of $M_iF_jD_kE_nG_r$, where F = fiscal policy, D = debt management policy, E = economic models, G = the political systems, and the subscripts indicate that each variable has a range of possible values (Culbertson 1968:407).

This expanded matrix is meant to suggest the complexity of policymaking. The monetary policymaker's decision is but one of many policy decisions and must be adaptable to changing circumstances.

COUNTING INSTRUMENTS

One instrument, many goals   Differences in instruments and operational and intermediate targets and goals make for a range of monetary policies each uniquely different. The goals of policy could be the same, for example, but two policies are distinct if in one case open-market operations are the chief instrument and in the other, the discount rate.

Two strategies are open to the policymaker: employ one bundle of instruments, targets, etc., in reaching all the goals or, alternatively, employ as many bundles as there are goals. In the first case, the policymaker is optimizing, getting as close to desired objectives as possible in an overall way but missing the individual goals (targets) by various distances.

We can refer to the bundle of instruments and operational and intermediate targets as the instrument, since any means to a further end can be considered a policy instrument. In this section we shall speak of instruments and targets, the latter being the ultimate goals of policy.

In this approach, the instrument (say the money stock) responds to both the desired and actual target values. The latter in turn are explained by the economic model. For example, in a simple autoregressive model, lagged values of real income, prices, and fiscal policy as reflected in the budget deficit may influence current values of real income, prices, unemployment, and the balance of payments. The policymaker then responds to lagged values of the target variables. The optimizing equation, which attempts to minimize disutility (maximize utility) with respect to changes in the instrument (the money stock), then might have this appearance:

$$M_t = A_1y_L - A_2P_L - A_3DEF_L + A_4y^* + A_5P_t^* - A_6U_t^* - A_7BP_t^*$$

The Fed increases the money supply in response to real income changes (y_L) and higher targeted values for real income (y^*) and the price level (p^*). But the monetary increase is negatively related to past price changes (P_L), past increases in the government deficit (DEF_L), increases in the target level of unemployment (U_t^*), and increases in the desired balance-of-payments surplus (BP_t^*). (The L subscript stands for lagged values.) Accommodation to the higher transactions requirements of higher incomes and higher targeted values of prices explain the positive signs. Resistance to higher current prices and to the inflationary effects of larger government deficits and the promotion of larger balance-of-payments surpluses explain the negative signs. The negative sign for the unemployment target means that policy can be less inflationary with higher targets. The net change in the money stock is then going to be the net outcome of all these influences, with no hitting of any single target.

The expression can be simplified by showing the Fed as reacting to actual values of target variables. In this form, the functon is known as a reaction function. Thus:

$$M = a_1 y_L - a_2 P_L + a_3 U_L - a_4 BP_L$$

The as indicate the relative importance attached to the goals, since they show how much the money stock will change in response to each. In an imperfect world where the policymaker has to compromise, the ratio of these weights indicates the trade-off between targets. For example, the ratio of the weights for unemployment and price increases (a_3/a_2) would indicate what a 1% reduction in unemployment would be worth in terms of more inflation. If the a_3 coefficient was 9 and the a_2 coefficient 3, this would tell us that a 1% reduction in the unemployment was worth an increase of 3 points in the price index ($9a_3 = 3a_2$). It would take a 3-point increase in the price index for the Fed to keep the money stock constant when the unemployment rate goes up by 1%. (The latter increase would result in an increase in the money stock by 9; the price increase of 3% would cause the money stock to decline by 9.)

Equal instruments and targets   The above approach is to be contrasted with another that tries to meet all targets with a matching number of instruments. Assume that we have target values for real income and prices (or changes in these variables). The policy model might then consist of the following two equations (cf. Dernburg and McDougall 1972:382–86):

$$y^* = a_1 DEF + b_1 M \qquad P^* = a_2 DEF + b_2 M$$

The target values are on the left-hand side of the equations. The unknowns are the instrumental variables – the government deficit (*DEF*) and the money stock (*M*). The two equations solved simultaneously determine the appropriate size of the deficit and the money stock to reach the target values for income and the price level. The contrast between forecasting and policy models is sharp. In econometric (forecasting) models the goal (target) variables are endogenous and the policy variables are exogenous. In policy models their roles are reversed. The goal values are now exogenous, the policy values endogenously determined.

The simultaneity requirement demonstrates what happens when policies are uncoordinated. Suppose that the Treasury has its primary interest in the income level, which is currently below the target value. At the same time, the price level is at its target level (Dernburg and McDougall 1972:385–86). The Treasury will increase spending, thus increasing the deficit. But since the deficit also increases the price level, the monetary authorities who are primarily interested in price stability will contract *M*, thus causing *y* to decrease since *y* is also related to *M*. This inconsistency in policies is illustrated in recent U.S. history. Fiscal policy has been easy and monetary policy has been tight. It is as if the policymakers had one foot on the accelerator and one on the brake. Fiscal and monetary policies must be coordinated, with simultaneous decisions made as to the magnitudes of the targets and the instruments.

Unfortunately, while coordination of policies is a possibility (with various interagency committees in Washington having this express function), the independence requirement for the equations is not easily met. This is violated if it is possible to derive the right-hand side of the first equation by multiplying the right-hand side of the second equation by a constant. For example, suppose the coefficients of the two equations were as follows:

$$y^* = 10DEF + 6M \qquad P^* = 5DEF + 3M$$

Multiplying the right-hand side of the second equation by 2 produces the right-hand side of the first. In effect, we have one equation and not two. Whatever changes take place in the values of DEF and M, the values of y and P will change in some fixed proportion. The two targets cannot be set independently. Perhaps the well-known Phillips curve, which states a relationship between real income and prices (see Ch. 21), demonstrates the difficulty in real life of solving two independent equations whose respective targets are real income and inflation.

Model of Fed behavior

Our previous models did not spell out the relationship between instruments (in the narrow sense), operational targets, intermediate targets, and ultimate goals. The simple model now offered will attempt this, going back to the first approach of having one intermediate target and many goals.

Assuming a certain economic structure, monetary policy works by influencing economic behavior as portrayed by this structure. The model of Fed behavior begins with two equations—the preference function and the economic structure:

$$\text{Maximize } SAT = F_1(X - X^*) \tag{12.5}$$

$$\text{Subject to } X = F_2(M_L, A_L) \tag{12.6}$$

Eq. 12.5 states that the central bank maximizes its utility (SAT) by approaching as close as it can to a series of target values (such as full employment), represented by the single symbol X^*. Eq. 12.6 is a "bare bones" statement of the economic model. Outcomes (X) are explained by the intermediate target variable, the money stock (M_L), and all other determinants of economic activity (A_L). The A variable is sufficiently comprehensive that it includes other policy influences (such as fiscal policy) and exogenous variables as varied as the price of oil or the psychology of the household and business sectors. The L subscript allows for the lagged effects of changes in M and A variables. The view of the economy in Eq. 12.6 is monetarist. But the other major view (Keynesian) could replace it by substituting R for M, where R stands for the interest rate structure (cf. Lombra and Torto 1976:428–29). The central bank would now be seen as aiming at controlling the interest rate.

The operational targets of the federal funds rate and a reserve aggregate (as suggested in Ch. 11) are interlinked in the determination of the intermediate target. The intermediate money stock target in turn is set on the basis of the effects that money is supposed to have on the ultimate policy goals. The following additional relationships show the linkages between the money stock and the operational targets:

$$M_d = F_3(Y_L, \; R_L) \tag{12.7}$$

$$R = F_4(RFF_L) \tag{12.8}$$

$$RFF = F_5(TR_d, \; TR_s) \tag{12.9}$$

Eq. 12.7 states that the public's demand for money (M_D) depends on nominal income (Y_L) and the interest rate (R_L). This equation is the cornerstone of monetary theory and, recently, of monetary policy. On the pivotal role of the demand-for-money function in policymaking, see Maisel (1973:56–61) and Wallich (1978:222–23). The first variable (Y_L) will have a positive effect on the demand for money, since it is highly correlated with monetary transactions. On the other hand, when the interest rate increases, the opportunity cost of holding money balances increases and the public will wish to hold less. Measuring opportunity cost is straightforward when the means of payment pay no interest. It is less straightforward when checking accounts pay interest on negotiable order of withdrawal (NOW) accounts. In that case, the opportunity cost is the excess of open-market interest rates over the interest paid on money.

If we think of a demand-for-money curve negatively sloping with respect to the interest rate (it will be drawn later), fixing the interest rate should determine the demand for money. At a higher interest the demand for money will decline. The public succeeds in reducing money holdings by switching into depository institution (DI) time deposits. In this way, the demand for money determines the supply. This theoretical point of view (which underlies Fed policymaking) is referred to as the "new view of the money supply" (see Gramley and Chase 1965:1380ff.). Its weakness is its reliance on a shift into time deposits as interest rates (including rates on time deposits) advance or on repayment of bank debt. Holders of money can shift into other assets with higher interest rates. In these cases, the "hot potato" analogy seems to apply to money. The ownership of checking accounts will change with such transactions but not the quantity. With the two provisions about time deposits and DI debt, the public does not have discretion over the money supply as the theory alleges. With respect to DI debt, when loans are paid off, DIs can replace them with other assets, including open-market securities (cf. also J. Cohen 1967:119–22).

Eq. 12.8 makes the interest rate structure (to which the public responds) depend on an operational target—the federal funds rate. The interest rate structure could be represented by a single interest rate, typically the Treasury bill rate. The federal funds rate is the interbank borrowing rate for reserve deposits. The manager of the Open-Market Account monitors this rate continuously in an effort to control the money supply. Finally, the federal funds rate in Eq. 12.9 is determined by the demand for and supply of DI reserves.

The supply of total reserves (TR) is another operational target of the Fed. The supply side can be stated as the sum of nonborrowed reserves (NBR) and DI borrowings (L). These sum to the demand elements—bank demand for excess reserves (ER) and bank demand for required reserves (RR):

$$TR = NBR + L = ER + RR \tag{12.10}$$

The DI borrowings can be subtracted from the ER to yield free reserves (FR).

Substituting *FR* for *ER*, the equilibrium condition now reads:

$$NBR = FR + RR \qquad\qquad (12.11)$$

The Fed controls *NBR* by its open-market purchases. Thus we can add:

$$OMO = \Delta NBR \qquad\qquad (12.12)$$

Since open-market operations (*OMO*) are a flow, they influence the change in *NBR*. The model can be simplified if the Fed controls *TR* rather than *NBR*. Eqs. 12.10 and 12.11 can be omitted and Eq. 12.12 written as $OMO = \Delta TR$. The pros and cons of the appropriate reserve target are considered later.

DEFENSIVE VS. DYNAMIC BEHAVIOR   The Fed must run just to stay in the same place. It must offset all other influences on DI reserves before it can change them. The offsetting of other influences is the Fed's defensive behavior. The net change effected in nonborrowed reserves (in accordance with the Fed's "dial setting" for the money stock) is its dynamic behavior.

The factors supplying and absorbing reserves are discussed in Chapter 10. The reserve equation (in stock terms) was there stated as:

$$DIRES = DEP + VC = GSEC + FAS + A + L + F + OA + GS + SDR$$
$$+ TCO - (CIP + TCH + TD + FD + OD + CA)$$

Transposing the reserve (*DIRES*) and government securities terms (*GSEC* + *FAS*) and expressing the equation in flow terms,

$$OMO = \Delta GSEC + \Delta FAS = \overset{1000}{\Delta DIRES} - \overset{50}{\Delta A} - \overset{200}{\Delta L} - \overset{100}{\Delta F} - \overset{60}{\Delta OA} - \overset{0}{\Delta GS}$$

$$\overset{100}{- \Delta SDR} \overset{500}{- \Delta TCO} \overset{2000}{+ \Delta CIP} \overset{30}{+ \Delta TCH}$$

$$\overset{300}{+ \Delta TD} \overset{100}{+ \Delta FD} \overset{75}{+ \Delta OD} \overset{50}{+ \Delta CA}$$

We have placed some hypothetical values above the variables in the second equation. The negative values identify factors supplying reserves. The appropriate defensive action is an open-market sale. But the factors absorbing reserves identified by positive values call for open-market purchases. By summing the positive values and subtracting the negative values, the defensive actions of the Fed come to $1445. Above $\Delta DIRES$ we have the desired increase in member bank reserves of $1000. Thus total open-market purchases to reach the target value will amount to $2445. A similar exercise could have been carried on for *NBR* by substituting $\Delta DIRES - \Delta L$ for the $\Delta DIRES$ term on the right-hand side. Empirically, most open-market operations are defensive in nature.

THE FEDERAL FUNDS RATE: END OR MEANS?   The ostensible strategy of policymaking is to decide on the desired money stock, given long-term policy goals, and then set the federal funds rate accordingly (Eqs. 12.7 and 12.8). The federal funds rate requires a consistent growth in reserves. These are supplied by the manager of the Open-Market Account (Eqs. 12.9, 12.10, 12.12).

This is a demand-determined approach to both the money stock and bank reserves (Lombra and Torto 1976:432–33). The money stock, once an interest rate level is selected, is determined by the demand for money; the supply of reserves at this interest rate is determined by the reserves demanded to support the desired amount of money. The implication is that the supply of reserves by the Fed at the selected federal funds rate is a horizontal line. Let us say that the monetary authorities have a target value for the money stock of M^*, as shown in Figure 12.2A. (Instead of absolute values of reserves and money, the horizontal axis in Fig. 12.2 and subsequent figures can be taken to measure growth rates in these variables. It is more realistic to have the growth rate decline than to have this happen to dollar values.) For the public to desire to hold M^* quantity of money, the market rate of interest must be r^*. The federal funds rate consistent with r^* is given by the term-structure relation (Eq. 12.8). Thus we can specify an equilibrium RFF^* (Fig. 12.2B), which the Fed aims for by its open-market operations. We now must assume that the demand for reserves (given a constant multiplier) is some fraction of the demand for money. The bank's demand curve for reserves is related

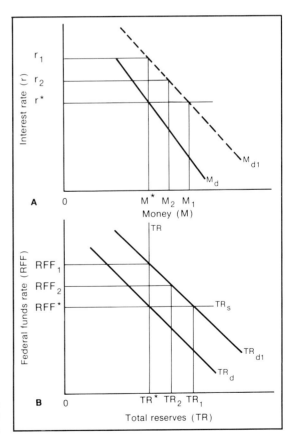

12.2. Demand vs. supply–determined approaches to money and bank reserves.

to both the federal funds rate and the demand for money. If the banks know the term-structure relation and have an idea as to the demand-for-money curve, for any *RFF* they could infer the demand for money and thus the appropriate amount of reserves. Given these assumptions, the demand for reserves will be some mirror image of the demand for money. We draw the demand for reserves so that the demand at *RFF** is sufficient to support *M**. In effect, the supply of reserves is perfectly elastic at *RFF**; the Fed supplies all that are necessary to keep the federal funds rate at *RFF** and thus, via the *r* and *RFF* relation, maintain the money stock at *M**.

In the supply-determined case, the supply of reserves is set independently of the federal funds rate, as depicted by the vertical *TR** curve (Fig. 12.2B). As drawn, the results for *RFF** are the same as before. The two cases part company, however, when we introduce an increase in the demand for money to M_{d1} and in reserves to TR_{d1}. Now, without a change in the targeted *RFF* value, the money stock will increase and so will the supply of reserves (to M_1 and TR_1 respectively) in Figures 12.2A and B. The Fed has apparently lost control of the money supply.

The Fed may have knowingly permitted this increase because it may be regarded as desirable, depending on the underlying reason for the shift in the demand curve. The demand for money may increase because of a rise in money income and thus in the transactions demand for money. In such a case, the Fed would like to restrain a potentially inflationary increase. On the other hand, the public may have become more uncertain about the future, leading to a greater demand for liquidity. Permitting more money in this case is not inflationary because an increase in the quantity is offset by a decrease in its velocity. A similar extenuating circumstance is an increase in financial transactions. Permitting interest rates to rise at such a time by controlling the money stock might have deflationary consequences (Maisel 1973:58–62).

The fundamental reason for restraining interest rate increases may be that the operational and intermediate targets of the Fed are money market conditions rather than monetary aggregates. Of the contrasting targets, the temptation is to say that the Fed leans to an interest rate target. Since 1979 this does not seem to have been the case, however. The target range has been so widened that staying within the range is no evidence for an interest rate target (Bryant 1983:95–99). In pursuing interest rate targets today (as many allege), the Fed would be following its oldest tradition. However, the truth may lie somewhere in between, with the Fed pursuing an eclectic monetary policy. In terms of Figure 12.1 the compromise is dictated by the infinity of economic models and potential strategies for the Fed. The Fed permits variation in both interest rates and the monetary aggregates.

This discussion of the reserve market has treated bank borrowing from the Fed (*L*) as if it were a fixed quantity. This cannot be so, however, because depository institutions (mainly commercial banks) will borrow more as the federal funds rate goes up. When this happens, assuming that the discount rate is unchanged, the inducement to borrow from the Fed increases. Introducing borrowed reserves means that we are now distinguishing between borrowed and nonborrowed reserves (Fig. 12.3).

The Fed supplies 0*N* nonborrowed reserves through open-market operations (as in Eq. 12.12). When the federal funds advance beyond the (fixed) discount rate

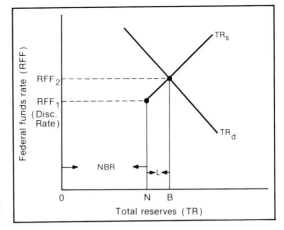

12.3. Introducing borrowed reserves.

at RFF_1, borrowing from the Fed begins and increases with increases in RFF as shown by the TR_s curve above the "kink." That is, the inducement to borrow is stronger (overcoming a reluctance to be in debt to the Fed), the greater the cost advantage of doing so. (When the discount rate is raised, the kink moves up so that with the same target for nonborrowed reserves the equilibrium federal funds rate rises, cutting back the amount of borrowed reserves.) Finally, at RFF_2, the supply of total reserves equals the demand. At equilibrium in the reserve market, total reserves are made up of NBR and L amounts of nonborrowed and borrowed reserves respectively.

The discussion of Figure 12.2 should not be taken as an endorsement of Fed theory. It lacks a supply-of-money function (based on the multiplier analyses of Ch. 6) and fails to relate the bank demand for reserves directly to the money stock.

In Figure 12.4A we have introduced a supply-of-money function. The money stock is now determined by the interaction of the supply and demand for money, not by the demand for money alone. If the money multiplier (m) is not responsive to the market interest structure (r), the money supply function is the vertical M_{s1} line. The supply of money is then a fixed multiple of the monetary base (mB).

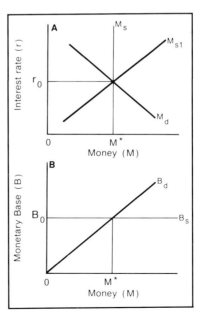

12.4. An alternative theory of money determination.

High-powered money (here the monetary base) is treated explicitly in Figure 12.4B. The supply is at the discretion of the Fed and is the horizontal B_s line. The demand for high-powered money (B_d) is now a function of the money stock (assuming a given value of m). The greater the money stock, the greater the demand for currency and reserves. Equilibrium is established when the demand for the monetary base is equal to the supply. This equality determines the money stock.

The M_{s1} curve in Figure 12.4A is based on a fixed value of m. As discussed in Chapter 6, the value of the m can be affected by many outside variables such as the market rate of interest. Assuming that banks keep less excess reserves the higher the interest rate, the supply curve of money will be positively sloping (the M_{s2} curve). The B_d curve in Figure 12.4B is based on the r interest rate of Figure 12.4A. If r increased because of an increase in the demand for money, desired excess reserves would decline, and the B_d curve would tilt downward (Fig. 12.5B). The greater value of m because of the increase in r means that less reserves are demanded for each level of the money stock. The tilt in the B_d curve coincides with a movement up the M_{s2} curve (Fig. 12.5A). Both sets of curves intersect at the M_2 quantity of money. An increase in the demand for money is responsible for the movement from M_d to M_{d1} (Fig. 12.5A), resulting in the movement up the M_{s2} curve and the downward tilt in the B_d curve. Thus there is an increase in the money supply from M_1 to M_2 without any increase in the supply of base money.

The advantages of introducing an M_s curve should now be apparent. A rise in the demand for money results in the money stock increasing without any growth in the monetary base. The demand for money affects the interest rate and thereby the value of m, $m = f(r)$. At higher interest rates the banking system is willing to acquire more assets and create more money.

Excess reserves are quantitatively unimportant, so we have to look elsewhere to explain the positive slope to the M_s curve. More of a slope will be introduced if the vertical scale in Figure 12.5B measures the "net source" base, which subtracts DI borrowings from the monetary base. Such borrowings are now incorporated in m by substituting the free reserves ratio (ratio of free reserves to demand deposits) for an excess reserves ratio in the multiplier formula. Borrowings will be more

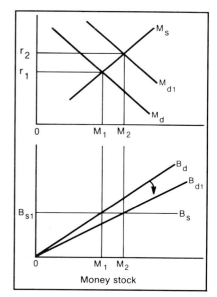

12.5. Introducing the supply-of-money curve: response to an increase in the demand for money.

responsive to market rates than excess reserves. The free reserves ratio declines with an increase in r, causing the m to increase in size as r rises. This imparts a positive slope to the M_{s2} curve. Simultaneously, the B_d curve is tilted downward as shown.

Choosing the reserve target

Many options are open to the Fed in choosing a reserve target. The requirement of a good operational target is controllability of the intermediate target, i.e., a stable relation between the two. Free or net borrowed reserves have the longest history as an operational target. This was the main target of the Fed in the 1950s and first half of the 1960s. (On this history, see Brunner and Meltzer 1965:197–209). Free reserves were seen as an indicator of the tightness of money. Less free reserves signaled less bank willingness to lend money in the same way that higher interest rates signaled a reduced willingness to borrow. This explains why it has been considered an indicator of money market conditions even though free reserves are the difference between two monetary aggregates: excess reserves and DI borrowings.

Free reserves can be a misleading signal of monetary tightness in the same way as movements in the federal funds rate. Assume that the Fed aims at a certain degree of monetary tightness and monitors the level of free reserves as an indicator. At the same time, the demand for credit is increasing. Banks borrow more from the Fed because of increased profitability. The Fed sees the level of free reserves declining; it interprets this as an unwanted increase in monetary tightness and supplies more reserves through open-market operations. This increases total bank reserves, the flow of credit, and the money supply. If such quantities determine economic activity (as critics allege), then free reserves fail as an indicator and thus as a policy target. It should be noted how easily free reserves could attain respectability. All the Fed has to do is keep an eye cocked on the demand for credit (cf. Knight 1970). Given an increase, it could decree a reduction in reserve availability by ordering a reduction in free reserves (Maisel 1973:83–84).

Free reserves fail as an instrument because of their endogeneity. They are determined not only by the Fed but by outside economic forces. In the context of policymaking, exogeneity is synonymous with discretion. Both interest rates and free reserves can vary because of forces on the demand-for-credit side rather than because of forces on the supply-of-credit side (controlled by the Fed).

Despite strong academic criticism of free reserves, money market conditions still dominated operational procedures until 1979. A minor departure was the adding of a so-called proviso clause to the Federal Open-Market Committee (FOMC) directive in 1966. The account manager was to aim at free reserves and money market conditions provided they did not conflict with the growth rate specified in the directive for some aggregate (e.g., bank credit) (Mayer et al. 1981:540–41). From 1972–75, at the initiative of Maisel (who served on the Federal Reserve Board 1965–72) (Maisel 1973:299–301) the operational target in the directive was reserves available for private deposits (RPD). Reserves kept against Treasury deposits and interbank deposits were subtracted from total reserves on the premise that the remainder (RPD) have a closer linkage with exogenous policymaking and economic activity. The volatility of this measure made it difficult to hit the target without sacrificing others such as the federal funds rate and monetary growth (Thomas 1979:310).

Targeting of the federal funds rate was succeeded in 1979 by the targeting of unborrowed reserves (Meek 1982:Ch. 6). A path for nonborrowed reserves on a week-to-week basis in the period between FOMC meetings is established by the joint deliberations of the Board staff and the New York Fed manager for domestic operations. This is how the FOMC directive is implemented. While open-market operations have nonborrowed reserves as their primary objective, the path cannot be estimated without estimating total reserves and borrowing at the Fed discount window. Total reserves are the sum of required and excess reserves. Estimates of required reserves are based on desired growth of money in the intermeeting period. Borrowing at the Fed discount window is estimated independently. Greater monetary restraint is achieved by forcing DIs to meet a larger fraction of their required reserves by borrowing. Such increased borrowing puts pressure on interest rates (see Fig. 12.3) leading to less expansion in money and credit. Subtracting targeted amounts of borrowing from estimated total reserves produces a weekly path for nonborrowed reserves. The path is continually revised on the basis of information received on money growth in past weeks. For example, stronger monetary growth than originally anticipated leads to upward revision of figures for borrowing given the maintenance of nonborrowed reserve targets.

The irony of targeting unborrowed reserves is that the more things change the more they are the same; for the use of the discount window in disciplining bank behavior restores the free reserves target to an earlier period. Increases in DI borrowing reduce free reserves and are expected to motivate DIs to tighten their lending policies. But targeting borrowed reserves instead of unborrowed reserves has the same effect of focusing on money market conditions. Since 1982, Fed policy has been interpreted as reverting to the targeting of the federal funds rate, a throwback to the policies of 1970–79. This allegedly is the result of the trading desk targeting borrowed reserves in response to the FOMC directive calling for more or less restraint. An increase in the demand for money and bank reserves, given the borrowed reserves target, results in an increase in nonborrowed reserves and a stabilization of the Fed funds rate (Gilbert 1985:13–21).

Reading the annual report submitted to the FOMC by the manager of the system open-market account (the report covers both Board and trading desk activities) leaves little doubt that central banking is an art rather than a science (Sternlight et al. 1984:39–56). The manager emphasizes the uncertainties and the need for flexibility and judgment rather than depending on mechanical procedures. Every element in policy implementation (monetary growth rates, factors influencing reserves other than open-market operations, excess reserves, discount window borrowing) poses forecasting problems. The setting of intermediate targets has similar problems.

Setting the intermediate targets

House Concurrent Resolution 133 (passed in 1975) required the chair of the Board to appear before congressional committees four times a year to announce projected growth ranges in the intermediate targets for the next four quarters. Under the Full Employment and Balanced Growth Act of 1978 (also called the

Humphrey-Hawkins Act), the Fed reports twice a year (see Auerbach 1982:344–45; Fed 1984f; Pierce 1984:692; Volcker 1984).

Ideally, the Fed would like to target transactions balances and rely on the velocity of such balances being stable. In this case, nominal gross national product (GNP), equal to $M(x)V$, is predictable. Predictability refers to a stable linkage between the intermediate target (M_1) and GNP. It depends on velocity (V) being stable. In contrast, the concept of controllability refers to the link between the operational instrument (e.g., unborrowed reserves) and M_1. A stable linkage here depends on a stable value for the money multiplier. Predictability has turned out to be a tall order. Velocity is unstable since the monetary aggregates (particularly M_1 and M_2) represent varying proportions of transactions balances. The logic of the linkages is better for the predictability achieved by monetary policy and worse for the controllability. Predictability (by widening the intermediate target) can only be bought at the expense of controllability and vice versa (Bryant 1983:82).

The nationwide introduction of negotiable order of withdrawal (NOW) accounts in 1981 meant that $M1$ gave a biased estimate of true transactions balances. The narrow money supply, the Fed's favorite target, now included savings balances. $M1$ was corrected briefly for the estimated flow of funds into NOW accounts from other types of savings accounts.

In the latter part of 1982, $M1$ was downgraded because its relation to income deviated sharply from past patterns (Sternlight 1984:44). During 1982, income velocity of $M1$ declined by the largest amount in any four-quarter span in the postwar period. The typical explanation is that the public's demand for money increased because of the decline in inflation and market interest rates. Falling rates lowered the opportunity cost of holding money balances. Since control of GNP via the monetary aggregates depends on a predictable velocity, the Fed began to place more emphasis on $M2$ and $M3$. The problem of velocity extends to these aggregates because of the changing mix of savings and transactions components; e.g., $M2$ velocity will increase with increase in transactions components.

The Fed protects itself against bad results and outside criticism by hedging its bets: (1) it targets various aggregates and can hail the one it comes closest to hitting; (2) the targets are stated as wide ranges, which makes them easier to hit; (3) it can change the fourth quarter ground rules and project the targets from a more convenient base within the calendar year; (4) it can change the definition of the aggregates in a helpful way; (5) since an annual target rate is announced, wide deviations are possible in shorter period growth rates that average out to the annual target rate.

Before 1979 the success in meeting targets was exaggerated because of the phenomenon of base drift. In successive quarters, the actual level of the monetary aggregates became the basis for setting targets for the coming quarter. Maintaining the same percentage range in successive quarters made for a higher growth rate in the monetary aggregate. Beginning in 1979, one-year growth rates were adopted in February and not adjusted every quarter. The base drift problem was eliminated within a calendar year but not between years because new ranges are established on the basis of actual values of the monetary aggregates at the beginning of the year (Gilbert and Trebing 1981:4).

HITTING THE TARGETS   Figure 12.6 plots target ranges expressed in dollars and

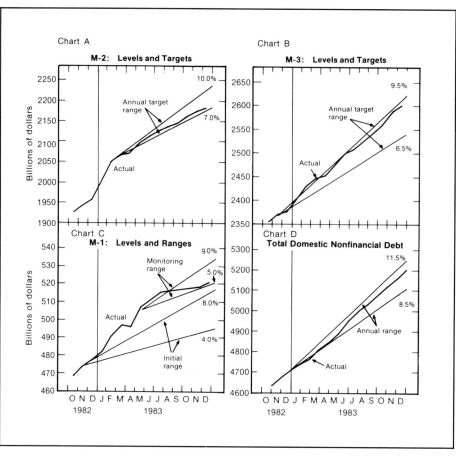

12.6. Levels and targets. (Sternlight 1984:41)

actual levels of the aggregates. The target range assumes the shape of a cone because different percentage growth rates are translated into absolute dollars. In addition to M1, M2, and M3, total domestic debt was targeted for the first time (Fig. 12.6D). This acknowledges the importance of external finance as the link between Fed policy and the real economy, an emphasis found throughout the text. The instability of money velocity has prompted wide support for the targeting of credit in the place of targeting the monetary aggregates (J. Cohen 1982:1–14; Morris 1982:5–14; B. Friedman 1982a:15–23; B. Friedman 1982b: 223–48; Kopcke 1983a:10–23). The credit variable reflects variations in money velocity and so provides a more reliable linkage with GNP. When households increase their demand for money, leading to a decline in money velocity, this is the other side of a decrease in their supply of loans to credit markets (Trehan 1985:28–39).

The nuance in the labeling of Figure 12.6D suggests that the Fed did not give its unconditional blessing to targeting credit. The uncertainty about M1 as a target explains "monitoring" instead of "target" in Figure 12.6C. When M1 growth (actual) fell outside the cone, the range was revised upward. If the test of successful implementation of the FOMC directive is a line of growth following the midpoint of the range, the trading desk fails the test. Accommodation to money growth rather than control (see Sternlight 1984:40) can explain some departures. Getting back on the desired path after movements beyond the upper limit poses a dilemma. Too fast a return invites sharp rises in interest rates, with upsetting effects on financial asset prices. On the other hand, too slow a return runs the danger of overshooting the ultimate GNP target.

The volatility of interest rates and money

The change in operating procedures since 1979 resulted in increased volatility in interest rates and money (Figs. 12.7, 12.8). The volatility of interest rates is understandable in the light of the theoretical framework outlined earlier (see Figs. 12.2–12.5). Reserve restraint will be responsible for sharp fluctuations in interest rates (most dramatically in the federal funds rate) in response to fluctuations in money demand.

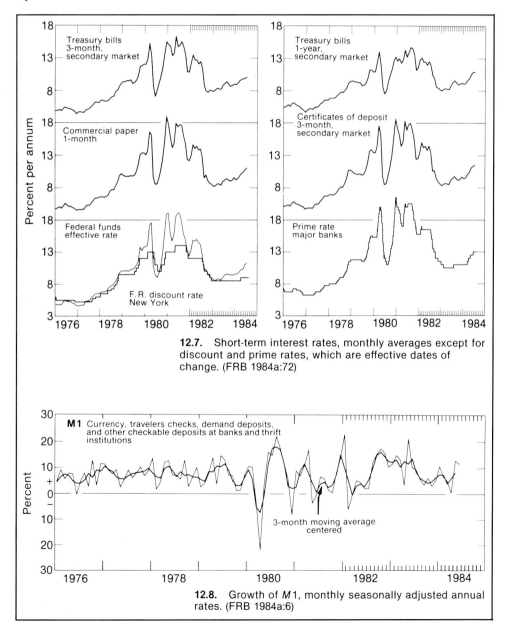

12.7. Short-term interest rates, monthly averages except for discount and prime rates, which are effective dates of change. (FRB 1984a:72)

12.8. Growth of *M*1, monthly seasonally adjusted annual rates. (FRB 1984a:6)

Following the efficient market hypothesis (discussed in Ch. 21), unanticipated changes in the money supply based on the Fed's weekly announcement of the money supply figures results in sharp changes in short-term interest rates (a second theory). Thirty-four percent of the volatility of the 3-month Treasury bill yield in 1980 and 1981 has been attributed to the market's response to unexpected changes in the money supply. The market attaches credibility to the Fed's intent to control money growth, and an unexpectedly large increase in the money stock leads to downward pressure on security prices as the market expects a tightening of the reserve market (Roley 1982:3–15). Greater emphasis on targeting borrowed reserves since 1982 and the shift to contemporaneous reserve requirements in 1984 has probably reduced announcement effects (Gavin and Karamouzis 1985:11–28).

A third theory of interest rate volatility focuses on the interest elasticity of the demand for money. Wider variations in interest rates since October 1979 have led to interest rate uncertainty and a more inelastic demand curve. A steeper money demand curve given the same money demand shocks (holding the supply curve constant) leads to larger interest rate changes (Walsh 1982:8–18). Interest rate volatility feeds on itself.

The volatility of the money stock is seen to be a leading factor explaining the volatility of interest rates. Behind this volatility lies financial innovation and deregulation, which are responsible for large shifts between $M1$ and other monetary aggregates. Another theory emphasizes the cyclical effects on money of lagged reserve requirements in combination with reserve targeting (Pierce 1984:741–45). The bank credit market is made the key factor explaining variations in the money stock in other accounts (Goodfriend 1982:3–18; Judd and Scadding 1981:21–44).

Sharp movements in interest rates have created serious management problems for financial institutions and firms. To reduce the risk of interest rate fluctuations (i.e., the cost of borrowing rising faster than the yields on their assets) they have resorted to a variety of hedging techniques that include interest-rate swaps, guaranteed commercial paper, money market loans, forward-priced loans, match-funded loans, and interest-rate caps. For definition of these terms, see Mellon Bank (1984). Interest rate swaps in particular have proven to be very popular (Loeys 1985:17–25).

The effectiveness of monetary policy

The effectiveness of monetary policy cannot be assessed until all the constraints under which the Fed operates can be considered. If we focus only on recent history, however, one important generalization might be that a restrictive monetary policy can be effective in reducing inflation. The record for 1979–82 shows success in reducing inflation by restricting aggregate demand. A high unemployment rate and unused capacity broke the wage-price spiral (Pierce 1984:733–38).

Summary

This chapter has emphasized four main elements in policymaking: goal setting, use of instruments to reach operational targets, use of operational targets to reach intermediate targets, and use of intermediate targets to reach ultimate goals.

The goals of the central bank are revealed in the preference function. The central banker labors under a variety of constraints in reaching these goals. A personal view of the workings of the economy, the influence of other public policies, and the political system all constrain central banking behavior. We suggest the complexity of policymaking by the device of a matrix, with the cells representing the outcomes of different policies, given different economic structures.

A monetary policy is represented by a single financial variable, usually the intermediate target variable such as the money stock. One approach to the theory of policy is to conceive the policymaker as achieving a vector of policy goals by manipulating this one target (in this case it can be considered an instrument). The policymaker, overall, tries to get as close as possible to the desired values of the ultimate target variables.

An alternative approach to policymaking is to match the number of goals with an equal number of policies (instruments). The appropriate model in this case is a simultaneous equation model. For policymaking to work, however, policies must be coordinated and the equations must be independent of each other.

A simple model of Fed behavior integrated the utility function with the Fed's economic model. A central feature of the model is the public's demand for money. Given that the money stock is the intermediate target (the financial variable closest to real economic activity) the Fed aims at controlling it via affecting the demand for money. This is done by influencing the interest rate structure, which in turn is related to the federal funds rate. By controlling the federal funds rate, the Fed affects the interest rate structure and the demand for money. In this fashion, the money stock is determined. An alternative theoretical formulation was offered, introducing a supply function of money so that the money stock and the interest rate structure are simultaneously determined by the interaction of supply and demand.

The confusion in a study of policymaking is whether the Fed is trying to influence a price variable (an interest rate) or a quantity variable (a reserve or monetary aggregate). The confusion occurs on the levels of the operational and of the intermediate targets. On the first level, the question is whether a reserve aggregate is being manipulated to reach a federal funds target or whether the federal funds rate is being monitored to reach a reserve target.

Even if reserves are the operational target, they could be an instrument for reaching an intermediate interest rate target. Until the fall of 1979 it was not clear from Fed behavior whether it was more interested in money supply targets than in interest rate targets. The announced change in operating procedures in October 1979 coupled with 1980–84 experience suggests that the Fed has stopped pegging the federal funds rate. When the Fed varies unborrowed reserves in order to maintain a given level of borrowing, however, this tends to stabilize the Fed funds rate.

The FOMC sets its monetary targets on an annual basis in February and revises them in July. Further modifications take place through the directives issued at the eight FOMC meetings to the manager of the open-market account. To reach the intermediate monetary targets (implementation of the directive) the trading desk at the Fed in New York develops a weekly nonborrowed reserve path based on a total reserve path and a level of discount window borrowing aimed at achieving the FOMC's preferred degree of reserve restraint. A study of target ranges and actual growth in the aggregates demonstrates the considerable difficulties in controlling the monetary aggregates. The intermediate target closest to our own emphasis on external finance is total domestic nonfinancial debt. Only recently introduced, it has not as yet been given the weight attached to the monetary aggregates. Because the velocity of $M1$ is unstable, considerable support has recently been given to targeting debt (credit) rather than the monetary aggregates.

The new operating procedures since 1979 have increased the volatility of interest rates and money. Various theories have been offered for interest rate volatility, but a major factor has been volatility in the money stock. Behind this volatility, in turn, lie financial innovation, deregulation, and variations in bank credit.

Despite problems in targeting and implementation, we should not let the trees obscure the forest. Monetary policy became restrictive after 1979 with visible effects on prices and unemployment.

Review questions

1. Show the Fed's disutility function in linear and quadratic form. Taking account of asymmetry in the preference function (for deviations from targeted values), write the equation for maximizing the Fed's utility.

2. Discuss the problems of decision making when the dimensions of choice are fully spelled out.

3. How is the expected value of a given monetary policy calculated?

4. Distinguish between maximax and minimax strategies.

5. Explain the difference between policy models with matching targets and instruments and models with more targets than instruments. Why is it difficult to satisfy the independence requirement for equations in the first case?

6. Develop a simple model of monetary policy beginning with the Fed's preference function.

7. "The demand-for-money equation is the key equation for understanding Fed policy." Explain, making use of diagrams.

8. Discuss the options in choosing a reserve target.

9. Identify the linkages between operational targets, intermediate targets, and ultimate goals in terms of controllability and predictability.

10. Discuss the implementation of FOMC directives by the Federal Reserve Bank of New York trading desk. What are the problems involved?

11. How successful is the Fed in hitting its targets?

12. Why have interest rates and money stock become more volatile since the new operating procedures of 1979?

13. Distinguish between defensive and dynamic behavior by the Fed.

13

Politics of money

This chapter marks the beginning of a critical appraisal of monetary policy. In Chapters 1–5 we emphasize the importance of finance in determining the level of economic activity. Some basic tools for measuring inflation and carrying on financial calculations are covered. Why financial intermediation has replaced direct finance is the theme of Chapter 4. After the first five chapters, the focus has been on the role of depository institutions, mainly commercial banking. Chapters 6–12 have concentrated on the Federal Reserve System. We now begin a discussion of the constraints on Fed behavior. The usual way of going beyond the Federal Reserve System is to tack on other financial institutions, introduce fiscal policy, provide a theoretical section centering on the demand for money function and "unclose" the economy by introducing the rest of the world. We shall cover the same territory but, it is hoped, in a more pointed way. Our perspective will be how these extensions affect the exercise of monetary policy. This involves exploring the linkages between the Fed and finance outside the system. Does the shifting of borrowers and lenders among financial markets strengthen or weaken the exercise of policy? Such shifts could be autonomous or could be in response to the price (interest rate) and quantity (flow of funds) effects of Fed action. Similarly, how does fiscal policy affect monetary policy? When an open economy is introduced, how does this constrain the pursuit of domestic policy objectives?

The role of theory will be approached in the same vein. Is the theory of stagflation, for example, a challenge to demand management by the Fed? Does the public's reaction to anticipated inflation, particularly the reaction called rational expectations, frustrate the monetary policymaker?

This chapter stays closer to home and considers the political pressures on the Fed from within and without. Do the politics of decision making make a mockery out of the game plan described in Chapters 11 and 12—an orderly sequence from lower to higher level targets?

The conflict of goals

Policymaking is frustrated by decision makers having different preferences. These differences are resolved by "golden mean" decisions, necessarily middle of the road and ambiguous. One former member of the Federal Reserve Board found that he could rank his colleagues according to how restrictive a policy they would advocate (Maisel 1973:48–49). Ironically, Board members did not take the logical next step of estimating their subjective trade-offs — how much of one goal they were willing to give up to achieve another. Behind their fixed positions were personal philosophies and value judgments that might variously emphasize the housing problem, high growth rates, or an aversion to inflation. Qualitative statements that, for example, call for moderate growth in money and credit over the months ahead are a way of reconciling conflicting opinion (Pierce 1979:486).

Theory of bureaucracy

Policymakers may disagree about the proper goals of policy, but they are more unanimous about their personal preference functions. Bureaucrats seek prestige, power, growth, and security for themselves (and their agencies). (For a comprehensive discussion of the theory of bureaucracy, see Culbertson 1968:Ch. 18). As a result, the policymaker leads two lives, the public life of nominal policy statements and the private life of action taken, dictated by the interests of the bureaucrat. On the basis of the personal preference function of its members, the agency "does what must be done and says what must be said." The more obscure the statements, the safer the central banker is from adverse criticism. "The public's interest lies in clearing the waters, the agency's interest in muddying them" (Culbertson 1968:411, 419).

The bureaucrat can resort to secrecy or "Kelly's constant" as a way of mystifying the public. Kelly's constant is the use of a variable with an unconstrained value to explain policy. It inevitably boils down to circular reasoning; e.g., unemployment may be explained by automation (Kelly's constant), but automation in turn is measured by unemployment (see Culbertson 1968:80-82, 419).

The Federal Reserve has long sought to suppress any rapid and detailed disclosure of its policy actions (Yohe 1976:591). Until the Freedom of Information Act of 1966, the policy actions were not made public until the *Annual Report* was published the following March. As discussed in Chapter 11, there is now a summary release following the next meeting of the committee. The full reports of the meeting are delayed for a number of years.

Various arguments have been made for secrecy. It is feared that speculators might profit from immediate disclosure and authorities would be hesitant to make policy changes if they had to defend them immediately. Finally, the Fed believes that uncertainty reinforces policy actions. But an opposing point of view is that uncertainty leads to misinterpretation and more disturbing results in securities markets (Horvitz 1979:380–81). The second Fed argument seems to concede that the Fed fears embarrassment if decisions turn out to be "wrong," a bureaucratic syndrome.

The desire for secrecy has resulted in the exclusion of key staff members from internal debates on monetary policy. The staff responsible for analysis and forecasting the gross national product, prices, and unemployment did not take part in monetary discussions under Chairman Burns (cf. Lombra 1979:500). Staff access to the "blue book," which analyzes alternative short-run paths laid out for $M1$ and $M2$, is limited.

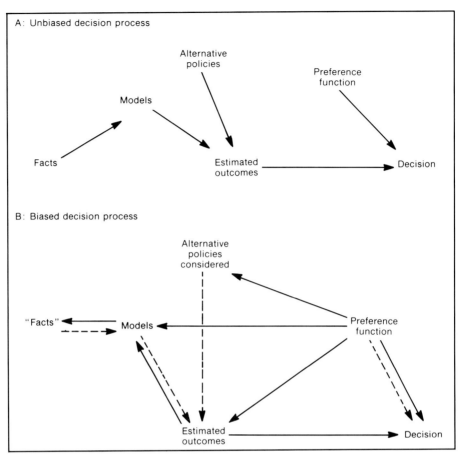

A: Unbiased decision process

Alternative policies

Preference function

Models

Facts

Estimated outcomes

Decision

B: Biased decision process

Alternative policies considered

"Facts"

Models

Preference function

Estimated outcomes

Decision

13.1. Unbiased and biased decision processes. (Used with permission from Culbertson 1968:416)

The classic example of Kelly's constant in current policymaking is frequent reference to the public's changing demand for cash balances. Variations in money growth are explained this way, with the Fed absolving itself of responsibility for unwanted fluctuations in the money supply (Lombra 1979:500). Since the money stock must be held by someone, increases in the money supply can always be explained this way even if it is supply determined. A partial escape from Kelly's constant is for the Fed (as Maisel did in Chapter 12) to argue that money demand unrelated to income is responsible for monetary changes. The problem here is that it is very difficult to identify such liquidity demand, which again saves the Fed from adverse criticism.

The bureaucratic decision process is a biased one in which prejudice determines decisions. Models, facts, alternative policies, and estimated outcomes serve to rationalize decisions made on nonobjective grounds. The unbiased decision process is compared in Figure 13.1 with the biased decision process, which reverses the causal order of the former. This unbiased process begins with facts and models, and on the basis of them outcomes of alternative policies are estimated.

Decisions are subsequently made on the basis of the policymaker's preference function, which contains the bona fide goals of economic stabilization. The dashed arrows in the lower half of Figure 13.1 repeat the solid arrows of the unbiased decision process. They are to be compared with the solid arrows. In every case, the unbiased arrows are reversed except for the arrows that go from the preference function to the decision. The preference function is central to the bottom diagram. It determines the alternative policies considered and the restricted set of estimated outcomes. Models and facts then rationalize the prior choice of outcomes.

Decision making at the Fed is not too far off this scenario. In the last quarter-century, two chairmen have dominated the decision process—William McChesney Martin (1951–69) and Arthur F. Burns (1970–77). They are a study in contrasting styles and philosophy. Martin was for intuition and the broad vision of a generalist. Burns believed in economic analysis and above all in measurement (Maisel 1973:114–15). It might have been expected that a difference between nominal policy and action would exist in both cases but that policy would be more biased under Martin. A student of both regimes says this is not so. While, qualitatively, policies were about the same (this would refer to nominal policy), quantitatively (this would refer to actions) Burns's policies were worse. The tragedy of his leadership, it is said, is that he did not put into place the monetary policy he advocated so vigorously (Poole 1979:473, 484). This opinion is concurred in by Pierce (1979:474–95) and by the discussants of the Poole and Pierce papers (496–504). The puzzle we wish to address is the paradox between what Martin and Burns said and what they did. The theory of bureaucracy is only part of the answer.

It is too early to evaluate the current regime of Paul A. Volcker, who became chairman in 1979. He has been accused, however, of the same activism pursued by previous chairmen (1965–79). Harsh policies to fight inflation were followed by easier policies. Policymakers produce cycles in inflation and unemployment of increasing magnitudes by abruptly changing the rules of the game (Pierce 1984:745–47). Beyond 1982 (where Pierce stops), monetary policy became much easier in 1983 with large increases in $M1$ following increases in the monetary base (Clark 1984:29).

Lender of last resort

The central banker faces pressure from the imminent collapse of a bank or a number of banks. A potential crisis occurred in 1970 with the Cambodian invasion, followed by the Penn Central Railroad bankruptcy (Maisel 1973:5–10). Penn Central had issued commercial paper that could no longer be repaid. (Commercial paper makes up the short-term IOU notes of large corporations and has a ready financial market because of its liquidity and low degree of risk.) This obviously upset the commercial paper market. The Fed informed the banks they could borrow from them if they had to make loans to their customers who were unable to roll over their commercial paper in the market.

The lender-of-last-resort function was on clear display in two major bank failures. Before Franklin National Bank of New York officially closed its doors in 1974, funds had to be available to meet large deposit withdrawals. At the time of the bank's closing, it had borrowed $1.5 bil. from the Federal Reserve Bank of New York, the largest single loan up to that time (Horvitz 1979:362–63). The Continental-Illinois collapse in 1984 set new records for Fed support (see Ch. 8).

Accommodating the Treasury

The solicitude of the central bank for the Treasury is most visible during Treasury debt operations. The central banks keep money and capital markets on an even keel during such periods. The Fed engages in open-market purchases before and after a financing operation to avoid disorderly conditions. This means that the Fed is sweetening the market so that the securities will be well received. In dollars-and-cents terms, Fed operations help to minimize the interest costs on the public debt. Turning to Canadian experience, the theory of bureaucracy has been applied ingeniously to expose the methods used by the Bank of Canada to hide its primary goal of minimizing interest costs on the public debt (Acheson and Chant 1973: 637ff.). Unlike the legal independence of the Fed, the Bank of Canada is responsible to the Canadian Minister of Finance. Nonetheless, the Bank of Canada has the same nominal goals of full employment and the like.

A weakening of the demand side as reflected in holders selling off their holdings or buying less new offerings at given interest rates will also increase central bank support of the market. The scenario begins with the private sector. An increase in economic activity leads to more private sector borrowing from financial institutions—bank and nonbank. Following the hypothesis that institutional holdings of governments are a residual asset, an increase in the private demand for credit will lead these institutions to sell off their securities. (On this hypothesis, see J. Cohen 1975a:23ff., 1975b:78, and McMillan and Beard 1980: 122ff.) This pressure on the government securities market leads to central bank support. Increases in bank reserves and the money supply are a by-product of this support.

The central bank's (*CEN*) reaction function reads as follows:

$$CEN = CEN(\overset{+}{BORR},\ \overset{-}{PRIV},\ \overset{-}{COMM})$$

The central bank will (as indicated by the signs above the variables) buy government securities in response to public borrowing (*BORR*) and buy less if the private sector (*PRIV*) and commercial banks (*COMM*) are buying them. If the private sector and the banking sector sell off government securities, the central bank will increase its purchases. These variables in statistical competition with stabilization targets offer a better explanation of open-market purchases. The empirical results in J. Cohen (1975a) were based on the experience of the United States, Canada, and the United Kingdom.

Further evidence in support of the accommodation hypothesis is given in the direct testimony of members of the Board of Governors and Bank presidents. Rapid money growth is inevitable, they have testified, when the Treasury borrows (see Weintraub 1978:359–60; Laney and Willett 1982).

Accommodating Congress

Despite pressures from Congress, the Fed does not accommodate that body. The pressures in part cancel out because of disagreements among members of the House and Senate; e.g., members of the Senate Banking Committee were for higher monetary growth rates in 1977, while their colleagues on the House side were against easing (Weintraub 1978:357). A more important reason is that Congress values the Fed too highly as a scapegoat to take responsibility for monetary policy (cf. Kane 1976:606–8).

The strongest attacks on the Fed came from the late Congressman Wright Patman of Texas who for years waged a one-man crusade against its high-interest policies. His strategy was to challenge the Fed's independent budgetary status and force it to depend on regular congressional appropriations (Kane 1976:602–4). Paradoxically, after 46 years of unremitting effort he was stripped of the chairmanship of the House Banking, Currency, and Housing Committee in the very year that Congress asserted itself by passing House Concurrent Resolution 133 (in 1975).

The reluctance of the House to take responsibility for errant policy explains the watered-down nature of the resolution. A more demanding procedure would have had the Fed request permission to operate within specified ranges of money growth. Robert Weintraub (1978:605), then a staff member on the House Banking Committee, was responsible for this proposal.

One test of congressional supervision is the before-and-after performance of the Fed in reaching quantitative targets. In the second quarter of 1975 the Fed announced a 5–7.5% annual growth rate for $M1$. In retrospect, from 1965 through the first quarter of 1975 the annualized quarterly growth rate was within this range 70% of the time (Pierce 1978:363–64). This sets a benchmark for evaluating later performance. The two-month target ranges set at 47 FOMC meetings (January 1974–November 1977) were met only 40% of the time. On the other hand, the Fed stayed within the federal funds rate range 100% of the time. The conclusion is that congressional surveillance has not produced closer control over the monetary aggregates.

It would be difficult for Congress to enforce monetary rules. Obfuscation can take many forms. So many targets are employed that the Fed can always choose the most favorable one. Base drift has not been entirely eliminated (e.g., $M1$ in 1983), making it difficult to keep track of growth rates. It has been suggested that the screams of harried participants in the money markets weigh more heavily on the psyches of the decision makers than possible congressional criticism (Kane 1976:610). The evidence seems to be that, at least until the change in policy in October 1979, the Fed placed even greater reliance on stabilizing the money market (i.e., interest rates) after the passage of Resolution 133 (Pierce 1978:366).

Accommodating the president

Presidential pressure is a different story. The thrust of monetary policy changes with changes in administrations. The Fed cannot fight the president, a former Governor of the Fed has pointed out. Monetary policy must give in to national policy (Maisel 1973:146–48).

References to the president or the administration must be interpreted as short-hand references to a great number of economic policymakers located in cabinet offices and various government agencies. The latter include the Office of Management and Budget, the Council of Economic Advisers, the National Security Council, and the Office of the Special Trade Representative. Efforts have been made repeatedly to secure unified policy stands (Flash 1965; Woolley 1984:Ch. 6). The most recent effort was the formation of the Economic Policy Council in April 1985 (Kilborn 1985b: 1F, 8F).

MEASURING CHANGES IN THE THRUST OF MONETARY POLICY   Monetary growth rates and unemployment rates can be compared for different administrations (see Table 13.1). Col. 1 gives the average monthly growth rate in $M1$ multiplied by 12, so that it is an annual rate. The other three columns allow for real growth potential and slack from unemployment. Both these factors reduce the inflationary implications of the monetary growth rate. In the formula for thrust 2 (see notes to Table 13.1), the increase in potential output based on productivity and labor force growth is taken to be 4% a year. It happens to be the same as the second 4 in the formula, which measures the normal unemployment rate. The other thrust figures are modifications to allow for feasible absorption of unemployment in any period (0.0625) and the secular rise in the nominal unemployment rate from 4 to 5.5% (the 1.5).

Table 13.1. Monetary policy thrust in each president's term, 1951-77

President	Dates	Thrust[a] (1)	(2)	(3)	(4)
Truman	3/51-12/52	4.75	0.80	0.81	0.77
Eisenhower	1/53-12/60	1.73	-2.32	-2.30	-2.28
Kennedy	1/61-10/63	2.31	-1.82	-1.78	-1.71
Johnson	11/63-12/68	4.78	0.77	0.82	0.79
Nixon	1/69- 7/74	6.17	2.11	2.18	2.17
Ford	8/74-12/76	4.76	0.53	0.61	0.74
Carter	1/77-11/77	6.61	2.41	2.50	2.59

Source: Weintraub 1978:351.
[a]Thrust 1 = percent change $M1$, monthly SA, at annual rate
Thrust 2 = thrust 1 - [4.0 + 0.0625(UN_{-1} - 4)]
Thrust 3 = thrust 1 - [4.0 + 0.0625(UN_{-1} - 4 + time × 0.003115 × 1.5)]
Thrust 4 = thrust 1 - [4.0 + 0.0625($\log UN_{-1}$ - log(4 + time × 0.003115 × 1.5))]

The smaller the figures, the tighter the monetary policy, with the reverse being true of bigger percentages. Truman was for support of the government securities market despite the famous accord of March 1951. This accord between the White House and the Fed presumably freed the Fed from supporting the bond market, but this is misleading (Weintraub 1978:353–54). Monetizing deficits was no longer necessary for the Fed when Eisenhower took office, since his concern was stopping inflation. The effective rates of money growth dropped sharply during this period. Kennedy's administration did not move as much the other way as might have been expected because of his concern with the international balance of payments. (Kennedy gets the best marks from Weintraub of all the presidents.) Johnson wanted an expansionist monetary policy and got it. Nixon did not believe that money caused inflation, and his incomes policy encouraged the Fed into monetary expansion.

Ford wanted to whip inflation "now," explaining lower growth rates for his administration. Carter, as Nixon did, regarded inflation as a nonmonetary phenomenon. The conclusion that Weintraub (1978:349,356) draws is that the dominant guiding force behind monetary policy is the president. Weintraub has an interesting discussion of personalities. Chairmen of the Federal Reserve Board (Eccles, McCabe) were removed when they acted independently. Close contact between the Fed and the administration is maintained by job shifting. Since the administration includes the Treasury, accommodation to the Treasury discussed earlier is accommodation to the president.

MEASURING THE REACTION FUNCTION   The Fed's reaction to different targets may differ under different administrations. This is another way of measuring accommodation to the president. A considerable number of empirical studies have estimated the reaction function. (For a bibliography, see Potts and Luckett 1978:532–34. The Wood study listed there was referred to in Ch. 12). One of these studies has estimated reaction functions for different administrations (Havrilesky et al. 1976:466ff.). The target variable (the federal funds rate) is made a function of the unemployment rate, the price level, and the foreign exchange rate vis-à-vis the deutsche mark.

For example, the period of monetary tightness when Johnson was president and Martin chairman of the Board (January 1964–November 1966) is represented by the following reaction function (Havrilesky et al. 1976:474):

$$\text{Federal funds rate}_t = -80.988 - 0.0365 U_{t-1} + 0.5577 P_{t-1} + 1.256 FX_{t-1}$$
$$(-10.342) \quad (-0.2603) \qquad (11.348) \qquad (3.593)$$

$$R^2 = 0.98, \; F^2 = 427.527, \; D/W = 1.759, \; N = 34$$

The results suggest that Martin was more concerned with inflation and the balance of payments than with unemployment (U). A one-point rise in the wholesale price index (P) in the previous month resulted in a 0.56% rise in the federal funds rate. A one-cent rise in the U.S. dollar price of the deutsche mark (FX_{t-1}) induced a 1¼% rise in the federal funds rate. In contrast, as indicated by the t-statistic below the coefficient, the response to the unemployment rate (U_{t-1}) was insignificant.

After November 1966 one of three monetary aggregates (the adjusted bank credit proxy, the narrow money supply, and reserves available to support private deposits) was tried as the target variable for different administrations (Havrilesky et al. 1976:475). None were statistically significant at the standard 5% level.

These results point out the difficulty in evaluating monetary policy under various administrations. Weintraub branded Johnson as the number one exponent of monetary ease; yet Martin under Johnson is characterized in the above reaction function as the number one inflation fighter. The problem is the choice of target or indicator. As discussed next, the weaknesses of indicators has led to another approach.

DISCRIMINANT ANALYSIS   A problem with reaction functions is that they are affected by the choice of policy target (e.g., federal funds rate or a monetary aggregate as the left-hand variable). If the wrong indicator is chosen (one failing to describe Fed behavior), the results are meaningless (Potts and Luckett 1978:526). Even if the correct target is selected, intended monetary policy may be obscured by the actual monetary policy as measured by the target. Outside factors may explain discrepancies between actual intentions and ex post values of the target.

The escape is to measure intentions directly on the basis of majority FOMC opinion. The FOMC may intend to stimulate the economy (easy money policy) or restrain the economy (tight money). Policy was classified monthly in this binary way, 1956–75 (Table 13.2). By the use of discriminant analysis, easy and tight money are related to the standard stabilization targets. This technique is discussed in Potts and Luckett (1978:533). The idea is to determine if differences in the values of the left-hand variable, which consists of the values of easy and tight money, have any significant relation to variations in the target variables of unemployment and the like. If, for example, an increase in the monthly unemployment rate increases the likelihood of an easy month, the unemployment rate is a significant variable explaining policy intentions.

Table 13.2.   Classification of intended monetary policy

Year	Jan.	Feb.	Mar.	Apr.	May	June	July	Aug.	Sept.	Oct.	Nov.	Dec.
1956	T	T	T	T	T	T	T	T	T	T	T	T
1957	T	T	T	T	T	T	T	T	T	T	E	E
1958	E	E	E	E	E	E	E	T	T	T	T	T
1959	T	T	T	T	T	T	T	T	T	T	T	T
1960	T	T	E	E	E	E	E	E	E	E	E	E
1961	E	E	E	E	E	E	E	E	E	E	E	E
1962	E	E	E	E	E	E	E	E	E	E	E	E
1963	E	E	E	E	E	F	T	T	T	T	T	T
1964	T	T	T	T	T	T	T	T	T	T	T	T
1965	T	T	T	T	T	T	T	T	T	T	T	T
1966	T	T	T	T	T	T	T	T	T	T	T	E
1967	E	E	E	E	E	E	E	E	E	E	E	T
1968	T	T	T	T	T	T	E	E	E	E	E	T
1969	T	T	T	T	T	T	T	T	T	T	T	T
1970	T	T	E	E	E	E	E	E	E	E	E	E
1971	E	E	E	T	T	T	T	T	E	E	E	E
1972	E	E	E	E	E	E	E	E	T	T	T	T
1973	T	T	T	T	T	T	T	T	E	E	E	E
1974	E	E	T	T	T	T	T	E	E	E	E	E
1975	E	E	E	E	E	E	E	E	E	E	E	E

Source: Used with permission from Glenn T. Potts and Dudley G. Luckett, Policy objectives of the Federal Reserve System, p. 530, copyright © 1978, *Quarterly Journal of Economics*.
Note: E = easy money; T = tight money.

The results of the analysis are presented in Table 13.3; U = percent of the civilian labor force that is unemployed, $IWPI$ = measure of prices based on the industrial commodities component of the wholesale price index, IIP = index of industrial production, and LBP = liquidity balance-of-payments surplus in millions of dollars. (The balance of payments will be discussed in Ch. 23.)

The results confirm Weintraub's analysis of presidential administrations. Prices are the most significant variable under Eisenhower. Under Kennedy-Johnson the shift is from a price-stability objective to a full-employment objective. The discriminating power of the U and IIP variables is the highest among the explanatory variables for this period. The Nixon-Ford results, while puzzling to Potts and

Luckett, would not be puzzling to Weintraub. The price variable loses all significance in this administration.

Reagan, Regan, and Volcker

Without quantitative studies as yet embracing the Reagan years, the relationship between the president and the second most powerful man in the country, as Paul Volcker has been regularly described (Kilborn 1984b:27), must be discussed in a less rigorous way. One can say that the restrictive monetary policies of Volcker were in tune with the policies of Reagan. They were the antiinflationary linchpin of Reagan's program (Alperovitz and Faux 1984:60). Despite this basic agreement, the first four years of the Reagan administration were characterized by sustained infighting with the White House, which was usually represented by former Secretary of the Treasury Donald Regan. The Treasury secretary, without sacrificing the White House antiinflation stance, first blamed high interest rates on the failure of the Fed to manage money properly (Fuerbringer 1983:18) and more recently on unnecessary tightness against a nonexistent inflation threat. By such "Fedbashing," Reagan aides hoped to put pressure on the central bank to ease its grip on the nation's credit (Jaroslovsky and Blustein 1984:1.17). The reappointment of Volcker as chairman by Reagan in June 1983 was over Regan's opposition. Volcker's support in the financial community and among the world's central bankers made the decision almost inevitable (Fuerbringer 1983:18).

Federal Reserve independence

Is the Fed independent? We have attempted to answer this question obliquely rather than head-on. A common distinction is made between de jure and de facto independence. The Federal Reserve System is said to be independent in a legal sense because it reports to Congress and not to the president. The analysis demonstrates that de facto the Fed is not independent. Paradoxically, however, it does not accommodate Congress, to whom it is responsible, but the president.

The de jure independence of the Fed is not the common pattern among the world's central banks. In most cases they are responsible to the administration via the minister of finance or the Treasury secretary. Does it make any difference in practice? The analysis would suggest not.

Summary

The Fed is subject to many constraints in the pursuit of stabilization targets. Most of the chapters that follow will be concerned with how the economy outside the Fed constrains its behavior. This chapter concentrates on the internal constraints and the external political constraints that frustrate ideal policy.

The three internal constraints discussed are conflicts over policy goals, bureaucratic shenanigans, and the function of lender of last resort. The external constraints focus on relationships with the Treasury, Congress, and the White House. The evidence seems strong that the Fed accommodates to the policies of

Table 13.3. Results of the discriminant analyses

Variable	Overall (1956-75)		Eisenhower		Kennedy-Johnson		Nixon-Ford	
	Coefficient	Discriminating power[a] (%)	Coefficient	Discriminating power[a] (%)	Coefficient	Discriminating power[a] (%)	Coefficient	Discriminating power[a] (%)
$U_{t-1}(-)$[b]	-0.162++	59.9	-0.100++	24.6	-0.108+	28.6	-0.175++	57.9
$\Delta_{t-1}IMPI(+)$	0.035	8.0	0.791++	38.8	0.547*	23.1	0.033	8.6
$\Delta_{t-1}IITP(+)$	0.108++	29.1	0.164+	28.0	0.212+	30.6	0.066*	18.7
$LPB(-)$[b]	(d)	3.0	(d)	8.7	(d)	17.65	(d)	14.8
Constant[c]	0.795++	...	0.469++	...	0.491++	...	0.874++	...
F-ratio	15.993++		9.471++		5.953++		9.398++	

Source: Used with permission from Glenn T. Potts and Dudley G. Luckett, Policy objectives of the Federal Reserve System, p. 530, copyright © *Quarterly Journal of Economics*.

Note: *, +, and ++ indicate significance at the 10%, 5%, and 1% levels respectively.
[a]The percentage discriminating power is a measure of the relative importance of each independent variable in the discriminant function. It is computed by forcing the sum of the standardized regression coefficients to be equal to one.
[b]The algebraic sign in parentheses is the theoretically "correct" sign. Thus, e.g., a negative sign on the coefficient for U_{t-1} means that an increase in unemployment will result in a smaller (or more negative) discriminant score, which in turn indicates easy money. That is, higher than average levels of unemployment are associated with easy money, and lower than average levels with tight money. Similar reasoning accounts for the other theoretically "correct" signs.
[c]The constant is a correction for the means of the raw data and is equal to the sum of the products of the estimated coefficients and the overall means of the independent variables.
[d]Less than 0.0005 in absolute value.

the Treasury and the White House. This is so whether accommodation is measured by central bank intentions or actual policies.

Congress has increased its supervision of monetary policy since 1975 with the passage of H.R. Resolution 133. Students of congressional supervision doubt, however, whether Congress wants to take responsibility for the conduct of monetary policy. As a result, Congress has not noticeably controlled Fed behavior.

Review questions

1. Describe the two lives of economic policymakers.

2. Compare the unbiased and biased decision process.

3. Identify the internal constraints that inhibit policymaking by the Board and FOMC.

4. Identify the external political constraints that inhibit monetary policymaking.

5. Is there any evidence that the Fed's preference function reflects the preference function of the White House?

6. What is Kelly's constant?

7. Should the Fed be integrated with the administration by being made responsible to the Secretary of the Treasury?

8. How would you evaluate the degree of independence exercised by the Fed?

9. Discuss the techniques of regression and discriminant analysis as a means for discovering the intentions of monetary policymakers.

14

Financial system
outside the Fed

The flow of credit (or external finance) is the linkage we have stressed between monetary policy and the real economy. Credit has so far been studied within the Federal Reserve System; now we go beyond it. This chapter develops a framework for explaining how sources and uses of funds vary for these outside institutions. Subsequent chapters will study the micro aspect of decision making.

The perspective here is the Fed responsibility for credit flows outside the system of depository institutions (DIs). A change in depository reserves affects other financial institutions. When checkable deposits increase with an increase in DI reserves, claims on money market, pension, and insurance funds may change in some fixed relation to the change in reserves and checkable deposits. The multiplier formula developed in Chapter 6 can be extended to allow for these outside flows. Monetary policy may also exert an interest rate effect that induces asset holders in DIs to switch between checkable accounts and other financial claims with lower reserve requirements. The volume of credit flowing through financial institutions (indirect finance) is thereby affected. In addition, direct finance is affected by interest rate changes. Checkable deposits, previously idle, are loaned directly to the nonfinancial sector. When interest rates are rising, the effect is to increase the financial velocity of money and the total volume of external finance. In this way, monetary policy aiming at a lower volume of credit may be frustrated.

This chapter provides an introduction to the main categories of private nonbank financial institutions (nonmember banks, thrift institutions, insurance and pension funds, direct finance), the latter including a variety of institutions such as finance companies, investment banking, and brokers and dealers in securities. Nonmember banks and thrift institutions have been previously discussed as DIs but not in a wider sources-and-uses-of-funds context.

The trick in working out multiplier formulas is to determine the proportions in which the public wishes to hold other assets when demand deposits increase by $1 and then estimate the reserves absorbed by these asset increases. The desired proportions of asset holdings constitute the numerator and the tied-up reserves, the denominator of the multiplier ratio.

The money multiplier (m) in Chapter 6 can be understood in these terms. This formula is now repeated with the addition of the ratio of Treasury deposits to checkable deposits. The reason for this is that Treasury deposits in DIs (mainly commercial banks) absorb reserves in the same way as checkable deposits but are not considered part of the money stock.

$$m = \frac{1 + c}{r_1(1 + g) + r_2 t + e + c} \tag{14.1}$$

where c = currency–checkable deposit ratio (0.28)
$\quad\ \ r_1$ = required reserve ratio against checkable deposits (0.12)
$\quad\ \ r_2$ = required reserve ratio against time deposits (0.03)
$\quad\ \ e$ = excess reserves–checkable deposit ratio (0.01)
$\quad\ \ t$ = time–checkable deposit ratio (3)
$\quad\ \ g$ = Treasury–checkable deposit ratio (0.001)

The $1 of checkable deposits absorbs $r_1(1 + g) + r_2 t + e$ in reserves. The currency in circulation per dollar of deposits absorbs an equal amount of reserves. Suppose the ratio was 1.28/0.50, using the values for the parameters shown in parentheses. This would tell us that $.50 in reserves or the monetary base supports an increase in the money supply of $1.28. One dollar increase in reserves (the way we ordinarily interpret the multiplier) will thus support 2 × 1.28 or $2.56 in new money.

Nonmember commercial banks

FINANCIAL BACKGROUND   We begin the odyssey outside the Fed with non-member commercial banks. The passage of the Depository Institutions Deregulation and Monetary Control Act (DIDMCA) in 1980 blurred the differences between member and nonmember banks, and separate data are no longer published in the *Federal Reserve Bulletin*. Some idea of the composition of assets and liabilities for nonmember banks as compared with member banks can be gained from an earlier detailed statement of assets and liabilities. In 1978 the footings of member banks were $904 bil., roughly three times the $295 bil. for nonmember banks. If we express individual items as percent of total footings, cash bank balances were 7 percentage points higher for member banks than for nonmember banks. Federal funds purchased on the liability side (a component of borrowed funds) were also 7 percentage points higher. Bank liquidity and short-term borrowing were relatively more important for member banks. The relative importance of the bank investment portfolio, total loans and investments, and total deposits was considerably greater for nonmember banks.

Thrift institutions

Thrift institutions are identified by the fixed-value redeemable claims they sell to households. In this way they are a safe outlet for personal saving. Into this category fall three well-known financial institutions — savings and loan associations (S&Ls), mutual savings banks (MSBs), and credit unions (CUs). Commercial banks provide a similar saving outlet via their time deposits. The heavy dependence of S&Ls and MSBs on mortgage investments has been responsible for deep financial distress in recent years.

SAVINGS AND LOAN ASSOCIATIONS   As seen from Tables 14.1 and 14.2, S&Ls are almost single-minded in the kind of assets they acquire and their dependence on deposits; they originated as building and loan societies. These societies had the cooperative idea of devoting the collective saving of members to finance each member's home building on a one-at-a-time basis. Subsequently, the saving and borrowing activities became divorced with no necessary relation between savers and home buyers. True to these origins, S&Ls finance new home purchases or purchases of existing homes. As a result of DIDMCA, this concentration on mortgages will probably lessen in the future. The powers of thrift institutions were expanded so that alternative investments in mutual funds, consumer loans, and business debt are now possible. The increase in consumer credit (line 4, Table 14.2) in 1983 reflects these new powers. The most remarkable recent development, however, is the upsurge in purchases of pool securities (line 10, Table 14.2) guaranteed by federal credit agencies (see discussion of federally sponsored credit agencies below). Funds flowing to S&Ls by their selling of mortgages no longer constitutes a revolving fund financing the purchase of new mortgages. In effect, S&Ls are swapping mortgages for safe securities guaranteed by the government.

Saving capital (deposits) dominates total liabilities. Depositors own 85% of the S&Ls; 15% are stock companies, which are more aggressive than depositor-owned companies (mutuals), making more construction and mobile home loans. Depositors are insured for $100,000 by the Federal Savings and Loan Insurance Corporation (FSLIC) in the same way that the Federal Deposit Insurance Corporation (FDIC) insures commercial and MSB depositors.

Table 14.1. Assets and liabilities of S&Ls (end of period)

Account	1981	1982	1983
		($ bil.)	
1 Assets	664,167	707,646	771,705
2 Mortgages	518,547	483,614	493,432
3 Cash and investment securities[a]	63,123	85,438	103,395
4 Other	82,497	138,594	174,878
5 Liabilities and net worth	664,167	707,646	771,705
6 Savings capital	525,061	567,961	634,076
7 Borrowed money	88,782	97,850	91,443
8 Federal Home Loan Bank Board	62,794	63,861	52,626
9 Other	25,988	33,989	38,817
10 Loans in process[b]	6,385	9,934	21,117
11 Other	15,544	15,602	15,275
12 Net worth[c]	28,395	26,233	30,911
13 *Memo:* Mortgage loan commitments outstanding[d]	15,225	18,054	32,996

Source: *Fed. Res. Bull.* 1984e:A26.
[a]Holdings of stock of the Federal Home Loan Banks are in "other assets."
[b]Beginning in 1982, loans in process are classified as contra-assets and are not included in total liabilities and net worth. Total assets are net of loans in process.
[c]Includes net undistributed income accrued by most associations.
[d]Excludes figures for loans in process.

Table 14.2. Flow of funds, S&Ls					
Funds	1979	1980	1981	1982	1983
			($ bil.)		
1 Current surplus	3.3	1.4	-5.2	-3.2	-1.2
2 Net acquisition of financial assets	56.6	52.6	35.8	56.9	120.9
3 Mortgages	44.0	28.3	18.0	-23.6	45.8
4 Consumer credit	3.7	2.6	0.7	4.2	7.5
5 Other assets	8.8	21.7	17.1	76.3	67.7
6 Demand deposits + currency	0.5	0.5	1.0	1.9	3.4
7 Time deposits	-2.2	2.5	-0.7	7.2	1.2
8 Federal funds + security repurchase agreements (RPs)	2.5	-0.7	4.2	0.4	5.9
9 U.S. Treasury securities	-2.9	5.7	-3.5	7.5	14.8
10 U.S. government agency securities	3.9	8.1	6.6	29.8	29.8
11 Tax-exempt obligations	-0.1	0.0	0.1	-0.5	0.1
12 Open-market paper	0.7	1.5	1.2	2.7	3.7
13 Miscellaneous	6.5	4.1	8.2	27.3	8.8
14 Net increase in liabilities	53.0	51.9	40.8	61.2	122.2
15 Deposits	39.1	41.8	20.0	46.8	101.4
16 Security RPs	0.5	2.1	3.0	-1.2	13.9
17 Credit market instruments	12.6	7.4	15.5	2.5	-2.7
18 Corporate bonds	1.4	0.4	-0.5	0.2	0.0
19 Bank loans n.e.c.	2.0	-0.1	-0.2	1.5	4.3
20 Federal home loan bank loans	9.2	7.1	16.2	0.8	-7.0
21 Profit taxes payable	-0.2	-0.3	-0.3	0.0	0.0
22 Miscellaneous liabilities	1.1	0.9	2.6	13.1	9.7
23 Discrepancy	-0.3	0.7	-0.3	1.2	0.1
24 *Memo:* Acquisition of credit market instruments	49.3	46.2	23.1	20.2	101.6
Source: FRB 1984e:23.					

The sharp rise in borrowed money in 1981 chiefly from the Federal Home Loan Bank Board (line 20, Table 14.2) reflects S&L difficulties in making both ends meet. Federally chartered S&Ls must belong to the home loan bank system, and most state-chartered institutions elect membership. The distress shows up in the decline in net worth in 1981 and 1982. It has its counterpart in a negative current surplus (negative saving) in the flow-of-funds statement of −$5.2 and −$3.2 bil. (line 1, Table 14.2). This negative saving summarizes current income less current expenses. Expenses of personnel, materials, etc., and interest payments have exceeded interest income. The dilemma of savings institutions is that they must pay competitive market rates of interest if they are not to be drained of their deposits. At the same time, rates of return on their mortgages are fixed. Savings institutions have little room to maneuver because their portfolios are dominated by old mortgages. Creative financing techniques, including variable rate mortgages, may modify the situation.

More than 80% of federally insured S&Ls (3756 in number) suffered net losses in 1981. At the time, it was predicted that 900 S&Ls could run out of capital (net worth) in another year (*New York Times* 1982:D8). Various bail-out schemes have been proposed, such as the government taking over low-rate mortgages. The continued decline in the net worth of the nation's S&Ls (line 12, Table 14.1) prompted new forms of assistance that were incorporated in the Garn–St. Germain Depository Institution Act of 1982 passed in October of that year. The regulatory agencies (FDIC, FSLIC) were given authority to bolster institutions with government-backed net worth certificates, which provide such institutions with additional funds. The assistance can range in amount up to 70% of operating losses. As an institution's earnings and net worth improve, the certificates are to be paid off (Johnston 1982).

An improvement is shown in 1983, with an increase in net worth (Table 14.1) and the current surplus becoming positive after two negative years (Table 14.2). (We should not expect consistency between increases in net worth and current surplus figures because of differences in the data and conceptual differences.) The upsurge of deposits in 1983 can in large part be attributed to the money market deposit accounts sanctioned by Garn–St. Germain.

As DIs do, S&Ls now must keep reserves against their transactions accounts. These can be in the form of cash in the vault or reserves held directly with the Fed or passed through to the Fed via commercial banks. They are included in line 6 of Table 14.2. S&Ls also maintain liquidity via their ownership of time deposits in commercial banks (line 7) and by lending federal funds and buying security repurchase agreements (RPs) (line 8). Borrowing by selling RPs has become an important short-term source of funds as can be seen from fluctuations in this item (line 16) when studied on a quarterly basis.

Thrifts were again prominent in the news in May 1985 when a run on privately insured S&Ls in Ohio was precipitated by the insolvency of the Home State Savings Bank of Cincinnati. The bank had large losses because of alleged fraud by a government securities dealer involving large repurchase agreements. When the private insurance fund could not cover these losses and other thrifts began suffering large deposit withdrawals, the governor declared a bank holiday for 71 private insured S&Ls. On a selective basis thrifts were reopened after a few weeks (Mayer et al. 1985:2).

Shortly afterward, similar runs on privately insured S&Ls took place in Maryland (Berg 1985:31, 35).

MUTUAL SAVINGS BANKS   Several institutional characteristics distinguish MSBs from S&Ls despite their common dependence on savings deposits. MSBs are concentrated in the northeastern part of the United States, although some are found in the far west. In contrast to the 18 states in which MSBs are found, S&Ls are found in all 50. MSBs are state chartered only, although federal chartering has been advocated to increase competition with S&Ls in the mortgage market. Besides the FDIC, to which about two-thirds of MSBs belong, insurance is provided for New York MSBs by a commercial bank, the Savings Bank Trust Company; MSBs in Massachusetts have created their own deposit insurance system.

As Table 14.3 indicates, MSBs have total assets about one-fourth those of S&Ls. Mortgages again dominate the portfolio, but not as overwhelmingly as the S&Ls. Corporate bonds and equities differentiate their portfolio. The decline in the general reserve account and the negative saving shown in Table 14.4 point out the problems MSBs were facing in 1981–82.

Like S&Ls, MSBs must now keep reserves against their transactions accounts. These include negotiable order of withdrawal (NOW) accounts and accounts subject to telephone or preauthorized transfers when the depositor is authorized to

Table 14.3. Assets and liabilities, MSBs (end of period)

Account	1981	1982	1983
		($ bil.)	
1 Assets	175,728	174,197	193,535
2 Loans			
3 Mortgage	99,997	94,091	97,356
4 Other	14,753	16,957	19,129
5 Securities			
6 U.S. government[a]	9,810	9,743	15,360
7 State and local government	2,288	2,470	2,177
8 Corporate and other[b]	37,791	36,161	43,580
9 Cash	5,442	6,919	6,263
10 Other assets	5,649	7,855	9,670
11 Liabilities	175,728	174,197	193,535
12 Deposits	155,110	155,196	172,665
13 Regular[c]	153,003	152,777	170,135
14 Ordinary savings	49,425	46,862	38,554
15 Time	103,578	96,369	95,129
16 Other	2,108	2,419	2,530
17 Other liabilities	10,632	8,336	10,154
18 General reserve accounts	9,986	9,235	10,368
19 *Memo:* Mortgage loan commitments outstanding[d]	1,293	1,285	2,387

Source: *Fed. Res. Bull.* 1984e:A26.
Note: The National Council reports data on member MSBs and savings banks that have converted to stock institutions and to federal savings banks.
[a]Beginning Apr. 1979, includes obligations of U.S. government agencies. Before that date, this item was included in "Corporate and other."
[b]Includes securities of foreign governments and international organizations and, before Apr. 1979, nonguaranteed issues of U.S. government agencies.
[c]Excludes checking, club, and school accounts.
[d]Commitments outstanding (including loans in process) of banks in New York State as reported to the Savings Banks Association of the state of New York.

Table 14.4. Flow of funds, MSBs

Funds	1979	1980	1981	1982	1983
			($ bil.)		
1 Current surplus	0.7	-0.4	-1.8	-1.3	0.6
2 Net acquisition of financial assets	5.2	8.2	4.2	4.4	19.3
3 Demand deposits and currency	-0.3	1.1	1.2	0.1	-0.7
4 Time deposits	-0.3	0.0	-0.1	1.4	0.0
5 Federal funds and security RPs	0.9	0.6	1.5	0.0	-0.6
6 Corporate equities	-0.1	-0.5	-0.6	-0.5	0.3
7 Credit market instruments	4.4	5.9	1.0	0.6	18.4
8 U.S. Treasury securities	-0.2	0.8	-0.2	0.7	3.8
9 U.S. government agency securities	1.3	2.5	1.2	1.2	6.0
10 Tax-exempt obligations	-0.4	-0.5	-0.1	0.2	-0.3
11 Corporate bonds	-1.1	0.7	-1.0	-1.1	3.0
12 Mortgages	3.6	0.6	-0.4	-2.6	3.3
13 Consumer credit	0.1	1.6	0.2	1.0	1.8
14 Commercial paper	1.1	0.3	1.3	1.2	1.0
15 Miscellaneous assets	0.5	1.0	1.1	2.7	1.8
16 Net increase in liabilities	4.6	8.3	5.5	5.0	18.2
17 Deposits	3.4	7.5	3.0	5.3	15.8
18 Miscellaneous liabilities	1.2	0.8	2.6	-0.3	2.4
19 Discrepancy	0.0	-0.2	-0.4	-0.7	-0.5

Source: FRB 1984e:23.

make no more than three transfers in a calendar month. The cash in an institution's vaults currently suffices to meet required reserves.

CREDIT UNIONS   CUs provide credit to their members who share a common bond, usually the same employer; the Navy and the Pentagon have the largest CUs. There are approximately 22,000 CUs, with membership of around 25 mil.

individuals; most have federal charters. CUs are regulated by the National Credit Union Administration (NCUA), which provides deposit insurance to all the federal CUs and to almost half of those with state charters. Between 1946 and 1977, CUs experienced the highest rate of growth compared with 14 different financial institutions. This can be explained by the importance of consumer durables (most notably the automobile) and their ability to offer lower rates on consumer loans than competing institutions. They are subsidized by free office space, utilities, and volunteer help. Assets and liabilities of credit unions are given in Table 14.5.

Table 14.5. Assets and liabilities, credit unions (end of period)			
Account	1981	1982	1983
		($ bil.)	
1 Total assets/liabilities and capital	60,611	69,585	81,961
2 Federal	39,181	45,493	54,482
3 State	21,430	24,092	27,479
4 Loans outstanding	42,333	43,232	50,083
5 Federal	27,096	27,948	32,930
6 State	15,237	15,284	17,153
7 Savings	54,152	62,990	74,739
8 Federal (shares)	35,250	41,352	49,889
9 State (shares and deposits)	18,902	21,638	24,850

Source: *Fed. Res. Bull.* 1984e:A26.
Note: As of June 1982, data include only federal or federally insured state credit unions serving natural persons.

As can be seen from the flow-of-funds statement, growth in net financial assets (line 2, Table 14.6) slowed down markedly in 1979 and 1981. Nevertheless, current surplus (saving) was still positive in these years. Consumer credit controls probably explain the net reduction in consumer credit in 1980 (line 9, Table 14.6). Many CUs have been liquidated by the NCUA because of insolvency (Auerbach 1982:78). Plant closings bode ill for future growth. Nonetheless, 1982 and 1983 show a sharp increase in financial assets, with the bulk of this increase going into government securities rather than consumer credit.

Table 14.6. Flow of funds, credit unions					
Funds	1979	1980	1981	1982	1983
			($ bil.)		
1 Current surplus	0.3	0.2	0.6	0.5	0.6
2 Net acquisition of financial assets	4.8	8.5	3.7	11.8	15.5
3 Demand deposits and currency	0.2	0.1	0.1	0.1	0.1
4 Time deposits	0.0	2.1	-0.7	0.0	0.0
5 Savings and loan deposits	1.8	3.9	0.6	1.1	-1.3
6 Credit market instruments	2.8	2.4	3.7	10.6	16.7
7 U.S. government securities	0.0	4.3	1.2	8.8	10.0
8 Home mortgages	0.6	0.5	0.5	0.5	0.5
9 Consumer credit	2.2	-2.5	1.9	1.3	6.2
10 Credit union shares	4.4	8.3	3.1	11.2	14.9

Source: FRB 1984e:23.

TIME DEPOSITS IN COMMERCIAL BANKS   Time deposits in commercial banks resemble similar claims on thrifts. Savings deposits (time deposits without fixed maturity dates) are similar in both types of institutions. The ceiling differential of 0.25 of 1% in favor of thrifts was phased out in January 1984 (Table 8.8). Time deposits of commercial banks and thrift institutions are compared in Table 14.7 in three categories: savings deposits and small- and large-denomination time deposits. Thrift institutions show larger amounts in the first two categories, but

Table 14.7. Time deposits in commercial banks and thrifts compared				
Item	Dec. 1980	Dec. 1981	Dec. 1982	Dec. 1983
	($ bil.)			
1 Savings deposits[a]				
2 Commercial banks	183.8	157.5	162.1	132.0
3 Thrift institutions	214.4	184.7	195.5	176.5
4 Small-denomination time deposits[b]				
5 Commercial banks	286.0	347.7	380.1	351.0
6 Thrift institutions	442.3	475.6	472.4	437.6
7 Money market mutual funds				
8 General purpose and broker/dealer	61.6	150.6	185.2	138.2
9 Institution-only	15.0	36.2	48.4	40.3
10 Large-denomination time deposits[c]				
11 Commercial banks[d]	218.5	252.1	266.2	229.0
12 Thrift institutions	44.3	54.3	66.2	100.7

Source: *Fed. Res. Bull.* 1984e:A13, A14.
[a]Savings deposits exclude money market deposit accounts.
[b]Small-denomination time deposits (including retail RPs) are those issued in amounts of less than $100,000. All individual retirement accounts (IRA) and Keogh accounts at commercial banks and thrifts are subtracted from small time deposits.
[c]Large-denomination time deposits are those issued in amounts of $100,000 or more, excluding those booked at international banking facilities.
[d]Large-denomination time deposits at commercial banks less those held by money market mutual funds, DIs, and foreign banks and official institutions.

commercial banks have far greater large-denomination liabilities. What is of interest is the amount still remaining in savings deposits at the end of 1983 despite the 5½% rate ceiling. The greater relative decline in bank saving deposits in 1980–83 may suggest more sensitivity in bank customers to changes in relative interest returns. (Money market mutual funds have a place in this table because household holdings, line 8, are a component of $M2$ like time deposits.)

Shifts out of $M1$ into time deposit components of $M2$ will have different consequences, depending on whether the shift is into a commercial bank time deposit versus a thrift institution or whether the deposit is a nonpersonal deposit and reservable. A shift out of checkable deposits ($M1$) into commercial bank time deposits will have the immediate effect of reducing the money stock. Because there currently are zero reserve requirements against personal time deposits, this will result in bank excess reserves. Under the simplest textbook multiplier conditions, $M1$ will be restored through loan expansion; e.g., assume that the reserve requirement is 12% against $M1$ deposits. A dollar shift into $M2$ personal time deposits will result in $.12 of excess reserves. The textbook multiplier will be the reciprocal of 12% or 8.33. Multiplying 8.33 by 0.12 equals $1 of new demand deposits. Since reserve requirements (3%) are imposed on nonpersonal time deposits such as large negotiable certificates of deposit (CDs), such a transfer would not restore the money stock even if the textbook multiplier was employed. This immediate reduction in the money stock will not take place if the transfer is into a thrift institution's $M2$ deposits. Now the thrift's ownership of $M1$ replaces the former ownership.

THRIFT INSTITUTIONS AND CREDIT MULTIPLIERS   In terms of the money multiplier formula (Eq. 14.1), thrift institutions, because of the importance of time deposits and credit union shares, increase the size of the t parameter as compared with commercial banking alone. The ratios of such claims in relation to the narrow money stock ($M1$) have risen steadily since 1946. For example, S&L

shares (deposits) were 7% of $M1$ in 1946, and at the end of 1982 they were 144% (FRB 1984b, c). In the calculation of asset multipliers the t and g parameters are now added to the numerator of Eq. 14.1. The size of asset multipliers is a good approximation of credit multipliers—the acquisition of interest earning assets by DIs (see Ch. 6).

The increase in credit extended in relation to the money stock as a result of thrifts means that they are responsible for an increase in the velocity of money. The gross national product (GNP) (financed by lending) rises faster than the money stock. As defined in Chapter 2, velocity is the ratio of these two variables. One way of picturing this velocity increase is to assume a shift of checkable deposits in commercial banks into time deposits in thrift institutions. Such a shift leaves the total of checkable deposits unchanged because thrifts now own checkable deposits in commercial banks formerly owned by their new time depositors. The resultant increase of lending by thrifts on the basis of their additional cash reserves and the subsequent spending on the GNP mean that monetary velocity increases.

When a tighter monetary policy results in higher market interest rates, the higher opportunity costs of holding money balances induce shifts into time deposits and increases in the numerator of the credit multiplier. In this way, monetary policy may have slippage effects. The increase in the credit multiplier offsets Fed tightening on reserves so that total DI lending may expand. (The increase in t also increases the denominator of the multiplier, tending to reduce its size, but the net effect is to increase the credit multiplier. In mathematical terms, the partial derivative of the credit multiplier with respect to t is positive.)

Contractual savings institutions

Contractual savings institutions are distinguished from thrift institutions by the fixed commitment that an insurance policy or retirement plan entails. Regular level payments must be made from one period to the next.

LIFE INSURANCE COMPANIES   The rationale of life insurance is that actuarial tables make it possible to estimate the probability of death of an individual in a certain demographic category (age, sex, occupation). On this basis premiums are charged to pay for the ultimate death benefits. The premiums and the interest earned less current expenses, including death benefits, constitute the policy reserves of life insurance companies. As can be seen from Tables 14.8 and 14.9, policy reserves are the major source of funds; life insurance companies administer private pension funds, and these reserves are the other major source.

The major uses of funds of life insurance companies are mortgages, bonds, and equities (stocks). The growing importance of direct investment in income-earning real estate is seen in line 2 of Table 14.9. No financial sector holds larger amounts of bonds than life insurance companies (line 9, Table 14.8). When interest rates go up, policyholders take advantage of the contractual borrowing privilege at bargain interest rates. This explains the growth in policy loans in recent years (line 12, Table 14.8; line 14, Table 14.9).

The first life insurance companies go back over 220 years (Harless 1975). The number of companies has since skyrocketed to about 1815. At the end of 1983,

Table 14.8. Financial assets and liabilities, life insurance
companies (end of period)

Account	1980	1981	1982	1983
		($ bil.)		
1 Total financial assets	464.2	507.5	567.5	633.3
2 Demand deposits and currency	3.2	4.3	4.6	4.0
3 Corporate equities	47.4	47.7	55.7	64.9
4 Credit market instruments	385.1	419.8	463.2	514.4
5 U.S. government securities	17.0	22.5	35.2	54.5
6 Treasury issues	5.8	8.2	16.5	28.6
7 Agency issues	11.1	14.3	18.6	25.9
8 Tax-exempt obligations	6.7	7.2	9.0	10.0
9 Corporate and foreign bonds	178.8	186.1	202.3	219.1
10 Mortgages	131.1	137.7	142.0	151.6
11 Open-market paper	10.1	17.6	21.7	25.2
12 Policy loans	41.4	48.7	53.0	54.1
13 Miscellaneous assets	28.5	35.8	44.0	50.1
14 Total liabilities	438.4	482.9	540.0	600.5
15 Life insurance reserves	207.4	216.3	223.3	231.1
16 Pension fund reserves	172.0	199.8	242.9	286.4
17 Profit taxes payable	1.2	0.7	0.7	0.6
18 Miscellaneous liabilities	57.9	66.1	73.1	82.4

Source: FRB 1984b:24.

Table 14.9. Flow of funds, life insurance companies

Funds	1979	1980	1981	1982	1983
			($ bil.)		
1 Current surplus	4.9	6.3	6.3	6.3	7.4
2 Physical investment	3.0	3.9	5.3	4.6	4.0
3 Net acquisition of financial assets	37.8	37.4	45.9	55.4	61.1
4 Demand deposits and currency	0.3	0.5	1.1	0.3	-0.6
5 Corporate equities	0.6	0.5	2.9	3.4	4.5
6 Credit market instruments	33.4	32.8	34.7	43.5	51.2
7 U.S. government securities	2.9	2.7	5.5	12.7	19.3
8 Treasury issues	0.1	1.0	2.3	8.4	12.1
9 Agency issues	2.8	1.8	3.1	4.3	7.2
10 Tax-exempt obligations	0.0	0.3	0.5	1.9	0.9
11 Corporate bonds	11.6	8.7	7.3	16.2	16.7
12 Mortgages	12.6	12.3	6.7	4.2	9.6
13 Open-market paper	1.6	2.2	7.4	4.2	3.4
14 Policy loans	4.7	6.6	7.3	4.3	1.1
15 Miscellaneous assets	3.5	3.6	7.3	8.1	6.1
16 Net increase in liabilities	35.1	35.5	46.1	53.7	57.2
17 Life insurance reserves	10.4	9.7	8.9	7.0	7.8
18 Pension fund reserves	19.4	22.3	29.5	39.7	40.2
19 Profit taxes payable	0.0	-0.4	-0.5	0.0	-0.1
20 Miscellaneous liabilities	5.3	3.8	8.2	7.0	9.2
21 Discrepancy	-0.7	0.5	1.2	0.0	-0.6

Source: FRB 1984e:25.

their total financial assets as shown in Table 14.8 amounted to $633 bil. This amount, while substantial, still greatly understates the face value of life insurance policies. Life insurance in force probably exceeds $3 tril. (Bishop and Hand 1981:135; this article has a comprehensive treatment of life insurance).

The high interest rates of the 1970s and 1980s placed life insurance companies at a competitive disadvantage because the typical policy (part protection and part savings) rewarded the holder with an annual interest rate between 3 and 5%. Life insurance companies are now advertising interest-sensitive insurance policies that pay market rates on accumulated savings (see two-page ad, *New York Times* 1984a:38–39).

A significant development is the takeover of well-known brokerage and investment companies by insurance companies. Thus, for example, Prudential takes over Bache, Aetna takes over Federal Investors. In this way, insurance companies aim at one-stop financial services. One-stop shopping has gone beyond financial shopping, with Sears Roebuck and Company (the world's largest retailer) buying the Dean Witter Reynolds brokerage firm in 1982. "Buy your stocks where you buy your socks" will soon be a reality, with Dean Witter financial service centers opening up in all the Sears stores (see Ch. 8 for earlier discussion of the emergence of a financial services industry).

PRIVATE PENSION FUNDS   Private pension funds described in Tables 14.10 and 14.11 are funds whose investment is entrusted to a bank or a nonbank trustee. In some cases, corporations may make their own investments. Internal management of this kind accounts for 22% of total assets. Banks manage two-thirds of pension fund assets, accounting for a large share of the business of trust departments (see Andrews and Eiseman 1981:167).

Table 14.10.   Assets of private pension funds

Account		1980	1981	1982	1983
			($ bil.)		
1	Total financial assets	412.7	431.0	518.1	607.8
2	Demand deposits and currency	2.8	3.0	2.8	3.4
3	Time deposits	17.2	18.5	17.2	21.6
4	Corporate equities	209.5	195.6	248.4	306.2
5	Credit market instruments	183.1	214.0	249.7	276.6
6	U.S. government securities	75.0	101.1	136.8	152.3
7	Treasury issues	49.6	65.5	90.9	101.1
8	Agency issues	25.4	35.7	45.9	51.2
9	Corporate and foreign bonds	82.0	85.4	86.5	92.3
10	Mortgages	3.7	3.7	4.1	5.2
11	Open-market paper	22.5	23.7	22.3	26.7
12	Miscellaneous assets	...	...	...	...
	Source: FRB 1984b:24.				

As far as investment policy is concerned, the uniqueness of pensions is the importance of their investments in stocks and bonds (lines 4, 9, Table 14.10). Of all the financial institutions considered, they are the largest investors in corporate equities. In 1983 they accounted for approximately half of total assets of $608 bil. Purchases of U.S. government securities are recently of importance, exceeding purchases of corporate equities, 1981–83 (line 6, Table 14.11).

Table 14.11.   Flow of funds, private pension funds

Funds		1979	1980	1981	1982	1983
				($ bil.)		
1	Net acquisition of financial assets	40.8	48.9	37.6	54.3	47.3
2	Demand deposits and currency	0.5	0.1	0.2	-0.2	0.6
3	Time deposits	2.8	0.4	1.2	-1.3	4.4
4	Corporate equities	9.3	17.7	5.4	20.1	15.3
5	Credit market instruments	28.2	30.8	30.8	35.7	27.0
6	U.S. government securities	11.6	19.5	26.2	35.7	15.5
7	Treasury issues	6.6	13.0	15.9	25.4	10.2
8	Agency issues	5.0	6.5	10.3	10.3	5.3
9	Corporate bonds	12.8	10.7	3.4	1.1	5.8
10	Mortgages	0.3	0.6	0.1	0.4	1.1
11	Open-market paper	3.5	-0.1	1.3	-1.5	4.5
12	Miscellaneous assets	0.0	0.0	0.0	0.0	0.0
	Source: FRB 1984e:25.					

STATE AND LOCAL GOVERNMENT RETIREMENT FUNDS   In comparison, state and local government retirement funds are more conservative in their investment policies. Legal restrictions explain the relatively lower significance of equities and the greater significance of bonds. Credit market instruments make up the bulk of holdings (Table 14.12). Nevertheless, as shown in Table 14.13 describing flows, purchases of corporate equities jumped sharply in 1983 (line 3).

Table 14.12. Assets of state and local government employee retirement funds

Account	1980	1981	1982	1983
	($ bil.)			
1 Total financial assets	198.1	224.2	263.8	316.1
2 Demand deposits and currency	4.3	4.4	7.0	10.4
3 Corporate equities	44.3	47.8	60.2	89.6
4 Credit market instruments	149.5	172.0	196.6	216.1
5 U.S. government securities	40.0	51.8	70.7	87.9
6 Treasury issues	20.9	27.6	36.9	50.2
7 Agency issues	19.1	24.3	33.8	37.7
8 Tax-exempt obligations	4.1	3.9	3.1	1.8
9 Corporate and foreign bonds	94.5	103.6	108.8	111.5
10 Mortgages	10.9	12.7	14.0	14.8

Source: FRB 1984b:24.

Figure 14.13. Flow of funds, state and local government employee retirement funds

Funds	1979	1980	1981	1982	1983
	($ bil.)				
1 Net acquisition of financial assets	16.2	26.5	31.0	37.3	44.5
2 Demand deposits and currency	1.3	0.3	0.2	2.5	3.4
3 Corporate equities	4.1	5.3	8.3	10.1	21.6
4 Credit market instruments	10.8	20.9	22.5	24.7	19.4
5 U.S. government securities	6.6	9.9	11.8	18.9	17.2
6 Treasury issues	5.3	6.2	6.6	9.3	13.3
7 Agency issues	1.4	3.7	5.2	9.5	3.9
8 Tax-exempt obligations	0.0	0.1	-0.2	-0.7	-1.3
9 Corporate bonds	3.2	9.5	9.1	5.2	2.7
10 Mortgages	1.0	1.3	1.8	1.3	0.8

Source: FRB 1984d:25.

The federal government's retirement programs (Federal Old Age and Survivors Insurance Trust Fund, Civil Service Retirement and Disability Program, Railroad Retirement Account) differ from previous pension plans, since they are automatically invested in special classes of government securities.

OTHER INSURANCE   Property-casualty companies are called the department stores of finance because they sell so many different kinds of policies (Harless 1975:19) (e.g., property coverage protects against fire, hail, and windstorm damage; casualty insurance against burglary and automobile liability). Their sources of funds are premium payments listed under policy payables in line 15, Table 14.14.

Table 14.14. Assets and liabilities, other insurance companies

Account	1980	1981	1982	1983
	($ bil.)			
1 Total financial assets	174.3	185.6	202.8	225.3
2 Demand deposits and currency	2.9	3.0	3.0	2.6
3 Security RPs	...	0.1	4.1	13.7
4 Corporate equities	32.3	32.4	38.5	48.1
5 Credit market instruments	123.5	132.0	137.0	138.6
6 U.S. government securities	18.4	20.5	22.6	28.1
7 Treasury issues	12.2	13.5	14.1	17.4
8 Agency issues	6.2	7.0	8.5	10.7
9 Tax-exempt obligations	80.5	83.9	87.0	86.7
10 Corporate and foreign bonds	23.6	26.3	25.8	21.6
11 Commercial mortgages	1.0	1.3	1.6	2.3
12 Trade credit	15.6	18.1	20.2	22.2
13 Total liabilities	123.0	133.7	144.2	156.2
14 Profit taxes payable	0.4	0.3	0.3	0.2
15 Policy payables	122.6	133.4	144.0	156.0

Source: FRB 1984b:24.

The payables are not as predictable as death benefits so other insurance follows a more conservative investment policy than life insurance. Most of its bonds are obligations of state and local governments (municipals). While equities are the second largest investment, they are made up of the common stock of less risky industries such as utilities, banks, and insurance companies. Casualty companies invest in more liquid securities than property companies, since casualty losses cannot be predicted as accurately as those for property.

MONETARY CONTROL AND CONTRACTUAL SAVINGS   The size of the credit multiplier (cm) is augmented by going beyond DIs. Now we add an extra term in the numerator of Eq. 14.1 without adding any terms in the denominator:

$$cm_{di+csi} = \frac{1 + c + t + g + s}{r_1(1 + g) + r_2 t + e + c} \tag{14.2}$$

This extra parameter (s) defines desired public holdings of claims on contractual savings institutions (CSIs). The reason for this asymmetry is that there are no legal reserve requirements for CSIs. The inflow of pension and insurance funds (which in turn can be linked to an initial expansion in checkable deposits) is free of reserve requirements. The expansion of claims on CSIs reflects the expansion of income and savings that results from an initial reserve increase owing to central bank action. We can write:

$$(\Delta D/\Delta R)(\Delta Y/\Delta D)(\Delta S/\Delta Y) = (\Delta S/\Delta D)(\Delta D/\Delta R)$$

where $\Delta S/\Delta D$ = s of Eq. 14.2
D = checkable deposits
Y = income
R = reserves

Compared with thrift institutions, we should expect that institutions depending on contractual savings would be more insulated from the effects of policy on income or interest rates. Flows into these institutions are geared to a household's conception of its average or permanent income. Aberrations in current income owing to policy are not likely to affect current flows. Nonetheless, policy loans do introduce some flexibility in household investment in life insurance. Rising interest rates caused by tight monetary policies encourage an increase in policy loans. Such funds will be spent or loaned in the open market. As discussed in the next section, shifts out of institutional claims into marketable securities will increase the flow of funds and frustrate monetary policy.

Direct finance

Direct finance companies issue variable-value instead of fixed-value claims and act as agents in the sale of such securities.

FINANCE COMPANIES   Finance companies are in the business of advancing both consumer and business credit. Companies that make personal loans are per-

Table 14.15. Assets and liabilities outstanding at finance companies by size of receivables, June 30, 1980

Balance sheet item	All finance companies	Size of company (short- and intermediate-term loans outstanding)					
		500 and over	100-499	25-99	5-24	1-4	Under 1
		($ mil.)					
Assets							
Consumer receivables	77,260	65,128	7,310	2,671	1,029	687	436
Retail passenger car paper	27,118	25,948	324	427	208	175	36
Mobile homes	4,832	4,363	248	153	56	10	2
Retail consumer goods	22,702	18,978	3,054	306	240	69	56
Revolving credit	16,161	13,766	2,257	3	135	0	0
Other retail consumer goods paper	6,541	5,212	797	303	105	69	56
Personal cash loans	22,609	15,838	3,684	1,784	525	434	343
Revolving credit	589	382	16	118	68	3	3
Other personal cash loans	22,021	15,457	3,668	1,667	457	432	340
Business receivables	86,067	65,157	14,743	4,620	1,211	264	71
Wholesale paper	21,741	18,952	2,036	674	28	44	7
Automobiles	12,373	12,226	118	6	8	15	0
Business, industrial, and farm equipment	5,072	3,983	585	495	4	5	0
All other	4,296	2,743	1,333	173	17	24	7
Retail paper	26,318	22,348	3,179	712	28	49	2
Commercial vehicles	10,088	9,241	780	49	2	14	2
Business, industrial, and farm equipment	16,230	13,107	2,399	663	26	35	0
Lease paper	23,261	14,916	5,277	2,042	949	62	16
Auto paper	6,194	5,858	151	17	161	5	3
Business, industrial, and farm equipment	16,937	9,058	5,064	2,001	744	56	13
All other	130	0	62	24	44	0	0
Other business credit	14,747	8,941	4,252	1,192	206	110	46
Short-term	8,325	3,614	3,550	931	146	54	31
Intermediate-term	6,422	5,328	702	262	61	55	15
Real estate loans	11,831	9,144	1,357	739	455	105	31
Secured by first liens	1,380	915	289	116	39	8	13
Secured by junior liens	10,451	8,229	1,068	623	415	97	19
Other accounts and notes receivable	8,183	7,590	313	216	25	16	23
Total receivables, gross	183,341	147,019	23,722	8,246	2,719	1,072	561
Less reserves for unearned income	21,251	16,404	3,122	1,096	470	111	49
Less reserves for losses	2,981	2,303	418	160	51	30	20
Total receivables, net	159,108	128,311	20,183	6,991	2,198	932	492
All other assets	15,917	11,636	2,535	954	329	147	316
Total assets, net	175,025	139,947	22,718	7,944	2,527	1,079	809
Liabilities and capital							
Loans and notes payable to banks	15,458	7,677	4,018	2,439	969	272	83
Short-term	7,885	4,036	1,691	1,456	477	168	58
Long-term	7,573	3,641	2,327	983	492	104	25
Commercial paper	52,328	45,662	5,277	1,227	143	14	4
Directly placed	43,232	41,537	1,320	262	95	14	4
Dealer placed	9,095	4,125	3,957	965	49	0	0
Other short-term debt	10,627	6,747	2,250	1,136	257	156	81
Other long-term debt	52,898	46,367	4,702	1,186	400	156	87
All other liabilities	18,363	14,574	2,615	719	283	136	36
Capital, surplus, and undivided profits	25,350	18,919	3,856	1,238	475	345	517
Total liabilities, capital, and surplus	175,025	139,947	22,718	7,944	2,527	1,079	809
Memo:							
Short-term debt	70,840	56,445	9,218	3,818	877	338	143
Long-term debt	60,471	50,008	7,029	2,169	892	260	112
Number of companies	2,775	48	100	156	239	484	1,749

Source: *Fed. Res. Bull.* 1981a:404.

sonal finance companies. Those that finance purchases of automobiles and other consumer durables are sales finance companies, which also finance automobile dealers by wholesale financing of their inventories. Companies that advance credit to business firms by buying their accounts receivable are called commercial finance companies. Table 14.15 presents the assets and liabilities of finance companies as of June 30, 1980. The end of 1983 data show total financial assets of $260 bil. (FRB 1983c).

Their dependence on equity finance and the sale of bonds and open-market commercial paper places them in the direct finance category of financial institutions. Finance companies are highly leveraged; their indebtedness is a large multiple of their net worth. The large companies are more highly leveraged than the small ones. As shown in Table 14.15, the largest companies show approximately a 6:1 ratio of debt (memo item) to capital and surplus as compared with a 0.5:1 ratio for the smallest companies.

It is a very concentrated industry with 11% of all finance companies (2775 in number) holding 97% of the value of all consumer receivables and 98% of the value of business receivables (*Fed. Res. Bull.* 1981a:402). The largest finance companies are captives of the major automobile manufacturing corporations.

REAL ESTATE INVESTMENT TRUSTS   Real estate investment trusts (REITs) date their first recorded statistics to 1966. They seemed to offer households the perfect inflation hedge — the purchase of real property or investment in high-yielding mortgages. They are trusts because of their unique tax exempt status. The Real Estate Investment Act of 1960 stipulated certain conditions such as 75% of assets being in real estate and 90% or more of income being distributed to stockholders.

Realty investments are the leading assets of REITs, with major sources of funds being bank loans, commercial paper, and shareholders' equity. The anticipated hedge against inflation failed to materialize for the shareholder in REITs. In 1973 and 1974 many of these companies suffered severe financial problems because of rising interest rates on loans, tighter credit, soaring construction costs, shortages of construction materials, and a generally depressed housing market. The decline and fall of REITs are demonstrated in the negative flow-of-funds figures in Table 14.16.

Table 14.16. Flow of funds, REITS

Funds	1979	1980	1981	1982	1983
			($ bil.)		
1 Physical investment	...	...	...	.3	.3
2 Net acquisition of financial assets	-0.6	-1.7	-0.7	.2	.2
3 Mortgages	-1.0	-0.7	-1.1	-.7	-.3
4 Miscellaneous assets	0.3	-1.0	0.4	.9	.4
5 Net increase in liabilities	-0.3	-1.5	-0.5	.6	.6
6 Corporate equity issues	0.9	0.6	-0.8	.6	.4
7 Credit market instruments	-1.3	-2.2	0.2	.1	.2
8 Mortgages	0.0	-0.1	-0.5	.1	.0
9 Corporate bonds	0.0	-0.2	-0.7	.0	.0
10 Bank loans n.e.c.	-1.4	-1.7	1.5	.1	.2
11 Open-market paper	0.1	-0.2	0.0	-.1	-.1
12 Miscellaneous liabilities	0.0	0.1	0.0	.0	.0

Source: FRB 1984e:27.

INVESTMENT COMPANIES   Investment companies or mutual funds sell shares and invest the proceeds in a wide variety of securities; in this way, the shareholder has the safety of diversification plus professional management. They began in Europe with the Société Générale de Belgique formed in 1822 being generally credited as the first investment company. In the United States the period of first growth covers the time between the end of World War I and the stock market crash of 1929. The investment company did not become significant until after World War II when the expansion of money income combined with the pooling of risk provided by mutual funds attracted unsophisticated first-time investors (Rose and Fraser 1985:558. Chapter 21 of Rose and Fraser provides comprehensive discussion of investment companies).

Investment companies are major holders of stocks, second only to private pension funds among nonbank financial institutions. Shareholders are free to cash in their holdings and be paid according to the market value of the portfolio at the time of redemption. Sales charges may be levied at the front (purchase) end or back (sale) end; or the fund may be a no-load fund, free of such charges. The mutual fund, apart from sales charges, receives compensation from a fixed management fee based on the market value of its assets.

Open-end investment companies are going concerns, continuously selling or redeeming shares. In contrast, the closed-end investment companies issue shares to be sold in the open market, and new shares are not issued regularly. Their assets are approximately 10% of those of open-end companies.

The assets held by open-end investment companies (see Table 14.17) are the net outcome of different portfolio strategies. Mutual funds may seek maximum capital gains, long-term growth, balanced portfolios, and income. Mutual funds seeking the first two objectives are common stock funds. The balanced funds mix bonds and common and preferred stock, while the income funds principally invest in long-term debt securities. Because equities satisfy most of these objectives, they account for 57% of total holdings of $129 bil. (end of 1983). This percentage has fallen sharply, however, since 1965 when it was 88%. Municipal bond funds carrying exemption from federal income tax have become increasingly attractive, with their percentage rising from 0 to 24% over this time (FRB 1984b).

Table 14.17. Assets and liabilities, open-end investment companies

Account	1980	1981	1982	1983
		($ bil.)		
1 Total financial assets	63.5	63.8	89.5	129.3
2 Demand deposits and currency	0.8	0.8	1.2	1.7
3 Corporate equities	42.2	37.2	48.9	73.5
4 Credit market instruments	20.5	25.7	39.4	54.1
5 U.S. government securities	1.9	2.8	5.1	5.7
6 Tax-exempt obligations	6.4	9.3	21.1	31.5
7 Corporate and foreign bonds	8.5	10.1	10.2	13.0
8 Open-market paper	3.8	3.6	3.0	4.0
9 Total shares outstanding	63.5	63.8	89.5	129.3
Source: FRB 1984b:26.				

MONEY MARKET FUNDS   Money market mutual funds (MMMFs) specialize in short-term investments, particularly negotiable CDs and open-market paper. Their attraction for shareholders has been high yields, check writing, wire transfer, float, and liquidity (Rose and Fraser 1985:433). (For the discussion of MMMFs by one of its pioneers, see G. Johnson 1978:4ff.; for a recent discussion, see Rose and Fraser 1985:Ch. 6.) Both the stock (Table 14.18) and the flow (Table 14.19) record the sharp rise in assets (1979–81) in response to a widening interest rate spread with the passbook savings rate. The decline in purchases in 1982 and the sell-off of assets in 1983 reflect the fall in interest rates and the effects of deregulation. The tables also reveal a decline in the relative importance of large CDs (in time deposits) in comparison with open-market commercial paper.

The strong competition offered by MMMFs to thrifts was a major impetus to financial deregulation. Innovations before DIDMCA in 1980 (applying to thrifts)

Table 14.18. Financial assets and liabilities, money market mutual funds
(end of period)

Account	1978	1979	1980	1981	1982	1983
				($ bil.)		
1 Total assets	10.8	45.2	74.4	181.9	206.6	162.5
2 Demand deposits and currency	0.1	0.1	0.2	0.5	0.3	-0.3
3 Time deposits	4.5	12.0	21.0	43.9	40.8	24.0
4 Security RPs	0.3	2.4	5.6	14.5	16.2	13.0
5 Foreign deposits	0.5	5.1	6.8	18.8	23.8	21.9
6 Credit market instruments	5.1	24.9	39.8	102.3	123.7	102.4
7 U.S. government securities	1.5	5.6	8.2	31.9	54.6	36.2
8 Open-market paper	3.7	19.3	31.6	70.4	69.1	66.2
9 Miscellaneous	0.3	0.7	1.1	2.9	1.8	1.5
10 Total shares outstanding	10.8	45.2	74.4	181.9	206.6	162.5

Source: FRB 1984b:26.

Table 14.19. Flow of funds, money market mutual funds

Funds	1979	1980	1981	1982	1983
			($ bil.)		
1 Net acquisition of financial assets	34.4	29.2	107.5	24.7	-44.1
2 Demand deposits and currency	0.0	0.1	-0.7	0.8	-0.6
3 Time deposits	7.5	9.0	22.8	-3.1	-16.8
4 Security RPs	2.1	3.2	8.9	1.7	-3.2
5 Foreign deposits	4.6	1.7	12.1	4.9	-1.8
6 Credit market instruments	19.8	14.9	62.5	21.4	-21.4
7 U.S. government securities	4.2	2.6	23.7	22.7	-18.4
8 Open-market paper	15.6	12.3	38.8	-1.3	-3.0
9 Miscellaneous	0.4	0.4	1.9	-1.1	-0.4
10 Net share issues	34.4	29.2	107.5	24.7	-44.1

Source: FRB 1984e:27.

included six-month money market certificates and two and one-half–year CDs, both tied to open-market rates. (see Table 8.8). The strongest counteraction was the introduction of money market deposit accounts late in 1982. The multiple uses of MMMFs argue for their survival, however. Not only are they a convenient way for households to park funds between stock and bond market investments but bank trust departments and corporations find them more economical for cash balance management than direct investment (Cook and Duffield 1979:15–31; see also Ch. 17).

INVESTMENT BANKING   New issues of primary securities are underwritten by investment banks and sold by brokers and dealers in securities. The latter also buy and sell old securities. Brokers buy and sell on account for their customers, earning a commission. Dealers, on the other hand, take a position in the security, buying and selling for their own accounts. In the flow of funds published data, the activities of security dealers, brokers, and investment banking are all subsumed under security brokers and dealers. Security credit is the primary asset and liability in the balance sheet (not shown). Banks are the principal source of such credit, and the customers of brokers are the principal users. Customers leave the proceeds of security sales with brokers (customer credit balances), and this is another important source of funds. The term "investment banking" is commonly used to refer to all these activities. Moreover, large investment houses will typically be vertically integrated, acting as underwriter-dealer-broker (Block and Hirt 1978:322).

The underwriting role is crucial in providing business with long-term financing. Investment banks function as intermediaries between borrowers and ultimate investors. They win the right to sell the security by bidding more than other underwriters. Their bid is a firm commitment to the borrower. They subsequently sell the securities to investors. The difference between the bid price and the selling price is the spread; e.g., if the bid price is $98 per share and it is resold to the public for $100, the spread is $2. As a percentage of proceeds, it will decline as the size of issue increases. In the past, for issues of less than $0.5 mil., it has amounted to 11.3% for common stock and 7.4% for debt. For issues of $50 mil. and over, the percentages fall to 2.3 and 0.8% respectively (Block and Hirt 1978:324). The underwriter is pulled by two opposing forces — winning the underwriting contract by offering a high bid and bidding low so as to sell the issue at a profit (Bloch 1964:72).

When the offering is sizable, an underwriting syndicate made up of many investment houses is formed. Managing the syndicate will be one of a half-dozen major investment houses. Now the price decision must be hammered out among members of the underwriting group. The jousting between the syndicate manager and the members reflects the conflict between winning the bid and making a profit. The syndicate members will be less aggressive than the manager, putting more weight on profitability than on losing the bid to a rival syndicate (Wayne 1982:3.1, 3.17).

TRUST DEPARTMENTS OF COMMERCIAL BANKS   Trust accounts have already been encountered in Chapter 7 when the activities of bank trust departments were briefly mentioned. They belong here because banks act as trustees or agents in the purchase of marketable securities for households or other estates. Table 14.20 shows the total assets over which banks have discretion to be $257 bil. at the end of 1982, with about half invested in equities. Personal trusts include common trust funds, which pool the assets of many small accounts, thereby achieving economies of scale. Employee benefit accounts, which include private pension funds and agency accounts, are also administered by banks as trustees. This means that pension funds administered by banks have been classified both as contractual savings and direct finance. Agency accounts are those for which banks provide advice only and do not engage in actual decision making.

Table 14.20. Personal trusts and estates administered by banks (asset holdings at end of period)

Account	1980	1981	1982
		($ bil.)	
1 Total assets	228.992	229.746	256.951
2 Deposits and credit market instruments	79.948	85.967	103.226
3 Total deposits	7.217	7.602	7.940
4 Demand deposits	1.881	2.003	1.638
5 Time and savings accounts	5.336	5.599	6.302
6 Credit market instruments	72.731	78.365	95.286
7 U.S. government securities	21.287	22.762	27.445
8 State and local government securities	20.994	20.469	27.010
9 Other security and time obligations	14.446	19.616	23.618
10 Other securities	12.070	11.327	12.880
11 Mortgages	3.934	4.191	4.333
	Corporate equities		
12 Common	124.765	116.044	125.161
13 Preferred	1.967	1.836	1.854
14 Real estate	18.347	21.062	21.828
15 All other assets	3.965	4.837	4.882

Source: FRB 1983c:66.
Note: Insured commercial and MSBs, Fed member trust companies, nonmember nondeposit trust companies owned by bank holding companies. Discretionary assets only. MSBs and trust companies introduced in 1979 held about 2% of total 1979 assets.

FEDERALLY SPONSORED CREDIT AGENCIES AND MORTGAGE POOLS   The purpose of federal lending agencies is to increase the flow of funds into certain sectors of the economy, primarily housing and agriculture. Table 14.21 covers the activities of the Federal Home Loan Bank (FHLB) system, sponsored credit agencies, and their mortgage pools. The FHLB system with 12 regional banks and a board in Washington, D.C., plays an analogous role for S&Ls to the Fed's role vis-à-vis the member banks. System securities are sold in the federal agency securities market, and they finance advances to the S&Ls. Federally sponsored credit agencies include the Federal National Mortgage Association (FNMA, or Fannie Mae), the Federal Home Loan Mortgage Corporation (FHLMC, or Freddie Mac), and the Government National Mortgage Association (GNMA, or Ginnie Mae). All three agencies aim at promoting new residential housing by supporting the buying side of the mortgage market.

The activities of the farm credit system that embrace the Bank for Cooperatives (BC) and Federal Intermediate Credit Banks (FICB) are reflected in lines 13 and 14. Farm mortgages in line 12 are extended by the Farmers Home Administration (FmHA) located in the U.S. Department of Agriculture. The depressed state of agriculture was responsible for placing the system in financial jeopardy in 1985 (Hershey 1985a:29, 36). A detailed description of government lending agencies will

Table 14.21. Federally sponsored credit agencies and mortgage pools, assets and liabilities (end of period)

Account	1980	1981	1982	1983
	($ bil.)			
Sponsored credit agencies				
1 Total financial assets	195.3	232.9	255.2	257.3
2 Demand deposits and currency	0.5	0.7	0.6	0.8
3 Federal funds and security RPs	6.0	9.5	14.9	12.6
4 Credit market instruments	184.2	217.4	233.1	236.2
5 U.S. government securities	2.5	2.9	4.3	3.1
6 Open-market paper	0.4	0.7	0.4	0.8
7 Student loans (SLMA)	2.6	4.8	6.4	7.9
8 Housing credit	113.5	134.6	145.6	147.8
9 Residential mortgages	64.5	69.4	79.6	88.9
10 Federal Home Loan Board (FHLB) loans to S&Ls	49.0	65.2	66.0	59.0
11 Loans to agriculture	65.3	74.4	76.3	76.6
12 Farm mortgages	36.0	43.7	47.3	48.1
13 Loans to co-ops (BC)	9.8	9.5	8.7	9.5
14 Loans to farmers (FICB)	19.4	21.2	20.4	19.0
15 Miscellaneous assets	4.5	5.3	6.7	7.8
16 Total liabilities	191.0	228.1	249.3	250.3
17 Credit market instruments	162.6	195.0	210.4	211.8
18 Sponsored agency issues	159.9	190.4	205.4	206.8
19 U.S. government loans	2.7	4.6	5.0	5.0
20 Miscellaneous liabilities	28.4	33.0	39.0	38.5
21 Deposits at FHLBs	10.1	11.9	14.7	11.8
22 Capital subscriptions	9.7	11.0	12.0	12.2
23 Other	8.6	10.1	12.3	14.5
Federally related mortgage pools[a]				
24 Total mortgage holdings	114.0	129.0	178.5	244.9
25 Home mortgages	107.1	124.8	174.1	239.4
26 Multifamily mortgages	6.0	3.4	3.8	5.0
27 Farm mortgages	0.9	0.7	0.6	0.5
28 Total pool securities	114.0	129.0	178.5	244.9
Memo:				
Totals for agencies and pools				
29 Housing credit	226.6	262.9	323.6	392.2
30 Loans to agriculture	66.1	75.1	76.9	77.2
31 Debt securities outstanding	273.9	319.4	383.9	451.7

Source: FRB 1984b:14.

[a]GNMA, FNMA, FHLMC, and FmHA pools. Excludes Federal Financing Bank holdings of pool securities, which are in U.S. government mortgages and other loans directly.

be found in Hand (1981:216–38). The distribution of farm debt by lender shows that in addition to the farm credit system and federal government agencies, banks, life insurance companies, and individuals hold substantial portions of the farm debt of $213 bil. (Benjamin 1985:12). (The entire issue of *Economic Perspectives,* November/December 1985, Fed, Chicago, is devoted to the farm credit crunch.)

Fannie Mae explains why the word "sponsored" is introduced before federal in the description of federal credit agencies. It was restructured in 1968 as a government-sponsored but privately owned corporation whose shares now trade on the New York Stock Exchange (Horvitz 1979:247).

Fannie Mae is the oldest agency, having been established in 1938. It principally buys mortgages insured by other government agencies – FmHA and Veterans Administration insured and guaranteed mortgages. The originators of mortgages (land developers, S&Ls, MSBs) then have funds to make more mortgage loans. There is something in it for originating institutions when they sell off their mortgages because they continue to service the mortgage (collecting the monthly mortgage payment) for which they are paid a servicing fee. Fannie Mae's activities are reflected in line 9, Table 14.21, amounting to $88.9 bil. at the end of 1983. Freddie Mac, established in 1970, buys conventional (noninsured) mortgages and also is involved with Ginnie Mae in mortgage pools, which refer to packages of mortgages whose purchase is financed by the sale of securities. These securities are guaranteed as to interest and principal by Ginnie Mae, although nominally they are issued by the originators of the mortgage package (such as S&Ls). The latter service the mortgages, with mortgage payments being passed through to the owners of the securities. For this reason they are called pass-through securities (Horvitz 1979:247–48; Light and White 1979:371). Ginnie Mae securities, because interest and principal are guaranteed and because of high yields, have turned out to be an attractive investment. The drawback is the early return of principal when mortgages are retired ahead of schedule.

Table 14.21 shows $244.9 bil. of such pool securities outstanding at the end of 1983 (line 28). The memorandum at the bottom of the table indicates that total housing credit advanced was $392.2 bil.; $77.2 bil. was advanced to agriculture via the BC, FICB, and FmHA. These amounts were financed by pool securities and the debt issued by sponsored credit agencies (the total of such securities is given in line 31).

The growth of pool securities in the 1980s means that federal credit agencies are not ultimate lenders but serve only as guarantors. Pass-through securities (collateraled by mortgages) are purchased by financial institutions and households. They are identified as agency securities in the flow-of-funds data for these sectors. When federal lending agencies issue their own debt, they take the demand side of the mortgage securities market and the supply side of the federal securities market. In this way, they affect relative yields on mortgages and bonds. The effect on the flow of funds into housing may be offsetting, however, because the purchasers of agency securities may be S&Ls or investors who otherwise put their money into the thrifts.

MORTGAGE COMPANIES   One more intermediary in the housing field is the mortgage company, also known as mortgage banking. The mortgage company responded to the development of a secondary market for mortgages made possible by the insuring of mortgages and Fannie Mae's standby role. Mortgage companies buy mortgages from their originators (such as S&Ls) and then sell them to more permanent holders, including federal credit agencies. The commitments to buy, which the mortgage company negotiates, facilitate their getting bank credit. In many cases the mortgage company is a subsidiary of a major bank holding company, with the commercial bank advancing credit. Yearly average originations by mortgage companies during 1970–76 were approximately $13 bil., or 18% of total mortgage originations (Light and White 1979:356–57).

DIRECT FINANCE AND THE SUPPLY OF CREDIT   Slippage in monetary control can result from shifts out of checkable deposits and intermediary claims into marketable securities. The institutional framework for such shifts has just been discussed. The analysis, compared with shifts into intermediary claims out of checkable deposits, is complicated by the availability of marketable securities. Intermediary claims are always on sale, whereas marketable securities must be offered as new issues or as existing issues in the secondary market. The analysis must be on an "as if" basis. It is as if the supply curve of securities is a horizontal line, so that the effect on the flow of credit (external finance) can be analyzed.

Looking at the financial system as a whole, a shift into marketable securities out of checkable deposits of say $1 mil. will have an equal effect on external finance. The volume of checkable deposits stays the same and so does the required reserves of DIs. A shift out of time deposits in DIs, however, will have a much smaller effect—possibly zero. The reason is that such purchases will involve the conversion of time deposits (sooner or later) into checkable deposits with their higher reserve requirements. In the limiting case where securities were purchased out of nonreservable personal time deposits, DIs would have to unload $100 of interest-earning assets to satisfy reserve requirements. This assumes that the Fed would not accommodate the increase in checkable deposits by furnishing more reserves.

Such increases in the flow of funds in credit markets offset the intended effects of monetary policy when it is responsible for increases in open-market interest rates. Because such rates are more volatile than the interest rates on intermediary claims, we should expect that disintermediation would be encouraged by tight policy. This seems to be the case. Figure 14.1 shows trends in the lender composition of net funds supplied. Figure 11.3 gives short-term interest rates that can be compared with the percentage composition of funds supplied in Figure 14.1, which is based on the data given in Table 4.2. The percentage of commercial banking in line 21 of that table to total funds advanced (line 1) underlies the commercial banking line in Figure 14.1. It overstates the importance of lending via the banking sector (indirect lending), since bank negotiable certificates of indebtedness (a major deposit source of funds) are more like marketable securities than time and savings deposits where they are classified. The remaining financial institutions (lines 22–24, Table 4.2) are the basis of private nonbank financial institutions in Figure 14.1. The solid line, private domestic nonfinancial sectors, is based on line 33 of Table 4.2. This includes lending to financial institutions—their credit market borrowing in line 27. So for all four components of the figure to add up to 100% of funds advanced, credit market borrowing is deducted from institutional

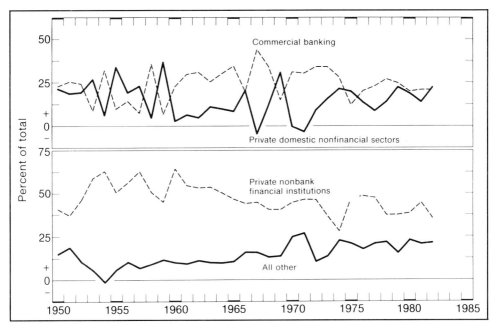

14.1. Net funds supplied by type of lender, annually. (FRB 1983d:48)

lending. If this was not done, direct lending would also show up in funds advanced by financial institutions. Finally, "all other" represents funds advanced by public agencies and the foreign sector (line 2, Table 4.2).

The first three curves in Figure 14.1 give the impression of an inverse relationship between financial and private domestic nonfinancial sector lending. The explanation lies in part in the procyclical behavior of interest rates. When interest rates advance in the expansion phase of the business cycle, a disintermediation process takes place. For example, Figure 11.3 shows short-term interest rates falling sharply in 1958, rising sharply in 1959, rising in 1966 and 1969, falling in 1972, and rising in 1974 and 1979. This interest rate pattern has its counterpart in intermediation and disintermediation. Disintermediation as measured by the second curve (Fig. 14.1) increases with increases in interest rates and declines (intermediation increases) with a fall in interest rates. Some DI sources of funds (most notably Super NOWs, money market deposit accounts, and large CDs) carry flexible rates, giving them the characteristic of open-market instruments. Disintermediation in periods of rising rates would be accentuated if DIs lacked this capacity to issue interest-sensitive claims. This flexibility was given them by the acts of 1980 and 1982.

Variations in commercial banks' share of the market may also be due to central bank behavior. Banks are not bona fide intermediaries, as discussed in Chapter 2. Rather than their deposits financing lending, it is closer to the truth that their lending generates deposits. Such lending in turn is related to bank reserves. When the central bank tightens credit, bank lending declines in relative terms at the same time that open-market rates go up.

Since 1973 the third curve for private nonbank financial institutions shows more sensitivity to open-market rates than commercial banks. They have been less successful in combating disintermediation. The relation of the fourth curve ("all other") to short-term rates is less systematic, since public agency and foreign lending will be dominated by other factors.

The effect of direct finance df on the credit multiplier when lending is financed by checkable deposits can be summarized by adding an additional term (the ratio of direct lending to checkable deposits d) to the numerator of Eq. 14.2. Again there is no absorption of reserves in the denominator of the multiplier formula. Thus:

$$cm_{di+csi+df} = \frac{1 + c + t + g + s + d}{r_1(1 + g) + r_2 t + e + c}$$

The flow of credit or external finance CR will be the overall credit multiplier (now simply cm) times total reserves: $CR = cm(R)$.

High-powered money and the flow of credit

A crude measure of the credit multiplier is provided by calculating the ratio of external finance to average reserves. When credit flows are related to the money stock, the financial velocity of money is suggested. The rise in interest rates and continued financial innovation have contributed to the long-run increase in both ratios since the 1950s (Table 14.22), because of the increase in size of the parameters of the credit multiplier.

In 1947, for every $100 in the money stock, $14.50 was raised in credit markets. This compares with $109 being advanced in 1983. Between 1947 and 1983, average bank reserves increased from $19 bil. to $44 bil. At the same time, "funds advanced" increased from $16 bil. to $411 bil. The approximate doubling of reserves accompanied a 30-fold increase in credit flows. This explains the increase in the ratio of external finance to average reserves from the initial 0.827 to 12.365 in 1983. Figure 14.2 carries the impact of high-powered money one step further by relating funds raised in credit markets to GNP. The message is that the upward movement in GNP has been accompanied by similar increases in the flow of credit, although until 1978 the latter was increasing somewhat faster. In more rigorous analysis the ratio has been said to be more or less stable, suggesting the dependence of GNP growth on the growth of external financing (Ch. 12; B. Friedman 1982).

Summary

Monetary policy has many obstacles to overcome. The financial system outside the Fed represents one such hurdle. Since the financial legislation of 1980 and 1982, nonmember banks and thrifts are part of the Federal Reserve System as far as monetary control is concerned.

Thrifts are discussed here for the first time in terms of their portfolio behavior. Contractual savings institutions and institutions involved in direct finance outside the Fed and their financial statements are analyzed.

	(1)	(2)	(3)	(4)=(3):(1)	(5)=(3):(2)
	Average	Average money	External	Ratio of external finance to	Ratio of external finance to average
Year	reserves	stock	finance	average reserves	money stock
	($ bil.)	($ bil.)	($ bil.)		
1947	19.1	109.1	15.8	.827	0.145
1948	21.2	112.0	13.0	.613	0.116
1949	20.5	111.7	16.3	.795	0.146
1950	19.2	112.6	24.4	1.271	0.217
1951	21.3	116.7	22.5	1.056	0.193
1952	22.7	122.2	30.8	1.357	0.252
1953	22.6	126.8	27.8	1.230	0.219
1954	22.0	129.3	25.8	1.173	0.199
1955	21.5	132.3	36.0	1.674	0.272
1956	22.0	135.2	27.5	1.250	0.203
1957	22.3	136.4	28.1	1.260	0.206
1958	22.0	137.5	40.0	1.818	0.291
1959	21.4	139.7	50.6	2.364	0.362
1960	20.8	141.4	37.1	1.784	0.262
1961	20.7	144.1	45.2	2.184	0.314
1962	21.5	147.8	54.4	2.530	0.368
1963	21.6	151.9	59.6	2.759	0.392
1964	21.8	158.2	67.9	3.115	0.429
1965	22.8	165.6	71.4	3.132	0.431
1966	24.2	171.6	68.3	2.822	0.398
1967	26.1	179.4	81.4	3.119	0.454
1968	28.0	192.2	98.3	3.511	0.511
1969	29.2	202.6	89.6	3.068	0.442
1970	30.3	211.1	94.9	3.132	0.449
1971	33.2	223.6	139.6	4.205	0.624
1972	34.8	241.3	166.4	4.782	0.689
1973	36.0	258.8	194.0	5.389	0.750
1974	37.6	271.6	190.3	5.061	0.701
1975	37.9	284.3	204.4	5.393	0.719
1976	37.8	300.7	262.8	6.952	0.874
1977	39.0	322.9	332.9	8.536	1.031
1978	43.7	349.3	403.6	9.236	1.155
1979	47.5	376.1	406.2	8.551	1.080
1980	47.8	401.5	371.8	7.778	0.926
1981	45.5	427.3	407.6	8.958	0.954
1982	44.9	459.4	419.8	9.350	0.914
1983	44.1	499.6	545.3	12.365	1.091

Table 14.22. High-powered money and external finance

Sources: External finance--FRB 1984e:3, line 31; average reserves--FRB 1984c:54, line 24; average money stock--(1947-59) U.S. Dep. Commer. 1975:pt. 2, 992; (1960-83) President 1984:21.

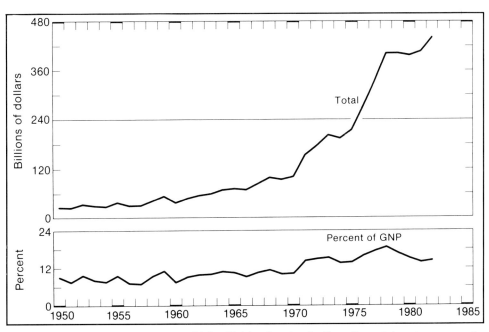

14.2. Net funds raised, all nonfinancial sectors, annually. (FRB 1983d:44)

The focus in this chapter is the effect of financial institutions outside the Fed on the total flow of credit. The leverage of the Fed is increased with additional institutions because the credit multipliers go up in value. Expressing the public's desired holdings of financial assets as ratios to checkable deposits and adding successive financial asset categories increase the numerator of the credit multiplier without increasing the denominator once we introduce institutions not subject to reserve requirements. Shifts into marketable securities take place through financial institutions that were identified as direct finance institutions. They themselves sell marketable securities or act as agents for purchases by the private nonfinancial sector.

Slippage results from autonomous shifts out of checkable deposits into other claims on thrift institutions or by shifts out of checkable deposits and intermediary claims into marketable securities. The connection with monetary policy is that a tighter policy may lead to higher interest rates, which then inspire these shifts out of money balances.

Historically, the relative importance of indirect and direct finance varies with cyclical movements in short-term interest rates. Direct finance (disintermediation) increases with increases in interest rates and goes down (intermediation goes up) with declines in interest rates. Whether intermediation or disintermediation is taking place, the long-run effect of higher interest rates is to increase the flow of external finance in relation to either the money stock or high-powered money. Since external finance is regarded here as the key linkage variable to the GNP, this complicates the problems of policymaking.

The increase in the size of the credit multiplier, when all financial flows are considered, means that high-powered money becomes more high-powered; a dollar increase in reserves can have a 12-fold effect on the expansion of credit. Such credit extension bears a close relation to variations in the GNP, which supports making credit the intermediate target of monetary policy.

Review questions

1. What is the difference between money and credit multipliers?

2. Contrast the leverage and slippage effects of monetary policy.

3. Distinguish between commercial banks, thrifts, contractual savings institutions, direct finance institutions. List the various members of these categories. Reference to their financial statements is necessary.

4. How and why does the expansion of the financial institution framework increase the size of the credit multiplier?

5. Compare commercial banks with thrifts in terms of the relative importance of different time deposit categories.

6. Describe the relationship between short-term interest rates and intermediation and disintermediation.

7. Why are reserves called high-powered money with respect to the flow of credit?

8. Does the relation between credit flows and the GNP strengthen the argument for credit targeting?

15

Finance and the allocative mechanism

Chapter 14 explored the flow of funds into nonbank financial institutions. Earlier chapters discuss the money-creating properties of depository institutions (DIs) (Ch. 6) and the response of banks to an intitial deposit increase (Ch. 7). Now we study the next linkage, that between portfolio behavior of financial institutions and borrowing by nonfinancial sectors. The interaction of many borrowers and lenders constitutes a financial market. The notion of interaction was less appropriate before because financial institutions (except those intermediating new security flotations) stood ready to accept all funds offered to them at posted interest rates. Now borrowers and lenders play an active role. The higher the interest rate, the more financial lenders lend. Borrowers borrow less the higher the interest costs are. In this way both borrowers and lenders interact, demonstrating their joint involvement in the determination of flows and interest rates.

The linkage between financial lender and nonfinancial borrower should be studied along with the linkage between borrowing and spending. This has already been covered in Chapter 2 and now again, since study of the two sets of linkages should show how finance affects the allocation of real resources.

Several approaches can be taken. One is to consider the nonbank financial institutions one by one, detailing the response to an inflow of funds in the same way as done earlier for the commercial banks (Ch. 7). A second approach is to take the point of view of the borrowing sector, where the various financial institutions would be discussed in relation to that sector and its uses of funds.

Fortunately, both approaches are reconciled in a flow-of-funds framework. A dummy statement of this matrix is given in Chapter 1. Now a more detailed matrix based on 1983 data is presented and analyzed. In succeeding sections the matrix will be analyzed from the standpoint of both financial and nonfinancial sectors.

Instead of the abbreviated sector-transactions breakdown of Chapter 1, the major sectors are disaggregated and many more lines of financial information are provided. Table 15.1 begins as before with the nonfinancial transactions of saving and investment, but with much more detail on investment. A new final row and

Table 15.1. The 1983 flow-of-funds matrix ($bil.)

	(1)	(2)	(3)	(4)	(5)	(6)	(7)	(8)	(9)	(10)	(11)	(1
					Nonfinancial sectors							
						State and						
	Private		Domestic		local				Foreign		U.S.	
	households		business		governments		Total		sector		governmen	
Funds	Uses	Sources	Uses	Sources	Uses	Sources	Uses	Sources	Uses	Sources	Uses	Sou
1 Gross saving	...	519.1	...	364.5	...	9.2	...	892.9	...	34.6	...	-19
2 Capital consumption	...	296.5	...	297.5	...	...	...	594.0	...	...	...	
3 Net saving, (1)-(2)	...	222.6	...	67.0	...	9.2	...	298.9	...	34.6	...	-19
4 Gross investment (5)+(11)	576.2	...	321.2	...	2.4	...	899.9	...	34.4	...	-202.0	.
5 Private capital expenditures	396.9	...	343.0	...	...	...	739.9	...	...	...	-7.8	
6 Consumer durables	279.4	...	...	...	...	...	279.4	...	...	...	...	
7 Residential construction	106.1	...	23.8	...	...	...	129.9	...	...	...	...	
8 Plant and equipment	11.3	...	317.9	...	...	...	329.2	...	...	...	...	
9 Inventory change	...	...	-6.4	...	...	...	-6.4	...	...	...	...	
10 Mineral rights	...	...	7.8	...	...	...	7.8	...	...	...	-7.8	
11 Net financial investment	179.4	...	-21.8	...	2.4	...	160.0	...	34.4	...	-194.2	.
12 Financial uses	368.5	...	138.6	...	47.1	...	554.1	...	69.3	...	11.5	.
13 Financial sources	...	189.1	...	160.4	...	44.6	...	394.2	...	34.9	...	20
14 Gold and official foreign exchange	...	...	...	...	...	...	...	...	0.0	0.5	2.7	.
15 Treasury currency	...	...	...	...	...	...	...	...	...	...	...	
16 Checkable deposits and currency	31.9	...	4.6	...	-2.0	...	34.6	...	1.6	...	-8.1	
17 U.S. government	...	...	...	...	...	...	...	...	...	...	-8.1	
18 Foreign	...	...	...	...	...	...	...	...	1.6	...	...	
19 Private domestic	31.9	...	4.6	...	-2.0	...	34.6	...	...	...	...	
20 Small time and savings deposits	215.5	...	...	...	5.3	...	220.8	..	...	...	-0.5	.
21 Money market fund shares	-44.1	...	...	...	...	...	-44.1	...	...	...	...	
22 Large time deposits	-9.8	...	16.6	...	-8.8	...	-1.9	...	0.5	...	...	
23 Federal funds and security RPs	...	...	5.5	...	3.0	...	8.5	...	...	...	...	
24 Foreign deposits	...	...	4.5	...	...	...	4.5	...	...	2.6	...	.
25 Life insurance reserves	15.8	...	...	...	...	...	15.8	...	...	...	...	
26 Pension fund reserves	126.9	...	...	...	...	...	126.9	...	...	...	...	1
27 Interbank claims	...	...	...	...	...	...	...	...	20.3	...	...	.
28 Corporate equities	9.9	...	...	28.3	...	...	9.9	28.3	5.4	3.9	...	.
29 Credit market instruments	73.0	166.7	16.7	126.3	50.1	43.7	139.8	336.8	27.8	17.7	9.7	18
30 U.S. Treasury securities	30.1	...	6.7	...	39.6	...	76.4	...	16.7	...	...	18
31 Federal agency securities	8.8	...	0.0	...	4.4	...	13.1	...	...	...	0.0	
32 State and local government securities	34.9	...	0.7	9.4	0.3	42.6	35.9	52.0	...	...	...	.
33 Corporate and foreign bonds	-3.3	...	...	14.9	...	...	-3.3	14.9	5.7	3.6	...	.
34 Mortgages	-2.3	108.1	...	62.6	5.9	...	3.6	170.7	...	...	1.2	-
35 Consumer credit	...	51.3	7.5	...	...	...	7.5	51.3	...	...	...	
36 Bank loans n.e.c.	...	3.6	...	22.5	...	...	...	26.1	...	3.8	...	
37 Open-market paper	4.8	...	1.9	-1.2	...	...	6.6	-1.2	5.4	6.0	...	
38 Other loans	...	3.8	...	18.1	...	1.1	...	23.0	...	4.3	8.5	.
39 Security credit	3.3	19.2	...	...	...	...	3.3	19.2	0.0	0.0	...	.
40 Trade credit	...	2.3	64.2	53.8	...	0.9	64.2	57.0	0.1	-0.2	1.8	
41 Taxes payable	...	...	...	3.4	-0.6	...	-0.6	3.4	...	...	5.3	(
42 Equity in noncorporate business	-61.0	...	...	-61.0	...	...	-61.0	-61.0	...	...	...	
43 Miscellaneous	6.9	0.9	26.5	9.5	...	...	33.4	10.4	13.6	10.4	0.6	
44 Sector discrepancies, (1)-(4)	-57.1	...	43.3	...	6.8	...	-7.0	...	0.2	...	6.2	

Source: FRB 1984i.

column (not in the original pro forma statement) measure discrepancies in debit and credit values for sectors (column discrepancies) and for transactions (row discrepancies). Data inadequacies explain such discrepancies; e.g., in the matrix, gross investment overall exceeds gross saving by $11.6 bil. (row 4, col. 25). This is

	(14)	(15)	(16)	(17)	(18)	(19)	(20)	(21)	(22)	(23)	(24)	(25)	(26)
				Financial sectors									
Sponsoring agency and marketing pools		Monetary authority		Commercial banking		Private nonbank finance		Total		All sectors		Discrepancy	National saving and investment
Uses	Sources	Uses	Sources	Uses	Sources	Uses	Sources	Uses	Sources	Uses	Sources	Uses	
.	1.7	...	0.6	...	12.0	...	7.7	...	21.9	...	753.6	...	719.1
.	...	...	...	...	10.3	...	3.1	...	13.4	...	607.4	...	607.4
.	1.7	...	0.6	...	1.7	...	4.6	...	8.5	...	146.2	...	111.7
9	...	0.6	...	22.3	...	9.2	...	33.0	...	765.2	...	-11.6	717.0
.	...	...	...	14.5	...	4.8	...	19.2	...	751.4	...	2.3	751.4
.	...	...	...	...	...	...	...	...	...	279.4	...	...	279.4
.	...	...	...	...	...	0.1	...	0.1	...	130.0	...	...	130.0
.	...	...	...	14.5	...	4.7	...	19.2	...	348.4	...	...	348.4
.	...	...	...	...	...	...	...	...	...	-6.4	...	...	-6.4
.	...	...	...	...	...	...	...	...	...	...	...	...	...
9	...	0.6	...	7.8	...	4.4	...	13.7	...	13.9	...	-13.9	-34.4
4	...	8.8	...	144.6	...	323.1	...	544.8	...	1179.7	...	-13.9	34.9
.	67.4	...	8.2	...	136.8	...	318.7	...	531.0	...	1165.8	...	69.3
.	...	-2.1	...	...	...	...	...	-2.1	...	0.5	0.5	...	...
.	...	0.0	...	...	...	...	...	0.0	...	0.0	0.5	0.5	...
2	...	...	12.3	2.2	15.8	6.7	10.6	9.1	38.7	37.2	38.7	1.5	...
.	...	...	-1.3	...	-5.3	...	...	...	-6.7	-8.1	-6.7	1.4	...
.	...	...	0.0	0.0	1.6	...	...	...	1.6	1.6	1.6	...	...
2	...	...	13.6	2.2	19.6	6.7	10.6	9.1	43.8	43.7	43.8	0.1	...
.	...	...	...	...	129.9	-1.4	89.0	-1.4	218.9	218.9	218.9	...	...
.	...	...	...	...	...	...	-44.1	...	-44.1	-44.1	-44.1	...	...
.	...	...	...	...	-53.4	-17.8	34.2	-17.8	-19.2	-19.2	-19.2	...	...
3	...	...	...	...	8.8	2.0	10.9	-0.3	19.7	8.2	19.7	11.5	...
.	...	...	...	...	...	-1.8	...	-1.8	...	2.6	2.6	...	...
.	...	...	...	...	...	...	15.7	...	15.7	15.8	15.8	...	...
.	...	...	...	...	...	...	112.9	...	112.9	126.9	126.9	...	...
.	...	-1.0	-3.6	-3.6	19.2	...	...	-4.6	15.7	15.8	15.7	-0.1	...
.	...	...	...	0.0	0.7	55.3	37.8	55.3	38.5	70.6	70.6	...	...
8	67.7	10.9	...	132.7	8.4	241.1	13.7	453.4	89.8	630.8	630.8	...	...
8	...	12.6	...	45.5	...	36.2	...	93.5	...	186.7	186.7	...	...
4	67.7	-0.7	...	0.7	...	55.0	...	54.6	67.7	67.7	67.7	...	...
.	...	...	...	3.8	...	12.4	...	16.2	...	52.0	52.0	...	...
.	...	...	...	3.8	4.9	29.3	12.2	33.1	17.1	35.6	35.6	...	...
3	...	...	...	28.7	...	60.8	0.0	165.8	0.0	170.6	170.6	...	...
.	...	...	...	22.7	...	21.1	...	43.8	...	51.3	51.3	...	...
.	...	0.0	...	28.9	...	...	-1.0	28.9	-1.0	28.9	28.9	...	...
4	...	-1.1	...	-1.4	3.5	7.9	9.5	5.8	13.0	17.8	17.8	...	...
7	0.0	...	...	...	...	18.4	-7.0	11.7	-7.0	20.2	20.2	...	...
.	...	...	...	2.4	...	18.2	4.6	20.6	4.6	23.8	23.8	...	...
.	...	...	...	...	...	2.0	...	2.0	...	68.0	59.4	-8.6	...
.	...	...	...	...	-0.1	...	0.1	...	0.0	4.7	3.4	-1.2	...
.	...	...	...	...	...	...	...	...	...	-61.0	-61.0	...	...
7	-0.3	1.0	-0.5	10.8	7.4	18.9	33.3	32.4	39.8	80.0	62.7	-17.4	...
8	...	0.0	...	-10.8	...	-1.5	...	-11.0	...	-11.6	...	-11.6	2.1

the total for the discrepancy column (col. 25). Since the debit and credit totals for all sectors correspond to the debit and credit totals for all transactions, the sum of the sector discrepancies similarly equals $11.6 bil. The large statistical discrepancy for the household sector ($57.1 bil.) is due to the transaction values in this sector to a considerable extent being the balancing item (residual) for differences in debit and credit entries along the transaction row for the remaining sectors for whom firmer statistical data are available.

Saving in the flow of funds differs from the more familiar personal saving concept in the national income accounts. Figures for 1983 are given in Table 15.2. The reason for the difference is that net saving adds on (principally) credits from government insurance and net durables in consumption. Capital consumption is an estimate of depreciation in homes and consumer durables. Gross saving is thus the appropriate concept for comparison with gross investment. In theory gross saving equals gross investment for each sector. In practice, as just indicated, a statistical discrepancy of $57 bil. exists in 1983 for households.

The addition of consumer durables makes for much higher personal saving rates than using national income (NIA) concepts. Further, while the NIA concept as a percent of disposable personal income has been falling in recent years (being at the rate of 5% in mid-1985) the flow-of-funds measure has been stable (21% in mid-1985) (FRB 1985b:7). While the NIA personal saving rate has been a cause for alarm, this is not the case for the broader flow-of-funds version (Hershey 1985a:1, 51).

Table 15.2. Reconciling personal saving (NIA) and saving in the flow of funds ($bil.)	
Item	1983
1 Personal income	2744.2
2 - Personal taxes and nontaxes	404.2
3 = Disposable personal income	2340.1
4 - Personal outlays	2222.0
5 = Personal saving, national income accounts (NIA) basis	118.1
6 + Credits from government insurance	58.7
7 + Capital gains dividends	4.4
8 + Net durables in consumption	61.5
9 = Net saving	242.7
10 + Capital consumption	280.4
11 = Gross saving	523.2
Source: FRB 1984e:7.	

The household sector

Our present interest is primarily with the financial sources of the household sector. As we learned in earlier chapters and can see from Table 15.1, the leading financial sources of funds for households are mortgages (line 34) and consumer credit (line 35). Other loans and security credit are noticeable sources of funds.

LINKAGES BETWEEN SOURCES AND USES OF FUNDS   The borrowing of the household sector and its financial dissaving (a kindred source of funds) can be explained by the sector's uses of funds and by interest rates. A higher interest rate on one source of funds encourages borrowers to seek out a cheaper source of funds. In estimating the explanatory relationships for households, we must avoid certain pitfalls. This means we should be mindful of the accounting constraints on borrowing-spending relations. For a full discussion of constrained estimation and the stacking of equations for this purpose, see Hendershott (1977:Ch. 4, 81–83).

A simplified flow-of-funds statement for households satisfies the following identity: increase in financial assets (FA) + consumer durables ($CDUR$) + housing expenditures ($HOUS$) = personal saving (PS) + increase in consumer credit (CC) + mortgage borrrowing (MOR). Transposing to the left-hand side the variables that we wish to explain:

$$CC + MOR = (FA - PS) + CDUR + HOUS$$

These variables are arranged in the form of a matrix in Figure 15.1 after reversing the signs on FA and PS. This matrix describes two equations, one for consumer credit and one for mortgage borrowing, with three explanatory variables across the columns.

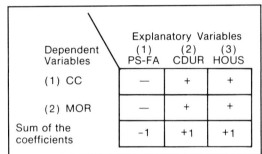

	Explanatory Variables		
Dependent Variables	(1) PS-FA	(2) CDUR	(3) HOUS
(1) CC	—	+	+
(2) MOR	—	+	+
Sum of the coefficients	-1	+1	+1

15.1. Constrained flow relations.

Personal saving net of increases in financial assets in the first column is expected to decrease both kinds of borrowing, as indicated by the signs in the column cells. The sum of the coefficients for net personal saving in the two equations is necessarily minus one. A $1 increase in net personal saving will mean an equal reduction in other sources of funds (consumer credit and mortgage borrowing) if we hold uses of funds constant. An increase in expenditures on consumer durables (col. 2) will mean an increase in borrowing with each $1 of increased expenditures resulting in a $1 increase in borrowing, as shown by the sum of coefficients. The same results hold for housing expenditures in col. 3.

When the explanatory variables go beyond flow of funds to include interest rate variables, the values of their coefficients are also constrained. Let us introduce the interest rates on consumer credit (CCI) and mortgages ($MORI$). Again the column variables are explanatory in equations explaining the row variables. (Fig. 15.2).

	Explanatory Variables	
Dependent Variables	CCI	MORI
(1) CC	—	+
(2) MOR	+	—
Sum of the coefficients	0	0

15.2. Constrained interest rate relations, with sources of funds only.

Higher interest rates on a given type of borrowing are expected to reduce borrowing there and induce more by alternate instruments. This substitution effect is shown by the signs in the cells of the matrix (Fig. 15.2). The coefficients necessarily sum to zero for each interest rate. This reflects the underlying sources-and-uses identity. The matrix assumes that total sources stay the same with an increase in interest rates. If, for example, an increase in the interest rate on consumer credit reduces consumer credit borrowing, it must increase mortgage borrowing by an equal amount.

In accordance with the identity, if total sources increase, uses of funds would also have to increase. The matrix in Figure 15.3 illustrates the equality by expanding the list of dependent variables. It now includes increases in financial assets and expenditures on consumer durables and housing. The interest rate on financial assets (*FAI*) has been added as an additional explanatory variable.

	CCI	MORI	FAI
(1) FA	0	0	+
(2) CD	−	−	−
(3) HOUS	−	−	−
(4) CC	−	+	−
(5) MOR	+	−	−
Sum of coefficients (1) + (2) + (3) − [(4) + (5)]	0	0	0

15.3. Constrained interest rate relations, with sources and uses of funds.

The sources–equal uses identity will only be satisfied if the interest rate change affects both sides of the identity equally. So once again, subtracting the coefficients in the borrowing equations from the coefficients in the uses-of-funds equations gives a sum of zero. The signs in the first two columns suggest that higher borrowing costs will discourage planned spending and borrowing, but with some substitution between the financial sources of consumer credit and mortgages. The signs in the final column show the response to higher interest returns on financial assets. They indicate that expenditures and borrowing decrease as financial assets are substituted for real assets. If households borrow to lend, the signs in rows 4 and 5 of the *FAI* column might be positive. Total flows might increase in this case. Otherwise the signs suggest a contraction in flows when interest rates go up. An exogenous increase in capital outlays (durables, housing), however, will be likely to increase total funds flows even though higher interest rates deter such expenditures.

Empirical estimates   Estimating similar equations by regression analysis (Hendershott 1977:Ch. 6) (quarterly 1957–74) gives empirical content to the earlier discussion of the linkages among sources and uses of funds as discussed in Chapter 2 (Fig. 2.1).

The results show that 97% of saving is allocated to financial assets (linkage 2, Fig. 2.1). To a slight extent such saving reduces borrowing. This illustrates linkage 6. Consumer durable expenditures are financed by a reduction in financial assets (linkage 5), by consumer credit (almost half of expenditures are financed in this way), and by mortgage credit (a third). Such borrowing exemplifies linkage 3. Similarly, new housing expenditures are financed in the same three ways, with mortgages accounting for two-thirds of the financing. The results indicate the fungibility of money. Money borrowed on a chattel mortgage, ostensibly to buy a car, may be used to finance housing. Similarly, money borrowed ostensibly to finance housing (on the basis of a mortgage loan) may go into consumer durables. The cushioning role of financial asset holdings is also noteworthy. Initially built up out of saving, they can later be used to finance capital expenditures. The fungibility of money and salability of financial assets dramatize the problems faced by monetary policy either in applying selective credit controls or general controls. Selective controls can be circumvented by using an acceptable collateral, or funds can be obtained for any spending whatsoever by selling off financial assets.

Interest-rate effects as distinct from the linkage effects specified in Figure 2.1 have also been estimated. The substitution effects of higher mortgage interest rates are reflected in less financial asset acquisition (as current spending on housing is increased out of current or past saving), more consumer credit borrowing, more policy loans, and (as expected) less mortgage borrowing. Higher open-market rates have the expected positive effect on policy loans. It is estimated that if the commercial paper rate advances by one percentage point, over the time of three quarters policy loans will go up by $500 mil. The proceeds in turn are invested in financial assets.

BREAKING DOWN FINANCIAL ASSETS   Financial asset purchases can be subdivided into four categories: money, savings accounts—commercial and mutual savings bank (MSB) deposits, large negotiable certificates of deposit (CDs), savings and loan (S&Ls), and credit union (CU) shares—short-term securities (commercial paper and Treasury bills), and long-term securities (equities and corporate, state and local, and federal government long-term debt) (Hendershott 1977:84ff.). The effect of the previous explanatory variables on financial assets can now be made more specific.

The first finding is that net sources of funds (savings less expenditures on durables, housing, and contractual saving) go largely into interest-bearing assets, with only 20% going into money holdings. One quarter later, half the increase in money holdings is shifted largely into savings accounts. Capital gains go into short-term assets, reducing liabilities, with the latter adjustment process taking longer than the asset adjustment. Runoffs of CDs, when interest rates reach ceiling levels, are shifted into open-market securities, two-thirds of which are short term, one-third long term.

Changes in the yields on savings accounts and short-term securities induce rapid movements out of money. Here for comparative purposes we speak in terms of relative percentage changes or elasticities. Thus the money elasticity with respect to the savings account rate is -0.43, and with respect to the short-term (commercial paper) rate it is -0.05. The first is an important elasticity indicating that a 1% increase in the savings account rate induces a 0.43% reduction in money holdings. Similarly, interest rate substitutions between saving accounts and open-market securities have low values. Moreover, the adjustment process takes longer than in the case of money.

Policy loans in response to higher short-term rates are invested in short-term security holdings. When mortgage rates are high, households reduce their mortgage borrowing and liquidate their savings accounts. Finally, an increase in income increases transactions balances and reduces the demand for open-market securities. The elasticity of transactions balances with respect to income is estimated to be 0.30; i.e., a 1% increase in income results in a 0.30% increase in money balances.

The business sector

The same kind of linkages between sources and uses can be established for the business sector. As before, the effect of interest rates can also be studied (Hendershott 1977:Ch. 7). The empirical analysis shows that fixed investment is largely financed by long-term debt issues. Inventories and trade credit are financed by short-term debt (mainly bank loans), liquidation of short-term debt, and money holdings. Residential construction in process has mortgages as its chief source of financing.

The business sector matches the maturity structure of its sources and uses. Such matching minimizes the interest and transactions costs of financing and it also makes the financing and interest more certain for long-term investments. Permanent short-term borrowing requires having to renew loans periodically, but long-term borrowing for short-term purposes entails expensive flotation costs. Substitution between financial and nonfinancial uses (see linkage 5, Fig. 2.1) takes place for inventories and trade credit. Money holdings and short-term assets are disposed of as these assets are acquired (or vice versa).

On the sources-of-funds side, linkages exist between gross internal funds (cash flow) and financial sources of funds. Total internal funds convert undistributed profits into a cash flow measure by adding imputed expenses (mainly capital consumption allowances) to profits and subtracting paper profits from inflated prices of inventories (inventory valuation adjustment). The derivation of internal funds for nonfinancial corporate business is given in Table 15.3.

Table 15.3. Derivation of internal funds for nonfinancial corporate business ($bil.)	
Item	1983
1 Profits before tax	148.9
2 - Profit tax accruals	58.0
3 - Domestic net dividends	72.2
4 = Domestic undistributed profits	18.6
5 + Capital consumption adjustment	33.0
6 + Depreciation charges, NIPA	215.2
7 + Earnings received from abroad	9.9
8 = U.S. internal funds, book	276.8
9 + Foreign earnings returned abroad	14.9
10 + Inventory valuation adjustment	-11.2
11 = Total internal funds and IVA	280.5
Source: FRB 1984e:11.	

The strong negative relationship with long-term borrowing indicates that cash flow is a closer substitute for long-term borrowing than short-term borrowing. Cash flow is viewed by the firm as a long-run source of funds having to be supplemented by long-term borrowing when it declines (Hendershott 1977:100). The linkage in Figure 2.1 between saving and financial assets (linkage 2) is also in evidence from the empirical estimates. Funds earmarked for tax payment purposes are invested in short-term assets (such as government securities) or used to retire short-term debts.

LONG-TERM SOURCES OF FUNDS   It is possible to divide the long-term category into commercial-type mortgages, term loans (exceeding a year in maturity), corporate equity, and corporate bonds. The long-term sources of corporate stocks and bonds are now seen as a substitute for cash flow (Hendershott 1977:113–14). Long-terms are issued when short-term debt exceeds desired levels, indicating a fear of illiquidity. An additional variable (stock market prices) helps to explain the issuance of corporate stock in the place of corporate bonds. More corporate stock will be issued the higher market prices are, with the proceeds possibly being used to retire long-term debt.

Capital outlays and the cost of capital

The interest rate affects business borrowing via its effects on planned business spending. The theory of investment emphasizes the relation between the cost of capital (the interest rate) and the expected return on capital. The traditional diagram is as shown in in Figure 15.4. The curve should initially be read from the horizontal axis to the vertical axis, with investment being related to the expected rate of return (also called the marginal efficiency of investment).

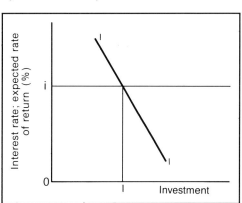

15.4. The investment decision.

The expected rate of return is found by solving a present-value equation of the kind discussed in Chapter 5. The rate of discount makes the present value of future returns from the investment equal to the cost of the investment. Thus:

$$PV = S_1/(1 + r) + S_2/(1 + r)^2 + \ldots + S_n/(1 + r)^n + SV/(1 + r)^n$$

where PV = present value (the purchase price of the investment)
$S_i = S_1, S_2 \ldots S_n$ = expected cash flow from the investment
                        SV = scrap value of the investment
                          r = rate of discount

PV, S_i, and SV are assumed to be known. Solving for r yields the expected rate of return or marginal efficiency of investment. As long as this rate exceeds the cost of borrowing, it pays to undertake additional investment. Alternatively, we can solve for PV, knowing the S_i and SV and substituting the market rate of interest (i) for r. As long as PV is greater than the purchase price of the capital good, the investment is worthwhile. A variant of this approach is to set a payout period of say $n - m$ years. Only the first $n - m$ terms in the expression will be discounted, and the requirement is that this sum equal or exceed the cost of the capital good.

The greater the planned investment, the lower the expected return (going from the horizontal to the vertical axis in Fig. 15.4). The law of diminishing returns (combining more capital with a given amount of other factors of production) results in a diminution of the S_i of the present-value equation. Also, more production might put downward pressure on product prices and upward pressure on input prices.

The curve (Fig. 15.4) is next interpreted as a planned investment curve, with investment responding to the market interest rate (proceeding from the vertical to the horizontal axis). Comparison of the expected rate of return with the market rate determines the investment decision. Assume that $0i$ is the market rate. Then $0I$ investment is decided on, since at this rate the interest cost equals the expected return on an additional unit of investment (say $1 bil.). Proceeding to the right down the curve until $0I$ investment is reached, the expected rate of return exceeds the market rate.

The market rate is some average of borrowing costs on alternative financial sources of funds; e.g., the sale of corporate stock will have a higher expected cost than corporate bonds. Because they are not guaranteed a return, investors will require compensation in the form of a higher yield when they buy stock. The market rate represents some weighted average of different borrowing costs.

Using the interest rate as synonymous with the cost of capital omits important elements of the latter. A more comprehensive cost-of-capital concept (also referred to as the rental or user price of capital) would consider capital consumption (depreciation), tax credits, corporate income tax, and the inflation rate. (We follow the modification of Dornbusch and Fisher 1978:179–96.) Thus the real cost of capital can be written as:

$$r_c = (1 - T)(i - \dot{P}^e + d)/(1 - t)$$

where r_c = rental cost of capital
$\quad\quad T$ = tax credit (a percentage of taxable income)
$\quad\quad i$ = market interest rate
$\quad\quad d$ = depreciation rate
$\quad\quad \dot{P}^e$ = expected rate of inflation
$\quad\quad t$ = corporate tax rate

The term $i - \dot{P}^e + d$ in the numerator measures real interest and depreciation expense. The rationale of subtracting the expected rate of inflation from the market interest rate is that inflation produces bonus dollars to meet these interest costs. Thus $10 interest on $100 borrowed for capital outlays becomes in effect zero interest if higher prices generate an extra $10 in revenues that are available for meeting interest expense. The first part of the expression reduces this real cost by the amount of the tax credit. If credit for depreciation expense or investment reduces the tax burden, the true cost is less by the T percentage. But the return on investment is reduced by corporate income taxes. In the above formulation, dividing by $1 - t$ shows this as an increase in the rental price of capital.

A further departure from the simplified investment function $I = f(i)$ that we started with is to think of investment as a stock adjustment process. Investment is a flow occasioned by a gap between the desired and actual capital stock. Thus:

$$I = \lambda(K^* - K_{-1})$$

where λ = speed of adjustment in filling the gap
K^* = desired stock of capital
K_{-1} = capital stock at the end of the previous period

The speed of adjustment coefficient λ can take on values between 1 and 0. The closer to 1, the quicker the adjustment will take place. In the limiting case of 1 the gap would be filled in a single period. The value of K^* is determined by the ratio of the productivity of capital to the cost of capital (which we have already discussed). The productivity of capital (actually its share of total output) can be represented by aY, where Y is total output and a measures capital's share of total output. Desired capital is then:

$$K^* = aY(1 - t)/(1 - T)(i - \dot{P}^e + d)$$

Because it does not consider the financial constraint, investment in this context should be interpreted as planned investment (ex ante investment). Actual investment (ex post investment) will depend on funds forthcoming for financing. This depends on the interaction between lenders and borrowers in financial markets (this affects the key linkage 3 of Fig. 2.1), the impact of borrowing on internal finance (linkage 6), and the extent to which investment expenditures are substitutes for financial assets (linkage 5). Hendershott (1977) considers financial flows and interest rates so that the analysis has both ex ante and ex post characteristics. He takes the capital expenditure variables as exogenous so that expenditures explain borrowing. In contrast, our approach would emphasize external finance as the necessary condition for expenditures without any such causal interpretation. A causal interpretation involves a complete model, which can distinguish between growth-induced and growth-inducing finance.

State and local government sector

The final nonfinancial sector to be considered is the state and local sector. Saving flows into financial assets (money, savings accounts, open-market securities) (Ch. 14; also Hendershott 1977:158). Part of the increase in money holdings is temporary, subsequently being shifted into savings accounts. Construction outlays are financed by issuing debt and liquidating financial assets in equal proportions. Interest rates appear to play a larger role in adjustments than for the household and business sectors. Expectations of lower interest rates lead to less debt financing and more asset liquidation. Liquid asset holdings respond quickly to interest rates. This finding of Hendershott runs counter to newspaper headlines that play up the failure of state and local governments to put their money out at interest.

Commercial bank sector

The other side of financial flows to the nonfinancial sectors includes the lending activities of the financial institutions. The Hendershott (1977:117ff.) study supplements our earlier findings on linkages for the commercial bank sector (see Ch. 7). Net demand deposits flow into short-term securities (a wide category including U.S. government securities, consumer credit, business loans, open-market paper, and security credit). In a subsequent quarter, a small part shifts into long-terms (U.S. government securities, state and local government securities, commercial mortgages, term loans). As in the Hester and Pierce (1975) study (discussed in Ch. 7), time deposits other than CDs flow more largely into long-terms and mortgages, with most of the funds that initially went into short-terms being transferred to long-terms. CDs finance increases in commercial loans responding to an increase in inventory investment.

Of significance for the commercial bank sector is how source-use linkages dominate the effect of interest rates in explaining bank allocations. Relative yields are found to have little influence on asset portfolios. Demand and time deposits follow certain paths, and CD issuance responds to the demand for funds by business. According to Hendershott (1977:128–29), more emphasis on linkages with expenditures (e.g., consumer credit for consumer durable spending, mortgage lending for home purchases) would strengthen the explanation of bank portfolio behavior.

Thrift institutions

SAVINGS AND LOAN ASSOCIATIONS   Mortgage investment dominates the portfolios of S&Ls. This was obvious from the data in Chapter 14. The empirical work shows that a decline in deposit inflows will be cushioned by advances from the Federal Home Loan Bank (FHLB) (the central bank for S&Ls) and by declines in purchases of long- and short-term securities. As for the effect of interest rates, higher mortgage rates encourage more mortgage lending and more borrowing from the FHLB (Hendershott 1977:139).

A problem of measuring interest rate effects is illustrated in this sector. It would be expected that the spread between the mortgage rate and the advances rate charged by the FHLB would be an important influence on borrowing from it. The problem is, however, that mortgage rates relative to the advances rate will be lowest when interest rates are at their peak, at which time short-term interest rates such as advances are at their highest level compared with long-term rates such as mortgages. But at just this moment, mortgage lending might be increasing because of expectations of falling mortgage rates. The interest rate is thus of limited usefulness in explaining mortgage lending. (Interest rates may influence borrower behavior, however. See Ch. 17.)

MUTUAL SAVINGS BANKS   MSBs show greater diversification in portfolios than S&Ls. They buy relatively more mortgages when the interest spread is favorable (Hendershott 1977:140–41). When the interest spread disappears, most deposit inflows are channeled into long-terms such as government securities. An acceleration of deposit inflows shows up in both short-terms and long-terms.

CREDIT UNIONS   The noteworthy linkage for CUs is from CU shares to consumer credit.

Contractual savings institutions

Four categories of contractual savings institutions (CSIs) have been distinguished: life insurance companies, private pension funds, state and local retirement funds, and other insurance companies (Hendershott 1977:150ff.). The difference in lending strategies reflects differences in investment objectives. Life insurance company benefits are fixed in nominal dollars, so they invest in corporate bonds and mortgages with fixed nominal returns. On the other hand, pension funds and state and local retirement funds (SLRFs) aim at maintaining the real value of benefits. As a result, pension funds (and to a lesser extent SLRFs) are heavy into equities as a hedge against inflation (see Ch. 14). SLRFs buy fewer equities as a percentage of their portfolio because of state restrictions on equity investment.

The greater significance of flow as opposed to stock adjustment is illustrated by life insurance companies. Stock adjustment means that an existing portfolio (as opposed to incoming funds) is adjusted in response to changes in relative interest rates. It is more expensive than flow adjustment because of the transactions cost in selling off securities and replacing them in the portfolio. New purchases out of incoming funds involve only one set of transaction costs. Testing for the two types of adjustment shows flow adjustment to be more significant. Life insurance companies adjust their new investments in response to changes in the long- and short-term interest spread (measured by the corporate bond rate and the commercial paper rates respectively). Lagged relations are more significant than current effects because acquisitions are based on earlier commitments to purchase bonds and mortgages (Cummins 1975:185). The preference for corporate bonds is of interest. With equal bond and mortgage rates and neutral interest expectations, 90% of funds flow into long-term bonds, with 10% into liquid assets (Hendershott 1977:153).

Direct finance

Direct finance ("other" in Hendershott) includes open-end investment companies, finance companies, and security brokers and dealers (Hendershott 1977:152–54). Open-end investment companies are in the equities market on both the sources and uses side. Finance companies make short-term loans to households and business and employ both short- and long-term sources in approximately equal proportions. Expectations of falling interest rates lead to more short-term borrowing, with the reverse being true of long-term borrowing. Mortgage companies buy long-term mortgages, which they finance through banks. Security brokers and dealers are in the short-term end of financial markets, lending short to their customers and borrowing from their customers (customers' credit balances) and from banks.

Federally sponsored credit agencies

Federally sponsored credit agencies support the mortgage market in keeping with the social goal of more family housing. During the 1960s market support, via the Federal National Mortgage Association (FNMA), was at the initiative of financial institutions who sold mortgages to Fannie Mae when interest rates were rising. To stabilize interest rates, Fannie Mae offered a favorable premium over market prices. On the other hand, no such premium was paid when interest rates were falling (Hendershott 1977:145).

Federal credit agencies became more active in the 1970s as a result of passage of the Housing and Urban Development Act of 1968. During this time mortgage pools were introduced and became substantial (see Ch. 14). Mortgage acquisitions by federal credit agencies occur with both rising and falling mortgage interest rates (Hendershott 1977:148). More mortgages, however, are acquired when interest rates are rising than when they are falling, which is consistent with earlier lending experience (FNMA).

Summary

The financial process has an essential rhythm. Funds flow back and forth between financial and nonfinancial sectors on the basis of linkages between each sector's sources and uses of funds and with linkages between sectors (one sector's use of funds is another's source of funds). The financial process takes time, as both nonfinancial and financial sectors shift from initial money holdings or reserves into less liquid assets. Speeds of adjustment may vary for different sectors from one quarter to several years.

The rhythm of financial flow is modified by the effect of changing interest rates. Lenders modify their portfolios in search of higher returns, and borrowers intent on capital expenditures substitute cheaper sources of funds for more expensive ones. Such substitutions on the borrowing side do not disturb the basic relationships between financial instruments and types of spending. In the household sector, consumer durables are financed by consumer credit and also to a surprising extent by mortgage credit. Housing is financed by mortgage credit and again to a surprising extent by consumer credit. In the business sector, increases in inventories are financed largely by bank credit, fixed investment by long-term securities.

The effect of higher interest rates will lead to substitutions among sources of funds, but the main safety valve is provided by financial asset holdings. Decreases in the purchase of financial assets is a key way that sectors maintain their planned expenditures in the face of higher borrowing costs or possibly in the face of funds not being available. A more expensive adjustment is the selling off of past acquisitions. Financial institutions adjust their portfolios in response to relative returns by adjusting flows rather than stocks, since this is a more economical procedure.

The most interest-sensitive nonfinancial sector as far as asset behavior is the household sector. Among financial sectors, the insurance sector (because of its balanced portfolio) shows the greatest interest sensitivity. Although its sources of funds are largely contractual, these will be negatively affected by policy loans in times of rising market interest rates.

Interest expectations will also affect the choice of assets and borrowing instruments. If it is expected that interest rates are going to fall in the future, borrowers will try to minimize their long-run costs by temporarily increasing their short-term borrowing. On the lending side, lenders will want to lend long to tie up their funds before rates fall. Such interest expectations may lead to borrower-lender behavior inconsistent with the current spread between rates on long- and short-term securities. Interest rates will be affected by such lender-borrower choices, as discussed in Chapter 16.

One-asset institutions are least sensitive to interest rates. The best examples are institutions (S&Ls, MSBs) in the mortgage field and CUs in the consumer credit field. On the sources side, thrift institutions are sensitive to interest rates. Flows into the mortgage market and thus into the housing market decline when open-market rates rise relative to "sticky" deposit rates. As mentioned in Chapter 14 and discussed further in Chapter 17, financial innovation has made deposit inflows less sensitive to open-market rates.

The insensitivity of bank portfolios to interest rates and their sensitivity to the demand for funds by ultimate spenders leads to this possible scenario. An increase in planned spending (depending in part on the cost of capital) leads to demands for bank credit and increased bank lending. Alternatively, an inflow of funds leads to an orderly sequence of portfolio selection based more on the type of liability than on interest rates.

Insofar as portfolios respond to interest rates, there is still the question as to how interest rates are determined. Chapter 16 attempts to answer various questions: When lenders and borrowers respond to interest rates (as in this chapter), what effect do they exert on current interest rates? What effect do interest expectations have on the term structure of interest rates? Is there any relationship between the volume of financial flows and interest rates? Answering the latter question might help to uncover the mainspring of the allocative mechanism. If financial flows correlate positively with interest rates, this suggests that the demand-for-credit side is calling the tune. On the other hand, if the relationship is negative, this will suggest that forces on the supply-of-credit side (the provision of bank reserves or autonomous shifts of deposits into thrift institutions) are dominant. This goes back to an earlier question as to whether finance is growth induced or growth inducing.

Review questions

1. Examining closely the flow-of-funds matrix for the United States in 1983, identify the sectors that dominate saving, the sectors that dominate capital outlays.

2. What are the chief financial flows (sources and uses or credits and debits) of the various private domestic nonfinancial sectors? What are the chief financial flows of the various financial sectors? In the same way analyze the financial flows for the U.S. government and the foreign sector.

3. The addition of a statistical discrepancy row and column distinguishes the statistical matrix of this chapter (Table 15.1) from the hypothetical matrix (Table 1.5) of Chapter 1. Why are such a row and column necessary? What sector shows the largest discrepancy? Why?

4. Does the empirical work of Hendershott throw light on the strength of the various linkages among sector sources and uses as first described in Chapter 2? Does the empirical estimation emphasize the relationship between expenditures and borrowing?

5. Compare the relative importance of financial sources and interest rates in determining the asset allocations of the various financial institutions.

6. Define the cost of capital and discuss its relevance for business decision making. What is meant by saying that business investment is a stock-adjustment process?

7. Which sector is most sensitive to relative interest rates in its portfolio decisions? Why in general would you expect more interest sensitivity when nonfinancial sectors acquire financial assets than when they borrow?

8. In what circumstances is it likely that nonfinancial sectors will dissave (sell off financial assets)?

16

Explaining interest rates

The way funds are allocated depends on interest rates. Decision-making sectors respond to interest rates. Collectively, they determine them. The "buzz words," as in much of economics, are demand and supply. The demand and supply of credit influence the level of interest rates and also their structure, which involves the relationship between rates on instruments of different maturities as well as the effect of the riskiness, tax liability, liquidity, and marketability of obligations.

Demand and supply measure a quantity response to a price (the interest rate). The quantity response usually takes a back seat to the interest rate. But as previous chapters have emphasized, the flow of finance is the key to understanding fluctuations in economic activity. For this reason, our focus will be not only on the price axis but on the quantity axis. We shall study their relationship to determine if the interest rate moves in the same or opposite direction to financial flows.

How lenders and borrowers make financial decisions

The important word in the discussion of lending and borrowing activity is substitution. Lenders will substitute interest-bearing assets for their money holdings in response to interest rate changes. They will similarly substitute among interest-bearing financial assets in accordance with relative changes in their returns. Borrowers on the other side of the market will behave in a symmetrical way, issuing financial claims that bear a lower interest cost for those bearing a higher cost. For example, when warranted, they will borrow from banks or issue short-term commercial paper in the place of stocks and bonds. Later, to rebuild liquidity, they may borrow long to repay short-term indebtedness.

Current interest returns or costs will not be the only determinants of investor-borrower choice. Interest rates expected in the future are an important determinant. Here it is necessary to introduce the concept of maturity of a financial claim. Some financial claims will have a short time to run (before they are paid off by the borrower), such as a three-month certificate of deposit (CD) issued by a commercial bank or a Treasury bill. Others, such as corporate and government bonds, may run for 25 years or more. A lender expecting that long-term yields will rise in the future will prefer to invest in short-terms. Otherwise, by investing long now it will not be possible to take advantage of later increases in yields (without suffering a capital loss when selling off the long investment). The borrower, assuming the same expectations, will prefer to borrow long to avoid the money market risk of higher interest costs when refinancing the debt.

The degree of risk attached to financial assets will influence decisions. Will the borrower fail to meet interest payments or skip (pass) a dividend payment? (It is convenient to treat common and preferred stock as a form of borrowing.) In the case of debt, what is the likelihood of default when the IOU falls due? The higher the risk, the higher the interest return expected by the lender.

The liquidity of an asset will affect the choice. Other characteristics being the same, the investor will prefer a liquid asset to a less liquid one. Liquidity is the ability to sell off an asset without appreciable capital loss. Near moneys (items in $M2$ but not in $M1$) are highly liquid assets. At the other extreme would be a long-term security not listed on major stock exchanges. Such securities are bought and sold in the over-the-counter market, a telephone market whose participants are stockbrokers and dealers. Such securities can fluctuate sharply in value, thus creating the risk of capital loss.

Finally, the tax features of a security affect its attractiveness. The securities sold by state and local governments (municipals) are exempt from federal income taxes and other taxes in the state in which they are issued. This is a great attraction, particularly the higher one's income tax bracket. If, for example, an individual was in a total tax bracket of 50%, a 6% yield on municipals would be equivalent to a 12% before-tax yield on a taxable security.

The investor then makes a choice on the basis of a number of criteria, most notably the yield on the security. On the other side of the market, borrowers are making similar choices. Lender and borrower choices taken collectively will determine the demand and supply of securities. In this way, they collectively influence interest yields.

Menu of markets and investments

There are literally millions of interest rates; e.g., each business loan may have a unique rate. Where the same nominal rate applies, effective interest rates will still vary because loan conditions such as compensating balance requirements or collateral requirements may be unique to each loan.

In discussing the level of interest rates, we abstract from individual loans and work with larger totals such as those given by financial uses and sources in Table 15.1. Financial uses are on the supply-of-funds side of the market. Financial sources stand for the demand for funds.

A convenient assumption is that the values for financial uses and sources are planned values associated with an equilibrium interest rate. In diagrammatic terms, equilibrium values occur at the intersection of demand and supply curves (r_0 and F_0, Fig. 16.1). The higher the market rate of interest, the greater the amount of funds supplied. Similarly, the demand-for-funds curve tells us that less will be borrowed as borrowing costs increase. (The totals for financial transactions shown in Table 15.1 exceed funds advanced to domestic nonfinancial sectors, as discussed in Ch. 4, because of the double counting of transactions intermediated by the financial sectors.)

Each sector is both a lender and borrower. Its surplus-deficit position is shown by its net financial investment (line 11, Table 15.1). In 1983 the positive value for households reveals that it was the major surplus sector among the non-financial sectors (state and local governments show a small positive value). On the other side of the market, businesses and the federal government are major demanders of funds. Financial sectors are seen as intermediaries because of the close matching of financial sources and uses.

INTEREST RATE THEORIES

Classical analysis   Demand and supply in financial markets can be interpreted in accordance with the classical savings-investment approach. It singles out gross saving (line 1) and private capital expenditures (line 5) in Table 15.1. The classical approach sees finance as allocating saving among real investment alternatives. The supply-side economics of President Reagan can be understood in terms of the classical model. Extensive tax incentives were introduced with the express purpose of shifting the saving curve to the right. In this way it was hoped to stimulate economic growth by increasing the volume of investment.

The trouble with the classical approach is that saving does not correspond to a supply of loanable funds, nor does investment correspond to a demand for loanable funds. The demand and supply of credit must be our yardstick, since market interest rates can be determined only by lenders and borrowers interacting in financial markets. Saving differs from lending because saving can be channeled into increases in money holdings. Lending can also exceed saving if monetary dissaving takes place (people using past money holdings to buy financial claims). Similarly, investment need not be a proxy for the supply of financial claims. Investment can be financed, for example, out of retained earnings or by means of financial dissaving (selling-off financial assets plus reductions in money holdings).

Keynesian liquidity preference   The modern approach to interest rates, known as the Keynesian liquidity preference theory, concentrates on the demand for and supply of money expressed in stock terms. The demand for money, according to

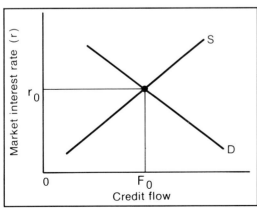

16.1   Demand and supply of credit.

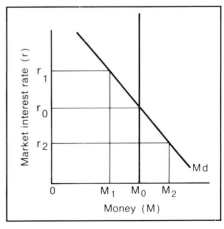

16.2.   Liquidity preference theory.

Keynes, is made up of transaction, precautionary, and speculative demands. (The transaction demand was the basis of the adjustment process after a monetary disturbance, Ch. 2.) The speculative demand is most closely related to the market rate. As the interest rate falls, the expectation might become stronger that it will go back up again. This is called a regressive or interest-inelastic type of expectation. As a result, the demand for money will increase with lower interest rates. The demand for money has a negative slope. A much debated question after the appearance in 1936 of Keynes's famous work, *A General Theory of Interest, Employment and Money,* was whether the demand for money could become infinitely elastic at some low rate of interest. This was known as the liquidity trap. Its policy importance was that increases in the money supply would be trapped without any lowering effect on the interest rate, thus rendering monetary policy impotent. A flow-of-funds approach is helpful in demonstrating the fallacy in the liquidity trap argument. An infinite demand for money would have to be financed by an infinite capacity to sell off other assets or to borrow.

The supply of money as shown in Figure 16.2 can be taken as perfectly inelastic (a vertical line). The interest rate is determined by equality of the demand for a given stock of money. At some different interest rate, an excess supply or demand for money will result in purchases or sales of interest-bearing securities, thus driving the rate down or up to an equilibrium level. For example, if the market rate happened to be r_1, desired money holdings would be M_1, which is less than actual money holdings M_0. Holding an excess quantity of money leads to extra purchases of securities. As the price of securities goes up, given fixed money returns on securities, the market yields will fall. It will fall until holders of the M_0 money balances (the money stock must be held by someone) are content to hold them (desired money holdings equal actual money holdings). Similarly, if the interest rate is below the equilibrium rate, desired money holdings M_2 will exceed actual money holdings. In this case, holders of securities will sell off their holdings, thus forcing down security prices and raising market yields.

If there are only two markets to consider, the securities market and the money market, the money market can be treated as the mirror image of the securities market. (The words "securities" and "bonds" are shorthand terms for all interest-bearing financial claims.) When one market is in equilibrium, so is the second. But solving for the interest rate indirectly via the money market becomes less tenable when we introduce a third major market, the commodity market. Now, credit and liquidity preference become equivalent theories only if the commodity market is assumed to be in equilibrium. Otherwise, an excess supply of money not only may mean an excess demand for bonds but may imply an excess demand for commodities. In such a case, commodity prices may increase rather than bond prices. An excess supply of money is no guarantee, therefore, that interest rates will fall to a clearing level in the money market. When several markets are considered, equilibrium requires clearing prices in all. When disequilibrium exists, excess demands in some of these markets necessarily match excess supplies in the remaining market. Further, if equilibrium is demonstrated for $n-1$ markets, equilibrium must exist (without separate proof) for the nth market. These theorems are associated with the name of the nineteenth-century French-Swiss economist Leon Walras.

Expressing the idea of excess demand-supply in symbols: $M_s - M_d = (B_d - B_s) + (X_d - X_s)$. This states that at any given time the excess supply of money will be equal to the excess demand for bonds plus the excess demand for commodities.

Neoclassical approach   The neoclassical extension of the classical theory combines the money market with saving-investment, creating special difficulties of its own. If the demand for money is aggregated with investment and the supply of money with saving to determine the interest rate, this would only accidentally be the same interest rate that clears the two individual markets. But if each market clears individually, we have the dilemma of two different interest rates.

Our credit market or bond market analysis is the most straightforward way to approach interest rates and is the one we shall follow.

Short-term interest rates

Short-term interest rates underlie the behavior of long-term rates. The factors explaining short-term rates are most visible in periods of sharply rising rates such as in 1974, 1979, and 1981. Short-term rates include those on bank loans, commercial paper, large negotiable CDIs, federal funds, Treasury bills, and short-term Treasury securities. In 1974 the business demand for credit was high. The financing of business inventories, commodity market speculative activity, and lending to foreigners were some of the causes (B. Friedman 1975:40).

Figure 16.3 graphs the upsurge in private borrowing in 1974 and 1979. The effect of such borrowing is manifested in the behavior of short-term interest rates (Fig. 12.7). As Figure 12.7 shows, short-term rates move together. Behind this

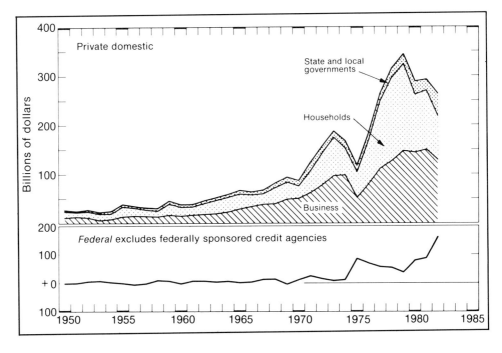

16.3. Net funds raised, major nonfinancial sectors, annually. (FRB 1983d:45)

covariation lies the principle of substitution. Borrowers, for example, switch between commercial paper and bank loans to save on interest.

Higher short-term rates in 1974 were also influenced by restrictive monetary policy on the supply side of the market (B. Friedman 1975:40–42). The Fed, well into the summer, followed a policy of sharply restricting the supply of reserves. It had a mistaken notion as to how fast the money stock was increasing. Because of inadequacies in data reporting for nonmember banks, the Fed estimated an 11.2% per annum increase in the money stock (M1) instead of the actual 8.7% increase.

Episodes of record high interest rates in 1979–80 and 1981 offer a more difficult puzzle. Again the business demand for credit as shown in Figure 16.3 was a pivotal factor. In 1979, household installment credit demand also surged. Chairman Paul Volcker on October 6 enunciated a stringent monetary policy to curb inflation. The events of that Saturday are now irreverently referred to as the "Saturday night special." The reference is to a poorly made handgun that may miss its mark, hit an innocent bystander, or even recoil on the holder. All of these suggest the possible consequences of the actions taken at special Saturday meetings of the Board of Governors and the Federal Open-Market Committee. The most prominent decision was abandoning the federal funds rate as the proximate target of policymaking in favor of aiming at reserve aggregates (see Ch. 12). The consequences were an upsurge in short-term rates to unprecedented levels. Again, miscalculations played a role. Computer errors by a large New York bank (Manufacturers Hanover) resulted in an overstatement of the money stock of $4.5 bil. in October 1979 (Rattner 1979: D1, D11). This helped to throw the securities market into chaos.

The persistence of high short-term rates in the face of a recession in 1981–82 and reduced fund flows to the private sector has led to various theories. Much weight is given to that intangible, expectations (the economist's safety net). Future government deficits are expected to put pressure on financial markets. A lack of confidence in the Fed staying on course leads to expectations of continued inflation. Surprisingly perhaps, high interest rates have little historical relation to record government deficits. The increased volatility of interest rates since the new Fed policy (Fig. 12.7) may have resulted in lenders demanding a risk premium of several percentage points. However, the tightness of monetary policy as a major contributing factor should be stressed (see Clark 1981:15; Kristol 1982:20; Rosenthal 1982:A22; R. Samuelson 1982:9). A theory that interest rates will fall with a subsidence in inflation because investors will move into financial assets out of tangibles has been advanced (see Rutledge 1981:18; 1982:19).

Long-term interest rates

Long-term interest rates have an obvious relationship to short-term rates. Both borrowers and lenders in the long-term market react to current and expected short-term rates. The mathematical relationship was explored in Chapter 5. The long-run interest rate was expressed as the geometric average of expected short-term rates. Although the expression is an identity and therefore a truism, it has considerable usefulness. A forecast of higher short-terms will require that the long-term rates go up so that investing in long-terms will be no less profitable than investing in a series of short-terms. One adjustment mechanism will be a movement out of long-terms into short-terms until equivalent returns are again established.

The expectations hypothesis helps to explain why long-term interest rates were high in 1974. The jump in current short-term rates led to expectations of higher future short-term rates. Long-term yields do not have to change in step with short-term yields, however. In fact, long-term yields fluctuate less than short-terms. One explanation might be sluggishness in adjusting future expectation when current rates change. Another explanation might be that short-term interest rates in the future are expected to decline below the current levels, although ending up higher than before.

The yield curve in Figure 16.4 helps to illustrate the different possibilities for expectations. This curve plots yields for securities with progressively longer maturities. As suggested by the discrete $a, b, c\ldots$ points on the A curve, not all maturities are available in the market. The points on the curve represent available maturities. The A curve shows uniform yields on all maturities $(a\ldots i)$. The inference is that future short-term rates are expected to be the same as the current ones. If the current short-term yield (represented by a) rises, constant expectations would result in the new A_1 curve; all yields will go up with increases in the current short-term rate.

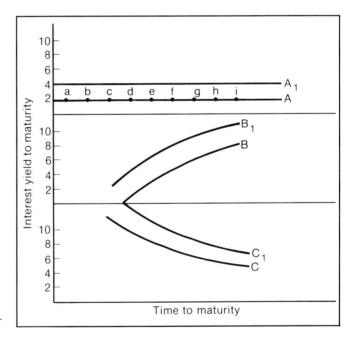

16.4. Interest yield curves.

Curve B describes rising interest expectations. Successive short-term rates are expected to be higher in future periods. An increase in the current short-term yield results in the curve moving up as described by B_1.

Curve C is appropriate for high-interest periods such as 1974 and 1979–81. An increase in the current short-term yield is accompanied by increases in yields on all maturities. Nonetheless, long-term yields are lower than short-term yields because of falling interest expectations. (When interest rates are high by historical standards, the market consensus is that they are likely to decline.) The onset of historically high rates will alter the yield pattern from B to C.

A mixture of type A and B yield curves is illustrated by the Treasury yield curve for June 29, 1984.

The term "callable issues" in Figure 16.5 means that the Treasury can call securities in for payment before their final maturity date. Plotting to the earliest call date when prices are above par is done because the Treasury will call in such a security as soon as possible because it can be refunded at lower interest yields.

Treasury securities are ideal for drawing yield curves, since they are all riskless securities. Rising yields for longer maturities until 1990 represent a forecast of increasing short-term yields until that time. The flattening out of the curve beyond 1989 is a prediction of stable short-term yields thereafter. The shape of the yield curve is protean in nature. For example, in September 1979 the yield curve forecast falling short-term yields between the middle of 1980 and 1983, with stable yields prevailing to 1989 (type C behavior).

UNBIASED EXPECTATIONS THEORY   The theory of interest expectations is founded on an identity. Mathematically, long-term rates (apart from liquidity and transactions costs) are a geometric average of expected short-term rates. We can always interpret changes in long-term rates in terms of the behavior of the current short-term rate and changes in the values of the expected forward rates.

The unbiased expectations hypothesis asserts that the expected (implicit) forward rates are unbiased (correct) estimates of future short-term rates; i.e., when year 2 rolls around, the observed one-year short-term rate should have been predicted by the implicit forward rate as calculated a year earlier. When tested this way, the unbiased expectations theory does very poorly. This is not too surprising and can be explained by forecasting errors. Higher levels of economic activity and a greater demand for finance than anticipated can result in higher interest rates than forecast by implicit rates, with the reverse being true for declining activity (Poole 1978:15ff.). Monetary and fiscal policy can upset expectations, and some behavioral function of considerable importance (e.g., the demand for money) can shift in an unexpected way.

The historical relationship between short- and long-term rates offers some indication of the difficulties of forecasting short-terms. As can be seen in Figure 16.6, short-term rates were substantially below long-terms throughout the 1930s and 1940s. Long-term rates were a forecast of rising short-terms that never materialized. Since the 1950s the short-term rate has fluctuated above and below the long-term rate. This is more consistent with correct forecasts, since the long-term rate may reflect expected movements in the short-term rate that differ from current fluctuations. When, as in recent years, the short-term rate exceeds the long-term rate, it provides the same information as the previous Treasury yield curve, an expectation of falling short-term rates. (A three-dimensional diagram has been constructed showing the yield curve at different points in time; see Homer 1977:387.) All the slopes suggested earlier in Figure 16.6, alone or in combination, have had their historical day.

Nonetheless, the application of learning theory to interest forecasts supports the hypothesis that changes in forward rates reflect changes in expectations. It has been found that forward rates are adjusted in response to differences between past

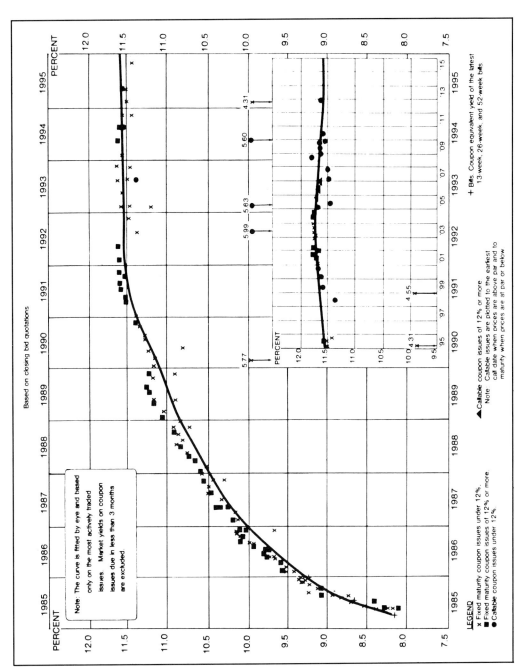

16.5. Yields of Treasury securities, Dec. 31, 1984. (U.S. Treasury 1985:33)

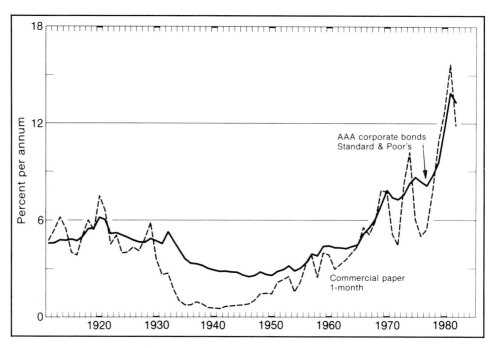

16.6. Long- and short-term interest rates, annually. (FRB 1983d:96)

short-term rates and the forecast of these rates as measured by earlier implicit rates. For example, if investor predictions of the current rate turn out to be on the low side, they revise upward their predictions of future rates. The forecaster learns from making mistakes (see Meiselman 1962; Kaufman 1981:220–21).

The development of a futures market in Treasury bills offers a less demanding test. Do forward rates have any relation to short-term forecasts? This market dates from January 1976, when Treasury bill futures contracts began to be traded on the International Monetary Market of the Chicago Mercantile Exchange (Rendleman and Carabini 1979:895). (Futures prices are regularly quoted in the *Wall Street Journal*.) Such contracts call for delivery of a Treasury bill in some future month. The maturity of the Treasury bill will be either 90, 91, or 92 days. The implicit forward rates calculated from different spot maturities of Treasury securities can be compared with market yields on Treasury bill futures; e.g., today's yield on a futures contract to be delivered 30 days hence and running for 90 days can be compared with the implicit forward rate calculated from today's yields on an outstanding Treasury bill running for 30 days and an outstanding Treasury bill maturing in 120 days. The evidence points to similar movements in forward rates and the yields on futures (Poole 1978:15ff.). Land and Rasche (1978:21ff.) present a mildly dissenting view that does not undermine the Poole argument once arbitrage costs are considered.

Unfortunately, the acid test cannot be made because of too much noise. This test would seek to determine if it paid to sell off a "spot" Treasury bill and invest in futures. Brokerage commissions, information costs, and the inability to match maturities in the spot and futures market inhibit such arbitrage, however. The implicit forward rate can depart from the futures rate without implying the failure of the forward rate as a proxy for the interest rate forecasts (Rendleman and Carabini 1979:913). In any case, interest rate forecasts via forward rates or via interest rate futures have not proved very accurate as predictors of future short-term rates (Craine, 1982).

LIQUIDITY PREMIUM   If interest expectations are as described by the A yield curve in Figure 16.5, observed yields may still be higher on long-terms because a premium must be paid the buyer for a sacrifice of liquidity. Therefore, a rising yield curve may reflect this liquidity premium in addition to expectations of rising short-term rates. Similarly, a C-type yield could have an even more pronounced negative slope if not for this liquidity premium.

The liquidity premium is the result of capital uncertainty outweighing income uncertainty in importance for the marginal investor, who is on the margin of indifference between choosing one maturity over another. Income uncertainty results from buying short-terms. When they mature, the investor may have to settle for a security paying less interest. This uncertainty is less compelling than the capital uncertainty associated with long-term securities. The investor forced to sell a long-term security before it falls due may have to take a substantial capital loss because of fluctuations in market interest rates. As explained in Chapter 5, such fluctuations produce a much smaller capital loss for short-term securities. A liquidity premium thus must be paid to the buyer of long-terms.

Uncertainty about the economic future increases the liquidity premium. This was the case in 1974–75 and 1981. An indicator is the interest spread between securities of different quality bonds. In these years the quality yield spread between *Aaa* and *Baa* corporate bonds increased dramatically (FRB 1983d:97).

MARKET SEGMENTATION   A third theory of interest rate determination emphasizes the supply of securities relative to the demand in different maturity ranges. The idea is that borrowers and lenders have preferred habitats. Banks prefer to lend short, insurance companies to lend long. Businesses financing inventories prefer to borrow short; public utilities financing a long-term investment prefer to borrow long. The theory then expects long-term securities to go down in price (yields to go up) when the supply of long-term securities increases relative to the demand. Yields on long-terms under these circumstances should rise relative to short-terms. The strongest evidence for market segmentation is probably in periods of sharply rising interest rates. Such increases can be explained by tight monetary policy restricting bank lending at the same time that the demand for bank credit is increasing to finance inventories.

USEFULNESS FOR FINANCIAL ANALYSIS   Yield curves are of use to corporate treasurers and portfolio managers of financial institutions as a forecast of the future. Rising curves mean that the market is predicting higher short-term rates in the future; falling curves mean the reverse. If individual predictions differ from the market, an opportunity for profit making exists. As a lender, a sector should lend long if a rising yield curve is expected to be replaced by a falling curve. Falling long-term yields will create a capital gain. Similar expectations on the part of borrowers will encourage them to borrow short, since postponement will lower long-term borrowing costs. Less dramatic forecasts can also lead to profitable action. One section of the yield curve may be thought to be out of line in the light of future security supply.

This advantage of studying yield curves depends on outguessing the market. If the market judgment is accepted, the long-term rate as a geometric average of short-term rates means that it is a matter of indifference whether one borrows or lends by means of a succession of short-term securities or a long-term security.

Yield curves might offer a chance for profit making by riding the yield curve or playing the pattern of rates. Assume that the yield curve is rising for the first three years and then flattens out. If the yield pattern persists, a capital gain can be made by buying a three-year security that with the passage of time becomes a two and one-half–year security, and so on. The lower yields on short-term maturities mean that the price of the three-year security will rise as it approaches maturity.

USEFULNESS FOR POLICYMAKING   Treasury officials managing the public debt can study the yield curve in the same way as a corporate treasurer, by looking for a soft spot in the curve. The Fed can try to influence the yield curve by concentrating open-market operations in certain maturity ranges. Thus "operation twist" in 1961–63 tried to keep long-term interest rates low to encourage real investment and short-term interest rates high to discourage capital outflows. The expectations theory would anticipate arbitraging between yields (selling long-terms, buying short-terms), thus frustrating Fed intentions. The evidence is that the yield differences did not respond significantly to Fed policy. While short-term rates increased relative to long-terms, this can be explained by factors unrelated to operation twist (Levy 1981:38–39).

Before and after operation twist the Fed followed a bills only policy. The reasoning in confining open-market operations to Treasury bills was operational efficiency and expectations theory. Procedurally, the Treasury bill market was the preferred market because of its depth, breadth, and resiliency.

Interest rate differentials

Securities have special characteristics that explain differences in their market yields. These include risk of default, callability, taxability, and marketability.

RISK OF DEFAULT   A corporate debtor may fail to meet interest payments or may default on the principal. Two services rate bonds according to their estimated risk. They are given in Table 16.1. Such ratings influence investors. The trade-off is clear: if one wishes more return, one must take a greater risk. Within broad risk categories, the informed investor may know of particular securities that deserve a

Table 16.1.	Bond rating classification	
Moody's	General description	Standard & Poor's
Aaa	Highest quality	AAA
Aa	High quality	AA
A	Upper medium grade	A
Baa	Medium grade	BBB
Ba	Lower medium grade	BB
B	Speculative	B
Caa	Poor standing (may be in default)	CCC–CC
Ca	Often in default	C for income bonds
C	Lowest grade (in default)	DDD–D

better rating. The analogy is to fire insurance premiums. While uniform premiums may be established (say on the basis of one home fire per 1000 homes), an individual home may be less likely to burn than the typical home because of the owner's special safeguards against fire (Henning et al. 1981:464).

The difference in the market yields of two securities otherwise comparable (such as the same maturity) is called the risk premium. Empirical evidence differs as to whether the risk premium compensates for loss from defaults by buying the risky security (Henning et al. 1981: 469), i.e., whether realized yields are higher on low-grade than high-grade securities. In any case, the higher realized yield is only an average. The individual security may indeed default, resulting in losses for its holder. The risk differential is the result of demand and supply forces, as for all yields. We can draw two sets of market curves, and the effect of risk will show up as a rate differential. The curves in the two markets could also have different elasticities. In the default-free market, the supply-of-funds curve is probably more elastic than in the risky funds market. In the latter market, suppliers demand some minimum rate of return, and beyond that the supply does not respond substantially to further increases in rates.

CALLABILITY   Both corporate bonds and government securities may have a call provision. The borrower can repay a debt before maturity if a penalty payment is made above the face value of the security. In addition, the coupon rate of interest will be higher as a result of the call feature. A corporation is willing to incur these extra costs so that it can take advantage of a fall in market rates, refunding its debt at these lower rates. The federal government, on the other hand, inserts call features so that it can better control the maturity structure of its debt (Henning et al. 1981:471–72).

TAXABILITY   The tax features applicable to securities affect relative yields. Capital gains taxes are lower than income taxes, so that a security offering a capital gain by selling at a discount will earn a higher yield to maturity than one not having this tax advantage. Bonds receivable for estate taxes at par have a similar tax advantage (these are called flower bonds because of their graveyard association). For example, a bond selling for $800 at the time of death will be accepted in payment for $1000 of estate taxes. Since 1977, as a consequence of the Tax Reform Act of 1976, the capital gain of $200 is subject to taxation.

Zero coupon bonds would seem to be the ideal discount bond since they pay no current interest and are sold at a heavy discount. Treasury and corporate zero coupon bonds, however, are subject to federal income tax on the imputed interest every year although holders receive no cash payments (Sloane 1985:22).

The most important tax feature is the exemption of state and local securities (municipals) from federal income tax. Increased supplies of state and local securities in recent years (the total outstanding has risen from $15 bil. in 1947 to over $400 bil. by the end of 1983) have made it worthwhile for taxpayers in relatively modest income brackets to buy municipals. Table 16.2 shows how advantageous buying a municipal bond can be with triple exemptions from federal, state, and local income taxes.

Looking at the 9% column in Table 16.2 (which represents a realistic tax-free rate in 1985 on 20-year general obligation bonds, an individual in the combined

46.1% personal income tax bracket (using 1985 tax schedules) would have had to earn 16.7% on a taxable issue to match the tax-free rate. Someone in the highest tax bracket (59.2%) would have to earn 22.06% on a taxable issue. The tax advantages are also substantial for banks and nonlife insurance companies, which hold the largest quantities of tax-exempts. Nonfinancial corporate business holds an insignificant amount. Why don't nonfinancial corporations invest in municipals when they pay the same taxes as banks? Their business is not financial claims; but when they do buy them, their interest is in liquidity. From a profit-maximizing point of view, however, these may not be convincing arguments.

The market for tax-free issues has been expanded by the Tax Reform Act of 1976, which permitted mutual funds to invest in municipals. Check-writing privileges have further enhanced their attractiveness. The rise in yields on tax-free issues has brought in investors in relatively low tax brackets. This has created a windfall gain for taxpayers in higher brackets. As a result, they save more in taxes than state and local governments save in interest. The net loser is the Treasury.

The Economic Recovery Act of 1981, "the biggest tax-cut bill ever passed," (*Concise...* 1981:2) introduced a new type of one-year certificate of deposit, the all-savers certificate paying interest that is exempt from federal tax. There was a lifetime ceil-

Table 16.2. Value of triple exemption from federal, New York State, and New York City income taxes

If your taxable income in 1985 is[a] (000s omitted)		Your combined federal NYS and NYC bracket will be[c] (%)	To match these tax-free rates — You would have to earn this much from a taxable investment (%)												
Married[b] (Joint return)	Single		5.00%	5.50%	6.00%	6.50%	7.00%	7.50%	8.00%	8.50%	9.00%	9.50%	10.00%	10.50%	11.00%
$19,000-$21,000		37.5	8.00	8.80	9.60	10.40	11.20	12.00	12.80	13.60	14.40	15.20	16.00	16.80	17.60
$21,000-$23,000		38.4	8.12	8.93	9.74	10.55	11.36	12.18	12.99	13.80	14.61	15.42	16.23	17.05	17.86
	$25,600-$31,120	38.7	8.16	8.97	9.79	10.60	11.42	12.23	13.05	13.87	14.68	15.50	16.31	17.13	17.94
$23,000-$24,460		39.5	8.26	9.09	9.92	10.74	11.57	12.40	13.22	14.05	14.88	15.70	16.53	17.36	18.18
	$31,120-$36,630	41.2	8.50	9.35	10.20	11.05	11.90	12.76	13.61	14.46	15.31	16.16	17.01	17.86	18.71
$24,460-$29,970		42.8	8.74	9.62	10.49	11.36	12.24	13.11	13.99	14.86	15.73	16.61	17.48	18.36	19.23
$29,970-$35,490	$36,630-$47,670	45.3	9.14	10.05	10.97	11.88	12.80	13.71	14.63	15.54	16.45	17.37	18.28	19.20	20.11
$35,490-$43,190		46.1	9.28	10.20	11.13	12.06	12.99	13.91	14.84	15.77	16.70	17.63	18.55	19.48	20.41
$43,190-$57,550	$47,670-$62,450	49.4	9.88	10.87	11.86	12.85	13.83	14.82	15.81	16.80	17.79	18.77	19.76	20.75	21.74
	$62,450-$89,090	52.6	10.55	11.60	12.66	13.71	14.77	15.82	16.88	17.93	18.99	20.04	21.10	22.15	23.21
$57,550-$85,130	$89,090-$113,860	55.1	11.14	12.25	13.36	14.48	15.59	16.70	17.82	18.93	20.04	21.16	22.27	23.39	24.50
	$113,860-$169,020	57.5	11.76	12.94	14.12	15.29	16.47	17.65	18.82	20.00	21.18	22.35	23.53	24.71	25.88
$85,130 and up		58.3	11.99	13.19	14.39	15.59	16.79	17.99	19.18	20.38	21.58	22.78	23.98	25.18	26.38
	$169,020 and up	59.2	12.25	13.48	14.71	15.93	17.16	18.38	19.61	20.83	22.06	23.28	24.51	25.74	26.96

Source: Used with permission from Lebenthal, Supplement to Municipal Bond Information Kit, copyright ©1985, Lebenthal Co., Inc., New York.

[a] Net taxable income after all exemptions, adjustments, and deductions.

[b] Assumes that all income is earned by one spouse.

[c] Your personal tax bracket is the combined federal and effective NYS and NYC rate, as a result of the federal tax law signed August 13, 1981, at which the next dollar of taxable income you earn will be taxed in 1985. Assumes (1) taxpayer itemizes deductions and deducts state and local taxes on his or her federal return and (2) that "maximum tax" in NYS on personal service income does *not* apply to the type of investment income being analyzed herein. The readjustment of tax brackets next year to reflect any changes this year in the cost-of-living may alter your bracket and the foregoing computations.

ing on exemptions of $1000 ($2000 in the case of a joint return), and they were only issued through the end of 1982. The certificates were in denominations of $500 and paid interest at a rate of 70% of the current investment yield on one-year Treasury bills (A. Bernstein 1982:138–39). When first issued, only those in tax brackets above 30% could achieve a higher after-tax yield by buying an all-savers certificate rather than a Treasury bill.

The act also encouraged investment in public utility companies providing gas or electric service. Starting in 1982 (and scheduled to expire in 1985), individuals could exclude up to $750 ($1500 on a joint return) on the reinvestment of dividends to purchase more shares of this stock (A. Bernstein 1982:415).

MARKETABILITY   A common reference in the financial literature is to the depth, breadth, and resiliency of financial markets. These add up to marketability, the ability to sell large amounts of a security without substantial price concessions (Henning et al. 1981:477–79). Marketability is a more comprehensive concept than liquidity. A security with a short time to run has liquidity in virtue of being near retirement. Treasury securities are highly marketable, while municipals and mortgages are at the other extreme. The thinness of the municipals market is reflected in the spread between bidding and asking prices. Someone buying a municipal and selling it the same day might lose 2% of the purchase price. The effect of sponsored federal credit agencies has been to create a secondary market for mortgages. Nonetheless, the mortgage instrument is still illiquid. The mortgage market may be a good example of a rationed market, one in which interest rates are below clearing levels. The availability of mortgage funds to savings institutions determines how much they loan (but see Ch. 18). Interest rates in the primary home mortgage markets are less variable, for example, than rates on newly issued corporate bonds. Behind the stickiness in interest rates are state usury laws (eliminated by the Depository Institutions Deregulation and Monetary Control Act of 1980) and institutional practices. Loan-to-value ratios, fees and special charges, and length of the mortgage will be varied in response to demand and supply rather than the stated interest rate. Nevertheless, the spread between rates on home mortgages and new issues of corporate bonds has greatly narrowed since 1965 (Light and White 1979:378,380; see also Ch. 18). Such narrowing reflects improved marketability of mortgages.

SEASONED VS. NEW ISSUES   Security issues that have been trading in the market have different interest yields from new issues of the same security. The explanation for higher yields on new issues seems to be higher coupon rates and market imperfections (Rea 1974:3–9). Higher coupon rates reflect the upward trend in interest rates and a desire to have a new issue succeed. The reluctance of institutional investors to sell off seasoned issues makes new issues a less perfect substitute. Despite these factors the spread is not a substantial one, being about 35 basis points (a third of a percentage) between 1951 and 1971 (Henning et al. 1981:479–81).

COMMON AND PREFERRED STOCKS   Preferred stock calls for fixed dividend payments and in this respect is more like bonds than equity issues. The yields have more in common with bonds than with the dividend yields on common stock. The

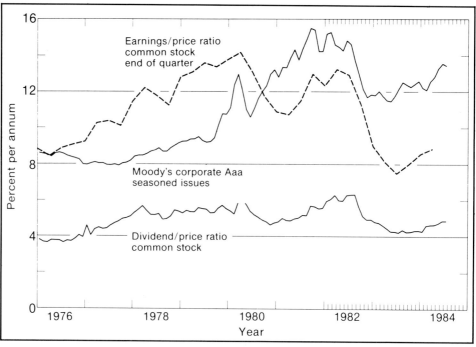

16.7. Stock and bond yields, monthly. (FRB 1984a:69)

dividend yield rate is the dividend-price ratio shown in Figure 16.7. It is below the bond yield and would also fall below the yield on preferred stock. Common stock yields are not a full measure of the return on equity because capital gains must be included. Such capital gains are in part measured by earnings, since retained earnings can be expected to affect the stock's market price. The earnings-price ratio shown in Figure 16.7 is not, however, an adequate measure of the full return on common stock. This ratio could be going up simply because stock market prices were falling, implying capital losses. Similarly, the ratio could be going down (as in 1980) because prices were rising. Capital gains must be calculated directly from stock market prices and added on to dividends to estimate the full return. When this is done, the average annual return on common stocks is greatly in excess of the returns on Treasury securities. The wider range of returns from common stock reflects the greater risk.

CONVERTIBLE BONDS   Since convertible bonds can be converted into common stock, they have the best of both worlds. A minimum return is guaranteed on the bonds, and advantage can be taken of appreciation in common stock prices. These advantages will be reflected in the higher price of convertible bonds (other factors being the same).

Interest rates move together

Interest rates move together because a change in the rate on one instrument will induce widespread adjustment in financial flows and the rates on other instru-

Table 16.3. Simple correlation coefficients of changes in market yields on three-month Treasury bills and other securities, 1955-1975

Other security	Same month	Change in yield on other security	
		One month later	Two months later
Bankers acceptances	.73	.47	.04
Finance company paper	.75	.61	.17
Nonfinance company paper	.71	.52	.06
Treasury bills: nine to twelve months	.87	.30	...
Treasury securities: three to five years	.70	.27	...
Treasury bonds: long term	.49	.07	...
State and local bonds: *Aaa*	.39	.14	.11
State and local bonds: *Baa*	.37	.12	.09
Corporate bonds: *Aaa*	.39	.27	...
Corporate bonds: *Baa*	.26	.30	...
Corporate bonds: public utility	.33	.24	...
Corporate bonds: industrial	.30	.18	...
Corporate bonds: railroad	.30	.29	...

Source: Used with permission from George G. Kaufman, *Money, the Financial System and the Economy*, p. 216, copyright © 1981, Rand McNally, Chicago.

ments. Movements in short-term yields will be more highly correlated with other short-term yields than with long-terms. The correlations of the Treasury bill rate with short- and long-term yields are given in Table 16.3. The closer relationship between yields in the same month points out the quickness with which an initial change in the Treasury bill yield spreads to others, particularly other short-term yields.

Interest rate: Demand or supply side?

We have pondered in earlier chapters whether discretion lies on the demand-for-funds or supply-of-funds side of financial markets. A simple test is whether interest rates move in the same or opposite direction to real financial flows. (The distorting effect of inflation on nominal dollar flows is handled by expressing flows in constant dollar prices.) In the first case, we surmise that the demand for credit is determining interest rates; in the second, the supply of credit is the critical factor. The evidence from Table 16.4 and Figure 16.8 is in favor of lender discretion, with real flows and rates moving in opposite directions 14 times and in the same direction 10 times between 1952 and 1983. This is not counting the years in which the short-term Treasury bill rate and the long-term bond rate give opposing signals. The presence of lender discretion in the crunch periods of 1966, 1969, 1974, and 1979–80 is a demonstration of the effects of restrictive monetary policy. (The increase in real flows is so slight in 1981 as to make the technically correct "B" designation suspect.) On the other hand, Fed policy in 1983 was on the easing side, with real borrowing going up at the same time that interest rates declined.

Forecasting interest rates

If interest rates are determined by demand and supply, forecasting interest rates entails forecasting demand and supply forces. Since everything depends on everything else in economics, complex econometric models are called for. A simpler approach is a judgmental model. It is known for sure that, ex post, credit demanded will equal credit supplied. Whether ex ante demand will exceed or fall short of supply at current interest rates must be forecast. If demand exceeds supply, the forecast will be that the gap will be closed by higher interest rates.

Year	(1) Borrowings ($ bil.)	(2) GNP deflator	(3)[a] Borrowings in 1972 ($)	(4) Aaa bond rate (ave.)	(5) Treasury bill rate (ave.)	(6)[b] Discretion
1952	30.8	58.0	53.1	2.96	1.77	
1953	27.8	58.8	47.3	3.20	1.93	L
1954	25.8	59.6	43.3	2.90	0.95	B
1955	36.0	60.9	59.1	3.06	1.75	B
1956	27.5	62.9	43.7	3.36	2.66	L
1957	28.1	65.0	43.2	3.89	3.26	L
1958	40.0	66.0	60.6	3.79	1.84	L
1959	50.6	67.5	75.0	4.38	3.40	B
1960	37.1	68.6	54.1	4.41-L	2.93-B	
1961	45.2	69.2	65.3	4.35	2.38	L
1962	54.4	70.5	77.2	4.33-L	2.78-B	
1963	59.6	71.5	83.4	4.26-L	3.16-B	
1964	67.9	72.7	93.4	4.40	3.55	B
1965	71.4	74.3	96.1	4.49	3.95	B
1966	68.3	76.7	89.0	5.13	4.88	L
1967	81.4	79.0	103.0	5.51-B	4.32-L	
1968	98.3	82.5	119.1	6.18	5.34	B
1969	89.6	86.7	103.3	7.03	6.68	L
1970	94.9	91.3	103.9	8.40-B	6.46-L	
1971	139.6	96.0	145.4	7.39	4.35	L
1972	166.4	100.0	166.4	7.21	4.07	L
1973	194.0	105.8	183.4	7.44	7.04	B
1974	190.3	116.0	164.0	8.57	7.89	L
1975	204.4	127.1	160.8	8.83-B	5.84-L	
1976	262.8	133.7	196.6	8.43	4.99	L
1977	332.9	141.6	235.1	8.02-L	5.26-B	
1978	403.6	152.0	265.5	8.73	7.22	B
1979	406.2	162.8	249.5	9.63	10.07	L
1980	371.8	177.4	209.6	11.94	11.43	L
1981	407.6	193.0	211.2	14.17	14.03	B
1982	419.8	207.5	202.3	13.79	10.61	B
1983	545.3	218.5	249.6	12.04	8.61	L

Sources: Col. 1--Fed, Flow of Funds Accounts, various issues; col. 2--U.S. Dep. Commer., *Surv. Curr. Bus.*, various issues; cols. 4, 5--Fed. Res. *Bull.*, various issues.

[a]The GNP deflator, 1972 = 100, converts the current dollar figures in col. 1 into the constant ("real") dollar figures of col. 3.

[b]A positive relationship between changes in col. 3 and cols. 4 and 5 indicates borrower discretion (B); a negative relation indicates lender discretion (L). When the bond and Treasury bill rates move in opposite directions, both B and L are indicated for the appropriate interest rate.

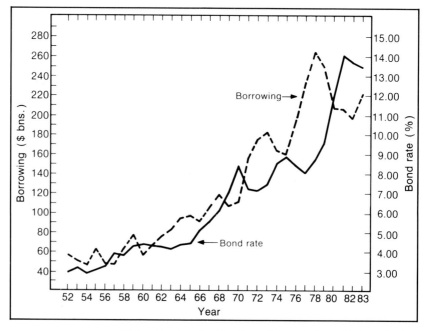

16.8. Funds raised in financial markets and interest rates.

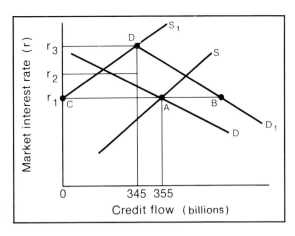

16.9. Forecasting interest rates.

As shown in Figure 16.9, because of demand and supply shifts (S_1 and D_1 replace S and D), an excess demand for credit is forecast at the current interest rate r_1. The CB gap will be closed by interest rates rising to r_3. Table 16.5 illustrates the Bankers Trust Company use of the flow of funds for forecasting purposes. Funds raised by sectors are equal to the uses-of-funds side of financial markets, as Table 16.5 is organized. These consist of short- and long-term (investment) funds

Table 16.5. Projection of funds raised and supplied, 1984, Bankers Trust

Funds	1978	1979	1980	1981	1982	1983 (est.)	1984 (proj.)
				($ bil.)			
Funds raised							
Investment	219.3	230.4	221.0	184.1	191.3	255.1	278.7
Short-term	124.1	139.7	77.4	115.5	52.4	96.5	134.3
U.S. government and budget agency							
securities, privately held	46.8	29.9	75.7	78.0	153.3	175.6	173.5
Total uses	390.2	400.1	374.1	377.6	397.0	527.2	586.5
Funds supplied							
Insurance companies and pension funds							
Life insurance companies	33.7	33.6	33.9	38.0	47.5	55.5	62.5
Private noninsured pension funds	16.0	16.0	20.3	21.1	26.5	31.7	32.3
State and local retirement funds	14.3	19.4	23.4	24.3	26.8	31.5	35.9
Fire and casualty insurance companies	19.2	17.5	14.5	12.7	11.0	9.9	8.9
Total	83.3	86.5	92.1	96.2	111.8	128.6	139.6
Thrift institutions							
Savings and loan associations	56.7	51.5	42.1	24.1	15.4	97.1	90.7
Mutual savings banks	8.4	4.7	5.3	-.2	...	15.8	12.1
Credit unions	8.3	2.4	-1.1	1.1	3.8	9.2	9.2
Total	73.5	58.6	46.3	25.0	19.2	122.1	112.0
Investment companies	5.2	22.4	22.5	73.0	50.6	24.6	41.3
Other financial intermediaries							
Finance companies	20.9	24.1	11.8	22.6	4.4	14.1	20.0
Mortgage companies	2.6	-1.4	2.8	.2	2.1	1.5	2.0
Real estate investment trusts	-1.1	-1.0	-.7	-1.1	-.7	-.3	-.3
Total	22.4	21.7	13.9	21.7	5.8	15.3	21.7
Commercial banks	126.2	122.2	101.8	108.8	108.5	140.0	148.0
Business							
Corporations	9.6	24.9	7.1	3.3	9.9	26.8	28.7
Noncorporate business	1.4	1.8	.5	2.6	1.7	3.7	3.8
Total	11.0	26.7	7.6	5.9	11.6	30.5	32.5
Government							
U.S. Government	3.1	6.2	6.9	4.3	1.9	1.5	1.8
Federally sponsored agencies	13.8	19.8	18.0	14.0	12.7	7.1	12.6
State and local general funds	11.5	8.1	14.5	9.8	24.9	30.1	26.5
Total	28.4	34.1	39.4	28.1	39.6	38.7	40.9
Foreign investors	40.4	-3.1	28.2	21.9	21.5	21.9	38.0
Individuals and others	47.4	81.2	59.6	54.3	49.6	39.1	55.2
Total gross sources	437.8	450.3	411.5	434.9	418.1	560.8	629.2
Less: Funds raised by financial							
intermediaries							
Investment	9.2	10.0	8.1	-1.0	3.6	17.6	11.7
Short-term	14.5	16.7	5.2	28.4	1.2	13.8	14.3
Federally sponsored agency							
securities, privately held	23.9	23.6	24.1	29.9	16.3	2.2	16.7
Total	47.6	50.3	37.4	57.3	21.1	33.6	42.7
Total net sources	390.2	400.1	374.1	377.6	397.0	527.2	586.5

Source: Bankers Trust 1984:T1.

in addition to government borrowing. Funds supplied by lenders describe the sources-of-funds side of financial markets.

Interest rates in 1984 cleared the market when $586 bil. of funds were projected to be demanded and supplied, about $60 bil. more than in 1983. A firming trend was predicted early in 1984 for 1984 interest rates because of tight monetary policy and an unprecedented fiscal environment (substantial government borrowing) (Bankers Trust 1984:11). In retrospect the forecast of higher interest rates turned out to be correct but borrowings were greatly underestimated (FRB 1985b:5). Tables similar to Table 16.5 are given for individual financial markets.

Long-term forecasting, using both judgmental and econometric approaches, involves more fundamental analysis of likely future sources and uses of funds; e.g., see Sametz and Wachtel (1977).

Credit rationing

Except for the case of mortgage lending, our analysis has assumed that credit markets clear. This may not be true of a number of markets where interest rates are traditionally sticky by law or custom. Not only mortgage lending but bank loans to business or consumer credit loans fall into this category. It is still true that ex post amounts supplied equal the amounts demanded.

The market model will show interest rates below the equilibrium level as in Figure 16.10. The interest rate is set by the lender at $0r$. The amount of credit rationing is AB, as lenders lend $0X$ amount of credit. Rationing techniques are now necessary to winnow out loan demand. For example, down payment requirements can be raised or loan maturities shortened (as in the case of mortgage or consumer credit). For business, compensating balance requirements can be varied. In a sense, prices are still involved; the lender has raised the noninterest price of loans.

If credit rationing takes place, the importance of credit availability in the determination of institutional lending is greatly enhanced. Lending is at the discretion of the lending institution and is not determined by the state of borrower demand. An increase in the inflow of funds will lead to more lending directly

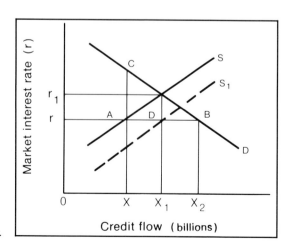

16.10. Credit rationing.

rather than indirectly by the effect this inflow has on the interest charged. In terms of Figure 16.10, the supply curve shifts to the right with $0X_1$ now being the amount of funds loaned at the stable interest rate r.

The work of Hester and Pierce (1975) supports this availability doctrine. Relative interest rates were not the allocational criterion in bank portfolio policy but rather deposit flows. Interest rates as the determinant of policy would work in two ways. Given higher interest rates in one market than in another, banks would lend in the market with the higher return. Given an inflow of funds, banks would lower interest rates charged in order to induce a greater demand for funds. Both these strategies are inconsistent with credit rationing. Demand and time deposits had close relationships to the kinds of assets acquired with certain time lags.

The policy implication is that monetary policy works by controlling the availability of funds rather than the cost; e.g., Regulation Q (setting interest ceilings on deposits) limits the ability of banks to attract funds and thus restricts their ability to lend (B. Friedman 1972:15). Similarly, an open-market purchase pumps reserves into the banking system and induces banks to make more credit available at current interest rates.

Interest rates and availability were interlinked in monetary policy when in the 1950s the Fed attempted to "lock in" bank holdings of government securities. It was thought that small price declines induced by open-market sales would discourage banks from selling their securities and lending the proceeds. (For a comprehensive discussion of this aspect of the availability doctrine see Melton 1985:19–28.)

While we have posed the cost of credit, interest rates, and availability as opposing theories in explaining bank behavior, in the long run they come together. In the short run, credit availability will dominate lending. In the long run, interest rates would be adjusted in response to changes in excess demand. An increase in funds would reduce excess demand, resulting in downward adjustments in rates. A decrease in funds would have the reverse effect.

Summary

Market interest rates vary in response to demand and supply forces. Not all interest rates constitute market rates in this sense. When interest rates are set at the discretion of the lender (mortgage loans, bank loans, consumer credit), the lending side of the market dominates the setting process. Even here, in the long run both sides of the market interact in determining interest rates.

The appropriate unit for expressing demand and supply is the dollar flow of credit. Alternatively, securities are supplied by borrowers and demanded by lenders. Historically, other approaches have been taken. Supply and demand have been expressed in terms of saving and investment and supply and demand for money. Only under very restrictive assumptions will these flows correspond to the supply and demand for credit or the demand and supply of interest-bearing securities.

Behind demand and supply in individual financial markets are borrower and lender preferences based on interest expectations. Expectations are the link between short- and long-term markets. The yield curve summarizes the effect of expectations on yields to maturity. Two additional theories besides the expectation theory lie behind the yield curve. These are liquidity premium and market segmentation.

Rate differentials on securities may be due to additional factors such as marketability, risk and tax features, the security carrying a call feature, being convertible into common stock, or being a seasoned versus a new issue. Common stocks were also considered as an alternative investment, with riskiness explaining higher average returns compared with debt instruments.

Interest rates move together. The flow of funds will be modified in all markets as sectors readjust their portfolios in search of higher interest returns. In so doing, an initial disturbance in one financial market will be transmitted to others.

The historical movement of real financial flow and interest rates suggests the presence of both lender and borrower discretion. The exercise of restrictive monetary policy (lender discretion) is clearly in evidence in the credit crunches of 1966, 1969, and 1974 and in Fed policy since 1979.

The demand-and-supply framework offers a simple judgmental model for forecasting interest rates. If at current interest rates it is expected that demand will exceed supply, the forecast will be for higher interest rates to close the gap.

Finally, we have dealt with the phenomenon of credit rationing. The assumption that financial markets always clear is not a realistic one. When interest rates are below equilibrium levels, alternative criteria to price become the basis for lending. In these circumstances, credit availability rather than the cost of credit is the transmission mechanism for monetary policy. An inflow of funds leads directly to more lending rather than indirectly via lower interest rates. Credit rationing is discussed further in Chapter 18.

Review questions

1. Why do financial instruments pay different market interest rates?

2. Why do interest rates move together?

3. Does discretion lie on the supply or demand side of financial markets?

4. Distinguish credit availability from the cost of credit as determinants of amounts loaned.

5. Compare and evaluate the main theories of interest rate determination.

6. Is there a fixed (unchanging) relationship between short- and long-term interest rates? Why would you not expect this to be the case? Which theory of term structure of rates comes closest to suggesting a fixed relationship?

7. How can the framework of demand and supply for credit be used as a tool for forecasting financial flows and interest rates?

8. Does monetary policy work by affecting the cost or the availability of credit — or by both avenues?

9. Define:

Liquidity trap	Ex post
Transactions demand for money	Ex ante
Speculative demand for money	Lender discretion
Interest inelastic expectations	Borrower discretion
Unbiased expectation theory	Credit rationing

Interest rates, financial innovation, and demand for money

Monetary control has velocity effects that tend to frustrate it. The linkage between the two is interest rates. To the extent that monetary policy affects interest rates, monetary velocity will increase. One reason is that the pace of financial innovation is quickened by higher interest rates.

The other side to monetary velocity is the holding of cash balances. High and rising interest rates encourage holders of cash to minimize their cash balance holdings. Every economic unit needs money to bridge the time gap between the receipts of income and the making of expenditures; e.g., a household may get paid monthly but makes cash outlays throughout the month. Business may have more frequent (daily) receipts, but these are not likely to be synchronized with their patterns of cash spending. If the return on liquid assets is sufficiently high, it pays to invest cash on a short-term basis and then cash in liquid assets when payments must be made. Analysis of the demand for money and the effects of higher interest rates necessarily begins with a discussion of the payments structure.

The payments matrix

The payments matrix shown in Table 17.1 estimates minimum cash balances for sectors with different patterns of receipts and payments. The figures in the columns represent payments; those in the rows, receipts. Expenditure patterns follow a five-day cycle. Households are represented by H, and firms by A, B, C, D, and E. Households pay daily for their purchases. Firms make payments at weekly intervals. Each transactor is represented by five columns and five rows; e.g., firm A makes intermediate payments of 60 on day 2 and 25 on day 4 to firms D and E respectively and income payments of 5 on day 5 to households H. Firm A receives receipts of 60 on day 1 and 20 on day 3 from firms C and B and daily

Table 17.1. The payments matrix

Payments

Receipts	A1	A2	A3	A4	A5	B1	B2	B3	B4	B5	C1	C2	C3	C4	C5	D1	D2	D3	D4	D5	E1	E2	E3	E4	E5	H1	H2	H3
A1											60															2		
A2																											2	
A3								20																				2
A4																												
A5																												
B1																					35					3		
B2												100															3	
B3																												
B4																												3
B5																												
C1																										5		
C2																											5	
C3																		100										
C4																								55				5
C5																												
D1	60																									6		
D2		60																									6	
D3								120																				
D4									120																			6
D5																												
E1																		70								4		
E2																											4	
E3			25																									
E4																												4
E5																												
H1																												
H2																												
H3																												
H4																												
H5				5						10			20						40					25				
TP			90					150					180					210					115					100
MB1	62	4	26	3	0	38	141	124	7	0	95	0	105	165	150	28	94	0	126	92	39	43	47	21	0	60	40	20
MB2	62	4	26	3	0	62	165	28	31	24	95	0	105	165	150	4	70	96	102	68	39	43	47	21	0	60	40	20
MB3	62	4	26	3	0	38	141	4	7	0	95	0	105	165	150	0	66	92	98	64	39	43	47	21	0	60	40	20
MB4	14	16	38	15	12	38	141	4	7	0	95	0	105	165	150	48	54	80	86	52	39	43	47	21	0	60	40	20
MB5	2	6	26	3	0	38	141	4	7	0	95	0	105	165	150	0	6	32	38	4	39	43	47	21	0	60	40	20

Source: Used with permission from Miles Fleming, The timing of payments and the demand for money, p. 134, copyright *Economica*.

receipts of 2 from *H*. (The underlined figures of 60 and 120 in the *A* and *B* columns are to be ignored at this time.) Total payments (TP) and receipts (TR) are shown at the bottom of the columns and at the end of the rows.

Table 17.1 records the weekly settlements for trade credit extended between business firms. The household sector in contrast pays daily for its purchases (there is no consumer credit) and is paid weekly on day 5 by the business sector for the services it has rendered during the week.

Below the total payments is a row showing minimum daily balances (MB). Given the payments structure, these are the least amount of balances that a transactor can hold during the week. On one day, minimum balances will be zero. Beyond this day the sum of payments and receipts (for the five-day cycle) will be equal. For example, firm *A* can end day 5 with zero balances because over the next five days total receipts match total expenditures. In the case of firm *C* this equality applies to total receipts and expenditures beginning on day 3. But on other days each transactor is seen to have positive money balances, which are inevitable in view of the timing pattern of receipts and expenditures. Adding up all minimum balances yields the economy's demand for money; initially, it is 322.

To economize further on cash balances, the timing of payments must be altered. If creditors could receive payment on low-cash days and debtors make

TR

90

150

180

210

115

100

845
322
322
294
294
234
4,

payment on high-cash days, minimum balances could be reduced. This can be illustrated in terms of the matrix. Now B agrees to pay 120 to D on day 3 (as shown by the underlined 120) instead of day 4. The week's trade credit from D to B starts and matures on day 3 rather than day 4. In the week the change is made, B pays $(120)(4/5) = 96$ to D on day 3 because only four days credit must be settled at this point. This leads to an increase of $120 - 96 = 24$ in the daily cash balance as shown by MB_2. Thereafter, B pays 120 to D on each succeeding day 3. The MB_2 row shows that B now has a positive money balance of 24 on day 5, and D has 4 on day 1. They can now reduce their money balances on all days by these amounts. This is shown by the MB_3 row. In the same way, if D changes its credit to A so that it gets paid on day 1 instead of day 2, the change in minimum balances is given by MB_4. The MB_5 row shows how the demand for money can be reduced in this case. Rearranging the timing of payments is not cost-free. Searches must be made for the necessary double coincidence of preferences. These involve the cost of time in addition to the money costs of acquiring information. Interest is saved by paying off bank debts, thus reducing the money supply.

Money balances are used not only to make payments for current purchases but also for investment purchases (capital outlays and financial investment). We can take the behavior of firm C in relation to households to illustrate this function of money balances. We now assume that firm C issues long-term securities every day 3, which are purchases by households on that day. This financial investment by households replaces previous consumption expenditures. The demand for money balances stays the same in row MB_1 despite the financing of investment in the place of consumption.

Rearranging the payments structure could be accomplished by a lending transaction. In terms of Table 17.1, it is as if A and B made one-day loans to D. This gives us a more general approach to optimizing cash balances. Knowing the payments structure, the transactor can temporarily dispose of excess cash by financial transactions. It will pay to do this as long as the cost of making such transactions (acquiring an asset and then disposing of it) is less than the interest gained.

The motive for holding cash is to bridge the gap between money receipts and money outlays. The demand for cash will depend on the payments structure and, as we have just seen, on the net return (interest minus costs) from the holding of financial assets. The more distant the future transaction, the smaller the cash holdings because of the net gain in holding an interest-bearing asset until that time. Additional motives for holding cash are the result of prohibitive costs of making transactions. This applies to the well-known precautionary and speculative motives. We hold cash for emergencies or because we anticipate that the bottom is going to drop out of the bond market. Exhausting financial assets far from home to pay for car repair, for example, is not feasible. This explains the precautionary motive for holding cash. The speculative or store-of-value function sees the demand for cash as influenced by the future behavior of interest rates. Increases in the rates will lower the value of fixed income assets. Such riskiness, particularly at a time of historically low rates encourages the holding of money rather than interest-bearing assets. Nevertheless, there is no reason to hold money unless transaction costs (including capital loss) exceed the interest return on financial assets. The motivation for holding money still boils down to the payment structure and the net return on financial assets.

The development of checkable deposits confuses the discussion. Now it is possible to hold money and earn interest. The question of choice between money (demand deposits and currency) and other assets is no longer clear-cut. Because of minimum average balance requirements, there is still a balancing of returns on checkable deposits against their costs. This balancing is the basis of a theory of optimal cash balances. Such a theory explains the investing of such cash, which cannot be shown in the payments matrix. The theory should apply to the choice of interest-bearing short-term liquid assets (savings accounts, money market funds) vs. checking accounts or in a broader framework to the choice of less liquid financial assets (e.g., long-term government bonds) instead of checkable deposits.

Optimal cash balances

When receipts occur at the beginning of a period (with regular payments being made throughout) and transaction costs (service charges) are known, the optimal value of cash balances can be estimated along with the optimal number of withdrawals. First, we identify average cash balances in the absence of financial investment. It can be generalized that when money is spent evenly over a period, the average cash balances will be half the receipts at the beginning of the period. In Figure 17.1 the average cash balance is identified as the midpoint between the initial cash receipt and 0 on the vertical axis. This will be the amount of money held in the middle of the period. If the period's income is spent early (Why is there so much month left at the end of the money?), the expenditure line will be steeper, hitting the horizontal axis before the end of the period and running along that axis until income is received again.

This analysis assumes that receipts are held in cash (checking accounts) until spent. The household sacrifices interest for maximum liquidity. (The market rate is assumed to be above the fixed rate on checkable deposits.) Instead, an inventory-theoretic approach can be applied to money holdings. Money can be treated as an inventory good. Parallel to batch-ordering inventories is the decision as to the optimal number of cash withdrawals after initially investing income (Baumol 1952:545ff.).

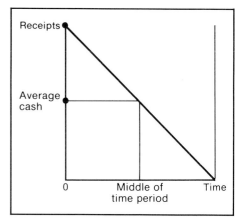

17.1. Average cash holdings when money is spent evenly.

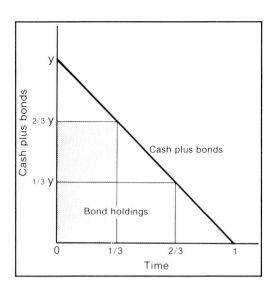

17.2. Optimal investment and withdrawals, three transactions. (Used with permission from Dernburg and McDougall 1972:166)

Figure 17.2 shows one initial investment of income (equal to two-thirds of income) and two withdrawals (three transactions in all). The more financial transactions, the greater the interest return from an initial investment of income. The greater the number of transactions, the greater the brokerage costs. Profitability then depends on how the number of transactions affects the difference between returns and costs (cf. Dernburg and McDougall 1972:167–70).

The relevant variables are:

$$P = [(n - 1)iy/2n] - na$$

where P = profits
n = number of transactions
i = interest return
y = income initially invested
a = brokerage costs per withdrawal

In calculating the revenue from financial investment, the average amount of investment must first be determined. This depends on the number of transactions n; e.g., if 10 transactions are made (counting the initial investment as a transaction), the initial investment would be nine-tenths of income (assuming that one-tenth of income was initially taken in cash). At the end of the time, the transactor will have zero financial holdings. Average holdings will then be:

$$\left[\frac{(9/10) + 0}{2}\right] y = (9/20)y$$

Generalizing this statement to n transactions, $[(n - 1)/2n)]y$ will be the average investment. The interest income at interest rate i will be i times this value, $[(n - 1)/2n]iy$. Given n transactions, the total brokerage cost will be $(n)(a)$, the brokerage cost per transaction.

Graphically, the cost and revenue relationship can be shown as in Figure 17.3. The revenue line R approaches the horizontal $iy/2$ line as the number of transactions n increases. The maximum-interest income is obtained when the average holding of bonds (as a result of continuous transactions) is $y/2$. Multiplying by the interest rate i equals $iy/2$. Profits are at a maximum when the slopes of the cost and revenue curves are equal. The slopes respectively measure marginal cost and

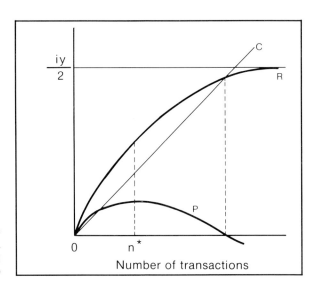

17.3. The optimal number of transactions. (Used with permission from Dernburg and McDougall 1972:169)

marginal revenue. This equality is marked by n^*.

A mathematical solution for n^* allows study of the effect of the individual variables. This solution is $n^* = \sqrt{iy/2a}$ and is arrived at by differentiating p with respect to n in the earlier equation and setting the resultant derivative equal to zero (Dernburg and McDougall 1972:169). It tells us that the optimal number of transactions will increase with increases in income and the interest rate and will decrease with increases in service charges.

The optimal cash balance can be found once the optimal number of transactions is determined (Dornbusch and Fischer 1978:216). Thus $M^* = \sqrt{ay/2i}$. The optimal amount of cash balances increases with increases in brokerage fees a and income y and decreases with increases in the interest rate. Hence the negative relation between the demand for money and the interest rate is confirmed.

More precisely, the square root rule suggests that if we double income, money balances will only go up by half. There are economies of scale in holding cash. Households manage with less average cash as income goes up because it pays to make more withdrawals. Assuming a fixed brokerage fee, the per dollar cost of withdrawals declines as they get larger in size. Since more withdrawals are made with increases in income, average money demand increases less than in proportion to such increases. But if both brokerage fees and income increase, proportionality still holds. This happens with an increase in the general price level. Transactions (money income) and brokerage fees both go up. These two changes together, as suggested by the formula, lead to a rise in the optimal demand for cash in the same proportion as a change in the price level (Baumol 1977:494).

FLUCTUATING CASH BALANCES   The pattern of receipts and disbursements underlying the square root model is more applicable to households than to business firms. As Figure 17.1 suggests, it is based on regular receipts and even cash disbursements. The cash balance pattern for businesses is more random. A cash balance strategy in these circumstances is to let the balance vary within certain limits. At an upper limit, securities will be bought; at the lower limit, securities will be liquidated (the classic article is Miller and Orr, 1966:413ff.; for a discussion, see Van Horne 1971:434–36). The optimal size of dollar transfers from securities to cash can be derived in a cubed root formula (Van Horne 1971:435).

Economizing on cash balances: Financial innovation

BUSINESS FIRMS   High interest rates have spawned new cash balance techniques. More generally, financial innovation can be induced by imposition of
regulatory constraints, exogenous decreases in a firm's rate of growth, an exogenous increase in the variability of major items on the balance sheet of the financial
firm, a change in the competitive nature of the markets facing the firm, sharply
rising yields, and a technological breakthrough. For a full discussion, see Silber
(1976: Ch. 2). Some of these causes have been discussed in previous chapters, most
notably Chapter 8. Deregulation, it was seen, has its own effects on innovation.
Both regulation and deregulation coupled with contributing factors help to explain
changing organizational forms and new financial instruments.

The dimensions of cash management by a major corporation are typified in
Figure 17.4. Short-term investments included Treasury bills and notes, certificates

17.4.   Flow-of-funds analysis, Gulf Oil Corporation. (Used
with permission from Gulf Oil Corporation 1984)

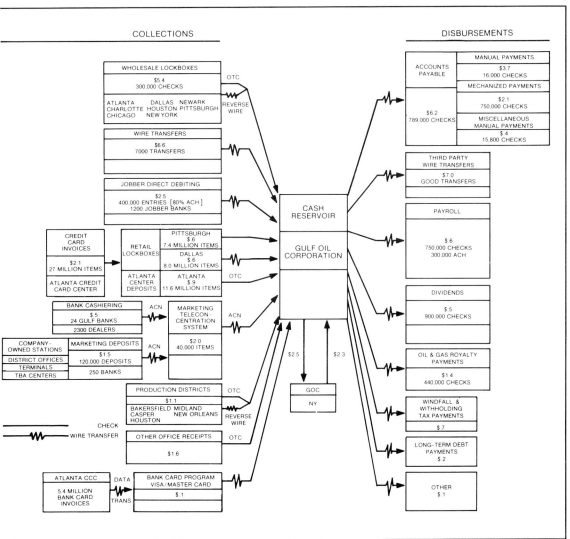

of deposit, time deposits, bankers' acceptances, and commercial paper. Recently, overnight "repos" have probably become a significant component of the portfolio. Repurchase agreements are a one-day sale of securities by banks to their corporate depositors. They are included in the *M*2 category (*Wall Street Journal* 1980:3). The importance of total investment income (including longer term financial investment) is dramatized by the size of a single day's interest, i.e., $500,000, or enough to keep a drilling rig operating in the Gulf of Mexico for nearly a month in 1977. In 1977 over $3 bil. of cash flow was processed monthly.

With so much at stake, the strategy of corporate cash management is to gather in cash receipts as quickly as possible and minimize idle cash. Computer models for forecasting cash flows have been used for some time by many corporations (Donaldson 1969:262ff.). While not discussed as openly and subject to more obstacles, corporate strategy also includes delaying payment. A favorite ploy is to have checks mailed from a remote location, thus increasing mail float. Several of the techniques for expediting cash receipts are displayed on the Gulf chart (Fig. 17.4): depository transfer checks (DTC), lock boxes, reverse wires, automated clearinghouses (ACHs), and collection concentration centers.

Concentration banking aims at shortening the period between the time a customer mails a check and the time the company has use of the funds. Thus collection centers may bill customers and deposit the checks in a local bank. The collection time is thereby reduced. DTCs transfer funds to the Treasury department in Houston. DTCs are an alternative to wire transfers; they are cheaper but do not give immediate funds. ACHs transfer funds between banks by the use of magnetic tape (see Ch. 10).

Lock box arrangements expedite collection of funds by having checks immediately deposited in a bank. The time between receipt by a collection center and its deposit in a bank is eliminated. Banks pick up mail from lock boxes in the local post office. Reverse wire permits one bank (say Mellon) to contact a number of banks and order them to wire transfer funds at Mellon Bank's direction. Funds flow to New York for investment at Gulf's New York Treasury office and flow from New York to Gulf for disbursement purposes.

The ultimate in cash management techniques for corporate customers is the cash sweep plan now being offered by major banks and brokerage houses. The amount of the customers' cash balance above a certain minimum is automatically invested in high-yielding liquid assets at the end of each business day. During the day they are available as transactions balances. Corporations finance transactions without any measured transactions balances. Since deposit balances are measured at the end of the business day, financial institutions benefit by avoiding reserve requirements (Higgins and Faust 1981:14). The statistics on transactions balances may have been temporarily distorted during a transitional settling-in period when such plans were initially adopted. Individuals get the equivalent benefits of such plans through NOW (negotiable order of withdrawal) or Super NOW accounts.

HOUSEHOLDS   Households have been confronted with the dazzling possibility of earning interest and having their money too. Turn the pages of any issue of the *Wall Street Journal* or the financial section of the Sunday *New York Times*. Merrill Lynch, Vanguard, Warwick, Fidelity, Dreyfus, Scudder, Oppenheimer, T. Rowe Price, take your pick—these money market funds promise constant share prices, daily income, check-writing privileges, and tax exemption. (A technical distinction is that a check drawn on a money market fund results in a debit to the fund's checking account at the custodian bank instead of a debit to the customer's transactions account as in the case of NOW accounts.) Early in 1980 the funds were promising yields as high as 17%, based on their own ownership of large denomination certificates of deposit (CDs).

In view of investors being able to have their cake and eat it too, it is surprising how long it took them to catch on to this sure thing. It took five years (1974–79) for money market assets to reach $11 bil. One year later, at the end of 1979, such assets had leaped to $49 bil. In 1981 assets grew by $107 bil. (see Ch. 14). The explanation might be that the typical small investor is used to walking into a bank or savings and loan (S & L). Money market funds lack this visibility. A spate of toll-free numbers in newspaper and radio advertising plus recognition that yields greatly exceeded earnings on fixed-maturity savings accounts may explain the stampede.

The options open to households were further multiplied by the passage of the Depository Institutions Deregulation and Monetary Control Act of 1980 and the Garn–St. Germain Depository Institutions Act in October 1982 (see also Ch. 6). Under the authority of the latter act, the Depository Institutions and Deregulation Committee (DIDC) authorized banks and S&Ls to offer money market deposit accounts competitive with money market mutual funds. Such accounts have no interest rate ceilings and until 1986 had a $1000 minimum balance requirement (Fed, Dallas 1982; table 8.8). With rates competitive (initially higher) with those paid by money market funds, these accounts had succeeded early in 1983 in siphoning large amounts away from the money market funds. The insurance feature of such accounts has been a big attraction offsetting the slight rate advantage (1985) on money market funds.

Deregulation of the banking industry continued to gain momentum with the establishment of a new Super NOW account by the DIDC beginning January 5, 1983. The major difference from the money market deposit accounts is that Super NOWs allow unlimited checking and are subject to the same reserve requirement as other types of transactions accounts. The money market deposit account is limited to six preauthorized and third-party transfers each month (Fed, Dallas 1983). Banks and thrifts have not been enthusiastic in pushing Super NOWs and the return and balance requirements have been below and above (respectively) those for money market deposit accounts.

Futher deregulation took place on October 1, 1983, when the DIDC allowed depository institutions to sell CDs (over 31 days) in any maturity, set interest rates (without their being tied to the Treasury bill rate), and determine minimum denominations. "You name the date. We've got the rate," "Say when CDs," and "have your own CD" have become the advertising slogans of banks and thrifts. Money market deposit accounts also became eligible for individual retirement accounts, thus giving them a tax exemption.

The ambiguity of the money concept supports its replacement by a less ambiguous target in the conduct of monetary policy. Instead of money (as suggested in Chapters 12 and 14), external finance provides an intermediate target free of the confusion of the money concept and with a close linkage to the gross national product.

Portfolio theory: The long-run demand for money

Money bridges the gap between receipts and expenditures. For households, the time horizon is the time between regular paychecks, say a month. In the long run (with retirement), disbursements continue but paychecks stop. The rationale of financial accumulation is to produce a balancing inflow of cash during retirement years. From this standpoint, building a portfolio constitutes a long-run demand for money. Estate building represents an even longer run demand for money extending into the next generation. Building a portfolio presents no problems if the long-run demand can be satisfied in the same way as the short-run demand. In the long run, however, the holding-period yield of liquid assets will not be as high as on other investments. The holding-period yield measures the average return until expected sale of the asset — now in the distant future. It includes capital gains or losses.

RISK   Once investors expand beyond liquid assets, they must contend with risk. The more risk taken, the greater the expected return. Instruments that give progressively more return in exchange for more risk are classified in Table 17.2.

```
Table 17.2.  Picking the right investment
Investor objective      Investment characteristics            Instruments
Safety of principal     Pretax income reflects       Money market funds
 (value of principal      inflation rate over long    Certificates of deposit
 preserved)               term                        Treasury bills
                        Zero volatility of principal  Commercial paper

Income                  Total pretax return of 3%     Government bonds
 (consistent              over inflation              Corporate or municipal bonds
 long-term income)      10% volatility of principal   Producing oil and gas wells
                                                      Income stocks

Growth                  Total pretax return of 6%     Common stock
 (long-term capital       over inflation              Stock-based annuities
 appreciation)          30% volatility of principal   Real estate
                                                      Oil and gas drilling

Aggressive growth       Total pretax return of 10%    Oil and gas exploration
 (potentially large       over inflation              Common stock of start-up
 return through tax     100% volatility of principal    companies
 benefits and/or                                      Equipment leasing
 appreciation)
```
Source: Blumstein 1984:66. Copyright © 1984 by The New York Times Company. Reprinted by permission.

Note: Portfolios reflect either conservative or aggressive investment strategies, with the rate of return corresponding to the amount of risk taken.

Risk and return both involve probabilities in their measurement. We begin with expected return: $E(r) = \sum_{i=1}^{n} p_i r_i$. The expected return is the sum of the probabilities (p_i) of different returns (r_1) times these returns. The probabilities are relative frequencies so they sum up to 1. For example, if a return of 10% has a 0.4 probability and a return of 15% has a 0.6 probability, the expected return would be 13%.

Risk is measured by the variability of returns. The standard deviation or its square, the variance, are standard measures of variability:

$$\sigma i^2 = \sum_{i=1}^{n} p_i[(r_i - E(r_i)]^2 \qquad \text{(variance)}$$

$$\sigma i = \sqrt{\sum_{i=1}^{n} p_i[(r_i - E(ri)]^2} \qquad \text{(standard deviation)}$$

Using our previous example:

$$\sigma i^2 = 0.4(0.10 - 0.13)^2 + 0.6(0.15 - 0.13)^2 = 0.0006$$
$$\sigma i = \sqrt{0.4(0.10 - 0.13)^2 + 0.6(0.15 - 0.13)^2} = 0.0245$$

A portfolio consists of many investments. Expected return and variance apply to the portfolio as a whole. The expected returns of the portfolio (p) is the weighted average of the expected returns of the individual securities. Thus, $E(r_p) = \sum_{i=1}^{n} w_i E(r_i)$, where the weights ($w_i$) indicate the proportions invested in the various securities. The sum of the weights equals 1.

The variance of the portfolio is more than the sum of the individual variances. Diversification (owning more than one security) affects the degree of risk. Returns may be negatively correlated with offsetting variations in returns, thus lowering the degree of overall risk. On the other hand, the returns may be positively correlated, accentuating the degree of risk. The formula for the variance of a two-security portfolio is:

$$\text{Var } (r_p) = w_1^2 \sigma 1 + w_2^2 \sigma 2 + 2 w_1 w_2 \sigma 12$$

where $\sigma 1$ and $\sigma 2$ = individual variances
$\sigma 12$ = covariance, which in turn is equal to $(r12)(\sigma 1)(\sigma 2)$
$r12$ = correlation coefficient for the two securities

The variance of the portfolio formula can be generalized to apply to n securities (see Francis and Archer 1979:28).

To illustrate, assume that investment A has an expected return of 5% and a σ of 20%. The second B investment has an expected return of 15% and a σ of 40%. Given certain weights, the expected return of the portfolio can be calculated. It is 8.3% if the weights are one-third and two-thirds for the A and B investments respectively. Different answers are obtained for Var(r_p), the variance of the portfolio, depending on the value of the correlation coefficient (r_{AB}). It can be worked out that an r_{AB} of -1 in this example produces a portfolio risk, Var (r_p), of zero value. On the other hand, an r_{AB} of $+1$ produces a portfolio risk of 25.4%.

The diversification recommended by portfolio theory goes beyond the injunction not to put all your eggs in one basket. Risk will not be reduced by simply investing in a great number of different securities if the returns are highly correlated.

Negative correlation coefficients are not easy to find, however. Taking the stock market as the basis of choice, studies show that about 50% of a security's risk is systematic. That means that only 50% is unsystematic risk and diversifiable. Changes in individual stock prices are correlated with each other and with the market as a whole. Research seems to suggest that an eight-security portfolio randomly selected does as well as much larger portfolios in reducing unsystematic risk to the systematic level (Francis and Archer 1979:197–98). While half of risk may be systematic, individual stocks can still vary sharply in their volatility. The risk ratio of the individual stock to the market index is called the beta coefficient (Friedland 1978:134).

Summary

This chapter emphasizes that the only reason to hold money is to bridge the gap between a transactor's receipts and expenditures. A payments matrix (Table 17.1) illustrates the pattern of payments for different sectors. Holding transactions balances means the sacrifice of interest even though a small amount may be received on such accounts. The amount of money held will be a simple question of whether it is worth holding. The cost of making financial transactions will be compared with the extra interest that can be earned by short-term investing. This was the basis for a discussion of optimal cash balances.

For business firms the trick is to gather in cash as quickly as possible and delay payments as long as possible. The use of collection centers, lock boxes, computer models for forecasting cash flows, and cash-sweep plans have contributed to a firm's maximizing interest income without sacrificing liquidity.

Longer term investment (portfolio policy) can be considered as long-run demand for money. At some future date, planned expenditures will exceed current receipts. At that time, assets accumulated over the life cycle will be liquidated from individual assets. Rational portfolio behavior calls for a diversified portfolio with returns (interest and capital gains) being negatively correlated. Unfortunately, most returns move together, making it difficult to reduce portfolio risk for a given expected return. The inevitable choice is between risk and return.

Review questions

1. Why do decision-making economic units hold money?

2. Describe a hypothetical pattern of payments and receipts by means of a payments matrix. How can rearrangement of this payment reduce overall minimum cash balances?

3. How do households determine their optimal cash balances? The key role of interest rates and transactions costs should be spelled out.

4. How are optimal cash balances determined for a business corporation (as opposed to households)?

5. How has financial innovation affected the management of cash balances?

6. Why can portfolio theory be identified as a long-run demand for money? How is this long-run demand to be distinguished from short-run demand?

7. "Risk and return is all that we know and all that we need to know about portfolio theory." Explain.

8. Describe the "inventory-theoretic" approach to money holdings.

9. Why is diversification so important in choosing a portfolio of assets?

18

Social priorities
and credit allocation

In Chapter 11 selective controls are discussed as instruments of monetary policy. In Chapter 16, credit rationing was the final topic. Here we expand on previous discussions by raising broader issues such as promoting good credit and discouraging bad credit by allocation (rationing) policies. Pursuing social priorities by monetary policy is closely allied to the politics of money discussed in Chapter 13.

The government's resort to credit control in March 1980 provides a case study. At that time, President Carter invoked the Credit Control Act of 1969. In contrast to the measures of October 6, 1979, which concentrated on the money supply, the new measures concentrated on the rate of growth of credit. The Fed was entrusted with drawing up and administering the new controls. (Press reports suggest that the Fed reluctantly took on the job of credit regulation; see Levine 1980:1). The policy steps had a 9-10-15-16 cadence (Burke 1980:1). Bank and other business lenders were asked to restrict the growth of business lending to no more than 9%; the reserve requirement on growth of managed liabilities was raised to 10%. Such managed liabilities included large certificates of deposit and dollars borrowed overseas (Eurodollar borrowing). This requirement was applied to nonmember banks for the first time. To slow consumer credit growth, a 15% noninterest-bearing deposit requirement on credit extensions was imposed on institutions such as banks, gasoline firms, and department stores. Credit card use was covered by this regulation. A similar 15% reserve requirement was imposed on increases in assets of money market mutual funds. All reserves had to be kept at the Fed. Three new lines were created on the liability side of Fed balance sheets: one for nonmember banks, one for consumer credit agencies, and one for money market funds. Finally, the Fed imposed a 3% surcharge on large banks (the 270 banks with deposits over $500 mil.), which resorted too frequently to the discount window (more than one week in a row or more than four weeks in a quarter). Added on to the prevailing 13% discount, this explains the 16 in the sequence of policy steps.

In addition to credit policy steps, President Carter's program aimed at balancing the federal budget. Fiscal policy has a relevance here, since budget balancing means a reduced allocation of credit to the federal government. Chapter 20 will consider the constraining effects of fiscal policy on monetary policy.

To appraise the whys and wherefores of credit allocation, including this recent case, we must question once again how financial markets work, the rationale of controls and their workability, and the evidence (both direct and indirect).

Prices as the regulator of the flow of funds

In earlier chapters we have emphasized the flow of outside finance as maintaining or increasing the gross national product. When money-creating DIs are involved, their lending adds to the total flow of credit. When checking accounts are shifted from banks to other lending institutions or to the purchase of open-market securities, the total flow of credit is again augmented (a velocity effect).

By means of financial flows, real resources are channeled among different uses. The lender lends where the highest return is earned. In this way real inputs are allocated to their most valuable use. Since some would-be bidders for funds are priced out of the markets, the market is discriminatory in its effects. To the market economists, discrimination is not a bad word. If prospective earnings are higher in one resource use than another, so be it. In a generalized conception of returns, the implicit earnings (rent) of a house are comparable with the explicit earnings from a business venture. The public at large or the politician monitoring social value judgments may assign a higher priority to the slighted activity than the market does. The discriminatory effects of the market are then "bad."

Other regulators of the flow of funds

The flow of funds will be modified by nonprice regulators (cf. Hood 1959:16ff.). Governments modify the flow of funds by their tax policies; e.g., state and local governments are subsidized by federal exemption of their interest payments. The deductibility of interest payments compared with dividend payments affects the way corporations raise outside funds. Depreciation allowances for tax purposes similarly affect investment activities.

The central bank affects the relative attractiveness of federal securities by its open-market operations. By manipulating the reserve base, the central bank influences the total footings of the depository system. The Fed administers a set of regulations running from A to Z. These include various selective controls that are exercised continuously (stock market margin requirements, interest ceilings) or sporadically (terms of mortgage and consumer credit). Similarly, public regulation of the portfolio practices of other financial institutions such as pension funds or insurance companies has allocational effects.

Tradition and custom regulate the flow of funds. Borrowers and lenders have preferred habitats. Borrowers, for example, match the maturities of their prospective assets and liabilities. Banks prefer large corporate customers because of the symbiosis of their loans and deposits. During tight money periods (but not exclusively) mortgage, business, and customer loans are rationed in various ways, including first priority to long-established depositors (Anderson and Ostas 1977:32–33).

Corporations regulate the flow of funds into financial markets by their decisions on self-finance. By the plowback of earnings they circumvent the judgment of the market (Hood 1959:269ff.; Thurow 1972:181). A rejoinder might be that corporate managers who ignore opportunity costs are replaced (Kane 1972:191), but at best this would be a long-drawn-out process.

Direct controls

It is an impossible task to analyze the discriminatory effects of government intervention and market imperfections. An overall generalization, however, is that financial markets operate to favor corporate borrowers at the expense of small business, housing, and state and local governments. In a less than perfect world, the second-best strategy may be to impose a layer of public regulation on top of existing regulation and private rationing. (The theory of the second best has to do with policymaking when one begins with a less than optimal situation.) This is a controversial question. While selective credit policies may improve the efficiency of existing credit markets, second-best policies may mean moving further away from the global optimum — free credit markets (Kaminow and O'Brien 1975:9).

The strongest argument against a second-best strategy is summarized in the old adage, "two wrongs don't make a right." Discrimination against housing, which is the outstanding example of alleged discrimination, may be due to existing regulation. For example, without Regulation Q more funds would flow into savings institutions. Removing usury ceilings and prohibitions on variable rate mortgages would also help flows into housing (Mayer 1975:72). (See, however, Ch. 8 on the dubious effect of deregulation on housing finance.)

But removing market imperfections would not meet the externalities argument. This points out that there are other-party benefits from better housing (e.g., less crime) that justify direct controls (cf. Thurow 1972:183; for a reply see Mayer 1975:66ff.). In addition to these sociological externalities, economic externalities must be considered. Some individuals in the neighborhood undermaintain their homes because the value depends, not on what they do, but on the neighborhood appearance as a whole. There is a "free ride" if neighbors maintain their property. Collective irrationality is the result of individual rationality. Too little is invested in housing maintenance than is warranted by economic rationality.

A major purpose of direct allocation is to increase investment in housing and other high-priority areas such as small business. In addition to increasing the capital stock, a second objective is stabilizing the level of such expenditures (Mayer 1975:48). Housing is a notoriously cyclical industry, and the periodic wastage caused by idleness of construction inputs is quite apparent.

When the aims are specific, nonetheless, the effect may be general. Thus the control of consumer credit, practiced on several occasions during and after World War II, is thought to have an effect on aggregate demand (Smith 1973:56). The reverse relationship is the reason for concern over the allocational effects of monetary policy. The exercise of general monetary controls has selective effects. Conceivably, a battery of selective controls may affect both aggregate demand and allocation of demand. In addition to the discussion in Chapter 11, see Guttentag (1975:58ff.).

Efficacy of controls

Can direct controls work? Three links must hold for the effectiveness of selective controls. First is the link between the instrument (e.g., an increase in the interest cost or other terms for consumer credit) and the amounts demanded of a particular kind of credit (here, consumer credit). (Cf. Kaminow and O'Brien 1975:19— if the market clears, "amounts demanded" applies; if rationing occurs "ex post supply" applies.) Second is the connection between the change in the amount of credit demanded and the demand of particular commodities (e.g., the purchase of a car). Third is the relation between the particular commodity and the output mix (car sales as a percent of total sales).

The third link implies that a particular effect can be exerted without influencing the relative allocation of resources. Other expenditures may be declining at the same time. A central concept is that of substitutability. It has primary relevance for the second link. Substitutability has three dimensions: among financial sources in the financing of a given expenditure (financial substitution), among expenditures in the use of a given financial source (capital expenditure substitution), and between borrowing and income (internal finance) (J. Cohen 1970:26–28).

For selective controls to be effective, the policymaker would hope for a strong one-to-one relation between the controlled financial instrument and the intended category of expenditure; e.g., if the intention is to restrict consumer durable expenditures, success depends on consumer loans going down but also on three other considerations. First, consumer credit should not be used for other kinds of capital outlays (capital expenditure substitution). If it is, restricting consumer credit will only affect other types of capital outlays. Second, the borrower who intended to buy consumer durables should not be able to find substitute financial sources (financial substitution). A third type of substitution is relevant to aggregate effects. If the objective is to increase aggregate demand, a high substitutability between external and internal finance would be appropriate. Making more consumer credit or mortgage credit available would increase aggregate demand if external finance was substituted for internal finance. Now more income would be available for current expenditures on food, education, travel, etc. On the other hand, for a reduction in aggregate demand, a substitution of internal for external finance would help to accomplish this objective even though the specific reduction in expenditures that was sought would not succeed. Consumer credit is a better example of restrictive credit control than mortgage credit because the latter has rarely been curbed by government action.

Two main categories of proposals to achieve credit changes are variations in the term of borrowing and in the supply of credit. Under conditions of perfect markets the two measures would be interrelated; a change of supply would affect the terms of credit. Under conditions of credit rationing, the amount supplied can increase without any change in the terms of credit.

Various proposals have been advocated for influencing credit terms (the price of credit) and the supply of credit (Guttentag 1975:38–40). Some of these have been implemented, such as interest rate and other subsidies paid to borrowers. In a strict sense, credit allocation should be limited to the proposals listed under the supply of credit. Selective credit controls can be viewed as a broader concept including regulations that operate on the price rather than the volume of debt claims. Considerable discussion has centered on variable asset reserve requirements to encourage mortgage lending. They are superior to mandatory floors or ceilings on certain types of loans (Mayer 1975).

Credit allocation must overcome a number of difficulties in order to work. Most importantly, the substitution requirements may not be met. The fungibility of money is a frequent criticism. This means that money borrowed for one purpose may be used for another. The problem of policing is particularly acute when the borrower has access to internal funds, as is the case for the large corporation (Merris 1975:15). A corporation may have been contemplating two projects, project A to be financed with internal funds and project B to be financed with a bank loan. If only project A qualifies as a priority use, the corporation will simply switch its plans. The goals of credit allocation are thwarted. Two of the three types of substitution discussed earlier are illustrated in this example. The borrower has engaged in capital expenditure substitution and has substituted internal for external finance. Had the corporation resorted to uncontrolled borrowing sources to finance the nonsanctioned project B, this would be an example of financial substitution. If only banks were controlled in their lending, borrowers could resort to other financial institutions, resulting also in financial substitution.

Apart from substitution, credit allocation faces serious problems of implementation and administration (Merris 1975:18; Mayer 1975:86). The preferred types of investment must be defined precisely and nonpriority uses translated into specific criteria. It would be difficult to avoid case-by-case decisions. If supplementary asset reserve requirements are adopted (lower reserve requirements on favored projects), decisions must be made about the percentages. Variations in percentages would be necessary over the business cycle. Administering the regulations would entail the costs of surveillance, including detailed reporting by lending institutions.

The question of efficient resource allocation resurfaces with the success of controls. A direct subsidy based on output (say housing starts) has the advantage over preferential treatment of mortgage finance. Subsidizing one input distorts the input mix. In the case of housing, low-interest costs may encourage capital-intensive techniques. As a result, new home building is favored at the expense of rehabilitating the existing housing stock (Mayer 1975:86).

Effectiveness of credit allocation

The evidence on the effectiveness of credit allocation is both direct and indirect. The direct evidence is in terms of U.S. experience with selective credit controls. The indirect evidence is based on what happens to credit availability and selected expenditures in periods of credit crunches.

DIRECT EVIDENCE   The chief direct evidence has to do with consumer credit and mortgage credit. One review of consumer credit controls (Regulation W) concludes that selective credit controls were effective in influencing the amount of credit used for expensive consumer durables, the level of expenditures, and the sales and output of these durables (Smith 1973:52–53; 1975:143). The most extensive use of Regulation W was during World War II. The direct regulation of consumer durables output in wartime clouds interpretation of its effectiveness.

The imposition of Regulation X on mortgage credit during the Korean War made for more restrictive down payment and maturity terms. This resulted in a decline in housing demand and construction. Federal mortgage credit programs (an example of credit allocation) since 1966 have probably dampened cyclical fluctuations in housing (Guttentag 1975:44–45, 51).

INDIRECT EVIDENCE   The indirect evidence on credit allocation is based on what happens in periods of tight money or credit crunches. Such periods simulate the financial substitution effects of direct controls. If the designated financial instrument loses its close connection to an expenditure category in these circumstances, controls are not likely to be successful.

The strongest case for low substitution and the effectiveness of credit availability is in the housing field (Berkman 1979:54ff.). A prima facie case is offered by Figure 18.1. Housing starts and net time deposits in banks and savings institutions (the supply of funds) move in tandem. The disintermediation process explains the variability of deposit flows. As the differential widens between open-market interest rates and time deposit rates, deposit holders withdraw their funds and purchase government and corporate debt. The interest rate differential is plotted in the lower half of Figure 18.1. Deposit flows mirror changes in the differential.

Variations in housing starts have a considerable significance for overall variations in economic activity. Table 18.1 shows how large a portion of the total decline in aggregate real output in three recessions is accounted for by the decline in residential investment.

While the availability of credit seems like a valid explanation of housing activity, a cost-of-credit theory offers a rival explanation. This theory of the housing cycle stresses the demand side of the market (Meltzer 1975:123ff.; Berkman 1979:60ff.). The demand for houses depends on the present value of the future services of the investment in housing. When the market rate is above the mortgage rate (which is possible because of the former's greater volatility or because of usury ceilings), the market rate is the opportunity rate and should be the discount factor applied to the value of these services. An increase in the mortgage rate means a decline in the present value of housing services and a decline in the

Table 18.1. Residential construction and the business cycle

(1) Date of National Bureau of Economic Research reference cycle	(2) Change in real GNP	(3) Change in real residential fixed investment	(4) (3):(2)	(5) Change in real residential fixed investment, peak to trough in corresponding housing cycle	(6) (5):(2)
	($ bil., 1972)		(%)	($ bil., 1972)	(%)
1953:3-1954:2	-16.8	1.9	...	- 8.0	48
1957:3-1959:1	-22.2	- 0.6	3	- 7.3	33
1960:1-1960:4	- 8.8	- 4.8	55	- 5.8	66
1969:3-1970:4	-12.0	- 3.3	28	- 6.9	58
1973:4-1975:1	-72.8	-17.7	24	-28.1	39
Memo:					
1965:4-1966:4	40.8	- 9.0	...	- 9.0	...

Source: Berkman 1979:57.

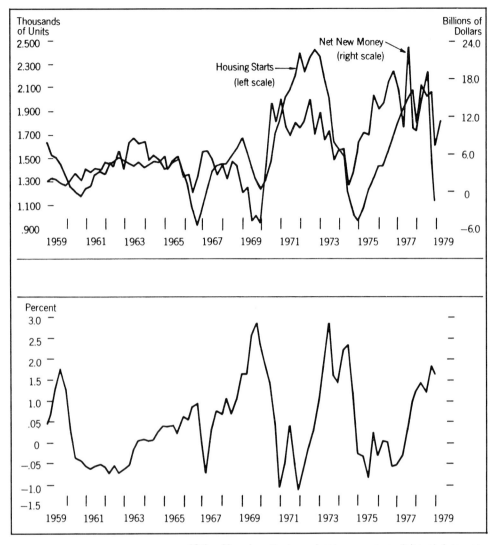

18.1. Housing starts and net new money (above); interest rate differential: 6-month Treasury bill minus time deposit rate (below). Net new money in any quarter was set equal to the difference between the net increase in household, personal trust, and nonprofit organizations time and savings accounts at commercial banks and savings institutions and the interest credited to these accounts during the quarter. (Berkman 1979:61)

amounts demanded of housing irrespective of the supply of mortgage funds. Although changes in the supply of mortgage funds (a change in availability) can affect mortgage interest rates, the change will not be significant. Increased federal agency borrowing to finance housing programs will exert an opposite effect on interest rates. Force-feeding of funds into the housing market will not work because of this counteracting effect.

According to this theory, the supply of mortgage funds indeed has an effect, but it is only one of financial substitution. Mortgage finance is substituted for equity finance in buying a home, without any effect on the volume of housing purchases. The loan-to-value ratio rises (Meltzer 1975:148–49).

Credit cost vs. credit availability has been tested for on the basis of the Federal Reserve Board econometric model. The results are summarized in Table 18.2. They support the hypothesis that credit availability plays a more important role than the mortgage rate in explaining the housing cycle (Berkman 1979:70ff.). Credit availability is defined as the supply of mortgage funds in crunch periods. Crunch periods begin when the rate of growth of the flow of funds into the mortgage market falls at least two percentage points below the flow in the previous year and end when they once again reach this previous level.

Table 18.2. Credit cost vs. credit availability in four housing cycles

	(1)	(2)	(3)	(4)	(5)	(6)	(7)
	Actual percentage decline in housing starts[a]		Percentage decline in housing starts predicted by FRB model, mortgage rate plus other factors operating[b]		Percentage decline in housing starts predicted by FRB model, mortgage rate effect only[c]		Percentage decline in housing starts predicted by FRB model, credit availability effect only
Date, peak to trough	Peak to trough	During credit crunch phase only[d]	Peak to trough	During credit crunch phase only	Peak to trough	During credit crunch phase only	During credit crunch phase only
1959:1-1960:4	-22.8	-16.0	-21.6	-10.8	-2.2	0.3	-15.3
1965:4-1966:4	-30.7	-16.6	-19.3	-17.0	-2.9	-1.6	-19.7
1967:4-1970:2	-29.7	-24.0	-26.5	-18.5	-7.8	-4.0	-28.1
1973:1-1975:1	-41.6	-34.0	-29.8	-26.4	-7.2	-7.2	-26.5

Source: Berkman 1979:73.
[a]The percentage decline in the real value (1972 dollars) of single-family housing starts as a percentage of total real personal consumption expenditures.
[b]Includes house prices, household formation, and household wealth.
[c]Derived from the mortgage rate elasticity of housing starts.
[d]Maximum percentage declines that occurred during the credit crunch periods 1960:1-3, 1966:3-1967:1, 1969:2-1970:1, and 1973:3-1975:1 respectively.

Comparison of cols. 1 and 2 in Table 18.2 shows that most of the decline in housing starts occurred during credit crunch phases (see note d). The percentage decline in housing starts predicted by the Board model during credit crunches via the mortgage rate (col. 6) is a great deal less than the effect of credit availability (col. 7).

The story may be quite different, however, since 1978. Instead of funds flowing into thrift institutions whose primary asset is mortgage loans, the mortgage market in the 1980s has become part of the bond market. The demand for mortgage credit is accommodated by an expansion in pass-through securities (secured by mortgages) that are bought by a wide variety of financial institutions and households attracted by high yields and federal guarantees. In effect, the purchase of mortgages is financed by their later sale — debit and credit entries on the asset side of the balance sheet. Deposit inflows, to a greater extent than before mortgage pools, may finance purchase of pass-through securities rather than outright investment in mortgages. The model tested by Berkman would have to be drastically revised to take account of recent institutional changes.

Foreign experience

In developed and developing economies, resort to direct credit controls has been extensive. In these contrasting economic environments, the appraisal has been largely negative. In general, the purpose of European controls has been to keep interest rates down, allocate funds to preferred uses, and impede rises in velocity by blocking channels of financial intermediation (Hodgman 1973:137ff.; 1974:218ff.). (For additional discussions of foreign experience in developed economies, see Holbik 1973; Lindbeck 1973:179ff.) In this way, control of the total volume of credit is combined with control over its allocation. The control of interest rates has a twofold purpose: to prevent the inflationary effects of capital inflows (such capital flows increase the reserve base for the banking system) and to stabilize the market for government bonds. In countries such as France and Italy, allocation measures include extensive control of nonfinancial intermediaries that may be publicly owned. In this way, medium and long-term investment credit is managed along with bank credit.

Hodgman (1973:159) is critical of overall credit ceilings because he sees the money supply or a comparable monetary aggregate as the appropriate target. Matters were not improved in England, however, when credit allocation techniques were abandoned in 1971 (M. Miller 1973:173ff.). One of the problems faced by the free-market Conservative government was the old bugaboo of monetary policy — the slippery concept of money. Hodgman is dubious about the applicability of European experience to the United States, which has much less concentration in banking and a greater variety of alternative financial institutions (for a defense of the housing priority in France, see David 1973:162ff.). The conclusions of an African study are equally negative (O. Johnson 1975:151ff.). Direct credit controls were found to distort relative prices and discourage the development of important financial institutions. An observer of a recent conference on economic development concluded that the greatest change in thinking among development economists is their respect for market forces (Silk 1985:26).

Recent U.S. experience

The recent U.S. credit-control program (1980) has both general and selective elements. While total bank credit growth has been an on-again, off-again target of monetary policy (see Ch. 12), business credit was temporarily given center stage. The aim was to curb aggregate demand (invite a recession). At the same time, some consumer credit was "bad credit." Because of the depressed state of the automobile industry, such credit was less bad than buying on time from Sears or J. C. Penney. Housing credit was in the same class as automobile credit, to be encouraged if possible. Because of the effect of money market funds in competing with thrift institutions, reserve requirements were imposed on the former. Financing corporate takeovers or mergers, financing purely speculative holdings of commodities or precious metals, or expanding commitments for back-up lines in support of commercial paper were also in the discouraged category. This is not a new concern of the Fed, which throughout its history has railed against so-called unproductive loans. The rash of takeovers financed by liberal lines of bank credit attests to the difficulties of allocating credit in this negative way.

The policy has had its most dramatic success in curbing consumer credit, particularly the use of credit cards. When the Fed imposed its controls, they were widely viewed as symbolic (Lohr 1980:A1, D6). Instead, the controls had a substantial impact on both the demand and supply of credit (Cox 1980). Faced with a 15% reserve requirement, lenders cut off or curtailed existing credit lines, stopped making new loans, shortened repayment periods, and required larger repayments. Oil companies and other credit-card issuers cut back on new cards. As a result of such actions and also because consumers altered their inflationary expectations (buy now before prices go up), total consumer installment debt declined by $571 mil. to $307.6 bil. during March 1980. A year earlier, installment debt had increased by $2.4 bil.

Attempts to discriminate in favor of and against certain kinds of consumer credit failed, however. The automobile and housing industries continued into deep depression after the March controls were announced. By May 1980 the Fed was beginning to worry about overkill. It removed the 3% surcharge on the discount rate. In June 1980 the March controls on credit were abandoned.

Summary

Governments may not defer to the market as to how resources are best allocated. The market from the government's point of view may favor big business or the consumer instead of housing, small business, or state and local governments. The government can always rationalize its priorities by reference to the externalities of increased housing or aid to small business and the farmer.

The U.S. central bank has traditionally been the designated agent for formulating and administering credit allocation. In the most recent instance, it appears to have done so reluctantly. This chapter details how social priorities add another major inhibition to Fed policymaking.

In theory, selective controls will not work if money borrowed ostensibly for one purpose is used for another. The direct evidence on selective controls is quite strong for the efficacy of consumer credit and residential mortgages. The indirect evidence (based on a study of credit crunches) is strongest in the housing field. Until 1978 the availability of mortgage credit appears to have been the decisive factor influencing the volume of housing starts. The restructuring of the mortgage market since that time, so that to all intents and purposes it is part of the bond market, modifies this conclusion.

Overall credit ceilings have as their objective the control of aggregate demand. Recent credit control operated in spectacular fashion. The ceilings had a significant psychological effect (via inflationary expectations), resulting in a sharp decrease in the demand for credit. At the same time, new reserve requirements also restricted the supply of credit.

Review questions

1. In what sense are unregulated markets discriminatory?

2. What do we mean when we say prices are the regulator of the flow of funds?

3. Explain and illustrate nonprice regulators of the flow of funds.

4. Why do governments resort to credit allocation?

5. Define the three links that must hold for direct controls (credit allocation) to be effective. Why is the use of the word "substitution" a "must"?

6. What is the direct evidence on the effectiveness of credit controls? What is the indirect evidence?

7. Distinguish between interest rate and credit availability theories of housing starts.

8. What are several authors' views on foreign experience with credit allocation?

9. Describe the U.S. experience with credit control, March–June 1980.

19

Prices, interest rates, and output: Leading theories

While prices, interest rates, and output have figured prominently in previous chapters, we have yet to make an attempt at a unified theory. Since they interact with one another, without such a theory one cannot claim an understanding of how the economy works. The task is made easier by the paucity of theories and their essential polarity.

Monetary theorists can be broadly classified as monetarists and Keynesians. One is tempted to paraphrase the Gilbert and Sullivan chorus about everyone born into this world is either a Liberal or Conservative. The rivalry has a long history, with the protagonists sparring under many aliases (see Wood 1972:3–12). The cleavage has obvious political overtones (monetarists support the Republicans, Keynesians the Democrats) and diverging implications for economic policy. Monetarists will be for a neutral monetary policy and minimal government intervention, Keynesians for an active fiscal policy and an accommodating monetary policy. (These distinctions were murky in 1984, with the Republicans behaving like traditional Democrats and Democrats talking like traditional Republicans.)

The monetarist position

Paradoxically, monetarists argue that money matters because it doesn't matter. Money is the root of inflation because the real sector is impervious to increases in money except when the economy has a potential for growth. When money increases faster than this growth rate, however, the effect is inflationary.

The anchoring point in the monetarists position is the labor market, which is assumed to clear, and output is determined by the employed labor force. The theoretical framework we sketch could also be called neoclassical. Its trademark, as we shall see, is an emphasis on flexible and market clearing prices. (For that matter, it could also be called a classical framework, since the economic literature does not offer a clear distinction.)

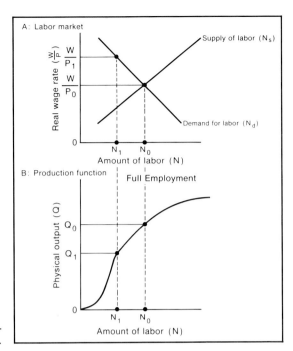

19.1. Employment and production.

In considering employment and production, one proceeds from Figure 19.1A
to 19.1B. In the latter, labor is the only input that varies in the short run and
therefore the only one that counts.

Once output is determined, the saving function in relation to the (physical)
investment function determines the rate of interest (Fig. 19.2). (For additional
discussion see Ch. 16.) Now the function of money as illustrated in Figure 19.3 is
simply to determine the price level. When output Q is given and the velocity of
circulation of money is similarly fixed, the quantity of money M determines the
price level P.

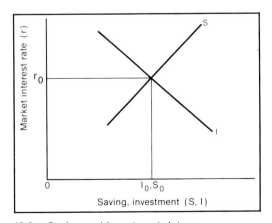

19.2. Saving and investment determine the interest rate.

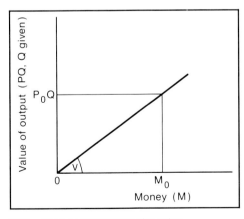

19.3. Money determines the price
level.

While what Keynes said is fraught with much controversy, its focus is unquestionably on aggregate demand. The starting point is thus the product market, with demand creating its own supply. Businesses produce whatever they expect to sell (the 45° helping line in Fig. 19.4). The standard diagram depicts equilibrium in the product market in terms of the overall market and in terms of saving and investment. Thus planned expenditure E equals planned supply Y at exactly the same level of output (income) that planned saving equals planned investment. The Keynesian model underlying Figure 19.4 consists of the following equations:

$$C = a + bY \qquad (19.1)$$
$$S = Y - C \quad \text{or} \quad S = -a + (1 - b)Y \qquad (19.2)$$
$$I = I^* \qquad (19.3)$$
$$C + I = E \qquad (19.4)$$
$$E = Y \qquad (19.5)$$

where C = consumption
Y = income
I = investment; I^* = exogenous investment
E = expenditures
S = saving

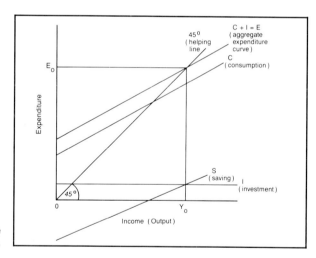

19.4. Equilibrium in the product market.

Eq. 19.1 is the famous Keynesian consumption function, which relates current consumption to income. The coefficient b is the marginal propensity to consume. In more advanced models many more variables are introduced. An alternative formulation (Eq. 19.2) expresses saving as a function of income. Eq. 19.3 makes (physical) investment exogenous. In a more complicated model, it is made dependent on the rate of interest and other costs of capital. Consumption and investment add up to total expenditures (Eq. 19.4). There is an identity between expenditures and output (Eq. 19.5).

In contrast to the monetarist (classical) approach, saving and investment determine output rather than determining the interest rate. Saving is a leakage,

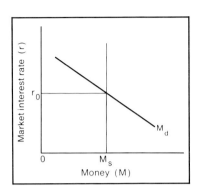

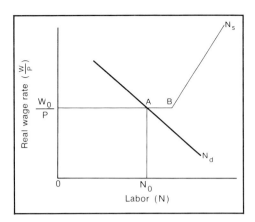

19.5. Keynesian interest rate determination in the money market.

19.6. The Keynesian labor market: perfectly elastic supply of labor.

investment an injection into the income stream. Since expenditures equal consumption plus investment (neglecting government) and saving equals income less consumption, the two intersections must occur at the same output level. Given that $Y = C + S$, or $C = Y - S$ and $E = C + I$; then $S = I$; and substituting for C, $E = Y - S + I = Y$.

In the Keynesian framework, the interest rate is determined by the demand for a given stock of money, with demand being conditioned by transaction requirements and speculation as to the future behavior of interest rates (Fig. 19.5). (See also Ch. 16.) The market interest rate can be considered to be the bond rate. The obverse to equilibrium in the money market is then equilibrium in the bond market (standing for all fixed-value financial assets), with desired bond holdings being equal to the stock of available assets.

The role of the interest rate is to affect investment. In terms of Figure 19.4, a lowering of the market rate (not measured directly in Fig. 19.4) will induce more investment. This raises the I and E curves, establishing a new equilibrium level of output.

The Keynesian analysis works its way back to the labor market. The distinguishing characteristic is a perfectly elastic supply curve of labor at the prevailing real wage rate above the market-clearing wage. The demand for labor will depend on the level of aggregate demand in the product market. As depicted in Figure 19.6, inadequate aggregate demand is seen to result in involuntary unemployment, a notion foreign to classical economics. Thus, at the real wage W_0/P, point A indicates the number of workers hired—less than B, which indicates the number of workers willing to work at that real wage rate.

The neoclassical synthesis

Keynes's *General Theory of Employment, Interest, and Money* (1936) is the great work of the twentieth century and a logical target for integration with neoclassical economics (see Dernburg and McDougall 1972:241–42). While the term "neoclassical synthesis" is much bandied about, clear definitions are hard to come by. The term evidently originates with Paul Samuelson, but his definition is not enlightening (cf. Hotson et al. 1976:14). Most simply, the neoclassical synthesis represents the stretching of the neoclassical framework based on price flexibility to fit (and swallow) Keynesian ideas.

The synthesis begins by showing that exactly the same equation system can describe both theories.

Monetarist sequence:

$$N_d(W/P) = N_s(W/P) \tag{19.6}$$
$$Y = X(N, K^*) \tag{19.7}$$
$$I(i) = Y - C(Y) \quad \text{or} \quad I(i) = S(Y) \tag{19.8}$$
$$M_s^*/P = L(i, Y) \tag{19.9}$$

Keynesian sequence:

$$I(i) = Y - C(Y) \quad \text{or} \quad I(i) = S(Y) \tag{19.10}$$
$$M_s^*/P = M_d/P = L(i, Y) \tag{19.11}$$
$$Y = X(N, K^*) \tag{19.12}$$
$$N = N_d = N_d(W^*/P) \tag{19.13}$$

where W = money wages; W^* = a fixed (given) level of money wages
P = price level
Y = real output (represented in the figures by Q)
N = employment; N_s = supply of labor; N_d = demand for labor
K^* = given capital stock
I = real investment
C = real consumption
S = real saving
i = interest rate
M_s^*/P = given money stock in real terms
M_d/P = demand for real money stock

The variables in parentheses are the explanatory variables.

In the monetarist sequence, the real wage (W/P) is first determined in Eq. 19.6 by equality of the demand (N_d) and supply (N_s) of labor. Both demand and supply depend on the real wage rate. Output is next determined by means of the production function. The interest rate is solved in Eq. 19.8 by saving and investment. Finally, the price level P is solved in Eq. 19.9 for the known values of i and Y (solved in previous equations) and for the given value of the money stock M_s^*. In the Keynesian sequence, Eqs. 19.6 and 19.7 jointly determine output and the interest rate; manpower requirements follow in Eq. 19.8 and the appropriate price level in Eq. 19.9. The price level brings about a real wage consistent with hiring the necessary labor to produce Y, as determined in Eqs. 19.6 and 19.7.

When the first two equations in the Keynesian sequence are drawn, the result is the trademark of monetary economics—the *IS-LM* diagram. Its fame derives from an ability to depict equilibrium conditions in two key markets (six different variables are involved) in two-dimensional space. Thus the *IS* curve in Figure 19.7 describes a series of equilibrium values in the product market. The negative slope

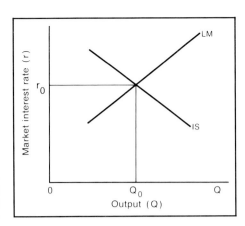

19.7. Simultaneous equilibrium in the product and money markets, *IS-LM* analysis.

is the standard one and states that as output levels rise, the interest rate will have to fall to equate saving and investment levels. The reasoning is that saving will increase with income (the obverse side of output) and, to induce a matching amount of investment, the cost of capital (the interest rate) must fall.

The *LM* curve denotes alternative interest rate and output combinations that equate the demand and supply of money. The conventional curve is positively sloped, indicating that as output rises, the interest rate must increase to equate the two variables. Such increases are necessary because the public's demand for money holdings is a function of its transactions, which in turn are measured by income. Given the money stock, this increased demand for money will be discouraged by market yields going up on financial investments (bonds). The latter yields adjust to whatever level is necessary to equate the demand for money to the existing supply.

The intersection of the two curves in Figure 19.7 simultaneously determines the interest rate and output. The underlying functions for saving, investment, demand, and supply of money enable us to determine their values as well.

To describe opposing theories by a common set of equations entailed one major change in the original Keynesian model: flexible prices replace rigid prices. It is then but a small step to a neoclassical "victory": replace fixed money wages in the original Keynesian model with flexible money wages. Prices and wages will now both fall in periods of economic slack and unemployment. This will generate a wealth effect. Associated with the name of the British economist A. C. Pigou, the wealth effect relates spending in the economy to real wealth holdings. Assuming that wealth is in fixed value claims, a fall in the price level will increase real wealth. Feeling wealthier, people will spend more and save less (the *IS* curve shifts to the right). At the same time, the *LM* curve shifts to the right because of the increase in the real supply of money balances (a given money stock is deflated by a lower price level). As long as unemployment exists, money wages will fall, bringing prices down with them. Real wages will fall to the level that clears the labor market. But now, because of the wealth effect in the product and money markets, these two markets will be consistent with full employment equilibrium in the labor market. The Keynesian thesis is seen to depend on an institutional quirk—fixed money wages, which in turn are responsible for rigid prices.

The power of monetary policy is restored in the neoclassical synthesis, even if money wages are rigid. An increase in the quantity of money can succeed in shifting the *LM* curve to the right, thus reaching a full employment level in the product market at the same time that it increases prices sufficiently to bring real wages down to a market-clearing level in the labor market. Thus, again in theory, monetary policy can achieve full employment despite fixed money wages.

The remaining, much chewed-over ideas of Keynesian theory are those of a liquidity trap and interest-inelastic investment demand. The liquidity trap is characterized by a horizontal *LM* slope; inelastic investment, by a vertical *IS* curve. Both slopes have important policy implications: monetary policy cannot work; only fiscal policy can increase aggregate demand.

The underlying money market curves in Figure 19.8 show how the *LM* curve in Figure 19.7 can have a horizontal slope. At a low rate of interest, the public is assumed to have an infinite desire to hold money, since they expect the interest rate to go back up. It is prudent under these circumstances to hold money rather than financial investments because a rise in the market rate of interest will cause bond prices to fall. A separate demand curve for money is drawn for each level of income (since the transactions demand for money depends on income). The crucial point is their convergence at point *A*. For a number of different levels of income on Figure 19.8, the demand for money equals the stock of money at the same rate of interest. Higher income levels shift the demand curve for money to the right so that the inelastic segments are distinct but the horizontal segments dominate the intersection with the money stock.

When Figure 19.8 is translated into interest rate–income space (the dimensions of the *IS-LM* diagram), the money market relationship between interest rates and real income shows up as a horizontal *LM* segment for all demand-for-money curves intersecting the money stock at the same rate of interest. The idea of infinite demand for money cannot stand the scrutiny of a flow-of-funds perspective, since it implies an infinite source of funds by disposal of assets or productive services in other markets.

The other limiting case is a vertical *IS* curve, which is associated with inelastic investment demand. The underlying product market diagram (Fig. 19.9) shows saving as responsive to real income and investment as unresponsive to the interest rate. Thus at a single income level but alternative interest rates, saving equals investment (the *IS* curve).

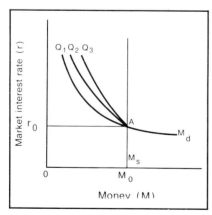

19.8. Derivation of the liquidity trap.

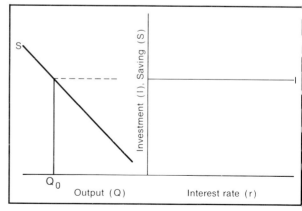

19.9. Derivation of the vertical *IS* curve.

Given these slopes, monetary policy is impotent. Thinking diagrammatically, a horizontal *LM* curve cannot be shifted to the right by increasing the money supply. A conventionally sloping *LM* curve can be shifted to the right but cannot increase income levels if it intersects a vertical *IS* curve. The only recourse is to fiscal policy, which will cause the *IS* curve (conventionally sloping or vertical) to move to the right, thus increasing income levels.

The antithetical situation, when only monetary policy is effective, obtains when the *LM* curve is vertical or the *IS* curve is horizontal. In these instances only a shift in the *LM* curve will result in a higher income level. Behind *IS-LM* lies a potentially complex equation system whose reduced form can be solved analytically for various policy multipliers. Reduced form means that the endogenous variables (interest rates and income) and the price level (when the production and employment sector is introduced) can be expressed as a function of all the exogenous variables. From this reduced form the partial derivatives can be solved; i.e., the effect of a one-unit change in the exogenous variables (such as the money supply, government expenditures, or taxes) on each of the endogenous variables can be estimated. These partial derivatives are called multipliers. Whether monetary policy or fiscal policy is more effective in influencing income can be demonstrated to be a function of the interest elasticities of saving, investment, cash hoarding, and bank money creation (e.g., see Smith and Teigen 1974: sect. 1).

It might be expected that empirical analysis will give a ready answer to the question of elasticities. This is not the case, unfortunately. As will be discussed in a later quantitative section, econometric analysis is not that straightforward. It is safe to say, however, that such extreme elasticities have never been verified.

Critique of the neoclassical synthesis

The neoclassical synthesis is vulnerable on several scores. First, its picture of the price adjustment process and movement to equilibrium fails to recognize the equilibrium nature of *IS-LM* analysis. The adjustment process features the latter curves plus a vertical line indicating the full employment output level established in the labor and production sector (Fig. 19.10).

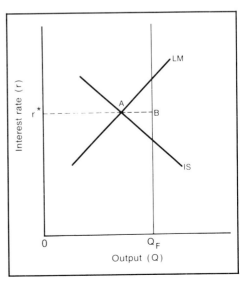

19.10. Adjustment process in the product and money markets when the labor market is introduced.

The horizontal distance AB denotes excess supply and leads to price and wage reductions that tend to shift the *IS-LM* curves to the right toward intersection with the vertical line. The *IS-LM* curves now measure effective demand without connotations as to planned output. This ignores that *IS* itself stands for planned equilibrium in the output market. Why should it be disturbed by the possibility of greater output? The neoclassical position, when it takes over *IS-LM* analysis, offers inconsistent explanations of the supply of output. In terms of the four-equation system, the problem with the neoclassical synthesis arises when the equation $I(i) = Y - C(Y)$ no longer determines the interest rate (the classical or monetarist interpretation) but instead, along with *LM*, jointly determines output and interest rates (the Keynesian sequence). At the same time, the neoclassical synthesis has the labor market clearing via wage-price flexibility so that output is at the full-employment level. By so doing, output determination is inconsistently based on both the labor and output markets.

The second major criticism is that the synthesis distorts the Keynesian position. It will be recalled that the Keynesian sequence of equations assumed flexible prices. In this way, the real wage adjusts so that the demand for labor will be consistent with equilibrium in the money and output markets (*IS-LM*). A more Keynesian approach would emphasize the importance of output levels (aggregate demand) in shifting the demand for labor. Thus in terms of Figure 19.6 a change in equilibrium output would cause the demand for labor to shift and intersect the horizontal portion of the labor supply curve at a different level of employment. Modern disequilibrium analysis makes much of the constrained nature of demand in the product and labor markets. The demand for labor is conditional on the sale of products; the demand for products, on the sale of labor. This is supposed to represent what Keynes "really meant." (The classic study is Leijonhufvud 1968.)

The neoclassical synthesis then seems to be a forced marriage rather than a genuine reconciliation. The Keynesian position is rightfully identified with less than full-employment situations, wage and price rigidities, and demand creating its own supply. On the other hand, the monetarist position should be equated with full employment and flexible wage and price situations. Needless to say, both positions may be quite irrelevant in the real world of stagflation.

Determination of the price level

Diagrammatically, the derivation of the demand curve for output can be represented as shown in Figure 19.11. Each *IS-LM* curve is identified by a price level. The curves shift to the left as the price level advances. Several reasons can be given for such leftward shifts in the *IS* curve. First, there is the familiar wealth effect. Real wealth will fall with a rise in the price level, causing the consumption curve to decrease. Second, real disposable income will fall, given a progressive tax system with increases in prices (discussed further below). The explanation of upward shifts in the *LM* curve is more direct. The real value of money balances declines so that money market equilibrium requires higher interest rates or lower real income. The aggregate demand curve in the top portion of Figure 19.11 is the locus of the intersectional points in the lower figure.

The supply curve of output in Figure 19.11 is derived by substitutions involving Eqs. 19.12 and 19.13 in the Keynesian sequence. Substituting for N in Eq.

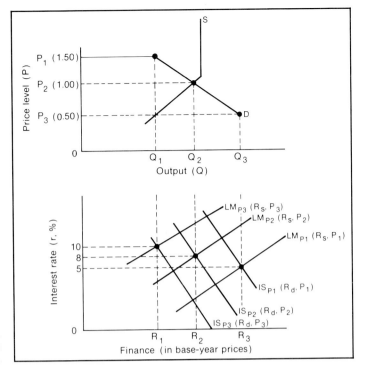

19.11.
Determination of the
price level.

19.12 yields $Y = X[N_d(W^*/P), K^*]$. The demand for labor increases as the real wage rate declines; an increase in the price level causes this. The parameter N_d measures the associated increase in employment N. The parameter X defines the increases in physical output associated with the increase in N. Combining the two equations then results in a price-output relationship that is upwardly sloping with respect to the price level.

In the neoclassical sequence, Eq. 19.6 indicates that the labor market clears. This is a full-employment world. Increases in P will be associated with proportional increases in flexible money wages. Higher prices will have no effect on output, since they have no effect on real wages. The supply curve in Figure 19.11 depicts both Keynesian and monetarist cases. It is positively sloping until the full-employment output is reached (Keynesian case). After that output, the curve becomes vertical, as in the market-clearing case. The price level is then determined by the intersection of the demand and supply curves for output.

Some reservations about the demand curve

Since the demand curve is derived from the *IS-LM* model, it is subject to the same basic criticism as before. Equilibrium in the product market (represented by *IS*) involves the supply side of the market, albeit in a passive, accommodating way. Supply therefore enters into the determination of effective demand as well as having its own curve based on the labor market. This inconsistency calls for a derivation of the demand curve in another way, one that is free of output considerations. This can be done by deriving the effective demand curve from the market for finance.

Now the market for finance is represented in the lower part of Figure 19.11. In the place of *IS*, the curve sloping downward from left to right is the demand for finance R_d, expressed in base-year prices. Behind the demand for finance lies planned expenditures. As planned expenditures increase, so does the demand for finance. Letting F = the dollar value of the demand for finance, $R_d = F/P$. The curve plots the demand for finance with respect to alternative interest rates. In functional form, $R_d = f(r)$.

Replacing LM is the supply-of-finance curve. Represented by R_s, the supply of funds is equal to the quantity of money M times its velocity of circulation V, corrected for the price level; i.e., $R_s = MV/P$. The R_s curve is drawn upward, sloping from lower left to upper right. As the market rate of interest increases, depository institutions (DIs) will lend more and thus add to the money supply. Holders of money balances will lend more of their money balances at high interest rates than at low rates. As a result, the money supply is more active at high rates. In functional language $R_s = f(\overset{+}{r})$.

Underlying this analysis is a version of the equation of exchange $MV = PQ$, with the terms suitably rearranged. Now the left-hand term MV/P denotes the planned supply of finance (in real terms); the right-hand term, $Q = R_d(= F/P)$, the planned demand for finance in real terms. Both depend on the interest rate. Thus, instead of the price level being determined as in the usual interpretation of this equation, it is the interest rate (given the price level) that is determined.

Given a price level of P_2, the market clears at the interest rate of 8%. At this rate the demand for finance is equal to the supply of finance. Planned expenditures are provided their finance, MV/P. This equilibrium situation in the purchasing power or finance market explains one point on the demand curve in the upper part of Figure 19.11. Using the values from Table 19.1, at a price of $1 ($P_2$), the effective demand for output Q_d is $150. This effective demand depends on the demand for finance R_d being matched by the supply of finance R_s. The demand for finance at 8% interest and a P_2 price level corresponds to the supply of funds at this interest rate and price level (Table 19.1). In similar fashion, using the data in Table 19.1, effective demand can be derived for prices P_1 and P_3 in Figure 19.1. The intersection of the R_s and R_d curves, which are marked with the same price labels, gives us the points for deriving the effective demand curves for output at that price.

Table 19.1.	Deriving the effective demand curve							
	(1)	(2)	(3)	(4)	(5)	(6)	(7)	(8)
						Increase in		
	Original curves				autonomous expenditures			
	Q_d	R_s	R_d	r	Q_d	R_s	R_d	r
	($)	($)	($)	(%)	($)	($)	($)	(%)
P_1=$1.50	100	100	100	10	140	140	140	12
P_2=$1.00	150	150	150	8	190	190	190	10
P_3=$.50	220	220	220	5	290	290	290	8

EFFECT OF A CHANGE IN PRICE LEVEL   As we have seen, when the price level changes, this will cause R_d and R_s to shift. Allowing for its effect, we should rewrite the functional relations:

$$R_d = F/P = f(\overset{-}{r}, \overset{-}{P}) \quad R_s = MV/P = f(\overset{+}{r}, \overset{+}{P})$$

An increase in the price level causes the two curves to shift to the left; a decrease causes them to shift to the right.

In the case of planned expenditures (the R_d curve), the reasons behind the leftward shift in the *IS* curve (discussed earlier) apply here also. As the price level goes up, the real value of financial assets such as money, time deposits, and bonds declines. We now feel poorer and plan to buy less at any specified market rate of interest. The demand for finance in real terms declines. This means that the money value of demand F increases by less than P so that F/P declines for any interest rate. Another reason is the tax structure. We give a bigger chunk of our income to the federal government as prices go up because of a progressive income tax structure. We move into a higher marginal tax bracket, which raises our average tax rate. Our take-home pay in real terms is less than before (see Ch. 3). We therefore plan to spend less at different interest rates. The R_d curve is now to the left of the original position.

In the case of the R_s curve, as the price level advances, the supply of purchasing power MV/P is less than before (at any interest) because MV is deflated by a new higher level of prices. (It is assumed that values of M and V are independent of the price level.)

The demand for finance is expressed in real terms in this analysis. In nominal dollars the demand for finance will be likely to increase with inflation. Inflationary expectations may cause the dollar demand to increase faster than current prices. The demand for real finance will then shift to the right (offsetting the leftward movement resulting from the wealth and tax effects of inflation). Such rightward movements in the real demand for finance could give the effective demand curve an upward slope (greater effective demand for output being associated with higher prices).

Setting aside the expectational effect, we can assume that the real supply of finance is more strongly affected by inflation than the real demand. Because of the definition of the real supply of finance as MV/P, this curve will shift to the left in proportion to price increases. On the other hand, the coefficients for wealth and disposable income in the demand-for-finance function are likely to be less than one, resulting in a less than proportional influence of price. Because of the respective movements leftward, the intersections in the finance market will trace out rising nominal rates (as shown in Fig. 19.11). At the same time, the real rate of interest (the nominal rate less the inflation rate) will be declining because nominal interest rates would not be keeping pace with inflation.

SHIFTS IN THE EFFECTIVE DEMAND CURVE   So far, we have derived the effective demand for output vis-à-vis prices. What will cause the effective demand curve itself to shift? It will shift whenever the R_d or the R_s curve shifts for reasons other than price changes. Let us distinguish three classes of shift variables for the effective demand curve. These will be additional variables to the tax rate (disposable income) and wealth, which (as discussed) are affected by the price level.

First, autonomous changes in planned expenditures may be responsible; e.g., regardless of interest rates, business may plan to increase its capital investment. Perhaps the utilities industry wishes to expand because of anticipated increases in energy demands. (We have not drawn these curves.) Their intersections with the original set of R_s curves will give us a new effective demand curve on Figure 19.11 to the right of the original. For any price level, the R_s and R_d curves will intersect at a greater amount of finance and thus a higher level of effective demand than before. The figures for such an autonomous increase in expenditures are exemplified in Table 19.1.

Another type of autonomous change may originate on the supply-of-funds side. Suppose that holders of money balances decide to reduce the size of their average monthly balances. Instead of holding an average of 20% of their monthly income in money, they decide to hold 15%. The effect will be an increase in the velocity of circulation. The supply of finance (purchasing power) will increase. Each R_s curve ($= MV/P$) will shift to the right. The effect will be a new set of intersections with the original R_d curves to the right of their previous intersection. Again the Q_d curve will lie to the right of the original.

Second, fiscal policy may be responsible for a shifting in the R_d curves. The federal government may plan to increase its expenditures (G) or reduce its taxes (T). This will lead to a new series of R_d curves (one for each alternative price level) to the right of the previous curves. The new set of intersections of R_s and R_d will be represented by a new effective demand curve to the right of the original curve.

Third, monetary policy may be responsible for the supply of finance (MV/P curves) shifting to the right. The central bank can increase the reserves available to DIs, which will lend more, increasing the money supply. A new series of MV/P curves will intersect the initial R_d curves to the right of the original intersections. The effective demand curve shifts to the right. Both the R_s and R_d curves may be shifting. If both shift in the same direction, the shift in the effective demand curve will be accentuated. If they shift in opposite directions, the shifts will be offsetting.

If we now allow for the additional variables mentioned, the functional relationships become as follows:

$$R_d = F/P = f\ [(\overset{-}{r},\ (\overset{+}{Y_p} - \overset{-}{tY_p}),\ \overset{+}{W/P},\ \overset{-}{AUT},\ \overset{+}{(G} - T)]$$
$$R_s = MV/P = f(\overset{+}{r},\ \overset{-}{P},\ \overset{+}{AUT},\ \overset{-}{RES})$$

where Y_p = personal income
t = tax rate
$Y_p - tY_p$ = disposable income
W/P = real wealth
AUT = autonomous factors
$G - T$ = government expenditures minus taxes
RES = DI reserves

Since AUT may include positive and negative effects, both signs are shown above this variable.

INTEREST RATE AS THE LINKAGE VARIABLE   The interest rate is emphasized in monetary economics as the linkage variable between the product market (expenditures) and financial markets. The implication is that the lower the cost of capital, as determined in financial markets, the more will be spent in the economy. The above analysis offers a critical perspective. Before planned expenditures can become effective demand (which is what counts), a supply of finance must be forthcoming. Those who stress the planned expenditure curves ignore the importance of the R_s curve as a precondition for effective demand. Once the R_s curves are introduced, it is apparent that interest rate is not a good indicator of effective demand. Thus, for example, increases in the R_d curves (shifts to the right) in Figure 19.11 (caused by the autonomous changes) will increase effective demand. But if we were to trace the path of intersections of the new R_d curves with the original R_s curves, the shift in the R_d curves would be responsible for higher interest rates compared with the previous set of intersections. The effective demand curve has increased despite the clearing of financial markets at higher interest rates than before. Higher interest rates are consistent with higher effective demand as long as the R_d curves increase. We illustrate this possibility in Table 19.1 in cols. 5–8. Thus Q_d is greater at every price level despite higher interest rates, (compare cols. 4 and 8). The increases in the R_d curves have increased the flow of finance by raising interest rates. Higher interest rates induce a greater supply of finance.

On the other hand, if the R_s curves shift to the right because of, say, a less restrictive monetary policy, the increase in the effective demand curve will be associated with a series of lower interest rates. (The reader should be able to demonstrate this by creating a table similar to Table 19.1 cols. 4–8.) The conclusion is that interest rates and effective demand may be negatively or positively related, depending on whether the underlying shift is in the R_s curve (resulting in a negative relation because of interest rates and effective demand) or in the R_d curve (resulting in a positive relation between interest rates and effective demand). Both shifts have occurred in the past, as seen in Chapter 16.

The implication for monetary policy is for the central bank not to take interest rates as the guide to policymaking. A better guide to the effects of policy on effective demand would seem to be the flow of external finance. The flow of credit has the more dependable relation with effective demand. The wary reader will notice that this is the first time we have mentioned external finance instead of merely finance. It has been necessary to speak throughout in terms of the market for finance instead of external finance because we wished to include total spending in the economy whether it was financed internally or externally. The other side of planned expenditures, then, is the demand for finance. Admittedly, there is a certain awkwardness in speaking of a demand for internal finance when this involves no recourse to a financial market. An alternative approach would be to limit the financial market to external finance and to make effective demand some multiple of the equilibrium supply of external finance. This would allow for the financing of expenditures by income. In this case, the output Q scale of Figure 19.11 would not match the R scale (see Ch. 20).

Some reservations about the supply curve of output

The supply curve of output with respect to price has been superimposed on the effective demand curve in Figure 19.11. Its derivation goes back to the earlier discussion of the labor market and production function. But such an approach is unduly restrictive. One that is more consonant with reality is an oligopolistic pricing point of view. Prices in this approach are seen as set by the major business corporations on the basis of their expected output, wages paid, fixed costs, taxes, and intermediate product costs. The relationship can be stated as:

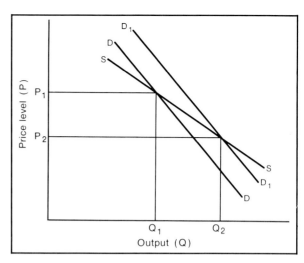

19.12. A falling supply curve of output.

$$P = P(\overset{-}{Q_s}, \overset{+}{WAGES}, \overset{+}{MAT}, \overset{+}{OC})$$

where Q_s = supply of output
$WAGES$ = wage rate
MAT = material costs
OC = other costs

Now the possible relationship is a negative one between output and prices; the curve can be negatively sloped (see Fig. 19.12). It describes the probable response of business firms to falling sales (output). As their sales fall, they will charge more for each unit they sell. This is the only way the firm can recoup its fixed (other) costs. The way we interpret the supply curve must now depart from its interpretation under competitive market conditions. It no longer denotes a reaction of producers' output to varying market prices but rather the reverse—the reaction of producers' prices to varying output.

According to this interpretation, prices charged will increase for any expected output if input costs of all kinds increase. Thus the high oil and wheat prices of the 1970s would have the effect of pushing the supply curve upward. The conventional supply curve based on the labor market cannot readily handle increases in costs, other than for labor. In terms of the limited number of shift variables it permits and its treatment of the supply curve as vertical or positively sloping, the conventional analysis is strongly misleading (for empirical evidence see Cohen and Kenkel 1979–80:255–66).

The revised model for aggregate demand and supply is represented by the following seven equations:

$$R_d = F/P = R_d(r, Y_p - tY_p, W/P, AUT, G - T) \tag{19.14}$$
$$t = t(P) \tag{19.15}$$
$$R_s = MV/P = f(r, P, AUT, RES) \tag{19.16}$$
$$R_d = R_s \tag{19.17}$$
$$P = P(Q_s, WAGES, MAT, OC) \tag{19.18}$$
$$Q_d = Q_s \tag{19.19}$$
$$Q_d = Q_d(R) \tag{19.20}$$

where R = equilibrium supply of finance. Eq. 19.15 states that the tax rate is a function of the price level. Eqs. 19.17 and 19.19 indicate that the product and financial markets clear. Eq. 19.20 shows that effective demand is a function of finance. Because of the availability of income to finance effective demand, this demand can be some multiple of external finance. Interpreting R as external finance, its coefficient will be in excess of 1. For any set of values of the exogenous variables (W, M, V, MAT, OC) a set of values for the endogenous variables (R_d, R_s, r, t, P, Q_d, Q_s) will be generated.

Some real-world applications

When we juxtapose the effective demand curve for output and the supply curve of output (drawn conventionally), the price level is determined by their interaction, as shown by point Q_1 in Figure 19.13. Now we have a useful apparatus for interpreting the real world. Let us say that business is buoyant and expanding its investment plans (the R_d curve of Fig. 19.11 is shifting to the right). The R_s curve may also be shifting in the same direction owing to an easy money policy. For both reasons, the effective demand curve will shift to the right. Both prices and employment will increase (point Q_2 on Fig. 19.13).

The second possibility is that labor will look askance at the higher cost of living represented by higher prices. It will seek higher money wages. The effect will be that the supply curve of output will decrease (shift up or to the left). Since money wages have gone up, for any output willingly produced before, the employer will now be willing to produce it only if prices are higher. In this way the real-wage cost will be the same for that output. We thus secure a series of new supply points above the original supply curve of output. These points constitute the new supply curve. The upward shifting of the supply curve of output will mean that demand and supply will now be equal at a higher price level than before but at a reduced output (point Q_3 on Fig. 19.13).

The rise in unemployment (which is the other side in the decline in output) will now be of considerable concern to the public policymakers. Monetary and fiscal policy will become easy. The federal government will start spending more or taxing less. The central bank will encourage credit flows by making more reserves available. As a result, the effective demand curve shifts once more to the right. Prices keep rising. If labor tries to keep up, the supply curve will shift once more to the left.

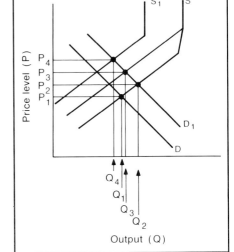

19.13. The inflationary spiral.

SLOWDOWN OF 1979   Aggregate demand and supply analysis have been applied to developments between 1978 and 1979 (Carlson 1979:15ff.). In Figure 19.14 the actual situation in the fourth quarter of 1978 (point A) is contrasted with a hypothetical situation in the second quarter of 1979 (point B) and the actual situation (point C). The hypothetical situation shows what would have happened had past trends continued. It is based on a growth rate for aggregate supply of 3.8% and, on the demand side, an 8% increase in the money supply (which affects the R_s curve of Fig. 19.11). The C point is up and to the left of the B point, reflecting higher prices and reduced real output. A slowdown in velocity and money growth lies behind the demand curve. On the supply side, nominal wages increased 8.9% in excess of trend productivity instead of the 8% implied by trends in prices and the money supply. Most important, energy prices (MAT costs are allowed for in this analysis) increased at a 30% annual rate (Carlson 1979:20).

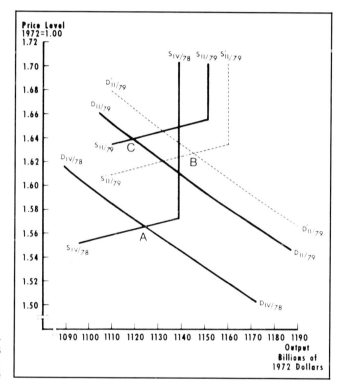

19.14. Economic developments, fourth quarter 1978 to second quarter 1979. (Carlson 1979:19)

Summary

This is a theoretical chapter devoted to the interrelationship of the key economic variables of prices, interest rates, and output. The neoclassical and Keynesian approaches are contrasted. The well-known neoclassical synthesis is an attempt at reconciliation. It may, however, be a procrustean technique, distorting Keynesian theory.

The difficulties with the neoclassical synthesis come to a head with aggregate demand and supply analysis. The derivation of these curves according to the synthesis is contrasted here with a different perspective, one that emphasizes finance and oligopolistic price behavior.

In keeping with a theme that began with Chapter 13 (the constraints on Fed policymaking), this chapter points out the inhibiting effects of supply-side factors on demand management. In terms of price-output (Fig. 19.11), cost-push factors (such as money wages and energy prices) have inflationary effects beyond the control of the Fed. If it resorts to demand management as it did in 1974–75 and 1979–82, the effect is to bring on recession. The Fed is between a rock and a hard place.

Review questions

1. According to classical, neoclassical, and monetarist schools of thought, explain the determination of output, interest rates, and price level.

2. According to Keynesians, how are output, interest rates, and price level determined?

3. Is it possible to express monetarist and Keynesian theories with the same set of equations, changing only the sequence of equations?

4. What is meant by the neoclassical synthesis?

5. What features of the Keynesian model were modified by the neoclassical synthesis? Do you agree with this modification?

6. Explain the derivation of *IS-LM* curves. Why has this analysis become the centerpiece of monetary theory?

7. Explain the derivation of the effective demand curve from *IS-LM* analysis. Can it be derived from an analysis of the demand and supply of finance? Show how this can be done.

8. "The supply of output is inconsistently explained in terms of the labor market and the product market in the neoclassical synthesis." Comment on this statement.

9. In Keynesian analysis, what are the consequences of the liquidity trap and interest-inelastic investment demand?

10. Distinguish between three classes of shift variables for the effective demand curve.

11. In equation form, show the functional relationships for the demand and supply of finance.

12. Compare and contrast the oligopolistic "prices charged" supply curve of output with conventional upward-sloping curves of output supply.

13. Apply the theoretical analysis of price and output determination to the real world.

20

Fiscal policy

"It's the government's fault." This is a common refrain, one joined at times by representatives of the Federal Reserve. We have already pointed out (Ch. 13) how the Fed is inhibited by Treasury debt operations. But the problems for economic stabilization (and monetary policymaking) go beyond such pressures. Overgenerous spending programs have been blamed for inflation. Heavy taxation is criticized as the culprit in discouraging investment and work incentives. High interest rates attributed to public borrowing are said to crowd out private investment.

We begin by describing the budget constraint of the federal government. Next we consider debt financing alternatives and consequences for high-powered money. We then go back to the analytical framework of Chapter 19 so that the financial and real effects of fiscal policy can be considered simultaneously. Here we compare various alternative approaches to the financing of government expenditures: borrowing from the banking system (the Fed, commercial banks), the nonbank public (including nonbank financial institutions), and taxation. Fiscal multipliers are calculated.

The public debt has wealth and distributional effects that must be considered. The changing of the maturity composition of the debt through debt management is another topic. The lags in fiscal policy are compared to the lags in monetary policy in evaluating the former's effectiveness. Finally, the fiscal activities of state and local government must be considered because they have economic effects.

The federal budget

Table 20.1 reproduces the flow-of-funds statement of the federal sector. What we call fiscal policy consists of the spending, taxing, granting, lending, and borrowing recorded in the government's budget. (For a description of the budgetary process, including the budgetary timetable, see Scherer 1978:285ff.; Henning et al. 1984:227–78.) Various budgetary concepts are included in this table, which combines the unified budget with certain off-budget transactions. The unified budget represents the grafting on of trust fund transactions (e.g., social security receipts and payments) to what used to be the regular budget, the so-called administrative budget.

320

Table 20.1. U.S. government flow-of-funds statement

Funds	1981	1982	1983
		($ bil.)	
1 Total receipts, national income accounts			
(NIA) basis	624.8	616.7	641.1
2 Personal taxes	298.7	306.2	295.2
3 Corporate profits tax accruals	65.7	46.6	59.8
4 Indirect taxes	56.4	48.4	52.4
5 Social insurance receipts	204.1	215.5	233.7
6 Total expenditures, NIA basis	689.1	764.9	819.7
7 Goods and services	228.9	258.9	269.7
8 Transfers, etc.	387.0	421.6	455.8
9 Net interest	73.3	84.4	94.2
10 Net surplus, NIA basis	-64.3	-148.2	-178.6
11 - Insurance credits to households	10.0	11.9	14.2
12 = Gross saving	-74.4	-160.1	-192.9
13 + Mineral rights sales[a]	4.8	7.8	7.8
14 = Nonfinancial surplus	-69.5	-152.3	-185.1
15 Net financial investment	-79.1	-155.5	-193.6
16 Net acquisition of financial assets	21.3	21.2	12.1
17 Gold, special drawing rights (SDRs)			
and foreign exchange	2.8	3.8	2.7
18 Demand deposits and currency	1.2	7.1	-8.1
19 Time deposits	-0.1	0.5	-0.5
20 Credit market instruments	24.1	16.0	9.7
21 Federal agency securities	0.0	0.0	0.0
22 Mortgages	4.9	2.4	1.2
23 Other loans	19.1	13.6	8.5
24 Taxes receivable	-10.0	-12.6	3.7
25 Trade credit	2.5	4.8	3.8
26 Miscellaneous	0.9	1.6	0.7
27 Net increase in liabilities	100.4	176.7	205.7
28 Treasury currency and SDR certificates	1.2	1.7	0.5
29 Credit market instruments	87.4	161.3	186.6
30 Savings bonds	-4.3	0.2	3.1
31 Other Treasury issues	92.2	162.0	183.5
32 Agency issues and mortgages	-0.5	-0.9	-0.1
33 Life and retirement reserves	10.0	11.9	14.2
34 Trade debt	0.7	1.7	2.4
35 Miscellaneous	1.0	0.2	2.0
36 Discrepancy	9.6	3.2	8.6
37 Memo: Corporate tax receipts, net	75.7	59.2	56.1

Source: FRB 1984e:15.
[a]Sales of Outer Continental Shelf leases.

The distinction between budget and off-budget operations is brought out in Table 20.2, which shows data on a fiscal year as well as a calendar year basis. The federal fiscal year begins on October 1 and runs through the following September. The unified budget for fiscal 1983 (ending September 30, 1983) shows receipts of $600.6 bil. and outlays of $795.9 bil. so that the deficit for the budget proper was $195.3 bil. The most important off-budget entity is the Federal Financing Bank, which accounts for $10.4 bil. of the total deficit of off-budget entities of $12.4 bil. These off-budget agencies are federally owned and controlled, but by law their transactions are excluded from the budget totals. Treasury borrowing to finance their operations is included in the national debt subject to statutory debt limits. Outlays financed by their own borrowing are not subject to debt limit (McElhattan 1980:1).

The Federal Financing Bank is part of the Treasury Department. It does not

Table 20.2. Federal fiscal and financing operations

Type of account or operation	Fiscal year 1983	Calendar year 1982 H1	1982 H2	1983 H1
		($ mil.)		
U.S. budget				
1 Receipts[a]	600,562	322,478	286,338	306,331
2 Outlays[a]	795,917	348,678	390,846	396,477
3 Surplus, or deficit (-)	-195,355	-26,200	-104,508	-90,146
4 Trust funds	23,056	-17,690	-6,576	22,680
5 Federal funds[b,c]	-218,410	-43,889	-97,934	-112,822
Off-budget entities [surplus, or deficit (-)]				
6 Federal Financing Bank outlays	-10,404	-7,942	-4,923	-5,418
7 Other[c,d]	-1,953	227	-2,267	-528
U.S. budget plus off-budget, including Federal Financing Bank				
8 Surplus, or deficit (-)	-207,711	-33,914	-111,699	-96,094
Source of financing				
9 Borrowing from the public	212,425	41,728	119,609	102,538
10 Cash and monetary assets [decrease, or increase (-)][d]	-9,889	-408	-9,057	-9,664
11 Other[e]	5,176	-7,405	1,146	3,222
Memo:				
12 Treasury operating balance (level, end of period)	37,057	10,999	19,773	100,243
13 Federal Reserve Banks	16,557	4,099	5,033	19,442
14 Tax and loan accounts	20,500	6,900	14,740	72,037

Source: *Fed. Res. Bull.* 1984f:A27.

[a]Effective Feb. 8, 1982, supplemental medical insurance premiums and voluntary hospital insurance premiums, previously included in other insurance receipts, have been reclassified as offsetting receipts in the health function.

[b]Half-year figures are calculated as a residual (total surplus/deficit less trust fund surplus/deficit).

[c]Other off-budget includes Postal Service Fund; Rural Electrification and Telephone Revolving Fund; Rural Telephone Bank; and petroleum acquisition and transportation and strategic petroleum reserve effective November 1981.

[d]Includes Treasury operating cash accounts; SDRs; gold tranche drawing rights; loans to IMF; and other cash and monetary assets.

[e]Includes accrued interest payable to the public; allocations of SDRs drawing rights; deposit funds; miscellaneous liability (including checks outstanding) and asset accounts; seigniorage; increment on gold; net gain/loss for U.S. currency valuation adjustment; net gain/loss for IMF valuation adjustment; and profit on the sale of gold.

operate programs but finances most of the federal government's direct loans. Its lending mainly supports rural housing and rural electrification programs. Loan assets are not considered in arriving at estimates of the off-budget deficit.

Measuring the federal deficit, however, is more complicated than simply adding up the deficits in the unified budget and the off-budget. Table 20.2, which shows a combined budget deficit of $207.7 bil. (fiscal year 1982) or $96.1 bil. for the first half of 1983 (line 8, H1), does not allow for the acquisition of credit market instruments. These are included, however, in the flow-of-funds statement (line 20, Table 20.1). Consideration of the assets arising from federal lending ($9.7 bil. in calendar 1983) modifies the size of the deficit.

The flow of funds has its own measures of the deficit—nonfinancial surplus (line 14, Table 20.1) or net financial investment (line 15, Table 20.1). Their theoretical equality is impaired, however, by statistical discrepancy. In calendar 1983 the discrepancy was $8.6 bil. (line 36). The flow-of-funds statement makes use of the nonfinancial (receipts and expenditures) data prepared by the Department of Commerce and is not comparable with the unified budget statement based on Treasury data. For example, the Commerce data is on an accrual basis, whereas the unified budget (Table 20.2) is on a cash basis. For the calendar year 1982, the flow-of-funds measure of the deficit was $152.3 bil. (line 14, Table 20.1) compared with $145.6 bil. in the combined budget shown in Table 20.2 (line 8).

In fact, two additional deficit concepts are shown in Table 20.1. There is the national income account (NIA) concept, −$178.6 bil. in 1983 (line 10), and the flow-of-funds gross saving concept, −$192.9 bil. (line 12). The gross saving concept is (algebraically) smaller than the NIA concept because government employee contributions to federal retirement programs (which are part of household gross saving in the flow-of-funds accounts) have been subtracted. Finally, federal revenues from mineral rights sales (line 13) are added to gross saving to yield the nonfinancial surplus concept in line 14.

To the unified budget and off-budget entities one has to add the "off-off−budget" transactions of sponsored credit agencies and mortgage pools. Their activities were discussed in Chapter 14 in stock terms. The borrowing of seven privately owned but government-sponsored agencies amounted to $1.2 bil. in calendar 1983, a sharp drop from 1982 (line 17, Table 20.3). These agencies provide

Table 20.3. Federally sponsored credit agencies and mortgage pools			
Sponsored credit agencies	1981	1982	1983
		($ bil.)	
1 Current surplus	1.2	1.9	1.5
2 Net acquisitions of financial assets	37.6	22.4	2.0
3 Demand deposits and currency	0.2	-0.2	0.2
4 Federal funds and security repurchase			
agreements (RPs)	3.5	5.4	-2.3
5 Credit market instruments	33.2	15.7	3.1
6 U.S. government securities	0.4	1.4	-1.3
7 Open-market paper	0.3	-0.3	0.4
8 Student loans (SLMA)	2.2	1.6	1.5
9 Housing credit	21.2	11.0	2.2
10 Residential mortgages	5.0	10.2	9.3
11 Federal Home Loan Board loans to S&Ls	16.2	0.8	-7.0
12 Loans to agriculture	9.1	2.0	0.3
13 Farm mortgages	7.6	3.6	0.8
14 Loans to coops (BC)	-0.3	-0.8	0.9
15 Loans to farmers (FICB)	1.8	-0.8	-1.3
16 Miscellaneous assets	0.7	1.4	1.1
17 Net increase in liabilities	37.1	21.3	1.2
18 Credit market instruments	32.4	15.3	1.4
19 Sponsored agency issues	30.5	14.9	1.4
20 U.S. government loans	1.9	0.4	0.0
21 Miscellaneous liabilities	4.7	5.9	-0.2
22 Discrepancy	0.7	0.8	0.7
Federally related mortgage pools[a]			
23 Net acquisitions of mortgages	15.0	49.5	66.4
24 Home mortgages	14.1	49.3	65.2
25 Multifamily mortgages	1.1	0.4	1.2
26 Farm mortgages	-0.1	-0.2	0.0
27 Net increments in pool securities	15.0	49.5	66.4
Memo: Totals for agencies and pools			
28 Housing credit	36.3	60.7	68.6
29 Loans to agriculture	9.0	1.8	0.2
30 Net security issues	45.5	64.5	67.8

Source: FRB 1984e:15.
[a]GNMA, FNMA, FHLMC, and FmHA pools. Excludes Federal Financing Bank holdings of pool securities, which are in U.S. government mortgages and other loans directly.

credit in the areas of housing, rural finance, and student loans. Most important are the three housing agencies—Federal Home Loan Banks, Federal National Mortgage Association (Fannie Mae) and the Federal Home Mortgage Corporation (Freddie Mac). The securities of these agencies are not guaranteed as to principal and interest by the Treasury. Nevertheless, their obligations sell at rates only slightly higher than those on Treasury securities (McElhattan 1980:2).

The role of the chief housing agencies has shifted from providing credit to guaranteeing pass-through securities, which are backed by mortgage pools. As seen under federally sponsored mortgage pools (line 23, Table 20.3) they financed $66.4 bil. of mortgages in calendar 1982 at the same time that housing credit amounted to only $2.2 bil. (line 9).

Including federal activity in the housing field greatly expands the size of the federal deficit, i.e., if we again ignore the acquisition of credit market instruments. Considering them, increases in liabilities for federally sponsored credit agencies and mortgage pools are initially matched by increases in financial assets, so there is no net effect on the size of the federal deficit.

The enormity of the dollar figures has resulted in the administration and economists turning to budgeting by percentage. Percentages are less alarming and the electronic calculators of congressmen and administration officials cannot accommodate numbers in the billions on their little screens (Kilborn 1984c:18). Using percentages, the current level of the budget deficit (Table 20.2 version) is 5% of the gross national product (GNP), which exceeds the percentage in most industrial countries.

President Reagan has set a deficit goal of 2–3% for 1988. Percentages are invariably resorted to in debating government spending and revenues. The administration argues for cutting the 24% of the GNP that represents spending; while on the Democrat side, the argument is made to raise the 19% that the government collects in taxes.

The budget identity

The budget identity explains the basis of the federal deficit: deficit = net borrowing − Δcash balances = expenditures + loans + net transfers − taxes. An increase in Treasury cash balances means that the deficit is less than net borrowing. (A decrease in Treasury cash balances means the opposite, that the deficit exceeds net borrowing.) A large amount of Treasury borrowing will be for refunding purposes, i.e., paying off old debts. Net borrowing is therefore the appropriate concept.

Next we define borrowings (*BORR*) in terms of the purchasers of Treasury debt. In this way the monetary implications of Treasury borrowing are brought out. The major investing categories are the government (*GOVT*) itself (via its agencies or trust funds), Federal Reserve Banks (*CEN*), the commercial banks (*COMM*), and other private investors (*PRIV*): *BORR = GOVT + CEN + COMM + PRIV*. Comprehensive data on the ownership of the public debt is provided in Table 20.4.

Table 20.4 initially divides the debt into marketable and nonmarketable debt. (This ignores the classification between interest-bearing and noninterest-bearing debt, since very little is in the latter category; some might argue for putting cur-

Table 20.4. Type and ownership of gross public debt (end of period)

Type and holder	1982	1983
	($ bil.)	
1 Total gross public debt	1,197.1	1,410.7
By type		
2 Interest-bearing debt	1,195.5	1,400.9
3 Marketable	881.5	1,050.9
4 Bills	311.8	343.8
5 Notes	465.0	573.4
6 Bonds	104.6	133.7
7 Nonmarketable[a]	314.0	350.0
8 State and local government series	25.7	36.7
9 Foreign issues[b]	14.7	10.4
10 Government	13.0	10.4
11 Public	1.7	.0
12 Savings bonds and notes	68.0	70.7
13 Government account series[c]	205.4	231.9
14 Noninterest-bearing debt	1.6	9.8
By holder[d]		
15 U.S. government agencies and trust funds	209.4	236.3
16 Federal Reserve Banks	139.3	151.9
17 Private investors	848.4	1,022.6
18 Commercial banks	131.4	188.8
19 Money market funds	42.6	22.8
20 Insurance companies	39.1	48.9
21 Other companies	24.5	39.7
22 State and local governments	113.4	n.a.
Individuals		
23 Savings bonds	68.3	71.5
24 Other securities	48.2	61.9
25 Foreign and international[e]	149.5	168.9
26 Other miscellaneous investors[f]	231.4	n.a.

Source: *Fed. Res. Bull.* 1984f:A29.
Note: n.a. = not available.
[a]Includes (not shown separately): securities issued to the Rural Electrification Administration; depository bonds, retirement plan bonds, and individual retirement bonds.
[b]Nonmarketable dollar-denominated and foreign currency-denominated series held by foreigners.
[c]Held almost entirely by U.S. government agencies and trust funds.
[d]Data for Federal Reserve Banks and U.S. government agencies and trust funds are actual holdings; data for other groups are Treasury estimates.
[e]Consists of investments of foreign and international accounts. Excludes noninterest-bearing notes issued to the International Monetary Fund.
[f]Includes savings and loan associations, nonprofit institutions, credit unions, mutual savings banks, corporate pension trust funds, dealers and brokers, certain U.S. government deposit accounts, and U.S. government-sponsored agencies.

rency outstanding in this category.) Of greater importance than savings bonds, which are well-known nonmarketable instruments, are the special issues to government agencies and trust funds and to state and local governments and foreign issues. From the breakdown by holder, it is seen that the government (including the Fed) is a major buyer of its own debt (lines 15, 16, Table 20.4). When these holdings are subtracted from the gross public debt, the remainder is referred to as the net public debt. The largest individual holders of the net public debt are commercial banks (line 18) and foreign and international (line 25).

BANKING SYSTEM PURCHASES   The purchase of debt by the Fed represents its open-market operations in existing debt. Direct lending to the Treasury is limited to $5 bil. and has been insignificant since 1979 (Fed, New York 1981:10–11).

When other factors supplying or absorbing the monetary base are allowed for, the equation connecting open-market operations and high-powered money is $CEN + OFC = MB$, where $OFC =$ other factors of change in the monetary base.

Open-market operations may be undertaken to offset OFC (defensive Federal Reserve policy). Open-market operations stabilize the government securities market when others are adding to or disposing of their holdings. When these influences are netted out, the relation between public borrowing and changes in high-powered money is a close one. The reaction function of the Fed becomes $CEN = f(BORR, PRIV, COMM, OFC)$. The central bank reacts positively to Treasury borrowing, buys less the more debt is absorbed (or less sold off) by the private sector and commercial banks, and reacts negatively to other factors increasing the monetary base. The observed relation between Fed debt holdings and the national debt need not be a close one (a lack of relationship has been noted by Dornbusch and Fischer 1978:444) because the other factors in the reaction function besides Treasury borrowing affect central bank holdings and thus obscure the net relationship between open-market operations and Treasury borrowing.

Purchases by the private sector and the commercial banking sector may be supported by central bank purchases. This was a well-known mechanism during World War II. The Fed pumped reserves into the system via its open-market operations, enabling banks to buy government securities with their excess reserves. Bank loans to the public to finance such purchases also increased. The reaction function above suggests that the greater the absorption of debt in this fashion, the less the central bank will have to intervene in the market. On the other hand, these purchases by the banking system were only made possible by the central bank open-market purchases. The action goes from CEN to $COMM$.

The acquisition of government securities by the banking system results in an equivalent increase in the assets held by the private nonfinancial sector. They may include money balances (currency and checkable deposits) and time and savings deposits. Thus a by-product of Treasury financing is an increase in private wealth. The increase in private loans and investments by the commercial banking system on the basis of an increase in high-powered money similarly increases deposit liabilities. Such deposits are defined as inside money as distinguished from the outside money associated with purchase of government securities. As such, they may not be deemed a net addition to private sector wealth because they are matched by the private sector's indebtedness to the banking system. This is a controversial idea, however, and it could be contended that wealth consists of all money holdings (see Pesek and Saving 1967).

PRIVATE SECTOR PURCHASES   The private sector (apart from financing its purchases through the banking system) can finance government security purchases through current saving or by shifting out of other assets. The overall supply of finance will only be increased if the shifting is out of inactive money balances.

The tangible result of an increase in activity of money balances is additional holding of government debt. The net wealth of the nonbank public goes up unless it is offset by the discounting of future tax payments. If we go on the basis of introspection, it does not seem likely that the average taxpayer offsets the discounted present value of future interest receipts with future tax payments. Nonetheless, the thesis that the government debt is irrelevant to economic decision making (here because of the capitalizing of future tax liabilities) has commanded considerable attention in the literature. It is also called the Ricardian equivalence principle after David Ricardo, a famous British economist of the nineteenth century who first suggested the idea of irrelevance (see Barro 1974:1095ff., 1984:Ch. 15; Webster 1983:19-28).

WEALTH EFFECT   The increase in private sector wealth (money, time deposits, holdings of government debt associated with deficit financing) exerts a wealth effect, which (in terms of the *IS-LM* framework of Ch. 19) affects both curves. The increase in wealth shifts the *IS* curve to the right by increasing consumption. The increase in wealth at the same time increases the demand for money, since holders of bonds will wish to balance their portfolios by adding money balances. Because of this latter effect it is argued that bond financing may be deflationary. The *LM* curve may shift to the left by a greater distance than the *IS* curve shifts to the right (see Silber 1978:279ff.).

DISTRIBUTIONAL EFFECTS   Debt holders are not likely to offset their public debt holdings with prospective tax payments. Nonetheless, the receipt of interest payments and tax payments do transfer income between households arranged by income classes. The question is complicated by indirect ownership of the debt. Households own debt via their ownership of government trust funds, financial institutions, and business corporations. Both the ownership of debt and tax liability by income classes must be estimated to determine distributional effects (J. Cohen 1951:267ff.). The finding was that in 1946 the distributional effect was in favor of households in the below $5000 income bracket. A more recent study confirms this redistribution effect in favor of lower income classes (see Vitaliano 1973:175ff.).

Intergenerational effects are a form of distributional effect. It has been commonly said that borrowing imposes a burden on future generations. The stock answer is that tomorrow's output cannot be shifted to the present through borrowing. In the sense of real output, future generations do not suffer. In terms of debt repayment, this is also true. Members of a future generation repay the debt to members of the same generation. But if the debt via a wealth effect results today in more consumption and less investment, future generations can suffer (cf. Ott and Ott 1978:302ff.).

Financing spending through the banking system

Financing through the banking system implies a mix of monetary and fiscal policy. Three cases can be distinguished. First, the Fed supplies reserves equal to Treasury bond sales. Second, the Fed supplies sufficient reserves for the commercial banks to buy the bonds not bought by it. Finally, the reserves for commercial bank expansion may not be sufficient to buy all the bonds.

These three cases differ in the effect of increased government expenditures on interest rates and aggregate demand. The analytical framework of Chapter 19 is apropos. The planned expenditures curve (R_d) in the lower part of Figure 19.11 shifts to the right as a consequence of fiscal policy (an increase in planned government spending). The curve is repeated in Figure 20.1. The open-market purchases

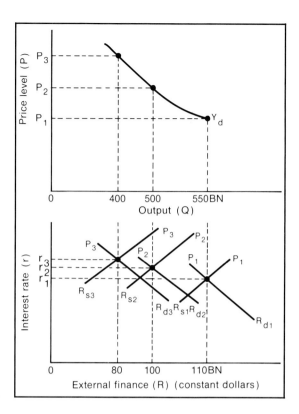

20.1. Multiplier analysis.

of the Fed increase reserves and shift the supply of finance function (MV/P) to the right. In the most generous case the supply shift will exceed the shift in the demand for finance, interest rates will fall, and effective demand will rise beyond the increase in government expenditures. (The fall in interest rates will stimulate investment demand.) In the intermediate case the shift in the two curves should be the same, and interest rates will be stable. In this case the increase in effective demand is limited to the increase in government expenditures. Finally, in the third case interest rates will rise, cutting off some private sector demand.

The controversy as to whether an increase in government expenditures inevitably leads to a crowding-out of private sector spending has heated up with accelerating federal government deficits. (For a standard discussion based on *IS-LM* analysis, see Pierce 1984:532–37.) The extent of nominal crowding-out of private demand depends on the slope of the supply-of-finance curve. If velocity is assumed to be invariant with respect to the interest rate (failing to increase with increases in the rate), the supply-of-finance curve will be a vertical line and nominal crowding out will be absolute. The supply of finance will only increase with an increase in the quantity of money made possible by an increase in reserves.

The upper portion of Figure 19.11 explains the division of effective demand between output and prices. The slope of the supply curve of output (derived independently of financial market analysis) determines this division. If we assume that the supply curve Q_s is vertical, for example, an increase in government demand will exert no effect on total output. Crowding-out in this case is real. The output of goods and services for the government is offset by a reduction in output for the private sector.

The conditions for nominal and real crowding-out of private expenditures can be summarized in terms of the slopes of the R_s (supply-of-finance) and Q_s (supply-of-output) curves. If the R_s curve is vertical, nominal crowding-out is absolute. If it is horizontal (or if policy-induced shifts have the same effect), there is no crowding-out. If the R_s curve shifts more to the right than the R_d curve (due again to monetary policy), there is the opposite situation in nominal terms of crowding-in; i.e., the decline in the interest rate induces an increase in expenditures beyond the increase in government expenditures.

Similarly, a vertical Q_s curve means that real crowding-out is absolute; a horizontal Q_s curve signifies the other extreme, no real crowding-out effects from public expenditure.

THE EVIDENCE   Whether government deficits raise nominal and real interest rates (nominal rates less the inflation rate) has been one of two testing grounds for the crowding-out thesis. If interest rates go up, this will discourage private investment. Despite a variety of empirical and statistical techniques, there is no consensus (Webster 1983:25-28). While some economists have found a small but statistically significant positive effect of government debt on nominal interest rates (e.g., Feldstein 1982:1-20), others have found support for the irrelevance hypotheses: it makes no difference to nominal interest rates whether the government finances expenditures by borrowing or taxation (Barro 1984:389-90; Plosser 1982:245-52).

In contrast to an emphasis on the constraining effects of interest rates, a flow-constrained approach has been taken to crowding out. Half the pool of saving is absorbed by the purchase of government securities, leaving an inadequate amount for investment by the private sector (see, e.g., B. Friedman 1983:73-95). As criticized in Chapter 1, this view of saving assumes that the amount is predetermined and is not affected by the level of external finance. The government deficit contributes to economic activity and the flow of saving, and it is misleading to offset the deficit against total private saving to estimate what is left over for private investment. Moreover, this approach to the deficit ignores the productive aspects of government spending.

Pure fiscal policy

Pure fiscal policy has two variants. First, the debt is sold outside the commercial banking system; second, additional expenditures are financed by an increase in taxes. In the first case the demand-for-finance curve that reflects government borrowing shifts to the right, producing an increased amount of finance supplied and a higher interest rate. In the second case the finance curves shift only if the taxpayer maintains consumption by borrowing, selling off assets, or reducing money balances. In the latter case, it is as if the demand-and-supply curves shift to the right by similar distances. Households demand more finance, which they satisfy by reducing their own holdings of cash balances. The supply curve of finance shifts in response to the demand. Holding money balances offers unique opportunities for self-finance.

In the first case of debt finance, the effective demand shifts to the right, but not by as much as the previous cases of mixed monetary and fiscal policy because the supply-of-finance curve is not shifting. In the case of taxation the effective demand curve shifts to the right only in case something happens to the flow of funds. If consumption declines by the increase in government expenditures, the effective demand curve will stay unchanged.

Multipliers

The idea of multipliers has been a staple of aggregate economic analysis since the time of Keynes. We discussed multipliers in Chapters 6 and 15 in connection with credit and deposit expansion. Now the concept is applied to real magnitudes. The theory is the same: that some outside disturbance variable will generate a change in an endogenous variable (here income and output) that is a multiple of the original disturbance variable. To illustrate the idea diagrammatically, we should use a different scale for the upper diagram of Figure 20.1—one that is a multiple of the scale for finance in the lower diagram. We can still locate effective demand points, as before. Figure 20.1 now denotes credit markets or external finance; e.g., an intersection at $100 bil. of sums raised in credit markets at a given price level might correspond to an effective demand point of, say, $500 bil. This gives an income multiplier of 5. (Fig. 14.2, which plots the historical values of the ratio of funds advanced to GNP, shows this ratio hovering around the 15% line, suggesting a multiplier of approximately 6%.) Similarly, $110 bil. of finance would correspond to an effective demand of $550 bil.

The multiplier works through the marginal propensities to consume and invest out of personal and business income. Borrowing generates household and business spending, which in turn generates income. On the basis of this increased income, consumption and business spending increase again. The process is a repetitive one.

The expansion process comes to an end (the multiplier has a finite value) when the money balances released by monetary and velocity changes are absorbed (income round by income round) in increased transaction balances. This explanation of the finite value of the multiplier differs from the conventional explanation, which emphasizes saving as the leakage rather than money holding. Saving is best seen as a source of funds in the capital account. The only nonuse of saving is an increase in money balances that short-circuits the process and represents a leakage. The process is similar to that described in Chapter 2. The analysis must be qualified by consideration of the wealth variable. If we allow for the holding of public debt as a result of public borrowing, this may have a complementary effect on the demand for money, as discussed earlier. Assuming that the economic agent aims at a balanced portfolio, the illiquidity of debt holdings will be compensated by increased holdings of money. This effect will tend to lower the value of the multiplier.

Using the model of Chapter 19, the multiplier can be stated with some precision. We distinguish between income-expenditure multipliers triggered by disturbances on the demand-for-credit side of the market and multipliers triggered by disturbances on the supply-of-credit sale.

On the demand side the multiplier $\Delta Q_d / \Delta AUT$ will represent the change in effective demand (for any given level of prices) that will be induced by a change in planned expenditures. The value of this multiplier will depend on the relationship between AUT and the flow of finance R and on the relationship between R and

Q_d. Representing the product of these impacts by K, $\Delta Q_d = K\Delta AUT$.

Looking at the model in Chapter 19, it might appear that K is the product of the coefficient (say a) of AUT in Eq. 19.14 and the coefficient of R in Eq. 19.20 (say b). This would exaggerate the value of the multiplier K, however, since it would be ignoring the slope of the supply-of-finance curve R_s (Eq. 19.16). The less elastic this curve is, the smaller the value of K.

Similarly, we can work out supply-side multipliers, say $\Delta Q_d / \Delta RES$. This will involve Eqs. 19.16 and 19.20 of the earlier model. Thus $\Delta Q_d = K_1 \Delta RES$. Symmetrically, the value of K is modified by the elasticity of the demand curve (R_d). The less elastic this curve is (the steeper its slope), the smaller the increase in effective demand pursuant to an increase in bank reserves.

The multipliers solve for the extent of horizontal shifts of the effective demand curve in the upper part of Figure 20.1. The output-price effects require that we bring in the prices-charged equation of the model (Eq. 19.18). The flatter this curve (not shown in Fig. 20.1), the greater the output effects of a fiscal disturbance as compared with its price effect.

BALANCED BUDGET MULTIPLIER   The analysis has stressed the presence of a monetary effect if multipliers are to have a positive value. This holds true in the so-called balanced budget multiplier case where increased expenditures are financed by taxes. However, conventional multiplier analysis (which treats saving as a leakage) comes to a different conclusion. Under simplifying conditions (as discussed below) the value of the balanced budget multiplier is one without a monetary effect being present.

Conventional multiplier models are built around the consumption function and the national income identity. Repeating with slight modification the equations of Chapter 19:

$$C = a + b\,(Y - T) \qquad Y = C + I^* + G^*$$

where C = consumption
Y = income
T = taxes (lump sum)
G^* = government expenditures (assumed given)
I^* = investment (assumed given)

The first equation states that consumption expenditures depend on an intercept value a and disposable income $Y - T$. (The analysis is complicated if taxes vary with income, as in the case of an income tax.) The parameter b depicts the positive slope of the consumption relation known as the marginal propensity to consume; e.g., if b had a value of 0.8, it would indicate that $.80 out of every additional $1 in income would be spent on consumption. The remainder $(1 - b)$, $.20, would be saved.

The second equation states that, in equilibrium, income Y is equal to consumption, investment, and government expenditures. We substitute for C in the second equation:

$$Y = a + bY - bT + I^* + G^*$$

Collecting the terms in Y:

$$Y - bY = a - bT + I^* + G^*$$
$$Y(1 - b) = a - bT + I^* + G^*$$
$$Y = (a - bt + I^* + G^*)/(1 - b)$$

The government expenditure multiplier is $\Delta Y/\Delta G$. Its value (upon differentiation) is $1/(1 - b)$ or $1/s$; e.g., if s (the marginal propensity to save) is 0.2, the value of the multiplier is 5. This means that an increase of $1 in government expenditures via its effect on income and on consumption (in successive rounds) will cause income to go up by $5.

If we differentiate Y with respect to taxes ($\Delta Y/\Delta T$), we secure the tax multiplier. Its value is $-b/(1-b)$. It will be noted that the difference between the two multipliers is the appearance of $-b$ in the numerator of the tax multiplier. The rationale is that a $1 increase in taxes causes consumption not to go down by the full $1 but by $.80. The other $.20 reduction will be a reduction in saving. When the two multipliers are combined into the balanced budget multiplier, $\Delta Y/\Delta G + \Delta Y/\Delta T = 1/(1 - b) + [-b/(1 - b)] = (1 - b)/(1 - b) = 1$.

Under the simplifying conditions of lump-sum taxes, a $1 increase in government expenditures financed by taxes will always increase income by $1. This magical result is due to government having an initial full $1 impact on income, while (owing to the impact of taxes being partly on saving) consumption does not initially decline by $1 but only by b. As a result, the combined multipliers have a value of 1 (regardless of the value of b).

Measuring Treasury discretion

Effective demand is increased when the government runs a deficit, with the effects magnified by mixing fiscal policy with monetary policy. The temptation is to interpret the size of the deficit as a measure of Treasury discretion. But taxes and expenditures may be automatically determined by the state of the economy rather than by deliberate Treasury action. If a recession develops, tax collections fall. The economy determines the state of the budget rather than the budget determining the state of the economy. Welfare payments also go up in recessionary times. These effects of the economy are referred to as automatic stabilizers. They occur automatically and help to stabilize the economy. Take-home pay goes down less rapidly than income or goes up less rapidly in times of economic expansion.

Some reference point is necessary to escape the vagaries of the business cycle. This point is the level of income at full or high employment. The full-employment surplus or deficit is estimated by extrapolating taxes and expenditures to their full-employment levels (Fig. 20.2).

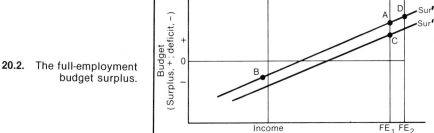

20.2.   The full-employment budget surplus.

The actual budget surplus (*SUR*) will be measured by:

$$SUR = tY - G - R$$

where t = tax rate
Y = income
G = government expenditures
R = net transfers

The full-employment surplus (FES) substitutes potential full-employment (*fe*) output Y_p for Y. Thus $SUR_{fe} = tY_p - G - R$. The difference between the two values SUR and SUR_{fe}, will be the higher amount of tax revenues at full employment: $SUR_{fe} - SUR = tY_p - tY$.

Points *A* and *B* on Figure 20.2 show the actual deficit (*B*) and the full-employment surplus (*A*). Treasury discretion shows up in a shifting of the budget surplus line. Thus if taxes are decreased or expenditures are increased by Treasury action, this will result in *SUR'* shifting to *SUR''*. The economic impact of Treasury discretion is the *AC* distance measured at full-employment income.

When economic growth is allowed for, the full-employment income line shifts to the right (from FE_1 to FE_2). The resultant increase in the full-employment surplus (from *A* to *D*) is called fiscal drag. The more elastic taxes are with respect to aggregate income, the greater the possibility of fiscal drag. The necessity for the government to offset fiscal drag by discretionary action was emphasized in the 1960s by the then chairman of the Council of Economic Advisers, Walter W. Heller (cf. Solow and Blinder 1978:251).

Instead of the FES terminology, in 1983 the government replaced it with a new one partitioning the federal budget into a cyclical component measuring the automatic responses of receipts and expenditures to economic fluctuations and a structural component measuring discretionary fiscal policy and other noncyclical factors affecting the budget (de Leeuw and Holloway 1983:1). Table 20.5 shows these components for 1980–89. The structural part corresponds to a full-employment deficit indicating a growing expansionary impact owing to government discretion. These projections of the structural component are much larger than the estimates of the Congressional Budget Office (Kopcke 1983b:1142).

Table 20.5. Cyclical and structural components of the deficit, fiscal years 1980-89

Fiscal year	Total	Cyclical	Structural
		($ bil.)	
Actual			
1980	60	4	55
1981	58	19	39
1982	111	62	48
1983	195	95	101
Estimates (current services)			
1984	187	49	138
1985	208	44	163
1986	216	45	171
1987	220	34	187
1988	203	16	187
1989	193	-4	197

Source: President 1984:36.

Suppose that increased tax rates increase the deficit instead of decreasing it? The FES concept assumes the opposite. The *SUR* curve in Figure 20.2 moves up with higher tax rates. Not only would the FES concept have to be thrown out if tax rates have this perverse effect but there is the more significant possibility of getting more by charging less. This is the position taken by the economist Arthur Laffer (see Wanniski 1978). Supply-side economics, which may be the heart of Reaganomics, has its philosophical origins in his analysis. In addition to the radical wing represented by Laffer, supply-siders included a mainstream group led by such economists as Martin Feldstein of Harvard, former chairman of the president's Council of Economic Advisers (Dornbusch and Fischer 1984:573–74). (A discussion of the *dramatis personae* of supply-side economics is found in Stubblebine and Willett 1983.)

The Laffer curve is drawn in Figure 20.3. A well-known anecdote is that Professor Laffer was having difficulty getting his tax-cut ideas across to an aide of Congressman Jack Kemp, a later sponsor of congressional tax cuts, and sketched his curve on a cocktail napkin. (For a delightful account of the origins of supply-side economics including this anecdote see Brooks 1982:96–150.) The extremes of the curve make obvious sense. If tax rates are zero, tax revenues shown on the vertical axis will be zero. If tax rates are 100%, revenues will fall to zero because of the lack of a work incentive. Laffer contends that when tax rates are beyond point *C* cutting back taxes will bring tax rates closer to the point of maximum revenue. No one knows, however, whether tax rates are presently to the right or to the left of *C*. Nevertheless, a Swedish study has some relevance here. Taking all taxes (federal, state, and local), the average tax for the United States of 32% in 1982 was a distance away from the average rate of 50% in Sweden where the Laffer argument has been said to apply (from a study cited in Barro 1984:358–59).

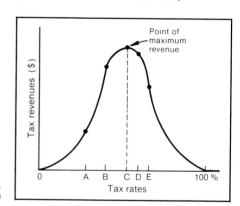

20.3. The Laffer curve. (Fed, Minneapolis 1979:8)

The huge cuts in personal and corporate taxes enacted in President Reagan's first year were intended to spur more saving and investment and as a result more output growth. The Economic Recovery Tax Act (ERTA) of 1981 permitted depreciation of equipment purchases over 5 years and structures over 15 years. The investment tax credit first introduced in the early 1960s was retained and provided for further acceleration of depreciation schedules in the mid-1980s. While modified in 1982 by the Tax Equity and Fiscal Responsibility Act (TEFRA), depreciation rules remained more favorable than before ERTA (Henning et al. 1984:532–33).

Personal income tax rates were reduced by 25% over a three-year period by ERTA. Marginal tax rates for the taxpayers in the highest bracket went down to 50% from 70%. The capital gains tax was reduced from a 28% maximum to a maximum of 20%.

Tax exemption of contributions to individual retirement accounts (IRAs) under ERTA up to a maximum of $2000 a year aimed at increasing savings. The deferring of taxes stimulated financial innovation that made possible low cash outlays and risk-free investments. Examples are the sale of Treasury investment growth receipts and certificates of accrual on Treasury securities. These are certificates with income accrual backed by Treasury securities (Henning et al. 1984:365). It was estimated that ERTA reduced potential tax revenues by close to $150 bil. over a three-year period (Brooks 1982:114).

The deep recession of 1981–82 cast a shadow over supply-side economics. The economy did not revive until an easing of monetary policy added to the stimulus of growing deficits (Davidson 1984:30).

The specific evidence on saving does not support the contentions of supply-siders. The personal saving rate, while increasing from 6 to 6.7% between 1980 and 1981 declined to 5% in 1983 (FRB 1985b:7; see also Ch. 15). Taxpayers switched existing asset holdings into tax-exempt or tax-deferred investments without adding to new saving. This is the early evidence on IRAs (DeMagistris and Palash 1982:24–32).

Politics of the deficit

The size of the current and projected deficits was a major debating point in the presidential campaign of 1984. The irony is that the Democrats have talked like traditional Republicans and Republicans have talked (or at least have acted) like traditional Democrats. President Reagan defended deficits as temporary until economic growth eliminated them (supply-side economics), and the Democratic presidential nominee Walter Mondale attacked deficits. Traditionally, the Democrats have been identified with Keynesian economics and the Republicans have been the party of the balanced budget.

The controversy over the deficit has not extended to monetary policy. Monetary policy may be too esoteric for the masses. Perhaps the independence of the Fed stultifies political debate, which may be an argument for making the Fed responsible to the president. The Reagan policy can be characterized as following an easy fiscal policy and a tight monetary policy (see Ch. 13). The Democrats in the campaign stood for tight fiscal policy and were not explicit about monetary policy.

The administration's concern with the deficit came out in the open after the president's victory in November 1984. A month after the election the Treasury published a detailed plan that would sharply lower corporate and individual income tax rates. By expanding the definition of what constitutes income and by eliminating many deductions, the plan would increase the base on which taxes are paid (Rosenbaum 1984:1). Major spending cuts were also proposed by the president for the fiscal year 1986 (Clines 1984:1, 14).

Congressional debate over the deficit late in 1985 delayed an increase in the federal debt ceiling of $1.8 tril. and created an embarrassing cash problem for the Treasury (Rogers 1985:3). Congress had imposed such a ceiling in 1917 in order to control the volume of federal debt (Prell 1971:9–16). While in the past Congress always "came through" voting for increases in the ceiling at the last moment, Treasury default on its obligations was avoided this time only by canceling securities in the social security trust fund thereby increasing the Treasury's borrowing power.

Lags in fiscal and monetary policy

Policy actions take time and this is a factor in evaluating their effectiveness. Economic policy has an inside and an outside lag. The outside lag is the time it takes for a policy change to affect the economy. The inside lag is made up of three parts—recognition, decision, and action.

RECOGNITION LAG   The recognition lag is the time between the economic disturbance and recognition by the policymakers. It is about the same for the Fed and the Treasury, since they and the Council of Economic Advisers are in constant contact with each other and share predictions (Dornbusch and Fischer 1978:278). The recognition lag exists because economic data takes time to collect, process, and analyze (Blinder and Solow 1978:258). Even with the computer it may take one or two quarters before it is recognized that something has happened. Inaccuracies in the data create a problem. Another is that a downturn in an economic series may quickly reverse itself and not be a harbinger of a longer run movement if left unchecked.

DECISION AND ACTION LAGS   The decision and action lags differ substantially for monetary and fiscal policy. The Fed Board meets daily; the Federal Open-Market Committee, approximately monthly. An instruction to the manager of the open-market account is required to implement policy (the action lag). In contrast, the decision lag for fiscal policy requires legislation. This must be prepared by the administration and steered through Congress. Three years were needed to reduce taxes in the early 1960s and three years for them to be raised in the late 1960s (Dernburg and McDougall 1976:398). To shorten the decision lag, it has been proposed that the president be given discretionary power over tax rates. Congress has not been sympathetic. The action lag that follows can be long, as in the case of public works expenditures, or short, as in the case of a change in the withholding tax.

OUTSIDE LAG   It has traditionally been thought that the outside lag is shorter for fiscal policy than for monetary policy. Changes in government expenditure have a direct effect on aggregate demand and output. The effect may be delayed if a "shelf" of public works must be organized, but the effect would be immediate in the case of transfer payments such as veterans' bonuses. Similarly, a reduction in taxes should lift the consumption function upward immediately. The indirectness of monetary policy was apparent in earlier chapters when it was pointed out that monetary policy works through financial variables.

It is therefore surprising that econometric studies point to average lags that are not greatly different. Fiscal policy multipliers suggest that 75% of the ultimate effect of nondefense spending is felt within the first year after initiation of the policy (Blinder and Solow 1978:259). A survey of monetary policy lags concludes that most of the effect of a change in the money supply, the monetary base, or total reserves occurs within four or five quarters. On the other hand, use of nonborrowed reserves as the exogenous monetary variable requires two and one-half years for the full effect to be exerted (Hamburger 1980:239ff.).

MULTIPLIER UNCERTAINTY   Econometric analysis gives a deceptive precision to the study of lags. They provide statistical averages based on historical data. The structure of the economy may not be understood and in any case it can change. At best, multiplier estimates are subject to a wide range of error. Policymakers cannot predict the future, and even if they could there are so many stochastic elements that success is only problematical. There is also the question of whether the private sector can neutralize government action by anticipating government moves. This is the "rational expectations" controversy to be reviewed in Chapter 21.

The difficulties in understanding the economy are well illustrated by controveries over determinants of investment and consumption (Blinder and Solow 1978: 262–66). Investment can be explained in terms of relative prices of inputs (the so-called neoclassical theory) or in terms of sources of funds (sales, retained earnings, external finance). In the case of consumption expenditures, the largest single component of aggregate demand, there are questions as to the effect of temporary variations in taxes versus permanent variation and whether tax payments or tax liabilities are the relevant concepts.

The policymakers can claim success for the tax cut of 1963. Evidence indicates that it indeed did have an expansionary effect. On the other hand, the tax surcharge of 1968 failed to cut down on demand and inflation. Here the rival effects of monetary policy may be responsible because monetary policy became easy during 1967–69. The growth rate in the money supply during this time (an average of 7%) was higher than in any two-year period since the 1940s (Dornbusch and Fischer 1978:237).

Allocational effects

Tax policies can aim at a desired social allocation of resources in the same way as credit allocation (see Ch. 18). When applied to the producing sectors of the economy, tax policies suffer from the same disadvantages as credit allocation; they distort relative input prices. Just as credit controls may cheapen capital inputs in house construction by lowering interest rates, so an investment tax credit limited to equipment distorts the relation between the prices of equipment and other factors of production. On the other hand, subsidies to final output, as in the case of a cash payment to home buyers, may avoid these distorting effects.

The tax cuts of 1981 were designed to increase investment at the expense of consumption. While nonresidential fixed investment grew rapidly in 1983–84, the evidence provides no support that cuts in business taxes produced a supply-side miracle. The overall fiscal package since 1980 has been proconsumption (via tax cuts for households) rather than proinvestment. High-tech investment and obsolescence of a portion of the capital stock have been cited as better explanations of the strength of investment (Throop 1984:1–3).

Debt management

Treasury debt management has to do with the composition of the public debt. The Treasury, in financing the deficit or rolling over the debt, has a choice between offering marketable and nonmarketable debt; its most important choice, however, affects the maturity. Table 20.6 analyzes the marketable debt by maturity. As col. 3 of the table shows, 44% of the debt of $862 bil. had a maturity of less than one year at the end of 1983. If we extend maturities to five years, the percentage of short-term securities rises to 78%. The average maturity of the debt reached its all-time low in 1976 (two years, seven months) and rose to four years, one month by the end of 1983. Average maturities have declined sharply since the 1946 average of nine years (Henning et al. 1984:639).

The shortness of average maturities is due to a congressional ceiling on the bond coupon rate. The ceiling rate of 4¼% forces the Treasury to issue short-term securities, since bonds are defined as securities running for 10 years or more. Currently $110 bil. of bonds are exempt from this legal restriction (Henning et al. 1984:281).

Table 20.6. Ownership of U.S. marketable debt by maturity

End of year	Amount out-standing, privately held	Within 1 year	Maturity class				Average length	
			1-5 years	5-10 years	10-20 years	20 years and over	Years	Months
			($ mil.)					
1967	150,321	56,561	53,584	21,057	6,153	12,968	5	1
1968	159,671	66,746	52,295	21,850	6,110	12,670	4	5
1969	156,008	69,311	50,182	18,078	6,097	12,337	4	2
1970	157,910	76,443	57,035	8,286	7,876	8,272	3	8
1971	161,863	74,803	58,557	14,503	6,357	7,645	3	6
1972	165,978	79,509	57,157	16,033	6,358	6,922	3	3
1973	167,869	84,041	54,139	16,385	8,741	4,564	3	1
1974	164,862	87,150	50,103	14,197	9,930	3,481	2	11
1975	210,382	115,677	65,852	15,385	8,857	4,611	2	8
1976	279,782	151,723	89,151	24,169	8,087	6,652	2	7
1977	326,674	161,329	113,319	33,067	8,428	10,531	2	11
1978	356,501	163,819	132,993	33,500	11,383	14,805	3	3
1979	380,530	181,883	127,574	32,279	18,489	20,304	3	7
1980	463,717	220,084	156,244	38,809	25,901	22,679	3	9
1981	549,863	256,187	182,237	48,743	32,569	30,127	4	0
1982	682,043	314,436	221,783	75,749	33,017	37,058	3	11
1983	862,631	379,579	294,955	99,174	40,826	48,097	4	1

Source: President 1984:313.
Note: All issues classified to final maturity. Through fiscal year 1976, the fiscal year was on a July 1-June 30 basis; beginning October 1976 (fiscal year 1977), the fiscal year is on an October 1-September 30 basis.

TREASURY TECHNIQUES   The Treasury must make decisions on the maturity of a new issue and the interest rate to be paid. It will be aware of current holders of maturing issues and try to tailor new offerings so that current holders will find them acceptable; e.g., life insurance companies are interested in long-terms, commercial banks in short-terms. As in the case of corporate bond issues, the Treasury must gauge the state of the market in setting interest rates. Too low an interest endangers the success of the issue. Too high a yield means more interest costs in the budget.

The auction technique is a way of influencing the market decision on interest rates. This method has traditionally been used for Treasury bills. The Treasury auctions off three-month and six-month bills weekly. (The Federal Reserve Banks are in charge of the auction.) The bills are sold to the highest bidder, with noncompetitive bids also being accepted at the average price of the competitive bids.

An alternative auction procedure, called the "Dutch auction" was tried in 1972 for 20-year bonds. Here bonds were awarded to all at the lowest accepted bid. The intention was to appeal to less knowledgeable investors (in the case of government securities these included pension funds, personal trusts, and savings banks). The effort was not successful, however (Henning et al. 1984:363–64). It might be thought that a Dutch auction would raise costs to the Treasury by lowering the average price received. But bidders, to have their bids accepted, might bid high knowing they could end up paying significantly less than their bid (Horvitz 1979:255).

In the 1960s the technique of advance refunding was employed. The idea was to stave off a shortening of average maturities with the passage of time. The average maturity is lengthened when debt holders accept longer term issues. Advanced refunding in more recent years has been stymied by interest-rate ceilings on long-term bonds being below market yields. Instead, Treasury offerings have been put on a regular basis. There are monthly auctions of one-year bills and regular offerings of notes and bonds (Horvitz 1979:266).

POLICY IMPLICATIONS   Variations in the maturity of the debt have liquidity and interest cost effects. Short-term debt is more liquid than long-term debt. As such, it provides a money substitute. Treasury bills and other short-term Treasury securities are part of the L monetary aggregate (see Ch. 6, Table 6.1). Ordinarily, the Treasury yield curve is a rising one. The interest costs of long-term debt as a result are greater than for short-term debt. This is no small consideration when it is realized that interest accounts for 11% of the U.S. budget ($90 bil. out of total outlays of $796 bil. in fiscal 1983).

The Treasury must weigh the liquidity effects of its actions against interest-saving effects. Such a choice has not been feasible because of the interest ceilings on bond interest. This has forced the Treasury to borrow short. Should the Treasury stay out of the way of the Fed or attempt to exert an economic effect?

Staying out of the way of the Fed would mean maintaining a neutral maturity structure. A countercyclical policy, on the other hand, would aim at lengthening the maturity of the debt and raising long-term interest rates in periods of expansion. In this way Treasury policy would fit in with monetary policy in curbing a boom. In contrast, in recession periods the Treasury should try to shorten the debt.

It is an interesting theoretical question as to how successful the Treasury can be in influencing the term structure of interest rates (the yield curve). The expectations hypothesis suggests that the rate structure will not respond to changes in the composition of the debt. Temporarily, yields may rise for long-terms when the Treasury supply increases. (Market practitioners believe that large issues do have a market impact.) The yield rise will be arbitraged away, however, if interest expectations are unchanged. It has been estimated that to twist the rate structure by a full percentage point would require a maturity switching operation of $50 bil. (Nordhaus and Wallich 1978:281).

State and local fiscal policy

State and local governments have a fiscal policy even if an unconscious one. Thus taxes and spending have a multiplier effect similar to the federal sector. Fiscal effects may be a better term because of the absence of any coordinated policy. The scope of state and local activities is given in Table 20.7.

Table 20.7. Flow-of-funds account, state and local government			
Funds	1981	1982	1983
	($ bil.)		
1 Total receipts, NIA basis	420.0	441.9	478.2
2 Tax receipts	299.4	322.2	352.9
3 Social insurance receipts	32.7	35.8	39.0
4 Grants-in-aid received	87.9	83.9	86.3
5 Total expenditures, NIA basis	382.4	409.0	434.1
6 Purchase of goods and services	367.6	391.5	415.8
7 Net interest and transfers	14.8	17.5	18.3
8 Net surplus, NIA basis	37.6	32.9	44.1
9 - Retirement credit to households	31.0	37.3	44.5
10 = Gross saving	6.6	-4.4	-0.4
11 Net financial investment	6.7	-2.1	0.6
12 Net acquisition of financial assets	13.9	30.1	38.1
13 Demand deposits and currency	-1.6	-3.7	-3.7
14 Time deposits	2.4	6.0	-3.5
15 Security RPs	2.5	0.1	3.0
16 Credit market instruments	9.6	29.1	40.4
17 U.S. government securities	1.9	22.6	33.6
18 Treasury issues	-1.0	15.0	28.2
19 Agency issues	2.9	7.6	5.3
20 Tax exempt obligations	0.1	1.6	0.9
21 Mortgages	7.6	4.9	5.9
22 Taxes receivable	1.0	-1.4	1.9
23 Net increase in liabilities	7.3	32.2	37.5
24 Credit market borrowing	6.2	31.3	36.7
25 Tax exempt obligations	4.9	30.3	35.6
26 Short-term	1.1	5.9	-6.6
27 Other	3.8	24.4	42.2
28 U.S. government loans	1.2	1.0	1.1
29 Trade debt	1.1	0.9	0.8
30 Discrepancy	0.0	-2.3	-0.9

Source: FRB 1984e:13.
Note: Employee retirement funds are in insurance sector.

Unlike the federal sector, states and localities run surpluses on a national income accounts (NIA) basis (line 8). When allowance is made for the equity of households (HH) in retirement funds (line 10), the surplus declines to more of a balanced budget situation. Purchases of goods and services (line 6) include significant capital expenditures. If these were excluded (as done for the private sector), gross saving would be vastly increased.

Purchases of goods and services by state and local governments have risen more rapidly than those of the federal government. This is reflected in federal spending on goods and services of $275 bil. in 1983 (Table 20.1) as compared with

$415 bil. of state and local spending. States and localities are closer to the people and spend money on basic services such as highways, education, sewage, health care, and water supply. Capital expenditures on such items in the growing states explain state and local borrowing.

State and local borrowing has steadily increased (the debt went up from $15 bil. at the end of 1945 to $392 bil. at the end of 1983). It would have gone up even faster without the growth in federal aid. One study estimated that grants-in-aid increased from 9 to 20% of the cost of capital expenditures between the 1952–57 and 1958–64 periods. As a result, borrowing and taxes declined in relative importance (Mitchell 1970:323). In 1983 federal aid constituted 18% of total receipts and can be assumed to finance a similar percentage of capital expenditures. The new federalism of the Reagan administration calls for a sharp decline in such transfers in coming years.

Because of federal aid the federal deficit overstates the true deficit. Without such payments, in many years the federal deficit would be converted into a federal surplus. If the federal sector is seen merely as a more efficient tax collection agency, at least the two sectors should be merged in estimating deficits.

The surplus states and localities are on the lending side of financial markets, particularly the market for federal securities (line 17, Table 20.7). The ploy of borrowing at tax-exempt rates and investing in higher yielding securities is frowned on by the Treasury.

The state and local sector has the great advantage of tax exemption in raising funds (at a net cost to the Treasury). On the other hand, it lacks access to the Fed. This is one reason for talking about state and local fiscal effects rather than fiscal policy. This sector's deficit financing is subject to financial market pressures in the same way as private sector borrowing.

Summary

The taxing, spending, and debt management powers of the federal government give it an economic power base that can either complement or thwart the exercise of monetary policy. With each divisible into tight and easy components, one can distinguish four gradations of ease and tightness. Going from tight to easy, the sequence is tight fiscal and monetary policy, tight fiscal and easy monetary policy, easy fiscal and tight monetary policy, and easy fiscal and monetary policy. Easy fiscal and tight monetary policy is easier than the reverse because tight monetary policy via higher interest rates can induce offsetting substitution effects on the flow of funds. Beginning with 1979, tight monetary policy and relatively tight fiscal policy have been succeeded by easy fiscal policy and tight money followed by both easy fiscal and monetary policies. Here we concentrate on the fundamentals of fiscal policy.

The federal budget is the beginning point. It summarizes government activities and defines the deficit. The financing of a deficit determines the intensity of fiscal policy. The greater the dependence on the banking system, particularly the central bank, the greater government influence on effective demand.

The analytical framework of Chapter 19 is useful in sorting out fiscal influences on interest rates, prices, and output. The greater the responsiveness of the supply-of-funds side of financial markets to an increase in government demand for funds, the greater the shift in the effective demand curve. Government effect on output will depend on the nature of the supply curve of output, i.e., how responsive supply is to an increase in effective demand. The conditions for nominal and real crowding-out of private expenditures can be summarized in terms of the slopes of the supply-of-finance and supply-of-output curves.

The national debt is a by-product of the borrowing activities of the federal government. Once created, it takes on a life of its own. It can exert a wealth effect on private sector demand and can also increase the demand for money balances. The debt has a distributional effect depending on who owns the debt and who pays the taxes. The effect may be intergenerational if current consumption demand is increased via the wealth effect.

The multiplier effects of fiscal policy estimate the effects of a shift in government expenditures or in taxes on effective demand. Using the analytical framework of Chapter 19, the value of such multipliers was shown to depend on the effect of such disturbances on the supply-and-demand curves for finance. A problem with conventional multiplier analysis is that it treats saving as a leakage instead of a source of funds for lending activities and capital expenditures.

The size of government deficits gives a biased measure of Treasury discretion. Deficits may be determined endogenously by the state of the business cycle rather than by the planned efforts of government. To correct for this bias, the FES concepts and later the structural deficit have been developed.

Another bias of the deficit concept is the presumed effect that an increase in taxes has on the deficit. An increase in taxes may increase rather than decrease the deficit because of its effect on the incentive to produce (the Laffer effect). Similarly, an increase in expenditures financed by increased taxation may succeed only in reducing output and increasing prices. The Laffer theory has had an important but controversial effect on federal tax policy.

Monetary and fiscal policies work with lags, and they are compared with respect to inside and outside lags. While fiscal policy has the longer inside lag, it has a shorter outside lag.

Fiscal policy is a substitute for credit allocation. Taxes and subsidies on the buyer of final output can avoid distorting the input mix, a potential failing of credit allocation.

Debt management affords the Treasury an opportunity to choose interest costs over liquidity or vice versa. It is a potential anticyclical device, but only if the Treasury places less emphasis on its housekeeping (minimizing interest cost) objective.

Finally, state and local governments are in the same league with the federal sector because of dependence on tax revenues. On the other hand, they are akin to the private sector when they borrow in financial markets. Their linkage with the federal sector via grants-in-aid is an argument for combining the two sectors in making estimates of government deficits and surpluses. The outlook is for tougher sledding for state and local governments as a result of a decline in the relative importance of federal aid.

Review questions

1. Distinguish among the various federal budget concepts and their respective effects on the size of the government deficit.

2. How does the government finance its deficit? Your answer should discuss the different kinds of financial instruments and the major purchasers of the debt.

3. Discuss the wealth and distributional effects of the public debt.

4. "Pure fiscal policy involves selling debt to the banking system." Is this statement true or false?

5. How can the analytical framework of Chapter 19 be applied to the nominal and real crowding-out controversies?

6. Compare and contrast the money multiplier of Chapter 6 with the income multipliers of this chapter.

7. Explain the balanced-budget multiplier.

8. Why did economists come up with a way for measuring Treasury discretion? Describe the FES concept (now called the structural component in the deficit).

9. Is the Laffer curve a "laugher" or is it to be taken seriously?

10. The role playing of Republicans and Democrats in 1984 seems confused. Explain.

11. Are the lags in fiscal and monetary policy of the same length?

12. Why should debt management be regarded as a distinct element in fiscal policy?

13. Is it correct to speak of state and local fiscal policies?

21

Expectations, stagflation, and monetary policy

Human behavior is complex. The way that economic agents react to events may not be predictable. On the other hand, behavior may be perfectly predictable given the assumption of economic rationality. Either way, the task of policymaking is made more difficult. In the first case, the government cannot predict the reaction to a policy action. In the second, the public anticipates policy actions and neutralizes their intended effect. The case of stagflation (inflation with unemployment) may be a classic example of how expectations frustrate policymaking.

Stagflation can be discussed in terms of the demand and supply for output (see Ch. 19). It can also be discussed in terms of the Phillips curve, a relationship between the inflation rate and level of unemployment. We shall emphasize the latter approach because it is the focus of discussions of stagflation and also discuss the two types of expectations (adaptive and rational) underlying movements in the Phillips curve. In view of its contemporary importance, special attention will be given to rational expectations. Finally, tax- and market-based income policies will be considered as untried but innovative approaches to stagflation.

Phillips curve

Almost thirty years ago, a British engineer-economist did path-breaking research on the relationship between unemployment and inflation (see Phillips 1958:283ff.; see also Santomero and Seater 1978:499ff.). What caught the eye of the profession was the negatively sloping nonlinear curve that he drew, as shown in Figure 21.1. The negative slope reflects the pressure of excess demand on wage rates. The labor market dynamics can be represented by the following equation (Santomero and Seater 1978:502):

$$\Delta W/W = \alpha[(D - S)/S]$$

where ΔW = change in money wage rate
W = money wage rate

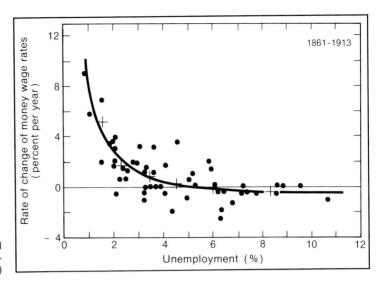

21.1. The original Phillips curve. (Humphrey 1979:62)

D = demand for labor
S = supply of labor
α = speed of adjustment

An excess demand for labor will generate a proportionate change in wage rates (the proportion depending on the speed of reaction). Unemployment is the proxy for excess demand. A decline in unemployment (moving to the left on Fig. 21.1) stands for an increase in excess demand and is associated with a higher rate of change in the wage rate.

The nonlinearity in the curve is explained by higher wages buying increasingly less employment. As unemployment decreases and the labor market tightens, the surplus pool of eligible workers declines so that the bidding is increased without corresponding gains in employment (Evans 1969:268).

INFLATION-UNEMPLOYMENT TRADE-OFF   The rate of inflation replaces the rate of change in money wages by allowing for productivity changes, as shown in Figure 21.2. The wage change less the productivity change yields the price change.

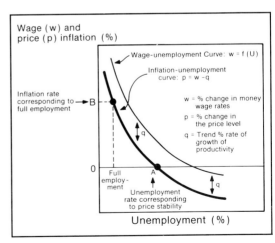

21.2. Deriving the inflation-unemployment trade-off. (Humphrey 1979:64)

The negative slope of the Phillips curve is of great significance. It means that a reduction in unemployment can be bought at the expense of more inflation. This is the objective trade-off determined by the way the economy works. The slope of the Phillips curve determines how much of one policy objective must be given up for the sake of another. The flatter the curve, for example, the lower the price of increased employment in terms of inflationary effects.

The subjective trade-off, in contrast, measures how much inflation a policy-maker is willing to tolerate for the sake of greater employment. Its shape is concave from below compared with the convex-from-below shape of the objective Phillips curve. Differences in subjective trade-offs are indicated by different shapes of the curve, as can be seen from Figure 21.3.

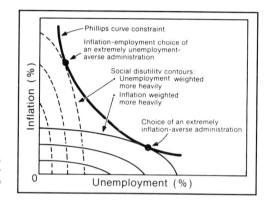

21.3. Different preferences, different policy choices. (Humphrey 1979a:66)

A liberal (Democratic?) administration might prefer a tangency point up in the northwest corner of the figure. An inflation-averse administration (Republican?) might prefer a southeasterly tangency position.

Shifting Phillips curve: Expectations

Trade-offs are complicated by shifts in the Phillips curve. Researchers have worked with a great number of variables (such as trade union membership, job vacancy rates, corporate profits, etc.) (Humphrey 1979a:68), but the dominant shift variable is expectations.

Excess product demand boosts prices and nominal wages. Prices initially go up faster than nominal wages. The result is a fall in real wages (nominal wages deflated by the price index). If we think of demand for labor in the labor market as responding to a fall in the real wage rate (assuming we are above the market-clearing rate), additional labor will be hired at the lower real wage rate. In Figure 21.4 we start at the W_0/P_0, real wage rate with N_0 workers being hired. Now the real wage falls to W_1/P_1, resulting in N_1 workers being hired.

Alternatively, if money wages (in the place of real wages) are being measured on the vertical axis, excess demand in the product market will shift the demand for labor in the labor market. Now the labor market is assumed to clear. At the higher equilibrium wage rate (the supply curve of labor not having shifted) more workers will be hired at a higher money wage rate. This adjustment is shown in Figure 21.5. Such an increase in employment accompanied by a higher inflation rate

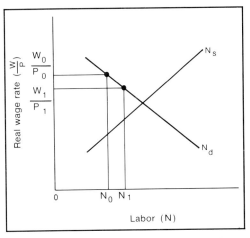

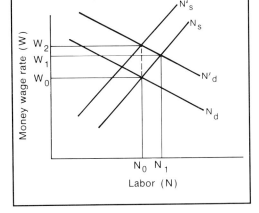

21.4. Labor market adjustment to a real wage change.

21.5. Labor market adjustment to price changes.

corresponds to a movement along the Phillips curve from *A* to *B* in Figure 21.6.

Figures 21.4 and 21.5 place different emphasis on the demand and supply sides of the labor market. In Figure 21.4 the employer's decision determines employment. In Figure 21.5 it is a shared responsibility. The supply side has been intensively analyzed under the topic of "search theory and information costs." Workers do not have the time or money to fully investigate other job offers. When wages start going up, they perceive their own wages as rising faster than wages in general. The effect is that fewer workers quit their jobs in any period, so that total employment goes up. Once they realize that all wages are going up and prices are advancing just as fast, the quit rate rises and employment goes back to an initial level. While such an interpretation is consistent with Figure 21.5, the problem with this approach is that quit rates historically go up with an increase in total employment and go down with a decrease. Figure 21.5 can be interpreted without search theory. The money reservation price of labor goes up with increases in the cost of living. On search theory, see Seater (1975:19ff.) and Santomero and Seater (1978:519ff.).

21.6. The shifting Phillips curve. Attempts to lower unemployment from the natural rate, U_n, to U_1 via movement along short-run trade-off curve S_0 will evoke wage bargaining and other adaptations to inflationary expectations. The economy will travel the path *ABCDE* to the new equilibrium, point *E*, where unemployment is the same but inflation is higher than it was originally. (Humphrey 1979a:68)

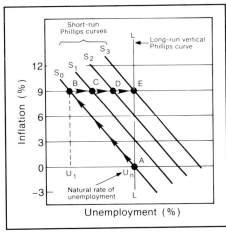

Workers have suffered a reduction in real wages as a price of increased employment. They do not suffer this reduction willingly. The initial money illusion (neglect of the price increase, concentration on the money wage increase) will not last. Workers will demand higher wages to keep up with inflation. In terms of Figure 21.5, the effect in the labor market will be a leftward shift in the supply curve to N_s'. In terms of Figure 21.6, the short-run Phillips curve shifts to the right. While in the labor market (Fig. 21.5) we have drawn only one new curve to show final equilibrium, the series of short-run curves in Figure 21.6 indicates a gradual adjustment to an assumed 9% rate of inflation. The S_1 curve indicates the shift in the curve when workers anticipate, say, a 3% increase in prices instead of the zero increase represented by the S_0 curve. In succession, the S_2 and S_3 curves show how the Phillips curve shifts as workers anticipations get more realistic. With the final S_3 curve the 9% inflation rate is fully anticipated. The result, shown by E, is a return to the original level of unemployment but with prices increasing at a 9% rate every year instead of 0%.

The implication of the return to the original level of unemployment is that the long-run Phillips curve is a vertical line. Different inflation rates accomplish only more or less inflation — no more employment. This persistent rate of unemployment (U_n) is called the natural rate of unemployment (a concept first introduced by Milton Friedman in his 1967 presidential address to the American Economic Association). It prevails whenever the actual rate of inflation corresponds to the anticipated rate. In this situation real wages are in equilibrium. Stated in symbolic form, which will be useful for later discussion (see Humphrey 1979b:79):

$$p - p^e = ax \quad \text{or} \quad x = (1/a)(p - p^e)$$

where p = rate of inflation
p^e = expected rate of inflation
x = excess demand in the labor and output markets
a = the numerical value of the trade-off between inflation and excess demand: the response of prices to excess demand or the response of excess demand to unexpected inflation (a is always greater than zero)

The equation states a relation between unexpected inflation ($p - p^e \neq 0$) and excess demand. It is referred to as the expectations-augmented Phillips curve. The first formulation of this equation shows that actual prices will exceed expected prices when excess demand exists (x is positive). The second formulation says that excess demand (output in excess of normal output) results from unexpected inflation. When unexpected inflation disappears ($p = p^e$), unemployment is at its natural rate and output is normal.

ACCELERATIONIST HYPOTHESIS   The long-run vertical Phillips curve can only be circumvented by accelerating inflation. This is the monetarist-accelerationist hypothesis. As shown in Figure 21.7, explosive ever accelerating inflation is necessary to keep the unemployment rate at U_1 (Humphrey 1979a:70).

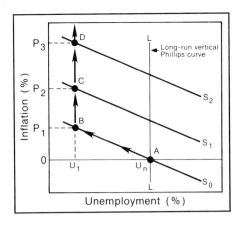

21.7. The accelerationist hypothesis. (Humphrey 1979:70)

Adaptive versus rational expectations

The gradual movement to the natural rate of unemployment reflects an adaptive theory of expectations. The more recent approach to the Phillips curve is founded on rational expectations, with which the speed of adjustment is greatly lessened. Although it challenges credulity, rational expectation argues that the adjustment is instantaneous. The consequences are that the natural rate of unemployment holds in both the short and long run.

ADAPTIVE EXPECTATIONS   The difference between the two kinds of expectations is that adaptive expectations are backward looking and rational expectations are forward looking. If expectations of wage earners are adaptive, the past behavior of prices is what influences expectations as to future price movements. Theories on the natural rate of unemployment focus on the expectations of wage earners, assuming that entrepreneurs successfully anticipate higher prices when making their decisions. Adaptive expectations can be expressed as a geometrically weighted average of past rates of inflation (Humphrey 1979b:75). Thus:

$$p^e = \Sigma w_i p_{-i}$$

where p^e = expected rate of inflation
w_i = weights for i years
p_{-i} = past rates of inflation
Σ = the summing up of past rates of inflation

The weights sum up to one. Assume that last year's weight is 50%. Then the previous year (two years earlier) will have a weight equal to some common ratio times 50%. If the ratio is high, say 80%, the weight given to the inflation rate two years earlier will be 40%. This means that only recent price history is relevant in determining people's price expectations. If last year's weight is low and the common ratio is low, the experience of many earlier years will be influencing current expectations.

A variant of this formulation is an error-learning mechanism. If people guess wrong one year about inflation, they will correct their forecast for next year in the light of the error (Humphrey 1979b:75). This form of the adaptive expectations hypothesis is expressed as $\dot{p} = b (p - p^e)$, where $\dot{p}$ = rate of change in the inflation rate and b = speed of adjustment. Suppose that expected inflation is 8%

but actual inflation turns out to be 18% and the speed of adjustment b was 0.6, the public will add 6% to the previously expected inflation rate of 8%, thus $\dot{p}$ will be 6%.

RATIONAL EXPECTATIONS   Rational expectations place the emphasis on the sophisticated transactor who makes use of all available information and whose forecasts go beyond extrapolations of past trends. Present prices reflect the market's assessment of future prices as well as past prices. This incorporation of all available data is written as $P_t = E_t(P_{t+1})$. The market does not wait until tomorrow to convert expected influences, $E_t(P_{t+1})$, but will act on this information today (P_t). This formulation highlights the forward-looking nature of rational expectations. A more conventional formulation is $p^e = E(p \mid I)$, where I is known information. Anticipated inflation is the expected value of the inflation rate conditional on the information available when the expectation was formed (Humphrey 1979b:75). Since present prices reflect all known information, prices change only when there is new information. This information is not reflected in current prices. Existing prices are therefore no guide to future ones. Prices follow a random walk. The random walk idea was originally applied to stock markets. It attacked the technical (chartist) approach to stock market prices. The chartists predicted stock market prices on the basis of past movements. The random walk school contended that past prices are no guide to future prices (the efficient market hypothesis). Rational expectations expanded the applicability of this hypothesis to behavior of economic agents in general. This has been called information-arbitrage efficiency. Three other deeper meanings can be given to efficiency, which cast doubt on its applicability to financial markets (Tobin:1984).

Rational expectations assume that the information available includes a knowledge of the "correct" economic model. As such $E(p \mid I)$ correctly identifies the inflation-generating process. Forecasting errors are still possible, however, owing to random disturbances (an error term in the price-forecasting equation). The forecast error z is then equal to the actual rate of inflation minus the expected value of the inflation rate: $z = p - E(p \mid I)$. On balance, errors cancel out so that, on the average, inflation is correctly forecast. This is another way of saying that forecasters do not keep making the same mistake.

Policy implications

The considerable attention given to rational expectations is due to its startling policy implications. Because economic agents know the policymakers' reaction function, they can forecast monetary growth rates and from that can forecast inflation. As a result, monetary policy is without real effects.

First, the inflation-generating mechanism is represented by a simple quantity-theory equation (cf. Humphrey 1979b:79–80): $p = m + e_p$, where m = rate of monetary growth and e_p = error term. Rational economic agents know how the monetary policymakers operate. The policy reaction function is written as $m = m(x_{-1}) + e_m$, where x_{-1} = lagged excess demand for labor (and output) and e_m = error term. The central bank determines the monetary growth rate with reference to excess demand. The greater excess demand, for example, the lower the monetary growth rate. Economic agents forecast prices on the basis of the expected monetary growth rate (the quantity theory). The monetary growth rate in turn is forecast from knowledge of the policy reaction function. The two equations are respectively $p^e = m^e$ and $m^e = m(x_{-1})$.

The existence of trade-off between output and inflation was described earlier by $p - p^e = ax$. We now substitute for p and p^e on the left-hand side of the equation, using the equations just discussed. This gives $[m(x_{-1}) + e_m + e_p] - [m(x_{-1})] = ax$. Cancelling out the $m(x_{-1})$ terms, we have $e_m + e_p = ax$. Only if there are error terms (without offsetting effects) will x have a value different from zero. If economic agents guess too low about the rate of monetary increase (the e_m error term is positive) and on the rate of price increase (e_p is also positive), unexpected inflation prevails with a positive effect on output.

The monetary policymaker has two alternatives. A random policy can be followed, thus manipulating the e_m error term. The reaction function becomes unpredictable. Or the reaction function can be changed secretly. Presumably e_p is not subject to the same variability; the relation between m and p is more dependable. So economic agents must be fooled by the policymaker if a short-run Phillips curve is to exist (Humphrey 1979b:80).

The policy implications of rational expectations are more restrictive than for adaptive expectations. Activist stabilization policies are less likely to generate a trade-off between unemployment and inflation. The natural rate of unemployment for rational expectations is both a short- and long-run phenomenon.

If the natural rate of unemployment is to be reduced, imperfections in the labor market must be overcome. The problem of teenage unemployment can be ameliorated by lowering the minimum wage and on-the-job training (Dornbusch and Fischer 1978:469ff.). Unemployment compensation schemes might be modified to offer less incentive for firms to lay off workers.

While the natural rate of unemployment view offers little scope for policy in the long run (perhaps more in the short run), a restrictive monetary policy, it is argued, will succeed in reducing the rate of inflation. The approach may be gradualist or "cold turkey" (Dornbusch and Fischer 1984:448–50). In either case, short-run unemployment will increase, since a tight monetary policy works through restricting aggregate demand. The burden of fighting inflation will be on the unemployed. This burden can be spread by WPA-type job programs. Nonetheless, anti-inflationary effects require that workers be paid something less than their original salaries (Seater 1975:27ff.). Financing the job program by taxes rather than deficit spending also has distributive effects. Those still employed will bear the burden of fighting inflation by paying higher taxes.

THE EVIDENCE   It is a simple matter to plot historical inflation and unemployment rates and observe whether the natural-rate hypothesis has more support than the trade-off relation. The results are mixed, as illustrated in Figure 21.8. The trade-off relation (a negatively sloping curve) is a phenomenon originally of the 1960s, appearing again in 1976–79 and 1981–83. Upward sloping relations are consistent with the Phillips curve shifting over time and support a natural-rate hypothesis. They are in evidence in 1973–76 and 1979–81 and signify the worst of both worlds, stagflation. The 1973–76 relationship, however, probably has little to do with the hypothesis. More likely it is the effect of OPEC oil prices on inflation and unemployment. Similar third-factor causes may be at work at other times.

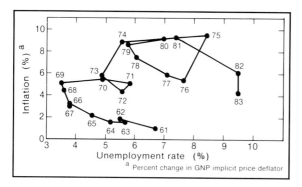

21.8. Inflation and unemployment. (President 1984)

Weakness and strength of rational expectations

The picture that rational expectations conjures up is one of instantaneous price adjustments following variations in the money supply. The real effects desired by the monetary authorities become price effects. The analysis too literally applies an efficient market hypothesis to the economy at large. This hypothesis confines its interest to price changes, neglecting quantity changes.

Rational expectations ignore the borrowing-spending effects of anticipated inflation. For the business firm, higher future prices mean a lower real cost of capital, thus stimulating real investment. For the households, it means paying 10–20% more for the same item later. This stimulation to effective demand is true even if the actual inflation rate equals the expected inflation rate ($p = p^e$ in our previous formulations). On the supply-of-output side, it ignores the other components of costs beside wages. As presented in Chapter 19, the supply (price) equation is described by

$$P = P \overset{-}{(}Q_s, \overset{+}{WAGES}, MAT, \overset{+}{OC})$$

Not only are there other cost elements besides wages, but wages themselves may respond with a lag to the state of the labor market. As the labor market tightens, so do wages. The state of the labor market (as reflected in excess demand x in the Phillips curve equation) must be considered along with price expectations. All these factors mean that an increase in the demand for output (owing in part to inflationary expectations) will not necessarily be offset by a decreased supply of output (a shift to the left in the prices charged curve).

The possibility of fluctuations to the right and to the left of the full-employment output associated with the natural rate of unemployment is suggested by Figure 21.9. Rational expectations (also called perfect foresight expectations) (cf.

21.9. Response to a monetary disturbance.

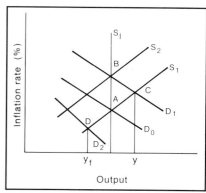

Dornbusch and Fischer 1978:423) would have the inflation rate move from A to B following a monetary disturbance that shifted the demand curve from D_0 to D_1. (As described in Ch. 19, we see the effective demand curve shifting because of underlying shifts in the demand and supply of credit in financial markets.) The supply curve adjusts instantaneously from S_1 and S_2 because of the perfect foresight of wage earners. More realistically, the short-run adjustment would be to point C. Similarly, a decline in demand would end up at point D. Whether the long-run adjustment is indeed to point B is a matter of futile debate. The shopworn expression "in the long run we are all dead" (attributed to Keynes) is still worth remembering. The real-financial interaction is slighted by rational expectations. Economic fluctuations can only be explained by random disturbances; the tail seemingly wags the dog.

The historical persistence of output levels to the left of full employment (the Great Depression of 1930–39 is the classic example) poses a major dilemma for rational expectations. Variations around an equilibrium value (here the natural rate) should be random rather than serially correlated as in this case. Rational expectations must either stumble over the facts (unconvincingly blame serial correlation on information lags) or argue that the 25% unemployment rate of the time was voluntary. (For an amusing discussion of the pros and cons of rational expectations including serial correlation see Maddock and Carter 1982.)

But this is not to deny to rational expectations an important virtue. The so-called Lucas critique (see Ch. 25 below and Attfield et al. 1985: Ch. 6) challenges the validity of econometric models. Because of rational expectations the coefficients of such models are not policy invariant. Changes in public policy affect the behavior of economic agents, so the behavioral (structural) equations of the econometrician become outmoded with such changes. The discussion in Chapter 12 of interest rate volatility provides an example. When the Fed stopped targeting the federal funds rate, interest rates became more volatile. As a result, one theory is that the public's money demand curve became more interest inelastic and as a result the volatility increased.

Remedies for stagflation

The phenomenon that sparked rational expectations is stagflation (Lucas 1981:558–67). While we question the logic of rational expectations, there is no denying that since the 1960s we have been frequently faced with rising inflation often associated with rising unemployment. The remedy of rational expectations is to control the rate of monetary growth. The natural rate of unemployment will then coexist with a low rate of inflation. The problem with tight monetary control, however, is "throwing the baby out with the bathwater." Monetary control works through demand management. As the slowdowns of 1980, 1981–82, and earlier recessions reveal, tight money takes its toll on output and employment. Moreover, it is questionable how much credit it can take for the admitted slowing down of inflation in 1981–82. Declining energy prices were a major factor.

The alternative approach is via the supply side. An incomes policy would curb the price-increasing effects of cost push. Wage and price controls come to mind when incomes policy is mentioned. The academic opposition to controls is based on the enforcement bureaucracy and black markets that it creates and its resource-distorting effects. If controls work at all, results are temporary. When controls are removed, pent-up demand asserts itself and prices rise sharply. Or prices may shoot up in anticipation of controls. In contrast to academic opposition, however, public opinion polls reveal that the public is in favor of them (Maital and Benjamini 1980:459–81). The one point in favor of controls on which all might agree is that they break the momentum of inflation. The disadvantage of wage and price controls has led to a great number of tax-based incomes policies (TIP) (see Okun and Perry 1978; Colander 1979). The intent is to allow the price mechanism to work through relative price and wage changes while controlling the level (Weintraub 1979:170).

The pioneer Wallich-Weintraub proposal (H. C. Wallich is a Governor of the Federal Reserve Board; S. Weintraub was a professor at the University of Pennsylvania) would tax major corporations (measured in terms of employees) on wage increases above a set norm, say 5% per annum. Firms that violated the norm would be subject to a penalty corporate income tax. The late Professor Weintraub consistently maintained that inflation is mainly the result of money wage rates rising faster than labor productivity and that the only way to control inflation is by controlling wages via an incomes policy (Bloomfield 1981–82:291–300).

The late Arthur Okun (Brookings Institution) proposed a "carrot variant" of TIP, which would offer a tax refund to union employees who accepted lower increases than the going inflation rate (Bloomfield 1981–82:172; Okun 1979:176ff.). The same carrot approach has recently been echoed by Sinai (1984a).

Lerner has proposed that the market, not the government, set the tax on wage increases (Lerner 1978:255ff.). Firms that wished to raise wages by more than estimated productivity increases (say 3%) would have to buy permits from firms who planned to reduce their wage bill by a similar amount. Permits would trade like shares of IBM. In this way, the national wage bill would rise by 3% a year, the productivity increase. The wage increase permit plan (WIPP) aims at two objectives—keeping the average wage rising at the same rate as output per worker and leaving individual wages free to vary (Lerner 1978:260). Inflationary pressure will be turned against itself (in jujitsu fashion) because the higher the price of the warrants, the stronger the counterinflationary incentive.

The drawback of TIP and WIPP is their confining pricing policies to wages. Labor can understandably argue that they are being discriminated against. Colander initially and then jointly with Lerner developed a value-added tax-based incomes policy, labeled as MAP (market anti-inflation plan)(Colander 1979:210ff.; Lerner and Colander 1979:210ff.). Value added refers to the payments to primary inputs at each stage of production (wages, profits, rents, interest payments). Initially, Colander proposed that inflationary increases in value added beyond that warranted by additional physical inputs should be subject to tax. Tax revenues will subsidize firms whose price changes are below the value-added guidelines. Later (with Lerner), MAP became market oriented. Firms buy and sell permits to enjoy net sales (value added) above or below the noninflationary levels.

Reforms of wage-fixing institutions have been advocated by the British Nobel Laureate J. E. Meade. A central representative body would announce a norm or average increase in the rate of pay aimed at promoting a high and stable level of employment. A national structure of pay tribunals would be instituted to which either party to a dispute about rates of pay could refer the case. This procedure could be combined with a special inflation tax on increases in rates of pay that exceeded the norm by some stated percentage (Meade 1983:9).

The TIP and the market-type proposals might minimize the administrative problems associated with wage and price controls. Guidelines still must be determined, however, and the books of companies (perhaps only the largest corporations) must be examined. Weintraub felt that the Internal Revenue Service could handle TIP with just a few extra lines of information on the corporate income tax form. According to Lerner-Colander, MAP could be administered by having the Fed set up an anti-inflation credit office. The schemes, particularly the market type, are intriguing substitutes for direct controls, and some daring administration should try them.

Summary

The leading economic puzzle of our times is the coexistence of inflation and unemployment. Economists used to believe that the monetary policymaker could reduce unemployment by courting inflation. Such a belief was given support by the original Phillips curve and subsequent studies. The persistence of both inflation and unemployment, increases in unemployment being associated with rising inflation, has led to a gloomier assessment. Underlying the pessimism is the potent effect of expectations. Product price changes are anticipated, and economic agents (most critically, workers) demand compensating factor payments. When expected and actual inflation rates match, the temporary gains in employment by inflationary policies are wiped out. The real wage rate, and as a consequence the original rate of unemployment (the natural rate), is restored. The two approaches to expectations differ only in the speed of adjustment back to a vertical Phillips curve. Adaptive expectations posit a slower speed of adjustment than rational expectations. The instantaneous speed of adjustment of rational expectations, based on the analogy to the workings of the stock market, defies reality. The real world is one of stickiness in prices and wages with time lags in adjustment to changes in expectations. Moreover, anticipated price changes may have real effects because they make current spending a bargain compared with later spending. Rational expectations are able to explain economic fluctuations only in terms of random disturbances, an unsatisfactory approach. The remedy of slower monetary growth may slow inflation, but it will also increase the unemployment rate. In Figure 21.8 the points for 1982 and 1983 are below and to the right of 1981 — the result of restrictive monetary policy. But when all this is said, the Lucas critique, borne of the rational expectations revolution, has serious merit.

Finally, a variety of incomes policies were explored as ways of combating inflation without sacrificing full employment. Most intriguing are proposals for selling permits to inflate. The inflationary effects of the permit buyers would be neutralized by the deflationary effects of the permit sellers. The administrative problems besetting direct wage-price controls might be reduced by these schemes. They deserve a try.

Review questions

1. What is the Phillips curve?

2. Explain money illusion.

3. Contrast adaptive and rational expectations.

4. Define the concept of stagflation.

5. Does the empirical evidence support the natural-rate hypothesis?

6. List the advantages and disadvantages of wage-price controls.

7. Distinguish between objective and subjective trade-offs of unemployment for inflation.

8. What difference(s) does it make in an analysis of the labor market to replace real wages on the vertical axis with money wages?

9. According to the natural-rate hypothesis, can monetary expansion succeed in increasing employment at the expense of more inflation?

10. What is the accelerationist hypothesis?

11. Describe some market-type approaches to an incomes policy.

12. Why is serial correlation in time-series variables (e.g., the unemployment variable) such a serious challenge to rational expectations?

13. Evaluate the merits of the Lucas policy critique.

22

Finance in the business cycle

Previous chapters have been interested in shocks to the economy (such as the effect of an increase in borrowing and the money stock in Ch. 2 or the effect of higher oil prices on the supply side of the market in Ch. 19). The analysis assumed that the economy settled down into an equilibrium situation after a period of adjustment.

The real world is one in which the balance sheets of economic agents are always out of kilter. Transactors may be heading for a stock equilibrium, but like the greyhound chasing the mechanical rabbit they never get there. One disequilibrium situation succeeds another, leading to the notion of a cycle (a regular alternation of good and bad times). The cycle has both real and financial characteristics. The point of this chapter is that the critical elements in the cycle are financial.

Disequilibrium will be interpreted here as stock disequilibrium, with markets in a flow sense always clearing. It can also be interpreted as flow disequilibrium in addition to stock disequilibrum. In the case of flow disequilibrium, markets do not clear; the minimum amounts demanded or supplied at nonclearing prices will be the amount sold. The analysis of flow disequilibrium has been systematically applied to the labor and product markets in a vast literature, e.g., see Muellbauer and Portes (1979:Ch.16).

We begin with a general description of the business cycle. Next we will develop a nonfinancial mechanical theory of the cycle. Its conversion to a financial flow-of-funds cycle takes up most of the chapter. In the last two sections we consider the stabilizing (or destabilizing) effects of the central bank and the federal deficit.

Business cycle

The business cycle is a phenomenon of a money-exchange economy. Before the widespread use of money, natural disasters such as floods and droughts accounted for economic disruption. The classic early study of the business cycle that makes this point is Mitchell (1913). The business cycle in this broad sense is man-made. Monetary disruptions (money as a leakage or disturbance variable) are at least a necessary condition for the business cycle. They are also a sufficient condition if they determine the turning points in the cycle.

Business cycle theories attempt to explain four successive phases: recovery (expansion), peak (boom), recession (contraction), trough (depression) (Fig. 22.1). The most formidable task is explaining the turning points, i.e., why booms turn into recession and why the trough is followed by recovery. Less challenging is the explanation of the snowball effect, i.e., expansion into boom then recession into depression.

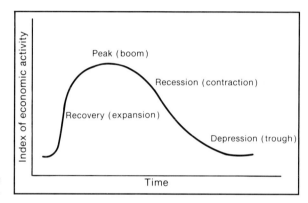

22.1. The four phases of the cycle.

Figure 22.2 traces fluctuations in prices and production since World War I. Fluctuations are measured as deviations from long-run upward trends (1902–28, 1929–83), with the trend line tilted to a horizontal position. The black line represents wholesale prices; the shaded areas measure industrial production (the Federal Reserve index of industrial production since 1919). The shaded areas show the variations in real economic activity. Indexes of employment and unemployment respectively would parallel and move inversely to the production index. On this parallelism after World War II, see McNees (1978:44ff.).

The Great Depression of the 1930s stands out. Since the trend line is a straight-line fit to the 1929–80 data, the Great Depression is the counterweight to the above-the-line behavior of business activity since World War II. But, nonetheless, the business cycle is still clearly visible.

The upward trend of wholesale prices since World War II is in sharp contrast to its cyclical behavior prior to that time (and going back to 1790). This is what causes so much difficulty in economic analysis. Since World War II it is no longer possible to lump real series such as production and employment with price behavior. The coincidence of downward physical movements and accelerating inflation in the recession phases of the cycle lies behind the concept of stagflation. An unambiguous discussion of the business cycle makes it necessary to ignore the long-run inflationary trend and concentrate on variations in the inflation rate.

The four stages of the business cycle in the United States are chronicled by the National Bureau of Economic Research (a leading nonprofit economic research organization). The timing of the stages is identified on the basis of statistical series describing real economic behavior. A five-stage sequence has been proposed to

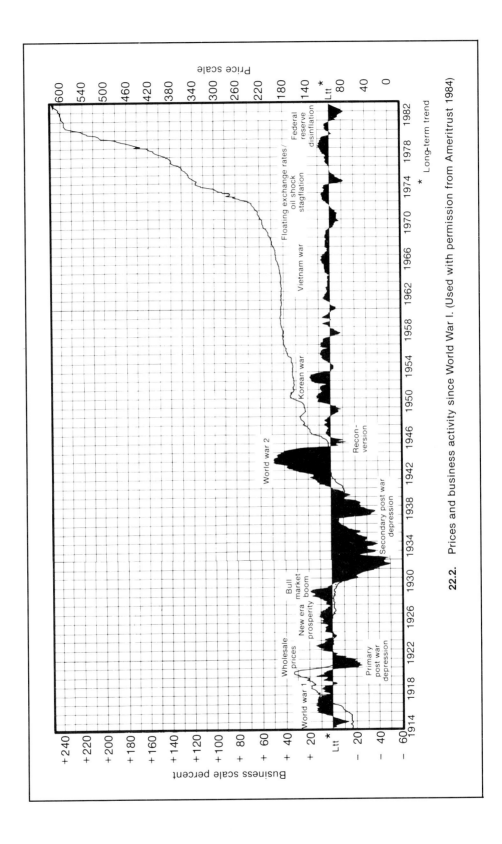

22.2. Prices and business activity since World War I. (Used with permission from Ameritrust 1984)

allow for associated financial phenomena (Eckstein and Sinai, forthcoming). These five stages are recovery (expansion), boom, precrunch period (credit crunch), recession (decline), and reliquefication. As shown in Table 22.1 the typical postwar cycle seems to run through all five stages. The new terminology emphasizes financial aspects of the cycle.

Table 22.1. Stages of postwar business cycles

Episode	Recovery/expansion	Boom	Recession	Precrunch period/ crunch	Reliquefication
I	1945:4-1948:4	...	1948:4-1949:4	...	...
II	1949:4-1953:2	1952:4-1953:2	1953:2-1954:2	...	...
III	1954:2-1957:3	1955:1-1955:4	1957:3-1958:2	1955:4-1957:4	1958:1-1958:2
IV	1958:2-1960:2	...	1960:2-1961:1	1959:2-1960:2	1960:3-1964:3
V	1961:1-1969:4	1964:4-1966:4	...	1966:1-1966:3	1966:4-1967:3
	...		1969:4-1970:4	1969:1-1970:1	1970:2-1971:2
VI	1970:4-1973:4	1972:2-1973:4	1973:4-1975:1	1973:1-1974:3	1974:4-1976:2
VII	1975:1-1980:1	1978:3-1979:1	1980:1-1980:3	1978:2-1980:1	1980:2-1980:3
VIII	1980:3-1981:3	...	1981:3-1982:4	1981:1-1981:4	1982:1-1983:2
IX	1982:4-	...	...	...	...

Not too long ago the question was raised whether the business cycle was obsolete (Bronfenbrenner 1969:vi). While the answer was in the negative, the conference conclusion was that the period and amplitude seemed to be decreasing and that recessions were largely, if not entirely, limited to decelerations in the rate of economic growth. Table 22.2, however, suggests that cyclical downturns have become more frequent and severe since 1969. As measured by the swings in industrial production, etc. (under amplitude), the business cycle has become more volatile.

The postwar cycles have an average length of four and one-half years, the median length being four years (Table 22.2). Average expansion length is more than four times average recession length. The so-called business cycle is to be distinguished from long cycles (called kondratieffs), said to be 50–60 years in length, and also from shorter inventory cycles.

The business cycle as fluctuations

The notion of a cycle suggests a regularity or rhythm in economic behavior. This is misleading because of the importance of shocks — exogenous disturbances on the supply or demand side of markets or in prices. Such shocks explain why some economists prefer the word "fluctuation" to "cycle." Examples of negative demand shocks are 1948 and 1960. The recession of 1948 accompanied the conversion of the American economy from a war to peacetime footing. Industrial production dropped sharply. President Eisenhower's achievement of a balanced federal budget in 1960 was a similar shock (Eckstein and Sinai, forthcoming).

Four supply shocks have been identified as playing a major role in particular business cycles. These are the steel strike of 1959, supply disruptions of world oil in 1973 and 1979–80, and the agricultural crisis caused by the poor crops of 1972. The imposition of wage price controls in 1971 and the hike in oil prices are exam-

ble 22.2. Dimensions of postwar business cycles

ough to peak peak to trough	Expansion (mo.)	Contraction (mo.)	Industrial production (% change)	Amplitude Real GNP ($ change)	Inflation (% change)	Unemployment rate (%)
:t. 1945 (T)- Nov. 1948 (P)	37	...	n.a.	n.a.	0.0 (T); 6.9 (P)	3.1 (T); 3.8 (P)
▸v. 1948 (P)- Oct. 1949 (T)	...	11	-8.5	-1.4	-6.9 (P); -4.1 (T)	3.8 (P); 7.9 (T)
:t. 1949 (T)- July 1953 (P)	45	...	50.1	27.2	-4.1 (T); 0.6 (P)	7.9 (T); 2.6 (P)
▸ly 1953 (P)- May 1954 (T)	...	10	-8.9	-2.6	0.6 (P); 3.3 (T)	2.6 (P); 5.9 (T)
▸y 1954 (T)- Aug. 1957 (P)	40	...	21.8	13.2	3.3 (T); 3.9 (P)	5.9 (T); 4.1 (P)
▸g. 1957 (P)- Apr. 1958 (T)	...	8	-12.6	-2.7	3.9 (P); 2.8 (T)	4.1 (P); 7.4 (T)
▸r. 1958 (T)- Apr. 1960 (P)	24	...	22.7	10.2	2.8 (T); 5.7 (P)	7.4 (T); 5.2 (P)
▸r. 1960 (P)- Feb. 1961 (T)	...	10	-6.1	-0.1	5.7 (P); 0.0 (T)	5.2 (P); 6.9 (T)
▸b. 1961 (T)- Dec. 1969 (P)	106	...	76.8	47.2	0.0 (T); 7.7 (P)	6.9 (T); 3.5 (P)
▸c. 1969 (P)- Nov. 1970 (T)	...	11	-5.8	-0.1	7.7 (P); 5.2 (T)	3.5 (P); 5.9 (T)
▸v. 1970 (T)- Nov. 1973 (P)	36	...	25.6	16.7	5.2 (T); 10.1 (P)	5.9 (T); 4.8 (P)
▸v. 1973 (P)- Mar. 1975 (T)	...	16	-15.1	-4.9	10.1 (P); 3.9 (T)	4.8 (P); 8.6 (T)
▸r. 1975 (T)- Jan. 1980 (P)	58	...	37.0	24.3	3.9 (T); 19.2 (P)	8.6 (T); 6.3 (P)
▸n. 1980 (P)- July 1980 (T)	...	6	-8.3	-2.2	19.2 (P); 1.0 (T)	6.3 (P); 7.8 (T)
▸ly 1980 (T)- July 1981 (P)	12	...	9.7	4.2	1.0 (T); 14.6 (P)	7.8 (T); 7.3 (P)
▸ly 1981 (P)- Nov. 1982 (T)	...	16	-12.3	-3.0	14.6 (P); 0.0 (T)	7.3 (P); 10.7 (T)

Recessions
Average length: 11.0 mo.
Median length: 10.5 mo.

Industrial production
Average decline: 9.7%
(P-T)
Median decline: 8.7%
(P-T)

Real GNP
Average decline: 2.1%
(P-T)
Median decline: 2.4%
(P-T)

Inflation (change in
percentage points)
(P-T)
Average: -5.4
Median: -4.8

Unemployment rate (change in
percentage points)
(P-T)
Average: 2.9
Median: 3.3

Expansions
Average length: 44.8 mo.
Median length: 38.5 mo.

Industrial production
Average rise: 34.8%
(T-P)
Median rise: 25.6%
(T-P)

Real GNP
Average rise: 20.4%
(T-P)
Median rise: 16.7%
(T-P)

Inflation (change in
percentage points)
(T-P)
Average: 5.4
Median: 4.1

Unemployment rate (change in
percentage points)
(T-P)
Average: -2.0
Median: -2.0

Source: From Otto Eckstein and Allen Sinai, The mechanisms of the business cycle in the postwar era, in Robert J. Gordon, ed., *The American Business Cycle Today: Continuity and Change*, forthcoming, copyright © 1986, The National Bureau of Economic Research. Reprinted with permission of the University of Chicago Press. All rights reserved.
Note: Consumer price index--all urban; annual rate at peak (P) or trough (T); n.a. = not available.

ples of price shocks. Because of the exogenous character of such shocks, they cannot be part of the theory of the business cycle based on endogeneity of the phases of the cycle. What follows are some of these theories.

Is it possible to show in rigorous fashion that one phase of the business cycle must necessarily emerge from the preceding phase? This is the attractiveness of the multiplier-accelerator model (see P. Samuelson 1944:261ff.).

The formal model is constructed from the following four equations:

$$Y_t = C_t + I_t \tag{22.1}$$
$$C_t = a + bY_{t-1} \tag{22.2}$$
$$I_t = \bar{I}_t + I_i \tag{22.3}$$
$$I_i = A(Y_{t-1} - Y_{t-2}) \tag{22.4}$$

Eq. 22.1 states the identity between income (Y) and consumption (C) and investment expenditures (I). Eq. 22.2 describes consumption as a function of lagged income. Eq. 22.3 expresses investment as a function of autonomous investment ($\bar{I}_t$) and induced investment (I_i). Eq. 22.4 expresses induced investment as a function of the change in income one period earlier (because of the Y_{t-2} term, it is called a second-order difference equation). If the following values are substituted, $a = 60$, $b = 8/10$, $\bar{I}_0 = 100$, $\bar{I}_1 = 110$, $A = 1$, Table 22.3 can be constructed.

Table 22.3. The multiplier-accelerator model

Period		Y	C	$\bar{I}$	I_i	I
	0	800	700	100	0	100
	1	810	700	110	0	110
	2	828	708	110	10	120
	3	850.4	722.4	110	18	128
	4	872.72	740.32	110	22.4	132.4
	5	890.50	758.18	110	22.32	132.32
P	6	900.18	772.40	110	17.78	127.78
	7	899.82	780.14	110	9.68	119.68
	8	889.49	779.85	110	-.36	109.64
	9	871.26	771.59	110	-10.33	99.67
	10	848.78	757.01	110	-18.23	91.77
	11	826.55	739.03	110	-22.48	87.52
	12	809.02	721.25	110	-22.23	87.77
T	13	799.70	707.23	110	-17.53	92.47
	14	800.45	699.77	110	-9.32	100.68
	15	811.12	700.37	110	0.75	110.75

Source: Used with permission from Carl A. Dauten and Lloyd M. Valentine, *Business Cycles and Forecasting*, p. 175, copyright © 1978, South-Western Publishing Co., Cincinnati, Ohio.

The cycle is generated by an increase in autonomous investment of 10 in period 1, leading to output (income) of 810 in this period by Eq. 22.1. Consumption (Eq. 22.2) in the third period is 708, based on the constant term of 60 and 80% of previous income of 810. Induced investment rises by 10, reflecting the difference between income in periods 0 and 1. An increase in output means an increase in the desired capital stock, which translates into induced investment in the period. An A value of 1 means that an increase in output of 10 will result in new investment of 10.

The assumed values of 0.8 for the marginal propensity to consume (b) and of 1 for the accelerator (A) produce a cycle. The peak occurs in period 6, the trough in period 13. The cycle does not stop there but repeats itself with slightly smaller swings in successive cycles. The B area in Figure 22.3 shows combinations of the

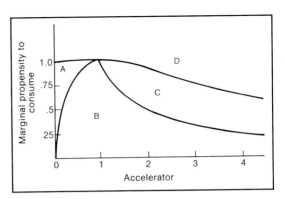

22.3. Model sequence of national income for selected values of marginal propensity to consume (B) and the accelerator (A). (Samuelson 1944:268)

two parameters that produce damped (convergent) cycles including the present values of $A = 1$ and $b = 0.8$. The values in the A area produce a steady (nonfluctuating) movement to a new equilibrium. The C area produces ever-widening cycles; D produces an even more explosive situation. If the accelerator is zero, only the multiplier is operative. In this case, there is a smooth adjustment to a new equilibrium, as shown by the A area.

The search for cause and effect in this model is frustrating. Perhaps the only statement that can be made is that the values are generated by solving a second-order difference equation. For if one blames the recession (the upper turning point) on the decline in induced investment in period 5 (Table 22.3), this decline in turn can be traced to the smaller increase in income from period 3 to 4 as compared with the increase between periods 2 and 3. All that one can say is that the structure of the model and the assumed value of the coefficients dictate the results (Dauten and Valentine 1978:176).

The mathematical model generates too regular a cycle. It must be complicated by introducing decision makers and their strategy. From the standpoint of money and finance, it must bring in the financial constraints affecting transactor behavior.

Investment and the cycle

Variations in investment must be given a key place in explaining the business cycle. The initial cycle in the multiplier-accelerator model (Table 22.3) was set off by an increase in autonomous investment. To understand investment, we must understand the constraining role of finance.

In Chapter 15, investment decisions were made on the basis of the cost of capital and the expected rate of return. An alternative (and equivalent) approach is to feature the demand and supply prices of physical (capital) assets (cf. Minsky 1975: esp. Chs. 4, 5, 6). The advantage is that now the investment decision can be integrated with the financing decision.

The demand price of capital assets is the present value of a prospective investment. Expected returns (as described in Ch. 5) are discounted at the appropriate market rate to yield a present value of the investment. The supply price of capital assets corresponds to the cost of production when financed internally. The supply price (as described below) rises when the capital good is financed externally.

In Figure 22.4, demand and supply prices are measured on the vertical axis; investment (in real units), on the horizontal axis. The dollar value of investment is determined by multiplying the demand price by the amount of investment. The dollar cost is equal to the supply price times investment. The *IF* curve is a rectangular hyperbola, indicating the amount of real investment that can be financed out of internal funds, given varying supply prices of investment goods. (All rectangles inscribed under the rectangular hyperbola have the same area, so they represent the same amount of internal finance.) The intersection of the *IF* curve and the *SP* curve shows that I_1 investment can be financed internally. Beyond I_1, investment must be financed externally. This means greater risk for both lender and borrower. Debt signifies a cash-flow commitment and possible bankruptcy if expectations do not materialize. For the borrower such uncertainty takes the form of progressively lower expected returns. As a result, the *DP* curve takes on a decided negative slope beyond I_1. In the same way, the *SP* curve starts rising beyond I_1. For the lender financing the purchase of capital goods, the effective interest charged goes up with the amount of financing and an increase in the debt/equity ratio. These interest changes are incorporated in the supply price of capital goods.

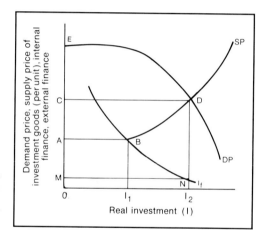

22.4. The investment and its financing. (Adapted from Minsky 1975:108. © 1975. Columbia University Press. By permission.)

The optimal amount of investment occurs when the demand price of investment corresponds to the supply price (at I_2). The amount of external financing is represented by the area *CDNM,* internal financing by MNI_20.

The resulting debt service payments must be met out of cash flows generated by investment. Figure 22.4 does not measure cash inflows; instead, it measures the present value of expected cash flows. This is the area under the *DP* curve (EDI_20). The present value of future debt payments (equals the amount of external financing) is *CDNM*. Equity investment via internal financing is given by MNI_20. Thus the owners enjoy a capital gain (measuring future profits) equal to the area *EDC*. The capital gain takes the form of higher stock market prices. Wall Street's mood becomes optimistic. The perception of risk falls, and both borrower and lender curves (*DP* and *SP*) shift and intersect further to the right than the present intersection. As a consequence the pace of investment quickens. Income expands in accordance with the multiplier-accelerator model. The upswing in investment is validated by rising cash flows. Holders of debt instruments also enjoy capital gains if the market revises its estimate of risk in a downward direction. The capital gain can also be called the net present value of the investment. Stock market valuations relative to the cost of capital goods play an important role in contemporary monetary theory beyond the work of Minsky (1975). Tobin's q-ratio is based on the ratio of market values to the reproduction cost of capital goods. A ratio greater than 1 encourages investment; a ratio less than 1 discourages it (e.g., see Tobin 1969; Ciccolo and Fromm 1980:294ff.). Minsky's discussion goes beyond Tobin's by the explicit introduction of external and internal finance and by the use of the model to explain the business cycle.

But a boom lives a precarious life (Minsky 1975:114). An important reason might be (Eckstein and Sinai, forthcoming) a slowing down of the rate of increase in consumption expenditures (a strategic element in the accelerator relation). Monetary policy could be the crucial factor. It becomes restrictive as the economy heats up (Sinai 1975:7; Eckstein and Sinai, forthcoming). Kindleberger (1978) has taken the Minsky thesis of financial instability (fragility) and illustrated it historically. Speculative excesses are found to be characteristic of the business cycle. They disprove the monetarist argument that markets are rational and that speculation is always stabilizing. Another important finding is that every time the authorities stabilize or control some quantity of M, some new type of money will be developed in response to credit demands. Monetary policy usually affects the household sector first (as discussed in Ch. 2), since corporate business is the favored customer of the banking sector. Despite the slump in housing and slowing of consumption, the corporate sector continues its capital investment programs as it reacts with a lag to previous favorable sales (Sinai 1975:7).

The business sector finds itself in a liquidity squeeze. Because of credit market stringencies, it relies increasingly on short-term borrowing and thus aggravates its repayment problems. Accompanying this increase will be worsening debt-equity ratios and an increase in the debt burden. This is measured by interest payments in relation to income. The effect will be a cutting back in planned investment projects. In terms of Figure 22.4, the demand-price curve shifts downward so that new investment is financed more out of internal funds.

The I_1 amount of investment in Figure 22.5 is now financed out of retained earnings, leaving BCI_1I_2 of such funds to rebuild liquidity. This is the beginning of a debt-deflation process whereby the burden of the debt leads to a reduction in real activity (see Fisher 1933:337ff.). In the Great Depression of the 1930s net investment turned negative. The DP curve fell outside the diagram.

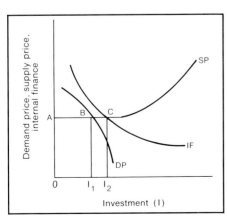

22.5. Downward adjustment in investment.

Liquidity cycle

Changes in liquidity of the household and business sectors over the course of the cycle is a key characteristic of the business cycle. The liquidity cycle consists of four distinct phases (overlapping the five stages of the business cycle discussed earlier): accumulation, precrunch, crunch, and reliquefication. In the accumulation phase, sectors rebuild their stocks of physical and financial assets. Times are booming, with strong consumer spending on housing and durables, followed by an acceleration in the rate of business spending (Sinai 1978:19). External financing requirements are at a minimum. In the precrunch period the credit demands of households, business, and government begin to outstrip available liquidity and external financing sources. The liquidity squeeze manifests itself in reduced expenditures for physical assets and less hiring of labor inputs. The monetary growth rate slows down.

In the crunch stage, sectors scramble for liquidity. Interest yields shoot up, asset holdings are liquidated. Many borrowers are unable to find funds at any price. Five ingredients have been identified: a boom economy with strong demand-side pressures, accelerating inflation, full employment, tight money and disintermediation, and financial instability. Liquid assets are relatively low, debt-service burden is high, and the structure of liabilities is predominantly short term (Sinai 1978:19).

In the final reliquefication stage (the cycle trough) sectors restore their balance sheet strength by restoring liquidity. Expenditures by households and business are reduced, outstanding liabilities are paid off, and financial assets rise sharply. Intermediation is restored, with financial institutions benefiting from high deposit inflows. Monetary policy eases as the central bank tries to stimulate the economy. The key role of the central bank in the business cycle has long been stressed; e.g., see Schumpeter (1964:Ch. 3), Lee (1971:Ch. 9), and Dauten and Valentine (1978:Ch. 6).

Political business cycle

Policymakers orchestrate their reelection by controlling the macroeconomic path of the economy. This is the theory of the political business cycle (Dornbusch and Fischer 1984:491–93). The theory predicts that politicians will use restraint early in an administration, raising unemployment but reducing inflation. With the approach of the four-year presidential election, policies become more expansionary so that unemployment will decline.

The evidence is not very convincing, however. Figure 22.6 plots inflation and unemployment rates in 1969–83. Perhaps the strongest evidence is the behavior of the time series on the eve of the presidential election. Thus unemployment is falling on the threshhold of the 1972, 1976, and (using data beyond Fig. 22.6) 1984 elections. President Reagan in 1984 also had the benefit of a long-run fall in the inflation rate.

The theory must overlook midterm congressional elections where the same motivations should be at work. The president cannot anticipate and prevent large macroshocks like oil prices and war. The independence of the Fed is also challenged in this theory. Chairman Burns indignantly denied that Fed expansionary policy before the 1972 election was politically motivated. His protestations are

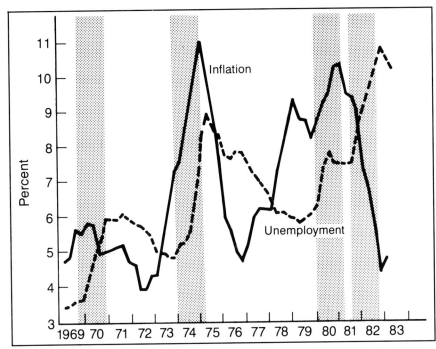

22.6. Inflation and unemployment, 1969–83. Shaded areas indicate recession periods. (Used with permission from Dornbusch and Fischer 1984:555)

supported by a Federal Open-Market Committee member who attended every meeting in 1972 (Morris 1983:142). But administration pressure on the Fed is not unknown (see Ch. 13; Foldessy 1984:26; *New York Times* 1984c:2E).

A more credible interpretation of public policy is that it alternates between control and accommodation. In both instances public policy is endogenous in the sense that it is reacting to the state of the private economy. The central bank plays a schizoid role, bringing on credit crunches in reaction to inflation. Financial deregulation with its velocity effects means that monetary policy has to become ever tighter to be effective (Wojnilower 1980:277–340). Accommodation takes the form of loosening up monetary policy with recession and functioning as a lender of last resort when money-center banks are failing.

The government deficit reflects the state of the economy and to some extent discretionary tax and expenditure policies. In either case the federal government performs a function of lender of last resort. On the basis of Kalecki-type relations, Minsky formulates the following identity (see Kalecki 1971): after-tax profits = investment + government deficit. In this formulation, whenever the deficit explodes (as in the second quarter 1975), the aggregate flow of profits to business increases (Minsky 1980:65). Recessions are mitigated because big government sustains business profits, enabling business to meet its cash flow commitments. This view of policymaking is a far cry from macromanipulation with an eye to the next presidential election.

Summary

The economy is always on the move from one disequilibrium situation to another. There is a certain rhythm to such activity, justifying the term cycle rather than fluctuations. The multiplier-accelerator model is a good beginning point to understanding the cycle, but it is too mechanical. The coefficients that trigger the model are subject to considerable variation because of outside disturbances and financial factors. A theory of investment is advanced that makes explicit the financial constraints of internal and external finance. Variations in cash commitments and cash inflows are the basis for defining the liquidity cycle. Inevitably, the central bank tightens monetary policy in response to inflation and full-employment situations, thus inducing credit crunches. While liquidity cycles can be documented for only the last 30 years, the crucial role of the central bank in business cycles has long been a basic ingredient in business cycle theories.

After precipitating crunches, the central bank is quick to neutralize their effects. Is so doing, it fulfills its function as lender of last resort. The explosion of financial innovation in recent years may have deferred the onset of crunches, but they still persist.

The federal government plays several stabilizing roles, such as maintaining the demand for goods and services and providing default-free liabilities. As a third function, it may also underwrite business profits because of the relation between profits and government deficits. Business is then better able to meet its cash flow commitments.

The political business cycle is a conspiracy theory that is hard to prove.

Review questions

1. In a historical context, what is unique about the behavior of prices since World War II?

2. Is there a business cycle? What is the difference between a cycle and fluctuations?

3. Describe the multiplier-accelerator model.

4. Define the liquidity cycle and relate it to the business cycle.

5. Variations in investment are an important ingredient in business cycle theory. Explain, using the Minsky analysis to show the constraining influence of finance.

6. Do you think there is a political business cycle — a cycle oriented to the next presidential election?

7. "Both the central bank and the U.S. Treasury function as lenders of last resort." Explain this statement.

8. In what sense does central banking display a split personality?

23

The United States in a world economy: The balance of payments

The United States is part of a world economy. The flow-of-funds matrix introduced in Chapter 1 and in greater detail in Chapter 15 contains a rest-of-the-world sector, which covers transactions with the United States by governments, individuals, businesses, and financial institutions in foreign countries. This activity is not coordinated and integrated by a single decision maker as the heading "rest of the world" might imply. In some instances, trade is indeed government controlled. But it is more accurate to think of the rest of the world as inhabited by millions of different transactors.

The rest-of-the-world sector does more than complete the U.S. flow-of-funds statement. Its credits and debits constitute the balance-of-payments statement of the rest of the world vis-à-vis the United States. When this statement is fully spelled out, it contains nonfinancial transactions such as exports and imports.

From the standpoint of the United States, its balance of payments is the same as the rest-of-the-world statement but with the entries reversed. For example, exports of commodities such as wheat from the United States are imports for the rest of the world. On the rest-of-the-world balance-of-payments statement, imports would be a debit; on the U.S. statement the corresponding exports would be a credit. Lending to the rest of the world on the U.S. statement is a debit; borrowing is a credit for the rest of the world.

The U.S. balance of payments is always in the news: the prices of the Organization of Petroleum Exporting Countries (OPEC) are killing the trade balance. The dollar is low; the dollar is high. Import quotas are necessary if the steel and automobile industries are to survive. The trade deficit set new records. Such are the daily news stories. Basic to an understanding of these headlines is an understanding of the balance of payments. We begin with some identities that link the domestic economy to the rest of world.

Table 23.1 presents a two-sector matrix with three transaction categories. The domestic economy has been consolidated into a single sector to highlight its relationship with the rest of the world.

Table 23.1. A two-sector flow-of-funds matrix

Transactions	Domestic (U.S.) sector		Rest-of-the world (foreign) sector	
	Debit	Credit	Debit	Credit
Nonfinancial	UD_1	UC_1	FD_1	FC_1
Financial claims	UD_2	UC_2	FD_2	FC_2
Monetary	UD_3	UC_3	FD_3	FC_3
	$\Sigma UD_{1,2,3}$	$\Sigma UC_{1,2,3}$	$\Sigma FD_{1,2,3}$	$\Sigma FC_{1,2,3}$

In each transaction row total credits equal total debits. That is,

$$UD_1 + FD_1 = UC_1 + FC_1$$
$$UD_2 + FD_2 = UC_2 + FC_2$$
$$UD_3 + FD_3 = UC_3 + FC_3$$

The nonfinancial market summarizes all transactions in goods and services. The financial claims or bond market summarizes all financial transactions. The money market summarizes increases (dr) or decreases in money holdings (cr). New money creation would also be on the credit side. Suppose that nonfinancial credits for the domestic sector exceed nonfinancial debits ($UC_1 > UD_1$). This can only mean that imports by the rest of the world exceed their exports: $UC_1 - UD_1 = FD_1 - FC_1$. Similarly, if U.S. borrowing exceeds U.S. lending ($UC_2 > UD_2$), foreign lending to the United States must exceed foreign borrowing: $UC_2 - UD_2 = FD_2 - FC_2$. The underlying identity between total sector credits and debits means that if credits on the first two lines exceed debits for the United States, with the reverse being true for the rest of the world, money holdings for the domestic sector will increase on balance and go down for the rest of the world: $UD_3 - UC_3 = FC_3 - FD_3$.

INTERNAL AND EXTERNAL EQUILIBRIUM   The concern of policymakers is with internal and external equilibrium. Internal equilibrium (the subject matter of earlier chapters) can be defined in terms of the nonfinancial row of the matrix. When planned demand for U.S. output equals the planned supply, internal balance is obtained. This can be defined as $UC_1 = UD_1 + (FD_1 - FC_1)$. Total planned sales ($UC_1$) equal the domestic demand for output (UD_1) plus net U.S. exports ($FD_1 - FC_1$). Domestic demand includes imports. The resultant overestimate of demand satisfied by domestic output is offset by subtracting U.S. imports (FC_1) from U.S. exports (FD_1).

External equilibrium is a more controversial concept. The focus might be on nonfinancial transactions, with an even balance of trade being the criterion ($FD_1 = FC_1$). Or the focus might be on the basic balance (the first two rows). In this case, external equilibrium is defined as $FD_1 + FD_2 = FC_1 + FC_2$. There is no problem with external equilibrium (it always exists) if now the money row is included. Total sector debits must equal total sector credits.

National policymakers are not consistent in their external goals. One country (e.g., U.S. in Table 23.1) may wish to have a favorable balance of trade, i.e., exports to exceed imports ($FD_1 > FC_1$) and capital outflows to exceed capital inflows ($FC_2 > FD_2$). While this is consistent with equilibrium in the basic balance for a single country, it will conflict with similar policies by the rest of the world aiming at an export surplus and net capital outflows. External disequilibrium has its roots in such conflicting objectives.

A more detailed look at the balance of payments will clarify the notions of deficit and surplus. It is a question of where we draw the line through the balance-of-payments statement.

Drawing the line through the balance of payments

We illustrate the meaning of above and below the line in Table 23.2. (Remember: we are now looking at the rest-of-the-world sector from the standpoint of the United States, i.e., what is a credit in the rest-of-the-world sector, such as its exports, will now be a debit for the United States, its imports.)

Table 23.2. Simplified U.S. balance-of-payments statement illustrating "above the line" and "below the line" concepts

Debit		Credit	
Imports	$100	Exports	$150
Current account totals	100		150
Current account balance[a]	[50]		
Long-term capital outflows	150	Long-term capital inflows	75
Basic account totals	$250		$225
		Basic balance[a]	[25]
Nonliquid short-term outflows	40	Nonliquid short-term inflows	30
Net liquidity account totals	$290		$255
		Net liquidity balance[a]	[35]
Increase in liquid claims on foreigners	30	Increase in liquid liabilities to foreigners	45
Official settlements account totals	$320		$300
		Official settlements balance[a]	[20]
Increase in U.S. reserve assets (gold, SDRs convertible currencies, gold holdings in IMF)	40	Increase in liabilities to foreign official holders	60
Total	$360		$360

[a]Balancing items not counted in totals.

Using imaginary numbers throughout and a limited number of transaction entries, the first line we draw is below exports and imports. Exports exceed imports by $50. This means that the balancing amount that makes debits equal to credits must be entered on the debit side. We call this first balancing amount the current account balance. (The balancing items themselves are not included when we cumulate debit and credit transactions.) When the balancing item is recorded on the debit side of the balance-of-payments account, it signifies that the balance of payments is in surplus. When the balancing item is entered on the credit side, it signifies a deficit in the balance of payments.

We next draw the line below long-term flows. These refer to investments made here by foreigners and investments made by U.S. nationals abroad. Capital flows are outflows when we invest abroad and inflows when foreigners invest here. They include investment in securities (paper claims) plus direct investment, i.e., foreigners building or buying branch plants here or Americans building or buying branch plants abroad. The second balancing item is called the basic balance. Since capital outflows exceed capital inflows ($150 − $75) by more than exports exceeded imports ($150 − $100), total debits exceed total credits and the basic balance indicates a deficit of $25.

Adding on short-term capital flows such as bank loans increases the deficit. Measuring this deficit is the balancing item net liquidity balance. This is because short-term capital outflows (debits) are assumed to exceed capital inflows (credits) by 10 (40 − 30) so that the net liquidity balance shows a value of $35, i.e., $10 larger than the basic balance. The final balancing item is the official settlements balance. This is determined by considering changes in liquid liabilities to foreigners (such as demand deposits in U.S. banks) and similar U.S. claims abroad. Because the increase in liabilities exceeds claims (credits exceed debits), when these transactions are added on to the previous entries, a deficit still exists but is now reduced by $15–$20. (The conventional terminology used for the balancing items is confusing. The first two, balance in the current account and basic balance, have reference to transactions recorded above the balancing item. However, the remaining terms, net liquidity balance and official settlements balance, have reference to transactions below the balancing item.)

Up to the official settlements balance, debits exceed credits by $20. This means that the remaining credit transactions must exceed the remaining debit transactions by 20, since overall total credits must equal total debits. So we see that the increase in liabilities to foreign official holders (e.g., foreign central banks) of $60 is greater than the increase in U.S. reserve assets − gold, special drawing rights (SDRs), etc. − of $40 by $20. Total debits cumulate to $360, equaling total credits of $360.

U.S. international transactions

The statistical data for the balance of payments is presented in a different form from the previous hypothetical table. Government recognition of the arbitrariness in drawing the line and establishing balancing items is a principal reason (for a discussion of this new format, see Stern et al. 1978:439ff.). The data in Table 23.3 are presented in single-column form, with credits being positive and debits negative. In 1983, merchandise exports (credits) were $200.3 bil. (line 4) and imports (debits) were $261.3 bil. (line 5). The balance on current account (line 1) includes military transactions, investment income, other service transactions, remittances, and U.S. government grants (lines 6, 7, 8, 9, 10). Residents of the United States receive interest and dividends from financial investments abroad. Since investment income is shown net, the receipts of the rest of the world from U.S. investments have been offset against U.S. income. Other service transactions reflect a variety of transactions such as tourist travel, or international freight shipments. Again, foreign receipts from U.S. tourists or from the use of ships to transport U.S. goods are offset against U.S. receipts. Remittances, pensions, and other transfers (line 9) along with government grants (line 10) are called unilateral transfers; no current economic service is rendered in return for such payments. They are debits because they are expense items. Alternatively (in the case of government transfers), they add to intangible assets, presumably creating goodwill.

Table 23.3. U.S. international transactions summary

Item credits (+) or debits (-)	1981	1982	1983
		($ mil.)	
1 Balance on current account	6,294	-9,199	-41,563
2 Not seasonally adjusted	...	...	...
3 Merchandise trade balance[a]	-28,001	-36,469	-61,055
4 Merchandise exports	237,085	211,198	200,257
5 Merchandise imports	-265,086	-247,667	-261,312
6 Military transactions, net	-1,116	195	515
7 Investment income, net[b]	34,053	27,802	23,508
8 Other service transactions, net	8,191	7,331	4,121
9 Remittances, pensions, and other transfers	-2,382	-2,635	-2,590
10 U.S. government grants (excluding military)	-4,451	-5,423	-6,060
11 Change in U.S. government assets, other than official reserve assets, net (increase, -)	-5,107	-6,143	-5,013
12 Change in U.S. official reserve assets (increase, -)	-5,175	-4,965	-1,196
13 Gold	0	0	0
14 Special drawing rights	-1,823	-1,371	-66
15 Reserve position in IMF	-2,491	-2,552	-4,434
16 Foreign currencies	-861	-1,041	3,304
17 Change in U.S. private assets abroad (increase, -)[b]	-100,694	-107,790	-43,281
18 Bank-reported claims	-84,175	-111,070	-25,391
19 Nonbank-reported claims	-1,181	6,626	-5,333
20 U.S. purchase of foreign securities, net	-5,714	-8,102	-7,676
21 U.S. direct investments abroad, net[b]	-9,624	4,756	-4,881
22 Change in foreign official assets in the United States (increase, +)	5,003	3,318	5,339
23 Treasury securities	5,019	5,728	6,989
24 Other U.S. government obligations	1,289	-694	-487
25 Other U.S. government liabilities[c]	-300	382	199
26 Other U.S. liabilities reported by U.S. banks	-3,670	-1,747	433
27 Other foreign official assets[d]	2,665	-351	-1,795
28 Change in foreign private assets in the United States (increase, +)[b]	76,310	91,863	76,383
29 U.S. bank-reported liabilities	42,128	65,922	49,059
30 U.S. nonbank-reported liabilities	917	-2,383	-1,318
31 Foreign private purchases of Treasury securities, net	2,946	7,062	8,731
32 Foreign purchases of other U.S. securities, net	7,171	6,396	8,612
33 Foreign direct investments in the United States, net[b]	23,148	14,865	11,299
34 Allocation of SDRs	1,093	0	0
35 Discrepancy	22,275	32,916	9,331
36 Owing to seasonal adjustments	...	...	...
37 Statistical discrepancy in recorded data before seasonal adjustment	22,275	32,916	9,331
Memo:			
Changes in official assets			
38 U.S. official reserve assets (increase, -)	-5,175	-4,965	-1,196
39 Foreign official assets in the United States (increase, +)	5,303	2,936	5,140
40 Change in OPEC official assets in the United States (part of line 22 above)	13,581	7,291	-8,639
41 Transfers under military grant programs (excluded from lines 4, 6, and 10 above)	675	593	205

Source: *Fed. Res. Bull.* 1984f:A50.
[a]Data are on an international accounts basis. Military exports are excluded from merchandise data and are included in line 6.
[b]Includes reinvested earnings.
[c]Primarily associated with military sales contracts and other transactions arranged with or through foreign official agencies.
[d]Consists of investments in U.S. corporate stocks and in debt securities of private corporations and state and local governments.

Instead of the liquid-illiquid breakdown of Table 23.2, a private vs. government ownership distinction is applied to financial flows. As a result, it is difficult to identify the means-of-payment side of balance-of-payment transactions. The United States can make payment by running down liquid assets abroad (included in line 18) or increasing dollar liabilities to foreigners (line 29). Similarly, foreigners settle by running down their liquid claims (line 29) or increasing liabilities to the United States (line 18). Checking accounts at any given time are a small part of U.S. assets abroad or foreign liquid assets here. Any increase in cash is quickly converted into interest-bearing investments that can be liquidated when cash balances must be built up.

The official settlements balance corresponds to the difference between change in U.S. official reserve assets (line 12) and change in foreign official assets in the United States (line 22). In 1983 the balance equaled $4.1 bil. If we single out the official settlements balance as the proper place to draw the line, the United States had a deficit of this amount in its balance of payments in 1983. This means that the United States had more debit transactions (e.g., imports and capital investments abroad) above the line than it had credit transactions (exports and foreign investments in the United States) and settled the difference principally by selling government securities to foreign governments (lines 23, 24). Below the line, credits exceeded debits. Both the U.S. budget deficit and the deficit in the balance of payments are financed this way by foreign purchases of U.S. government debt. In contrast, the surplus in the official settlements balance in 1979 of $14.7 bil. can be explained by official foreign holders selling off $22 bil. of U.S. Treasury securities (*Fed. Res. Bull.* 1982:A54). The excess of debits over credits below the line corresponds to an excess of credits over debits above the line in 1979. One major factor was the large amount of bank-reported liabilities in that year.

The SDRs appear both as a component of official U.S. reserve assets (line 14) and in a separate allocation (line 34). The International Monetary Fund hands out these "poker chips" to member countries, and they show up on line 34 as an allocation to the United States (credit). Simultaneously, the increased holdings appear as debits in line 14. When the United States disposes of them to other countries, SDRs are credited on this line.

The large statistical discrepancy as high as $32.9 bil. in 1982 (line 37) casts doubt on the accuracy of the balance-of-payments data. Since the discrepancy is a credit, its value indicates that recorded debits exceed recorded credits. The discrepancy results from international transactions going unreported and valuation mistakes. Purchases and sales of short-term financial claims go unreported. Errors and omissions arise, for example, from differences in the export documentation and the amount eventually paid by the foreign importer (Fieleke 1976:10–11). Bank reports of decrease in U.S. short-term liabilities (a debit) then differ from the credit to merchandise exports. The official assets balance is the one balance free from error, since it is based on correct below the line figures. Statistical discrepancy reconciles the imbalance of credits and debits above the official settlements line with the imbalance below the line.

Line 40 (a memo item) is noteworthy because it shows how much of OPEC oil revenues results in claims on the United States. The figures show a sharp change between 1981 when OPEC assets increased by $13.6 bil. and 1983 when they declined by $8.6 bil.

CAPITAL MOBILITY   Money can be transferred in a matter of seconds from one financial center to another at opposite ends of the globe. Financial transactions in the balance of payments are the outcome of choices between domestic and foreign markets. Currency substitution makes portfolio diversification possible so that a given expected return will be associated with a lower degree of risk. Foreign assets may be held in checkable deposit form for payment purposes (this is the strict meaning of currency substitution), or they may be held in a wide spectrum of interest-bearing assets (portfolio diversification). The internationalization of capital markets has proceeded at a rapid pace in the postwar period with the relaxation of domestic controls over foreign payments. The resultant mobility of capital might have been expected to eliminate international differences in nominal interest rates. This does not necessarily follow, however. Reasons include differences in asset risk and exchange rate expectations (Levich and Hawkins 1981:402; Dornbusch and Fischer 1984:682–86). Expectations, for example, of depreciation of the foreign currency at the time of repatriation of the foreign investment will make for higher foreign interest rates. Relative inflation rates may be behind expectations. When interest rates are "covered" for future depreciation and assets have comparable risk (e.g., Canadian and U.S. commercial paper), evidence is that rates do move in tandem, although a small differential still exists (Dornbusch and Fischer 1984:549–51).

Where to draw the line

How do we choose among the various balancing entries for *the* measure of deficit or surplus? A favorable balance of trade has been a national policy goal since the British mercantilists of the seventeenth century. More exports than imports meant more incoming gold, the mark of economic power. The same sentiment exists today, not for gold's sake, but to increase gross national product (GNP) via the component of net exports of goods and services.

A broader yardstick for drawing the line is whether an entry is autonomous or accommodative. An autonomous entry records a planned transaction. An accommodative entry records a balancing item, e.g., when foreign checking accounts go up in the United States because this is the way that exports to the United States are paid for.

A strong argument can be made for considering long-term capital flows as autonomous flows similar to goods and services. From this point of view, the basic balance becomes the preferred balance. A surplus is an excess of credits in the basic account. From this standpoint, the United States is just as well off if foreign investment is made here as if it sells more goods abroad. But one can go further and include short-term capital flows. Illiquid short-term flows can be treated in the same way as long-term flows. But what about liquid short-term claims. Do they have a strictly means-of-payment character? This may not be so. If the U.S. dollar serves as the international medium of exchange, increases in foreign holdings of the dollar may be planned increases; U.S. short-term liquid liabilities in this case are as much of an export as coal and airplanes.

Indeed, the United States has been most fortunate in the postwar period ever since a dollar surplus superseded a dollar shortage. From the standpoint of welfare (if not the size of the GNP) the U.S. situation improved. For now we paid for imports and foreign investments in a costless way — by creating paper claims against ourselves. The rub comes, however, when the rest of the world feels oversupplied with dollars. Flexible exchange rates replace fixed exchange rates. Potential pressure on the U.S. dollar means a depreciation in the rate of exchange (to be discussed in Ch. 24), which means a higher cost of imports.

This brings us to the official settlements balance. Perhaps the strongest case can be made here that such transactions are accommodative. An excess of debits over credits above the line suggests that foreign central banks are deliberately adding to their assets to stabilize foreign exchange rates. But this balance may also include autonomous transactions, e.g., official OPEC reserves may largely represent investment decisions based on considerations of income, liquidity, and risk rather than exchange stabilization (Kemp 1975:21).

MONETARY APPROACH   The official settlements balance (Table 23.4) has another argument in its favor. It comes closest to a money account balance, summarizing the international transactions that affect the monetary base. Those who take the monetary approach to the balance of payments disdain deficit-surplus concepts. Instead, the preferred balance-of-payments concept is one that summarizes transactions affecting domestic and foreign money supplies (Kemp 1975:17).

Conventional analysis according to the monetary approach fails to see deficits and surpluses as symptoms of monetary imbalance. An increase in the money stock in country A results in an excess supply of money. This leads to an increase in demand for goods, services, and securities. Prices rise in country A for domestic real and financial assets relative to foreign prices. As a result, spending on foreign real and financial assets increases. Debit entries above the official settlements line exceed credit entries. The official settlements account then records the imbalance.

Not all the entries in the U.S. official settlements account correspond to a money account. The test is whether transactions affect the U.S. monetary base. All the debit entries are factors supplying reserves, so they qualify. On the other hand, only one slight component of other U.S. liabilities reported by U.S. banks (Table 23.3, l. 26) would be a factor absorbing reserves, i.e., foreign official accounts in Federal Reserve Banks. (Such deposits amounted to only $242 mil. at the end of August 1984.)

Table 23.4. Official settlements account (United States)	
Change in U.S. official reserve assets (debit)	Change in foreign official assets in the United States (credit)
Gold	Treasury securities
Special drawing rights	Other U.S. government obligations
Reserve position in IMF	Other U.S. government liabilities
Foreign currencies	Other U.S. liabilities reported by U.S. banks
	Other

From the perspective of a "reserve currency" country such as the United States the money account would not be very significant. Moreover, by means of open-market operations the Fed can offset their effects. From the standpoint of the rest of the world, however, it is quite a different matter; for changes in official claims on the United States are factors supplying reserves in foreign countries. The customers of foreign commercial banks convert their dollar claims into local currencies. Their banks in turn convert dollar foreign exchange into reserves at the central bank. The central bank acquires interest-bearing assets with its foreign deposits at the Fed. The upshot of this sequence is that U.S. balance-of-payments deficits bear a good deal of responsibility for foreign inflation.

The significance of the monetary approach is that it has influenced the lending activities of the International Monetary Fund (IMF) (Dornbusch and Fischer

1984:639–42). A balance sheet identity for foreign central banks can be written simply as $\Delta NFA = \Delta H - \Delta DC$, where NFA = net foreign assets (an asset item on the balance sheet), H = high-powered money (a liability item), and DC = domestic credit (an asset item). NFA constitutes a summary of the official settlements balance from the standpoint of the foreign country. The IMF, in arranging stabilization packages (see Ch. 24), sets the ΔNFA target (in effect the permissible balance-of-payments deficit) and also determines the appropriate money stock based on ΔH and the money multiplier. Once these two variables are set, the tolerable expansion in net domestic credit (DC) is automatically determined.

The problem with the monetary approach is that it makes the money market the key in explaining external disequilibrium. The metamorphosis in the U.S. balance of payments since World War II (to which we now turn) may be better explained by above-the-line developments in the current and capital accounts.

A long-term perspective

Studying the U.S. balance of payments over a long stretch of time indicates some significant shifts. For this purpose the focus should be on the net exports of goods and services (lines 3 + 6 + 7 + 8 of Table 23.3), net financial transfers (lines 9 + 10 + 17 + 28 + 35), and official reserve transactions (lines 12 + 22). As can be seen from Figure 23.1, until recently the U.S. acquisition of

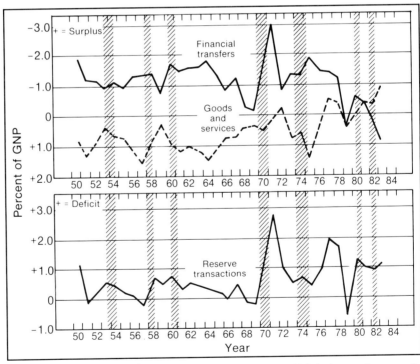

23.1. Cyclical movements in the U.S. balance of payments, 1950–79. Shaded areas indicate recession periods. (Clarke 1980:24)

foreign assets has exceeded foreign acquisition of U.S. assets. This is shown by the curve for financial transfers being most of the time in the negative part of the upper diagram. (In accordance with Table 23.3 increases in U.S. assets have minus signs, foreign acquisitions have plus signs; i.e., debits are recorded with a minus sign, credits with a plus sign.) The flows in Figure 23.1 are expressed as a percent of GNP, providing a comparison with economic activity as a whole. The statistical discrepancy in the balance of payments is included in financial transfers (see Clarke 1980:Table 1.24).

In recent years the sign of financial transfers has more largely turned positive, with 1983 being marked by a flood of foreign investment. By the end of 1983 the United States was on the verge of becoming a debtor nation. The total assets of the foreign sector were $572.6 bil. as opposed to liabilities to the United States of $580.5 bil. (FRB 1984b:12). The goods and services line has followed an opposite path to financial transfers, with the average annual surplus declining to 0.3% of the GNP, 1975–79, from almost 1% in the 1950s and 1960s (Clarke 1980:25). In 1983 the dwindling surpluses became a resounding deficit of $33 bil. The worsening merchandise trade balance ($61 bil., line 3, Table 23.3) was no longer offset by rising net investment and service income (lines 7 and 8). The deficit in goods and services in 1983 amounts to 1% of the GNP in that year. Projections are that the United States will owe the world a net $357 bil. at the end of 1987 (Sterngold 1984:F24).

The progressive weakness of the merchandise trade balance has many explanations. These include more rapid growth and technological advance abroad based on higher investment rates; the exchange rate structure; import prices rising more rapidly than export prices; and increased dependence on imported raw materials, particularly petroleum (Hawkins and Levich 1981:126). The dramatic differences in investment rates for both industrial and developing countries in comparison with the United States can be seen in Table 23.5. In more recent years the high value of the U.S. dollar in relation to other currencies has been a major factor.

An excess of financial transfers over net exports of goods and services represents the transfer gap and is balanced by official reserve transactions. When the 1950s and 1960s are compared with the 1970s, the average for the transfer gap has risen from 0.25% to over 1% of GNP (Clarke 1980:24). The transfer gap has become less important in recent years, with the highest figure for reserve transactions being 0.12% of the GNP in 1983 (Fig. 23.1).

By plotting periods of recession, Figure 23.1 indicates cyclical movements in the balance of payments. In periods of monetary stringency prior to recessions, net financial outflows fall (interest rates rise in the United States relative to foreign rates). As can be seen in Figure 23.1 there are five occasions when net reserve transactions are negative, indicating a surplus in the official settlements account. Despite the flood of foreign investment in 1983, the transfer gap was still positive because of the huge trade deficit.

U.S. FINANCIAL STRENGTH   The paradox is that the decline in the U.S. creditor status has turned out to be a measure of U.S. financial strength. The foreign exchange value of the dollar has reached new highs (see Ch. 24). This demonstrates that the foreign supply of credit to the United States has shifted to the right

Table 23.5. Gross domestic investment in selected countries (as percentage of gross domestic product)

Country	1960	1976	1977	1978	1979	1980	1981	1982	1983
Industrial countries									
France	24	23	24	21	21	22	21	21	16
Germany	27	24	22	21	22	23	22	20	20
Italy	24	18	21	19	19	20	20	19	18
Japan	34	33	32	31	32	32	31	30	28
United Kingdom	19	17	19	18	18	17	15	15	15
United States	18	16	18	19	20	18	18	17	17
Developing countries									
Brazil	22	26	22	21	20	21	19	19	18
Egypt	13	24	24	27	27	31	26	23	24
India	17	19	21	19	19	19	20	20	20
Korea, Republic of	11	25	26	30	32	32	27	28	29
Mexico	20	26	20	21	23	24	26	23	21
Philippines	16	31	30	24	26	25	26	25	24
Spain	21	24	23	20	19	19	20	19	19
Taiwan	20	28	27	26	29	31	28	26	23

Source: Clarke 1980:30 (for 1960, 1976, 1977); 1978-83: Bus. Int. Corp.

rather than the U.S. demand for credit. (If the United States took the initiative in seeking foreign credit, the exchange rate would have depreciated instead of appreciating.)

Another measure of financial strength is the heavy dependence of the world economy on dollar financing. Almost three-fourths of the world's financing (bank loans and bonds) is denominated in dollars (information supplied by Norman Klath, Morgan Guaranty Trust Co., Nov. 9, 1984).

The efficiency of the world financial system may in large part be due to the dollar providing an international medium of exchange. The oil shock of 1974–76 is an outstanding example of the channeling of funds from surplus to deficit sectors via U.S. and Eurodollar deposits. With the quadrupling of oil prices in 1973, OPEC nations found themselves with enormous surplus revenues. Banks gaining OPEC deposits increased their syndicate loans to deficit countries. In the period 1974–80 the nonoil-producing less developed countries had cumulative current account deficits of 210 bil. U. S. dollars and borrowed a net total of $93 bil. from Eurocurrency banks. Over the same period the OPEC countries invested $82 bil. in these same banks (N. Cameron 1984:600).

Table 23.6 shows how petrodollars were parceled out between deposits and nonbank investments. The liquidation of assets in 1983 is a commentary on the current account deficits of OPEC countries, a possibility that would not have been dreamed of a decade earlier.

Table 23.6. Parceling out the petrodollars

Funds	1974	1980	1981	1982	1983	End 1983 level
			($ bil.)			
Identified financial surplus	56.0	87.4	48.3	1.6	-18.7	345.5
Deposits in banks	28.7	41.2	1.1	-16.0	-13.2	123.5
United States (domestic)[a]	4.2	-1.2	-2.1	4.7	0.7	17.6
United Kingdom (sterling)	1.7	1.4	0.5	1.2	0.4	5.4
Eurocurrency and other	22.8	41.0	2.7	-21.9	-14.3	100.5
U.S. bank foreign branches	n.a.	0.8	-2.8	-6.4	-2.0	18.8
Other investments	27.3	46.2	47.2	17.6	-5.5	222.0
United States (domestic)[a]	7.3	16.2	17.0	5.4	-9.2	68.1
Portfolio[b]	6.6	14.3	15.0	6.8	-8.6	54.3
Other[c]	0.7	1.9	2.0	-1.4	-0.6	13.8
United Kingdom	5.5	1.4	1.1	-0.5	-0.3	7.4
Other industrial countries[d]	11.0	17.0	19.5	6.7	-1.3	125.4
Loans to LDCs		6.7	7.2	3.9	1.1	
International organizations and gold	3.5	4.9	2.4	2.1	4.2	21.1

Source: Ghalib 1984:7.
Note: n.a. = not available.
[a]Includes investments by Bahrain and Oman.
[b]Includes Treasury bills and bonds, federal agency bonds, corporate bonds and stocks.
[c]Includes direct U.S. investment, prepayment for U.S. military exports, and nonbank liabilities.
[d]Before 1979, LDC loans were not reported separately.

The international payments mechanism is seen to work through checking accounts, just as for domestic payments. A groundless fear was that OPEC surpluses would disappear from the financial system, driving oil-importing countries to financial panic and bankruptcy (Fieleke 1974:51). Horvitz (1979:569) has amusingly spoken of neat stacks of $100 bills being placed in attaché cases and carried off to the desert by Arab sheiks.

Financing U.S. investment

Paradoxically, the U.S. deficit in goods and services may have helped to finance domestic investment (capital expenditures) and the government deficit. The identity for saving and nonfinancial investment (see the top rows in Table 1.5 or Table 15.1) is based on the following national income identity:

$$I + G + X = S + T + M$$

where I = domestic investment
G = government expenditures
T = taxes
S = domestic saving
X = U.S. exports of goods and services (current account)
M = U.S. imports (current account)

This is converted into a saving-investment statement, using $G - T$ = government deficit (S_g) and $M - X$ = rest-of-the-world saving (S_{row}). Thus $I - S + S_g = S_{row}$. An excess of domestic investment over domestic saving plus the government deficit are both financed by S_{row}.

This is the common interpretation of the national income identity when suitably arranged (see, e.g., Krugman 1983). But the identity tells us nothing about causality, which can be interpreted as running in the opposite direction.

The accounting matrix of Table 1.5 or Table 15.1 illustrates the possibilities of two-way causality. With net financial investment as the bridge between the financial and nonfinancial rows, rest-of-the-world saving can be determined from the "bottom up" via financial debits and credits (capital flows), or capital flows can be determined from the "top down" by the current account balance (gross saving). According to the "bottom up" theory an increase in the U.S. government deficit (as discussed in Ch. 24) puts pressure on interest rates and attracts an inflow of foreign investment. Nonresidents sell off local assets and buy dollars. The dollar appreciates vis-à-vis foreign currencies. The strong dollar leads to an excess of U.S. imports and corresponding amounts of gross saving for the rest of the world. This is the causal sequence for the "bottom up" interpretation. It is supported when the dollar appreciates in value. If an increase in imports (top-down theory) was directly responsible for rest-of-the-world saving, the evidence would have to be depreciation in the value of the dollar. Whatever the propelling force, the exchange rate as discussed in Chapter 24 plays a critical role in adjusting trade and capital flows. (The word adjustment occurs frequently in discussions of an open economy, affirming the persistence of external disequilibrium.)

Summary

This chapter moves the analysis from a closed to an open economy. The objective of external equilibrium must now be added to internal equilibrium as a goal of monetary policy. A simplified two-sector matrix demonstrates the conditions for the equilibria. While internal equilibrium has an unequivocal meaning (under simplified assumptions), external equilibrium is more ambiguous. The definition depends on a detailed study of the U.S. balance of payments. This statement is anticipated in Chapter 1 when the rest-of-the-world sector is introduced. The U.S. balance of payments is the mirror image of this statement.

A pro forma balance-of-payments statement shows the different ways that a line can be drawn to generate deficits or surpluses. The actual balance-of-payments statement (called a statement of international transactions) follows. The criteria for drawing the line are posed, and it is suggested that drawing the line as far down in the statement as possible makes the most sense. This points to the official settlements balance. The items constituting this balance approximate the monetary account, which summarizes international influences on the monetary base.

Historical developments since World War I show a dramatic increase in the transfer gap. This growing gap signifies the failure of net exports of goods and services to pay for net financial investment abroad. Behind this failure lie many factors such as more rapid technological advances abroad, oil shocks, and the exchange rate structure. National efforts to handle deficits are the topic of Chapter 24.

Review questions

1. Why is it necessary to have a "rest-of-the-world" sector to complete the U.S. flow-of-funds matrix?

2. What is the relation between the U.S. balance of payments and the rest-of-the-world sector in the flow of funds?

3. Distinguish between internal and external equilibrium.

4. Why is there a problem in defining a country's balance-of-payments surplus or deficit? Your answer should indicate an understanding of the anatomy of the balance-of-payments statement and the problem of drawing the line.

5. Describe the monetary approach to the balance of payments. Contrast this approach with approaches that emphasize above-the-line transactions.

6. Define the transfer gap and explain its determination. How has it changed over time? Can you detect an oncoming recession through changes in the transfer gap?

7. Why has the U.S. balance of trade weakened over the last 15 years?

8. How does the hypothetical balance-of-payments statement of this chapter differ from the Fed's table of international transactions?

9. "The U.S. deficit on goods and services accounts helps to finance domestic investment and the government deficit." Explain this statement. Is it possible to reverse this reasoning and say that capital inflows are responsible for the trade deficit?

The United States in a world economy: Dealing with a deficit

Now that the balance of payments has been introduced and deficits defined, our interest is in policy. The appropriate framework is the foreign exchange market because international transactions and foreign exchange rates are both represented there.

Policymaking aims at affecting the foreign exchange market in a way that is consistent with internal equilibrium. So internal and external equilibrium must be achieved simultaneously. Foreign exchange rates, interest rates, and monetary and fiscal policy are among the policy instruments. Depending on whether capital flows are interest sensitive or whether flexible or fixed exchange rates are assumed, the desired aggregate demand effects can be better attained by either monetary or fiscal policy.

International monetary cooperation is shown to be an inevitable outcome of mutually inconsistent (and destructive) national policies. The events of the last decade also make it clear that international organizations must keep up with changing times. Oil shocks are one of the more dramatic of these changes. Finally, the United States, with its economic regions, can be viewed as a microcosm of the world economy.

Foreign exchange rates

The exchange rate is the price of a unit of foreign money; e.g., if it takes $.3916 to buy the German deutsche mark, this is the foreign exchange rate between the United States and Germany. Exchange rates are given for a number of countries in Table 24.1. Before 1982 the *Federal Reserve Bulletin* presented exchange rates as they were previously defined in terms of the amount of U.S. dollars equal to a unit of foreign money. Table 24.1 shows how many foreign currency units a U.S. dollar will buy (except for selected countries). The current format is more

Table 24.1. Foreign exchange rates (currency units per dollar)

Country/currency	1981	1982	1983
1 Australia/dollar[a]	114.95	101.65	90.14
2 Austria/schilling	15.948	17.060	17.968
3 Belgium/franc	37.194	45.780	51.121
4 Brazil/cruzeiro	92.374	179.22	573.27
5 Canada/dollar	1.1990	1.2344	1.2325
6 China, P.R./yuan	1.7031	1.8978	1.9809
7 Denmark/krone	7.1350	8.3443	9.1483
8 Finland/markka	4.3128	4.8086	5.5636
9 France/franc	5.4396	6.5793	7.6203
10 Germany/deutsche mark	2.2631	2.428	2.5539
11 Greece/drachma	n.a.	66.872	87.895
12 Hong Kong/dollar	5.5678	6.0697	7.2569
13 India/rupee	8.6807	9.4846	10.1040
14 Ireland/pound[a]	161.32	142.05	124.81
15 Israel/shekel	n.a.	24.407	55.865
16 Italy/lira	1138.60	1354.00	1519.30
17 Japan/yen	220.63	249.06	237.55
18 Malaysia/ringgit	2.3048	2.3395	2.3204
19 Mexico/peso	24.547	72.990	155.01
20 Netherlands/guilder	2.4998	2.6719	2.8543
21 New Zealand/dollar[a]	86.848	75.101	66.790
22 Norway/krone	5.7430	6.4567	7.3012
23 Philippines/peso	7.8113	8.5324	11.0940
24 Portugal/escudo	61.739	80.101	111.610
25 Singapore/dollar	2.1053	2.1406	2.1136
26 South Africa/rand[a]	114.77	92.297	89.85
27 South Korea/won	n.a.	731.93	776.04
28 Spain/peseta	92.396	110.09	143.500
29 Sri Lanka/rupee	18.967	20.756	23.510
30 Sweden/krona	5.0659	6.2838	7.6717
31 Switzerland/franc	1.9674	2.0327	2.1006
32 Taiwan/dollar	n.a.	n.a.	n.a.
33 Thailand/baht	21.731	23.014	22.991
34 United Kingdom/pound[a]	202.43	174.80	151.59
35 Venezuela/bolivar	4.2781	4.2981	10.6840
Memo:			
United States/dollar[b]	102.94	116.57	125.34

Source: *Fed. Res. Bull.* 1984g:A68.
Note: Averages of certified noon buying rates in New York for cable transfers. n.a. = not available.
[a]Value in U.S. cents.
[b]Index of weighted-average exchange value of U.S. dollar against currencies of other G-10 countries plus Switzerland. March 1973 = 100. Weights are 1972-76 global trade of each of the 10 countries. Series revised as of August 1978.

readily interpreted as the foreign value of the dollar. (For a recent discussion of the mechanics of the foreign exchange market including spot and forward markets, foreign exchange options, interest arbitrage, triangular or space arbitrage, and the dominance of the dollar as the money of foreign exchange markets, see Chrystal 1984a.)

The convention is to say that the rate of exchange decreases when less dollars must be paid for a unit of the foreign money; e.g., the foreign exchange rate vis-à-vis Canada decreased between 1981 and 1983 from $.83 to $.81 (the reciprocal of the values in Table 24.1). While the U.S. dollar strengthened against all currencies in this period, this was not true in earlier years; e.g., the rate increased vis-à-vis the United Kingdom from $1.97 to $2.32 between 1978 and 1980.

The foreign exchange rate is a key price because it affects all international prices. And the price of the U.S. dollar may be the most important price in the world economy (Emminger 1985:17–24). Whatever the prices of internationally traded items before the exchange rate change, foreign prices will uniformly rise in the depreciating country's currency and uniformly fall in the appreciating country's currency.

Each country's balance of payments is stated in terms of that country's currency, even though transactions may be denominated in terms of a foreign currency. Does it make any difference as to which country's currency is the basis of the international transaction? No, not insofar as the balance-of-payments statement is concerned. But it does make a difference to the mechanics of exchange rate determination. It also means that the currency functioning as an international medium of exchange will be demanded for its own sake, i.e, for transactions purposes.

The U.S. dollar will be taken to be the international unit of account and medium of exchange. For this reason it is convenient to study exchange rate determination from the standpoint of a second country.

Figure 24.1 is a demand-supply analysis of the foreign exchange market in a hypothetical country named Alpha. On the horizontal axis, the commodity being bought and sold (U.S. dollars) is measured. The vertical axis measures the price of U.S. dollars in terms of the native Alpha currency (alphas). As one goes up the vertical scale, the exchange rate increases; it takes more alphas to buy one U.S. dollar.

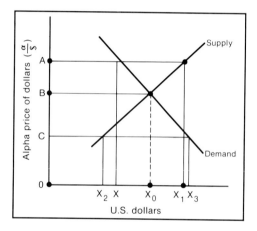

24.1. The foreign exchange market in Alpha country.

The demand and supply curves for dollars cover the autonomous (planned) transactions shown in the balance-of-payments statement of Chapter 23. Initially, we shall assume that these include commodity and service flows and long-and short-term (illiquid) capital flows (in both directions). Alpha's planned purchases in the United States will increase with changes in the value of U.S. dollars in terms of alphas. As the exchange rate falls, U.S. goods become cheaper and the demand for dollars will be greater. Thus the demand curve in Alpha is downward sloping. For the demand for dollars to increase as the exchange rate falls, it must be assumed that the quantity of imports goes up by more than the price in the local Alpha currency goes down. Without an assumption that the elasticity of the demand for imports is greater than one, the demand curve would be positively sloping.

The supply curve of dollars in Figure 24.1 measures the transactions of Alpha on the credit side of the balance of payments. The higher the foreign exchange rate, the greater the sales to the United States of both commodities and financial claims because one U.S. dollar will convert into more alphas. Seen from the standpoint of the United States, the higher the foreign exchange rate in Alpha, the lower it is in the United States. The rate of exchange is decreasing from the point of view of the United States. Thus it plans to buy more, meaning that it will be supplying more U.S. dollars to Alpha as the rate of exchange increases there. The supply of U.S. dollars in Alpha is thus an upward sloping curve, as shown in Figure 24.1. The elasticity assumption now must be that foreign demand increases relatively more than the decline in price owing to the depreciation in alphas.

If the exchange rate is fixed by government at the $0A$ level, the supply of U.S. dollars ($0X_1$) will exceed the demand ($0X$). This means that Alpha is supplying more goods and services and illiquid financial claims to the United States than it is acquiring. The difference (XX_1) will be an increase in Alpha's net liquidity balance. Alpha, either as individuals, businesses, or its government, will be increasing its liquid claims on the United States more than the other way around. On a liquidity balance basis, Alpha will have a surplus in its balance of payments. As already pointed out, as long as this state of affairs goes on, the United States is being subsidized by Alpha. The United States is able to import more goods and services than it exports, render economic and military aid to Alpha (such aid is called a transfer payment in the balance of payments), and acquire ownership of factories and time deposits in commercial banks and short-term Alpha government securities (liquid paper claims).

In a free market, the foreign exchange market will clear at the $0B$ exchange rate, at which rate the demand for dollars will match the supply. The balance of payments will be in balance above the line. We have assumed initially that the line is drawn above the liquidity balance. But if Alpha plans for increased liquidity balances in the same way that it plans for imports, the line should be drawn above the official settlements balance.

The $0A$ rate undervalues alphas. As compared with the equilibrium $0B$ rate, a dollar is worth more alphas than warranted by market forces. In the same way, if the rate had been set by government at $0C$ below $0B$, the rate would have been overvalued. Too few alphas are required to buy a dollar than is warranted by the market. In such a case, the balance of payments would be in deficit, with the excess demand for dollars having to be handled in a variety of ways. Foreign exchange controls with licensing requirements for imports, tariffs, or quotas can restrict the effective demand for foreign exchange. The effect of such controls is to reduce the demand for dollars to $0X_2$ in Figure 24.1. Alternatively, the $0X_3$ demand can be met (or some amount between $0X_2$ and $0X_3$) out of foreign exchange reserves of dollars.

Historically, after World War II when there was a dollar shortage in the world, foreign exchange rates in the major trading countries would resemble the $0C$ case. Subsequently, in the 1960s and 1970s, when foreign exchange rates vis-à-vis the dollar were undervalued, the situation is suggested by $0A$.

Policies of fixed exchange rates with frequent changes (adjustable pegs) blend into contemporary practices of dirty or managed float. Since 1973 central banks have intervened to buy and sell foreign currencies. Such intervention is reflected in official reserve transactions in the balance of payments.

The 1984 strength of the dollar belied the weakness of the dollar as recently as 1979. Figure 24.1, which looks only at Alpha in terms of a demand and supply of dollars, is an incomplete picture of U.S. participation in the foreign exchange market. It would be appropriate to have a corresponding diagram of the United States, with foreign currencies demanded and supplied and the vertical axis measuring the dollar cost of foreign currencies. To carry on managed float, the Fed first swaps dollars for foreign currencies. The Fed swap network consists of reciprocal credit arrangements with fourteen central banks and the Bank for International Settlements (a central bank to central banks) (Kubarych 1978:17). Sometimes surreptitiously, the Fed supports the dollar by supplying foreign exchange. More recently it supports foreign currencies by supplying dollars. Foreign central banks will be carrying on similar support operations for their currencies. Arbitrage guarantees that exchange rates will be the same in all foreign exchange markets. If the British pound trades for $1.30 in the United States, the dollar trades for its reciprocal (0.77 of a pound in England). Any discrepancy will be ironed out by arbitrageurs buying and selling the respective currencies; e.g., if the pound traded for $1.30 in New York but at the equivalent of $1.29 in London, pounds would be sold in New York for dollars and bought for dollars in London. The increased supply of pounds in New York and increased demand for pounds in London would force the rates to parity.

DEMAND AND SUPPLY SHIFTS   Strengthening or weakening of the dollar apart from intervention can be achieved by shifting the underlying demand-and-supply curves for foreign exchange in the appropriate direction. Our perspective is the U.S. demand for and supply of foreign exchange. The supply of foreign exchange is equal to (cf. Kaufman 1973:360):

$$FE_s = X + CI$$

where FE_s = supply of foreign exchange
   X = value of current account exports (credits)
   CI = capital inflows (credits)

The value of X will depend on foreign demand for exports:

$$X = f[\overset{+}{y_{row}}, \overset{-}{(P/P_{row})}\ \overset{+}{E}]$$

where y_{row} = real income of the rest of the world
   P/P_{row} = relative prices at home and abroad
   E = foreign exchange rate

As the signs above the variables suggest, an increase in foreign real income, the foreign exchange rate, and foreign prices will increase the U.S. supply of foreign exchange. On the other hand, if U.S. prices rise relative to foreign prices, this will discourage foreign demand (foreign purchases in the United States).

Capital inflows (CI) will depend on relative real interest rates (in the case of debt flows), profitability (equity investments), and exchange rate risk. The profit potential is represented by the rate of change in real income (a proxy for the accelerator effect). Real interest rates equal nominal rates less expected inflation rates.

386

$$CI = f(\overset{+}{r/r_{\text{row}}}, \overset{+}{\dot{y}/y_{\text{row}}}, \overset{-}{E_{\text{var}}})$$

where r = real interest rate
      $\dot{y}$ = rate of change in real gross national product (GNP)
    E_{var} = exchange rate risk

On the side of demand for foreign exchange:

$$FE_d = M + CO$$

where FE_d = demand for foreign exchange
     M = value of imports
   CO = capital outflows

The U.S. demand for imports is similar to the export equation with obvious adjustments:

$$M = f(\overset{+}{y}, \overset{+}{P/P_{\text{row}}}, \overset{-}{E})$$

Now it is the U.S. income that matters, and the next two signs are reversed. The same factors that influence capital inflows influence capital outflows but with the signs reversed except for exchange rate risk (equation not shown).

Policymaking in an open economy

FIXED EXCHANGE RATE REGIME   As the above equations suggest, the economic policymaker, in addition to influencing the foreign rate, can work on the real national income and the price level. In doing so, the policymaker wishes to achieve both internal and external balance. Variations in national income and the foreign exchange rate are two policy tools for achieving two policy goals. Figure 24.2 shows the possibilities.

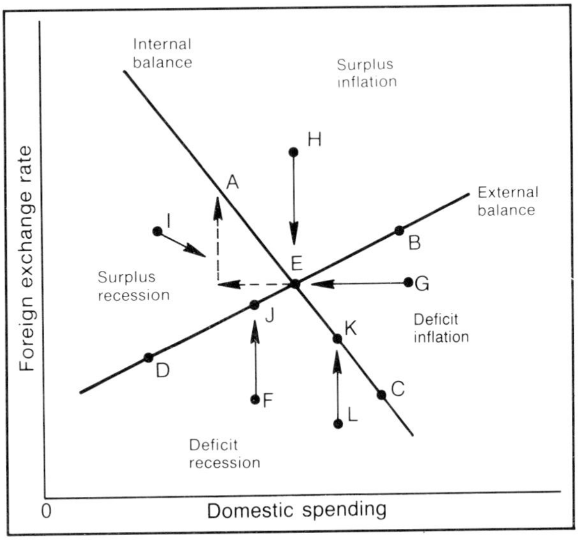

24.2. Internal and external balance.

The vertical axis in Figure 24.2 denotes the foreign exchange rate, the horizontal axis, domestic spending. External balance can be achieved by various combinations of exchange rates and domestic spending. Assume an initial external balance (equilibrium in the balance of payments) at point E. If income increases, this will lead to a greater demand for imports. To maintain balance in the balance of payments, the exchange rate must increase. This will stimulate exports and sales of financial instruments abroad and discourage imports and purchases of foreign instruments (expenditure switching will be encouraged, i.e., the substitution of domestic output for imports). Thus point B might represent an alternative equilibrium point. The locus of external equilibrium is the positively sloping line shown in Figure 24.2. Any combination of exchange rates and domestic spending below the external balance line will represent a deficit in the balance of payments (such as point G). Points above the line mark a surplus.

The internal balance line is negatively sloping because an increase in domestic spending will have to be offset by an appreciation of the exchange rate to encourage imports. Since the GNP can be expressed as domestic spending ($C + I + G$) plus net exports ($X - M$), internal (full employment) equilibrium requires a decline in net exports to compensate for the increase in domestic spending. Points such as C are alternative equilibrium points to E. To the right of the internal balance line, full employment and inflation prevail; to the left, unemployment and recession. The two intersecting lines form four quadrants, each with a unique disequilibrium situation.

The aim of policy is to move toward overall equilibrium at point E. Going counterclockwise around the quadrants beginning with external deficit-inflation, the dominant policy should be domestic retrenchment via monetary-fiscal policy, as suggested by point G. The problem with expenditure switching via exchange depreciation is that it will stimulate the economy. In the external surplus-inflation case (H), the appropriate policy is one of exchange appreciation. In the surplus-recession case (I), monetary-fiscal expansion is called for. The worst of all possible states might be deficit-recession (F, L) because concern with external balance inhibits expansionist policies. A policy of expansion, because of the income-elasticity of imports, will worsen the external deficit.

Deficit-recession might also describe the dilemma posed by stagflation. Instead of increasing real income, domestic expansion may succeed only in raising prices. This lack of real effect will not help the balance-of-payments deficit because of the adverse effect of inflation on U.S. competitiveness.

Choosing between exchange rate and monetary-fiscal policies is least difficult when the economy is on either one of the two functions. Points B, A, D, and C illustrate these possibilities. At B, a combination of the two policies (appreciation and restriction) will move the economy toward E. As another example, if the economy is at point A, a policy of appreciation should be followed. The adverse effect on employment calls for expansionary policies. In this way, we continue to move down the internal balance curve.

Monetary vs. fiscal policy   Let us assume that the appropriate policy calls for expansion of domestic output. Should the policymaker choose monetary or fiscal policy or does it make any difference? The standard theory points to a preference for fiscal policy under fixed exchange rates and for monetary policy under flexible rates. (The classic article is Mundell 1962.)

An increase in government spending creates a balance-of-payments deficit. The demand for imports exceeds exports as income increases. Given a constant money stock, an increased demand for money following the increase in income will put pressure on interest rates. Higher rates will attract capital inflows, offsetting the current account deficit. On the other hand, the use of monetary policy to increase output might depress interest rates, inducing capital outflows rather than inflows. The assumption in this analysis is that an increase in the money stock will cause the interest rate to go down. According to today's rational expectationists, this is not necessarily so. Market reports of an increase in $M1$ above the anticipated increase result in a rise in interest rates and vice versa.

FLOATING RATES   The exchange rate is a policy instrument in a fixed exchange rate regime. (While fixed, at any time the "peg" is adjustable.) What happens if exchange rates are allowed to fluctuate freely? We have no experience with market-determined rates (clean float), since central banks continued to intervene after 1973. In that year, fixed exchange rates based on a linkage with the U.S. dollar were supplanted by flexible rates. Nonetheless, the later experience is illuminating in terms of the effect of fluctuating rates on the balance of trade and the underlying determinants of foreign exchange rates.

Exchange rate depreciation after 1973 did not bring about an equilibrium in the U.S. balance of trade. After 1975 net exports declined sharply despite a drop in the trade-weighted currency value of the dollar and the price-adjusted dollar through 1979 (see Fig. 24.3). The trade-weighted exchange rate is an average of the value of the dollar against ten other currencies, with these being weighted by their shares in trade with the United States. The price-adjusted (real) dollar is the trade-weighted nominal dollar multiplied by relative consumer prices—the U.S. consumer price index divided by a weighted average index of foreign consumer prices.

24.3.   Nominal and real effective exchange rate of the U.S. dollar. (President 1984:46)

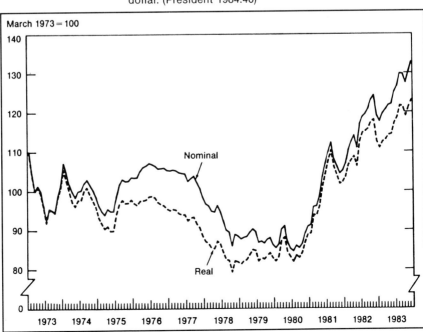

According to one major theory of exchange rates (the purchasing power parity or monetary theory of exchange rates), the exchange rate in nominal terms reflects its domestic purchasing power in comparison with the purchasing power of the foreign currency; i.e., $E = P/P_{row}$. Assume that initially $1 in the United States buys as much as 10 alphas in Alpha and the foreign exchange value of the dollar is $1 = 10 alphas ($E = \$1/10$ alphas). If the exchange rate increases and it takes $2 to buy 10 alphas (the foreign exchange, value of the dollar E, falls, by half), the purchasing power parity theory would explain this change in terms of the price level in the United States (P) rising twice as far as the price level in Alpha (P_{row}). According to this theory, the real value of the dollar always stays the same; the nominal exchange rate compensates for changes in relative prices. The number of dollars represented in the exchange rate buys the same basket of goods and services at home and abroad ($EP_{row} = P$). Figure 24.3 casts doubt on this theory (at least in the short run), since the real value of the dollar is far from a horizontal line. (For the thesis that purchasing power parity holds in the long run, see Batten 1981.) Between 1974 and 1979 the price-adjusted line has its widest distance below the nominal dollar. This tells us that the dollar fell in nominal value more than warranted by relative inflation rates. (The real value of foreign currencies rose.)

During this time U.S. exports should have become better bargains relative to German and Japanese exports; yet their trade accounts showed continued surpluses alongside U.S. deficits. Factors other than price (such as quality and delivery time), which may have been decreasing the relative demand for U.S. imports, must be considered. The lag in adjustment in response to exchange rate depreciation must also be allowed for. The so-called j theory points out that the trade gap can be increasing with depreciation as exports in the pipeline take on a lower foreign exchange value and imports a higher one.

Depreciating and appreciating exchange rates aggravate or mitigate the domestic inflation problem, so that a vicious circle is created. Deficit countries with depreciating rates (such as the United States) suffered more inflation as the price of imports rose. The rise in the price of imports spreads to the prices of import substitutes. The rising price level then contributes to a rising deficit, to a weakening exchange rate, etc. (the poor get poorer, but the rich get richer). Surplus countries such as Germany or Japan, which had appreciating rates, experienced lower inflation rates because inflation was dampened by falling import prices. This made them more competitive internationally, leading to larger trade surpluses.

An appreciating rate, however, did not work in favor of the United States. While cheaper imports did indeed keep down the cost of living, the deficit on the goods-and-services account (see Ch. 23) kept growing. After 1979, the dollar began a dramatic rise. From the fourth quarter of 1980 through March 1984, the dollar appreciated in nominal terms 45% (Isard 1984:270). In real or price-adjusted terms, the weighted average value of the dollar rose almost as much, 40% over three years, 1981–83. This represented a level roughly 25% above its average value for the entire 11-year period of floating rates (1973–83). The dollar continued to rise through March 1985 when the real value of the dollar stood 47.5% above its 1980 value. Subsequently, through October the real value declined 10% (Hakkio and Whittaker 1985:5).

If we consider the balance of payments as a whole, however, flexible exchange rates moved the United States closer to external equilibrium. The criterion is the size of the transfer gap. As shown in Figure 23.1, the size of the transfer gap has declined with flexible rates.

Explaining the strong dollar   Purchasing power parity fails as an explanation of variations in the nominal value of the dollar on the downside and the upside as well. The dollar rose more than warranted by relative inflation rates, as shown by the real value of the dollar paralleling the nominal value. Then what explains the strong dollar? The origin is to be found principally in the U.S. policy mix. A tight monetary policy and an easy fiscal policy produced high real interest rates. Beyond interest rates, the decline in inflation, U.S. economic recovery, and a perception of the United States as a safe haven for funds have all contributed to a net inflow of capital and a surplus on capital account.

Care must be taken, however, in attributing appreciation to interest rates. More often than not, from the beginning of managed floating rates in 1973 to the last quarter of 1979, increases in the interest differential went hand in hand with currency depreciation instead of in the opposite direction. The dramatic steps to rescue the dollar in November 1978, in part by increasing local interest rates, failed (Batten 1981:22–30; Mudd 1979:9ff.). From the middle of 1982 to early 1984 the real value of the dollar appreciated more than 10% at the same time that the real interest differential declined one percentage point (Isard 1984:271). An expectation of rising long-term interest rates because of the federal fiscal deficit may be behind the strong dollar so that the current interest differential is not the relevant interest variable (Sinai 1984b).

Capital transactions based on the substitution of foreign for domestic assets now dominate the foreign exchange market (President 1984:50–51). The relevant theory is called portfolio balance (an extension to an open economy of the portfolio theory discussed in Ch. 17). Despite its credibility, it is of note that empirical models based on portfolio balance are equally at a loss to explain exchange rate movements as purchasing power parity theory (see, e.g., Meese and Rogoff 1983; Bergstrand 1983).

The exchange rate as a guide to monetary policy   Variations in the exchange rate have an information value for policymaking (Bergstrand 1985:5–18). A focus on the behavior of interest rates and the money stock may give misleading signals. It has been pointed out that in the first half of 1984 the $M1$ was growing near the top of its range and the one-year Treasury bill rate rose from 9.2 to 10.9%. On these criteria alone the Fed might suspect inflationary pressures and clamp down on money growth. At the same time, however, the value of the dollar was rising. The message was one of foreign confidence in the U.S. economy and anticipations of high rates of return on investment in the United States. Similarly, late in 1984 the fall in the rate of growth of $M1$ was misleading because of the continued strength of the dollar. Empirical studies also show that the exchange rate has been a better predictor of inflation than $M1$ since 1981 (Bergstrand 1985:15).

MONETARY CONTROL AND THE EURODOLLAR MARKET   A global financial market with relatively free movement of financial capital across national borders poses problems for monetary policy beyond those of a closed economy. Alternative financial sources of funds abroad can frustrate central bank efforts at restraint. The Eurodollar market (first discussed in Ch. 8) is a case in point.

The size of the Eurodollar market is a matter of much conjecture. Reasonable estimates are that the gross size of the market had reached $1310 bil. by 1980. When interbank deposits are subtracted, the net size is cut in half (Henning et al. 1984:318).

Because of the importance of interbank deposits and because private sector holdings are time deposits of the $M2$ variety, the Eurodollar market has a velocity effect rather than a monetary effect. The lending in this market causes foreign bank demand deposits in the United States (the ultimate basis of this lending) to turn over more rapidly. The velocity effect is also the consequence of U.S. banks borrowing in the Eurodollar market. Eurodollar borrowing is part of the managed liabilities of commercial banks as discussed in Chapter 8. The effect of such borrowing (modified when reserve requirements were imposed on Eurodollar borrowing) was to increase the excess reserves of U.S. banks and thus total lending. Eurodollar borrowing has the effect of transferring reserves from the U.S. banks in which Eurobanks have their deposits to U.S. banks doing the borrowing. Because of reserve requirements against foreign deposits, the net effect is to cause required reserves in the borrowing banks to go up by less than they go down in the depository banks. The shuffling of reserves also has the effect of increasing cash items in process of collection, which reduces net demand deposits and required reserves. The history of reserve requirements against Eurodollar borrowing will be found in the *Federal Reserve Bulletin* as a footnote to the table on reserve requirements of depository institutions.

European banks' Eurodollars provide the base for multiple expansion of credit. Assume that one Eurobank makes a Eurodollar loan (based on its foreign dollar deposit) that ends up as a Eurodollar deposit in a second European bank. The process can then repeat itself. The extent of multiple expansion, however, is a controversial question. If the Eurodollar borrower deposited the proceeds in a U.S. bank, the European reserve base would disappear and the expansion process would instantly end. Eurodollars can be the outcome of balance-of-payments transactions as foreign exporters or borrowers take payment in the form of dollar balances abroad. They can also increase if U.S. residents transfer dollars in checking accounts to foreign banks (see Balbach and Resler 1980:2ff.). The Eurobank (it can be a foreign branch of some U.S. bank or an unaffiliated foreign bank) forwards the checks to the United States, where its account is credited. At the same time, the U.S. resident's account is debited at some U.S. bank. Under the $M1$ definition, which excludes interbank deposits, including those of foreign banks such a Eurodollar transaction reduces $M1$. With the introduction of international banking facilities Eurodollar deposits may be physically located in the United States (see Ch. 8). A wider concept than that of a Eurodollar market is the Eurocurrency market, which encompasses currencies such as the Dutch guilder or the German mark. Nonetheless, U.S. dollars make up approximately 75% of the Eurocurrency market. Finally, Eurobonds are the long-run counterpart of the Eurodollar market (see Henning et al. 1984:356–58).

Eurodollar deposits can also result if U.S. owners convert large certificates of deposit (CDs) into Eurodollars. Again $M1$ will contract for the additional reason, besides the exclusion of interbank deposits, that reserve requirements are lower against CDs than against foreign demand deposits.

The reinvestment of foreign deposits in interest-bearing assets means that their effect on the money supply is temporary. This is reflected in bank demand deposit liabilities to all foreigners at the end of 1981 being $20 bil., about 5% of the $364 bil. of demand deposits outstanding. Foreign deposits at the Fed were only $500 mil. In any case, the Fed can always compensate for such increases by expanding the monetary base.

Does a U.S. balance-of-payments deficit automatically mean that Eurodollars are increasing? The answer is no, as it is to the reverse proposition—that an increase in Eurodollars necessarily results in a larger deficit. Only when a foreign exporter takes a Eurodollar deposit (rather than a deposit in the local currency) will the U.S. deficit be associated with an increase in Eurodollars.

Suppose Eurodollars result from a portfolio shift; i.e., a U.S. resident increases Eurodollar deposits by liquidating CDs (Resler 1979:12). Now liquid claims held against the United States increase, since a European bank has additional deposits in U.S. banks. But at the same time, the balance of payments would record more U.S. liquid claims on foreigners, i.e., the Eurodollar deposit made by an American. The net liquidity balance will be unaffected; the same amount has been added to both U.S. liquid claims on other countries and to U.S. liabilities.

The Eurodollar market can in either case affect the size of official settlements balance. If a central bank, for example, acquires Eurodollars by purchasing them from its own citizens (banks or the nonbank public), official reserves will increase. If it supplies its citizens with dollars (to prevent the dollar from appreciating in relation to the domestic currency), official reserves decrease.

Policy dilemmas

Strong dollar or weak dollar, the global economy is always in an upset state. Floating exchange rates may have helped to bring the balance of payments closer to an overall balance for individual countries (such as the United States), but for the major industrial countries as a whole (the so-called group of ten), the magnitude of official reserve movements gives more evidence of disequilibrium under floating rates than under adjustable pegs (IMF 1984a:9–10). In times of the strong dollar, the dilemma of the major trading countries is to resist the strong dollar or give in to it. If they attempt to resist capital outflows by their own high-interest policy, they invite unemployment and output decline, but if they let the exchange rate depreciate, they import inflation.

Exchange rates since 1973 have not only been flexible but volatile. The resultant exchange rate uncertainty affects both import demand and export supply (Abrams 1980:4; Hakkio 1984:20–21). In terms of economic performance for the seven largest industrial countries, the comparison is not favorable to floating rates versus the adjustable peg. On average, inflation rates have been twice as high, unemployment rates almost twice as high, real income growth less than half as rapid, excess capacity more than twice as large, and growth in labor productivity only half as rapid (IMF 1984a:10). These differences must in part, however, be attributed to other features of the global economic environment besides floating rates.

Somehow the world economy totters on through endless vicissitudes. How have past difficulties been resolved, and what are some current proposals?

International cooperation

If nations go their own way and attempt to beggar their neighbors through protectionist policies, the end result will be less international trade, and all trading countries suffer. While sometimes the lesson is forgotten, there is a long history of international monetary cooperation.

EARLY HISTORY   Before the 1930s the major trading countries followed the rules of the international gold standard. Each country defined its monetary unit in terms of gold and committed itself to buying and selling gold at a fixed price so that the gold value of the circulating media could be maintained. With each currency being defined in terms of gold, the mint par of exchange between currencies was automatically defined. The actual rate under balance-of-payments pressure could depart from the mint par, but only as far as the gold points, which measured the cost of shipping gold. This cost set the limit as to what an importer would pay for a bank draft. For example, suppose that the U.S. dollar was defined as 23.23 grains of gold and the British pound was defined as 113 grains (historically the case). The mint par of exchange between the two currencies was \$4.86 = £1, since these amounts contained the same quantity of gold. If the cost of shipping gold was \$.02, it would pay to export gold if the rate increased to \$4.88 = £1 and to import it if the rate fell to \$4.84 = £1.

Movements of gold provided an automatic corrective mechanism for deficits or surpluses. Countries who played the gold standard game were committed to expanding the money supply when gold flowed in. Similarly, a loss of gold produced a monetary contraction. The expected results were substitution and income effects, both working to restore external equilibrium. When gold flowed in, the expansion process would result in higher prices, higher incomes, and lower interest rates. An initial surplus in the balance of payments (which generated the gold inflow) thus is corrected as debits increase from the substitution of cheaper foreign imports for domestic goods and from the income elasticity of imports. Reverse effects would take place as gold flowed out of the deficit country.

But the strength of the gold standard was also its weakness. The rules of the game tied a country's domestic fate to its gold stock; in the 1930s, the gold standard countries no longer could afford to play. Bank runs in Austria in 1931 led to abandonment of the gold standard by Austria, Germany, England, and later the United States. Abandoning gold did not prevent worldwide depression and unemployment (possibly because of faulty monetary policies), but it dissuaded countries from ever again going back to a metallic standard. The monetary discipline of the gold standard still has its admirers, however, as a way of fighting inflation (see Silk 1980:D2; for arguments against revival, see E. Bernstein 1980:8ff.). The great interest in gold prompted the formation of a gold commission made up of government, congressional, and private-sector figures. The majority opinion expressed in the commission's 1982 report was to favor no change in the present role of gold

(Report of the Gold Commission 1982). The report also stated the obvious, that price instability in the future would strengthen the political influence of the "gold bug."

INTERNATIONAL LENDING AGENCIES   The lessons of the 1930s were clear-cut: competitive devaluation and foreign exchange controls have disastrous effects on world trade and finance. Could the fixed rate advantage of the gold standard be captured without imposing limits on discretionary policy? A solution was produced at the well-known Bretton Woods (New Hampshire) conference of 1944 attended by 44 nations. Bretton Woods was revisited in 1984 for a conference on the international monetary system (Fed, Boston 1984).

The articles of the International Monetary Fund (IMF) defined each country's monetary unit in terms of the dollar or in terms of gold, thus determining a fixed structure of exchange rates. After the IMF began operating in 1946, member countries had some discretion in varying par values in case of balance-of-payments difficulties (for a detailed account of the early years of the IMF, see Yeager 1966:Ch. 19). But the raison-d'être of the IMF was to minimize such changes by its lending activities. In this way, the best of both worlds was to be achieved: fixed exchange rates and adjustments by temporary borrowing rather than gold flows.

The IMF lends by buying currencies from the treasuries or central banks of member countries. The member country pays off the loan (buys back its own currency) with gold or foreign exchange. Country borrowing is limited by quotas based on member contributions of gold and IOUs to the IMF. These quotas are periodically revised.

The IMF's influence and visibility has risen sharply in the 1980s as a result of the international lending crisis. It filled an international void by prevailing upon banks and governments to reschedule debts and by arranging consultations and economic adjustment programs for debtor countries (Bergstrand 1984:14). The conditions that the IMF imposes on debtor countries made "conditionality" a hot issue. While austerity has improved the external accounts in some countries (Mexico is a leading example), the IMF has been held responsible for substantial decline in per capita incomes and social unrest in developing countries.

A companion lending agency is the International Bank for Reconstruction and Development (IBRD, the World Bank). The IBRD makes long-term loans so that member countries can repair deep-seated balance-of-payments problems by increasing productive capacity. Additional international agencies engaged in long-term investment are the International Financial Corporation (IFC) (1956) and the International Development Association (IDA) (1959). The IFC makes loans to private business firms in developing countries. The IDA provides loans on easier terms to less developed countries (LDCs). Because of their interrelated activities the IBRD, IFC, and IDA are referred to as the World Bank Group. In turn, their activities are closely allied to those of the IMF. The IMF and World Group occupy connecting buildings in Washington, D.C. A central bank to central banks is the Bank of International Settlements (BIS) in Basel, Switzerland. In 1980 the BIS held $50 bil. in central bank deposits and managed 10% of $340 bil. of official currency reserves (Janssen 1980:1). While the U.S. central bank is not one of its owners, it makes use of its services, such as swap arrangements among central banks.

The IMF is more of a bank than a fund, and the IBRD is more of a fund than a bank (Horvitz 1979:294). Initially, the IMF did function as a fund consisting of gold and local IOUs (currencies), with foreign currency being loaned to borrowing members (remember that "currency" is used metaphorically). But in 1970 special drawing rights (SDRs) were credited to member accounts in the manner of commercial banking. In contrast, IBRD still functions as a fund, depending on the contributions of its members or raising funds in international capital markets.

BREAKDOWN OF BRETTON WOODS

Special drawing rights   The story of SDRs mirrors the breakdown of Bretton Woods after a quarter-century of tolerable success (Sobol 1979:42). The chronic problem was that world liquidity depended on the United States running a deficit in its balance payments. As a result, the overhang of dollars became so large that it endangered the U.S. promise to redeem official foreign reserves in gold. Finally, in 1971 the United States withdrew this promise. At the same time, the United States made efforts to reduce its payments deficits. The SDRs were a move toward a new international currency whose volume could be varied at the discretion of a world central bank (the IMF). In so doing, the IMF revived an earlier proposal made by Lord Keynes at the Bretton Woods conference to create a new international currency unit called the bancor. The SDR is valued as the average of a basket of currencies and as a result is more stable than the individual currency in the basket. More technically, the value of the SDR vis-à-vis the U.S. dollar is determined as the sum of the dollar values (based on market exchange rates) of specified quantities of five currencies—the U.S. dollar, the Japanese yen, the British pound, the German mark, and the French franc. The value of the SDR in terms of any currency other than the U.S. dollar is derived from that currency's exchange rate against the dollar and the U.S. dollar value of the SDR (IMF 1984a:356). When the dollar rises in value, the dollar value of SDRs decreases. In November 1984 the SDR was worth one U.S. dollar, a decline in value from $1.27 in December 1980 (IMF 1980:390). Holders of SDRs earn interest based on world interest rates (a weighted average) and borrowers of SDRs pay a slightly higher fraction of this rate (Laney 1980:8).

Managed float   The dollar surplus helps to explain managed floating after 1973. The role of the United States under Bretton Woods was to redeem dollars for gold for official holders at $35 an ounce. A lack of confidence resulted in a rise in the price of gold in the free market. Official support action failed, with the result that in 1968 a two-tier system was established. One tier was the free market with prices determined by demand and supply, the other consisted of official transactions at the official $35 price. Deterioration in the balance of payments, however, caused President Nixon to abandon convertibility in 1971. Devaluation of the dollar was inevitable, and the Smithsonian agreements (conferees met at the Smithsonian Institution in Washington, D.C.) changed the price of gold to $38. In 1973 the price of gold was further increased to $42.22. Such alterations were of only symbolic value because the U.S. Treasury was no longer buying or selling gold. This devaluation ushered in an era of dirty float. The volatility of the U.S. dollar has since occupied center stage.

The short-run solution to world disequilibrium might be for central banks to give more weight to the exchange rate in formulating monetary policy. The real value of the major currencies conveys important information about relative financial ease or tightness. Currently (1984) this might call for central bank intervention to effect a lower value of the dollar. The long-run recommendation, say by the year 2010 (Cooper 1984:30–38), is for a single world currency. The analogy might be to the United States with many different economic regions employing the same monetary unit.

IN THE SHORT RUN   The straightforward solution to a strong dollar and high real interest rates is an easier monetary policy in the United States. Two birds could be killed with one stone if the central bank intervened in the foreign exchange market. The dollar would be cheapened and at the same time the monetary base increased.

The standard response is that the Fed is hostage to the fiscal deficit. An easy money policy would court inflation if coupled with a soft budget. It would not succeed in lowering interest rates because the market would demand ever-larger inflation premiums. While one can be skeptical about the wickedness of the deficit (see Ch. 20), the attraction of sterilized intervention is that it bypasses the controversy over policy mix. Sterilized intervention purportedly is neutral in its monetary effects by offsetting purchases of foreign exchange (reserve increasing) with open-market security sales (reserve decreasing).

A comparison of sterilized and unsterilized intervention is possible as shown in Figure 24.4. The *MM* curve describes alternative equilibrium points in the domestic money market and by inference in the domestic securities market—the mirror image of the money market. With a given stock of money, depreciation of the local currency requires an increase in the domestic interest rate if equilibrium is to be maintained (see Boughton 1983). This positive slope implies that the demand for money is negatively related to the interest rate and positively related to the foreign exchange rate. (Reminder: an increase in the foreign exchange rate means that the local currency has depreciated in value in relation to other moneys.) Depreciation increases the excess demand for local money (increases excess supply

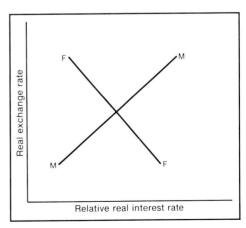

24.4. Unsterilized vs. sterilized intervention.

in the domestic securities market) because foreign purchases become more expensive. If domestic securities are good substitutes for local money, the necessary increase in the local interest rate to cut back the demand for money (increase demand in the securities market) will be less than if they were poor substitutes. Good substitutes will make the *MM* curve steeper. Similarly, the curve will be steeper the less attractive foreign securities are in relation to money holdings. The weaker this substitute relation, the less will be the competition faced by the domestic securities market from foreign securities and the less will interest rates have to rise for equilibrium to be restored in that market. More ambiguous is the case of poor substitutability between money and both foreign and domestic securities and good substitutability between securities. Because of poor substitutability, interest rates with excess supply in the domestic securities market will have to rise more than before, but such increases will be dampened by the movement between the foreign and domestic securities market in response to higher domestic interest rates.

The *FF* curve describes equilibrium in the foreign exchange market. A decrease in the foreign exchange rate increases the demand for foreign exchange because of the lower effective prices of foreign commodities and securities. Such excess demand has to be countered by an increase in the domestic interest rate. For this reason, the *FF* curve is negatively sloping. The greater the substitutability of domestic securities for foreign ones, the steeper the *FF* curve. (This is the reverse of the *MM* case where greater substitutability made the *MM* curve flatter.) The reason for this is that a slight increase in the domestic interest rate is enough to induce investors to buy fewer foreign securities (reducing the amounts demanded of foreign exchange), buying local securities instead.

With perfect substitution, the *FF* curve would approach the vertical. This possibility is emphasized by those who take the monetary approach to the balance of payments (monetarists). The significance is that sterilized intervention alters the composition of outstanding securities (foreign and domestic) without altering the total stock. The consequence is that sterilized intervention cannot shift a vertical *FF* curve and cannot affect the exchange rate.

The intersection of the *MM* and *FF* curves determines the equilibrium interest and foreign exchange rates. Three comparisons can be made with Figure 24.4. First, a conventional open-market purchase by the Fed will increase the supply of money and shift the *MM* curve to the left. Given the *FF* curve, the effect will be to raise the exchange rate and lower the relative interest rate. In contrast, with sterilized intervention aimed at depreciating the currency, *MM* stays unchanged *but* FF shifts to the right as a result of part of the stock of foreign exchange being taken off the market. The result is an increase in the foreign exchange rate and the interest rate. The third case would be unsterilized intervention. It differs from an open-market operation in that the asset acquired is foreign exchange. Now the *MM* and *FF* curves shift in opposite directions, so that the net effect is on the exchange rate rather than the interest rate. In the light of world-wide criticism of high U.S. interest rates, unsterilized intervention, in theory at least, seems the preferred alternative.

The evidence   The evidence points to the relative ineffectiveness of sterilized intervention: the study by the Working Group on Exchange Market Intervention

(Batten and Ott 1984:25); the Japanese experience (Hutchison 1984), and the U.S. experience (Nguyen 1984). But for unsterilized intervention to work, the market must be convinced that central banks "mean business." This translates into a conviction that the Fed plans to follow an easy money policy. With such expectations, the market would reinforce downward movements in interest rates following monetary increases instead of betting against them in anticipation of tighter monetary policies. The Fed may be forced to follow an easy money policy as a result of the international debt situation. But a positive policy statement rather than a negative defense in terms of being the lender of last resort would better elicit the support of the market.

It is possible that the decline in the dollar that began in March 1985 may be due in part to threats of the major industrial countries to intervene. In September the United States along with Britain, West Germany, France, and Japan made a formal commitment to work in concert to drive the dollar down (Kilborn 1985a:1, 36). Underlying economic and financial trends such as a sluggish U.S. economy may be the more decisive influences, however.

A final caveat about the strong dollar is that exchange rates fluctuate in unpredictable ways because of shifts in market psychology. Only a few years ago the dollar was weak even though many of the same factors were at work as now. Suppose world financial markets become panicky about U.S. fiscal deficits or they lose confidence in American know-how because of mounting current-account deficits. The strong dollar might quickly become the weak dollar and probably remain the target of world criticism. (An amusing cartoon in the *New York Times* [June 17, 1984, p. 4E] had a U.S. dollar saying to a female Europe: "You hate me when I'm strong and despise me when I'm weak.")

IN THE LONG RUN   The United States serves as a likely model for a world monetary system. If we consider the United States as organized by Federal Reserve Districts, each region has its own central bank. The Board in Washington, D.C., functions as a super central bank, exercising major power over the system but allowing some discretion to the district banks, such as control of the discount window. The circulation of dollars in all regions at par is equivalent to fixed exchange rates among political entities.

The balance of payments of each region summarizes its relations with other regions. A growth in the Sun Belt in relation to the Snow Belt (e.g., as a result of tourism or the distribution of Treasury expenditures) will show up as a deficit in the Snow Belt account and a surplus in the Sun Belt account. Higher interest rates in the Sun Belt might attract investment funds on capital account, further contributing to the Snow Belt's deficit. The deficit will be settled by a movement of dollars between regions. Deposits and reserves will go up in the Sun Belt and down in the Snow Belt. Based on regional money multipliers, secondary money expansions and contractions will occur. These will affect regional economic activity and feed back on the balance of payments.

The regional reserve (monetary) base will be affected by all the variables summarized in the reserve equation (see Ch. 10). It is not likely that their effects will be uniform over all the regions; e.g., assume that defensive open-market purchases are undertaken in Washington to offset increased Treasury deposits at the Fed (a factor absorbing reserves). Because the regional impacts of open-market operations and Treasury deposit increases are not likely to be symmetrical, reserves will go up in one region, down in another (cf. R. Miller 1977). More than this, because the regional money multipliers are not uniform, the money supply changes will not balance out overall. The regional dimension renders the national outcome uncertain. In administering global policy, a world central bank would have to be mindful of these differential effects as it attempts to control the world's money supply.

Let us now assume that each region has its own monetary unit (cf. Dernburg and McDougall 1968:160ff.). Suppose the Appalachian region is depressed, but wages and prices are downwardly rigid. Appalachia will then experience a balance-of-payments deficit and unemployment. Introducing flexible exchange rates would help because it provides such a key price. Appalachia output (say coal and tourism) now becomes cheaper; imports become more expensive. Fluctuations in the rate of exchange serve as a substitute for cost-price flexibility. The great weakness, however, is that flexibility becomes a substitute for efficiency. Fixed exchange rates impose more of an economic discipline on a region (or a country) than flexible ones. This is putting the best light on flexible rates—that they respond to real factors. Their unpredictability is proof that they vary without regard to underlying economic fundamentals, including inflation rates. Government macroeconomic planning is disrupted by volatile rates, and the temptation is to impose trade and capital controls, thus diminishing global commerce. A common currency, possibly a variant of SDRs or European Currency Units, is an idea for the future (Cooper 1984:30–38; Lewis 1984:29, 50).

Summary

In an open economy the economic policymaker must worry about both internal and external equilibrium. Internal equilibrium has been the focus in Chapters 1–22. Now Chapters 23 and 24 have introduced international transactions. Does external equilibrium deserve equal billing with internal equilibrium?

Suppose exchange rates are fixed and the United States runs deficits on the official transactions basis (the most plausible deficit concept). We assume that the transfer gap is the result of a trade deficit as well as capital outflows. The scenario might run as follows. An expansion of credit in the United States leads to an increase in income and an excess of imports over exports. Foreigners sell their dollar balances to their central banks. Official reserves are invested in interest-bearing assets in the United States. Instead of being indebted to U.S. residents, the indebtedness of the private and public sectors is to foreign owners. In effect foreigners have swapped goods and services for paper claims. Suppose further that their investment income is reinvested. The result is an enhancement in the welfare of U.S. residents. Imports are enjoyed without having to be paid for in similar goods and services. This is assuming that full employment can still be maintained in the United States despite problems in the export industries. Welfare effects of net imports are obscured by conventional national income measures, since net imports are subtracted from total output. External disequilibrium is beneficial under these circumstances. The scenario fits the United States in the postwar years until 1973. It is difficult to be critical of external disequilibrium under these circumstances.

The rub comes when foreigners are unhappy with their large dollar claims, and the dollar overhang shatters the fixed rate system. Flexible exchange rates, however, have not proved to be a panacea. They have created a set of new problems centering on the volatility of exchange rates. Short-run solutions might call for concerted central bank action based on the signalling value of exchange rates. Rapid appreciation of exchange rates (the recent case of the U.S. dollar) is evidence of an overly tight money policy. With the United States following an easy monetary policy, the other major trading countries should be less reluctant to do likewise. The banking system provides an ideal analogy. When banks expand in step, the likelihood of each bank losing reserves to other banks through the clearinghouse is reduced. Internationally, in-step expansion reduces the risk of individual countries aggravating current account deficits by their expansionary policies.

In the long run (the year 2010?) a common world currency would create a world monetary system that matches the burgeoning global market for goods and services and financial claims.

Review questions

1. Why is the foreign exchange market the key to an analysis of external equilibrium and disequilibrium?

2. When we say that the exchange rate decreases, does that mean that the value of the currency vis-à-vis other currencies appreciates or depreciates?

3. If foreigners prefer dollar paper claims to goods and services, how does this increase U.S. welfare? Is the conventional measure of GNP misleading from this standpoint?

4. Can you draw the diagram that pictures the conditions for both internal and external disequilibrium?

5. Why did floating (clean and dirty) replace fixed exchange rates in 1973?

6. Describe the international lending organizations established after World War II. Why were they set up?

7. What have proven to be the weaknesses of flexible exchange rates after 1973?

8. When the U.S. dollar is called overvalued, is there any evidence? Your answer should bring in the purchasing power parity theory.

9. Why did the U.S. dollar become so strong after 1980?

10. Distinguish between sterilized and nonsterilized intervention. The diagram showing equilibrium in the domestic money market and the foreign exchange market should be helpful.

11. "The United States Federal Reserve System provides the model for a world monetary system." Explain.

25

Finance in econometric models: Hope lies in quantitative analysis— or does it?

The late Nobel Laureate, Enrico Fermi, once explained to his colleagues his preference for studying physics over the social sciences: "In social sciences there are too many variables." Econometric models are the economist's way of coping with a maze of interrelated economic variables. The reader has already been exposed to the basic building block of econometric models, the multiple regression equation. In Chapter 2 we express output as a function of external finance. In Chapter 15 linkages between sector uses and sources of funds are explored in regression form. Some of the basic terms are introduced, such as dependent variable, independent variable, regression coefficient, coefficient of multiple determination, standard error, exogenous, and endogenous.

The next step is to work with a system of equations, a model. The identifying characteristic of a model is that an exogenous independent variable in one equation is an endogenous dependent variable in another; a variable explains another variable in one equation but is itself explained by other variables in a second. For example, consumption expenditures may be a function of the rate of interest among other variables; the rate of interest in turn may depend on the supply of money among other variables. When the model is in symbolic form, it is a theoretical model, such as the models discussed in Chapter 19. In quantitative form the theoretical model becomes an econometric model.

Econometric models

An econometric model provides an intriguing crystal ball. By feeding certain information into the computer, we get quantitative answers. We can test hypotheses about economic relationships in this way, both for the period of observed behavior (ex post forecasting) and for the period beyond the observation period (ex ante forecasting). Thus, for example, we may study the effect of business borrowing on business (private) investment for the period 1951–84. We fit a relation to the time series data by means of multiple regression analysis. In this way a value is estimated for investment in each year 1951–84. This value of investment is the ex post forecast value. (A modified ex post forecast is to drop off a year or two from the statistical fit and test, say 1983–84, using historical (known) values of the right-hand variables.) When we plug in values of the independent variables expected to prevail in a future period, say 1986, and estimate the resultant value of the dependent variable, this is an ex ante forecast of the dependent variable (private investment). To determine how well the model works, we compare the values estimated by means of the regression equation with actual historic values. (Of course, for ex ante forecasting we will have to wait until the end of 1986 to see how well the model predicted that value.)

Models that pass the ex ante forecasting test are made of sterner stuff than those that pass the ex post test. The coefficients (parameters) of the equations are based on the sample period data. They summarize an average relationship between the data for the independent variables and the dependent variable. It is therefore not surprising that inserting the observed values for the independent variables during the sample period will generally succeed in reproducing an estimated or predicted value for the dependent variable that is close to its true value for the period. On the other hand, beyond the familiar terrain of the sample period, the results are subject to changes in the initial structural relationships (the parameters are unstable) or to errors in forecasting the independent variables. For both these reasons, the ex ante forecast is the more demanding. (The ex post forecast is also referred to as the conditional forecast, the ex ante as the unconditional forecast.)

Unconditional forecasts run the gamut from pure "mechanical" forecasts to pure "judgmental" forecasts (see McNees 1975:13). The mechanical forecast takes the estimated econometric model as is and generates expected values solely on the basis of assumptions about the future values of the exogenous variables. At the other extreme, judgmental forecasts make subjective adjustments to the parameters of the model when the model "doesn't look right." Judgment shows up in a model by "intercept adjustments, add factors and tender loving care" according to one model builder who eschewed these techniques (see Andersen and Carlson 1976:54). An even purer judgmental model would be a noneconometric one where forecasts are based upon hunches or some extrapolation of past trends. Judgment to a degree enters even mechanical models because the forecaster must estimate future values of the exogenous variables.

The necessity for judgment springs from an unstable world where (1) past behavioral (structural) relations between variables may not hold, and (2) where the economic system is continually shocked in unexpected ways. As an example of (1), continuous inflation may change consumer and business behavior in product and financial markets compared with the effect of a one-shot increase in prices. As an example of (2), one can wonder whether any well-known economist anticipated the major shocks of recent years. From Penn Central's collapse, the Organization of Petroleum Exporting Countries (OPEC), New York City finances, the overthrow of the Shah and the taking of American hostages in Iran, and Continental-

Illinois to repudiation of Marxist economics in mainland China, the world is full of surprises. On a more mundane level there are strikes, embargoes, economic controls, and shortages. In such a world exogenous disturbance variables cannot be anticipated, let alone measured.

The use of judgment in such circumstances is inevitable. The researcher who is attuned to fast-breaking developments (imminence of strikes in a key industry, likely price decisions of OPEC) can feed valuable inputs into the econometric forecast. When, however, the researcher changes the parameters of the model because of poorness of fit, it is an admission that the behavioral relations no longer hold. Because econometrics is always fighting the last war and fails to allow for the learning ability of transactors, rational expectationists are highly critical of such models. Their argument is based on the structural effects of policy changes. As discussed in Chapter 21, the decisions of consumers and producers depend on their perceptions of the rules being followed by economic policymakers. If policymakers change direction, decision making in the marketplace changes and the structure of the economy is altered (Lucas 1976:41; Lucas and Sargent 1978:69; Lang 1983:9). The parameters of econometric models are now obsolete. Many leading economists, however, regard the Lucas-Sargent criticisms as an overstatement of the problems of standard econometric models (Lang 1983:12).

Before rational expectations, other estimation problems were debated among econometricians. In the specification problem, different sets of economic variables may be equally adept at explaining a given dependent variable, say the demand for money. The policy implications, however, can be quite different depending on which equation is preferred. Two Fed models, one of the Board of Governors and one of San Francisco were studied in depth (Anderson and Rasche 1982:796–826). The two models suggest very different trade-offs between close short-run control of the money supply and the volatility of money market interest rates. The San Francisco model, by having an additional argument (variable) in the money demand function (changes in bank loans), implies much less interest volatility (Judd and Scadding 1982:868–77). Using their model, the policymakers would be less cautious in getting back on the targeted money growth path, assuming the money stock strayed on the high side.

Another technical problem is identification. It is best illustrated in terms of demand-and-supply analysis. Unless the stringent requirements for identification are satisfied, it is not a straight forward matter to know whether a change in price is the result of a shift on the demand or supply side. Finally, the econometrician must be careful to correct for simultaneous equation bias. In a regression equation the action runs from the right-hand variables to the left-hand (dependent) variable. But the causality may just as well run in the opposite direction, invalidating the results.

Despite the problems besetting econometric models, they give us numbers and at worst ballpark estimates of the likely effects of economic policy. If they fail in forecasting ability, they can qualify as cliometrics, the use of econometric models to explain past history.

We have described hypothesis testing and forecasting in terms of a single relation. The same procedure applies to a multiple-equation model. Now we introduce values for all exogenous variables of the model; by the magic of computer solutions (these involve deriving a reduced form by matrix inversion) we secure values for a series of dependent variables (one for each equation of the model).

We can also simulate the model, thereby testing for the potential effects of fiscal and monetary policy. When the equations of the model are linear in form, multiplier values can be calculated from its reduced form. These can be used to estimate the effect of varying the instrumental variables on the endogenous variables of the model. Simulation, as described in this paragraph, is necessary when the model has nonlinearities. In this case, the model must be put through its paces a second time so that a dynamic solution can be compared with the control solution. First, we get the estimated values of the dependent variables as described in the previous paragraphs. We call this the control solution or the basic simulation. Next, we vary the exogenous policy variables (the instrumental variables) from their historical values (we increase the monetary base by, say, $1 bil. in all periods above its historical value) and determine the dynamic or alternative solutions. By comparing the control simulation with the dynamic solution, we can pinpoint the quantitative effects of policymaking; e.g., we can estimate the effects on gross national product (GNP), interest rates, and prices.

It is easier to simulate than to forecast. Simulation works with historic data, genuine forecasting with new. Moreover, by working with the control solution and the dynamic simulation, the discrepancies between the control solution and historic values are ignored. One must work with estimated values rather than actual historic values in evaluating the effects of changes in economic policy because the differences between historic values and dynamic simulations reflect not only the effect of policy but also the errors inherent in the model.

Characteristics of econometric models

Table 25.1 lists some of the leading econometric models and distinguishes them in terms of time frame (whether the data is quarterly, monthly, annual), size of model, disaggregation by number of producing sectors, and financial and real interaction. These characteristics boil down to different degrees of disaggregation. The more frequent the observations and the greater the number of endogenous variables considered (by sector, market), the more disaggregated the model. A disaggregated model offers certain advantages: a greater number of economic variables can be forecast, new information can easily be incorporated into the model, policy decisions are more flexible (the shorter the time frame), and weaknesses in the model are easier to discover (Miller and Kaatz 1974:15). On the other hand, as models get larger, data maintenance becomes increasingly difficult as well as programming them for the computer and solving them. The added complexity of large-scale models creates a "black box." Results emerge by "magic." We shall focus on three models that illustrate differences in size, and theoretical underpinnings. Most econometric models are Keynesian; some (most notably the St. Louis model in Table 25.1) are monetarist. In the past, the flow of funds were prominent in the DRI model. The FRB-MIT antecedent of the MPS model (MIT stands for Massachusetts Institute of Technology) will illustrate Keynesian models, the St. Louis model will illustrate the monetarist model, and the DRI flow-of-funds model will be presented.

Table 25.1. Some leading models

Model[a]	Time frame	Scale[b]	Disaggregation of production[c]	Endogenous financial-real interaction[d]
BEA	Quarterly	Medium	Limited	Weak
Brookings	Quarterly	Very large	Medium	Medium
MQEM	Quarterly	Small	Limited	Weak
DRI	Quarterly	Very large	Medium (recursive)	Strong[e]
Fair	Quarterly	Small	Limited	None
St. Louis	Quarterly	Very small	None	Strong
MPS	Quarterly	Large	Limited	Strong
Wharton	Quarterly	Large	Medium	Medium
H-C	Annual	Medium	Limited	Weak
Wharton annual	Annual	Very large	High	Medium
Liu-Hwa	Monthly	Medium	Limited	Medium

Source: Used with permission from Gary Fromm and L. R. Klein, The NBER/NSF model comparison seminar: An analysis of results, in L. R. Klein and E. Burmeister, *Econometric Model Performance*, pp. 380-81, copyright © 1976, University of Pennsylvania Press, Philadelphia.

[a]Bureau of Economic Analysis Model (BEA)--A.A. Hirsch, Bruce Grimm, and G. V. L. Narasimham; Brookings Model--G. Fromm, L. R. Klein, and G. Schink; University of Michigan (MQEM) Model--S. Hymans and H. Shapiro; Data Resources Inc. (DRI) Model--O. Eckstein, E. Green, and A. Sinai; Fair Model, Princeton and Yale Universities--R. Fair; Federal Reserve Bank of St. Louis Model (Fed, St. Louis)--L. Andersen and K. Carlson; M.I.T., Pennsylvania, S.S.R.C. Model (MPS)-- A. Ando and R. Rasche; Wharton Model (Mark III and Anticipations Version)--M. D. McCarthy, L. R. Klein, F. G. Adams, G. R. Green, and V. Duggal; Stanford University (H-C Annual) Model--B. Hickman and R. Coen; Wharton Annual Model--R. S. Preston; Cornell University (Liu-Hwa Monthly) Model--T. C. Liu and E. C. Hwa.

[b]Based on number of equations: very small = 9 or less; small = 10-49; medium = 50-119; large = 120-199; very large = 200 or more.

[c]Based on sector detail: limited = 2-5 sectors; medium = 6-20 sectors; high = 21 or more sectors.

[d]Based on qualitative judgments on pervasiveness of financial variables in real sector equations and real variables in financial sector equations.

[e]This classification is on the basis of more recent DRI models. The original classification was "medium."

Keynesian econometric models

Econometric models are Keynesian when the interest rate is the link between monetary policy and economic activity. It will be remembered that Keynes explained interest rates in terms of the interaction of the demand and supply for money. Keynesian models are nonmonetarist because money exerts its effect on output indirectly via the rate of interest rather than directly as in monetarist models.

In the FRB-MIT model (first published in 1968), a series of interest rates are solved for in a kind of succession based on portfolio adjustment. Figure 25.1 makes a distinction between instruments, financial markets, and real-sector links. The instruments are open-market operations and the Fed discount rate (discussed in Ch. 11). The initial disturbance is assumed to be an open-market purchase that affects unborrowed reserves (RU on the left-hand side of Fig. 25. 1). The commercial banks now have free reserves (RF), which are equal to excess reserves minus member bank borrowings. The banks seek balance in their portfolios (actual free reserves exceed desired free reserves) and acquire short-term interest-earning assets, leading to a decline in yields on Treasury bills (R_{TB}), commercial paper (R_{CP}), and bank loans (R_{CL}).

Demand deposits increase via a substitution for short-term assets. As yields

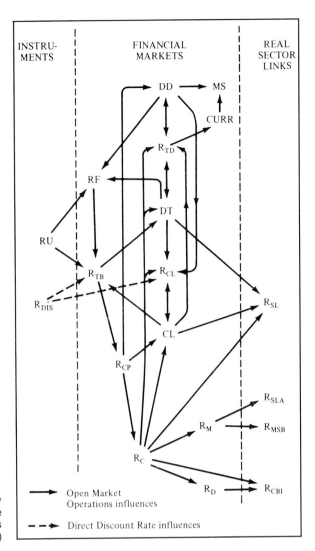

25.1 The monetary policy process of the FRB-MIT model. (Crews 1973)

fall on these assets, the opportunity cost of holding interest-free deposits declines. The supply of money is seen as determined by the demand for money, which in turn depends on the rate of interest. Increases in time deposits are also conditioned by relative interest rates. Feedback from the real sector as incomes increase (not shown on Fig. 25.1) will increase both time and demand deposits. As bank deposits increase because of substitution and income effects, so do required reserves. In this way, an initial increase in excess reserves is transformed into required reserves, actual reserves now match desired reserves, and the bank reserves market is in balance.

Current monetary policy departs from the FRB-MIT model in the determination of money (*MS*). Before October 1979 (as in the above analysis) the supply of money was controlled via the interest rate. Since then (ostensibly) it has been controlled via the control of unborrowed reserves. As a result, current monetary policy has a closer affinity to the monetarist St. Louis model than its own econometric model.

As Figure 25.1 shows, the increase in the money stock *MS* (made up of *DD* and *CURR*) goes nowhere in the original model. Instead, a decline in short-term rates (via term-structure relations) leads to a decline in long-term rates — corporate bond rate (R_C), mortgage rate (R_M), and stock market yield (R_D). The stimulus of the open-market purchase is then transmitted to the industrial bond rate (R_{CBI}), the state and local government bond rate (R_{SL}), and the deposit rates of nonbank savings insititutions (R_{SLA}, R_{MSB}).

Figure 25.2 shows how interest rates affect the real sector of the economy. The diagram begins with the *Aaa* corporate rate (the equivalent of R_C in Fig. 25.1). The fall in this basic rate is channeled in three directions. The cost of capital for long-term borrowers (the industrial bond rate) falls, thus influencing long-term borrowing and capital expenditures. For this transmission effect follow the lower part of Figure 25.2. Open-market purchases (in the complex way described in Fig. 25.1) succeed in lowering the corporate bond rate, followed by declines in the industrial bond rate. This means that cost of capital falls for both structures and equipment. The minimum required rate of return on investment (quasi-rent) falls concurrently with the fall in the cost of capital. Investment must earn less to cover the lower interest and related costs. The consequence is a change in the desired capital-output ratio; e.g., for each unit of output that businesses produce they will wish to employ more physical capital: capital has become a less expensive input compared with other inputs such as labor. New orders for plant and equipment will follow, to be succeeded by expenditures on GNP.

A second channel of effects is the wealth effect (top strip of Fig. 25.2). Equities (common and preferred stock) in household portfolios advance in value with declines in the market interest rate because future earnings from stock are discounted at a lower interest rate. Alternatively, one can say that stocks are a better bargain when interest rates on fixed-value securities are falling. (If interest rates are rising, there will be a reverse effect on the stock market as in 1972–73, 1977–81.) The effect of increased consumer wealth is that consumers spend more. They finance such spending by selling off part of their financial wealth or saving less in financial form (see Ch. 15).

The third channel (in the middle of Fig. 25.2) describes the credit rationing effect of a change (decline) in the long-term interest rate. Assume stickiness in the interest rate on mortgage loans and the yield on savings deposits. More funds will now flow into savings institutions because the rate of return on deposits has risen relative to open-market yields (the yields, say, on corporate bonds). Intermediation (discussed in Ch. 14) will increase. The expanded flow of funds will mean more mortgage financing, more housing starts, and again a rise in the GNP (see Ch. 18). Initially, an increased flow of funds means a relaxing of nonprice credit terms. Down payments are lowered; maturity terms are lengthened. But this will be a short-run phenomenon only. Progressively, the mortgage loan rate (the price of credit) will be lowered and the effects on mortgage loans will be via this cost-of-capital effect. The credit rationing effect (the effect of nonprice credit terms) will become progressively less, as borne out by the simulation results of a change in unborrowed reserves.

The simulation results are shown in Table 25.2, which analyzes the effect of an increase in $1 bil. unborrowed reserves (above their historical level) on components of the GNP, with each component explained by the three channels. Percentage of total effect and the dollar magnitudes are both given. The table gives

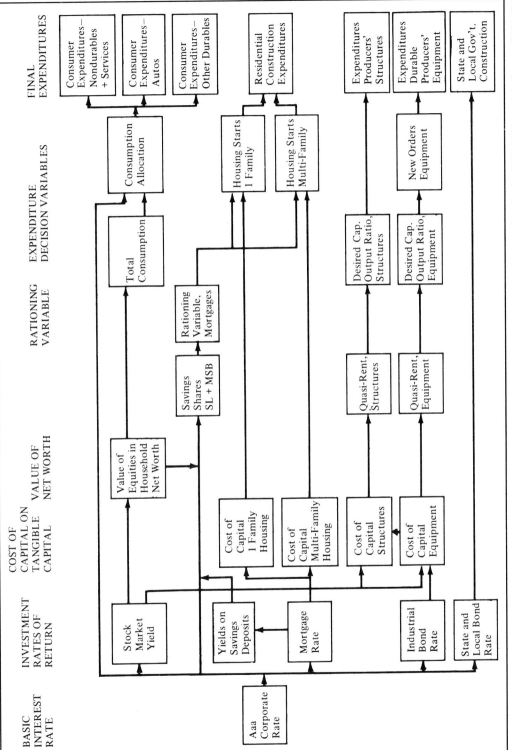

25.2. First-round effects of monetary policy in the FRB-MIT model. (Crews 1973:230)

immediate effects, without allowing for feedback effects from the goods market to financial markets or induced multiplier-accelerator effects (see Ch. 22). The effect of 16 quarters of simulation are recorded in the table. The cost of capital is seen to be the main channel, followed by wealth. The credit-rationing effect turns out to be negative by the sixteenth quarter. The wealth effect dominates consumption expenditures; the cost-of-capital effect dominates residential construction, plant and equipment, and state and local construction expenditures. Credit rationing is relevant only to residential construction expenditures. The figures in the upper strip of Table 25.2 measure the effect in each period of an extra $1 bil. in unborrowed reserves.

Table 25.2. Direct effects of a $1-bil. step increase in unborrowed reserves (initial conditions of 1964:1)

Billions of current dollars

Quarter	Personal consumption expenditures			Residential construction expenditures			Plant and equipment	State and local construction	Total			
	Cost of capital	Wealth	Total	Cost of capital	Credit rating	Total	Cost of capital	Cost of capital	Cost of capital	Wealth	Credit rating	Total
4	0.3	1.2	1.5	1.0	0.6	1.6	0.2	0.2	1.7	1.2	0.6	3.5
8	0.4	2.3	2.7	1.3	0.5	1.8	0.6	0.3	2.6	2.3	0.5	5.4
12	0.5	3.0	3.5	1.5	0.3	1.8	1.1	0.4	3.5	3.0	0.3	6.2
16	0.4	3.2	3.6	2.2	-0.8	1.4	1.5	0.5	4.6	3.2	-0.8	7.0

Percentages of total effect

Quarter	Construction	Residential construction	Plant and equipment	State and local	Channel		
					Cost of capital	Wealth	Credit rationing
4	43	45	6	6	49	34	17
8	50	33	11	6	48	43	9
12	51	26	16	7	51	44	5
16	51	20	21	8	66	45	-11

Source: De Leeuw and Gramlich 1969:487. Crews's discussion of the FRB-MIT model is based on this article.
Note: The results shown describe only the effect of unborrowed reserves in financial markets and, through financial markets, on final demand for goods and services. They do not include multiplier-accelerator interactions or feedback from goods markets to financial markets.

The complete policy effects have also been worked out for the FRB-MIT model, including feedback effects of the real sector. What stands out is the lack of real effects after 16 quarters (de Leeuw and Gramlich 1969:488). Real GNP is only slightly above its original level (despite unborrowed reserves being $1 bil. higher in every quarter), with the long-run effect being on the price level. In the long run the Keynesian model yields similar effects to those of the monetarist model.

The monetarist model

The St. Louis model is the best-known monetarist model. First published in 1970 (Andersen and Carlson 1970:4ff.), it has many points of difference from the FRB-MIT model. Its theoretical frame of reference is the quantity theory long applied by the St. Louis Bank to the analysis of economic developments (Andersen and Carlson 1976:48). It uses a reduced-form approach, which means that key endogenous variables are explained by a few key exogenous variables. The relationships in the model are direct and unambiguous. It is highly aggregative and does not attempt to explain individual sector behavior. Figure 25.3 illustrates the model.

Changes in the money stock and high employment federal expenditures determine the total spending (changes in federal expenditures are measured at their full-

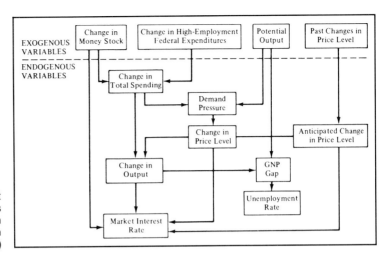

25.3. Flow chart of the St. Louis model. (Andersen and Carlson 1970:10)

employment value so that they represent government discretion; see Ch. 20.) These exogenous variables work with lags that are ignored in the flow chart (but they show up in later equations). The price level advances with an increase in total spending, declines with an increase in potential (real) output, and increases with anticipated increases in the price level. The unemployment rate is related to the GNP gap, which in turn is the difference between potential and actual output (expressed as ratio to potential output). Finally, the interest rate is the outcome of changes in the money stock, output, and current and anticipated price changes.

Money replaces interest rates in the Keynesian model as the linkage variable. One model's linkage becomes another's cul de sac. Money went nowhere in the nonmonetarist Keynesian model (see Fig. 25.1). Similarly, in the monetarist model (Fig. 25.3), changes in the market interest rate fail to feed back into the real sector. The exact form of the equations and two sets of statistical estimates of the coefficients are given in Andersen and Carlson 1976:67-68. The St. Louis model supports monetarist propositions. Money swamps fiscal policy in importance. Not supported by the equations is the contention that monetary actions have little if any lasting effect on real variables, with lasting effect only on nominal variables (price and interest rates). Such a hypothesis must be supported by simulation exercises, where money is varied above its historic value. This is done elsewhere (see Andersen and Carlson 1970:15ff.).

Despite the credibility of the equations, the St. Louis model does not forecast well (McNees 1973a:3–27; 1973b:29–34). In defense, it is pointed out that it is a mechanical model (Andersen and Carlson 1976:54).

Flow-of-funds models

Flow-of-funds models give center stage to credit markets and the actors in these markets. Balance sheets take on great importance because real and financial assets and financial liabilities affect flow-of-funds behavior. Our approach to money and finance has been a flow-of-funds approach.

Many flow-of-funds models have appeared. In addition to the Hendershott model discussed in Chapter 15, see Bosworth and Duesenberry (1973:39ff.), Backus et al. (1980:259ff.), Sinai (current study in process), and Cohen and Kenkel (1979–80:255ff.). (Elements of the Cohen-Kenkel model have been described in Ch. 19.) We shall now consider the large-scale Data Resources Incorporated (DRI) model.

THE LARGE-SCALE DRI MODEL   The financial instability theory outlined in Chapter 22 is incorporated in the DRI econometric model, the largest of all large-scale econometric models. The DRI quarterly model of the U.S. economy was once described as requiring 25 full-time professionals to develop and operate it on a continuing basis, as well as general-purpose computers at the top of the available range. The following material is a preliminary version of Sinai's current study begun when he was a leading economist for DRI (he is now chief economist at Shearson/Lehman).

Table 25.3 summarizes the variables and equations included in Sinai's version of the financial system. The financial model has 201 equations, 61 of which explain sector sources-and-uses behavior. Another 62 equations capture the information provided by flow-of-funds sector and transaction identities.

Table 25.3. Financial system of the DRI model

Sectors	Behavioral	Identities	Total	
I. Financial sector	44	17	61	
A. Monetary and reserve aggregates	8	13		21
B. Interest rates	24	1		25
1. Short-term	15	–		15
2. Intermediate-term	1	–		1
3. Long-term	8	1		9
C. Loans and investments of commercial banks	6	1		7
D. Stock market	6	2		8
II. Flow-of-funds	61	62	123	
A. Households	20	16		36
B. Nonfinancial corporations	24	34		58
C. Mortgage activity	17	12		29
1. Commercial banks	1	1		2
2. Savings and loan associations	3	2		5
3. Mutual savings banks	4	2		6
4. Life insurance companies	6	2		8
5. Mortgage rates, aggregate concepts, and miscellaneous	3	5		8
III. Miscellaneous: Inflation expectations, installment credit at all financial institutions, new issues of U.S. government debt, new issues of state and local government debt	11	6	17	
Total	116	85	201	

Source: Used with permission from Allen Sinai, *The Financial System in the U.S. Economy*, p. 171, forthcoming.

The financial and real linkages in the Sinai version of the DRI model rely heavily on a flow-of-funds framework (Sinai, current study in process: 176). Each transactor sector has in mind long-run values (targets) for financial assets, physical assets, and financial liabilities. Rates of return and costs for each balance sheet item help to determine the long-run targets. Adjustment takes place through acquisition of assets (uses of funds) and financing activity (sources of funds). The result of interaction of sources and uses activities is a new balance sheet position. (A recent conversation with DRI economists reveals that the Sinai model was too

Table 25.4. Monetary policy and spending: major channels in the Sinai model

I. Monetary policy
   A. High-powered money
   B. Federal funds rate

II. Interest rates
   A. Money market
      1. Federal funds
      2. Treasury bills
      3. Commercial paper
      4. Eurodollars
      5. Large CDs
   B. Deposits
      1. Commercial banks
      2. Savings & loan assocs.
      3. Mutual savings banks
      4. Credit unions
   C. Loans
      1. Prime business
      2. Auto installment
      3. Mortgage
   D. Long-term
      1. Corporate bond
      2. U.S. government
      3. Municipal

III. Stock market
   A. Stock market
      1. S&P 500 common stock index
      2. Dividend yield on S&P 500

IV. Rental prices
   A. Avg. cost of financial capital
      1. Weighted avg. cost of short- and long-term financing; after tax
      2. Expected return on stock: dividend yield plus growth in earnings per share
      3. Capital structure: proportion of debt and equity
   B. Rental price of capital
      1. Supply prices of capital goods
      2. Avg. cost of financial capital; after tax
      3. Tax parameters
         a. Investment tax credit
         b. Tax savings for depreciation expense rate
         c. Profits tax rate
         d. Tax allowable lifetimes for depreciation
   C. Rental price of autos
      1. Supply prices of automobiles
      2. Auto installment rate
      3. Price of gasoline

V. Sectoral portfolio behavior: balance sheet and flow-of-funds adjustments in response to changing yield differentials, "new money" flows, and existing portfolio positions
   A. Households (new money-disposable income)
      1. "Financial risk":
         a. Debt service burden with components interest rates, outstanding debt, disposable income
         b. Loan repayment burden relative to disposable income
      2. Financial wealth
         a. Market value-equity
         b. Market value-bonds
         c. Money and deposits
   B. Commercial banks (new money-deposit inflows and repayments)
      1. Mortgages outstanding
   C. Savings & loan assocs. (new money-deposit inflows and loan repayments)
      1. New mortgage commitments
      2. Mortgages outstanding
   D. Mutual savings banks (new money-deposit inflows and loan repayments)
      1. New mortgage commitments
      2. Mortgages outstanding

   E. Life insurance cos. (new money-reserves less policy loans and loan repayments)
      1. New mortgage commitments
      2. Mortgages outstanding
   F. Corporations (new money-cash flow)
      1. "Financial risk" debt service burden with components interest rates, outstanding debt, cash flow
   G. State and local govts. (new money-tax receipts)
      1. "Financial risk" debt service burden with components interest rates, outstanding debt

VI. Real final demands
   A. Consumption
      1. Durables
         a. Real hh. financial wealth
         b. Hh. debt service burden
         c. Loan repayment burden
         d. Rental price of autos
      2. Nondurables
         a. Real hh. financial wealth
         b. Loan repayment burden
      3. Services
         a. Real hh. financial wealth
         b. Loan repayment burden
   B. Housing and residential construction
      1. Demand
         a. Mortgage rate
         b. Mortgage debt service
         c. Treasury bill rate
      2. Supply
         a. Mortgage rate
         b. New mortgage commitments
         c. Outstanding mortgages
   C. Investment
      1. Business fixed
         a. Rental price of capital
         b. Debt service burden
      2. Inventories
         a. Debt service burden
   D. Government spending--state and local; public construction
      1. Outstanding state Local government bonds
      2. Municipal bond rate

Source: Used with permission from Allen Sinai, *The Financial System in the U.S. Economy*, pp. 186-87, forthcoming.

complex and has been replaced with simpler forecasting tools.)

A linear description of linkages is given in Table 25.4. It begins with monetary policy and ends with final spending (real final demands). In a general way, without going into a detailed description, an initial change in high-powered money affects interest rates and stock prices. These in turn affect the cost of capital (in item IV). Sector portfolios in V and VI respond to interest rates and money flows. While real final demands are treated sequentially in VI, they can be considered as decisions made at the same time that financial decisions are made in V. The effect of balance sheet adjustments on financial risk (section V) is a unique feature of the DRI model. DRI (modestly) has left the evaluation of its forecasts to third-party scholars. The flow-of-funds detail in the DRI model pays off, with its forecasts of short-term interest rates being the best of four—DRI, Wharton, Chase, and General Electric (McNees 1979a:48).

How good are forecasts from an econometric model? We turn to outside evaluations.

Forecasting with an econometric model

Because there has been relatively little attention in the literature to forecasts of financial variables, the emphasis here will be on forecasting of nonfinancial variables.

FORECASTING THE BUSINESS CYCLE   One yardstick in evaluating econometric forecasts is business cycle turning points (Behravesh 1975:21ff.). A turning point occurs when the economy shifts from a positive to a negative growth period and vice versa. The former points are peaks and the latter, troughs. (The National Bureau of Economic Research is responsible for such cycle dating.) A detailed study of 1957–61 is not too kind to forecasts. As Table 25.5 shows, the average of all forecasts (made at different times ahead of the turning points) hit the turning points 35% of the time. The shorter the forecast period, the better the forecast. The forecasts shown are historic, meaning that actual values of the exogenous variables were plugged into the model to generate forecasts of troughs and peaks. Knowing the values of the exogenous variables in advance does not guarantee success in forecasting.

Table 25.5.   Spotting turning points, 1957-61

Averages	Too soon	Too late	On time
Forecasts starting 3 quarters ahead of turning point	43%	26%	31%
Forecasts starting 2 quarters ahead of turning point	37	28	35
Forecasts starting 1 quarter ahead of turning point	28	33	39
All forecasts	36	29	35

Source: Behravesh 1975:22.
Note: The three models in question are the 1969 versions of the Wharton, BEA, and MIT-Penn-Fed models.

Table 25.6.   Predicting sizes of peaks and troughs, 1957-61

Averages	Too large	Too small	Correct
Forecasts starting 3 quarters ahead of turning point	21%	54%	25%
Forecasts starting 2 quarters ahead of turning point	15	62	23
Forecasts starting 1 quarter ahead of turning point	15	55	30
All forecasts	17	57	26
Forecasts during contractions	14	57	29
Forecasts during expansions	21	56	23

Source: Behravesh 1975:23.

Econometric models have the tendency to smooth out business cycles, thus undershooting the size of both peaks and troughs. This can be seen from Table 25.6. The models on average were right only 26% of the time.

ONE-YEAR-AHEAD FORECASTS IN THE 1970s AND 1980s   Instead of turning points, another test is one-year-ahead forecasts. The hectic 1970s provide a more demanding test of forecasting models than the long, relatively smooth expansion of the 1960s (in the 1950s, forecasting was in its infancy) (McNees 1973a:26).

Twelve leading forecasting models are described in Table 25.7. With one exception, their forecasts were generated with the help of an econometric model. The third organization (BMARK) produced its forecasts using autoregressive integrated moving average time series equations. This technique forecasts on the basis of past historic values of the predicted variable (NcNees and Ries 1983:5). Judgmental forecasts are part of the forecasting techniques (second to last col., Table 25.7). The relative weights given the forecasting techniques are arbitrary

Table 25.7. Summary information on forecasting organizations studied

Forecasting organization, (abbreviated title), contact for further information	Number of macroeconomic variables forecasted	Typical forecast horizon, quarters	Frequency of release year	Date forecast first issued regularly	Forecasting technique(s) (approximate weights)	Published reference(s)
American Statistical Association and National Bureau of Economic Research Survey of regular forecasts, median, (ASA), Victor Zarnowitz	17	5	4	1968	Most participants rely primarily on an "informal" GNP model; the majority also consider econometric model results	V. Zarnowitz chapter in Butler, Kavesh, and Platt, eds., *Methods and Techniques of Business Forecasting*, Prentice-Hall, 1974 and NBER *Reporter*, Summer, 1982.
Bureau of Economic Analysis, U.S. Commerce Department, (BEA), Michael McKelvey	About 900	10 to 12	8	1967	Econometric model (70%), judgment (20%), current data analysis (5%), interaction with others (5%)	A. Hirsch, et al., ch. 10 in Klein & Burmeister, *Econometric Model Performance*, U. of Pa. Press, 1976.
Charles R. Nelson Associates, Inc., Benchmark forecast, (BMARK), Charles R. Nelson	3	4	4	1976	Time-series methods (100%)	C. Nelson, *Applied Time Series Analysis*, Basic Books, 1973.
Chase Econometrics, (Chase), Lawrence Chimerine	About 700	10 to 12	12	1970	Econometric model (70%), judgment (20%), time-series methods (5%), current data analysis (5%)	None
Data Resources, Inc., (DRI), Roger Brinner	About 1000	10 to 12	12	1969	Econometric model (55%), judgment (30%), time-series methods (10%), current data analysis (5%)	O. Eckstein, *The DRI Model of the U.S. Economy*, McGraw-Hill, Inc., 1983.
Economic Forecasting Project, Georgia State University, (GSU), Donald Ratajczak	300	8	12	1973	Econometric model (60%), judgment (30%), current data analysis (10%)	None
Kent Economic and Development Institute, (KEDI), Vladimir Simunek	1699	10	12	1974	Econometric model (60%), judgment (20%), time-series methods (10%), interaction with others (10%)	V. Simunek, *Kent Model of the U.S. Economy*, Kent Econometric Associates, Inc., Kent, Ohio, 1974.
Manufacturers Hanover Trust, (MHT), Irwin Kellner	37	4 to 5	3	1970	Econometric model (50%), judgment (50%)	None
Research Seminar in Quantitative Economics, University of Michigan, (RSQE), Saul Hymans	About 100	8	9	1969	Econometric model (80%), judgment (20%)	Harold T. Shapiro and George A. Fulton, Appendix in *A Regional Econometric Forecasting System: Major Economic Areas of Michigan*. Univ. Mich. Press, 1983.
Townsend-Greenspan & Co., Inc., (TG), Alan Greenspan	About 1400	6 to 10	4	1965	Econometric model (30%), judgment (50%), current data analysis (20%)	None
University of California at Los Angeles, School of Business, (UCLA), Larry J. Kimbell	About 1000	8 to 12	4	1968	Econometric model (70%), judgment (20%), interaction with others (10%)	None
Wharton Econometric Forecasting Associates, Inc., (WEFA), Lawrence R. Klein	About 1200	12	12	1963	Econometric model (60%), judgment (30%), current data analysis (10%)	Lawrence R. Klein and Richard M. Young, *An Introduction to Econometric Forecasting and Forecasting Models*, Lexington, Mass., Heath, 1980.

Source: McNees and Ries 1983:6.

because of the two-way interaction between the use of a model and the forecaster's judgment. The models show considerable variation in the number of macroeconomic variables forecast, how far ahead they forecast, and the frequency of their releases.

Are academic economists more successful than business economists at forecasting? For the first time, the fourth annual Silbert Economic Forecasting Award was given to an academic economist (Saul H. Hymans, item 9 in Table 25.7). The honor was given for his 1983 projections of economic growth, inflation, and unemployment rate (*New York Times* 1984a:32).

Table 25.8 presents the errors of the median (among five) one-year-ahead forecasts of four macroeconomic variables: nominal GNP growth, real GNP growth, inflation rate, and unemployment rate. For example, the GNP value for 1971:2 of -1.6 indicates that actual GNP growth was 1.6% higher than the value predicted in 1970:2. Large errors (those greater than the root-mean-squared error for the entire period) are in italic. Virtually all these large errors occurred in four episodes: the 1973–75 recession, late 1978–early 1979 acceleration of inflation, recovery from the 1980 recession, and the 1981–82 recession (McNees and Ries 1983:10–12).

The errors for 1973–75 are due to both supply-side shocks and overestimates of real demand. The oil embargo and subsequent price increases in the fall of 1973 had significant price-output effects. In the late April 1974 forecasts made after the embargo was ended there was still no appreciation of the severity of the 1974–75 recession. Forecasts of final sales were overestimated because the heavy liquidation of automobile inventories in 1975:1 was not anticipated and also because of fixed investment errors. Here a significant overestimate of the monetary growth rate and underestimate of interest rates may have been partly responsible (McNees 1979b:235, 238–39).

Forecasters systematically underestimated the acceleration of the inflation rate for mid-1977 through early 1978. As a result they made large errors in 1978 and 1979. At the same time Table 25.8 reveals large underestimates in the first half of 1980 of 1981 GNP and real growth. The 1980 recession was briefer than forecasters had anticipated (NcNees and Ries 1983:11).

The severity of the 1981–82 recession was underestimated in forecasts made in 1981 and early 1982. Predicted values for GNP growth are in excess of actual values. The same overprediction applies to the inflation rate for the first time. The 1981–82 experience has been characterized as a "demand shock" with an overestimate of both output and prices. This is in contrast with the 1973–74 supply shock when nominal GNP errors were reduced by offsetting price and output errors.

One might wonder whether the best forecaster can be singled out. This is of obvious interest to forecast users. The McNees-Ries study skirts this delicate issue by pointing out that the answer would depend on the relative importance that the user attaches to each variable being forecast. Predictive performance varies among forecast horizons. Although Table 25.8 describes one-year-ahead forecasts, the forecast horizon can be shorter or as long as eight quarters ahead (NcNees and Ries 1983:12–18).

ECONOMETRICS VS. PURE JUDGMENT AND NO CHANGE   Another way of gauging the effectiveness of econometric forecasts is to compare them with

Source: McNees and Ries 1983:10.

Table 25.8. Episodes of "large" forecast errors (based on the median 1-year-ahead forecasts of five prominent forecasters)

Forecast period ending in	GNP	Real GNP	Implicit price deflator	Unemployment rate
1971:2	-1.6	-0.3	-1.3	-0.8
:3	-1.3	0.2	-1.5	-0.5
:4	-1.3	-0.1	-1.1	-0.3
1972:1	-0.3	0.7	-0.7	-0.1
:2	-0.7	-0.7	0.1	0.2
:3	-0.4	0.2	-0.6	-0.1
:4	-1.4	-0.8	-0.5	0.0
1973:1	-2.3	-1.3	-0.8	0.4
:2	-1.7	0.2	-1.8	0.1
:3	-2.1	0.8	-2.8	0.3
:4	-2.4	0.9	-3.3	0.2
1974:1	0.1	3.5	-3.5	-0.4
:2	-0.8	2.4	-3.1	-0.1
:3	-1.3	2.7	-4.4	-0.3
:4	0.1	3.2	-3.6	-0.5
1975:1	3.5	6.0	-4.0	-2.5
:2	2.7	4.4	-1.9	-2.8
:3	0.8	-0.4	0.5	-1.5
:4	-0.3	-1.4	0.6	-0.1
1976:1	-1.7	-2.4	-0.1	0.8
:2	1.6	1.1	0.4	0.5
:3	2.8	1.2	1.3	-0.1
:4	2.1	0.8	1.2	-0.6
1977:1	2.0	1.1	0.9	-0.6
:2	-0.3	-0.2	0.1	-0.2
:3	-2.1	-1.3	-0.5	0.0
:4	-0.7	-0.2	-0.4	0.0
1978:1	1.7	1.5	0.1	0.5
:2	-1.8	-0.7	-1.1	0.4
:3	-2.1	-0.1	-1.9	0.6
:4	-3.9	-1.4	-2.2	0.6
1979:1	-3.2	-0.4	-2.5	0.3
:2	-1.3	0.7	-1.8	0.7
:3	-2.1	-0.6	-1.6	0.6
:4	-1.3	-1.0	-0.9	0.8
1980:1	-1.8	-1.5	-0.1	0.5
:2	-0.5	-0.1	-0.6	0.0
:3	-1.1	-0.4	-0.7	-0.1
:4	-1.5	-0.1	-1.1	0.1
1981:1	-4.1	-3.6	-0.7	0.7
:2	-4.6	-3.9	-0.2	0.9
:3	-1.8	-1.8	0.1	0.3
:4	1.3	-0.1	1.5	-0.8
1982:1	6.9	4.2	2.0	-1.5
:2	5.9	4.1	1.3	-2.0
:3	6.2	3.6	2.3	-1.7
:4	6.9	3.9	2.8	-2.0
1983:1	5.2	3.2	1.4	-1.7
:2	3.0	1.2	1.9	-1.1
Average error	0.0	0.5	-0.7	-0.3
Average absolute error	2.2	1.6	1.4	0.7
Root mean square error	2.8	2.1	1.8	0.9

Source: McNees and Ries 1983:10.
Note: 1-year-ahead errors are calculated from the median of early quarter forecasts by the ASA/NBER survey, Chase, DRI, Wharton, and BEA.
Errors for GNP, real GNP, and the implicit price deflator are calculated as predicted minus actual growth at compound rates. Unemployment rate errors are the difference between predicted and actual unemployment rate levels.

judgmental and statistical forecasts. Econometric forecasts that are not mechanical reflect judgment. So the first comparison is between a purely judgmental forecast and a mixed econometric forecast. The results here are not conclusive because surveys of judgmental forecasters (e.g., the American Statistical Association/National Bureau of Economic Research Survey of Forecasts) do not distinguish sharply between noneconometricians and those who base their forecasts on econometric models. Also in doubt is whether forecasts generated by statistical rules (the simplest rule would be to forecast no change; more complex rules regress the variable on past values of the same variable in time series equations) are not indeed superior to econometric models (McNees 1979b:224–46).

Forecasting and policymaking

THE PUBLIC SECTOR   Government agencies and departments have their own models as well as making use of commercial forecasting services. Forecasting errors aggravate the problems of making policy. A small error in percentage terms can mean a large absolute error in dollar terms; e.g., in a $3 tril. economy a 2% error amounts to $60 bil. For "price" variables, such as the inflation rate, a seemingly small percentage error can loom large relative to the actual value. A real-life example is the forecast error for inflation in 1974. The actual value of the GNP deflator in 1974 was 8.7%. The average downside error (averaging the four 1974 quarters) according to Table 25.8 was 3.6%, or 41% of the actual price increase.

An underestimate of inflation will be coupled with an underestimate of nominal GNP (a function of both the price level and real quantities). If the policy-makers had their preference, they would prefer to overestimate inflation and underestimate real GNP. Unhappily, economic control is not so dependable that nominal growth can be directed to real changes and away from inflation.

Monetary forecasts and uncertainty   The Federal Reserve money market models are the basis of econometric forecasts (Anderson and Rasche 1982:796–826; Tinsley et al. 1982:829–56). How robust the models are will condition the policy-makers confidence. Robustness is a question of error, the uncertainty of forecasts. The Fed can simulate the effects of random disturbances (so-called white noise) on the choice of any operating procedure. The results display wide deviations from monetary or interest rate targets. For example, assuming a regime of lagged reserve requirements and nonborrowed reserves as the proximate target, the chances are seven out of ten that monthly changes in the money stock will fall as far away as 11 standard deviations (plus or minus) from the targeted monthly change in the money stock (Tinsley et al. 1982:846–47). Furthermore, the model of the Federal Reserve Bank of San Francisco gives results sharply at variance with the Board of Governors model.

The volatility of bank deposits, interest rates, personal income, and excess reserves underly forecast errors (Tinsley et al. 1982:851–52). It is no wonder that Anderson and Rasche (1982:816) conclude that current models provide little reliable information regarding monetary control. Nor is it too surprising that policy-makers place little faith in their staffs' models.

THE PRIVATE SECTOR   The private sector increasingly depends on econometric models for policymaking. The uncertainty of the 1970s has stimulated the demand for forecasts. The private sector can buy prepackaged forecasts and access to econometric models or customized models. With access, the client can tinker with the commercial model and explore different possible scenarios. Customized models are specially built for the client. Satellite models are tied to existing models (Behravesh and Mulhern 1979:15, 16).

Econometric models may be an unnecessary extravagance. Suppose that the business firm wishes to forecast interest rates. Futures markets in government securities produce a weighted average forecast, taking account of all available information. Paying for a forecast in such a case is of doubtful worth. Disenchantment with forecasting services has affected their income (Clark and Malabre 1984:1, 15; Wayne 1984:F4).

Summary

All the tools of the trade are reflected in econometric models, so discussion of them is a fitting way to end a text on money and finance. Theory, mathematics, statistical methods, and economic data are integrated in such models. Great expectations naturally arise. Such models should sort out the bad theories from the good. This has not turned out to be the case. Keynesian, monetarist, and flow-of-funds models flourish side by side. Perhaps all can survive because they all breathe the same economic air. Whether small or large scale, the monetary base via some transmission mechanism influences aggregate economic activity. The high correlation of economic time series guarantees similar results regardless of what variables are chosen as the transmission mechanism.

When forecasting ability is tested, all econometric models fare badly when confronted with severe outside shocks. The 1973–75 period dominated by oil shocks is a classic example. Models such as the St. Louis can place part of the blame on their mechanical nature—no tampering with the underlying equations when testing the model beyond its observation period. The crucial importance of judgment for forecasting success is disturbing. It suggests that hidden inside every model there is an economist pulling the levers to keep it running. This points to the inherent instability of the parameters of an econometric model. The structural (behavioral) equations become obsolete as sectors revamp their behavior in light of new circumstances (which means continuously). The limited forecasting ability of econometric models results from unexpected shocks and other such behavior modifications. This affects the ability of policymakers to fine-tune the economy. Short-run policy adjustments can make matters worse if forecasts are inaccurate.

But the weakness in forecasting ability is not a convincing argument against further use and development of econometric models. We know more about the workings of the economy (the transmission mechanisms) as a result of such models. Models force us to be precise in our formulation and testing of hypotheses. Students will probably learn their money and finance to an increasing extent by the study of large-scale econometric models.

Review questions

1. Why can econometrics be regarded as the highest stage of development of the subject of economics?

2. Discuss some of the identifying characteristics of an econometric model.

3. Why is judgment an indispensable element in model-building?

4. Discuss four technical problems that challenge the validity of econometric models.

5. "Models are distinguished by their degree of disaggregation." Explain this statement.

6. Compare and contrast Keynesian, monetarist, and flow-of-funds models.

7. Econometric models are put through their paces by means of simulation. Explain what this concept means.

8. How successful has forecasting been with econometric models? Discuss some of the leading episodes of forecast errors for GNP, real GNP, inflation, and the unemployment rate.

9. Explain the limited usefulness of econometric models for monetary policy-making.

10. How do you explain the survival of so many different models based on different economic theories?

11. Suppose you are running your own business. Would you use econometric forecasting models? Would you buy this service or produce it in-house?

Abrams, Richard K. 1980. International trade flows under flexible exchange rates. *Econ. Rev.,* March. Fed, Kansas City.

Acheson, K., and J. F. Chant. 1973. Bureaucratic theory and the choice of central bank goals: The case of the Bank of Canada. *J. Money, Credit, Banking,* May.

Ackley, Gardner. 1978. *Macroeconomics: Theory and Policy.* New York.

Alperovitz, Gar, and Jeff Faux. 1984. *Rebuilding America.* New York.

AmeriTrust. 1984. American business activity from 1790 to today. Cleveland.

Andersen, Leonall C., and Keith M. Carlson. 1970. A monetarist model for economic stabilization. *Review,* April. Fed, St. Louis.

———. 1976. St. Louis model revisited. In L. R. Klein and E. Burmeister, eds., *Econometric Model Performance,* Philadelphia.

Anderson, Paul S., and James R. Ostas. 1977. Private credit rationing. *N. Engl. Econ. Rev.,* May-June. Fed, Boston.

Anderson, Richard G., and Robert H. Rasche. 1982. What do money market models tell us about how to implement monetary policy? *J. Money, Credit, Banking,* suppl., November.

Andrews, Victor L., and Peter C. Eiseman. 1981. Insurance-type intermediaries: Pension funds. In M. E. Polakoff et al., *Financial Institutions and Markets.* Boston.

Ascheim, J. 1959. Open-market variation versus reserve requirement variation. *Econ. J.,* December.

Attfield, C. L. F., D. Demery, and N. W. Duck. 1985. *Rational Expectations in Macroeconomics.* Oxford, England.

Auerbach, Robert D. 1982. *Money, Banking, and Financial Markets.* New York.

Bach, G. L., and James B. Stephenson. 1974. Inflation and the distribution of wealth. *Rev. Econ. Stat.,* February.

Backus, David, William C. Brainard, Gary Smith, and James Tobin. 1980. A model of U.S. financial and nonfinancial economic behavior. *J. Money, Credit, Banking,* spec. iss., May.

Balatsos, Dimitri N. 1978. Not by debt alone. Manufacturers Hanover Trust Company. New York.

Balbach, Anatol B., David H. Resler. 1980. Eurodollars and the U.S. money supply. *Review,* June-July. Fed, St. Louis.

Bankers Trust Co. 1980. Report, March 17. New York.

———. 1984. *Credit and Capital Markets.* New York.

Barro, Robert, J. 1974. Are government bonds net wealth? *J. Polit. Econ.,* November-December.

———. 1984. *Macroeconomics.* New York.

Barth, James R., and Joseph Pelzman. 1984. *International Debt Conflict and Resolution.* Fairfax, Va.

Batten, Dallas S. 1981. Foreign exchange markets: The dollar in 1980. *Review,* April. Fed, St. Louis.

Batten, Dallas S., and Mack Ott. 1984. What can central banks do about the value of the dollar? *Review,* May. Fed, St. Louis.

Baumol, William J. 1952. The transactions demand for cash: An inventory theoretic approach. *Q. J. Econ.,* November.

———. 1977. *Economic Theory and Operations Analysis.* Englewood Cliffs, N.J.

Behravesh, Nariman. 1975. Forecasting the economy with mathematical models: Is it worth the effort? *Bus. Rev.,* July-August. Fed, Philadelphia.

Behravesh, Nariman, and John J. Mulhern. 1979. Econometric forecasting: Should you buy it? *Bus. Rev.,* May-June. Fed, Philadelphia.

Benjamin, Gary L. 1985. The financial distress in agriculture. *Econ. Perspect.,* November-December. Fed, Chicago.

Bennett, Robert A. 1978. Foreigners' takeovers irk banks. *New York Times,* March 12.

———. 1983. Deregulation alters banking. *New York Times,* December 5.

———. 1984a. Chilling specter at Continental. *New York Times,* May 20.

———. 1984b. Argentine loans hurt 4 banks. *New York Times,* July 13.

———. 1984c. U.S. will invest $4.5 billion in rescue of Chicago bank, vowing more aid if needed. *New York Times,* July 27.

Berg, Eric N. 1985. Maryland's unflappable chief. *New York Times,* May 17.

Berger, Allen N., Joanna H. Frodin, and David B. Humphrey. Forthcoming. Interstate banking and the payments system. FED, Financial Studies Working Paper, Washington, D.C.

Bergstrand, Jeffrey H. 1983. Selected views of exchange rate determination after a decade of "floating." *N. Engl. Econ. Rev.,* May-June.

_____. 1984. Summary. In *International Monetary System: Forty Years after Bretton Woods,* conf. ser. 28. Fed, Boston.

Bergstrand, Jeffrey H. 1985. Exchange rate variation and monetary policy. *N. Engl. Econ. Rev.,* May-June. Fed, Boston.

Berkman, Neil G. 1979. Mortgage finance and the housing cycle. *N. Engl. Econ. Rev.,* September-October. Fed, Boston.

Bernstein, Allen. 1982. *1982 Tax Guide for College Teachers.* Washington, D.C.

Bernstein, Edward M. 1980. Back to the gold standard? *Brookings Bull.,* fall.

Bishop, George, and Thomas R. Hand. 1981. Insurance-type intermediaries: Insurance companies. In M. E. Polakoff et al., *Financial Institutions and Markets,* 2nd ed. Boston.

Bleakley, Fred R. 1984. Continuing plight of brokers. *New York Times,* August 8.

Bleakley, Fred R. 1985. How Hutton scheme worked. *New York Times,* May 17.

Blinder, Alan S., and Robert M. Solow. 1978. Lags and uncertainties in fiscal policy: General considerations and the 1968–1970 experience. In R. L. Teigen, ed., *Readings in Money, National Income, and Stabilization Policy,* 4th ed. Homewood, Ill.

Bloch, Ernest. 1964. Pricing a corporate bond issue: A look behind the scenes. *Essays in Money and Credit,* Fed, New York.

Block, Stanley B., and Geoffrey A. Hirt. 1978. *Foundations of Financial Management.* Homewood, Ill.

Bloomfield, Arthur I. 1981–82. Sidney Weintraub: A profile. *J. Post Keynesian Econ.,* winter.

Blumstein, Michael. 1984. Investing for changing steps of life. *New York Times,* May 20.

Bosworth, Barry, and James S. Duesenberry. 1973. A flow of funds model and its implications. *Issues in Federal Debt Management,* conf. ser. 10. Fed, Boston.

Boughton, James. 1983. Alternatives to intervention: Domestic instruments and external objectives. In Donald Hodgman, ed., *Political Economy of Monetary Policy,* conf. ser. 26. Fed, Boston.

Brimmer, Andrew F., and Frederick R. Dahl. 1976. Growth of American international banking: Implications for public policy. In T. M. Havrilesky and J. T. Boorman, *Current Perspectives in Banking.* Chicago.

Broaddus, Alfred. 1972. Linear programming: A new approach to bank portfolio management. *Mon. Rev.,* November. Fed, Richmond.

_____. 1985. Financial innovation in the United States – Background, current status and prospects. *Econ. Rev.,* January-February. Fed, Richmond.

Bronfenbrenner, Martin, ed. 1969. *Is the Business Cycle Obsolete?* New York.

Brooks, John. 1982. The supply side. *New Yorker,* April 19.

Brundy, James, David B. Humphrey, Myron L. Kwast. 1979. Check processing at Federal Reserve offices. *Fed. Res. Bull.,* February.

Brunner, Karl, and Allan H. Meltzer. 1965. Development of the free reserve conception of monetary processes. In W. L. Smith and R. L. Teigen, *Readings in Money, Income, and Economic Stabilization Policy,* 1st ed., Homewood, Ill.

_____. 1968. Liquidity traps for money, bank credit, and interest rates. *J. Polit. Econ.,* January-February.

Bryant, Ralph C. 1983. *Controlling Money.* Washington, D.C.

Burger, Albert E. 1969. A historical analysis of the credit crunch of 1966. *Review,* September. Fed, St. Louis.

_____. 1971. *The Money Supply Process.* Belmont, Calif.

_____. 1975. Monetary effects of the treasury sale of gold. *Review,* January. Fed, St. Louis.

Burke, William. 1980. Countering the threat. *Wkly. Lett.,* March 21. Fed, San Francisco.

Business International Corporation Data Base: 1978–1983. 1984. New York.

Cacy, J. A., and Mary Hamblin. 1974. Trends and cycles in credit market borrowing. *Mon. Rev.,* March. Fed, Kansas City.

Cacy, J. A., and Scott Winningham. 1980. Reserve requirements under the depository institutions deregulation and monetary control act of 1980. *Econ. Rev.,* September-October. Fed, Kansas City.

Cameron, Norman E. 1984. *Money, Financial Markets, and Economic Activity.* Don Mills, Ontario, Canada.

Cameron, Rondo. 1967. *Banking in the Early Stages of Industrialization.* New York.

Carlson, Keith N. 1979. Explaining the economic slowdown of 1979: A supply and demand approach. *Review,* October. Fed, St. Louis.

Carron, Andrew S. 1984. Banking on change: The reorganization of financial regulation. *Brookings Rev.,* spring.

Chandrasekhar, Ashok. 1984. Gauging living standards in '84. *Wall Street Journal,* July 24.

Cheng, Hang-Sheng. 1983. International debt management. *Wkly. Lett.,* December 23. Fed, San Francisco.

Chrystal, K. Alec. 1984a. A guide to foreign exchange markets. *Review,* March. Fed, St. Louis.

_____. 1984b. International banking facilities. *Review,* April. Fed, St. Louis.

Ciccolo, John, and Gary Fromm. 1980. "q" corporate investment and balance sheet behavior. *J. Money, Credit, Banking,* spec. iss., May.

Clark, Lindley H., Jr. 1981. What's been buffeting interest rates? *Wall Street Journal,* December 22.

_____. 1984. The Fed is unlikely to tighten policy any time soon. *Wall Street Journal,* April 10.

Clark, Lindley H., Jr., and Alfred L. Malabre, Jr. 1984. Business forecasters find demand weak in their own business. *Wall Street Journal,* September 7.

Clarke, Stephen V. O. 1980. Perspective on the United States external position since World War II. *Q. Rev.,* summer. Fed, New York.

Clines, Francis X. 1984. Reagan proposes $34 billion saving and pay cut of 5%. *New York Times,* December 6.

Cloos, George W. 1978. Indexation and inflation. *Econ. Perspect.,* May-June. Fed, Chicago.

Clymer, Adam. 1984. Poll finds most say they're better off than in '80. *New York Times,* August 17.

Cohen, Jacob. 1951. Distributional effects of the federal debt. *J. Finance,* September.

_____. 1965a. Federal reserve margin requirements and the stock market. *J. Fin. Quant. Anal.,* September.

_____. 1965b. The impact of the stock market on the flow of funds. *Riv. Int. Sci. Econ. Commer.,* September.

_____. 1967. Comment on Gaines and Smith papers. In G. Horwich, ed., *Monetary Process and Policy.* Homewood, Ill.

_____. 1970. Direct versus indirect control as instruments of monetary policy. *Q. Rev. Econ. Bus.,* fall.

_____. 1975a. Borrower discretion, the government securities market, and monetary policy. *J. Econ. Bus.,* spring.

_____. 1975b. Borrower discretion, the government securities market and monetary policy — errata. *J. Econ. Bus.,* fall.

_____. 1982. Beyond IS-LM. *Malay. Econ. Rev.,* April.

Cohen, Jacob, and James L. Kenkel. 1979–80. A credit model featuring external finance and scale economies. *J. Post Keynesian Econ.,* winter.

Cohen, Jerome B. 1979. *Personal Finance,* 6th ed. Homewood, Ill.

Colander, David C. 1979. A value-added tax-based incomes policy. In D. C. Colander, ed., *Solutions to Inflation.* New York.

Concise Explanation of the Economic Recovery Tax of 1981. 1981. Englewood Cliffs, N.J.

Cook, Timothy, and Jeremy Duffield. 1979. Money market mutual funds: A reaction to government regulations or a lasting financial innovation? *Econ. Rev.,* July-August. Fed, Richmond.

Cooper, Richard N. 1984. Is there a need for reform? *International Monetary System: Forty Years after Bretton Woods,* conf. ser. 28. Fed, Boston.

Corrigan, E. Gerald. 1984. Statement to Congress. *Fed. Res. Bull.,* May.

Cox, Donald. 1980. The March 14 credit controls, consumer credit and spending: Progress report, res. pap. 8010. Fed, New York.

Craine, Roger. 1982. Volatility and unpredictability. *Wkl. Lett.,* October 1, Fed, San Francisco.

Crews, Joseph M. 1973. Econometric models:

The monetarist and nonmonetarist views compared. In T. M. Havrilesky and J. T. Boorman, *Current Perspectives in Banking,* Chicago.

Culbertson, John M. 1968. *Macroeconomic Theory and Stabilization Policy.* New York.

Cummins, J. David. 1975. *An Econometric Model of the Life Insurance Sector of the U.S. Economy.* Lexington, Mass.

Dauten, Carl A., and Lloyd M. Valentine. 1978. *Business Cycles and Forecasting.* Cincinnati, Ohio.

David, Jacques H. 1973. In *Credit Allocation Techniques and Monetary Policy,* conf. ser. 11. Fed, Boston.

Davidson, Paul. 1984. Who's afraid of the big bad federal deficits? *New York Times,* August 23.

De Leeuw, Frank, and Edward Gramlich. 1969. The channels of monetary policy. *Fed. Res. Bull.,* June.

De Leeuw, Frank, and Thomas H. Holloway. 1983. Measuring and analyzing the cyclically adjusted budget. *Economics of Large Government Deficits,* conf. ser. 27. Fed, Boston.

DeMagistris, Robin C., and Carl J. Palash. 1982. Impact of IRAs on saving. *Q. Rev.,* winter. Fed, New York.

DePamphilis, Donald M. 1974. The short-term commercial bank adjustment process and Federal Reserve regulation. *N. Engl. Econ. Rev.,* May-June. Fed, Boston.

Dernburg, Thomas F., and Duncan M. McDougall. 1968. *Macroeconomics,* 3rd ed. New York.

_____. 1972. *Macroeconomics,* 4th ed. New York.

_____. 1976. *Macroeconomics,* 5th ed. New York.

Donaldson, Gordon. 1969. *Strategy for Financial Mobility.* Boston.

Donoghue, William. 1984. Headaches combine with convenience in age of electronic banking. *Pittsburgh Press,* August 20.

Dornbusch, Rudiger, and Stanley Fischer. 1978. *Macroeconomics,* 1st ed. New York.

_____. 1984. *Macroeconomics,* 3rd ed. New York.

Eastburn, David P., and W. Lee Hoskins. 1978. The influence of monetary policy on commercial banking. *Bus. Rev.,* July-August. Fed, Philadelphia.

Eckstein, Otto, and Allen Sinai. 1986. The mechanisms of the business cycle in the postwar era. In Robert J. Gordon, ed., *The American Business Cycle Today: Continuity and Change.* Chicago.

Emminger, Otmar. 1985. The international role of the dollar. *Econ. Rev.,* September-October. Fed, Kansas City.

Erb, Richard D., ed. 1978. *Federal Reserve Policies and Public Disclosure.* Washington, D.C.

Evanoff, Douglas D., ed. 1985. Financial industry deregulation in the 1980s. *Econ. Perspect.,* September-October. Fed, Chicago.

Evans, Michael K. 1969. *Macroeconomic Activity.* New York.

Fallek, Evelyn C., and Richard W. Nelson. 1978. Bank holding company financial structure and bank capital supervision: An economic appraisal, res. pap. 7810. Fed, New York.

Federal Deposit Insurance Corporation (FDIC). 1979. Annual report. Washington, D.C.

————. 1980. Annual report. Washington, D.C.

————. 1982. Statistics on banking. Washington, D.C.

————. 1983. Data book. Washington, D.C.

————. 1984. Annual report. Washington, D.C.

Federal Open Market Committee (FOMC). 1984. Report, July 25. Washington, D.C.

Federal Reserve Bank (Fed), Boston. 1984. *International Monetary System: Forty Years after Bretton Woods,* conf. ser. 28.

Federal Reserve Bank (Fed), Chicago. 1975. Modern money mechanics.

————. 1980. The Depository Institutions Deregulation and Monetary Control Act, 1980. *Econ. Perspect.* September-October.

————. 1983. *Leveling the Playing Field.* Chicago.

Federal Reserve Bank (Fed), Dallas. 1982. Reagan signs landmark banking law. *Roundup,* November.

————. 1983. "Super NOW" accelerates deregulation trend. *Roundup,* January.

Federal Reserve Bank (Fed), Minneapolis. 1979. The tax-cut illusion. Annual report.

Federal Reserve Bank (Fed), New York. 1974. *A Day at the Fed.* New York.

————. 1981. Statistical facts. New York.

————. 1982. C.H.I.P.S. Public Information Dept., March.

————. 1983. The story of checks. New York.

Federal Reserve Bank (Fed), Philadelphia. 1964. *50 Years of the Federal Reserve Act.*

————. 1984. *Depository Institutions and Their Regulators.* New York.

Federal Reserve Bank (Fed), Richmond. 1974. *The Federal Reserve at Work.*

Federal Reserve Board (FRB). n.d. *Truth in Lending Regulation Z Annual Percentage Rate Tables,* vol. 1. Washington, D.C.

————. 1970. Annual report. Washington, D.C.

————. 1974. *The Federal Reserve System, Purposes and Functions.* Washington, D.C.

————. 1978a. Annual report. Washington, D.C.

————. 1978b. *A Guide to Federal Reserve Regulations.* Washington, D.C.

————. 1980a. *Introduction to Flow of Funds.* Washington, D.C.

————. 1980b. The new Federal Reserve technical procedures for controlling money, memo, February 1. Washington, D.C.

————. 1981. *A Guide to Federal Reserve Regulations.* Washington, D.C.

————. 1982. Annual statistical digest. Washington, D.C.

————. 1983a. Annual report. Washington, D.C.

————. 1983b. *Credit Cards in the U.S. Economy.* Washington, D.C.

————. 1983c. *Flow of Funds Accounts, Assets and Liabilities Outstanding, 1959–82.* Washington, D.C.

————. 1983d. *Historical Chart Book.* Washington, D.C.

————. 1983e. Reduction and pricing of Federal Reserve float, press release, May 4. Washington, D.C.

————. 1984a. *Chart Book.* Washington, D.C.

————. 1984b. *Flow of Funds Accounts, Assets and Liabilities Outstanding, 1960–83.* Washington, D.C.

————. 1984c. *Flow of Funds Accounts, Balance Sheets for the U.S. Economy, 1945–83.* Washington, D.C.

————. 1984d. *Flow of Funds Accounts, 1st Quarter, 1984.* Washington, D.C.

————. 1984e. *Flow of Funds Accounts, 2nd Quarter, 1984.* Washington, D.C.

————. 1984f. *Monetary Policy Objectives for 1984 with Tentative Monetary Growth Ranges for 1985.* Summary of Report to Congress on Monetary Policy pursuant to Full Employment and Balanced Growth Act of 1978.

————. 1984g. Statistical release H.6. Washington, D.C.

————. 1984h. *Structure Data for U.S. Offices of Foreign Banks by Type of Institution.* Washington, D.C.

————. 1984i. Flow of Funds Section, Div. Res. and Stat. May.

————. 1985a. Flow of Funds Section, Div. Res. and Stat. January.

————. 1985b. Flow of Funds Accounts, 2nd Quarter, 1985. Washington, D.C.

Federal Reserve Bulletin. 1940. Sources of a bank's lending power. February.

————. 1976. Federal Reserve operations in payment mechanisms: A summary. June.

————. 1978. June.

————. 1981a. Survey of finance companies. May.

————. 1981b. August.

————. 1982. February.

————. 1983a. May.

————. 1983b. July.

————. 1983c. September.

————. 1984a. May.

————. 1984b. June.

————. 1984c. Record of policy actions of the Federal Open Market Committee. June.

————. 1984d. June.

————. 1984e. August.

————. 1984f. September.

————. 1984g. December.

————. 1985a. January.

————. 1985b. February.

Feldstein, Martin. 1982. Government deficits and aggregate demand. *J. Monetary Econ.,* January.

Fieleke, Norman S. 1974. Oil and international payments. *N. Engl. Econ. Rev.,* November-December. Fed, Boston.

————. 1976. What is the balance of payments? *N. Engl. Econ. Rev.,* July. Fed, Boston.

Fisher, Irving. 1930. *The Theory of Interest Rates.* New York.

————. 1933. The debt-deflation theory of great

depressions. *Econometrica,* vol. 1.

Flash, Edward S., Jr. 1965. *Economic Advice and Presidential Leadership.* New York.

Fleming, Miles. 1964. The timing of payments and the demand for money. *Economica,* May.

Foldessy, Edward P. 1984. Bonds surge again as administration turns up pressure on Fed to ease policy. *Wall Street Journal,* November 24.

Francis, Jack Clark, and Stephen H. Archer. 1979. *Portfolio Analysis,* 2nd ed. Englewood Cliffs, N.J.

Frankel, Allen. 1974. International banking—Structural aspects of regulation. *Bus. Cond.,* October. Fed, Chicago.

Friedland, Seymour. 1966. *The Economics of Corporate Finance.* Englewood Cliffs, N.J.

———. 1978. *Principles of Financial Management.* Cambridge, Mass.

Friedman, Benjamin M. 1972. Credit rationing: A review. *Staff Economic Studies,* no. 72. Washington, D.C.

———. 1975. The determination of long-term interest rates: Why were bond yields so high in 1974? *N. Engl. Econ. Rev.,* May-June. Fed, Boston.

———. 1982a. Time to reexamine the monetary targets framework. *New Engl. Econ. Rev.,* March-April. Fed, Boston.

———. 1982b. Using a credit aggregate target to implement monetary policy in the financial environment of the future. In *Monetary Policy Issues in the 1980s.* Fed, Kansas City.

———. 1983. Implications of the government deficit for U.S. capital formation. *Economics of Large Government Deficits,* conf. ser. 27. Fed, Boston.

Friedman, Lisa. 1984. Bank card system expands capabilities. *Pittsburgh Post-Gazette,* August 22.

Friedman, Milton, and Anna Jacobson Schwartz. 1963. *A Monetary History of the United States, 1867–1960.* Princeton, N.J.

Fromm, Gary, and L. R. Klein. 1976. The NBER/NSF model comparison seminar: An analysis of results. In L. R. Klein and E. Burmeister, *Econometric Model Performance,* Philadelphia.

Fuerbringer, Jonathan. 1983. Choice of Volcker seen as based on experience. *New York Times,* June 19.

Furlong, Frederick T. 1984. FDIC's modified payout plan. *Wkly. Lett.,* May 18. Fed, San Francisco.

Furlong, Frederick T., and Michael W. Keran. 1984. The federal safety net for commercial banks: Part II. *Wkly. Lett.,* August 3. Fed, San Francisco.

Gavin, William T., and Nicholas V. Karamouzis. 1985. The reserve market and the information content of *M*1 announcements. *Econ. Rev.,* quarter 1. Fed, Cleveland.

Ghalib, Sharif. 1984. OPEC's sea of red. *Chase Economic Observer,* September-October.

Gilbert, R. Alton. 1979. Benefits of borrowing from the Federal Reserve when the discount rate is below market interest rates. *Review,*

March. Fed, St. Louis.

———. 1983. Two measures of reserves: Why are they different? *Review,* June-July. Fed, St. Louis.

———. 1985. Operating procedures for conducting monetary policy. *Review,* February. Fed, St. Louis.

Gilbert, R. Alton, and A. Steven Holland. 1984. Has the deregulation of deposit interest rates raised mortgage rates? *Review,* May. Fed, St. Louis.

Gilbert, R. Alton, and Jean M. Lovati. 1978. Bank reserve requirements and their enforcement: A comparison across states. *Review,* March. Fed, St. Louis.

Gilbert, R. Alton, and Michael E. Trebing. 1981. The FOMC in 1980: A year of Reserve targeting. *Review,* August-September. Fed, St. Louis.

Gold Commission. 1982. *Report to the Congress of the Commission on the Role of Gold in the Domestic and International Monetary Systems,* 2 vols. Washington, D.C.

Goldsmith, Raymond W. 1958. *Financial Intermediaries in the American Economy Since 1900.* Princeton, N.J.

Goodfriend, Marvin. 1982. A model of money stock determination with loan demand and a banking system balance sheet constraint. *Econ. Rev.,* January-February. Fed, Richmond.

Gordon, Robert J. 1981. *Macroeconomics,* 2nd ed. Boston.

Gramley, Lyle E., and Samuel B. Chase. 1965. Time deposits in monetary analysis. *Fed. Res. Bull.,* October.

Gregorash, Sue F. 1983. First year experience: Illinois multibanks shop carefully. *Econ. Perspect.,* May-June. Fed, Chicago.

———. 1984. The Midwest prepares for interstate banking. *Econ. Perspect.,* March-April. Fed, Chicago.

Guttentag, Jack M. 1975. Selective credit controls on residential mortgage credit. In I. Kaminow and J. M. O'Brien, *Studies in Selective Credit Policies.* Fed, Philadelphia.

Hakkio, Craig S. 1984. Exchange rate volatility and Federal Reserve policy. *Econ. Rev.,* July-August. Fed, Kansas City.

Hakkio, Craig S., and J. Gregg Whittaker. 1985. The U.S. dollar—Recent developments, outlook and policy options. *Econ. Rev.,* September-October. Fed, Kansas City.

Hamburger, Michael J. 1980. The lag in the effect of monetary policy: A survey of recent literature. In T. M. Havrilesky and J. T. Boorman, *Current Issues in Monetary Theory and Policy,* 2nd ed., Arlington Heights, Ill.

Hand, John H. 1981. Government lending agencies. In M. E. Polakoff et al., *Financial Institutions and Markets,* 2nd ed. Boston.

Harless, Doris E. 1975. *Nonbank Financial Institutions.* Fed, Richmond, Va.

Havrilesky, Thomas M., Robert H. Sapp, and Robert L. Schweitzer. 1976. Tests of the Federal Reserve's reaction to the state of the economy: 1964–1974. In T. M. Havrilesky and J. T. Boorman, *Current Perspectives in Banking,* Chicago.

Hawkins, Robert G., and Richard W. Levich. 1981. International financial policy. In M. E. Polakoff et al., *Financial Institutions and and Markets,* 2nd ed., Boston.

Hendershott, Patric H. 1977. *Understanding Capital Markets,* vol. 1: *A Flow-of-Funds Financial Model.* Lexington, Mass.

Henning, Charles N., William Piggot, and Robert Haney Scott. 1981. *Financial Markets and the Economy,* 3rd ed. Englewood Cliffs, N.J.

———. 1984. *Financial Markets and the Economy,* 4th ed. Englewood Cliffs, N.J.

Hershey, Robert D., Jr. 1985a. Savings rate in U.S. lowest since 50's, despite incentives. *New York Times,* October 29.

———. 1985b. Farm debt aid is said to emerge. *New York Times,* October 31.

Hertzberg, Daniel. 1984. FDIC action on failed banks continues effort to increase "market discipline." *Wall Street Journal,* March 21.

Hertzberg, Daniel, Tim Carrington, and John Andrew. 1984. Confidence game. *Wall Street Journal,* May 25.

Hervey, Jack L. 1983. Bankers' acceptances revisited. *Econ. Perspect.,* May-June. Fed, Chicago.

Hester, Donald D., and James L. Pierce. 1975. *Bank Management and Portfolio Behavior.* New Haven, Conn.

Higgins, Byron. 1978. Velocity: Money's second dimension. *Econ. Rev.,* June. Fed, Kansas City.

Higgins, Byron, and Jon Faust. 1981. Velocity behavior of the new monetary aggregates. *Econ. Rev.,* September-October. Fed, Kansas City.

Hodgman, Donald R. 1963. *Commercial Bank Loan and Investment Policy.* Urbana, Ill.

———. 1973. Credit controls in western Europe: An evaluative review. *Credit Allocation Techniques and Monetary Policy,* conf. ser. 11. Fed, Boston.

———. 1974. *National Policies and International Monetary Cooperation.* Boston.

Holbik, Karel, ed. 1973. *Monetary Policy in Twelve Industrial Countries.* Fed, Boston.

Homer, Sydney. 1977. *A History of Interest Rates.* New Brunswick, N.J.

Hood, William C. 1959. *Financing of Economic Activity in Canada.* Ottawa.

Horvitz, Paul M. 1974. *Monetary Policy and the Financial System,* 3rd ed. Englewood Cliffs, N.J.

———. 1979. *Monetary Policy and the Financial System,* 4th ed. Englewood Cliffs, N.J.

———. 1984. Discussion. *J. Finance,* July.

Hotson, John H., et al. 1976. *Stagflation and the Bastard Keynesians.* Waterloo, Ontario.

Houpt, James V., and Michael G. Martinson. 1982. Foreign subsidiaries of U.S. banking organizations, Fed staff studies 120. Washington, D.C.

Howell, James E., and Daniel Teichroew. 1963.

Mathematical Analysis for Business Decisions. Homewood, Ill.

Humphrey, Thomas M. 1979a. Some recent developments in Phillips curve analysis. *Essays in Inflation.* Fed, Richmond.

———. 1979b. Changing views of the Phillips curve. *Essays in Inflation.* Fed, Richmond.

Hutchison, Michael M. 1984. Intervention, deficit finance, and real exchange rates: The case of Japan. *Econ. Rev.,* winter. Fed, San Francisco.

Ibbotson, R., R. A. Sinquefield, and L. B. Siegel. 1984. Historical returns on principal types of investment. Cited in J. J. Pringle and R. S. Harris, *Essentials of Managerial Finance.* Glenview, Ill.

International Monetary Fund (IMF). 1980. Survey, December 15. Washington, D.C.

———. 1984a. *Exchange Rate System: Lessons of the Past and Options for the Future.* Washington, D.C.

———. 1984b. Survey, November 26. Washington, D.C.

———. 1984c. *World Economic Outlook.* Occ. paper 27. Washington, D.C.

Isard, Peter. 1984. U.S. international transactions in 1983. *Fed. Res. Bull.* April.

Janssen, Richard F. 1980. Bankers' bank. *Wall Street Journal,* October 18.

Jaroslovsky, Rich, and Paul Blustein. 1984. Gathering storm, climb in interest rates clouds sunny outlook for Reagan strategists. *Wall Street Journal,* May 11.

Johnson, Glen R. 1978. Money market funds. In Jacob Cohen, ed., *Money Management in Pittsburgh.* Pittsburgh, Pa.

Johnson, Omotunde. 1975. Direct controls in a development context: The case of African countries. In T. Mayer: *Government Credit Allocation,* Institute of Contemporary Studies, San Francisco.

Johnston, Verle B. 1982. Sero sed serio. (Late but earnest). *Wkly. Lett.,* October 15. Fed, San Francisco.

———. 1983. Moratorium? *Wkly. Lett.,* June 3. Fed, San Francisco.

———. 1984. Reorganization? *Wkly. Lett.,* March 2. Fed, San Francisco.

Jordan, Jerry L. 1969. Elements of money stock determination. *Review,* October. Fed, St. Louis.

Judd, John P., and Brian Motley. 1984. Ending the lag. *Wkly. Lett.,* March 30. Fed, San Francisco.

Judd, John P., and John L. Scadding. 1981. Liability management, bank loans and deposit "market" disequilibrium. *Econ. Rev.,* summer. Fed, San Francisco.

———. 1982. Comment on "What do money market models tell us about how to implement monetary policy?" *J. Money, Credit, Banking,* November.

Kalecki, M. 1971. *Selected Essays on the Dynamics of the Capitalist Economy, 1933–1970.* Cambridge, England.

Kaminow, Ira, and James M. O'Brien. 1975. Issues in selective credit policies: An evaluative essay. In I. Kaminow and J. M. O'Brien, eds., *Studies in Selective Credit Policies.* Fed, Philadelphia.

Kane, Edward J. 1972. Discussion in *Policies for a More Competitive System,* conf. ser. 8. Fed, Boston.

_____. 1976. How much do new congressional restraints lessen Federal Reserve independence? In T. M. Havrilesky and J. T. Boorman, *Current Perspectives in Banking.* Chicago.

_____. 1984. Technological and regulatory forces in the developing fusion of financial-services competition. *J. Finance,* July.

Kaufman, G. C. 1973. *Money, the Financial System and the Economy,* 1st ed. Chicago.

_____. 1977. *Money, the Financial System and the Economy.* 2nd ed. Chicago.

_____. 1981. *Money, the Financial System and the Economy,* 3rd ed. Chicago.

Kaufman, George G., Larry R. Mote, and Harvey Rosenblum. 1984. Consequences of deregulation for commercial banking. *J. Finance,* July.

Keeley, Michael C. 1984. Interest-rate deregulation. *Wkly. Lett.,* January 13. Fed, San Francisco.

Keeley, Michael C., and Gary C. Zimmerman. 1984. Deregulation and bank profitability. *Wkly. Lett.,* July 13. Fed, San Francisco.

Kemp, Donald S. 1975. Balance-of-payments concepts: What do they really mean? *Review,* July. Fed, St. Louis.

Keran, Michael W., and Frederick T. Furlong. 1984. The federal safety net for commercial banks: Part I. *Wkly. Lett.,* July 27. Fed, San Francisco.

Kilborn, Peter T. 1984a. After years of absence, deflation causes worries. *New York Times,* July 23.

_____. 1984b. Appraising Volcker's record. *New York Times,* June 15.

_____. 1984c. Computing a budget. *New York Times,* November 19.

_____. 1985a. U.S. and 4 allies plan move to cut value of dollar. *New York Times,* September 23.

_____. 1985b. How the Big Six steer the economy. *New York Times,* November 17.

Kindleberger, Charles P. 1978. *Manias, Panics, and Crashes,* New York.

Klise, Eugene S. 1955. *Money and Banking.* Cincinnati, Ohio.

Knight, Robert E. 1970. *Federal Reserve System Policies and Their Effects on the Banking System.* Fed, Boston.

_____. 1972. The impact of changing check clearing arrangements on the correspondent banking system. *Mon. Rev.,* December. Fed, Kansas City.

_____. 1974a. Reserve requirements, Part 1: Comparative reserve requirements at member and nonmember banks. *Mon. Rev.,* April. Fed, Kansas City.

_____. 1974b. The changing payments mecha-nism: Electronic funds transfer arrangements. *Mon. Rev.,* July-August. Fed, Kansas City.

Kopcke, Richard W. 1978. The decline in corporate profitability. *N. Engl. Econ. Rev.,* May-June. Fed, Boston.

_____. 1983a. Must the ideal "money stock" be controllable? *New Engl. Econ. Rev.,* March-April. Fed, Boston.

_____. 1983b. Will big deficits spoil the recovery? *The Economics of Large Government Deficits,* conf. ser. 27. Fed, Boston.

Kristol, Irving. 1982. The focus is on the Fed. *Wall Street Journal,* February 12.

Krugman, Paul. 1983. International aspects of U.S. monetary and fiscal policy. *Economics of Large Government Deficits,* conf. ser. 27. Fed, Boston.

Kubarych, Roger M. 1978. *Foreign Exchange Markets in the United States.* Fed, New York.

Kvasnicka, Joseph G. 1976. International Banking: Part II. Reprinted in Fed, Chicago, *Readings in International Finance,* 1983.

Land, Richard W., and Robert H. Rasche. 1978. A comparison of yields on futures contracts and implied forward rates. *Review,* December. Fed, St. Louis.

Laney, Leroy O. 1980. SDR substitution, the dollar or multiple reserve assets: Where are we bound from here? *Voice,* July. Fed, Dallas.

_____. 1984. The strong dollar, the current account, and federal deficits: Cause and effect. *Econ. Rev.,* January. Fed, Dallas.

Laney, Leroy O., and Thomas D. Willett. 1982. Presidential politics, budget deficits, and monetary policy in the United States: 1960–1976. *Claremont Work. Pap.,* January.

Lang, Richard W. 1979. TTL note accounts and the money supply process. *Review,* October. Fed, St. Louis.

_____. 1983. Using econometric models to make economic policy: A continuing controversy. *Bus. Rev.,* January-February. Fed, Philadelphia.

Laporte, Anne Marie. 1973. ABC's of figuring interest. *Bus. Cond.,* September. Fed, Chicago.

Lebenthal. 1985. *Supplement to municipal bond information kit.* New York.

Lee, Maurice W. 1971. *Macroeconomics: Fluctuations, Growth, and Stability,* 5th ed. Homewood, Ill.

Leijonhufvud, Axel. 1968. *On Keynesian Economics and the Economics of Keynes.* New York.

Lerner, Abba P. 1978. A wage-increase permit plan to stop inflation. In A. M. Okun and G. L. Perry, *Curing Chronic Inflation,* Washington, D.C.

Lerner, Abba, and David C. Colander. 1979. MAP: A cure for inflation. In D. C. Colander, ed., *Solutions to Inflation.* New York.

Levich, Richard M., and Robert G. Hawkins. 1981. Foreign investment. In M. E. Polakoff et al., *Financial Institutions and Markets,* 2nd ed. Boston.

Levine, Richard J. 1980. Fed pitches money down the middle. *Wall Street Journal,* May 12.

Levy, Michael. 1981. Fiscal and debt management policies. In M. E. Polakoff et al., *Financial Institutions and Markets,* 2nd ed. Boston.

Lewis, Paul. 1984. Europe currency units may play bigger role. *New York Times,* December 6.

Light, Jay O., and William L. White. 1979. *The Financial System.* Homewood, Ill.

Lindbeck, Assar. 1973. Some fiscal and monetary policy experiments in Sweden. *Credit Allocation Techniques and Monetary Policy,* conf. ser. 11. Fed, Boston.

Loeys, Jan G. 1985. Interest rate swaps: A new tool for management risk. *Bus. Rev.,* May-June. Fed, Philadelphia.

Lohr, Steve. 1980. Buying habits found unexpectedly curbed by controls on credit. *New York Times,* May 9.

Lombra, Raymond E. 1979. Discussion. *J. Finance,* May.

Lombra, Raymond E., and Raymond C. Torto. 1976. The strategy of monetary policy. In T. M. Havrilesky and J. T. Boorman, *Current Perspectives in Monetary Theory and Policy.* Chicago.

Lucas, Robert E, Jr. 1976. Econometric policy evaluation: A critique. *The Phillips Curve and Labor Markets,* Carnegie-Rochester Conf. Ser. on Public Policy. Amsterdam, Holland.

————. 1981. Tobin and monetarism: A review article. *J. Econ. Lit.,* June.

Lucas, Robert E., and Thomas J. Sargent. 1978. After Keynesian economics. *After the Phillips Curve: Persistence of High Inflation and Unemployment,* conf. ser. 19. Fed, Boston.

McCarthy, Edward J. 1975. *Reserve Position: Methods of Adjustment.* Fed, Boston.

McElhattan, Rose. 1980. Budgets and borrowing. *Wkly. Lett.,* April 11. Fed, San Francisco.

Machlup, Fritz. 1940. *The Stock Market, Credit and Capital Formation.* London.

McMillan, W. Douglas, and Thomas R. Beard. 1980. The short-run impact of fiscal policy on the money supply. *South. Econ. J.,* July.

McNees, Stephen K. 1973a. The predictive accuracy of economic forecasts. *N. Engl. Econ. Rev.,* September-October. Fed, Boston.

————. 1973b. A comparison of the GNP forecasting accuracy of the Fair and St. Louis econometric models. *N. Engl. Econ. Rev.,* September-October. Fed, Boston.

————. 1975. An evaluation of economic forecasts. *N. Engl. Econ. Rev.,* November-December. Fed, Boston.

————. 1978. The current business cycle in historical perspective. *N. Engl. Econ. Rev.,* January-February. Fed, Boston.

————. 1979a. The forecasting record for the 1970s. *N. Engl. Econ. Rev.,* September-October. Fed, Boston.

————. 1979b. Lessons from the track record of macroeconomic forecasts in the 1970s. In S. Madridakis and S. C. Wheelwright, eds., *Forecasting: Studies in Management Sciences,* vol. 13. Amsterdam.

McNees, Stephen K., and John Ries. 1983. The track record of macroeconomic forecasts. *N. Engl. Econ. Rev.,* November-December. Fed, Boston.

Maddock, Rodney, and Michael Carter. 1982. A child's guide to rational expectations. *J. Econ. Lit.,* March.

Maisel, Sherman J. 1973. *Managing the Dollar.* New York.

————. 1982. *Macroeconomics.* New York.

Maital, S., and Yael Benjamini. 1980. Inflation as prisoner's dilemma. *J. Post Keynesian Econ.,* summer.

Mansfield, Edwin. 1977. *Economics,* 2nd ed. New York.

Martin, A. E. 1985. The book-entry system for Treasury securities. *Econ. Rev.,* September. Fed, Atlanta.

Mayer, Thomas. 1975. Credit allocation: A critical view. *Government Credit Allocation,* Institute of Contemporary Studies. San Francisco.

Mayer, Thomas, James S. Duesenberry, and Robert Z. Aliber. 1981. *Money, Banking, and the Economy,* 1st ed. New York.

————. 1984. *Money, Banking, and the Economy,* 2nd ed. New York.

————. 1985. *Newsletter, vol 2,* September, New York.

Meade, James. 1983. A new Keynesian approach to full employment. *Lloyds Bank Rev.,* October.

Meek, Paul 1982. *Open Market Operations.* Fed, New York.

Meese, Richard A. and Kenneth Rogoff. 1983. Empirical exchange rate models of the seventies. *J. Int. Econ.,* vol. 14.

Meiselman, D. 1962. *The Term Structure of Interest Rates.* Englewood Cliffs, N.J.

Mellon Bank. 1984. *Corporate Finance: Taming Today's Interest Rates,* 10th of a series. Pittsburgh.

Melton, William C. 1985. *Inside the Fed.* Homewood, Ill.

Meltzer, Allan H. 1975. Credit availability and economic decisions: Some evidence from the mortgage and housing markets. *Government Credit Allocation,* Institute of Contemporary Studies. San Francisco.

Merris, Randall C. 1975. Credit allocation and commercial banks. *Bus. Cond.,* August. Fed, Chicago.

Miller, Marcus. 1973. *Credit Allocation Techniques and Monetary Policy,* conf. ser. 11. Fed, Boston.

Miller, Merton H., and Daniel Orr. 1966. A model of the demand for money by firms. *Q. J. Econ.,* August.

Miller, Norman C. 1983. *Macroeconomics.* Boston.

Miller, Preston, and Ronald Kaatz. 1974. *Intro-*

duction to the Use of Econometric Models in Economic Policy Making. Fed, Minneapolis.

Miller, Randall J. 1977. *The Regional Impact of Monetary Policy in the United States.* Lexington, Mass.

Minarik, Joseph J. 1978. Who wins, who loses from inflation? *Brookings Bull.,* summer.

Minsky, Hyman P. 1975. *John Maynard Keynes.* New York.

———. 1980. Finance and profits: The changing nature of American business cycles. In *Business Cycles and Public Policy 1929–1979,* Joint Economic Committee of the U.S. Congress.

Mitchell, Wesley C. 1913. *Business Cycles.* New York.

Mitchell, William E. 1970. State and local government borrowing. In Murray Polakoff et al., *Financial Institutions and Markets.* Boston.

Modigliani, France, and Merton H. Miller. 1958. The cost of capital, corporation finance and the theory of investment. *Am. Econ. Rev.,* June.

———. 1963. Corporate income taxes and the cost of capital: A correction. *Am. Econ. Rev.,* June.

Moore, Thomas G. 1966. Stock market margin requirements. *J. Polit. Econ.,* April.

Morris, Frank. 1982. Do the monetary aggregates have a future as targets of Federal Reserve policy? *N. Engl. Econ. Rev.,* March-April. Fed, Boston.

———. 1983. Discussion of paper by James S. Duesenberry, The political economy of monetary policy. In Donald Hodgman, ed., *Political Economy of Monetary Policy,* conf. ser. 26. Fed, Boston.

Mudd, Douglas R. 1979. Do rising U.S. interest rates imply a stronger dollar? *Review,* June. Fed, St. Louis.

Muellbauer, John, and Richard Portes. 1979. Macroeconomics when markets do not clear. In W. H. Branson, *Macroeconomic Theory and Policy,* 2nd ed. New York.

Muir, Frederick M. 1984. Ailing money brokers seek new products. *Wall Street Journal,* July 25.

Mundell, Robert. 1962. The appropriate use of monetary and fiscal policy under fixed exchange rates. *IMF Staff Papers,* March.

Nash, Nathaniel C. 1985. Adjusting to a hundred failed banks. *New York Times,* November 16.

New York Times. 1978. June 6, 7, 23.

———. 1982. Plight of thrifts. March 25.

———. 1984a. October 25.

———. 1984b. Michigan professor wins Silbert Prize. November 14.

———. 1984c. Time again for a little Fed-bashing. December 14.

Nguyen, An Vinh. 1984. U.S. government intervention in foreign exchange markets. Ph.D. dissertation, University of Pittsburgh.

Nichols, Dorothy M. 1977. Banking insights: The truth about member bank reserves deposits as a source of Federal Reserve Bank

earnings. *Econ. Perspect.,* May-June. Fed, Chicago.

Noble, Kenneth B. 1984. FDIC may consider rise in bank premiums. *New York Times,* July 31.

Nordhaus, William D., and Henry C. Wallich. 1978. Alternatives for debt management. In R. L. Teigen, ed., *Readings in Money, National Income, and Stabilization Policy,* 4th ed. Homewood, Ill.

O'Brien, James M. 1984. The information value of the FOMC policy directive under the new operating procedures. *J. Money, Credit, Banking,* May.

Okun, Arthur M. 1979. A reward TIP. In D.C. Colander, ed., *Solutions to Inflation.* New York.

Okun, Arthur M., and George L. Perry, eds. 1978. *Curing Chronic Inflation.* Washington, D.C.

Opper, Barbara Negri. 1983. Profitability of insured commercial banks in 1982. *Fed. Res. Bull.,* July.

Ott, David J., and Attiat F. Ott. 1978. Federal budget policy. In R. L. Teigen, ed., *Readings in Money, National Income, and Stabilization Policy,* 4th ed. Homewood, Ill.

Pasztor, Andy. 1985. Top Hutton aide urged overdrafts in company note. *Wall Street Journal,* August 6.

Pear, Robert. 1984. Rate of poverty found to persist in face of gains. *New York Times,* August 3.

Pesek, Boris P., and Thomas R. Saving. 1967. *Money, Wealth, and Economic Theory.* New York.

Phillips, A. W. 1958. The relation between unemployment and the rate of change of money wage rates in the United Kingdom, 1861–1957. *Economica,* November.

Pianalto, Sandra. 1984. Reorganizing the U.S. banking and regulatory structure. *Econ. Comment.,* April. Fed, Cleveland.

Pierce, James L. 1978. The myth of congressional supervision of monetary policy. *J. Monetary Econ.,* vol. 4, April.

———. 1979. The political economy of Arthur Burns. *J. Finance,* May.

———. 1984. *Monetary and Financial Economics.* New York.

Plosser, Charles. 1982. Government financing decisions and asset returns. *J. Monetary Econ.,* May.

Poole, William. 1978. Using T-bill futures to gauge interest-rate expectations. *Econ. Rev.,* spring. Fed, San Francisco.

———. 1979. Burnsian monetary policy: Eight years of progress? *J. Finance,* May.

Potts, Glenn T., and Dudley G. Luckett. 1978. Policy objectives of the Federal Reserve System. *Q. J. Econ.,* August.

Prell, Michael J. 1971. The Treasury debt and bond rate ceilings. *Monthly Rev.,* April. Fed, Kansas City.

President, U.S. 1984. Economic report. Washington, D.C.

Rattner, Steven. 1979. $800 million error cited by Fed. *New York Times,* October 30.

Rea, John D. 1974. The yield spread between newly issued and seasoned corporate bonds. *Mon. Rev.,* June. Fed, Kansas City.

Reif, Arnold E. 1978a. TIAA or CREF? *AAUP Bull.,* March.

———. 1978b. Correspondence. *AAUP Bull.,* May.

Rendleman, Richard J., Jr., and Christopher E. Carabini. 1979. The efficiency of the Treasury bill futures market. *J. Finance,* September.

Resler, David H. 1979. Does Eurodollar borrowing improve the dollar's exchange value? *Review,* August. Fed, St. Louis.

Rhoades, Stephen A. 1984. The implications for bank merger policy of financial deregulation, interstate banking, and financial supermarkets, FRB staff study 137. Washington, D.C.

Rogers, David. 1985. *Wall Street Journal,* November 14.

Roley, V. Vance. 1982. Weekly money supply announcements and the volatility of short-term interest rates. *Econ. Rev.,* April. Fed, Kansas City.

Roosa, Robert V. 1956. *Federal Reserve Operations in the Money and Government Securities Market.* Fed, New York.

Rose, Peter S., and Donald R. Fraser. 1985. *Financial Institutions,* 2nd ed. Plano, Tex.

Rosenbaum, David E. 1984. Regan foresees final tax plan like Treasury's. *New York Times,* November 4.

Rosenblum, Harvey, Diane Siegel, and Christine Pavel. 1983. Banks and nonbanks: A run for the money. *Econ. Perspect.,* May-June. Fed, Chicago.

Rosenthal, Benjamin. 1982. The Fed can cut interest rates. *New York Times,* March 17.

Ruebling, Charlotte E. 1969. The administration of regulation. *Q. Rev.,* September. Fed, St. Louis.

Rukeyser, Louis. 1978. Stocks are best bet, investors finding out. *Pittsburgh Post-Gazette,* July 18.

Runyon, Herbert. 1983. The new CPI. *Wkly. Lett.,* March 4. Fed, San Francisco.

Rutledge, John. 1981. Why interest rates will fall in 1982. *Wall Street Journal,* December 14.

———. 1982. What lower yield on tangibles means. *Wall Street Journal,* January 20.

Sametz, Arnold W., and Paul Wachtel. 1977. *Understanding Capital Markets,* vol. 2: *The Financial Environment and the Flow of Funds in the Next Decade.* Lexington, Mass.

Samuelson, Paul A. 1944. Interactions between the multiplier analysis and the principle of acceleration. In Haberler, ed., *Readings in Business Cycle Theory.* Philadelphia.

Samuelson, Robert. 1982. Your interest rate guess is as good as anyone's. *Pittsburgh Post-Gazette,* March 9.

Sandler, Linda. 1984. U.S. banks prepare for possibility of third-world debt repudiation. *Wall Street Journal,* July 6.

Santomero, Anthony M., and John J. Seater. 1978. The inflation-unemployment tradeoff: A critique of the literature. *J. Econ. Lit.,* June.

Savage, Donald T. 1982. Developments in banking structure, 1970–1981. *Fed. Res. Bull.,* February.

Scherer, Joseph. 1978. New directions for the federal budget. In R. L. Teigen, ed., *Readings in Money, National Income, and Stabilization Policy,* 4th ed. Homewood, Ill.

Schroeder, Frederick J. 1983. Developments in consumer electronic fund transfers. *Fed. Res. Bull.,* June.

Schumpeter, Joseph A. 1964. *Business Cycles.* New York.

Seater, John J. 1975. A perspective on stagflation. *Bus. Rev.,* May. Fed, Philadelphia.

Segala, John P. 1979. A summary of the International Banking Act of 1978. *Econ. Rev.,* January-February. Fed, Richmond.

Sellon, Gordon H., Jr. 1984. The instruments of monetary policy. *Econ. Rev.,* May. Fed, Kansas City.

Sellon, Gordon H., Jr., and Diane Seibert. 1982. The discount rate: Experience under reserve targeting. *Econ. Rev.,* September-October. Fed, Kansas City.

Shoven, John B., and Jeremy I. Bulow. 1976. Inflation accounting and nonfinancial corporate profits: Financial assets and liabilities. *Brookings Pap. Econ. Act.,* vol. 1.

Silber, William L. 1976. Towards a theory of financial innovation. In W. Silber, ed., *Financial Innovation.* Lexington, Mass.

———. 1978. Fiscal policy is IS-LM analysis: A correction. In R. L. Teigen, ed., *Readings in Money, National Income, and Stabilization Policy,* 4th ed. Homewood, Ill.

Silk, Leonard. 1980. Gold standard as inflation curb. *New York Times,* December 26.

———. 1985. Economic scene. *New York Times,* November 4.

Simpson, Thomas O., et al. 1979. A proposal for redefining the monetary aggregates. *Fed. Res. Bull.,* January.

Sinai, Allen. 1975. The integration of "financial instability" in large-scale macroeconomic models: Theory, practice, problems. Paper, Midwest Economic Association annual meetings, April. Chicago.

———. 1978. Credit crunch possibilities and the crunch barometer. *Data Resources U.S. Rev.,* June.

———. 1984a. Buying time for a TIP. *Challenge,* March-April.

———. 1984b. Deficits, interest rates, and the economy. Paper, Money Workshop, University of Pittsburgh, March 14.

———. Forthcoming. *The Financial System in the U.S. Economy.*

Sloane, Leonard. 1985. A zero coupon has its risks. *New York Times,* November 9.

Smith, Paul F. 1971. *Economics of Financial Institutions.* Homewood, Ill.

———. 1973. Controlling the terms on consumer credit. *Credit Allocation Techniques and Monetary Policy,* conf. ser. 11. Fed, Boston.

_____. 1975. A review of the theoretical and administrative history of consumer credit controls. In I. Kaminow and J. M. O'Brien, *Studies in Selective Credit Policies.* Fed, Philadelphia.

Smith, William L., and Ronald L. Teigen, eds. 1974. *Readings in Money, National Income, and Stabilization Policy,* 3rd ed. Homewood, Ill.

Sobol, Dorothy Meadow. 1979. A substitution account: Precedents and issues. *Q. Rev.,* summer. Fed, New York.

Solow, Robert M., and Alan S. Blinder. 1978. The analytical foundations of fiscal policy. In R. L. Teigen, ed. *Readings in Money, National Income, and Stabilization Policy,* 4th ed. Homewood, Ill.

Stern, Robert M., et al. 1978. *The Presentation of the U.S. Balance of Payments: A Symposium.* In R. L. Teigen, ed., *Readings in Money, National Income, and Stabilization Policy,* 4th ed. Homewood, Ill.

Sterngold, James. 1984. A nation hooked on foreign funds. *New York Times,* November 18.

Sternlight, Peter D. 1984. Monetary policy and open market operations in 1983. *Q. Rev.,* spring. Fed, New York.

_____. 1985. Monetary policy and open market operations in 1984. *Q. Rev.,* spring. Fed, New York.

Stubblebine, W. C., and T. D. Willett, eds. 1983. *Reaganomics: A Midterm Report.* San Francisco.

Taggart, William R. 1978. The "Fed" in Pittsburgh. In Jacob Cohen, ed., *Money Management in Pittsburgh.* Pittsburgh, Pa.

Talley, Samuel H. 1983. Bank capital trends and financing. FRB staff study 122. Washington, D.C.

Terrell, Henry S., and Rodney H. Mills. 1983. International banking facilities and the Eurodollar market, FRB staff study 124. Washington, D.C.

Thomas, Lloyd B., Jr. 1979. *Money, Banking, and Economic Activity,* 1st ed. Englewood Cliffs, N.J.

_____. 1982. *Money, Banking, and Economic Activity,* 2nd. ed. Englewood Cliffs, N.J.

Thorndike, David. 1980. *The Thorndike Encyclopedia of Banking and Financial Tables.* Boston.

Throop, Adrian W. 1984. A "Supply-side miracle"? *Wkly. Lett.,* November 2. Fed, San Francisco.

Thurow, Lester C. 1972. Proposals for rechanneling funds to meet social priorities. *Policies for a More Competitive Financial System,* conf. ser. 8. Fed, Boston.

Tinsley, Peter A., Helen T. Farr, Gerhard Fries, Bonnie Barrett, and Peter von zur Muehlen. 1982. Policy robustness: Specification and simulation of a monthly market model. *J.*

Money, Credit, Banking, suppl., November.

Tobin, James. 1969. A general equilibrium approach to monetary theory. *J. Money, Credit, Banking,* February.

_____. 1984. On the efficiency of the financial system. *Lloyds Bank Rev.,* July.

Trehan, Bharat. 1985. The information content of credit aggregates. *Econ. Rev.,* spring. Fed, San Francisco.

U.S. Congr., Committee on Government Operations. 1984. *Thirty-Fifth Report.* Washington.

U.S. Department of Commerce. 1975. Historical Statistics of the United States Colonial Times to 1970. Washington, D.C.

U.S. Department of the Treasury. 1985. *Bulletin,* 1st quarter.

U.S. Statistical Abstract. 1982.

_____. 1984.

Van Horne, James C. 1971. *Financial Management and Policy,* 2nd ed. Englewood Cliffs, N.J.

Vitaliano, D. 1973. The payment of interest on the federal debt and the distribution of income. *J. Econ. Bus.,* spring-summer.

Volcker, Paul A. 1984. Monetary policy objectives for 1984. July 25. Washington, D.C.

Waage, Thomas O. 1979. 1978 banking legislation: Logjam into useful lumber. *Financier,* February.

Wallace, William H., and William E. Cullison. 1979. *Measuring Price Changes,* 4th ed. Fed, Richmond.

Wallich, Henry C. 1978. Innovations in monetary policy. In R. L. Teigen, ed., *Readings in Money, National Income, and Stabilization Policy,* Homewood, Ill.

Wall Street Journal. 1980. February 8.

_____. 1985a. French banks unveil program to circulate "smart" credit cards. March 6.

_____. 1985. Banking deregulation benefits many people but stirs some worry. September 30.

Walsh, Carl E. 1982. The Federal Reserve's operating procedures and interest rate fluctuations. *Econ. Rev.,* May. Fed, Kansas City.

Wanniski, Jude. 1978. *The Way the World Works: How Economies Fail—and Succeed.* New York.

Wayne, Leslie. 1982. The heat's on Morgan Stanley. *New York Times,* March 21.

_____. 1984. Dismantling the innovative D.R.I. *New York Times,* December 16.

Webster, Charles E., Jr. 1983. The effects of deficits on interest rates. *Econ. Rev.,* May. Fed, Kansas City.

Weintraub, Robert E. 1970. *Introduction to Monetary Economics.* New York.

_____. 1978. Congressional supervision of monetary policy. *J. Monetary Econ.,* vol. 4, April.

_____. 1979. TIP, a tax-based incomes policy to stop stagflation. In D. C. Colander, ed., *Solutions to Inflation.* New York.

White, Betsy Buttrill. 1982. Foreign banking in

the United States: A regulatory and supervisory perspective. *Q. Rev.,* summer. Fed, New York.

Winn, Willis J. 1970. The role of the director: The ideal and the real. In D. P. Eastburn, ed., *Men, Money, and Policy: Essays in Honor of Karl R. Bopp.* Fed, Philadelphia.

Wojnilower, A. M. 1980. The central role of credit crunches in recent financial history. *Brookings Pap. Econ. Act.,* vol. 2.

Wood, John H. 1967. A model of Federal Reserve behavior. In G. Horwich, ed., *Monetary Process and Policy.* Homewood, Ill.

———. 1972. Money and output: Keynes and Friedman in historical perspective. *Bus. Rev.,* September. Fed, Philadelphia.

Woolley, John T. 1984. *Monetary Politics.* Cambridge, England.

Yeager, Leland B. 1966. *International Monetary Relations.* New York.

Yohe, William P. 1976. Federal Reserve behavior. In T. M. Havrilesky and J. T. Boorman, *Current Perspectives in Banking.* Chicago.

Zweig, Phillip L. 1985. Fed rules on overdrafts worry firms. *Wall Street Journal,* November 12.

Free publications may be obtained from the following sources:

Administrative Services Department, Federal Reserve Bank of San Francisco, San Francisco, CA 94120.

Bank and Public Relations Department, Federal Reserve Bank of Richmond, Richmond, VA 23261.

Finance and Development, International Monetary Fund Building, Washington, DC 20431.

Library, Federal Reserve Bank of Chicago, Chicago, IL 60690.

Manufacturers Hanover Trust, *Economic Report,* 350 Park Avenue, New York, NY 10022.

Publications Services, Division of Administrative Services, Board of Governors of the Federal Reserve System, Washington, DC 20551.

Public Information Department, Federal Reserve Bank of Boston, Boston, MA 02106.

Public Information Department, Federal Reserve Bank of Kansas City, Kansas City, MO 64198.

Public Information Department, Federal Reserve Bank of Minneapolis, Minneapolis, MN 55480.

Public Services Department, Federal Reserve Bank of Philadelphia, Philadelphia, PA 19101.

Research Department, Federal Reserve Bank of Atlanta, Atlanta, GA 30303.

Research Department, Federal Reserve Bank of Cleveland, Cleveland, OH 44101.

Research Department, Federal Reserve Bank of Dallas, Dallas, TX 75222.

Exchange rates
  fixed and free, 385, 387–91
  international economy, 379–81, 382–94
  volatility, 393
Exchange Stabilization Fund (ESF), 154, 161–62
Expectations hypothesis. *See* Interest rates
External finance. *See also* Credit
  direct versus indirect, 58–59, 61
  importance, 22–23, 26, 239
  investment, 56–57, 364–65
  spending, 16

"**F**annie Mae." *See* Federal National Mortgage Association
Farmers Home Administration (FmHA), 234
Federal agency obligations, 157
Federal Deposit Insurance Corporation (FDIC), 107, 119, 125–27
Federal Financing Bank, 321
Federal Home Loan Bank (FHLB), 119, 234, 324
Federal Home Loan Board (FHLB), 119
Federal Home Loan Mortgage Corporation (FHLMC, "Freddie Mac"), 235
Federal Home Mortgage Association, 324
Federal Intermediate Credit Banks (FICB), 234
Federal lending agencies, 234
Federal National Mortgage Association (FNMA, "Fannie Mae"), 234–35, 254, 324
Federal Old Age and Survivors Insurance Trust Fund, 227
Federal Open-Market Committee (FOMC), 131–33, 175–78, 197–98, 213–14
Federal Reserve
  adjustment credit, 154
  agent for foreign governments, 148–49
  balance sheet, 151
  bankers' acceptances, 156–57
  capital accounts, 159–60
  conflicting policy goals, 205–6
  Congress, 210
  cost of operation, 149
  counting instruments and targets, 188–90
  credit availability policy, 277
  defensive versus dynamic behavior, 160, 192
  deposits, 158–59, 164
  discount rate, 104, 154, 168–72
  distribution of currency, 144
  disutility function, 184–85
  economic impact on "real" economy, 167
  economic policy, 184–87, 190–91, 197–99, 202–3, 205–6
  electronic funds transfer, 144–45
  extended credit, 154
  fiscal agency function, 148–49
  float, 143–44, 148, 149
  gold holdings, 161–62
  independence, 214, 366–67
  instruments, 166–83, 291
  interest rates, 187, 262

lender of last resort, 208–9
lending to Treasury, 325–26
liability accounts, 158–59
loans, 154, 208–9
monetary control and contractual savings institutions, 228
money demand, 193–94
notes, 144, 158, 160, 169
open-market operations, 157, 174–75
organization, 4, 131–33, 135, 175–76
payments mechanism (clearing of checks), 135–42
and the president, 210–14
publications, 14
reaction function, 189, 212, 326
regulations on international banking, 116–17
repurchase agreements, 156–57
reserve balances, 162
social welfare function, 184–85
supervision of DIs, 119–20, 128
transmission mechanism, 168
Treasury Department, 209, 320, 325–26
U.S. government securities, 158
volatility of interest rates, 262
Federal Reserve Act of 1913, 106, 132, 168, 169
  1919 amendment (Edge Act), 113
Federal Reserve Bank of Chicago, 125
Federal Reserve Banks
  districts, 134–35
  quasi-public nature, 131–32
  suppliers of reserves, 78–79, 81
Federal Savings and Loan Insurance Corporation (FSLIC), 119, 126
Fermi, Enrico, 402
FIFO accounting, 45
Finance, 13, 27, 357–68
Finance companies, 228–30
Financial asset purchases, 247–48
Financial claims, 257–58
Financial innovations, 112–13, 123–24, 285
Financial institutions, 216–40
Financial Institutions Examination Council, 107
Financial Institutions Regulatory and Interest Rate Control Act of 1978, 107
Financial intermediation, 59
Financial markets
  analysis, 312–13
  defined, 241
  derivation of effective demand, 311–14
  discriminating effects, 293
  primary versus secondary, 59–61
Financial services, 129
Financial substitutability, 294
Fiscal and monetary policy, 336–37, 341
Fiscal drag, 333
Fiscal policy
  neoclassical synthesis, 308
  "pure," 329–30
  state and local, 340–41
Fisher, Irving, 47
Fisher effect, 47

Fisher index, 35
Float
  Federal Reserve, 143–44, 148, 149
  mail, 142
  managed ("dirty"), 385, 396
Flow of funds, 292–95
Flow-of-funds accounts, 3–13
  econometric modeling, 411–14
  forecasting interest rates, 273–76
  matrix, 13
  public debt, 322
Foreign Direct Investment Program (FDIP),
  113
Foreign exchange markets, 382–83, 386–87
  intervention, 397
FRB-MIT model, 405–7
"Freddie Mac." *See* Federal Home Loan
  Mortgage Corporation
Free reserves, 196–97
Friedman, Milton, 170, 348
Full Employment and Balanced Growth Act of
  1978 (Humphrey-Hawkins Act), 198–99
Full-employment surplus, 332–33

Garn–St. Germain Depository Institutions Act
  of 1982, 92, 110, 219–20, 287
Glass, Carter, 169
Glass-Steagall Act of 1932, 110, 117, 169
GNP deflator, 39–40
Gold
  market prices, 153
  monetary gold stock, 161
  standard, 151, 153
Gold certificates, 151–54
Gold stock, monetary, 161–62
Government deficit. *See* Public debt
Government expenditure multiplier, 330–32,
  337
Government National Mortgage Association
  (GNMA, "Ginnie Mae"), 235
Great Depression, 358
Gross National Product (GNP), 16, 21, 239
Growth-induced versus growth-inducing
  finance, 27
Gulf Oil Corporation, 286

Hand, John M., 235
Hendershott model, 411–12
Hester, Donald D., 277
High-powered money, 238–39
Holding companies, 108–10
  multibank (MBHC), 108–9
  one-bank (OBHC), 108–9
Holding period yield, 288
House Banking, Currency, and Housing
  Committee, 210
House Concurrent Resolution 133 of 1975, 198,
  210, 215
Household sector

accrued comprehensive income (ACI), 44
balance sheet, 28
borrowing, 244–48
economic group, 4–5
financial asset purchases, 247–48
financial substitution, 30
interest rates, 244, 245–48
linkage between sources of uses of funds,
  244–47
Housing starts, significance, 296–98
Humphrey-Hawkins Act of 1978, 198–99

Identities, 6
Income
  inflation, 41
  velocity, 20
Income determination, 304
Income-expenditure multiplier, 330–32, 337
Income policy, 353–54
Indexation, 50–51
Indifference curves, 53–54, 56–58
Indirect finance. *See* External finance
Individual Retirement Account (IRA), 335
Inflation
  control, 202
  debtor versus creditor firms, 46
  distributive effects via wealth, 42–43
  effects, 40–41, 45–46, 50
  employment, 345
  government as beneficiary, 49–50
  hedges, 43
  indexation, 50–51
  leverage ratio, 44–45
  poverty, 41
  premium, 47–49
  price indexes, 34
  tax revenues, 50
  wealth effect, 44–45, 46–49
Information-arbitrage efficiency, 350
Information costs, 13, 347
Installment loans, 70
Insurance
  life, 228
  property-casualty, 227–28
Interest
  components, 64
  yield calculation, 69
Interest equalization tax (IET), 113
Interest rates
  business sector, 248–49
  call provisions, 269
  cash balances, 279
  ceilings, 120–23
  common versus preferred stock dividends,
    271–72
  compound, 69
  convertible bonds, 272
  credit availability, 277
  credit-market analysis, 261
  discounts, 70
  econometric modeling, 408